SHORT STORY
WRITERS
REVISED EDITION

MAGILL'S CHOICE

SHORT STORY WRITERS

REVISED EDITION

Volume 1
Chinua Achebe — Louise Erdrich
1 – 378

edited by
CHARLES E. MAY
CALIFORNIA STATE UNIVERSITY, LONG BEACH

SALEM PRESS, INC.

Pasadena, California   Hackensack, New Jersey

Cover photo: Shawn Gearhart/©iStockphoto.com

Some essays in these volumes originally appeared in *Critical Survey of Short Fiction, Second Revised Edition*, 2001. New material has been added.

∞ The paper used in these volumes conforms to the American National Standard for Permanence of Paper for Printed Library Materials, Z39.48-1992 (R1997).

Library of Congress Cataloging-in-Publication Data

Short story writers / edited by Charles E. May. — Rev. ed.
        v. cm. — (Magill's choice)
    Includes bibliographical references and index.
    ISBN 978-1-58765-389-6 (set : alk. paper) — ISBN 978-1-58765-390-2 (vol. 1 : alk. paper) — ISBN 978-1-58765-391-9 (vol. 2 : alk. paper) — ISBN 978-1-58765-392-6 (vol. 3 : alk. paper) 1. Short story. 2. Short stories—Bio-bibliography—Dictionaries. 3. Novelists—Biography—Dictionaries. I. May, Charles E. (Charles Edward), 1941-

PN3373.S398 2008
809.3'1—dc22

                                                                  2007032789

First printing

PRINTED IN CANADA

Contents – Volume 1

Publisher's Note

Short Story Writers, Revised Edition, is the first revision of a Magill's Choice set published in 1997. To that earlier edition's collection of 102 articles, this edition adds 44 more articles on important authors of short fiction. The revised three-volume set thus has 146 articles on the most frequently taught, most frequently read, most acclaimed, and most often researched short-fiction writers studied in American schools and colleges. The essays in these volumes have been culled from the 480 author essays in Salem Press's *Critical Survey of Short Fiction, Second Revised Edition* (2001) and have been updated. They collectively provide an essential look at the best in short-fiction writing in an easy-to-use and student-friendly format.

Any list of contents in a work such as this is necessarily subjective, making the inclusion of one author over another open to debate. Nevertheless, the editors have done their best to meet the needs of core-literature curricula in schools by including the authors who most commonly appear on basic reading lists. Thanks to the greater than 40-percent expansion of coverage in *Short Story Writers, Revised Edition,* users are more likely than ever to find articles on the authors whom they are studying.

The selection of authors in these volumes focuses mainly on modern short-story writers, with a brief nod to the classic fourteenth century writings of Giovanni Boccaccio (*The Decameron*) and Geoffrey Chaucer (*The Canterbury Tales*). The set also takes into account the influence of the *contes* or *Märchen,* represented here by Germany's Brothers Grimm. More than two dozen of the authors did most of their writing during the nineteenth century. Among the best known of these are Nathaniel Hawthorne, Edgar Allan Poe, Ivan Turgenev, Mark Twain, Bret Harte, Henry James, Guy de Maupassant, Kate Chopin, and Anton Chekhov. By the middle of the nineteenth century, two distinct types of short fiction existed: the tale and the essay-sketch. The modern short story brings together the best of these two traditions. Although questions of how, when, and where short fiction developed have generated lively debate, most scholars of the genre agree that the modern short story began in the United States and specifically in the writings of Washington Irving. Indeed, it is often conceded that Irving's "Rip Van Winkle" (1809) was the first *great* modern short story.

Although Irving is often regarded as the inventor of the short story form, modern short stories appeared at almost exactly the same time he was writing—in Russia, France, Germany, and elsewhere in the United States. Consequently, credit for creating the form has also been attributed to Russia's Nikolai Gogol, France's Prosper Mérimée, and America's Nathaniel Hawthorne and Edgar Allan Poe. Among these other writers, Poe stands out; he not only wrote short stories but also wrote *about* the short story form in theory. He addressed it as a distinct genre, advancing the thesis that a story should have a unified effect and be compact—principles that still guide short-story criticisms.

Many outstanding writers of the genre followed the nineteenth century pioneers. Other authors covered in this set reflect the range and diversity of nineteenth and twentieth century short-story writing. More than half of those covered (87) are from the United States, reflecting the strength of the genre in one of its most important birthplaces. These American writers include 10 African Americans, 4 Native Americans, and 3 Latinos. The second largest national grouping is England (19), added to which are some of the great authors of Ireland (7) and Scotland (3). Readers will also find some of the cornerstone short fiction writers of Canada, the Continent, Russia, Asia, Africa, and South America. Women authors have excelled in the genre, and of the 49 surveyed in these volumes, 21 are new to this edition.

Organization

The essays are arranged alphabetically, by authors' surnames, in the three volumes, and their concise and accessible formats follow an easy-to-use template. Each essay begins with the author's name, birth date and place, death date and place when appropriate, and a chronological list of the subject's major publications of short fiction. The text of the essay is divided into four subsections:

- **Other literary forms** describes other genres in which the author has worked
- **Achievements** addresses what the author has contributed to the genre and mentions any important honors and awards the author has received
- **Biography** summarizes the author's life
- **Analysis**, the main body of the text, is a detailed examination of the author's short-story writing that usually includes three or four subheaded sections focusing on individual stories that help explain the author's work

The back matter of each essay includes "Other major works," which lists the author's publications in genres other than the short story, and a solid annotated bibliography. All the bibliographies—which average ten citations—have been substantially updated. More than half the titles cited have been published since 1994, and nearly one-third have been published since the first edition of *Short Story Writers* was issued.

Volume 3 concludes with a glossary of 118 terms and techniques relevant to the study of short fiction, a time line listing all the covered authors by their dates of birth, and a comprehensive index.

Achnowledgments

Salem Press would like to thank the nearly 170 scholars who contributed their time and knowledge to writing the essays and providing updates for this set. Their names and affiliations are listed the pages that follow this note. Salem especially wishes to thank Dr. Charles E. May of California State University at Long Beach for lending his expertise on the short-story genre to this project by serving as its Editor.

List of Contributors

Michael Adams
*City University of New York, Graduate
    Center*

Thomas P. Adler
Purdue University

Karen L. Arnold
Independent Scholar

Marilyn Arnold
Independent Scholar

Robert W. Artinian
University of Virginia

Stanley S. Atherton
Original Contributor

Bryan Aubrey
Independent Scholar

Jane L. Ball
Wilberforce University

Mary Baron
University of North Florida

Melissa E. Barth
Appalachian State University

Bert Bender
Original Contributor

Alvin K. Benson
Utah Valley State College

Dorothy M. Betz
Georgetown University

Cynthia A. Bily
Adrian College

Margaret Boe Birns
New York University

Nicholas Birns
Eugene Lang College, New School

Carol Bishop
Indiana University, Southeast

Lynn Z. Bloom
University of Connecticut

Julia B. Boken
*State University of New York, College at
    Oneonta*

Jo-Ellen Lipman Boon
Independent Scholar

Jerry Bradley
Original Contributor

Harold Branam
Savanna State University

Gerhard Brand
California State University, Los Angeles

Laurence A. Breiner
Boston University

Keith H. Brower
Salisbury State University

Mary H. Bruce
Monmouth College

Louis J. Budd
Duke University

Rebecca R. Butler
Dalton College

Edmund J. Campion
University of Tennessee

John Carr
Original Contributor

Warren J. Carson
University of South Carolina, Spartunburg

Mary LeDonne Cassidy
South Carolina State University

Thomas Cassidy
South Carolina State University

Hal Charles
Eastern Kentucky University

Lisa-Anne Culp
University of South Florida

Bill Delaney
Independent Scholar

Joan DelFattore
University of Delaware

Kathryn Zabelle Derounian
University of Arkansas, Little Rock

John F. Desmond
Whitman College

Grace Eckley
Independent Scholar

Wilton Eckley
Colorado School of Mines

Robert P. Ellis
Worcester State College

Thomas L. Erskine
Salisbury University

Walter Evans
Augusta College

James Feast
Baruch College, City University of New York

John W. Fiero
University of Louisiana, Lafayette

Edward Fiorelli
St. John's University, New York

James K. Folsom
University of Colorado, Boulder

Carol Franks
Portland State University

Timothy C. Frazer
Western Illinois University

Terri Frongia
University of California, Riverside

Miriam Fuchs
Independent Scholar

Jean C. Fulton
Malarishi University of Management

Kenneth Funsten
Independent Scholar

Ann D. Garbett
Averett University

Linda S. Gordon
Worcester State College

Peter W. Graham
Virginia Polytechnic Institute and State University

Julian Grajewski
Original Contributor

James L. Green
Arizona State University

William E. Grim
Ohio University

David Mike Hamilton
Independent Scholar

Stephen M. Hart
University College London

Terry Heller
Coe College

Diane Andrews Henningfeld
Adrian College

Allen Hibbard
Middle Tennessee State University

Jane Hill
Independent Scholar

Nika Hoffman
Crossroads School

William Hoffman
Independent Scholar

Theodore C. Humphrey
California State Polytechnic University, Pomona

Archibald E. Irwin
Indiana University, Southeast

Eunice Pedersen Johnston
North Dakota State University

Theresa Kanoza
Lincoln Land Community College

Karen A. Kildahl
South Dakota State University

Sue L. Kimball
Methodist College

Cassandra Kircher
Elon College

Carlota Larrea
Pennsylvania University

Eugene S. Larson
Los Angeles Pierce College

Donald F. Larsson
Mankato State University

Norman Lavers
Arkansas State University

Leon Lewis
Appalachian State University

Douglas Long
Independent Scholar

R. C. Lutz
CII, Jüterbog, Germany

Joanne McCarthy
Independent Scholar

Richard D. McGhee
Arkansas State University

Victoria E. McLure
Texas Tech University

Bryant Mangum
Independent Scholar

Barry Mann
Alliance Theatre

Patricia Marks
Valdosta State College

Karen M. Cleveland Marwick
Independent Scholar

Paul Marx
University of New Haven

Charles E. May
California State University, Long Beach

Laurence W. Mazzeno
Alvernia College

Kenneth W. Meadwell
University of Winnipeg

Martha Meek
University of North Dakota

Ann A. Merrill
Emory University

Vasa D. Mihailovich
University of North Carolina

Paula M. Miller
Biola University

Robert W. Millett
Original Contributor

Christian H. Moe
Southern Illinois University, Carbondale

S. S. Moorty
Southern Utah State College

Robert A. Morace
Daemen College

Sherry Morton-Mollo
California State University, Fullerton

Earl Paulus Murphy
Harris-Stoew State University

Brian Murray
Youngstown State College

John M. Muste
Ohio State University

Susan Nayel
Original Contributor

William Nelles
University of Massachusetts, Dartmouth

Evelyn Newlyn
Virginia Polytechnic Institute and State University

Emma Coburn Norris
Troy State University

George O'Brien
Georgetown University

Keri L. Overall
University of South Carolina

Cóilín Owens
George Mason University

Janet Taylor Palmer
Caldwell Community College & Technical Institute

Robert J. Paradowski
Rochester Institute of Technology

Leslie A. Pearl
Independent Scholar

David Peck
California State University, Long Beach

Susan L. Piepke
Bridgewater College

Constance Pierce
Miami University, Ohio

Mary Ellen Pitts
Rhodes College

Victoria Price
Lamar University

Karen Priest
Lama University, Orange

Norman Prinsky
Augusta State University

Jere Real
Lynchburg College

Peter J. Reed
University of Minnesota

Rosemary M. Canfield Reisman
Charleston Southern University

Martha E. Rhynes
Independent Scholar

Mary Rohrberger
University of Northern Iowa

Jill Rollins
Trafalgar College

Paul Rosefeldt
Delgado Community College

Ruth Rosenberg
Original Contributor

Gabrielle Rowe
McKendree College

David Sadkin
Nigara University

Chaman L. Sahni
Boise State University

David N. Samuelson
California State University, Long Beach

Victor A. Santi
University of New Orleans

Barbara Kitt Seidman
Linfield College

D. Dean Shackelford
Concord College

Allen Shepherd
Original Contributor

Jan Sjåvik
University of Washington

Roger Smith
Willamette University

Ira Smolensky
Monmouth College

Katherine Snipes
Independent Scholar

Jean M. Snook
Memorial University of Newfoundland

George Soule
Carleton College

Madison V. Sowell
Brigham Young University

Sandra Whipple Spanier
Pennsylvania State University

John Stark
Original Contributor

Karen F. Stein
University of Rhode Island

Judith L. Steininger
Milwaukee School of Engineering

Louise M. Stone
Bloomsburg University

W. J. Stuckey
Purdue University

Alvin Sullivan
Southern Illinois University

Eileen A. Sullivan
Original Contributor

James Sullivan
California State University, Los Angeles

Catherine Swanson
Independent Scholar

Roy Arthur Swanson
University of Wisconsin, Milwaukee

Terry Theodore
University of North Carolina, Wilmington

Lou Thompson
Texas Woman's University

Christine Tomei
Columbia University

Richard Tuerk
Texas A&M University, Commerce

Scott D. Vander Ploeg
Madisonville Community College

Dennis Vannatta
University of Arkansas, Little Rock

Barbara Wiedemann
Auburn University, Montgomery

Albert Wilhelm
Tennessee Technological University

Patricia A. R. Williams
Texas Southern University

Judith Barton Williamson
Sauk Valley Community College

Michael Witkoski
University of South Carolina

Anna M. Wittman
University of Alberta

Mary F. Yudin
Pennsylvania State University

Gay Annette Zieger
Independent Scholar

Complete List of Contents

Volume 1

Volume 2

Volume 3

SHORT STORY WRITERS
REVISED EDITION

Chinua Achebe

Born: Ogidi, Nigeria; November 16, 1930

Principal short fiction • "Dead Men's Path," 1953; *The Sacrificial Egg, and Other Stories*, 1962; *Girls at War*, 1972.

Other literary forms • In addition to his short-story collections, Chinua Achebe is known for essays, children's literature, and collections of poetry, which include *Collected Poems* (2004). He is best known, however, for his novel *No Longer at Ease* (1960), which became a modern African classic. The book is the second in a trilogy about change, conflict, and personal struggle to find the "New Africa." The first is *Things Fall Apart* (1958) and the third is *Arrow of God* (1964). Achebe's fourth novel, *A Man of the People* (1966), was followed twenty-one years later by *Anthills of the Savannah* (1987), his fifth novel. In 1984 he became the founder and publisher of *Uwa Ndi Igbo: A Bilingual Journal of Igbo Life and Arts*. Achebe edited volumes of African short fiction, including *African Short Stories* (1985) and *The Heinemann Book of Contemporary African Short Fiction* (1992), both with C. L. Innes.

Achievements • Chinua Achebe received awards or award nominations for each of his novelistic works, from the Margaret Wrong Memorial Prize for *Things Fall Apart* to a Booker McConnell Prize nomination for *Anthills of the Savannah*. He was also awarded a Rockefeller travel fellowship in 1960 and the United Nations Educational, Scientific, and Cultural Organization (UNESCO) Fellowship for creative artists in 1963. In 1979 he received the Nigerian National Merit Award and was named to the Order of the Federal Republic of Nigeria. Achebe received honorary doctorates from universities around the world, including Dartmouth College in 1972 and Harvard University in 1996.

Biography • Chinua Achebe, christened at birth Albert Chinualumogu Achebe, was born in Ogidi in Eastern Nigeria on November 16, 1930, near the Niger River. His family was Christian in a village divided between Christians and the "others." Achebe's great-grandfather served as the model for Okonkwo, the protagonist of *Things Fall Apart*. Because he was an Ibo and a Christian, Achebe grew up conscious of how he differed not only from other Africans but also from other Nigerians. Achebe was one of the first graduates of University College at Ibadan in 1953. In 1954, he was made producer of the Nigerian Broadcasting Service and in 1958 became the founding editor of Heinemann's African Writers series; this position and the publication, in that series, of *Things Fall Apart*, account for his vast influence among writers of his and the following generation.

Achebe married Christie Chinwe Okoli in 1961 and became the father of four children. When a civil war began in Nigeria in 1966 with the massacre of Achebe's fellow tribesmen in the northern part of the country, Achebe returned to the east, hoping to establish in the new country of Biafra a publishing house with other young Ibo writers. One of this band was the poet Christopher Okigbo, killed later that year in action against federal forces. After Biafra's defeat in the civil war, a defeat which

Rocon/Enugu, Nigeria

meant for many of his compatriots imprisonment in camps and "reeducation," Achebe worked as an educator as well as a writer. He traveled to the United States on several occasions to serve as a guest lecturer or visiting professor, and he visited many countries throughout the world. In addition, his interest in politics led to his serving as the deputy national president of the People's Redemption Party in 1983 and then as the president of the town union in Ogidi, Nigeria, in 1986.

Achebe served as visiting professor on an international scale. Universities at which he taught include Cambridge University, the University of Connecticut, and the University of California, Los Angeles. A 1990 car accident injured Achebe's spine, confining him to a wheelchair. He spent six months recovering, then accepted an endowed professorship at New York's Bard College. He continued to teach and write throughout the 1990's.

Analysis • Chinua Achebe is an African English-language writer. As an author, Achebe uses the power of English words to expose, unite, and reveal various aspects of Nigerian culture. His subjects are both literary and political. In general, Achebe's writings reflect cultural diversity in twentieth century African society. He focuses on the difficulty faced by Africans who were once under the rule of British colonials but later had to struggle with issues of democracy, the evils of military rule, civil war, tribal rivalries, and dictatorship.

Achebe seeks to preserve the proverbs and truths of his Ibo tribal heritage by incorporating them into his stories, whether they be in his contemporary novels or his children's tales. His works do more, however, than entertain; they reveal truths about human nature and show the destructiveness of power corrupted. Achebe's writing does not cast blame but delivers a message to his readers, concerning unity and the necessity for political stability in Nigerian culture.

"Vengeful Creditor" • Achebe's "Vengeful Creditor" is a story that seems to be about what a misconceived government decree guaranteeing free education to all can lead to, including some rather comic developments. It appears to be a story about class struggle, and then, as readers see layer after layer of meaning stripped away and one theme leading directly to another, it seems to be—and is—about something really quite different from either education or the class system.

Mr. and Mrs. Emenike are part of the Nigerian upper class: He is a parliamentary secretary, and he and his wife own a Mercedes and a Fiat and employ servants from the still-uneducated masses, most of them from the village of their birth, to which the Emenikes return periodically to shower largesse upon the populace. At the beginning of the story, a free-education bill has caused a mass desertion of servants, even those of college age, all of whom wish to go back to their villages and qualify for an education. Apparently many others have the same idea, for the turnout for free schooling is double what the government statisticians had predicted. Readers see Emenike and his running buddies at the cabinet meeting at which it is decided to make everyone pay, after all, because the army might have to be called out if new taxes are announced to pay for the unexpected costs of the program.

The Emenikes, finding themselves with this "servant problem," return to their native village and ask Martha, a village woman known to them, if her daughter Vero will be their baby nurse for the princely sum of five pounds per year. Martha has led a rather sad life: She was educated at a Christian school whose reason for being was the education of African girls up to the standards expected of the wives of native pastors. The woman in charge of her school, however, by way of furthering her own romantic aspirations, persuaded Martha to marry a carpenter being trained at an industrial school managed by a white man. Carpentry never came into its own, however, at least not as much as preaching and teaching, and Martha had a "bad-luck marriage," which eventually left her a widow with no money and several children to support, although she was a Standard Three (beginning of high school) reader and her classmates were all married to prosperous teachers and bishops.

The withdrawal of the free-education decree has cast Martha's daughter, Vero, back onto the streets. When Mr. Emenike says that one does not need education to be great, Martha knows he is patronizing her; she knows exactly what the fate of an uneducated person usually is, but she needs the money from this job. Mr. Emenike rounds out his recruiting pitch by saying he thinks there is plenty of time for the ten-year-old girl to go to school. Martha says, "I read Standard Three in those days and I said they will all go to college. Now they will not even have the little I had thirty years ago." Vero turns out to be quick, industrious, and creative, but there also begins to be a connection between her charge's maturing and her own chance of an education. Finally, as she comes to realize the child will need care until hope of an education has passed her, she tries to poison him by making him drink a bottle of red ink.

Mrs. Emenike, one of the least sympathetic Africans in any short story ever written by an African, beats Vero unmercifully. They drive back to the village where they were all born and pull her out of the car. Martha hears from Vero that she has been fired, sees the blood on her daughter, and drags her to the Emenikes. Called one who taught her daughter murder, she retorts to Mrs. Emenike that she is not a murderer. Mr. Emenike, trying to break up this confrontation, says, "It's the work of the devil. . . . I have always known that the craze for education in this country will one day ruin all of us. Now even children will commit murder in order to go to school."

"Uncle Ben's Choice" • "Uncle Ben's Choice" is a ghost or magical story which involves the element of human choice. A succubus-goddess known as the Mami-Wota, capable of many disguises, is both a seducer and a betrayer. She makes it possible for a young girl who offers herself to a man to guarantee not only sexual relations but also success, riches, and whatever material things the man desires. The only condition is that the Mami-Wota prevents the man from marrying her.

"Uncle Ben's Choice" is a monologue told by Uncle Ben in a tone that is skeptical yet simultaneously sincere and ingenuous. Uncle Ben is a clerk determined not to marry, whose passions are scotch, a brand-new phonograph, and his bicycle. His affluence brings him to the attention of the Mami-Wota because he not only lives better than the average African but also is much more concerned with the material rewards of life than even his fellow clerks.

A "light" girl who is Roman Catholic falls for him, and he tries to stay out of her way. However, he comes home one night after some heavy drinking and falls into bed, only to find a naked woman there. He thinks at first that it is the girl who has been making a play for him, then he feels her hair—it feels European. He jumps out of bed, and the woman calls to him in the voice of the girl who has a crush on him. He is suspicious now and strikes a match, making the most fateful decision of his life: to abjure wealth gotten from being the exclusive property of the Mami-Wota, her lover and her slave. "Uncle Ben's Choice" is about the innate morality of men in society. Uncle Ben honors his society by suppressing his own urges and fantasies in favor of remaining a part of his family, clan, and tribe, whose rewards he values more than riches.

"Girls at War" • "Girls at War" is a story about the war between the seceding state of Biafra and Nigeria, and both the theme and the plot are foreshadowed in the spare sentence introducing the principal characters: "The first time their paths crossed nothing happened." The second time they meet, however, is at a checkpoint at Akwa, when the girl, Gladys, stops Reginald Nwankwo's car to inspect it. He falls back on the dignity of his office and person, but this fails to impress her, which secretly delights and excites him. He sees her as "a beautiful girl in a breasty blue jersey, khaki jeans and canvas shoes with the new-style hair plait which gave a girl a defiant look." Before, in the earlier stages of the war, he had sneered at the militia girls, particularly after seeing a group recruited from a high school marching under the banner "WE ARE IMPREGNABLE." Now he begins to respect them because of the mature attitude and bearing of Gladys, who seems both patriotic and savvy, knowing and yet naïve.

The third time they meet, "things had got very bad. Death and starvation had long chased out the headiness of the early days." Reginald is coming back to Owerri after using his influence as an official to obtain some food, unfortunately under the eyes of a starving crowd who mock and taunt him. He is something of an idealist, and this embarrasses him, but he has decided that in "such a situation one could do nothing at all for crowds; at best one could try to be of some use to one's immediate neighbors." Gladys is walking along in a crowd, and he picks her up, but not because he recognizes her. She has changed: She is wearing makeup, a wig, and new clothes and is now a bureaucrat and no doubt corrupt. She reminds him that she was the one who searched him so long ago; he had admired her then, but now he just wants her, and as soon as they get into town he takes her into an air-raid bunker after Nigerian planes fly over, strafing.

Later, they go to a party, where in the midst of Biafran starvation there is scotch, Courvoisier, and real bread, but a white Red Cross man who has lost a friend in an air crash tells them all that they stink and that any girl there will roll into bed for a fish or a dollar. He is slapped by an African officer who, all the girls think, is a hero, including Gladys, who begins to appear to the protagonist—and to the readers—as the banal, improvident child she really is. Finally, Gladys goes home and to bed with Reginald, who is shocked by the coarseness of her language. He has his pleasure and writes her off. Then he begins to think she is nothing but a mirror reflecting a "rotten, maggoty society" and that she, like a dirty mirror, needs only some cleaning. He begins to believe she is under some terrible influence. He decides to try to help her;

he gives her food and money, and they drive off together to her house. He is determined to see who is there and who her friends are, to get to the bottom of her life of waste and callousness.

On the way he picks up a soldier who has lost part of one leg. Before, he would not have picked up a mere private, not only sweaty but also an inconvenience with his crutches and his talk of war. Then there is another air raid. He pushes past Gladys, who stops to go back to help the disabled soldier, and, terrified, goes into the timberline, where a near-miss knocks him senseless. When he awakes, he finds the driver sobbing and bloody and his car a wreck. "He saw the remains of his car smoking and the entangled remains of the girl and the soldier. And he let out a piercing cry and fell down again." With Gladys's horrible death, the protagonist understands the potential for nobility within the heart and soul of even the most banal and superficial of human beings. "Girls at War" confirms Achebe's faith in humanity and in Africa.

"Civil Peace" • Because of the remarkable portrayal of Nigerian culture, Achebe's works, like the three stories analyzed above, are frequently anthologized. Achebe himself edited and published the collection *African Short Stories* (1985). It is subdivided by regions of the African continent. In the West African section, Achebe included his own work "Civil Peace," originally published in *Girls at War.*

This story takes place in the time period just after the Biafran War. It points out with the ironic title that there may not be much difference between civil war and civil peace. Jonathan Iwegbu feels fortunate that he, his wife, and three of their four children have survived the war. As an added bonus, so has his bicycle, which Jonathan had cleverly buried in his yard to keep it from the marauding troops. After the war, Jonathan's entrepreneurial instincts can flourish because he has the bicycle.

Jonathan's business ventures do well and, in addition, he receives a cash payment of Nigerian money (called the *ex-gratia* award or egg-rasher by the Nigerians struggling with the foreign term) for turning in rebel money coined during the conflict. Unfortunately, a band of thieves, many of them former soldiers, armed with machine guns and other weapons, learn of his windfall and terrorize Jonathan and his family in a way reminiscent of wartime, until Jonathan gives them the money. Fatalistically, yet realistically, Jonathan realizes he is back to square one, and, at the end of the story, he and his family are once again preparing to go out and start all over again. In Jonathan's own words, "I say, let egg-rasher perish in the flames! Let it go where everything else has gone."

This story illustrates one of Achebe's major themes, a portrayal of both the problems or weaknesses and the strengths of the Nigerian people. The society has been vicious and cruel to itself, yet the strength and spirit of individuals will carry it onward.

John Carr
With updates by Paula M. Miller and Judith L. Steininger

Other major works

CHILDREN'S LITERATURE: *Chike and the River,* 1966; *How the Leopard Got His Claws,* 1972 (with John Iroaganachi); *The Drum,* 1977; *The Flute,* 1977.

ANTHOLOGIES: *The Heinemann Book of Contemporary African Short Stories,* 1992 (with C.L. Innes); *Aka Weta: An Anthology of Ibo Poetry,* 1978; *Don't Let Him Die: An Anthology of Memorial Poems for Christopher Okigbo, 1932-1967,* 1978 (with Dubem Okafor); *African Short Stories,* 1985 (with C. L. Innes); *Beyond Hunger in Africa,* 1990 (with others).

NOVELS: *Things Fall Apart,* 1958; *No Longer at Ease,* 1960; *Arrow of God,* 1964; *A Man of the People,* 1966; *Anthills of the Savannah,* 1987.

MISCELLANEOUS: *Another Africa,* 1998 (poems and essay; photographs by Robert Lyons).

NONFICTION: *Morning Yet on Creation Day,* 1975; *The Trouble with Nigeria,* 1983; *Hopes and Impediments,* 1988; *Conversations with Chinua Achebe,* 1997 (Bernth Lindfors, editor); *Home and Exile,* 2000.

POETRY: *Beware: Soul Brother, and Other Poems,* 1971, 1972; *Christmas in Biafra, and Other Poems,* 1973; *Collected Poems,* 2004.

Bibliography

Achebe, Chinua. "The Art of Fiction CXXXIX: Chinua Achebe." Interview by Jerome Brooks. *The Paris Review* 36 (Winter, 1994): 142-166. In this interview, Achebe discusses his schooling, work as a broadcaster, and views on other writers, as well as the nature of his writing process and the political situation in Nigeria.

_____. *Home and Exile.* New York: Oxford University Press, 2000. Exploration, based on Achebe's own experiences as a reader and a writer, of contemporary African literature and the Western literature that both influenced and misrepresented it.

Booker, M. Keith, ed. *The Chinua Achebe Encyclopedia.* Westport, Conn.: Greenwood Press, 2003. Helpful reference in an encyclopedia format.

Ezenwa-Ohaeto. *Chinua Achebe: A Biography.* Bloomington: Indiana University Press, 1997. Full-length biography of Achebe, this book benefits from its author's insights as a former student of Achebe's, a native of Nigeria, and a speaker of Igbo. Ezenwa-Ohaeto examines Achebe's life and literary contributions and places them within their social, historical, and cultural contexts. Written with the cooperation of Achebe and his family, the book includes several rare and revealing photographs. Includes bibliographical references and an index.

Gikandi, Simon. *Reading Chinua Achebe: Language and Ideology in Fiction.* Portsmouth, N.H.: Heinemann, 1991. Analyzes Achebe's short stories and novels.

Joseph, Michael Scott. "A Pre-modernist Reading of 'The Drum': Chinua Achebe and the Theme of the Eternal Return." *Ariel* 28 (January, 1997): 149-166. In this special issue on colonialism, postcolonialism, and children's literature, Achebe's "The Drum" is discussed as a satirical attack on European colonial values and a text dominated by nostalgia for a lost Golden Age.

Lindfors, Bernth, ed. *Conversations with Chinua Achebe.* Jackson: University Press of Mississippi, 1997. Twenty interviews with Achebe in which he discusses African oral tradition, the need for political commitment, the relationship between his novels and his short stories, his use of myth and fable, and other issues concerning being a writer.

Olubunmi Smith, Pamela J. "Dead Men's Path." In *Masterplots II: Short Story Series,* edited by Charles E. May. Rev. ed. Vol. 2. Pasadena, Calif.: Salem Press, 2004. Analysis of "Dead Men's Path" with sections on themes and meaning and style and technique. Also includes a detailed synopsis of the story.

Petersen, Kirsten Holst, and Anna Rutherford, eds. *Chinua Achebe: A Celebration.* Portsmouth, N.H.: Heinemann, 1991. Compilation of essays analyzing Achebe's work to honor his sixtieth birthday.

Alice Adams

Born: Fredericksburg, Virginia; August 14, 1926
Died: San Francisco, California; May 27, 1999

Principal short fiction • *Beautiful Girl*, 1979; *To See You Again*, 1982; *Molly's Dog*, 1983; *Return Trips*, 1985; *After You've Gone*, 1989; *The Last Lovely City: Stories*, 1999; *The Stories of Alice Adams*, 2002.

Other literary forms • Though Alice Adams was first successful in short fiction, she also published several novels, including *Careless Love* (1966), *Families and Survivors* (1974), *Listening to Billie* (1978), *Rich Rewards* (1980), *Superior Women* (1984), *Second Chances* (1988), *Caroline's Daughters* (1991), *Almost Perfect* (1993), *A Southern Exposure* (1995), *Medicine Men* (1997), and *After the War* (2000). In addition, her story "Roses, Rhododendrons" appeared as an illustrated gift book.

Achievements • Alice Adams did not publish her first collection of stories until she was in her fifties, but she quickly assumed a place among the leading practitioners of the genre. Twenty-two of her stories have appeared in *Prize Stories: The O. Henry Awards*. A full collection of her stories appeared in 2002, three years after her death. In 1976, Adams received a grant from the National Endowment for the Arts and, in 1978, she received a John Simon Guggenheim Memorial Foundation Fellowship. In 1982, Adams received the O. Henry Special Award for Continuing Achievement, given for only the third time; her predecessors were Joyce Carol Oates (in 1970) and John Updike (in 1976). She also received the American Academy of Arts and Letters Award in literature in 1992.

Biography • Alice Boyd Adams was born in Fredericksburg, Virginia, on August 14, 1926, the daughter of Nicholson Adams, a professor, and Agatha (née Boyd) Adams, a writer. Shortly after her birth, the family moved to Chapel Hill, North Carolina, where Adams spent her first sixteen years. After receiving her bachelor's degree from Radcliffe College in 1946, she married Mark Linenthal, Jr. Two years later, they moved to California, and in 1951, their only child, Peter, was born. Their marriage ended in divorce in 1958, following which Adams held a number of part-time clerical, secretarial, and bookkeeping jobs while rearing her son and writing short stories.

It was not until 1969 that she broke into the magazine market when *The New Yorker* bought her story "Gift of Grass." Since then, her stories have continued to appear in *The New Yorker* as well as *Redbook, McCall's*, and *The Paris Review*. In addition, Adams taught at the University of California at Davis, the University of California at Berkeley, and Stanford University. She died on May 27, 1999, in San Francisco after being treated for heart problems.

Analysis • Most of Alice Adams's stories revolve around common themes, and her characters, mostly educated, upper-middle-class women, are defined by a set of common traits and situations which reappear in somewhat different combinations. They find their lives flawed, often by unhappy relationships with lovers, husbands, parents, friends, sometimes with combinations of these, usually with a living antagonist, occasionally with one already dead. Often, they resolve these problems, but sometimes they do not.

Frequently, the tensions of Adams's plots are resolved when her central female characters learn something new or find a new source of strength, which enables them to part with unsatisfactory husbands, lovers, or friends. Claire, in "Home Is Where" (in *Beautiful Girl*), leaves both an unsatisfactory marriage and a miserable love affair in San Francisco, where she feels "ugly—drained, discolored, old," to spend the summer with her parents in her North Carolina hometown, where she had been young and "if not beautiful, sought after." Refreshed and stimulated by the sensual landscape and a summertime affair, Claire returns to San Francisco to divorce her husband, take leave of her unpleasant lover, and, eventually, to remarry, this time happily. Cynthia, in "The Break-in" (*To See You Again*), finds herself so different from her fiancé Roger, when he automatically blames the burglary of his home on "Mexicans," that she leaves him without a word. The narrator of "True Colors" (*To See You Again*) discovers, in Las Vegas, David's ugly side as an obsessive gambler and leaves him: "From then on I was going to be all right, I thought." Clover Baskerville in "The Party-Givers" (*To See You Again*) leaves behind her malicious friends when she realizes that she need not call them if she does not want to see them. All these characters have learned that "home is where the heart" not only "is" but also chooses to be.

Adams's heroines sometimes reach out from their lonely and isolated lives to find sympathetic bonds with poor or troubled people from other cultures. In "Greyhound People" (*To See You Again*), a divorced, middle-aged woman's discovery of kinship with her (mostly black and poor) fellow commuters, along with her discovery that her commuter ticket will take her anywhere in California, is so liberating that she can finally break free of her repressive, domineering roommate and friend Hortense. In "Verlie I Say unto You" (*Beautiful Girl*), Jessica Todd's sensitivity to her black maid Verlie's humanity underscores a fundamental difference between herself and her insensitive husband (see also "The Break-in" in this regard).

In "Mexican Dust" (*To See You Again*), Marian comes to prefer the company of the Mexican peasants to that of her husband, friends, and other Americans as they bus through Mexico on vacation; she abandons her party and returns to Seattle, where she plans to study Spanish, presumably to prepare for a return to Mexico alone. In fact, one sign of a strong character in Adams's stories is a marked sensitivity to other cultures. Elizabeth, in the story by that name, purchases her Mexican beach house in the name of her Mexican servant Aurelia and leaves Aurelia in full possession of the house at her death. The central focus in "La Señora" (*Return Trips*) is the friendship between a wealthy, elderly American woman, who vacations annually at a Mexican resort, and Teodola, the Mexican maid in charge of her hotel room. Adams's own concern for the human plight of those of other cultures can be seen in "Teresa," in *Return Trips*, a story about the privation, terror, and grief of a Mexican peasant woman.

"Molly's Dog" and "A Public Pool" • In two of Adams's most effective stories, female protagonists learn to live confidently with themselves: "Molly's Dog" and "A Public Pool" (both from *Return Trips*). In the former, Molly returns with her homosexual friend Sandy to a small cabin by the ocean, where she experienced a love affair so intense she cannot think of it without weeping. A friendly dog attaches itself to them on the beach and follows them as they leave; Molly pleads with Sandy to go back for the dog, but he drives faster, and the dog, though running, falls back and shrinks in the distance. Molly and Sandy quarrel over the dog, and Molly, realizing that she is much too dependent on men, comes to see less of Sandy back in San Francisco. She finally learns to think of the dog without pain but cannot forget it, and the place by the ocean becomes in her memory "a place where she had lost, or left something of infinite value. A place to which she would not go back."

In "A Public Pool," the protagonist, though working class, neither part of the literary or artistic world nor so well educated as many of Adams's female characters, shares with many of them a dissatisfaction with her body and a sense of being cut off and alone. She cannot bear to meet people or even look for a job ("We wouldn't even have room for you," she imagines an employer saying), so that life at the age of thirty is a grim existence in a cold apartment with a penurious mother. Though swimming offers an escape from home and a chance for meeting new people, it also has its fears: of exposing her body in the locker room and enduring the rebukes of strangers, of the faster swimmers whose lane she blocks, of the blond-bearded man who goes by so swiftly that he splashes her, and of a large black woman who tells her that she should stay by the side of the pool.

After a few months of lap swimming, her body changes and her fear of others lessens. An early remark of the blond-bearded man made her babble nervously, but now she responds to his conventional questions with brief assent. On the day the black lady compliments her on her stroke and they leave the pool together, she is finally able to find a job and thinks of moving out of her mother's apartment. She walks happily about the neighborhood, thinking that she and the black woman might become friends. At that moment, she meets in the street the blond-bearded man, who smells of chewing gum and is wearing "sharp" clothes from Sears. He invites her for coffee, but, "overwhelmed" by the smell of gum and realizing that "I hate sharp clothes," she makes her excuses. Like other Adams women, she has experienced loneliness, but, also like many other women in these stories, she finds new strength that will mitigate her isolation by giving her independence. Yet it is primarily achieved by herself, and Adams's always masterful use of language here is especially striking. As Adams's character goes off independently from the blond-bearded man, she says confidently, "I leave him standing there. I swim away."

"You Are What You Own" and "To See You Again" • Not all these stories, however, end so conclusively; in others, it is unclear whether the heroines' chosen resolutions to the problems confronting them will be satisfactory. The young housewife of "You Are What You Own: A Notebook" (*Return Trips*) lives in a house crammed with her domineering mother's furniture, which the girl seems doomed to polish for all eternity. Her boring graduate-student husband complains that she does not polish the furniture enough and even starts to do it himself. She escapes in fantasy, fictionalizing the artists who live in a house down the street from her, assigning them her own names (not knowing their real ones), and indulging in imagined conversations with them. At the end of the story—recorded in her notebook—she tells her husband in a letter that she is leaving him the furniture and going to look for a job in San Francisco. Does she go? Is she capable? Similarly, the lonely young wife in "To See You Again" uses the image of a beautiful adolescent boy in her class to re-create the image of her husband as he was when they fell in love—slim and energetic, not as he is now, overweight and frequently paralyzed by chronic, severe depression. The story ends with her fantasizing that somehow she has escaped her grim life with him, that things are as they once were, her husband somehow reclaimed in the body of the young student.

"Beautiful Girl" • The story plots summarized here raise a possible objection to Adams's fiction—that many of her female characters are too obsessed with the attention of men, even to the point where the women's own highly successful careers seem to matter little. This issue, however, must be placed in historical perspective. Most of the women in her stories, like Adams herself, grew up and entered adulthood during the period after World War II, when women's roles in American society were constricted, when women were sent home from their wartime jobs to take on what then seemed an almost patriotic duty: submitting themselves to the roles of wife and mother. From this point of view, Adams's female characters are victims of that culture, dependent on men and falling desperately in love with them because they were expected to do just that. Given these crushing expectations, it is no wonder that Adams's heroines feel lost when bereft, by divorce or widowhood, of the men in their lives. The young people in these stories often reach out to surrogate parents, usually mothers, when the incredible strain on the postwar nuclear family cracks and splinters it (a character in "Roses, Rhododendrons," in *Beautiful Girl*, says "we all need more than one set of parents—our relations with the original set are too intense, and need dissipating").

Emblematic of the plight of this generation is Ardis Bascombe in "Beautiful Girl," an ironic title because Ardis, though in her youth beautiful and popular, is now fleshy, drinking herself to death in her San Francisco apartment. She has failed as a wife and, as her filthy kitchen attests, failed as a homemaker. She had been independent enough to leave her unhappy marriage, but, like other women of her generation, despite her intelligence, idealism, courage, and sophistication, she was unable to make a new life. The life of this beautiful girl demonstrates graphically the destructive pressures on postwar women.

The Last Lovely City • In this, her final collection of stories, Alice Adams also focuses on sophisticated contemporary women dealing with wandering husbands, belligerent children, and the tribulations of being divorced or widowed; however, because Adams was in her late sixties when she wrote most of these stories, her protagonists are older, albeit not always wiser, veterans of the domestic wars of the 1960's and 1970's.

Adams was always a favorite of the judges of *Prize Stories: The O. Henry Awards*, and three of these stories were chosen for that prestigious collection: "The Islands" in 1993, "The Haunted Beach" in 1995, and "His Women" in 1996. Two of these are among the best stories in the collection, for they economically and without self-indulgence focus on futile efforts to repeat the past. What "haunts" the beach in "The Haunted Beach" is one woman's previous marriage. Penelope Jaspers, a San Francisco art dealer, takes her new lover, a middle-aged superior court judge, to a West Coast Mexican resort that she and her dead husband used to visit. Although she remembers it as charming, she now sees it as "unspeakably shabby" and returns to San Francisco, having decided not to marry the judge.

The persistence of the past also haunts "His Women," as a university professor cannot reconcile with his lover because of memories of the previous women in his life. In the title story, Benito Zamora, a Mexican cardiologist and "sadhearted widow," is forced to dredge up unpleasant moments from his past by an attractive young reporter who he mistakenly thinks is interested in him sexually. In "Old Love Affairs," a woman's living room is filled with keepsakes that remind her only that she is growing old and can no longer hope for love in her life.

The last four stories in the book—"The Drinking Club," "Patients," "The Wrong Mexico," and "Earthquake Damage"—are linked stories, somewhat like chapters of a novella, in which two Bay Area psychiatrists, who are sometimes lovers, move in and out of various affairs. Both are passive professionals, as are many Adams characters— watchers rather than active participants, caught in a recurrent round of unhappy marriages and unfulfilling affairs.

The weakest stories in the collection—"The Islands," "Raccoons," and "A Very Nice Dog"—are simple paeans to pets. The most interesting, "The Islands," begins with the sentence: "What does it mean to love an animal, a pet, in my case a cat, in the fierce, entire and unambivalent way that some of us do?" Although readers who share such a pet passion might find the question intriguing, many others will view this story about the death of a beloved cat as sentimental rather than sensitive. Although the fact that Adams died at the age of seventy-two, a few months after this book appeared, gives it some poignancy, on a purely critical level, these stories represent a falling off from the crisp and sophisticated stories of the writer in her prime.

Timothy C. Frazer
With updates by Louise M. Stone and Charles E. May

Other major works

NOVELS: *Careless Love*, 1966; *Families and Survivors*, 1974; *Listening to Billie*, 1978; *Rich Rewards*, 1980; *Superior Women*, 1984; *Second Chances*, 1988; *Caroline's Daughters*, 1991; *Almost Perfect*, 1993; *A Southern Exposure*, 1995; *Medicine Men*, 1997; *After the War*, 2000.

NONFICTION: *Mexico: Some Travels and Some Travelers There*, 1990.

Bibliography

Adams, Alice. Interview by Patricia Holt. *Publishers Weekly* 213 (January 16, 1978): 8-9. In talking about her life with interior designer Robert McNee, Adams emphasizes the importance of her work as the foundation for the self-respect necessary in a long-term relationship.

Blades, L. T. "Order and Chaos in Alice Adams' *Rich Rewards.*" *Critique: Studies in Modern Fiction* 27 (Summer, 1986): 187-195. In an issue devoted to four women writers—Adams, Ann Beattie, Mary Gordon, and Marge Piercy—Blades explores the artificially imposed order created by Adams's female characters and the world of chaos that threatens it. Like Jane Austen's characters, Adams's women enter into unstable relationships but eventually realize that they must concentrate on work and friendships, not romance, to have a healthy self-respect.

Bolotin, Susan. "Semidetached Couples." Review of *The Last Lovely City: Stories. The New York Times*, February 14, 1999. Detailed review of Adams's collection, commenting on several of the stories, particularly the characters and the social world in which they live.

Chell, Cara. "Succeeding in Their Times: Alice Adams on Women and Work." *Soundings* 68 (Spring, 1985): 62-71. Work is the catalyst that enables Adams's characters to realize their self-worth. Chell provides an interesting treatment of this theme throughout Adams's career.

Flower, Dean. "Picking Up the Pieces." *The Hudson Review* 32 (Summer, 1979): 293-307. Flower sets Adams among other American storytellers who look to the past for explanations and intensification of feelings. He explores how this orientation leads to a preoccupation with growing old.

Herman, Barbara A. "Alice Adams." In *Contemporary Fiction Writers of the South*, edited by Joseph M. Flora and Robert Bain. Westport, Conn.: Greenwood Press, 1993. Brief biography and discussion of Adams's novels and short stories; suggests her two major themes are the maturation of middle-class women seeking self-respect, identity, and independence and women's relationships with husbands, lovers, and friends. Includes a survey of Adams's own criticism and a bibliography of works by and about her.

May, Charles E., ed. *Masterplots II: Short Story Series, Revised Edition.* 8 vols. Pasadena, Calif.: Salem Press, 2004. Designed for student use, this reference set contains articles providing detailed plot summaries and analyses of these four short stories by Adams: "Greyhound People" (vol. 3); "Roses, Rhododendron" (vol. 6); and "Snow" and "Truth or Consequences" (vol. 7).

Pritchard, William H. "Fictive Voices." *The Hudson Review* 38 (Spring, 1985): 120-132. Pritchard examines Adams's narrative voice in the context of other contemporary writers. Though the section on Adams is not long, it provides a useful approach to analyzing her stories.

Upton, Lee. "Changing the Past: Alice Adams' Revisionary Nostalgia." *Studies in Short Fiction* 26 (Winter, 1989): 33-41. In the collection of stories, *Return Trips*, Adams's female characters turn to memories of the past as their most valued possessions. Upton isolates three different relationships with the past and shows how each enables Adams's characters to interpret nostalgic images so that they produce more satisfying relationships with the present.

Woo, Elaine. "Alice Adams." *Los Angeles Times*, May 29, 1999, p. B8. Biographical and critical sketch and tribute; notes Adams's specialization in contemporary relationships among white, urban, middle- and upper-class women; charts her career and her critical reception.

Conrad Aiken

Born: Savannah, Georgia; August 5, 1889
Died: Savannah, Georgia; August 17, 1973

Principal short fiction • *The Dark City*, 1922; *Bring! Bring!, and Other Stories*, 1925; *Costumes by Eros*, 1928; "Silent Snow, Secret Snow", 1932; *Impulse*, 1933; *Among the Lost People*, 1934; "Round by Round", 1935; *Short Stories*, 1950; *Collected Short Stories*, 1960; *Collected Short Stories of Conrad Aiken*, 1966.

Other literary forms • Best known as a poet, Conrad Aiken published dozens of volumes of poetry from 1914 until his death in 1973. He also published novels, essays, criticism, and a play. In addition, he edited a considerable number of anthologies of poetry.

Achievements • Conrad Aiken's reputation as a writer of short fiction rests on two frequently anthologized short stories: "Silent Snow, Secret Snow," which has twice been adapted to film, and "Mr. Arcularis," which was adapted to a play. Although he published several collections of short stories—they were collected in one volume in 1950—he did not contribute significantly to the development of the short story.

Biography • When Conrad Aiken was eleven, his father killed his mother and then committed suicide. This incident could very well have influenced the subject matter of a great number of his stories, where one step more may take a character to an immense abyss of madness or death. After graduating from Harvard University in 1911, Aiken became a member of the famous Harvard group that included T. S. Eliot, Robert Benchley, and Van Wyck Brooks. He published his first volume of poems in 1914. A contributing editor of *The Dial* from 1917 to 1919, Aiken later worked as London correspondent for *The New Yorker*. Through the course of his career he was the recipient of many awards, including the Pulitzer Prize in 1930 for *Selected Poems* (1929), the National Book Award in 1954 for *Collected Poems* (1953), and the Bollingen Prize in Poetry in 1956. He died in 1973 at the age of eighty-four.

Analysis • The fictional "voice" in Aiken's stories so closely approximates his poetic "voice" that his stories are often seen as extensions of his more famous poems. His best-known stories, "Silent Snow, Secret Snow" and "Mr. Arcularis" are both "poetic" expressions of characters' psychological states. "Silent Snow, Secret Snow," in fact, is often read as the story of a creative artist, a "poet" in a hostile environment. Aiken's Freudian themes, his depiction of a protagonist's inner struggle and journey, and his portrait of the consciousness—these are perhaps better expressed in lengthy poetic works than in prose or in individual poems, which are rarely anthologized because they are best read in the context of his other poems.

"Silent Snow, Secret Snow" • In "Silent Snow, Secret Snow," a story once included in almost every anthology of short fiction, Conrad Aiken describes a young boy's alienation and withdrawal from his world. The story begins one morning in December when Paul Hasleman, aged twelve, thinks of the postman, whom the boy hears every morning. The progress of the postman as he turns the corner at the top of the hill and makes his way down the street with a double knock at each door is familiar to the boy, and, as he slowly awakens, he begins to listen for the sounds on the cobblestones of the street of heavy boots as they come around the corner. When the sounds come on this morning, however, they are closer than the corner and muffled and faint. Paul understands at once: "Nothing could have been simpler—there had been snow during the night, such as all winter he had been longing for." With his eyes still closed, Paul imagines the snow—how it sounds and how it will obliterate the familiar sights of the street—but when he opens his eyes and turns toward the window, he sees only the bright morning sun. The miracle of snow has not transformed anything.

The moment and his feelings about the snow, however, remain with him, and later in the classroom as his geography teacher, Miss Buell, twirls the globe with her finger and talks about the tropics, Paul finds himself looking at the arctic areas, which are colored white on the globe. He recalls the morning and the moment when he had a sense of falling snow, and immediately he undergoes the same experience of seeing and hearing the snow fall.

As the days go by, Paul finds himself between two worlds—the real one and a secret one of peace and remoteness. His parents become increasingly concerned by his "daydreaming," inattentive manner, but more and more he is drawn into the incomprehensible beauty of the world of silent snow. His secret sense of possession and of being protected insulates him both from the world of the classroom, where Deidre, with the freckles on the back of her neck in a constellation exactly like the Big Dipper, waves her brown flickering hand, and from the world at home where his parents' concern and questions have become an increasingly difficult matter with which to cope.

Aiken's presentation of the escalation of Paul's withdrawal is skillfully detailed through the use of symbols. The outside world becomes for Paul fragmented: scraps of dirty newspapers in a drain, with the word Eczema as the addressee and an address in Fort Worth, Texas; lost twigs from parent trees; bits of broken egg shells; the footprints of a dog who long ago "had made a mistake" and walked on the river of wet cement which in time had frozen into rock; the wound in an elm tree. In the company of his parents Paul neither sees them nor feels their presence. His mother is a voice asking questions, his father a pair of brown slippers. These images cluster together in such a way as to foreshadow the relentless progress of Dr. Howells down the street to Paul's house, a visit which replicates the progress of the postman.

The doctor, called by the parents because their concern has now grown into alarm over Paul's behavior, examines the boy, and, as the examination and questioning by the adults accelerate, Paul finds the situation unbearable. He retreats further into his secret world where he sees snow now slowly filling the spaces in the room—highest in the corners, under the sofa—the snow's voice a whisper, a promise of peace, cold and restful. Reassured by the presence of the snow and seduced by its whisperings and promises, Paul begins to laugh and to taunt the adults with little hints. He believes they are trying to corner him, and there is something malicious in his behavior:

> He laughed a third time—but this time, happening to glance upward toward his mother's face, he was appalled at the effect his laughter seemed to have upon her. Her mouth had opened in an expression of horror. This was too bad! Unfortunate! He had known it would cause pain, of course—but he hadn't expected it to be quite as bad as this. . . .

The hints, however, explain nothing to the adults, and, continuing to
feel cornered, Paul pleads a head-
ache and tries to escape to bed. His
mother follows him, but it is too
late. "The darkness was coming in
long white waves," and "the snow
was laughing; it spoke from all sides
at once." His mother's presence in
the room is alien, hostile, and brutal. He is filled with loathing, and he
exorcizes her: "Mother! Mother! Go
away! I hate you!" With this effort,
everything is solved, "everything became all right." His withdrawal is
now complete. All contact with the
real world is lost, and he gives himself over to a "vast moving screen of
snow—but even now it said peace, it
said remoteness, it said cold, it said
sleep." Paul's withdrawal is, as the

Library of Congress

snow tells him, a going inward rather
than an opening outward: "It is a flower becoming a seed," it is a movement toward
complete solipsism and a closure of his life.

"Strange Moonlight" • "Strange Moonlight," another story of a young boy's difficulty in dealing with the realities of life and death, could be a prelude to "Silent
Snow, Secret Snow." In "Strange Moonlight" a young boy filches a copy of Poe's tales
from his mother's bookshelf and in consequence spends a "delirious night in inferno." The next day the boy wins a gold medal at school which he later carries in his
pocket, keeping it a secret from his mother and father. The desire to keep a secret recalls Paul's need to keep from his parents his first hallucination of snow. The gold
medal is "above all a secret," something to be kept concealed; it is like a particularly
beautiful trinket to be carried unmentioned in his trouser pocket.

The week's events include a visit to a friend's house where the boy meets Caroline
Lee, an extraordinarily strange and beautiful child with large pale eyes. Both Caroline Lee and the house in which she lives, with its long, dark, and winding stairways,
excite and fascinate him. Within a few days, however, the boy learns that Caroline
Lee is dead of scarlet fever. He is stunned: "How did it happen that he, who was so
profoundly concerned, had not been consulted, had not been invited to come and
talk with her, and now found himself so utterly and hopelessly and forever excluded—from the house as from her?" This becomes a thing he cannot understand.

The same night he is confronted with another disturbing mystery. He overhears
an intimate conversation between his father and mother. Filled with horror, the boy
begins at once to imagine a conversation with Caroline Lee in which she comes back
from the grave to talk with him. The next day his father unexpectedly takes the family
to the beach, and the boy wanders away and finds a snug, secret hiding place on a
lonely hot sand dune. He lies there surrounded by tall whispering grass, and Caroline's imagined visit of the night before becomes real for him. Rather than ending in

unreality as one would expect, however, Aiken inexplicably brings the boy back to reality without resolving any of the problems set up in the story. He thus leaves a gap between the protagonist's conflicts with sexuality, reality, and unreality, and their final resolution.

"Your Obituary, Well Written" • In another story, however, "Your Obituary, Well Written," Aiken presents a young man identified only as Mr. Grant, who confronts a similar circumstance. Told in the first person by the protagonist, Mr. Grant, the story repeats what is basically the same pattern of events. Although supposedly a portrait of Katherine Mansfield, to whom Aiken is strongly indebted for the forms his stories take, the character of Reiner Wilson is also strongly reminiscent of Caroline Lee, the little girl in "Strange Moonlight." The narrator says of Reiner Wilson: "I was struck by the astonishing frailty of her appearance, an otherworld fragility, almost a transparent spiritual quality—as if she were already a disembodied soul." Knowing from the first that she is not only married but also fatally ill, he manages to see her one time and fall in love with her, and then he almost simultaneously withdraws. "At bottom, however, it was a kind of terror that kept me away. . . . The complications and the miseries, if we did allow the meetings to go further might well be fatal to both of us."

The same conflicts which Paul, the child in "Silent Snow, Secret Snow," experienced are again faced by the man who is not able to resolve the riddles of sex and love, life and death. The narrator never sees Reiner again, and at her death he is left on a park bench under a Judas tree wanting to weep, but unable to: "But Reiner Wilson, the dark-haired little girl with whom I had fallen in love was dead, and it seemed to me that I too was dead." Another similarity between "Silent Snow, Secret Snow" and "Your Obituary, Well Written" is Aiken's use of a natural element as major metaphor. In "Your Obituary, Well Written," rain functions in the same manner that snow does in "Silent Snow, Secret Snow." During Grant's one meeting alone with Reiner Wilson, the room had suddenly darkened, and rain fell, sounding to him as though it were inside the room. The sensations the man feels in response to the rain are similar to those Paul feels in response to the snow. Grant tells Reiner about a time when as a boy he went swimming, and it began to rain:

> The water was smooth—there was no sound of waves—and all about me arose a delicious *seething*. . . [T]here was something sinister in it, and also something divinely soothing. I don't believe I was ever happier in my life. It was as if I had gone into another world.

Reiner calls Grant "the man who loves rain," and her estimate of him is correct. Unable to open up himself, unable to make himself vulnerable and live in the real world, he is at the end of the story as withdrawn from reality as is Paul, who chooses the silent and secret snow.

"Thistledown" • Besides dealing with various subconscious desires projected by means of hallucinating visions, many of Aiken's stories reflect preoccupations of the times in which the stories were written. Chief among these themes is the changing roles of women and sexual mores of the 1920's. In most of Aiken's stories, these conflicts are presented through the male point of view.

"Thistledown," a first-person narrative told by a man who is married and living with his wife, opens with private musings of the narrator, wherein he associates a young woman named Coralyn with thistledown, which is being swept in every direction by the wind but which is ultimately doomed for extinction. Coralyn had been his wife's secretary, and, attracted to her, Phillip, the narrator, became bent on seduction. Far from being "frighteningly unworldly," Coralyn is a "new woman" who has had numerous lovers. He finds her cynical and detached, she finds him an old-fashioned and sentimental fool. The affair is brief. Coralyn leaves, and as the years pass she is in and out of his life, until she disappears altogether, leaving him bitter, disappointed, and angry. The irony that marks "Thistledown" is characteristic of the stories in which Aiken examines the conventional sexual mores, holding a double-faced mirror to reflect the double standard by which men and women are judged.

"A Conversation" • In "A Conversation," the theme of double standards is examined within the framework of a conversation between two men, probably professors, taking place on a train in a sleeping car. The conversation is overheard by a visiting lecturer at the University who occupies the adjacent sleeping car. The lecturer is tired of "being polite to fools" and wants desperately to go to sleep; but the conversation he overhears keeps him awake, as do clock bells that ring marking every quarter hour. The conversation concerns the fiancée of one of the men, and the other is trying to convince his friend that the woman is not as innocent as she looks; indeed, she has been "manhandled." The engaged man keeps trying to protect his own views of the woman: her central idealism, her essential holiness—views that attach themselves to women who are not prostitutes. By the end of the story, however, the point is made; the engagement will not last, and the woman will be put aside like a used razor or a cork that has been tampered with, images used earlier in the story. The clock bells do not ask a question; they simply continue to toll. In the end, the men cannot accept a female sexuality which is not exclusively directed toward a husband, although there is never a question about their own sexual behavior.

Mary Rohrberger
With updates by Thomas L. Erskine

Other major works

PLAYS: *Fear No More*, 1946, pb. 1957 (as *Mr. Arcularis: A Play*).

ANTHOLOGIES: *A Comprehensive Anthology of American Poetry*, 1929, 1944; *Twentieth Century American Poetry*, 1944.

NOVELS: *Blue Voyage*, 1927; *Great Circle*, 1933; *King Coffin*, 1935; *A Heart for the Gods of Mexico*, 1939; *Conversation: Or, Pilgrim's Progress*, 1940; *The Collected Novels of Conrad Aiken*, 1964.

NONFICTION: *Skepticisms: Notes on Contemporary Poetry*, 1919; *Ushant: An Essay*, 1952; *A Reviewer's ABC: Collected Criticism of Conrad Aiken from 1916 to the Present*, 1958; *Selected Letters of Conrad Aiken*, 1978.

POETRY: *Earth Triumphant, and Other Tales in Verse*, 1914; *The Jig of Forslin*, 1916; *Turns and Movies, and Other Tales in Verse*, 1916; *Nocturne of Remembered Spring, and Other Poems*, 1917; *Senlin: A Biography, and Other Poems*, 1918; *The Charnel Rose*, 1918; *The House of Dust*, 1920; *Punch: The Immortal Liar*, 1921; *Priapus and the Pool*, 1922; *The Pilgrimage of Festus*, 1923; *Changing Mind*, 1925; *Priapus and the Pool, and Other Poems*, 1925; *Prelude*, 1929; *Selected Poems*, 1929; *Gehenna*, 1930; *John Deth: A Metaphysical Legend, and Other Poems*, 1930; *Preludes for Memnon*, 1931; *The Coming Forth by Day of Osiris Jones*, 1931; *And in the Hanging Gardens*, 1933; *Landscape West of Eden*, 1934; *Time in the Rock: Preludes to Definition*, 1936; *And in the Human Heart*, 1940; *Brownstone Eclogues*, *and Other Poems,* 1942; *The Soldier: A Poem by Conrad Aiken,* 1944; *The Kid,* 1947; *Skylight One: Fifteen Poems,* 1949; *The Divine Pilgrim,* 1949; *Wake II,* 1952; *Collected Poems,* 1953, 1970; *A Letter from Li Po, and Other Poems,* 1955; *The Fluteplayer,* 1956; *Sheepfold Hill: Fifteen Poems,* 1958; *Selected Poems,* 1961; *The Morning Song of Lord Zero,* 1963; *A Seizure of Limericks,* 1964; *Cats and Bats and Things with Wings: Poems,* 1965; *The Clerk's Journal,* 1971; *A Little Who's Zoo of Mild Animals,* 1977.

Bibliography

Aiken, Conrad. *Selected Letters of Conrad Aiken.* Edited by Joseph Killorin. New Haven, Conn.: Yale University Press, 1978. Includes a representative sample of 245 letters (from some three thousand) written by Aiken. A cast of correspondents, among them T. S. Eliot and Malcolm Lowry, indexes to Aiken's works and important personages, and a wealth of illustrations, mostly photographs, add considerably to the value of the volume.

Butscher, Edward. *Conrad Aiken: Poet of White Horse Vale.* Athens: University of Georgia Press, 1988. This critical biography emphasizes Aiken's literary work, particularly the poetry. Butscher's book nevertheless contains analyses of about fifteen Aiken short stories, including his most famous ones, "Silent Snow, Secret Snow" and "Mr. Arcularis." Includes many illustrations, copious notes, and an extensive bibliography that is especially helpful in psychoanalytic theory.

Dirda, Michael. "Selected Letters of Conrad Aiken." *The Washington Post,* June 25, 1978, p. G5. A review of Aiken's *Selected Letters,* with a brief biographical sketch; suggests that the letters will help redress the neglect Aiken has suffered.

Hoffman, Frederick J. *Conrad Aiken.* New York: Twayne, 1962. The best overview of Aiken's short fiction. Hoffman's volume contains careful analyses of several individual stories, including "Mr. Arcularis," which receives extensive discussion. Hoffman, who believes Aiken's short stories are more successful than his novels, stresses "Aiken's attitude toward New England, his obsession with "aloneness," and his concern about human relationships. Contains a chronology, a biographical chapter, and an annotated bibliography.

Lorenz, Clarissa M. *Lorelei Two: My Life with Conrad Aiken.* Athens: University of Georgia Press, 1983. Lorenz, Aiken's second wife, discusses the 1926-1938 years, the period when he wrote his best work, including the short stories "Mr. Arcularis" and "Silent Snow, Secret Snow." She covers his literary acquaintances, his work habits, and the literary context in which he worked. The book is well indexed and contains several relevant photographs.

May, Charles E., ed. *Masterplots II: Short Story Series, Revised Edition.* 8 vols. Pasadena, Calif.: Salem Press, 2004. Designed for student use, this reference set contains articles providing detailed plot summaries and analyses of these four short stories by Aiken: "The Dark City" (vol. 2); "Impulse" (vol. 4); "Round by Round" (vol. 6); and "Silent Snow, Secret Snow" (vol. 7).

Seigal, Catharine. *The Fictive World of Conrad Aiken: A Celebration of Consciousness.* De Kalb: Northern Illinois University Press, 1993. Chapters on the Freudian foundation of Aiken's fiction, on his New England roots, and on many of his novels. Concluding chapters on Aiken's autobiography, *Ushant,* and an overview of his fiction. Includes notes, selected bibliography, and index.

Spivey, Ted R. *Time's Stop in Savannah: Conrad Aiken's Inner Journey.* Macon, Ga.: Mercer University Press, 1997. Explores Aiken's thought processes and how they translate to his fiction.

Spivey, Ted R., and Arthur Waterman, eds. *Conrad Aiken: A Priest of Consciousness.* New York: AMS Press, 1989. Though their focus is on Aiken's poetry, Spivey and Waterman include essays on the short stories and a review of criticism of the short stories. Contains an extensive chronology of Aiken's life and a lengthy description of the Aiken materials in the Huntington Library.

Womack, Kenneth. "Unmasking Another Villain in Conrad Aiken's Autobiographical Dream." *Biography* 19 (Spring, 1996): 137. Examines the role of British poet and novelist Martin Armstrong as a fictionalized character in Aiken's *Ushant*; argues that Aiken's attack on Armstrong is motivated by revenge for Armstrong's marriage to Aiken's first wife.

Sherman Alexie

Born: Spokane Indian Reservation, Wellpinit, Washington; October 7, 1966

Principal short fiction • *The Lone Ranger and Tonto Fistfight in Heaven,* 1993; *The Toughest Indian in the World,* 2000; *Ten Little Indians,* 2003.

Other literary forms • A prolific writer, Sherman Alexie has published more than three hundred stories and poems. His poetry and poetry/short fiction works include *The Business of Fancydancing* (1992), *I Would Steal Horses* (1992), *First Indian on the Moon* (1993), *Old Shirts and New Skins* (1993), *Seven Mourning Songs for the Cedar Flute I Have Yet to Learn to Play* (1994), *Water Flowing Home* (1994), *The Summer of Black Widows* (1996), *One Stick Song* (2000), and *Dangerous Astronomy* (2005). He has also written the novels *Reservation Blues* (1995), *Indian Killer* (1996), and *Flight* (2007), a contemporary story about an adolescent boy who is half Irish and half Native American.

Achievements • Sherman Alexie began accruing his numerous accolades and awards while in college, including a Washington State Arts Commission poetry fellowship (1991) and a National Endowment for the Arts poetry fellowship (1992). He also won Slipstream's fifth annual Chapbook Contest (1992), an Ernest Hemingway Foundation Award Citation, a Lila Wallace-*Reader's Digest* Writer's Award (1994), an American Book Award (1996), and The Ernest Hemingway Foundation/PEN Award for First Fiction. His first novel, *Reservation Blues* (1995), won the Before Columbus Foundation's American Book Award, the Murray Morgan Prize, and prompted Alexie to be named one of *Granta*'s Best of Young American Novelists. *Indian Killer* (1996), his second novel, was listed as a *New York Times* notable book.

Biography • A self-described Spokane/Coeur d'Alene Indian who believes "Native American" is a "guilty white liberal term," Sherman Joseph Alexie, Jr., grew up in Wellpinit, Washington, on the Spokane Indian Reservation. His father, an alcoholic, spent little time at home, and his mother supported the family by selling hand-sewn quilts at the local trading post. Born hydrocephalic, Alexie spent most of his childhood at home voraciously reading books from the local library. He later attended high school outside the reservation. His academic achievements there secured him a place at Spokane's Jesuit Gonzaga University in 1985. While there, he turned to alcohol as a means of coping with the pressure he felt to succeed. His goal to become a medical doctor was derailed by fainting spells in human anatomy class, and Alexie later transferred to Washington State University in 1987, where he began writing and then publishing his poetry and short stories. During a 1992 National Endowment for the Arts fellowship, he wrote his award-winning *The Business of Fancydancing* and *The Lone Ranger and Tonto Fistfight in Heaven*. With this success came sobriety.

Drawing on his collection of short stories in *The Lone Ranger and Tonto Fistfight in Heaven*, Alexie wrote and directed the award-winning *Smoke Signals* (1998), the first feature film ever made with an all-Native American cast and crew. Alexie, his child, and wife Diane, a member of the Hidatsa nation and college counselor, settled in Seattle, Washington.

Analysis • According to Sherman Alexie in an interview with *CINEASTE*, the five major influences on his writing are "my father, for his nontraditional Indian stories, my grandmother for her traditional Indian stories, Stephen King, John Steinbeck, and *The Brady Bunch.*" It is no wonder then that Alexie's work, in particular the short stories in *The Lone Ranger and Tonto Fistfight in Heaven*, has been described by *American Indian Quarterly* as resembling a "casebook of postmodernist theory" that revels in such things as irony, parody of traditions, and the mingling of popular and native cultures. The result is a body of work that allows Alexie to challenge and subvert the stereotypes of Native Americans seen in the mass media (the warrior, the shaman, the drunk) and explore what it means to be a contemporary Native American.

In commenting on Native American poets and writers, writers such as Leslie Marmon Silko describe how Native American artists often create their strongest work when they write from a position of social responsibility. In Alexie's case, his work is often designed to effect change by exposing other Indians and whites to the harsh realities of reservation life. In Alexie's early work—work influenced by his own alcoholism and father's abandonment (as seen in *The Lone Ranger and Tonto Fistfight in Heaven*)—he uses the Spokane Indian community as a backdrop for his characters, who often suffer from poverty, despair, and substance abuse. Yet it is his use of dark humor and irony that enables these characters to survive both their own depressions and self-loathing and the attitude and activities of the often ignorant and apathetic white society. Alexie writes in his short story "Because My Father Always Said He Was the Only Indian Who Saw Jimi Hendrix Play 'The Star-Spangled Banner' at Woodstock":

> On a reservation, Indian men who abandon their children are treated worse than white fathers who do the same thing. It's because white men have been doing that forever and Indian men have just learned how. That's how assimilation works.

With sobriety, Alexie claims that from *The Business of Fancydancing* in 1992 to *Smoke Signals* in 1998, his personal vision of Indian society has brightened and his writing has moved from focusing on the effects to the causes of substance abuse and other selfdestructive behaviors. In *CINEASTE*, Alexie describes his growth as a writer in this way:

> As I've been in recovery over the years and stayed sober, you'll see the work gradually freeing itself of alcoholism and going much deeper, exploring the emotional, sociological, and psychological reasons for any kind of addictions or dysfunctions within the [Indian] community. . . . It's more of a whole journey, you get there and you get back.

The Lone Ranger and Tonto Fistfight in Heaven • Alexie's first collection of (only) short stories, *The Lone Ranger and Tonto Fistfight in Heaven*, received much critical acclaim. Many of the Native American characters that he introduced in his earlier poetry—like the storyteller Thomas Builds-The-Fire and his friend Victor Joseph—appear here as vehicles through which Alexie illustrates how Indians survive both the hardships they face on reservations and the gulfs between similar and dissimilar cultures, time periods, and men and women.

In a number of the twenty-two often autobiographical stories in this collection, Alexie infuses irony into tales that illustrate the destructive effects of alcohol on both children and adults on reservations. For example, in "The Only Traffic Signal on the

© Marion Ettlinger

Reservation Doesn't Flash Red Any More" he weaves the tradition of storytelling with the contemporary issue of how cultures create their own heroes. In this story, the narrator and his friend Adrian, both recovering alcoholics, are sitting on a porch playing Russian roulette with a BB gun. They stop and watch a local high school basketball player walk by with his friends. As the narrator talks, readers learn that contemporary heroes on the reservation are often basketball players, and stories about their abilities are retold year after year. Yet, these heroes, including the narrator himself, often succumb to alcoholism and drop off the team. From the narrator's reminiscences, it becomes clear that, while all people need heroes in their lives, creating heroes on a reservation can be problematic.

In "A Drug Called Tradition," the narrator tells the story of Thomas Builds-The-Fire and the "second-largest party in reservation history" for which he pays with money he receives from a large utility company land lease. Although the narrator claims that "we can all hear our ancestors laughing in the trees" when Indians actually profit in this way, who the ancestors are truly laughing at is unclear. Are they laughing at the white people for spending a lot of money to put ten telephone poles across some land or the Indians for spending that money on large quantities of alcohol? Later in the story, Victor, Junior, and Thomas go off and experience a night of drug-induced hallucinations about the faraway past, the present, and future. In the present, the boys return to a time before they ever had their first drink of alcohol. From this story, readers learn that it is best for people to stay in the present and keep persevering and not become stuck in the past or an imagined future.

Several of the stories in *The Lone Ranger and Tonto Fistfight in Heaven* that were eventually adapted for the film *Smoke Signals* explore both the connections and fissures between people of different genders and similar or dissimilar cultures. In "Every Little Hurricane," readers are introduced to nine-year-old Victor, who is awakened from his frequent nightmares by one of the many family fights, this one occurring between his uncles during a New Year's Eve party. Memories of other seasonal alcohol and poverty-induced "hurricanes" ensue, such as that of the Christmas his father could not afford any gifts. At the end of the story, as all the relatives and neighbors pick themselves up and go home, Victor lies down between his father and mother, hoping that the alcohol in their bodies will seep into his and help him sleep. This story is about how Indians continue to be "eternal survivors" of many types of storms.

In "Because My Father Always Said He Was the Only Indian Who Saw Jimi Hendrix Play 'The Star-Spangled Banner' at Woodstock," the narrator details the love-hate relationship between his mother and his father (who would later leave the family), while using a popular music icon to illustrate how Native Americans and whites share at least one common culture. The narrator of this story, the abandoned Victor, later teams up with former childhood friend and storyteller Thomas in "This Is What It Means to Say Phoenix, Arizona," to collect Victor's father's ashes in Phoenix. In their ensuing journey, the characters grow spiritually and emotionally, while exploring what it means today to be a Native American.

Lisa-Anne Culp

Other major works

NOVELS: *Reservation Blues*, 1995; *Indian Killer*, 1996; *Flight*, 2007.

MISCELLANEOUS: *The Business of Fancydancing: Stories and Poems*, 1992; *First Indian on the Moon*, 1993; *The Summer of Black Widows*, 1996 (poems and short prose).

POETRY: *I Would Steal Horses*, 1992; *Old Shirts and New Skins*, 1993; *The Man Who Loves Salmon*, 1998; *One Stick Song*, 2000; *Dangerous Astronomy*, 2005.

SCREENPLAYS: *Smoke Signals*, 1998; *The Business of Fancydancing*, 2002.

Bibliography

Alexie, Sherman. "Sending Cinematic Smoke Signals: An Interview with Sherman Alexie." Interview by Dennis West. *CINEASTE* 23, no. 4 (1998): 28-32. Discusses both the film *Smoke Signals* and short stories in *The Lone Ranger and Tonto Fistfight in Heaven*, followed by an interview with Alexie about his early influences and work.

Andrews, Candace E. "This Is What It Means to Say Phoenix, Arizona." In *Masterplots II: Short Story Series*, edited by Charles E. May. Rev. ed. Vol. 7. Pasadena, Calif.: Salem Press, 2004. Analysis of "This Is What It Means to Say Phoenix, Arizona," with sections on themes and meaning and style and technique. Also includes a detailed synopsis of the story.

Baxter, Andrea-Bess. "Review of *Old Shirts and New Skins, First Indian on the Moon*, and *The Lone Ranger and Tonto Fistfight in Heaven*." *Western American Literature* 29, no. 3 (November, 1994): 277-280. A review of the three works with commentary on the appeals of Alexie's writing and its strengths.

Bogey, Dan. Review of *The Lone Ranger and Tonto Fistfight in Heaven*, by Sherman Alexie. *Library Journal* 118 (September 1, 1993). Admires Alexie's narrative voice.

Lincoln, Kenneth. *Native American Renaissance*. Berkeley: University of California Press, 1983. Gives a general social and literary overview of American Indian writers.

Low, Denise. *The American Indian Quarterly* 20, no. 1 (Winter, 1996): 123-125. In examining Alexie's work through a postmodern lens, Low discusses his characters and rhetorical strategies in *The Lone Ranger and Tonto Fistfight in Heaven* and *The Business of Fancydancing*.

May, Charles E. "The Toughest Indian in the World." In *Masterplots II: Short Story Series*, edited by Charles E. May. Rev. ed. Vol. 7. Pasadena, Calif.: Salem Press, 2004. Student-friendly analysis of "The Toughest Indian in the World" that covers the story's themes and style and includes a detailed synopsis.

Schneider, Brian. Review of *The Lone Ranger and Tonto Fistfight in Heaven*, by Sherman Alexie. *Review of Contemporary Fiction* 13 (Fall, 1993). Praises Alexie's passionate lyrical voice.

Silko, Leslie Marmon. "Bingo Man—*Reservation Blues* by Sherman Alexie." *The Nation* 260, no. 23 (June 12, 1995): 856-860. A review, by a celebrated Native American writer, of Alexie's short stories and poems with special focus on his first novel, *Reservation Blues*.

Isabel Allende

Born: Lima, Peru; August 2, 1942

Principal short fiction • *Cuentos de Eva Luna,* 1990 (*The Stories of Eva Luna,* 1991).

Other literary forms • Although greatly respected as a writer of short stories, Isabel Allende is probably better known for her writing in other genres. She published eight novels through 2006. These include *La casa de los espíritus* (1982; *The House of the Spirits,* 1985), which established her reputation, *De amor y de sombra* (1984), *Eva Luna* (1987), *El plan infinito* (1991), *Hija de la fortuna* (1999), *Portrait sépia* (2000; *Portrait in Sepia,* 2001), *Zorro* (2005; English translation, 2005), and *Inés del alma mía* (2006; *Inés of My Soul,* 2006).

Allende has also published an account of her daughter's death in *Paula* (1994); a memoir about her homeland, *Mi país inventado* (2003; *My Invented Country: A Nostalgic Journey Through Chile,* 2003); and a collection of humorous pieces poking fun at machismo, originally published in the magazine *Paula,* entitled *Civilice a su troglodita* (1974). In 1984 she published a collection of children's stories in Spanish, *La gorda de Porcelana.* Two decades later, she returned to that genre with *Ciudad de las bestias* (2002; *City of the Beasts,* 2002), *El reino del dragón de oro* (2003; *Kingdom of the Golden Dragon,* 2004), and *El bosque de los Pigmeos* (2004; *Forest of the Pygmies,* 2005).

Achievements • Isabel Allende has been the recipient of numerous prestigious literary prizes, including the Panorama Literario Novel of the Year (1983), Author of the Year in Germany (1984 and 1986), and the Grand Prix d'Évasion in France (1984), as well as the Colima prize for best novel in Mexico (1985). A 1993 film version of *La casa de los espíritus,* directed by Bille August, was a box-office success.

Biography • Though Chilean by nationality, Isabel Angelica Allende was born in Lima, Peru, on August 2, 1942. The niece of the former Chilean president Salvador Allende, who died in September, 1973, during the military coup d'état engineered by Augusto Pinochet, Allende attended a private high school in Santiago, Chile, from which she graduated in 1959. She worked as a secretary at the United Nations Food and Agricultural Organization until 1965. She married Miguel Frías in 1962, had a daughter, Paula, and a son, Miguel. In Santiago, she worked as a journalist, editor, and advice columnist for *Paula* magazine from 1967 to 1974 and as an interviewer for a television station from 1970 to 1975. She was also an administrator for Colegio Marroco, in Caracas, from 1979 to 1982. Allende divorced her husband in 1987 and married William Gordon in 1988. Her daughter died in 1993, and this event formed the basis of the novel named after her.

Analysis • Isabel Allende's literary career is notable in that it stands outside the shifting fashions of the Latin American literary scene. Since the 1960's in Latin America the literary fashion has tended to favor intricate, self-conscious novels that test readers' interpretive powers. Flying in the face of this trend, however, Allende's novels favor content over form, reality over novelistic devices. Though her fiction has been dismissed by some critics as simply an imitation of Gabriel García Márquez's work, especially his so-called Magical Realist style, it is clear that Allende enjoys unparalleled popularity. Her novels and short stories have attracted an enormous readership in Spanish as well as in English, French, and German. Allende tends to write plot-centered, reader-friendly fiction. Her stories often focus on love and sex as seen from a feminine perspective.

The Stories of Eva Luna • The short-story collection *The Stories of Eva Luna* is essentially a sequel to her novel *Eva Luna* (1987), published three years earlier; thus the narrator of *The Stories of Eva Luna* is the Eva Luna who appeared in the earlier novel, that is, a resourceful, bright young woman who, though born to poverty, rises to riches as a result of becoming a famous soap-opera writer. Two of the stories provide a direct link to *Eva Luna* the novel. "El huésped de la maestra," for example, finishes a story that was left unresolved in the novel. The novel describes how Inés, the schoolmistress of Santa Agua, saw her son brutally murdered at the hands of a local man, who caught him stealing mangoes in the garden. Riad Halabí, by an ingenious plan, managed to force the murderer to leave town. In the short story, readers learn that the murderer returns many years later to Santa Agua and is then killed by Inés in an act of revenge; much of the short story is taken up by a description of the ingenious way in which Halabí disposes of the body. Also related to the novel is the short story "De barro estamos hechos." The novel introduces Rolf Carlé, a cameraman, who eventually becomes Eva's companion. Here readers see firsthand his experience of the floods that ravaged the country and that caused a young girl called Azucena to die slowly and painfully, even while he was filming her. The short story focuses on how this experience has changed Rolf's life. These two short stories can be seen as sequels to Allende's long fiction and show continuity of theme and character.

There are twenty-three short stories in *The Stories of Eva Luna* and only two of them, as described above, use the same characters that the novels do. In other words, above all, they are new stories that Eva Luna has invented for the enjoyment of her lover, Rolf Carlé. The overriding structure is provided by the theme of *Alf layla walayla* (fifteenth century; *The Arabian Nights' Entertainments*, 1706-1708), in which the female narrator, Scheherazade, must tell a story each night in order to avoid being executed by the king. The collection of short stories opens, indeed, with Rolf Carlé asking the narrator, who, though unnamed, is obviously Eva Luna, to tell him a story that has never been told to anyone else. The first story, "Dos palabras," explores the same theme. Here the protagonist, Belisa Crepusc…, wrote a speech for a man who wanted to become president; and she also gave him two secret words. The speech was an enormous success, but the Colonel soon discovers that he is fatally attracted to Belisa as a result of the linguistic spell she has cast over him.

There are a number of themes that run through the stories. The most obvious one is that of sexuality and love, which forms the focus for nineteen of the twenty-three stories in the collection. Love is often presented as occurring purely through chance. In "Tosca," for example, a love relationship begins in this short story as a result of the apparently insignificant fact that Leonardo is seen by Laurizia reading the score of the work *Tosca* by the famous Italian composer Giacomo Puccini. From this chance encounter a passionate affair develops. Of the nineteen stories that focus on love and sexuality, ten focus on illicit sex. A good example is "Si me tocaras el corazón," which tells the story of Amadeo Peralta, who, while on a visit to Santa Agua, seduces a fifteen-year-old girl called Hortensia; when he tires of her, he decides to lock her up permanently in the basement of a sugar refinery. Years later, some children hear monstrous noises coming from the basement, and Hortensia is discovered, diseased and at the brink of death, which leads to Amadeo's discomfiture. The moral of this short story seems to be that unbridled sexual passion can have disastrous consequences. Some of the stories, such as "Boca de sapo," "María, la boba," and "Walimai," explicitly allude to prostitution.

Other themes covered in the stories include vengeance, as in "Una venganza," in which revenge for rape is enacted on the rapist; the clash between cultures, as in "Walamai," which describes the struggles between the tribe of the Sons of the Moon and the white man, told from an Indian perspective; the miracle, as in "Un discreto milagro," which tells how Miguel, a priest, has his sight restored by a local saint, Juana de los Lirios; as well as predestination, as in "La mujer del juez," a well-written, suspense story which focuses on the protagonists, Nicolás Vidal and Casilda Hidalgo, who conduct an illicit affair even though they know beforehand that it will lead to their deaths. One particularly powerful story, "Un camino hacia el norte," contains a strong social critique. It describes how Claveles Picero, and her grandfather, Jesús Dionisio Picero, are tricked into giving up Claveles's illegitimate son Juan to a United States adoption agency, which is later discovered to be a front for a contraband agency which sells human organs. The story ends with a description of their journey to the capital in an attempt to discover Juan's fate; they, like the readers, fear the worst. The message is that poverty leads to exploitation and death.

A common technique in the stories involves the story opening with a scene (whose import is not understood) and then cutting to the past, at which point the narrative of the lives of the main protagonists is told. This occurs in a number of stories, including "El camino hacia el norte" and "El huésped de la maestra." Most of the stories are told in the third person, although some, such as "Walimai," are told in the first person.

Stephen M. Hart

Other major works

CHILDREN'S LITERATURE: *La gorda de porcelana*, 1984; *Ciudad de las bestias*, 2002 (*City of the Beasts*, 2002); *El reino del dragón de oro*, 2003 (*Kingdom of the Golden Dragon*, 2004); *El bosque de los Pigmeos*, 2004 (*Forest of the Pygmies*, 2005).

NOVELS: *La casa de los espíritus*, 1982 (*The House of the Spirits*, 1985); *De amor y de sombra*, 1984 (*Of Love and Shadows*, 1987); *Eva Luna*, 1987 (English translation, 1988); *El plan infinito*, 1991 (*The Infinite Plan*, 1993); *Hija de la fortuna*, 1999 (*Daughter of Fortune*, 1999); *Portrait sépia*, 2000 (*Portrait in Sepia*, 2001); *Zorro*, 2005 (English translation, 2005); *Inés del alma mía*, 2006 (*Inés of My Soul*, 2006).

MISCELLANEOUS: *Afrodita: Cuentos, recetas, y otros afrodisiacos*, 1997 (*Afrodite: A Memoir of the Senses*, 1998).

NONFICTION: *Civilice a su troglodita: Los impertinentes de Isabel Allende*, 1974; *Paula*, 1994 (English translation, 1995); *Conversations with Isabel Allende*, 1999; *Mi país inventado*, 2003 (*My Invented Country: A Nostalgic Journey Through Chile*, 2003).

Bibliography
Allende, Isabel. *Conversations with Isabel Allende*. Austin: University of Texas Press, 1999. Edited by John Rodden. A collection of interviews from the University of Texas's Pan-American series.

Correas Zapata, Celia. *Isabel Allende: Life and Spirits.* Houston, Tex.: Arte Público, 2002. The first biographical discussion of Allende in book form. This intimate glimpse of Allende's life is written by her admiring but scholarly friend.

De Carvalho, Susan. "The Male Narrative Perspective in the Fiction of Isabel Allende." *Journal of Hispanic Research* 2, no. 2 (Spring, 1994): 269-278. Shows that "Walimai" is different from the other short stories in *Los cuentos de Eva Luna* in that it is written in the first person and from a male perspective. Argues that the first-person, male perspective in this story represents the ideal narrative voice.

García Pinto, Magdalena, ed. *Women Writers of Latin America: Intimate Histories.* Austin: University of Texas Press, 1991. Contains an excellent interview with Allende with a great deal of insight into the way she views her writing. It is here that Allende mentions that she sees herself as a troubadour going from village to village, person to person, talking about her country.

Hart, Stephen M. *White Ink: Essays on Twentieth-Century Feminine Fiction in Spain and Latin America.* London: Tamesis, 1993. Sets Allende's work within the context of women's writing in the twentieth century in Latin America. Examines the ways in which Allende fuses the space of the personal with that of the political in her fiction and shows that, in her work, falling in love with another human being is often aligned with falling in love with a political cause.

Levine, Linda Gould. *Isabel Allende.* New York: Twayne, 2002. This volume from Twayne's World Authors series includes useful bibliographical references and an index.

Marketta, Laurila. "Isabel Allende and the Discourse of Exile." In *International Women's Writing, New Landscapes of Identity,* edited by Anne E. Brown and Marjanne E. Gooze. Westport, Conn.: Greenwood Press, 1995. This book is helpful both for Marketta's analysis of Allende's use of the language of exile and for other Allende materials in the collection.

May, Charles E., ed. *Masterplots II: Short Story Series, Revised Edition.* 8 vols. Pasadena, Calif.: Salem Press, 2004. Designed for student use, this reference set contains articles providing detailed plot summaries and analyses of these three short stories by Allende: "Clarisa" (vol. 2), "Toad's Mouth" (vol. 7), and "Wicked Girl" (vol. 8).

Roof, Maria. "W. E. B. Du Bois, Isabel Allende, and the Empowerment of Third World Women." *CLA Journal* 39, no. 4 (June, 1996): 401-416. A good source for readers interested in the feminist elements in Allende.

Hans Christian Andersen

Born: Odense, Denmark; April 2, 1805
Died: Rolighed, near Copenhagen, Denmark; August 4, 1875

Principal short fiction • *Eventyr*, 1835-1872 (*The Complete Andersen*, 1949; also *Fairy Tales*, 1950-1958; also *The Complete Fairy Tales and Stories*, 1974); *It's Perfectly True, and Other Stories*, 1937; *Andersen's Fairy Tales*, 1946; *Hans Andersen's Fairy Tales*, 1953.

Other literary forms • Hans Christian Andersen's first publication was a poem in 1828, and his first prose work, a fantasy of a nightly journey titled *Fodreise fra Holmens Canal til Østpynten af Amager* (1829; a journey on foot from Holman's canal to the east point of Amager), was an immediate success. He wrote six novels, of which *Improvisatoren* (1835; *The Improvisatore*, 1845) securely established his fame. His nine travel books began with *En digters bazar* (1842; *A Poet's Bazaar*, 1846) and mainly concern his European travels. Other works are *Billebog uden billeder* (1840; *Tales the Moon Can Tell*, 1855) and *I Sverrig* (1851; *In Sweden*, 1852). His autobiographies are *Levnedsbogen, 1805-1831* (1926; *Diaries of Hans Christian Andersen*, 1990), discovered fifty years after his death; *Mit Livs Eventyr* (1847; *The Story of My Life*, 1852); and the revised *The Fairy Tale of My Life* (1855). Other publications include his correspondence, diaries, notebooks and draft material, drawings, sketches, paper cuttings, and plays.

Achievements • Although hailed as the greatest of all fairy-tale writers in any language, throughout most of his life, Hans Christian Andersen considered his fairy tales to be of far less importance than his other writings. He considered himself much more of a novelist, playwright, and writer of travel books. It was his fairy tales, however, that spread his fame across Europe and, immediately upon publication, were translated into every European language. Andersen was much more famous, courted, and honored abroad than in his native Denmark. In his later years, however, his compatriots did at last recognize Andersen's greatness. He became a friend and guest to royalty, was made a state councillor, and had a touching tribute paid to him in the form of the statue of the Little Mermaid, which sits in the Copenhagen harbor.

Biography • The son of a shoemaker, who died when Hans was eleven, and an illiterate servant mother, Hans Christian Andersen from his early childhood loved to invent tales, poems, and plays and to make intricate paper cuttings; he loved to recite his creations to any possible listener. Later he yearned to be a creative writer of divine inspiration and an actor. In 1819 he journeyed to Copenhagen where he lived through hard times but developed a talent for attracting benefactors. Among them was Jonas Collin, whose home became Andersen's "Home of Homes," as he called it, who acted as a foster father, and whose son Edvard became a close friend. Through Jonas's influence and a grant from the king, Andersen attended grammar school (1822-1827) and struggled with a difficult headmaster as well as with Latin and Greek. Andersen never married, although he was attracted to several women, among them the singer Jenny Lind. Although he was very tall and ungainly in appearance, with large feet, a large nose, and small eyes, and although he was sentimental and exceptionally concerned with himself, his fears and doubts, Andersen enjoyed the company of Europe's leading professionals and nobility, including kings and queens; in later life many honors were bestowed on him. His last nine years he lived at the home of the Moritz Melchiors, just outside Copenhagen, and he died there on August 4, 1875.

Analysis • Following publication of his 1844 collection of tales, Hans Christian Andersen explained in a letter that he wanted his tales to be read on two levels, offering something for the minds of adults as well as appealing to children. Three examples of such adult tales, "The Snow Queen," "The Shadow," and "The Nightingale," demonstrate how, as Andersen said, in writing from his own breast instead of retelling old tales he had found out how to write fairy tales.

"The Snow Queen" • Comprising seven stories, "The Snow Queen" begins with a mirror into which people can look and see the good become small and mean and the bad appear at its very worst. Andersen could remember, in later years, that his father had maintained that "There is no other devil than the one we have in our hearts"; and this provides a clue to the plot and theme of "The Snow Queen." Only when the demon's followers confront heaven with the mirror does it shatter into fragments, but unfortunately those fragments enter the hearts of many people.

The second story introduces Little Kay and Gerda, who love each other and the summer's flowers until a fragment of the evil mirror lodges in Little Kay's eye and another pierces his heart. Having formerly declared that if the Snow Queen visited he would melt her on the stove, Kay now views snowflakes through a magnifying glass and pronounces them more beautiful than flowers. He protests against the grandmother's tales with a *but* for the logic of each one, and, apparently arrived at adolescence, transfers loyalty from the innocent Gerda to the knowing Snow Queen. He follows the visiting queen out of town and into the snowy expanses of the distant sky.

The journey from adolescence to maturity becomes for Gerda her quest for the missing Kay, her true love and future mate. Fearing the river has taken Kay, she offers it her new red shoes; but a boat she steps into drifts away from shore, and, riding the river's current, she travels far before being pulled ashore and detained by a woman "learned in magic." Gerda here forgets her search for Kay until the sight of a rose reminds her. In one of the story's most abstract passages, she then asks the tiger lilies, convolvulus, snowdrop, hyacinth, buttercup, and narcissus where he might be; but each tells a highly fanciful tale concerned with its own identity. The narcissus, for example, alludes to the Echo and Narcissus myth in saying "I can see myself" and fails to aid Gerda. Barefoot, Gerda runs out of the garden and finds that autumn has arrived.

A crow believes he has seen Kay and contrives a visit with the Prince and Princess, who forgive the invasion of their palatial privacy and then outfit Gerda to continue her search. All her newly acquired equipage attracts a "little robber girl," a perplexing mixture of amorality and good intentions, who threatens Gerda with her knife but provides a reindeer to carry Gerda to Spitsbergen, where the wood pigeons have reported having seen Kay. At one stop, the reindeer begs a Finnish wise woman to give Gerda the strength to conquer all, but the woman points out the great power that Gerda has already evidenced and adds, "We must not tell her what power she has. It is in her heart, because she is such a sweet innocent child." She sends Gerda and the reindeer on their way, with Gerda riding without boots or mittens. Eventually the reindeer deposits her by a red-berry bush in freezing icebound Denmark, from which she walks to the Snow Queen's palace.

Here she finds a second mirror, a frozen lake broken into fragments that is actually the throne of the Snow Queen; the queen calls it "The Mirror of Reason." Little Kay works diligently to form the fragments into the word "Eternity," for which accomplishment the Snow Queen has said he can be his own master and have the whole world and a new pair of skates. Gerda's love, when she sheds tears of joy at finding Kay, melts the ice in his heart and the mirror within his breast; and Kay, himself bursting into tears at recovering Gerda and her love, finds that the fragments magically form themselves into the word "Eternity." The two young people find many changes on their return journey but much the same at home, where they now realize they are grown up. The grandmother's Bible verse tells them about the kingdom of heaven for those with hearts of children, and they now understand the meaning of the hymn, "Where roses deck the flowery vale,/ There Infant Jesus, thee we hail!" The flowers of love, not the mirror of reason, make Kay and Gerda inheritors of the kingdom of heaven, the Snow Queen's elusive eternity.

Only the style makes such stories children's stories, for "The Snow Queen," with devices such as the snowflakes seen under a microscope, obviously attacks empiricism; at the same time, the story offers the symbol of the foot, important to folklore, and the journey of Gerda through obstacles and a final illumination constitutes a "journey of the hero" as delineated by the mythologist Joseph Campbell.

"The Shadow" • Andersen's "The Shadow" presents an alter-ego with psychic dimensions well beyond the ken of children. The setting with which "The Shadow" begins reflects Andersen's diary entries from his trip to Naples in June, 1846, when he found the sun too hot for venturing out of doors and began writing the story. With the hot sun directly overhead, the shadow disappears except in morning and evening and begins to assume a life of its own. Its activities, closely observed by its owner, the "learned man from a cold country," leads him to joke about its going into the house opposite to learn the identity of a lovely maiden. The shadow fails to return, but the learned man soon grows a new shadow. Many years later, once more at home, the original shadow visits him but has now become so corporeal that it has acquired flesh and clothes. Further, it divulges, it has become wealthy and plans to marry. Its three-week visit in the house opposite, it now reveals, placed it close to the lovely maiden Poetry, in whose anteroom the shadow read all the poetry and prose ever written. If the learned man had been there, he would not have remained a human being, but it was there that the shadow became one. Emerging thence he went about under the cover of a pastry cook's gown for some time before growing into his present affluence.

Later, the learned man's writing of the good, the true, and the beautiful fail to provide him an income; only after he has suffered long and become so thin that people tell him he looks like a shadow does he accede to the shadow's request that he become a traveling companion. Shadow and master have now exchanged places, but the king's daughter notices that the new master cannot cast a shadow. To this accusation he replies that the person who is always at his side is his shadow. When the new master cannot answer her scientific inquiries, he defers to the shadow, whose knowledge impresses the princess. Clearly, she reasons, to have such a learned servant the master must be the most learned man on earth.

Against the upcoming marriage of princess and shadow, the learned man protests and threatens to reveal the truth. "Not a soul would believe you," says the shadow, and with his new status as fiancé he has the learned man cast into prison. The princess agrees that it would be a charity to deliver the learned man from his delusions and has him promptly executed.

The fact that Poetry would make a human being divine or "more than human" gives Poetry the identity of Psyche, whose statue by Thorvaldsen Andersen had admired in 1833 in the Danish sculptor's studio. (Also, Andersen in 1861 wrote a story called "The Psyche.") In "The Shadow," the human qualities with which Poetry's presence infuses the shadow function for him as a soul. Thereafter, his incubation under the pastry cook's gown provides him a proper maturation from which, still as shadow, he looks into people's lives, spies on their evils and their intimacies, and acquires power over them. This phase of his existence explains the acquisition of wealth, but as the shadow grows human and powerful the learned man declines.

The shadow, the other self of the learned man, reflects the psychic stress Andersen suffered in his relationship with Edvard Collin. What Andersen desired between himself and Collin has been recognized by scholars as the *Blütbruderschaft* that D. H. Lawrence wrote about—a close relationship with another male. Collin persisted, however, in fending off all Andersen's attempts at informality, even in regard to the use of language. In the story the shadow is obviously Collin, whose separate identity thrives at the expense of the learned man's—Andersen's—psyche. Writing in his diary of the distress and illness brought on by a letter from Edvard Collin, Andersen contemplated suicide and pleaded "he must use the language of a friend" (1834); so also the story's shadow rejects such language and commits the learned man to prison and to death. The problem of language appears twice in the story, although various translations diminish its effect. On the shadow's first visit to his former master, his newly acquired affluence provides him with the daring to suggest that the learned man speak "less familiarly" and to say "sir" or—in other translations—to replace "you" with "thee" and "thou." Frequently argued between Andersen and Collin as the question of *Du* versus *De,* the problem reappears in the story when the learned man asks the shadow, because of their childhood together, to pledge themselves to address each other as *Du.* (In some translations, this reads merely "to drink to our good fellowship" and "call each other by our names.") In the shadow's reply, Andersen improved on Collin's objection by having the shadow cite the feel of gray paper or the scraping of a nail on a pane of glass as similar to the sound of *Du* spoken by the learned man.

"The Emperor's New Clothes" • Such touches of individuality made Andersen's writing succeed, as evidenced by a tale he borrowed from a Spanish source, the tale of "The Emperor's New Clothes," which he said he read in a German translation from Prince don Juan Manuel. Andersen's version improved on the original in several respects, including his theme of pretense of understanding as well as ridicule of snobbery and his ending with the objection of the child—an ending which Andersen added after the original manuscript had been sent to the publisher.

Andersen's talent for universalizing the appeal of a story and for capitalizing on personal experiences appears time and again throughout his many tales. Because of his grotesque appearance, which interfered with his longed-for stage career, Andersen knew personally the anguish of "The Ugly Duckling," but his success as a writer made him a beautiful swan. His extreme sensitivity he wrote into "The Princess and the Pea," detailing the adventures of a princess who could feel a pea through twenty mattresses. Andersen in this story borrowed from a folktale in which the little girl understands the test she is being put to because a dog or cat aids her by relaying the information; however, Andersen contrived that her sensitivity alone would suffice. Nevertheless, some translators could not accept the idea of her feeling a single pea and changed the text to read three peas and the title to read "The Real Princess."

Andersen's stories thus objectify psychic conditions, and among these his frequent association with nobility enabled him to depict with humor the qualities of egotism, arrogance, and subservience found at court. In "The Snow Queen" the crow describes court ladies and attendants standing around; the nearer to the door they stand the greater is their haughtiness. The footman's boy is too proud to be looked at. The princess is so clever she has read all the newspapers in the world and forgotten them again.

"The Nightingale" • One of Andersen's best depictions of court life and, at the same time, one of his best satires is "The Nightingale," which he wrote in honor of Jenny Lind, the singer known as the Swedish Nightingale. The story's theme contrasts the artificial manners and preferences of the court with the natural song of the nightingale and the ways of simple folk. Far from the palace of the emperor of China where bells on the flowers in the garden tinkle to attract attention to the flowers, the nightingale sings in the woods by the deep sea, so that a poor fisherman listens to it each day and travelers returning home write about it. The emperor discovers this nightingale from reading about it in a book, but his gentleman-in-waiting knows nothing about it because it has never been presented at court. Inquiring throughout the court, he finds only a little girl in the kitchen who has heard it and who helps him find it. Brought to the court, it must sing on a golden perch, and, when acclaimed successful, it has its own cage and can walk out twice a day and once in the night with twelve footmen, each one holding a ribbon tied around its leg.

When the emperor of Japan sends as a gift an artificial nightingale studded with diamonds, rubies, and sapphires, the two birds cannot sing together, and the real nightingale flies away in chagrin. The court throng honors the mechanical bird with jewels and gold as gifts, and the Master of Music writes twenty-five volumes about it. The mechanical bird earns the title of Chief Imperial Singer-of-the-Bed-Chamber, and in rank it stands number one on the left side, for even an emperor's heart is on the left side.

Eventually the mechanical bird breaks down, and the watchmaker cannot assure repair with the same admirable tune. Five years later the emperor becomes ill, and his successor is proclaimed. Then, with Death sitting on his chest and wearing his golden crown, he calls on the mechanical bird to sing. Although it sits mute, the nightingale appears at the window and sings Death away and brings new life to the emperor. With the generosity of a true heroine, it advises the king not to destroy the mechanical bird, which did all the good it could; however, it reminds the emperor, a little singing bird sings to the fisherman and the peasant and must continue to go and to return. Although it loves the emperor's heart more than his crown, the crown has an odor of sanctity also. The nightingale will return, but the emperor must keep its secret that a little bird tells him everything.

Andersen's comment comparing the heart and the crown of the emperor may be his finest on the attraction of the great, an attraction which he felt all his life. Early in 1874, after visiting a count in South Zealand, he wrote to Mrs. Melchior that no fairy tales occurred to him any more. If he walks in the garden, he said, Thumbelina has ended her journey on the water lily; the wind and the Old Oak Tree have already told him their tales and have nothing more to tell him. It is, he wrote, as if he had filled out the entire circle with fairy-tale radii close to one another. On his seventieth birthday, April 2, 1875, the royal carriage was sent to fetch him to the castle, and the king bestowed another decoration. It was his last birthday celebration, for in a few months Andersen had filled out the circle of his life.

Grace Eckley
With updates by Leslie A. Pearl

Other major works

PLAYS: *Kjærlighed paa Nicolai Taarn: Elle, Hvad siger Parterret,* pr. 1829; *Agnete og havmanden,* pr. 1833; *Mulatten,* pr. 1840.

NOVELS: *Improvisatoren,* 1835 (2 volumes; *The Improvisatore,* 1845); *O. T.,* 1836 (English translation, 1845); *Kun en Spillemand,* 1837 (*Only a Fiddler,* 1845); *De To Baronesser,* 1848 (*The Two Baronesses,* 1848); *At være eller ikke være,* 1857 (*To Be or Not to Be,* 1857); *Lykke-Peer,* 1870 (*Lucky Peer,* 1871).

MISCELLANEOUS: *The Collected Works of Hans Christian Andersen,* 1870-1884 (10 volumes).

NONFICTION: *Fodreise fra Holmens Canal til Østpynten af Amager,* 1829; *Skyggebilleder af en reise til Harzen, det sachiske Schweitz,* 1831 (*Rambles in the Romantic Regions of the Hartz Mountains, Saxon Switzerland, etc.,* 1848); *Billebog uden billeder,* 1840 (*Tales the Moon Can Tell,* 1855); *En digters bazar,* 1842 (*A Poet's Bazaar,* 1846); *I Sverrig,* 1851 (*In Sweden,* 1852); *Mit Livs Eventyr,* 1855 (*The True Story of My Life,* 1847; also as *The Fairy Tale of My Life,* 1855); *I Spanien,* 1863 (*In Spain,* 1864); *Et besøg i Portugal,* 1866 (*A Visit to Portugal,* 1870); *Levnedsbogen, 1805-1831,* 1926 (*Diaries of Hans Christian Andersen,* 1990).

POETRY: *Digte,* 1830.

Bibliography

Andersen, Jens. *Hans Christian Andersen: A New Life.* Woodstock, N.Y.: Overlook Press, 2005. Highly readable and useful biography examining the writer's life and literary work.

Book, Frederik. *Hans Christian Andersen.* Norman: University of Oklahoma Press, 1962. This biography studies Andersen's personal and literary history. It considers how psychiatry, folklore, and the history of religion affected Andersen's life. Andersen's autobiographies are examined in the light of what was real and what was the fairy tale he was creating about his life. Contains illustrations of his fairy tales and photographs.

Bresdorff, Elias. *Hans Christian Andersen: The Story of His Life and Work, 1805-1875.* New York: Noonday Press, 1994. This book is divided in two sections: The first part is a biographical study of Andersen's complex personality; the second is a critical study of his most famous fairy tales and stories.

Dollerup, Cay. "Translation as a Creative Force in Literature: The Birth of the European Bourgeois Fairy-Tale." *The Modern Language Review* 90 (January, 1995): 94-102. Discusses the European bourgeois fairy tale's development as the result of translation of the stories of the Brothers Grimm into Danish and the stories of Hans Christian Andersen into German because children would not be familiar with foreign languages. Argues that the Grimms and Andersen were adapted to European middle-class values.

Grobech, Bo. *Hans Christian Andersen.* Boston: Twayne, 1980. Grobech provides a solid introduction to Andersen's life told in entertaining narrative style. The book includes studies of Andersen's fairy tales, his international influence, and his influence in the twentieth century. It can be read by the general reader as well as literary specialists.

Johansen, Jorgen Dines. "The Merciless Tragedy of Desire: An Interpretation of H. C. Andersen's *Den lille Havfrue.*" *Scandinavian Studies* 68 (Spring, 1996): 203-241. Provides a psychoanalytic interpretation of "The Little Mermaid," focusing on the tension between earthly love and religious reparation in the story. Discusses the themes of love and salvation in an extensive analysis of love and sexuality in the tale.

Nassaar, Christopher S. "Andersen's 'The Shadow' and Wilde's 'The Fisherman and His Soul': A Case of Influence." *Nineteenth-Century Literature* 50 (September, 1995): 217-224. Argues that Oscar Wilde's tale is a Christian response to Andersen's nihilistic tale. Claims that, while Andersen's tale is about the triumph of evil, Wilde's story is about the triumph of Christian love.

_____. "Andersen's 'The Ugly Ducking' and Wilde's 'The Birthday of the Infanta.'" *The Explicator* 55 (Winter, 1997): 83-85. Discusses the influence of Andersen's "The Ugly Duckling" on Wilde's story. Argues that, in spite of the surface differences, Wilde's story is a direct reversal of Andersen's.

Rossel, Sven Hakon, ed. *Hans Christian Andersen: Danish Writer and Citizen of the World.* Amsterdam: Rodopi, 1996. This scholarly collection of essays establishes Andersen as a major European writer of the nineteenth century. Special attention is given to his biography as well as his travel writing and fairy tales.

Spink, Reginald. *Hans Christian Andersen and His World.* New York: G. P. Putnam's Sons, 1972. Excellent overview of Andersen's life. Emphasizes how his background and childhood affected his art. Extensively illustrated with photographs, drawings, and reprints of the illustrated fairy tales in several foreign-language editions.

Wullschlager, Jackie. *Hans Christian Andersen: The Life of a Storyteller.* New York: Alfred A. Knopf, 2001. Thorough biography of the writer.

Sherwood Anderson

Born: Camden, Ohio; September 13, 1876
Died: Colón, Panama Canal Zone (now in Panama); March 8, 1941

Principal short fiction • *The Triumph of the Egg*, 1921; *Horses and Men*, 1923; *Death in the Woods, and Other Stories*, 1933; *The Sherwood Anderson Reader*, 1947.

Other literary forms • Sherwood Anderson published seven novels, collections of essays, memoirs, poetry, and dramatizations of *Winesburg, Ohio*, as well as other stories. He was a prolific article writer and for a time owned and edited both the Republican and Democratic newspapers in Marion, Virginia. In 1921, he received a two-thousand-dollar literary prize from *The Dial* magazine. While employed as a copywriter, Anderson wrote many successful advertisements.

Achievements • Sherwood Anderson, a protomodernist, is generally accepted as an innovator in the field of the short story despite having produced only one masterpiece, *Winesburg, Ohio*. In his work, he not only revolutionized the structure of short fiction by resisting the literary slickness of the contrived plot but also encouraged a simple and direct prose style, one which reflects the spare poetry of ordinary American speech. Anderson's thematic concerns were also innovative. He was one of the first writers to dramatize the artistic repudiation of the business world and to give the craft of the short story a decided push toward presenting a slice of life as a significant moment. His concern with the "grotesques" in society—the neurotics and eccentrics—is also innovative as is the straightforward attention he pays to his characters' sexuality. Anderson's contemporaries Ernest Hemingway, William Faulkner, and John Steinbeck were influenced by his work, as were several later writers: Carson McCullers, Flannery O'Connor, Saul Bellow, Bobbie Ann Mason, and Raymond Carver.

Biography • Sherwood Anderson was the third of seven children of a father who was an itinerant harness maker, house painter and a mother of either German or Italian descent. His father was a Civil War veteran (a Southerner who fought with the Union), locally famed as a storyteller. His elder brother, Karl, became a prominent painter who later introduced Sherwood to Chicago's Bohemia, which gained him access to the literary world. Declining fortunes caused the family to move repeatedly until they settled in Clyde, Ohio (the model for Winesburg), a village just south of Lake Erie. The young Anderson experienced a desultory schooling and worked at several jobs: as a newsboy, a housepainter, a stableboy, a farmhand, and a laborer in a bicycle factory.

After serving in Cuba during the Spanish-American War (he saw no combat), he acquired a further year of schooling at Wittenberg Academy in Springfield, Ohio, but remained undereducated throughout his life. Jobs as advertising copywriter gave him a first taste of writing, and he went on to a successful business career. In 1912, the central psychological event of his life occurred. He suffered a nervous breakdown, which led him to walk out of his paint factory job in Elyria, Ohio. He moved to

Chicago, where he began to meet writers such as Floyd Dell, Carl Sandburg, and Ben Hecht, a group collectively known as the Chicago Renaissance. A significant nonliterary contact was Dr. Trigant Burrow of Baltimore, who operated a Freudian therapeutic camp in Lake Chateaugay, New York, during the summers of 1915 and 1916. It should be noted, however, that Anderson ultimately rejected scientific probing of the psyche, for he typically believed that the human mind is static and incapable of meaningful change for the better. Publication of Winesburg, Ohio catapulted him into prominence, and he traveled to Europe in 1921, where he became acquainted with Gertrude Stein, Ernest Hemingway, and James Joyce. In 1923, while living in New Orleans, he shared an apartment with William Faulkner.

Anderson married and divorced four times. He and his first wife had three children. His second wife, Tennessee Mitchell, had been a lover to Edgar Lee Masters, author of the *Spoon River Anthology* (1915). His last wife, Eleanor Copenhaver, had an interest in the southern labor movement, which drew Anderson somewhat out of his social primitivism, and, for a time in the 1930's, he became a favorite of communists and socialists. His death, in Colón, Panama Canal Zone, while on a voyage to South America, was notable for its unique circumstances: He died of peritonitis caused by a toothpick accidentally swallowed while eating hors d'œuvres.

Analysis • Sherwood Anderson's best-known and most important work is the American classic, *Winesburg, Ohio*. It is a collection of associated short stories set in the mythical town of Winesburg in the latter part of the nineteenth century. The stories catalog Anderson's negative reaction to the transformation of Ohio from a largely agricultural to an industrial society, which culminated about the time he was growing up in the village of Clyde in the 1880's. Its twenty-five stories are vignettes of the town doctor; the voluble baseball coach; the still attractive but aging-with-loneliness high school teacher; the prosperous and harsh farmer-turned-religious fanatic; the dirt laborer; the hotel keeper; the banker's daughter, and her adolescent suitors; the Presbyterian minister struggling with temptation; the town drunk; the town rough; the town homosexual; and the town "half-wit." The comparison to Masters's *Spoon River Anthology* is obvious: Both works purport to reveal the secret lives of small-town Americans living in the Middle West, and ironically both owe their popular success to the elegiac recording of this era, which most Americans insist on viewing idyllically. Anderson's work, however, differs by more directly relating sexuality to the bizarre behavior of many of his characters and by employing a coherent theme.

That theme is an exploration of psychological "grotesques"—the casualties of economic progress—and how these grotesques participate in the maturing of George

Willard, the teenage reporter for the *Winesburg Eagle,* who at the end of the book departs for a bigger city to become a journalist. By then his sometimes callous ambition to get ahead has been tempered by a sense of what Anderson chooses to call "sophistication," the title of the penultimate story. The achievement of George's sophistication gives *Winesburg, Ohio* its artistic movement but makes it problematic for many critics and thoughtful Americans.

"The Book of the Grotesque" • The prefacing story defines grotesques. A dying old writer hires a carpenter to build up his bed so that he can observe the trees outside without getting out of it. (While living in Chicago in 1915 Anderson had his own bed similarly raised so that he could observe the Loop.) After the carpenter leaves, the writer returns to his project—the writing of "The Book of the Grotesque," which grieves over the notion that in the beginning of the world there were a great many thoughts but no such thing as a "truth." People turned these thoughts into many beautiful truths such as the truth of passion, wealth, poverty, profligacy, carelessness, and others; a person could then appropriate a single one of these truths and try to live by it. It was thus that a person would become a grotesque—a personality dominated by an overriding concern which in time squeezed out other facets of life.

This epistemological fable, which involves a triple-reduction, raises at least two invalidating questions: First, Can there be "thoughts" without the truth to establish the self-differentiating process which generates thought?, and second, If universals are denied and all truths have equal value (they are *all* beautiful), then why should a person be condemned for choosing only one of these pluralistic "truths"?

"Hands" • The stories in *Winesburg, Ohio* nevertheless do grapple with Anderson's intended theme, and a story such as "Hands" clearly illustrates what he means by a grotesque. The hands belong to Wing Biddlebaum, formerly Adolph Myers, a teacher in a Pennsylvania village who was beaten and run out of town for caressing boys. Anderson is delicately oblique about Wing's homosexuality, for the story focuses on how a single traumatic event can forever after rule a person's life—Wing is now a fretful recluse whose only human contact occurs when George Willard visits him occasionally. George puzzles over Wing's expressive hands but never fathoms the reason for his suffering diffidence. "Hands," besides giving first flesh to the word grotesque, makes readers understand that a character's volition is not necessarily the factor that traps him into such an ideological straitjacket; sympathy can therefore be more readily extended.

"The Philosopher" • "The Philosopher" provides a more subtle illustration of a grotesque and introduces the idea that a grotesque need not be pitiable or tragic; in fact, he can be wildly humorous, as demonstrated at the beginning of the story with the philosopher's description:

> Doctor Parcival, the philosopher, was a large man with a drooping mouth covered by a yellow moustache . . . he wore a dirty white waistcoat out of whose pocket protruded a number of black cigars . . . there was something strange about his eyes: the lid of his left eye twitched; it fell down and it snapped up; it was exactly as though the lid of the eye were a window shade and someone stood inside playing with the cord.

It is George Willard's misfortune that Dr. Parcival likes him and uses him as a sounding board for his wacky pomposity. He wishes to convince the boy of the advisability of adopting a line of conduct that he himself is unable to define but amply illustrates with many "parables" which add up to the belief (as George begins to suspect) that all men are despicable. He tells George that his father died in an insane asylum, and then he continues on about a Dr. Cronin from Chicago who may have been murdered by several men, one of whom could have been yours truly, Dr. Parcival. He announces that he actually arrived in Winesburg to write a book. About to launch on the subject of the book, he is sidetracked into the story of his brother who worked for the railroad as part of a roving paint crew (which painted everything orange); on payday the brother would place his money on the kitchen table—daring any member of the family to touch it. The brother, while drunk, is run over by the rail car housing the other members of his crew.

One day George drops into Dr. Parcival's office for his customary morning visit and discovers him quaking with fear. Earlier a little girl had been thrown from her buggy, and the doctor had inexplicably refused to heed a passerby's call (perhaps because he is not a medical doctor). Other doctors, however, arrived on the scene, and no one noticed Dr. Parcival's absence. Not realizing this, the doctor shouts to George that he knows human nature and that soon a hanging party will be formed to hang him from a lamppost as punishment for his callous refusal to attend to the dying child. When his certainty dissipates, he whimpers to George, "If not now, sometime." He begs George to take him seriously and asks him to finish his book if something should happen to him; to this end he informs George of the subject of the book, which is: Everyone in the world is Christ, and they are all crucified.

Many critics have singled out one or another story as the best in *Winesburg, Ohio*; frequently mentioned are "The Untold Lie," "Hands," and "Sophistication." However, aside from the fact that this may be an unfair exercise—because the stories in *Winesburg, Ohio* were written to stand together—these choices bring out the accusation that much of Anderson's work has a "setup" quality—a facile solemnity which makes his fictions manifest. "The Philosopher" may be the best story because Dr. Parcival's grotesqueness eludes overt labeling; its finely timed humor reveals Anderson's ability to spoof his literary weaknesses, and the story captures one of those character types who, like Joe Welling of "A Man of Ideas," is readily observable and remembered but proves irritatingly elusive when set down.

"Godliness" • Anderson exhibits a particular interest in the distorting effect that religious mania has on the personality, and several stories in *Winesburg, Ohio* attack or ridicule examples of conspicuous religiosity. "Godliness," a tetralogy with a gothic flavor, follows the life of Jesse Bentley, a wealthy, progressive farmer who poisons the life of several generations of his relatives with his relentless harshness until he becomes inflamed by Old Testament stories and conceives the idea of replicating an act of animal sacrifice. Because of this behavior, he succeeds in terrifying his fifteen-year-old grandson, the only person he loves, who flees from him never to be heard from again, thus breaking the grandfather's spirit.

"The Strength of God" • Two stories, "The Strength of God" and "The Teacher," are juxtaposed to mock cleverly a less extravagant example of piety. The Reverend Curtis Hartman espies Kate Swift, the worldly high school teacher, reading in bed and smoking a cigarette. The sight affronts and preoccupies him and plunges him into a prolonged moral struggle, which is resolved when one night he observes her kneeling naked by her bed praying. He smashes the window through which he has been watching her and runs into George Willard's office shouting that Kate Swift is an instrument of God bearing a message of truth. Kate remains entirely oblivious of the Reverend Hartman, for she is preoccupied with George, in whom she has detected a spark of literary genius worthy of her cultivation. Her praying episode—an act of desperation which Hartman mistook for a return to faith—was the result of her realization, while in George's arms, that her altruism had turned physical.

"Sophistication" • It is exposure to these disparate egoisms, the death of his mother and a poignant evening with Helen White, the banker's daughter, which are gathered into the components of George's "sophistication," the achievement of which causes him to leave town. George's departure, however, has a decidedly ambivalent meaning. Anderson as well as other writers before and after him have shown that American small-town life can be less than idyllic, but *Winesburg, Ohio* is problematic because it is not simply another example of "the revolt from the village." In the story "Paper Pills," the narrator states that apples picked from Winesburg orchards will be eaten in city apartments that are filled with books, magazines, furniture, and people. A few rejected apples, however, which have gathered all their sweetness in one corner and are delicious to eat, remain on the trees and are eaten by those who are not discouraged by their lack of cosmetic appeal. Thus the neuroses of Anderson's grotesques are sentimentalized and become part of his increasingly strident polemic against rationality, the idea of progress, mechanization, scientific innovation, urban culture, and other expressions of social potency. Anderson never wonders why pastorals are not written by pastors but rather by metropolitans whose consciousnesses are heightened by the advantages of urban life; his own version of a pastoral, *Winesburg, Ohio*, was itself written in Chicago.

Anderson published three other collections of short stories in his lifetime, and other stories which had appeared in various magazines were posthumously gathered by Paul Rosenfeld in *The Sherwood Anderson Reader*. These are anthologies with no common theme or recurring characters, although some, such as *Horses and Men*, portray a particular milieu such as the racing world or rustic life. Many of the stories, and nearly all those singled out by the critics for their high quality, are first-person narratives. They are told in a rambling, reminiscent vein and are often preferred to those in *Winesburg, Ohio* because they lack a staged gravity. The grotesques are there, but less as syndromes than as atmospheric effects.

"Death in the Woods" • The gothic nature of the later stories becomes more pronounced, and violence, desolation, and decay gain ascendancy in his best story, "Death in the Woods," from the collection of the same name. This work also has another dimension: It is considered "to be among that wide and interesting mass of creative literature written about literature," for, as the narrator tells the story of the elderly drudge who freezes to death while taking a shortcut through the snowy woods, he explains that as a young man he worked on the farm of a German who kept a bound servant like the young Mrs. Grimes. He recalls the circular track that her dogs made about her body while growing bold enough to get at her bag of meat when he himself has an encounter with dogs on a moonlit winter night. When the woman's body is found and identified, the townspeople turn against her ruffian husband and son and force them out of town, and their dwelling is visited by the narrator after it becomes an abandoned and vandalized hulk.

Because Mrs. Grimes is such an unobtrusive and inarticulate character, the narrator is forced to tell her story, as well as how he gained each aspect of the story, until the readers' interest is awakened by the uncovering of the narrator's mental operations. This process leads the narrator to ponder further how literature itself is written and guides him to the final expansion: consciousness of his own creative processes. The transfer of interest from the uncanny circumstances of Mrs. Grimes's death to this awareness of human creativity lends some credibility to Sherwood Anderson's epitaph, "Life, Not Death, Is the Great Adventure."

"The Man Who Became a Woman" • "The Man Who Became a Woman," from *Horses and Men*, is another critic's choice. A young horse groom is sneaking a drink at a bar and imagines that his image on the counter mirror is that of a young girl. He becomes involved in an appalling barroom brawl (its horror contradicts the popular image of brawls in Westerns), and later, while sleeping nude on top of a pile of horse blankets, he is nearly raped by two drunken black grooms who mistake him for a slim young woman. The several strong foci in this long story tend to cancel one another out, and the built-in narrative devices for explaining the reason for the telling of the story succeed only in giving it a disconnected feel, although it is the equal of "Death in the Woods" in gothic details.

"I Am a Fool" • "I Am a Fool," also from *Horses and Men*, is Anderson's most popular story. Here a young horse groom describes a humiliation caused less by his own gaucheness with the opposite sex than by the gulf of social class and education which separates him from the girl. The story re-creates the universe of adolescent romance so well presented in *Winesburg, Ohio* and brings a knowing smile from all manner of readers.

"The Egg" • In "The Egg" (from *The Triumph of the Egg*), a husband-and-wife team of entrepreneurs try their hand at chicken-raising and running a restaurant. They fail at both, and the cause in both instances is an egg. This is a mildly humorous spoof on the American penchant for quick-success schemes, which nevertheless does not explain the praise the story has been given.

"The Corn Planting" • "The Corn Planting" (from *The Sherwood Anderson Reader*) is Anderson without histrionics. An elderly farm couple are told that their city-dwelling son has been killed in an automobile accident. In response, the pair rig a planting machine and set about planting corn in the middle of the night while still in their nightgowns. At this concluding point, a generous reader would marvel at this poignant and internally opportune description of a rite of rejuvenation. An obdurate one would mutter Karl Marx's dictum on the idiocy of rural life (not quite apropos since Marx was referring to European peasants, not technologically advanced American farmers); but this reader shall remark that the story itself functions within its confines and breezily add that Anderson's favorite appellation (and the title of one of his short stories) was "An Ohio Pagan."

Julian Grajewski
With updates by Cassandra Kircher

Other major works

PLAYS: *Plays: Winesburg and Others*, pb. 1937.

NOVELS: *Windy McPherson's Son*, 1916; *Marching Men*, 1917; *Winesburg, Ohio*, 1919; *Poor White*, 1920; *Many Marriages*, 1923; *Dark Laughter*, 1925; *Beyond Desire*, 1932; *Kit Brandon*, 1936.

NONFICTION: *A Story Teller's Story*, 1924; *The Modern Writer*, 1925; *Sherwood Anderson's Notebook*, 1926; *Tar: A Midwest Childhood*, 1926; *Hello Towns!*, 1929; *Perhaps Women*, 1931; *No Swank*, 1934; *Puzzled America*, 1935; *Home Town*, 1940; *Sherwood Anderson's Memoirs*, 1942; *The Letters of Sherwood Anderson*, 1953; *Sherwood Anderson: Selected Letters*, 1984; *Letters to Bab: Sherwood Anderson to Marietta D. Finley, 1916-1933*, 1985.

POETRY: *Mid-American Chants*, 1918; *A New Testament*, 1927.

Bibliography

Appel, Paul P. *Homage to Sherwood Anderson: 1876-1941*. Mamaroneck, N.Y.: Paul P. Appel, 1970. Collection of essays originally published in homage to Anderson after his death in 1941. Among the contributors are Theodore Dreiser, Gertrude Stein, Thomas Wolfe, Henry Miller, and William Saroyan. Also includes Anderson's previously unpublished letters and his essay "The Modern Writer," which had been issued as a limited edition in 1925.

Bassett, John E. *Sherwood Anderson: An American Career*. Selinsgrove, Pa.: Susquehanna University Press, 2006. Biography of Anderson that focuses on his nonfiction and journalistic writing and takes a look at how he coped with cultural changes during his time.

Campbell, Hilbert H. "The 'Shadow People': Feodor Sologub and Sherwood Anderson's *Winesburg, Ohio*." *Studies in Short Fiction* 33 (Winter, 1996): 51-58. Discusses parallels between some of Sologub's stories in *The Old House, and Other Tales* and the stories in *Winesburg, Ohio*. Suggests that the Sologub stories influenced Anderson. Cites parallels to Sologub's tales in such Anderson stories as "Tandy," "Loneliness," and "The Book of the Grotesque."

Ellis, James. "Sherwood Anderson's Fear of Sexuality: Horses, Men, and Homosexuality." *Studies in Short Fiction* 30 (Fall, 1993): 595-601. On the basis of biographer Kim Townsend's suggestion that Anderson sought out male spiritual friendships because he believed that sexuality would debase the beauty of woman, Ellis examines Anderson's treatment of sexuality as a threat in male relationships in "I Want to Know Why" and "The Man Who Became a Woman."

Hansen, Tom. "Who's a Fool? A Rereading of Sherwood Anderson's 'I'm a Fool.'" *The Midwest Quarterly* 38 (Summer, 1997): 372-379. Argues that the narrator is the victim of his own self-importance and is thus played for a fool. Discusses class consciousness and conflict in the story.

May, Charles E., ed. *Masterplots II: Short Story Series, Revised Edition*. 8 vols. Pasadena, Calif.: Salem Press, 2004. Designed for student use, this reference set contains articles providing detailed plot summaries and analyses of these seven short stories by Anderson: "Death in the Woods" and "The Egg" (vol. 2), "Hands" (vol. 3), "I Want to Know Why" and "I'm a Fool" (vol. 4), "The Man Who Became a Woman" (vol. 5), and "Sophistication" (vol. 7).

Papinchak, Robert Allen. *Sherwood Anderson: A Study of the Short Fiction*. New York: Twayne, 1992. Introduction to Anderson's short stories that examines his search for an appropriate form and his experimentations with form in the stories in *Winesburg, Ohio*, as well as those that appeared before and after that highly influential book. Deals with Anderson's belief that the most authentic history of life is a history of moments when we truly live, as well as his creation of the grotesque as an American type that also reflects a new social reality.

Rideout, Walter B., ed. *Sherwood Anderson: A Collection of Critical Essays.* Englewood Cliffs, N.J.: Prentice-Hall, 1974. Treats Anderson from a variety of perspectives: as prophet, storyteller, and maker of American myths.

Small, Judy Jo. *A Reader's Guide to the Short Stories of Sherwood Anderson.* New York: G. K. Hall, 1994. Provides commentary on every story in *Winesburg, Ohio, The Triumph of the Egg, Horses and Men,* and *Death in the Woods.* Small summarizes the interpretations of other critics and supplies historical and biographical background, accounts of how the stories were written, the period in which they were published, and their reception. Ideally suited for students and general readers.

Townsend, Kim. *Sherwood Anderson.* Boston: Houghton Mifflin, 1987. In this biography of Sherwood Anderson, Townsend focuses, in part, on how Anderson's life appears in his writing. Supplemented by twenty-six photographs and a useful bibliography of Anderson's work.

Maya Angelou

Born: St. Louis, Missouri; April 4, 1928

Principal short fiction • "Steady Going Up," 1972; "The Reunion," 1983.

Other literary forms • Maya Angelou is known primarily as a poet and autobiographer. She has produced more than a dozen volumes of poetry, ranging from *Just Give Me a Cool Drink of Water 'fore I Diiie* in 1971 to *Amazing Peace* in 2005 and *Mother: A Cradle to Hold Me* in 2006. She has also published six volumes of autobiography and autobiographical essay, starting with *I Know Why the Caged Bird Sings* in 1970 and ranging through *A Song Flung Up to Heaven* in 2002 and *Hallelujah! The Welcome Table: A Lifetime of Memories with Recipes* in 2004. The latter is both a memoir and a cookbook. Her other writings include six published plays, many screenplays, and nine books for children. The latter include *Angelina of Italy, Izak of Lapland, Mikale of Hawaii,* and *Renie Marie of France,* all of which she published in 2004.

Achievements • *I Know Why the Caged Bird Sings* was nominated for the National Book Award in 1970, and Maya Angelou's first volume of poetry (*Just Give Me a Cool Drink of Water 'fore I Diiie*) was nominated for the Pulitzer Prize in 1972. Angelou was also nominated for Tony Awards for her performances in *Look Away* in 1973 and *Roots* in 1977, and she won a Grammy Award for best spoken word or nontraditional album for "On the Pulse of Morning," the poem she read at the first inauguration of President Bill Clinton in 1993. She holds more than two dozen honorary doctorates, among numerous other awards.

Biography • Maya Angelou was born (as Marguerite Johnson) in St. Louis, Missouri, and spent time as a young girl in Arkansas (in Stamps, near Hope, where Clinton grew up) and California. She was raped at the age of eight by her mother's boyfriend (a story that is retold in *I Know Why the Caged Bird Sings*), had a son by the time she was sixteen, and worked at a number of jobs before she became an artist. In her early career, she was a singer and an actor, appearing in plays and musicals around the world through the 1950's and 1960's. She has since directed plays and films, recorded music and spoken word, and appeared on television as both a narrator and a series host. She has also taught at various American universities since the 1960's and at Wake Forest University since 1981. She has been an outspoken advocate of civil and human rights most of her adult life, and she has lectured and written widely about these issues for decades.

Analysis • Maya Angelou has produced only a few short stories, but those stories, like her multiple volumes of autobiography, deal directly and poignantly with issues of African American life in America. Since her early years, Angelou has been a political activist and educator, and she is knowledgeable and articulate about civil rights and related issues. Her fiction, like her poetry and her nonfiction, reflects social issues and conditions in the second half of the twentieth century, when racial barriers were falling, but the problems behind them continued. In this sense, Angelou must be con-

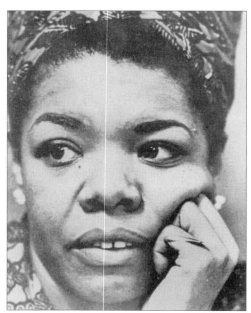

Courtesy, Central Arkansas Library

sidered a social realist, for her stories demonstrate the difficulties of growing up an African American woman in an America still riven by racism and sexism. Dozens of anthologies and other collections of contemporary literature have excerpted pieces from one or another of Angelou's autobiographies because they raise so many important issues about modern America—about identity, education, gender, and race. Her short stories are only marginally more fictional and raise many of the same issues.

"Steady Going Up" • "Steady Going Up" was first published in the collection *Ten Times Black* in 1972 and has since been reprinted several times, including in Gloria Naylor's *Children of the Night: The Best Short Stories by Black Writers, 1967 to the Present* (1995).

The story seems more dated than "The Reunion" but raises several important questions nonetheless. As the story opens, a young black man, Robert, is traveling by bus from his home in Memphis to Cincinnati. He has never before been out of Tennessee, but this is hardly a pleasure trip, for he is rushing to pick up his younger sister at the nursing school where she has suddenly become ill (possibly from kidney trouble). Robert has raised Baby Sister since their parents died within six months of each other: "He was three years older than she when, at the age of fifteen, he took over as head of the family." Getting a job as a mechanic at a local garage, he has been able to support Baby Sister, see her through high school, and send her to nursing school. He has had to put his own life on hold (he plans to marry Barbara Kendrick when Baby Sister is finished with school), and now her illness may further complicate his life. The bus ride is full of understandable anxiety for Robert.

When the bus makes its last stop before Cincinnati, Robert gets off to relieve himself but is cornered in the "colored" bathroom by two white men, who have also been traveling on the bus. An older black woman, who was sitting across the aisle from Robert during the trip, has already warned him about the two men, who have been drinking and staring at him. Now they confront him, accusing him of going north to find white women. Robert cannot "stand the intention of meanness" in the two men, and he decides to act so that he will not miss the bus: "He wasn't going to get left with these two crazy men." When one tries to force him to drink the bourbon that has made them both drunk, Robert kicks him in the groin and then hits the other man over the head with the bottle. Robert manages to get back on the bus, hiding the blood on his hands and shirt, and the bus pulls away with the two men still sprawled in the bathroom. There is no resolution to the story except this escape. Robert has left "those crazy men"—at least for now—but readers wonder what will happen to him. He may be free of them for the moment, but the hatred and violence they represent will continue to follow him. The story ends with a neutral description of the continuing bus trip: "Then he felt the big motor turn and the lights darkened and that old big baby pulled away from the sidewalk and on its way to Cincinnati." Robert's problems—as for so many African Americans at this time—still lie before him.

"The Reunion" • "The Reunion" has been collected several times, first in the Amina and Amiri Baraka collection *Confirmation: An Anthology of African American Women*. The story is short (only five pages) but is a much more positive short fiction than the earlier "Steady Going Up," with its lack of resolution. The story is set in 1958 and is narrated by a jazz pianist named Philomena Jenkins, who is playing the Sunday matinee at the Blue Palm Café on the South Side of Chicago with the Cal Callen band. It is a club filled with other African Americans, but suddenly on this day Philomena spots Miss Beth Ann Baker, a white woman sitting with Willard, a large black man. The sight sends Philomena back in memory to her painful childhood growing up in Baker, Georgia, where her parents worked for the Bakers, and she lived in the servants' quarters behind the Baker main house.

The memories are painful because these were "years of loneliness," when Philomena was called "the Baker Nigger" by other children, and she has moved a long way from "the hurt Georgia put on me" to her present success in jazz music. She fantasizes about what she will say to Beth Ann when she meets her, but when they finally face each other at the bar a little later in the story, it is Beth Ann who does all the talking. She is going to marry Willard, who is a south side school teacher, she tells Philomena, and she claims she is very happy. However, her parents have disowned her and even forbidden her to return to Baker. It is clear that she is with Willard to spite her parents, for she sounds to Philomena like "a ten-year-old just before a tantrum," "white and rich and spoiled." When Beth Ann invites "Mena" to their wedding, the narrator replies simply, "'Good-bye Beth. Tell your parents I said go to hell and take you with them, just for company.'" When she returns to her piano after this break, she realizes that Beth Ann

> had the money, but I had the music. She and her parents had had the power to hurt me when I was young, but look, the stuff in me lifted me up above them. No matter how bad times became, I would always be the song struggling to be heard.

Through her tears, Philomena has had an epiphany and experienced a form of reconciliation with her true self, in the recognition that art can transcend social inequity. In the story's last lines, "The piano keys were slippery with tears. I know, I sure as hell wasn't crying for myself." Like a number of other artists (James Baldwin and Amiri Baraka, among them), Maya Angelou posits art—and thus literature—as one way of getting above and beyond the social injustices that her society has created. Philomena cannot erase the painful childhood memories, but her music can lift her and others above them to another, healthier human plane. The hurt may remain, but the "song struggling to be heard" is stronger.

David Peck

Other major works

CHILDREN'S LITERATURE: *Mrs. Flowers: A Moment of Friendship*, 1986 (illustrated by Etienne Delessert); *Life Doesn't Frighten Me*, 1993 (poetry; illustrated by Jean-Michel Basquiat); *Soul Looks Back in Wonder*, 1993; *My Painted House, My Friendly Chicken, and*

Me, 1994; *Kofi and His Magic*, 1996; *Angelina of Italy*, 2004; *Izak of Lapland*, 2004; *Mikale of Hawaii*, 2004; *Renie Marie of France*, 2004.

PLAYS: *Cabaret for Freedom*, pr. 1960 (with Godfrey Cambridge; musical); *The Least of These*, pr. 1966; *Encounters*, pr. 1973; *Ajax*, pr. 1974 (adaptation of Sophocles' play); *And Still I Rise*, pr. 1976; *King*, pr. 1990 (musical; lyrics with Alistair Beaton, book by Lonne Elder III; music by Richard Blackford).

NONFICTION: *I Know Why the Caged Bird Sings*, 1970 (autobiography); *Gather Together in My Name*, 1974 (autobiography); *Singin' and Swingin' and Gettin' Merry Like Christmas*, 1976 (autobiography); *The Heart of a Woman*, 1981 (autobiography); *All God's Children Need Traveling Shoes*, 1986 (autobiography); *Wouldn't Take Nothing for My Journey Now*, 1993 (autobiographical essays); *Even the Stars Look Lonesome*, 1997; *A Song Flung Up to Heaven*, 2002 (autobiographical essays); *Hallelujah! The Welcome Table: A Lifetime of Memories with Recipes*, 2004 (memoir and cookbook).

POETRY: *Just Give Me a Cool Drink of Water 'fore I Diiie*, 1971; *Oh Pray My Wings Are Gonna Fit Me Well*, 1975; *And Still I Rise*, 1978; *Shaker, Why Don't You Sing?*, 1983; *Poems: Maya Angelou*, 1986; *Now Sheba Sings the Song*, 1987 (Tom Feelings, illustrator); *I Shall Not Be Moved: Poems*, 1990; *On the Pulse of Morning*, 1993; *Phenomenal Woman: Four Poems Celebrating Women*, 1994; *The Complete Collected Poems of Maya Angelou*, 1994; *A Brave and Startling Truth*, 1995; *Amazing Peace*, 2005; *Mother: A Cradle to Hold Me*, 2006.

SCREENPLAYS: *Georgia, Georgia*, 1972; *All Day Long*, 1974.

TELEPLAYS: *Black, Blues, Black*, 1968 (ten epidsodes); *The Inheritors*, 1976; *The Legacy*, 1976; *I Know Why the Caged Bird Sings*, 1979 (with Leonora Thuna and Ralph B. Woolsey); *Sister, Sister*, 1982; *Brewster Place*, 1990.

Bibliography

Bair, Barbara J. "Steady Going Up." In *Masterplots II: Short Story Series*, edited by Charles E. May. Rev. ed. Vol. 7. Pasadena, Calif.: Salem Press, 2004. Analysis of "Steady Going Up" with sections on themes and meaning and style and technique. Also includes a detailed synopsis of the story.

Bloom, Harold, ed. *Maya Angelou*. Philadelphia: Chelsea House, 1999. This selection of essays dealing with Angelou's poetry and prose broaches, among other subjects, the singular relationship of Angelou to her audience and her distinctively African American mode of literary expression.

Ducksworth, Sarah Smith. "The Reunion." In *Masterplots II: Short Story Series*, edited by Charles E. May. Rev. ed. Vol. 6. Pasadena, Calif.: Salem Press, 2004. Student-friendly analysis of "The Reunion" that covers the story's themes and style and includes a detailed synopsis.

Elliott, Jeffrey M., ed. *Conversations with Maya Angelou*. Jackson: University Press of Mississippi, 1989. Part of the University Press of Mississippi's ongoing Literary Conversations series, this work is a collection of more than thirty interviews with Angelou that originally appeared in various magazines and newspapers, accompanied by a chronology of her life. Provides a multifaceted perspective on the creative issues that have informed Angelou's work as an autobiographer and a poet.

Guntern, Gottlieb, ed. *The Challenge of Creative Leadership*. London: Shepheard-Walwyn, 1997. Guntern's criteria for those who inspire others to move beyond mediocrity are explored in these philosophical pieces. Among these criteria are originality, elegance, and profundity.

Hagen, Lynn B. *Heart of a Woman, Mind of a Writer, and Soul of a Poet: A Critical Analysis of the Writings of Maya Angelou*. Lanham, Md.: University Press of America, 1996.

Although a number of scholarly works address the different literary forms Angelou has undertaken (most devoted to autobiography), few critical volumes survey her entire opus, and Hagen's is one of the best. Chapters include "Wit and Wisdom/Mirth and Mischief," "Abstracts in Ethics," and "Overview."

King, Sarah E. *Maya Angelou: Greeting the Morning.* Brookfield, Conn.: Millbrook Press, 1994. Includes biographical references and an index. Examines Angelou's life, from her childhood in the segregated South to her rise to prominence as a writer.

Lisandrelli, Elaine Slivinski. *Maya Angelou: More than a Poet.* Springfield, N.J.: Enslow, 1996. Lisandrelli discusses the flamboyance of Angelou, comparing her to the earlier African American author Zora Neale Hurston. Their hard work, optimism, perseverance, and belief in themselves are extolled.

Lupton, Mary Jane. *Maya Angelou: A Critical Companion.* Westport, Conn.: Greenwood Press, 1998. Although focusing mainly on the autobiographies, Lupton's study is still useful as a balanced assessment of Angelou's writings. The volume also contains an excellent bibliography, particularly of Angelou's autobiographical works.

O'Neale, Sondra. "Reconstruction of the Composite Self: New Images of Black Women in Maya Angelou's Continuing Autobiography." In *Black Women Writers* (1950-1980), edited by Mari Evans. Garden City, N.Y.: Anchor Press, 1983. O'Neale argues that Angelou's primary contribution to the canon of African American literature lies in her realistic portrayal of the lives of black people, especially black women. O'Neale goes on to demonstrate the ways in which Angelou successfully destroys many of the stereotypes of black women.

Williams, Mary E., ed. *Readings on Maya Angelou.* San Diego, Calif.: Greenhaven Press, 1997. This collection of essays by literary scholars and noted faculty offers diverse voices and approaches to Angelou's literary canon.

Margaret Atwood

Born: Ottawa, Ontario, Canada; November 18, 1939

Principal short fiction • *Dancing Girls, and Other Stories*, 1977; *Bluebeard's Egg*, 1983; *Murder in the Dark: Short Fictions and Prose Poems*, 1983; *Wilderness Tips*, 1991; *Good Bones*, 1992 (pb. in U.S. as *Good Bones and Simple Murders*, 1994); *Moral Disorder: Atwood Stories*, 2006.

Other literary forms • Margaret Atwood's publishing history is a testimonial to her remarkable productivity and versatility as an author. She is the author of numerous books, including poetry, novels, children's literature, and nonfiction. In Canada, she is most admired for her poetry, which has been collected in more than two dozen volumes, ranging from *Double Persephone* in 1964 to *Eating Fire* in 1998.

Outside Canada, Atwood is better known as a novelist, particularly for *Surfacing* (1972) and *The Handmaid's Tale* (1985). Her other novels include *The Edible Woman* (1969), *Lady Oracle* (1976), *Bodily Harm* (1981), and *Alias Grace* (1996). Among her volumes of poetry are *The Circle Game* (1964), *The Animals in That Country* (1968), *The Journals of Susanna Moodie* (1970), *Interlunar* (1984), *Morning in the Burned House* (1995), *The Blind Assassin* (2000), *Oryx and Crake* (2003), and *The Penelopiad* (2005).

In 1972, Atwood published *Survival: A Thematic Guide to Canadian Literature*, a controversial critical work on Canadian literature, and in 1982, *Second Words: Selected Critical Prose*, which is in the vanguard of feminist criticism in Canada. She later followed those nonfiction works with *Negotiating with the Dead: A Writer on Writing* (2002) and *Moving Targets: with Intent: Essays, Reviews, Personal Prose, 1983-2005* (2005). Her published interviews have been collected in several volumes, including *Waltzing Again: New and Selected Conversations with Margaret Atwood* (2006).

Atwood has also written for television and theater, one of her successful ventures being "The Festival of Missed Crass," a short story made into a musical for Toronto's Young People's Theater. Atwood's conscious scrutiny, undertaken largely in her nonfiction writing, turned from external political and cultural repression to the internalized effects of various kinds of repression on the individual psyche. The same theme is evident in her fiction; her novel *Cat's Eye* (1988) explores the subordination of character Elaine Risley's personality to that of her domineering "friend" Cordelia.

Achievements • Margaret Atwood is a prolific and controversial writer of international prominence whose works have been translated into many languages. She has received several honorary doctorates and is the recipient of numerous honors, prizes, and awards, including the Governor-General's Award for Poetry in 1967 for *The Circle Game*, the Governor-General's Award for Fiction in 1986 and the Arthur C. Clarke Award for Best Science Fiction in 1987 for *The Handmaid's Tale*, the Ida Nudel Humanitarian Award in 1986 from the Canadian Jewish Congress, the American Humanist of the Year Award in 1987, and the Trillium Award for Excellence in Ontario Writing for *Wilderness Tips* in 1992 and for her 1993 novel *The Robber Bride* in 1994. The French government honored her with the prestigious Chevalier dans l'Ordre des Arts et des Lettres in 1994.

Two of Atwood's novels have been selected for CBC Radio's *Canada Reads* competition: *The Handmaid's Tale*, supported by former prime minister Kim Campbell in 2002, and *Oryx and Crake* (2003), supported by Toronto city councillor Olivia Chow in 2005.

Biography • Margaret Eleanor Atwood was born in Ottawa, Ontario, Canada, on November 18, 1939. She grew up in northern Ontario, Quebec, and Toronto. Following graduation from Victoria College, University of Toronto, she attended Radcliffe College at Harvard University on a Woodrow Wilson Fellowship, receiving a master's degree in English in 1962. She taught at a number of Canadian universities and traveled extensively. During the early 1990's Atwood was a lecturer of English at the University of British Columbia at Vancouver. She later settled in Toronto with writer Graeme Gibson and their daughter, Jess.

Courtesy, Vancouver International Writers Festival

Atwood's output was steady in fiction and particularly in nonfiction. She made successful forays into the fields of script writing for film and musical theater, and she also produced notable novels. It is her prolific, passionate essay and article writing on a variety of national and international social issues, however, of which human rights is her central concern, that made her a bellwether of Canadian opinion. Her involvement with world political and social issues became evident in her vice leadership of the Writers' Union of Canada and her presidency of the International Association of Poets, Playwrights, Editors, and Novelists (PEN), where she waged a vigorous battle against literary censorship. Her association with Amnesty International prompted an increasingly strong expression of her moral vision.

Analysis • One of Margaret Atwood's central themes is storytelling itself, and most of her fiction relates to that theme in some way. The short-story collections each focus on key issues. *Dancing Girls* is primarily concerned with otherness, alienation, and the ways in which people estrange themselves from one another. *Bluebeard's Egg* revolves around a favorite theme of Atwood's, the Bluebeard tale of a dangerous suitor or husband. The title story explores Sally's excessive concern with her husband and lack of awareness of herself. *Wilderness Tips* centers on the explanatory fiction people tell themselves and one another, on the need to order experience through such fiction, and on the ways in which humans are posing threats to the wilderness, the forests, and open space.

"The Man from Mars" • In *Dancing Girls*, a gift for comic and satiric invention is evident from the first story, "The Man from Mars." Christine, an unattractive undergraduate at a Canadian university, is literally pursued by an odd-looking, desperately poor exchange student. The daily chases of a bizarre, small, Asian man in hot pursuit of a rather large Christine (a mouse chasing an elephant, as Atwood describes it) attract the attention of other students and make Christine interesting to her male acquaintances for the first time. They begin to ask her out, curious as to the mysterious sources of her charm. She begins to feel and actually to be more attractive. As months pass, however, Christine begins to fantasize about this strange man about whom she knows nothing. Is he perhaps a sex maniac, a murderer? Eventually, through the overreactions and interventions of others, complaints are made to the police, and the inscrutable foreigner is deported, leaving Christine with mingled feelings of relief and regret. She graduates and settles into a drab government job and a sterile existence. Years pass. A war breaks out somewhere in the Far East and vividly revives thoughts of the foreigner. His country is the scene of fighting, but Christine cannot remember the name of his city. She becomes obsessed with worry, studying maps, poring over photographs of soldiers and photographs of the wounded and the dead in newspapers and magazines, compulsively searching the television screen for even a brief glimpse of his face. Finally, it is too much. Christine stops looking at pictures, gives away her television set, and does nothing except read nineteenth century novels.

The story is rich in comedy and in social satire, much of it directed against attitudes that make "a person from another culture" as alien as a "man from Mars." Christine's affluent parents think of themselves as liberal and progressive. They have traveled, bringing back a sundial from England and a domestic servant from the West Indies. Christine's mother believes herself to be both tolerant and generous for employing foreigners as domestic servants in her home; she observes that it is difficult to tell whether people from other cultures are insane. Christine also typifies supposedly enlightened, liberal attitudes, having been president of the United Nations Club in high school, and in college a member of the forensics team, debating such topics as the obsolescence of war. Although the story is on the whole a comic and satiric look at the limits of shallow liberalism, there is, however, also some pathos in the end. It seems that the encounter with the alien is the most interesting or significant thing that has ever happened to Christine and that her only feeling of human relationship is for a person with whom she had no real relationship. At the story's conclusion, she seems lost, now past either hope or love, retreating into the unreal but safe world of John Galsworthy and Anthony Trollope.

"Dancing Girls" • Another encounter with the alien occurs in the collection's title story, "Dancing Girls," which is set in the United States during the 1960's. Ann, a graduate student from Toronto, has a room in a seedy boardinghouse. Mrs. Nolan, its American proprietor, befriends Ann because a Canadian does not look "foreign." Mrs. Nolan's other tenants are mathematicians from Hong Kong and an Arab who is becoming crazed with loneliness and isolation. Ann's only other acquaintances are Lelah, a Turkish woman studying Russian literature, and Jetske, a Dutch woman studying urban design. Ann also is studying urban design because she has fantasies of rearranging Toronto. She frequently envisions the open, green spaces she will create, but she seems to have the same limitation as "The City Planners" in Atwood's poem of that name. People are a problem: They ruin her aesthetically perfect designs, cluttering and littering the landscape. Finally, she decides that people such as Mrs. Nolan, Mrs. Nolan's unruly children, and the entire collection of exotics who live in the boardinghouse will have to be excluded from urban utopia by a high wire fence.

Yet an event in the story causes Ann to change her mind. The Arab whose room is next to hers throws a rowdy party one night for two other Arab students and three "dancing girls." Ann sits in her room in the dark, fascinated, listening to the music, drinking sherry, but with her door securely bolted. As the noise level of the party escalates, Mrs. Nolan calls the police but cannot wait for them to arrive. Overcome by xenophobic and puritanical zeal, she drives the room's occupants out of her house and down the street with a broom.

Ann finally sees Mrs. Nolan for what she evidently is, a "fat crazy woman" intent on destroying some "harmless hospitality." Ann regrets that she lacked courage to open the door and so missed seeing what Mrs. Nolan referred to as the "dancing girls" (either Mrs. Nolan's euphemism for prostitutes or a reflection of her confused ideas about Middle Eastern culture). The story concludes with Ann again envisioning her ideal city, but this time there are many people and no fence. At the center of Ann's fantasy now are the foreigners she has met, with Lelah and Jetske as the "dancing girls." The implication is clear: Ann has resolved her ambivalent feelings about foreigners, has broken out of the need for exclusion and enclosure, and has rejected the racism, tribalism, and paranoia of Mrs. Nolan, who sees the world in terms of "us" versus "them."

"Polarities" • The question of human warmth and life and where they are to be found is more acutely raised in "Polarities," a strange, somewhat abstract story which also comments on the theme of alienation. Louise, a graduate student of literature, and Morrison, a faculty member, are both at the same western provincial university (probably in Alberta). Both are "aliens": Morrison is American and therefore regarded as an outsider and a usurper of a job which should have been given to a Canadian; Louise is a fragile person searching for a place of refuge against human coldness. Louise, a student of the poetry of William Blake, has developed her own private mythology of circles, magnetic grids, and north-south polarities. Her friends, who believe that private mythologies belong in poetry, judge her to be insane and commit her to a mental institution. At first Morrison is not sure what to believe. Finally, he discovers that he loves Louise, but only because she is by now truly crazy, defenseless, "drugged into manageability."

Examining his feelings for Louise and reflecting on her uncanny notebook entries about him, Morrison is forced to confront some unpleasant realities. He realizes that his own true nature is to be a user and a taker rather than a lover and a giver and that all his "efforts to remain human" have led only to "futile work and sterile love." He gets in his car and drives. At the story's end, he is staring into the chill, uninhabitable interior of Canada's far north, a perfect metaphor for the coldness of the human heart that the story has revealed and an ironic reversal of the story's epigraph, with its hopeful reference to humans who somehow "have won from space/ This unchill, habitable interior." The polarities between Louise's initial vision of a warmly enclosing circle of friends and Morrison's final bleak vision of what poet William Butler Yeats called "the desolation of reality" seem irreconcilable in this story.

"Giving Birth" • The final story in *Dancing Girls* is the most ambitious and complex in this collection. "Giving Birth" is about a physical process, but it is also about language and the relationship between fiction and reality. The narrator (possibly Atwood herself, who gave birth to a daughter in 1976) tells a story of a happily pregnant woman named Jeanie. Jeanie diligently attends natural-childbirth classes and cheerfully anticipates the experience of birth and motherhood. A thoroughly modern woman, she does "not intend to go through hell. Hell comes from the wrong attitude." Yet Jeanie is shadowed by a phantom pregnant woman, clearly a projection of the vague apprehensions and deep fears that Jeanie has repressed. When the day arrives, Jeanie calmly rides to the hospital with her husband and her carefully packed suitcase; the other woman is picked up on a street corner carrying a brown paper bag. As Jeanie waits cheerfully for a room, the other woman is screaming with pain. While Jeanie is taken to the labor room in a wheelchair, the other woman is rolled by on a table with her eyes closed and a tube in her arm: "Something is wrong."

In this story, Atwood suggests that such mysterious human ordeals as giving birth or dying can never be adequately prepared for or fully communicated through language: "When there is no pain she feels nothing, when there is pain, she feels nothing because there is no *she*. This, finally, is the disappearance of language." For what happens to the shadowy woman, the narrator says, "there is no word in the language." The story is concerned with the archaic ineptness of language. Why the expression, "giving birth"? Who gives it? And to whom is it given? Why speak this way at all when birth is an event, not a thing? Why is there no corollary expression, "giving death"? The narrator believes some things need to be renamed, but she is not the one for the task: "These are the only words I have, I'm stuck with them, stuck in them." Her task is to descend into the ancient tar pits of language (to use Atwood's metaphor) and to retrieve an experience before it becomes layered over by time and ultimately changed or lost. Jeanie is thus revealed to be an earlier version of the narrator herself; the telling of the story thus gives birth to Jeanie, just as Jeanie gave birth to the narrator: "It was to me, after all, that birth was given, Jeanie gave it, I am the rez senses: the biological birth of an infant, the birth of successive selves wrought by experience and time, and the birth of a work of literature which attempts to rescue and fix experience from the chaos and flux of being."

"Bluebeard's Egg" • A frequent theme in Atwood's fiction and poetry is the power struggle between men and women. At times, the conflict seems to verge on insanity, as in "Under Glass," "Lives of the Poets," "Loulou: Or, The Domestic Life of the Language," and "Ugly Puss." The title story in *Bluebeard's Egg*, however, seems less bleak. In a reversal of sexual stereotypes, Sally loves her husband, Ed, because he is beautiful and dumb. She is a dominating, manipulating woman (of the type seen also in "The Resplendent Quetzal"), and her relationship to her husband seems to be that of doting mother to overprotected child, despite the fact that he is a successful and respected cardiologist, and she has no meaningful identity outside her marriage. Bored, Sally takes a writing class in which she is admonished to explore her inner world. Yet she is "fed up with her inner world; she doesn't need to explore it. In her inner world is Ed, like a doll within a Russian wooden doll and in Ed is Ed's inner world, which she can't get at." The more she speculates about Ed's inner world, the more perplexed she becomes. Required to write a version of the Bluebeard fable, Sally decides to retell the story from the point of view of the egg, because it reminds her of Ed's head, both "so closed and unaware." Sally is shocked into a new assessment of Ed, however, when she witnesses a scene of sexual intimacy between her husband and her best friend. Ed is after all not an inert object, a given; instead, he has a mysterious, frightening potential. Sally is no longer complacent, no longer certain she wants to know what lies beneath the surface.

"Significant Moments in the Life of My Mother" • The first and last stories in *Blue-beard's Egg* reveal Atwood in an atypically mellow mood. "Significant Moments in the Life of My Mother" is a loving celebration of the narrator's (presumably Atwood's) mother and father and of an earlier, simpler time. Yet it is never sentimental because Atwood never loses her steely grip on reality. Looking at an old photograph of her mother and friends, the narrator is interested in

> the background . . . a world already hurtling towards ruin, unknown to them: the theory of relativity has been discovered, acid is accumulating at the roots of trees, the bull-frogs are doomed. But they smile with something that from this distance you could almost call gallantry, their right legs thrust forward in parody of a chorus line.

The "significant moments" of the title inevitably include some significant moments in the life of the narrator as well. Amusing discrepancies between mother's and daughter's versions of reality emerge, but not all are funny. For example, the narrator sees that her compulsive need to be solicitous toward men may be the result of early, "lethal" conditioning; her mother sees "merely cute" childhood behavior. The narrator recalls the shock she felt when her mother expressed a wish to be in some future incarnation an archaeologist—inconceivable that she could wish to be anything other than the narrator's mother. Yet when the narrator becomes a mother herself, she gains a new perspective and "this moment altered for me." What finally emerges between mother and narrator-daughter is not communication but growing estrangement. Recalling herself as a university student, she feels as though she has become as unfathomable to her mother as "a visitor from outer space, a time-traveler come back from the future, bearing news of a great disaster." There are distances too great for maternal love to cross. Atwood is too much of a realist to omit this fact.

"Unearthing Suite" • The final story, "Unearthing Suite," another seemingly auto-biographical reminiscence, begins with the parents' pleased announcement that they have purchased their funeral urns. Their daughter is stunned—they are far more alive than she. Mother at the age of seventy-three figure skates, swims daily in glacial lakes, and sweeps leaves off steeply pitched roofs. Father pursues dozens of interests at once: botany, zoology, history, politics, carpentry, gardening. From her torpor, the narrator wonders at their vitality and, above all, at their enviable poise in the face of life's grim realities, those past as well as those yet to come. Perhaps the answer is that they have always remained close to the earth, making earthworks in the wild, moving granite, digging in gardens, and always responding joyously to earth's little unexpected gifts such as the visit of a rare fisher bird at the story's end, for them the equivalent of a visit "by an unknown but by no means minor god." The narrator appreciates her parents' wise tranquillity. She cannot, however, share it.

Wilderness Tips • Atwood's stories are frequently explorations of human limitation, presentations of people as victims of history, biology, or cultural conditioning. The theme of isolation and alienation recurs: There are borders and fences; generational gaps, which make parents and children strangers to each other; failed communication between women and men; gaps between language and felt experience. It is easy to overstate the pessimism which is present in her writings, to see only the wreckage of lives and relationships with which her work is strewn. It is therefore important not to lose sight of the human strength and tenacity (a favorite Atwood word) which also informs her work.

Eight years later, the stories in Atwood's short-fiction collection *Wilderness Tips* ultimately celebrated (still grudgingly) the same human strength and tenacity. This and related themes that shaped Atwood's vision over her writing life are embodied in the sometimes humorous and self-deprecating, often grim and urgent, seekings of the (mostly) female protagonists both to liberate and to preserve themselves in an increasingly ugly world. The conflicts that oppress these characters are rendered more nastily brutish by the realities of middle-class Canadian society in the late twentieth century. The predominant setting is Toronto, no longer "the Good" but now the polluted, the unsafe, the dingy, the dangerous, and, worst, the indifferent.

The battle between the sexes is again the focus of most of the ten stories, the combatants ranging from youth through middle age. For the most part, the battles are lost or at best fought to a draw; the victories are Pyrrhic. In "True Trash," the consequences of adolescent sexual and social betrayals at a wilderness summer camp are dealt with only by escape into the banal anonymity of adulthood in the city. In "Hairball," Kat, who is in her thirties, is betrayed by both a previously acquiescent lover and her own body. Stripped of the brittle security she had carefully built for herself, she hits back with a spectacularly gross act of revenge. In "Isis in Darkness," conventional, secretly romantic Richard invests the poet Selena with a spiritual transcendence totally at odds with her real-life alienation and pathetic descent to early death over the years of their tenuous relationship. In "Weight," the narrator, a woman of substance, lives by compromise, paying defiant homage to the memory of her scrappy, optimistic friend Molly, who was battered to death by her mad husband. For many of these protagonists (as in Atwood's other works), language is a weapon of choice: In "Uncles," Susanna, though emotionally unfulfilled, is a successful, ambitious journalist; in "Hack Wednesday," Marcia is a freelance columnist; in "Weight," the narrator and Molly, aggressive lawyers, play elaborate word games to ward off threatening realities; in "The Bog Man," middle-aged Julie mythologizes her disastrous youthful affair with Connor. Nevertheless, as it does so often in Atwood's works, the gulf between language and understanding yawns, exacerbating the difficulties of human connections.

In two of the collection's most successful stories, however, that gulf is bridged by messages spoken, ironically, by the dead. In "The Age of Lead," a television documentary chronicles the exhumation from the Arctic permafrost of the body of young John Torrington, a member of the British Franklin Expedition, killed like his fellows by lead poisoning contracted through their consumption of tinned food. The documentary, which protagonist Jane is sporadically watching, weaves in and out of her recollections of Vincent, a friend from her childhood, recently dead. All their lives, his identity was ephemeral and undefined, but as Jane recalls his slow decline and death of an unnamed disease and ponders his enigmatic nature, the television offers the 150-years-dead Torrington, emerging virtually intact from his icy grave to "speak" eloquently to the living. Similarly, in "Death by Landscape," Lois's childhood acquaintance Lucy, who vanished on a camp canoe trip, slyly returns to haunt the adult Lois in Lois's collection of wilderness landscape paintings, assuming a solidity she never had as a live child.

Still, despite the pessimism, inadequacies, and guilt of many of the stories' characters, the readers' lasting impressions are positive ones. "Hack Wednesday," the last story, speaks the same grumpy optimism that informs much of Atwood's poetry and prose. Marcia knows she will cry on Christmas Day, because life, however horrific at times, rushes by, and she is helpless to stop it: "It's all this hope. She gets distracted by it, and has trouble paying attention to the real news."

Good Bones and Simple Murders • *Good Bones and Simple Murders* incorporates some material from *Murder in the Dark*. The short pieces in this collection have been termed *jeux d'esprit* and speeded-up short stories. They showcase Atwood's wit, control, and wordplay as she speculates about hypothetical situations, such as "What would happen if men did all the cooking?", and revises traditional tales, such as "The Little Red Hen." In Atwood's version, the hen remains "henlike" and shares the loaf with all the animals that refused to help her produce it. In these pieces, characters who were silent in the original tales get to tell their side of the story. In "Gertrude Talks Back," Hamlet's mother explains matter-of-factly to her son that his father was a prig and that she murdered him. In "Simmering," the women have been cast out of the kitchens and surreptitiously reminisce about the good old days when they were allowed to cook.

Many of the short pieces here are explicitly about storytelling. The first story, "Murder in the Dark," describes a detective game and presents the writer as a trickster, a spinner of lies. "Unpopular Gals" tells of the mysterious women of traditional stories, the witches and evil stepmothers who tell their own side of the story here. "Let Us Now Praise Stupid Women" explains that it is not the careful, prudent, rational women who inspire fiction but rather the careless "airheads," the open, ingenuous, innocent women who set the plots in motion and make stories happen. "Happy Endings" plays with variations on a simple plot, answering in different ways what happens after a man and a woman meet. "The Page" explores the blank whiteness of an empty page and the myriad stories that lurk beneath it.

Atwood does not imply that human experience is beyond understanding, that evil is necessarily beyond redemption, or that human beings are beyond transformation. Her wit, humor, irony, imagination, and sharp intelligence save her and her readers from despair, if anything can. To write at all in this negative age seems in itself an act of courage and affirmation, an act Margaret Atwood gives no sign of renouncing. Though her readers already know Atwood's message, it bears repeating.

Karen A. Kildahl
With updates by Jill Rollins and Karen F. Stein

Other major works

NOVELS: *The Edible Woman*, 1969; *Surfacing*, 1972; *Lady Oracle*, 1976; *Life Before Man*, 1979; *Bodily Harm*, 1981; *The Handmaid's Tale*, 1985; *Cat's Eye*, 1988; *The Robber Bride*, 1993; *Alias Grace*, 1996; *The Blind Assassin*, 2000; *Oryx and Crake*, 2003; *The Penelopiad: They Myth of Penelope and Odysseus*, 2005.

POETRY: *Double Persephone*, 1961; *The Circle Game*, 1964 (single poem), 1966 (collection); *Kaleidoscopes Baroque: A Poem*, 1965; *Talismans for Children*, 1965; *Expeditions*, 1966; *Speeches for Dr. Frankenstein*, 1966; *The Animals in That Country*, 1968; *What Was in the Garden*, 1969; *Procedures for Underground*, 1970; *The Journals of Susanna Moodie*, 1970; *Power Politics*, 1971; *You Are Happy*, 1974; *Selected Poems*, 1976; *Two-Headed Poems*, 1978; *True Stories*, 1981; *Snake Poems*, 1983; *Interlunar*, 1984; *Selected Poems II: Poems Selected and New, 1976-1986*, 1987; *Selected Poems, 1966-1984*, 1990; *Poems, 1965-1975*,

1991; *Poems, 1976-1989*, 1992; *Morning in the Burned House*, 1995; *Eating Fire: Selected Poems, 1965-1995*, 1998.

NONFICTION: *Survival: A Thematic Guide to Canadian Literature*, 1972; *Second Words: Selected Critical Prose*, 1982; *The CanLit Foodbook: From Pen to Palate, a Collection of Tasty Literary Fare*, 1987; *Margaret Atwood: Conversations*, 1990; *Deux sollicitudes: Entretiens*, 1996 (with Victor-Lévy Beaulieu; *Two Solicitudes: Conversations*, 1998); *Negotiating with the Dead: A Writer on Writing*, 2002; *Moving Targets: Writing with Intent, 1982-2004*, 2004 (pb. in U.S. as *Writing with Intent: Essays, Reviews, Personal Prose, 1983-2005*, 2005); *Waltzing Again: New and Selected Conversations with Margaret Atwood*, 2006 (with others; Earl G. Ingersoll, editor).

CHILDREN'S LITERATURE: *Up in the Tree*, 1978; *Anna's Pet*, 1980 (with Joyce Barkhouse); *For the Birds*, 1990; *Princess Prunella and the Purple Peanut*, 1995 (illustrated by Maryann Kowalski); *Rude Ramsay and the Roaring Radishes*, 2004 (illustrated by Dusan Petricic).

ANTHOLOGY: *The New Oxford Book of Canadian Verse in English*, 1982.

MISCELLANEOUS: *The Tent*, 2006.

Bibliography

Bloom, Harold, ed. *Margaret Atwood*. Philadelphia: Chelsea House, 2000. Collection of critical essays about Atwood that have been assembled for student use, from the series Modern Critical Views. Includes an introduction by Bloom.

Brown, Jane W. "Constructing the Narrative of Women's Friendship: Margaret Atwood's Reflexive Fiction." *Literature, Interpretation, Theory* 6 (1995): 197-212. In this special journal issue on Atwood, Brown argues that Atwood's narrative reflects the struggle of women to attain friendship. Maintains Atwood achieves this with such reflexive devices as embedded discourse, narrative fragmentation, and doubling. Discusses the difficulty women have in creating friendships because few women think such friendships are important.

Cooke, Nathalie. *Margaret Atwood: A Critical Companion*. Westport, Conn.: Greenwood Press, 2004. Part of the publisher's series of reference books on popular contemporary writers for students, this volume provides detailed plot summaries and analyses of Atwood's major works, along with character portraits, a biography of Atwood, and an extensive bibliography. Nathalie Cooke is also the author of *Margaret Atwood: A Biography* (1998).

Deery, June. "Science for Feminists: Margaret Atwood's Body of Knowledge." *Twentieth Century Literature* 43 (Winter, 1997): 470-486. Shows how the themes of feminine identity, personal and cultural history, body image, and colonization in Atwood's fiction are described in terms of basic laws of physics. Comments on Atwood's application of scientific concepts of time, space, energy, and matter to the experience of women under patriarchy in an adaptation of male discourse.

Howells, Coral Ann. *Margaret Atwood*. New York: St. Martin's Press, 1996. In this lively critical and biographical study, Howells elucidates issues that have energized all of Atwood's work: feminist issues, literary genres, and her own identity as a Canadian, a woman, and a writer. Focuses on the fiction.

May, Charles E., ed. *Masterplots II: Short Story Series, Revised Edition*. 8 vols. Pasadena, Calif.: Salem Press, 2004. Designed for student use, this reference set contains articles providing detailed plot summaries and analyses of these three short stories by Atwood: "The Man from Mars" (vol. 5), "Rape Fantasies" (vol. 6), and "The Sin-Eater" (vol. 7).

Meindl, Dieter. "Gender and Narrative Perspective in Atwood's Stories." In *Margaret Atwood: Writing and Subjectivity*, edited by Colin Nelson. New York: St. Martin's Press, 1994. Discusses female narrative perspective in Atwood's stories. Shows how stories such as "The Man from Mars" and "The Sin Eater" focus on women's failure to communicate with men, thus trapping themselves inside their own inner worlds.

Nischik, Reingard M., ed. *Margaret Atwood: Works and Impact*. Rochester, N.Y.: Camden House, 2000. Solid collection of original (not reprinted) criticism of a wide variety of aspects of Atwood's writing.

Stein, Karen F. *Margaret Atwood Revisited*. New York: Twayne, 1999. Lucid and thorough overview of Atwood's writing in all genres. Includes references and a selected bibliography. This volume supersedes an equally fine volume in the same series, Jerome Rosenberg's *Margaret Atwood* (1984).

Suarez, Isabel Carrera. "'Yet I Speak, Yet I Exist': Affirmation of the Subject in Atwood's Short Stories." In *Margaret Atwood: Writing and Subjectivity*, edited by Colin Nelson. New York: St. Martin's Press, 1994. Discusses Atwood's treatment of the self and its representation in language in her short stories. Demonstrates how in Atwood's early stories characters are represented or misrepresented by language and how struggle with language is a way to make themselves understood; explains how this struggle is amplified in later stories.

Sullivan, Rosemary. *The Red Shoes: Margaret Atwood, Starting Out*. Toronto: Harper-Flamingo Canada, 1998. Biography focusing on Atwood's early life through the 1970's. Attempts to explain how Atwood became a writer and to describe the unfolding of her career.

Isaac Babel

Born: Odessa, Ukraine, Russian Empire (now in Ukraine); July 13, 1894
Died: Butyrka prison, Moscow, Soviet Union (now in Russia); January 27, 1940

Principal short fiction • *Rasskazy*, 1925; *Istoriia moei golubiatni*, 1926; *Konarmiia*, 1926 (*Red Cavalry*, 1929); *Odesskie rasskazy*, 1931 (*Tales of Odessa*, 1955); *Benya Krik, the Gangster, and Other Stories*, 1948; *The Collected Stories*, 1955; *Izbrannoe*, 1957, 1966; *Lyubka the Cossack, and Other Stories*, 1963; *You Must Know Everything: Stories, 1915-1937*, 1969.

Other literary forms • Although Isaac Babel spent most of his career writing short stories, he tried his hand at other genres without making significant contributions to them. He wrote two plays: *Zakat* (1928; *Sunset*, 1960) and *Mariia* (1935; *Maria*, 1966). He also wrote several screenplays, most of which remain unpublished. Babel was known to have worked on several novels, but only a few fragments have been published. If he ever completed them, either he destroyed them or they were confiscated by police when he was arrested in 1939, never to be seen in public again. Because of their fragmentary nature, the tendency among critics is to treat them as short fiction. He also wrote a brief autobiography, a diary, reminiscences, and newspaper articles.

Achievements • Isaac Babel's greatest achievement lies in short fiction. From the outset, he established himself as a premier short-story writer not only in Russian but also in world literature as well. He achieved this reputation not only through his innovative approach to the subject matter—the civil war in Russia, for example, or the Jewish world of his ancestry—but also through his stylistic excellence. His mastery of style earned for him, early in his career, a reputation of an avant-garde writer—a model to be emulated, but at the same time difficult to emulate. He elevated the Russian short story to a new level and attracted the attention of foreign writers such as Ernest Hemingway, who read him in Paris. At the same time, it would be unjust to attribute his greatness only to the uniqueness of his subject matter or to his avant-garde style. Rather, it is the combination of these and other qualities that contributed to his indisputably high reputation among both critics and readers, a respect that seems to grow with time.

Biography • Isaac Emmanuilovich Babel was born in Odessa on July 13, 1894, into a Jewish family that had lived in southern Russia for generations. Soon after his birth, the family moved from this thriving port on the Black Sea to the nearby small town of Nikolayev, where Babel spent the first ten years of his life. His childhood was typical of a child growing up in a colorful Jewish environment and, at the same time, in a Russian society replete with prejudices against Jews. In his stories, Babel describes the difficult lessons of survival that he had to learn from childhood on, which enabled him not only to survive but also to keep striving for excellence against all odds. He was a studious child who read under all conditions, even on his way home, and his imagination was always on fire, as he said in one of his stories. Among many other subjects, he studied Hebrew and French vigorously, becoming more proficient in them than in Russian.

After finishing high school in Odessa—which was difficult for a Jewish child to enter and complete—Babel could not attend the university, again because of the Jewish quota. He enrolled in a business school in Kiev instead. It was at this time that he began to write stories, in French, imitating his favorite writers, François Rabelais, Gustave Flaubert, and Guy de Maupassant. In 1915, he went to St. Petersburg, already thinking seriously of a writing career. He had no success with editors, however, until he met Maxim Gorky, a leading Russian writer of the older generation, who published two of his stories and took him under his wing. This great friendship lasted until Gorky's death in 1936. Gorky had encouraged Babel to write and had protected him but had published no more of his stories, and one day Gorky told Babel to go out into the world and learn about real life. Babel heeded his advice in 1917, setting off on a journey lasting several years, during which he volunteered for the army, took part in the revolution and civil war, married, worked for the secret police, was a war correspondent, and finally served in the famous cavalry division of Semyon Mikhaylovich Budenny in the war against the Poles. Out of these dramatic experiences, Babel was able to publish two books of short stories, which immediately thrust him into the forefront of the young Soviet literature. The period from 1921 to 1925 was the most productive and successful of his entire career.

By the end of the 1920's, however, the political climate in the Soviet Union had begun to change, forcing Babel to conform to the new demands on writers to serve the state, which he could not do, no matter how he tried. His attempts at writing a novel about collectivization never materialized. His inability (or, more likely, unwillingness) to change marks the beginning of a decade-long silent struggle between him and the state. Refusing to follow his family into emigration, he tried to survive by writing film scenarios, unable to publish anything else. In May, 1939, he was arrested and sent to a concentration camp. On January 27, 1940, he was shot for espionage. His confiscated manuscripts—a large crate of them—were never found.

Analysis • Isaac Babel's short stories fall into three basic groups: autobiographical stories, tales about Jews in Odessa, and stories about the Russian Revolution and civil war. Even though the stories were written and published at different times, in retrospect they can be conveniently, if arbitrarily, classified into these three categories. A small number of stories do not fall into any of these groups, but they are exceptions and do not figure significantly in Babel's opus.

Although it is true that many of Babel's stories are autobiographical, even if indirectly, a number of them are openly so. Several refer to his childhood spent in Nikolayev and Odessa. In one of his earliest stories, "Detstvo: U babushki" ("Childhood: At Grandmother's"), Babel pays his emotional due to his kind grandmother, who kept quiet vigil over his studying for hours on end, giving him her bits of wisdom every now and then: "You must know everything. The whole world will fall at your feet and grovel before you. . . . Do not trust people. Do not have friends. Do not lend them money. Do not give them your heart!" Babel loved his childhood because, he said, "I grew up in it, was happy, sad, and dreamed my dreams—fervent dreams that will never return." This early wistful realization of the inevitable transience of all things echoes through much of his writings. The mixture of happiness and sadness is reflected in one of his best stories, "Istoriia moei golubiatni" ("The Story of My Dovecot"), where a child's dream of owning a dovecote is realized during a pogrom, but the dove, which his father had promised him if he was accepted to high school, is squashed against his face. The trickling of the dove's entrails down his face symbolizes the boy's loss of innocence and a premature farewell to childhood.

Babel's discovery of love as the most potent feeling of humankind came to him rather early. As he describes in "Pervaia liubov" ("First Love"), he was ten years old when he fell in love with the wife of an officer, perhaps out of gratitude for her protection of Babel's family during the pogrom in Nikolayev. The puppy love, however, soon gave way to fear and prolonged hiccuping—an early indication of the author's rather sensitive nervous system that accompanied him all his life. This innocent, if incongruous, setting points to a sophisticated sense of humor and to irony, the two devices used by Babel in most of his works. It also foreshadows his unabashed approach to erotica in his later stories, for which they are well known.

As mentioned already, Babel lived as a child in a world of books, dreams, and rampant imagination. In addition, like many Jewish children, he had to take music lessons, for which he had no inclination at all. He had little time for play and fun and, as a consequence, did not develop fully physically. He was aware of this anomaly and tried to break out of it. During one such attempt, as he describes it in "Probuzhdenie" ("Awakening"), he ran away from a music lesson to the beach, only to discover that "the waves refused to support" him. Nevertheless, this experience made him realize that he had to develop "a feel for nature" if he wanted to become a writer. Another experience of "breaking out" concerns Babel's awareness of his social status, as depicted in the story "V podvale" ("In the Basement"). In the story, he visits the luxurious home of the top student in his class and has to use his power of imagination to convince the rich boy that socially he is on equal footing with him. When the boy visits the apartment of Babel's family, "in the basement," however, the truth becomes obvious, and the little Isaac tries to drown himself in a barrel of water. This realization of the discrepancy between reality and the world of dreams and the need and desire to break out of various imposed confines were constant sources of aggravation in Babel's life. Other autobiographical stories, as well as many other stories seemingly detached from the author's personal life, attest this perennial struggle.

Tales of Odessa • The stories about the life of Jews, in the collection *Tales of Odessa*, demonstrate Babel's attachment to his ethnic background as well as his efforts to be objective about it. In addition to being an economic and cultural center, Odessa had a strong underground world of criminals made mostly of Jews, which fueled the imagination of the growing Isaac; later, he used his reminiscences about the Jewish mafia in some of his best stories. He immortalized one of the leaders, Benya Krik, alias the King, in "Korol" ("The King"). Benya's daring and resourcefulness are shown during the wedding of his elderly sister, whose husband he had purchased. When the police plan to arrest Benya's gang during the wedding celebration, he simply arranges for the police station to be set on fire. He himself married the daughter of a man he had blackmailed in one of his operations.

An old man who saw in Babel a boy with "the spectacles on the nose and the autumn in the heart" told him the story of Benya's rise to fame in "Kak eto delalos v Odesse" ("How It Was Done in Odessa"). Here, Benya orders the liquidation of a man who did not give in to blackmail, but Benya's executioner kills the wrong man, a poor clerk who had very little joy in life. Benya orders a magnificent funeral for the unfortunate clerk and a lifelong financial support for his mother, thus showing his true nature and revealing that it is not crime that attracted him to the underground life but rather a subconscious desire to right the wrongs and help the downtrodden. Through such characters and their motives, Babel is able to lend his stories a redeeming grace, neutralizing the mayhem saturating them.

Loyalty is another quality that binds these lawbreakers, as illustrated in the story "Otec" ("The Father"), where Benya helps an old gangster, who had given him his start, to marry off his daughter to the son of a man who had rejected the marriage. They are assisted by another legendary figure, Lyubka, known also from the story "Liubka Kazak" ("Lyubka the Cossack"). Lyubka, a middle-aged shop and whore-house keeper, reigns supreme in her dealings with customers, who, in turn, help her wean her baby from breast-feeding. This interdependency in a life fraught with danger and risks gives Babel's characters a human face and his stories a patina of real drama.

Not all stories about Jews in Odessa deal with the underground world, as "Di Grasso," a colorful tale about theater life in Odessa, shows. Di Grasso, a Sicilian tragedian, and his troupe flop the first night of the show. After a favorable newspaper review praising Di Grasso as "the most remarkable actor of the century," the second night the theater is full and the spectators are so enthralled that the wife of the theater "mogul," to whom the fourteen-year-old Isaac had pawned his father's watch, makes the husband return the watch, sparing Isaac much trouble. Babel's uncanny ability to intertwine high aspirations and small concerns, pathos with bathos, turns seemingly insignificant events into genuine human dramas. This is even more evident in the story "Konets bogadel'ni" ("The End of the Old Folks' Home"), where the inmates of a poorhouse near the Jewish cemetery make a living by using the same coffins again and again, until one day the authorities refuse to allow a used coffin for the burial of a revolutionary hero. The ensuing rebellion by the inmates leads to their dispersal and to the end of their life-sustaining scheme. Thus, what began as a clever business proposition turns into tragedy, making Babel's story a timeless statement of the human condition.

Red Cavalry • Babel uses a similar technique in the collection *Red Cavalry*. Although the stories here are based on Babel's real-life experiences in the war between the Russian revolutionaries and the Poles, their real significance lies beyond the factual presentation of a historical event, as the author endows every gesture, almost every word, with a potential deeper meaning. It is not coincidental that the entire campaign is seen through the eyes of, and told by, a baggage-train officer named Liutov (a persona standing for Babel), not by a frontline participant. Readers learn about the general nature of the conflict, recognize the place names, and even follow the course of the battles, but they cannot piece together the exact history of the conflict simply because that was not the author's intention. Babel gives readers single episodes in miniature form instead, like individual pieces of a mosaic; only after finishing the book are readers able to take in the complete picture.

The first story, "Perekhod cherez Zbruch" ("Crossing into Poland"), sets the tone for the entire collection. The opening lines reveal that a military objective has been taken, but Liutov's baggage train that follows sinks into a hazy, dreamy, impressionistic atmosphere, as if having nothing to do with the campaign:

> Fields flowered around us, crimson with poppies; a noontide breeze played in the yellowing rye; on the horizon virginal buckwheat rose like the wall of a distant monastery. The Volyn's peaceful stream moved away from us in sinuous curves and was lost in the pearly haze of the birch groves; crawling between flowery slopes, it wound weary arms through a wilderness of hops. . . .

This passage shows a poetic proclivity of Babel, but it is also his deliberate attempt to take his readers away from the factual course of events and move them to what he considers to be more important—the human perception of the events. Many of the stories in the collection bear the same trademark.

Although many stories deserve detailed comment, several stand out for their "message" or meaning that can be culled from the story. Nowhere is the brutal nature of the civil war depicted more poignantly than in "Pis'mo" ("A Letter"). A young, illiterate cossack, Vasily, dictates to Liutov a letter to his mother. He inquires about his beloved foal back home, and only after giving detailed advice about handling him does he tell how his father, who is on the other side, killed one of his sons and was then killed in return by another. This most tragic piece of news is relayed matter-of-factly, as if to underscore the degree of desensitization to which all the participants have fallen prey through endless killing.

The cruelty of the civil war is brought into sharp focus by an old Jewish shopkeeper in "Gedali." Gedali reasons like a legitimate humanitarian and libertarian: "The Revolution—we will say 'yes' to it, but are we to say 'no' to the Sabbath? . . . I cry yes to [the Revolution], but it hides its face from Gedali and sends out on front naught but shooting." He understands when the Poles commit atrocities, but he is perplexed when the Reds do the same in the name of the revolution. "You shoot because you are the Revolution. But surely the Revolution means joy. . . . The Revolution is the good deed of good men. But good men do not kill." Gedali says that all he wants is an International of good people. Liutov's answer that the International "is eaten with gunpowder," though realistic, falls short of satisfying the old man's yearning for justice, which, after all, was the primary driving force of the revolution. It is interesting that, by presenting the case in such uncompromising terms, Babel himself is questioning the rationale behind the revolution and the justification of all the sacrifices and suffering.

A similar moral issue is brought to a climactic head in perhaps the best story in *Red Cavalry*, "Smert' Dolgushova" ("The Death of Dolgushov"). Dolgushov is wounded beyond repair and is left behind the fighting line to die. He is begging Liutov to finish him off because he is afraid that the Poles, if they caught him alive, would mutilate his body. Liutov refuses. The commander gallops by, evaluates the situation, and shoots Dolgushov in the mouth. Before galloping away, the commander threatens to kill Liutov, too, screaming, "You guys in specks have about as much pity for chaps like us as a cat has for a mouse." Aside from the revolutionaries' mistrust of Liutov (alias Babel) and the age-old question of euthanasia, the story poses a weighty moral question: Has a human being the right to kill another human being? Even though Babel seems to allow for this possibility, he himself cannot make that step, making it appear that he is shirking his responsibility (after all, he is fighting alongside the revolutionaries). More likely, he is hoping that there should be at least someone to say no to the incessant killing, thus saving the face of the revolution (as if answering Gedali's mournful plea). More important, this hope hints at Babel's real attitude toward the revolution. For such "misunderstanding" of the revolution he was criticized severely, and it is most likely that through such attitudes he sowed the seeds of his own destruction two decades later.

Not all stories in *Red Cavalry* are weighed down with ultimate moral questions. There are stories of pure human interest, colorful slices of the war, and even some genuinely humorous ones. In "Moi pervyi gus'" ("My First Goose"), Liutov is faced with the problem of gaining the respect of the illiterate cossacks in his unit. As a bespectacled intellectual ("a four-eyed devil," as they called him), and a Jew at that, he knows that the only way to win them over is by committing an act of bravery. He thinks of raping a woman, but he sees only an old woman around. He finally kills a goose with his saber, thereby gaining the respect of his "peers." Only then are they willing to let him read to them Vladimir Ilich Lenin's latest pronouncements. With this mixture of mocking seriousness and irony, Babel attempts to put the revolution in a proper perspective. His difficulties at adjusting to military life are evident also in the story "Argamak," where he ruins a good horse by not knowing how to handle it.

The Jews are frequently mentioned in these stories because the war was taking place in an area heavily populated by them. Babel uses these opportunities to stress their perennial role as sufferers and martyrs, but also to gauge his own Jewish identification. In "Rabbi" ("The Rabbi"), he visits, with Gedali, an old rabbi, who asks him where he came from, what he has been studying, and what he was seeking—typical identification questions. Later, they and the rabbi's son, "the cursed son, the last son, the unruly son," sit amid the wilderness of war, in silence and prayers, as if to underscore the isolation of people threatened by an alien war. In "Berestechko," a cossack is shown cutting the throat of an old Jewish "spy," being careful not to stain himself with blood. This one detail completes the picture of a Jew as an ultimate victim.

Many characters are etched out in these miniature stories. There is Sandy the Christ in the story by the same title ("Sashka Khristov"), a meek herdsman who at the age of fourteen caught "an evil disease" while carousing with his stepfather and who later joined the Reds and became a good fighter. There is Pan Apolek ("Pan Apolek"), an itinerant artist who painted church icons in the images not of the saints but of local people. There is Afonka Bida ("Afonka Bida"), the commander who almost shot Liutov because of Dolgushov, who loses his horse Stepan and disappears hunting for another. After several weeks, he reappears with a gray stallion, but the loss of Stepan still makes him want to destroy the whole world. In "So" ("Salt"), a woman carrying a bundled baby uses him to gain sympathy and hitch a train ride. It turns out that the bundle is nothing but a two-pound sack of salt; she is thrown out of the moving train and then shot from the distance. The man who killed her pronounces solemnly, "We will deal mercilessly with all the traitors that are dragging us to the dogs and want to turn everything upside down and cover Russia with nothing but corpses and dead grass," which is exactly what he has just done. Finally, in one of the best stories in the book, "Vdova" ("The Widow"), a lover of the dying commander is bequeathed all of his belongings, with the request that she send some of them to his mother. When the widow shows signs of not following the will of the deceased, she is beaten, and, if she forgets the second time, she will be reminded again in the same fashion. These stories are perfect illustrations of Babel's ability to create unforgettable but credible characters, to set up dramatic scenes, and to conjure a proper atmosphere, while endowing his creations with a truly human pathos—qualities that characterize most of his stories but especially those in *Red Cavalry*.

Among the stories outside the three groups, several are worth mentioning. An early story, "Mama, Rimma, i Alla" ("Mama, Rimma, and Alla"), resembles an Anton Chekhov story in that the domestic problems in a family (a mother finds it difficult to cope with her daughters in absence of her husband) are not solved and the story dissolves in hopelessness. "Iisusov grekh" ("The Sin of Jesus") is a colorful tale of a woman whose husband is away at war and who goes to Jesus for advice about loneliness. When Jesus sends her an angel, she accidentally smothers him to death in sleep. She goes again to Jesus, but now he damns her as a slut, which she resents, for it is not her fault that she lusts, that people drink vodka, and that he has created "a woman's soul, stupid and lonely." When finally Jesus admits his error and asks for forgiveness, she refuses to accept it, saying, "There is no forgiveness for you and never will be." The story displays Babel's exquisite sense of humor along with a keen understanding of human nature and the complexities of life. A variant, "Skazka pro babu" ("The Tale of a Woman"), another Chekhovian story, again depicts the plight of a widow who, in her loneliness, asks a friend to find her a husband. When she does, he mistreats her and walks out on her, which causes her to lose her job. Finally, "Ulitsa Dante" ("Dante Street") is a Paris story in the tradition of Guy de Maupassant, showing Babel's versatility and imagination.

Babel's stylistic excellence has been often praised by critics. His style features a Spartan economy of words, and he is known to have spent years reworking and revising his stories. Babel's attention to detail, especially to line and color, often result in fine etchings. There is a pronounced poetic bent in his stories, whether they are located in a city milieu or in the countryside. This is reinforced by a prolific use of images and metaphors in the style of the following passages, quoted at random:

> A dead man's fingers were picking at the frozen entrails of Petersburg.... The gentleman had drooping jowls, like the sacks of an old-clothes man, and wounded cats prowled in his reddish eyes.

One finds in Babel also a surprising amount of humor, as if to offset the cruelty and gruesome injustice of his world.

Babel's artfulness is especially noticeable in his treatment of irony as his strongest device. He refuses to accept reality as one perceives it. He also plays games with readers' perceptions, as he says openly, "I set myself a reader who is intelligent, well educated, with sensible and severe standards of taste.... Then I try to think how I can deceive and stun the reader." This cool intellectual approach, coupled with the strong emotional charge of his stories, gives his stories an aura of not only skillfully executed works of art but also pristine innocence of divine creation.

Vasa D. Mihailovich

Other major works

PLAYS: *Zakat*, pb. 1928 (*Sunset*, 1960; also known as *Sundown*); *Mariia*, pb. 1935 (*Maria*, 1966).

MISCELLANEOUS: *Isaac Babel: The Lonely Years, 1925-1939, Unpublished Stories and Private Correspondence*, 1964, 1995; *The Complete Works of Isaac Babel*, 2001 (short stories, plays, screenplays, and diaries).

NONFICTION: *1920 Diary*, 1995.

POETRY: *Morning in the Burned House*, 1996.

SCREENPLAYS: *Benia Krik: Kinopovest'*, 1926 (*Benia Krik: A Film Novel*, 1935); *Bluzhdaiushchie zvezdy: Kinostsenarii*, 1926.

Bibliography

Avins, Carol J. "Kinship and Concealment in *Red Cavalry* and Babel's 1920 Diary." *Slavic Review* 53 (Fall, 1994): 694-710. Shows how a diary Babel kept during his service in the 1920 Polish campaign was a source of ideas for his collection of stories, *Red Cavalry*. Claims that Babel's efforts to conceal his Jewishness, recounted in the diaries, is also reflected in the stories.

Carden, Patricia. *The Art of Isaac Babel.* Ithaca, N.Y.: Cornell University Press, 1972. In this discerning study of Babel's art, Carden combines biography and analysis of his main works and themes, especially his search for style and form, and philosophical, religious, and aesthetic connotations. The meticulous scholarship is accompanied by keen insight and empathy, making the book anything but cut-and-dried. Includes a select bibliography.

Charyn, Jerome. *Savage Shorthand: The Life and Death of Isaac Babel.* New York: Random House, 2005. Fascinating, critically lauded account of Babel's work and life.

Ehre, Milton. "Babel's *Red Cavalry:* Epic and Pathos, History and Culture." *Slavic Review* 40 (1981): 228-240. A stimulating study of Babel's chief work, incorporating its literary, historical, and cultural aspects. No attention to detail, but rather a sweeping overview.

Falen, James E. *Isaac Babel, Russian Master of the Short Story.* Knoxville: University of Tennessee Press, 1974. Falen's appraisal of Babel is the best overall. Following the main stages of Babel's life, Falen analyzes in minute detail his works, emphasizing the short stories. Lucidly written and provided with the complete scholarly apparatus, the study offers an exhaustive bibliography as well.

Luplow, Carol. *Isaac Babel's Red Cavalry.* Ann Arbor, Mich.: Ardis, 1982. This detailed, full-length study of Babel's most famous collection focuses on the narrative perspective of the stories, the basic dialectic between the spiritual and the physical which they embody, their style and romantic vision, and the types of story structure and epiphanic vision they reflect.

May, Charles E., ed. *Masterplots II: Short Story Series, Revised Edition.* 8 vols. Pasadena, Calif.: Salem Press, 2004. Designed for student use, this reference set contains articles providing detailed plot summaries and analyses of these eight short stories by Babel: "Crossing into Poland" and "Di Grasso: A Tale of Odessa" (vol. 2), "Guy de Maupassant" (vol. 3), "How It Was Done in Odessa" and "In the Basement" (vol. 4), "Lyubka the Cossack" and "My First Goose" (vol. 5), and "The Story of My Dovecot" (vol. 7).

Mendelson, Danuta. *Metaphor in Babel's Short Stories.* Ann Arbor, Mich.: Ardis, 1982. Scholarly discussion, drawing from linguistic and psychological studies as well as structuralist studies of narrative.

Shcheglov, Yuri K. "Some Themes and Archetypes in Babel's *Red Cavalry.*" *Slavic Review* 53 (Fall, 1994): 653-670. Discusses initiatory and otherworldly thematic patterns in "My First Goose," showing how Babel used archetypes subtly and selectively. Concludes that "My First Goose," with its density reinforced by archetypal connotations, is an emblematic prototype of later works of Soviet fiction that focus on similar themes.

Sicher, Efraim. *Style and Structure in the Prose of Isaak Babel.* Columbus, Ohio: Slavica, 1986. Primarily a formalist study of the style of Babel's stories. In addition to discussing Babel's lyrical prose, the book analyzes setting, characterization, narrative structure, and point of view in Babel's stories.

Terras, Victor. "Line and Color: The Structure of I. Babel's Short Stories in *Red Cavalry.*" *Studies in Short Fiction* 3, no. 2 (Winter, 1966): 141-156. In one of the best treatments of a particular aspect of Babel's stories, Terras discusses his style in terms of line and color and of his poetic inclination.

James Baldwin

Born: New York, New York; August 2, 1924
Died: St. Paul de Vence, France; December 1, 1987

Principal short fiction • *Going to Meet the Man*, 1965.

Other literary forms • In addition to one edition of short stories, James Baldwin published more than twenty other works, including novels, essays, two plays, a screenplay on Malcolm X, one play adaptation, a children's book, two series of dialogues, and a collection of poetry, as well as numerous shorter pieces embracing interviews, articles, and recordings.

Achievements • James Baldwin received numerous awards and fellowships during his life, including the Rosenwald, John Simon Guggenheim Memorial Foundation, and Partisan Review fellowships, a Ford Foundation Grant, and the George Polk Memorial Award. In 1986, shortly before his death, the French government made him a Commander of the Legion of Honor.

Biography • James Arthur Baldwin grew up in Harlem. While he was still attending DeWitt Clinton High School in the Bronx he was a Holy Roller preacher. After high school, he did odd jobs and wrote for *The Nation* and *The New Leader*. A turning point for him was meeting Richard Wright, who encouraged him to write and helped him obtain a fellowship that provided income while he was finishing an early novel. After moving to Paris in 1948 he became acquainted with Norman Mailer and other writers. His first major work, *Go Tell It on the Mountain*, appeared in 1953 and was followed by a long list of books. He moved back to New York in 1957, and during the 1960's his writing and speeches made him an important force in the Civil Rights movement. Following the assassination of Martin Luther King, Jr., Baldwin returned to Europe several times and again settled in France in 1974, where he lived until his death. He continued his productivity in the 1980's. In 1985, for example, Baldwin wrote three works, including his first book of poetry. He died in 1987 of stomach cancer and is buried near Paul Robeson's grave at Ferncliff Cemetery, Ardsley, New York.

Analysis • James Baldwin is widely regarded as one of the United States' most important writers in the latter part of the twentieth century. Baldwin's writing career spanned more than four decades and is remarkable for its wide diversity of literary expression, encompassing fiction, nonfiction, poetry, and plays. He was considered the most important American writer during the 1950's, 1960's, and 1970's on the issue of racial inequality. The repeated thrust of his message, centered on being black in a white America, touched a responsive chord. Disgusted with American bigotry, social discrimination, and inequality, he exiled himself in France, where he poured out his eloquent and passionate criticism. Baldwin also wrote with compelling candor about the Church, Harlem, and homosexuality. He often fused the themes of sex and race in his work. Today, Baldwin's essays are considered his most important contribution to literature.

"The Man Child" • Baldwin's "The Man Child," the only story in *Going to Meet the Man* that has no black characters, scathingly describes whites, especially their violent propensities. The central character is Eric, an eight-year-old. The story opens as he, his mother, and his father are giving a birthday party for Jamie, his father's best friend. In the next scene Eric and his father walk together and then return to the party. After a brief summary of intervening events, the story moves forward in time to a day when Jamie meets Eric, entices him into a barn, and breaks his neck. The story described thus, its ending seems to be a surprise, and it certainly is a surprise to Eric. In fact, his sudden realization that he is in grave danger is an epiphany. "The Man Child" is thus a coming-of-age story, an account of a young person's realization of the dark side of adult existence. Eric, however, has little time to think about his realization or even to generalize very much on the basis of his intimation of danger before he is badly, perhaps mortally, injured.

© John Hoppy Hopkins

The story, however, contains many hints that violent action will be forthcoming. A reader can see them even though Eric cannot because Eric is the center of consciousness, a device perfected, if not invented, by Henry James. That is, Eric does not narrate the story so the story does not present his viewpoint, but he is always the focus of the action, and the story is in essence an account of his responses to that action. The difference between his perception of the events he witnesses (which is sometimes described and sometimes can be inferred from his actions) and the perception that can be had by attending carefully to the story encourages a reader to make a moral analysis and finally to make a moral judgment, just as the difference between Huck Finn's perception and the perception that one can have while reading *The Adventures of Huckleberry Finn* (1884) at first stimulates laughter and then moral evaluation. Eric's lack of perception is a function of his innocence, a quality that he has to an even larger extent than has Huck Finn, and thus he is less able to cope in a threatening world and his injury is even more execrable. If the measure of a society is its solicitude for the powerless, the miniature society formed by the three adults in this story, and perhaps by implication the larger society of which they are a part, is sorely wanting.

To be more specific about the flaws in this society and in these persons, they enslave themselves and others, as is suggested very early in the story: "Eric lived with his father . . . and his mother, who had been captured by his father on some faroff unblessed, unbelievable night, who had never since burst her chains." Her husband intimidates and frightens her, and his conversation about relations between men and women indicates that he believes she exists at his sufferance only for sex and procreation. Her role becomes questionable because in the summary of events that happen between the first and last parts of the story one learns that she has lost the child she had been carrying and cannot conceive anymore. The two men enslave themselves with their notions about women, their drunkenness (which they misinterpret as male companionship), their mutual hostility, their overbearing expansiveness, in short, with their machismo. Eric's father is convinced that he is more successful in these terms. He has fathered a son, an accomplishment the significance of which to him is indicated by his "some day all this will be yours" talk with Eric between the two party scenes. Jamie's wife, showing more sense than Eric's mother, left him before he could sire a son. Jamie's violent act with Eric is his psychotic imitation of the relation of Eric's father to Eric, just as his whistling at the very end of the story is his imitation of the music he hears coming from a tavern. Eric is thus considered by the two men to be alive merely for their self-expression. His father's kind of self-expression is potentially debilitating, although somewhat benign; Jamie's version is nearly fatal.

"Going to Meet the Man" • "Going to Meet the Man" is a companion to "The Man Child," both stories having been published for the first time in *Going to Meet the Man.* Whereas the latter story isolates whites from blacks in order to analyze their psychology, the former story is about whites in relation to blacks, even though blacks make only brief appearances in it. The whites in these stories have many of the same characteristics, but in "Going to Meet the Man" those characteristics are more obviously dangerous. These stories were written during the height of the Civil Rights movement, and Baldwin, by means of his rhetorical power and his exclusion of more human white types, helped polarize that movement.

The main characters in "Going to Meet the Man" are a family composed of a southern deputy sheriff, his wife, and his son, Jesse. At the beginning of the story they are skittish because of racial unrest. Demonstrations by blacks have alternated with police brutality by whites, each response escalating the conflict, which began when a black man knocked down an elderly white woman. The family is awakened late at night by a crowd of whites who have learned that the black has been caught. They all set off in a festive, although somewhat tense, mood to the place where the black is being held. After they arrive the black is burned, castrated, and mutilated—atrocities that Baldwin describes very vividly. This story, however, is not merely sensationalism or social and political rhetoric. It rises above those kinds of writing because of its psychological insights into the causes of racism and particularly of racial violence.

Baldwin's focus at first is on the deputy sheriff. As the story opens he is trying and failing to have sexual relations with his wife. He thinks that he would have an easier time with a black, and "the image of a black girl caused a distant excitement in him." Thus, his conception of blacks is immediately mixed with sexuality, especially with his fear of impotence. In contrast, he thinks of his wife as a "frail sanctuary." At the approach of a car he reaches for the gun beside his bed, thereby adding a propensity for violence to his complex of psychological motives. Most of his behavior results from this amalgam of racial attitudes, sexual drives, fear of impotence, and attraction to violence. For example, he recalls torturing a black prisoner by applying a cattle prod to his testicles, and on the way to see the black captive he takes pride in his wife's attractiveness. He also frequently associates blacks with sexual vigor and fecundity. The castration scene is the most powerful rendition of this psychological syndrome.

The deputy sheriff, however, is more than a mere brute. For example, he tries to think of his relation to blacks in moral terms. Their singing of spirituals disconcerts him because he has difficulty understanding how they can be Christians like himself. He tries to reconcile this problem by believing that blacks have decided "to fight against God and go against the rules laid down in the Bible for everyone to read!" To allay the guilt that threatens to complicate his life he also believes that there are a lot of good blacks who need his protection from bad blacks. These strategies for achieving inner peace do not work, and Baldwin brilliantly describes the moral confusion of such whites:

> They had never dreamed that their privacy could contain any element of terror, could threaten, that is, to reveal itself, to the scrutiny of a judgment day, while remaining unreadable and inaccessible to themselves; nor had they dreamed that the past, while certainly refusing to be forgotten, could yet so stubbornly refuse to be remembered. They felt themselves mysteriously set at naught.

In the absence of a satisfying moral vision, violence seems the only way to achieve inner peace, and the sheriff's participation in violence allows him to have sex with his wife as the story ends. Even then, however, he has to think that he is having it as blacks would. He is their psychic prisoner, just as the black who was murdered was the white mob's physical prisoner.

Late in this story one can see that Jesse, the sheriff's eight-year-old son, is also an important character. At first he is confused by the turmoil and thinks of blacks in human terms. For example, he wonders why he has not seen his black friend Otis for several days. The mob violence, however, changes him; he undergoes a coming of age, the perversity of which is disturbing. He is the center of consciousness in the mob scene. His first reaction is the normal one for a boy: "Jesse clung to his father's neck in terror as the cry rolled over the crowd." Then he loses his innocence and it becomes clear that he will be a victim of the same psychological syndrome that afflicts his father: "He watched his mother's face . . . she was more beautiful than he had ever seen her. . . . He began to feel a joy he had never felt before." He wishes that he were the man with the knife who is about to castrate the black, whom Jesse considers "the most beautiful and terrible object he had ever seen." Then he identifies totally with his father: "At that moment Jesse loved his father more than he had ever loved him. He felt that his father had carried him through a mighty test, had revealed to him a great secret which would be the key to his life forever." For Jesse this brutality is thus a kind of initiation into adulthood, and its effect is to ensure that there will be at least one more generation capable of the kind of violence that he has just seen.

"Sonny's Blues" • Whereas "The Man Child" has only white characters and "Going to Meet the Man" is about a conflict between whites and blacks, "Sonny's Blues" has only black characters. Although the chronology of "Sonny's Blues" is scrambled, its plot is simple. It tells the story of two brothers, one, the narrator, a respectable teacher and the other, Sonny, a former user of heroin who is jailed for that reason and then becomes a jazz musician. The story ends in a jazz nightclub, where the older brother hears Sonny play and finally understands the meaning of jazz for him. The real heart of this story is the contrast between the values of the two brothers, a contrast that becomes much less dramatic at the end.

The two brothers have similar social backgrounds, especially their status as blacks and, more specifically, as Harlem blacks. Of Harlem as a place in which to mature the narrator says, "boys exactly like the boys we once had been found themselves encircled by disaster. Some escaped the trap, most didn't. Those who got out always left something of themselves behind, as some animals amputate a leg and leave it in a trap." Even when he was very young the narrator had a sense of the danger and despair surrounding him:

> When lights fill the room, the child is filled with darkness. He knows that every time this happens he's moved just a little closer to that darkness outside. The darkness outside is what the old folks have been talking about. It's what they've come from. It's what they endure.

For example, he learns after his father's death that his father, though seemingly a hardened and stoical man, had hidden the grief caused by the killing of his brother.

At first the narrator believes that Sonny's two means for coping with the darkness, heroin and music, are inextricably connected to that darkness and thus are not survival mechanisms at all. He believes that heroin "filled everything, the people, the houses, the music, the dark, quicksilver barmaid, with menace; and this menace was their reality." Later, however, he realizes that jazz is a way to escape: He senses that "Sonny was at that time piano playing for his life." The narrator also has a few premonitions of the epiphany he experiences in the jazz nightclub. One occurs when he observes a group of street singers and understands that their "music seemed to soothe a poison out of them." Even with these premonitions, he does not realize that he uses the same strategy. After an argument with Sonny, during which their differences seem to be irreconcilable, his first reaction is to begin "whistling to keep from crying," and the tune is a blues. Finally the epiphany occurs, tying together all the major strands of this story. As he listens to Sonny playing jazz the narrator thinks that

> freedom lurked around us and I understood, at last, that he could help us be free if we would listen, that he would never be free until we did. Yet, there was no battle in his face now. I heard what he had gone through, and would continue to go through.

The idea in that passage is essentially what Baldwin is about. Like Sonny, he has forged an instrument of freedom by means of the fire of his troubles, and he has made that instrument available to all, white and black. His is the old story of suffering and art; his fiction is an account of trouble, but by producing it he has shown others the way to rise above suffering.

John Stark
With updates by Terry Theodore

Other major works

CHILDREN'S LITERATURE: *Little Man, Little Man,* 1975.

PLAYS: *The Amen Corner,* pr. 1954, pb. 1968; *Blues for Mister Charlie,* pr., pb. 1964; *A Deed from the King of Spain,* pr. 1974.

NOVELS: *Go Tell It on the Mountain,* 1953; *Giovanni's Room,* 1956; *Another Country,* 1962; *Tell Me How Long the Train's Been Gone,* 1968; *If Beale Street Could Talk,* 1974; *Just Above My Head,* 1979.

NONFICTION: *Notes of a Native Son,* 1955; *Nobody Knows My Name: More Notes of a Native Son,* 1961; *The Fire Next Time,* 1963; *Nothing Personal,* 1964 (with Richard Avedon); *A Rap on Race,* 1971 (with Margaret Mead); *No Name in the Street,* 1971; *A Dialogue,* 1975 (with Nikki Giovanni); *The Devil Finds Work,* 1976; *The Evidence of Things Not Seen,* 1985; *The Price of the Ticket,* 1985; *Conversations with James Baldwin,* 1989; *Collected Essays,* 1998; *Native Sons: A Friendship That Created One of the Greatest Works of the Twentieth Century,* "*Notes of a Native Son,*" 2004 (with Sol Stein).

POETRY: *Jimmy's Blues: Selected Poems,* 1983.

SCREENPLAY: *One Day, When I Was Lost: A Scenario Based on "The Autobiography of Malcolm X,"* 1972.

Bibliography

Hardy, Clarence E. *James Baldwin's God: Sex, Hope, and Crisis in Black Holiness Culture.* Knoxville: University of Tennessee Press, 2003. Brief exploration of some the most troubling themes in Baldwin's writing.

Kinnamon, Keneth, ed. *James Baldwin: A Collection of Critical Essays.* Englewood Cliffs, N.J.: Prentice-Hall, 1974. Good introduction to Baldwin's early work featuring a collection of diverse essays by such well-known figures as Irving Howe, Langston Hughes, Sherley Anne Williams, and Eldridge Cleaver. Includes a chronology of important dates, notes on the contributors, and a select bibliography.

Leeming, David. *James Baldwin: A Biography.* New York: Alfred A. Knopf, 1994. Biography of Baldwin written by one who knew him and worked with him for the last quarter century of his life. Provides extensive literary analysis of Baldwin's work and relates his work to his life.

McBride, Dwight A. *James Baldwin Now.* New York: New York University Press, 1999. Stresses the usefulness of recent interdisciplinary approaches in understanding Baldwin's appeal, political thought and work, and legacy.

May, Charles E., ed. *Masterplots II: Short Story Series, Revised Edition.* 8 vols. Pasadena, Calif.: Salem Press, 2004. Designed for student use, this reference set contains articles providing detailed plot summaries and analyses of these five short stories by Baldwin: "Come Out the Wilderness" (vol. 2); "Going to Meet the Man" (vol. 3); and "Sonny's Blues," "Tell Me How Long the Train's Been Gone," and "This Morning, This Evening, So Soon" (vol. 7).

Miller, D. Quentin, ed. *Re-Viewing James Baldwin: Things Not Seen.* Philadelphia: Temple University Press, 2000. Explores the way in which Baldwin's writing touched on issues that confront all people, including race, identity, sexuality, and religious ideology.

Sanderson, Jim. "Grace in 'Sonny's Blues.'" *Short Story,* n.s. 6 (Fall, 1998): 85-95. Argues that Baldwin's most famous story illustrates his integration of the personal with the social in terms of his residual evangelical Christianity. Argues that at the end of the story when the narrator offers Sonny a drink, he puts himself in the role of Lord, and Sonny accepts the cup of wrath; the two brothers thus regain grace by means of the power of love.

Scott, Lynn Orilla. *James Baldwin's Later Fiction: Witness to the Journey.* East Lansing: Michigan State University Press, 2002. Analyzes the decline of Baldwin's reputation after the 1960's, the ways in which critics have often undervalued his work, and the interconnected themes in his body of work.

Sherard, Tracey. "Sonny's Bebop: Baldwin's 'Blues Text' as Intracultural Critique." *African American Review* 32 (Winter, 1998): 691-705. A discussion of Houston

Baker's notion of the "blues matrix" in Baldwin's story; examines the story's treatment of black culture in America as reflected by jazz and the blues. Discusses how the "blues text" of the story represents how intracultural narratives have influenced the destinies of African Americans.

Tomlinson, Robert. "'Payin' One's Dues': Expatriation as Personal Experience and Paradigm in the Works of James Baldwin." *African American Review* 33 (Spring, 1999): 135-148. A discussion of the effect life as an exile in Paris had on Baldwin. Argues that the experience internalized the conflicts he experienced in America. Suggests that Baldwin used his homosexuality and exile as a metaphor for the experience of the African American.

Tsomondo, Thorell. "No Other Tale to Tell: 'Sonny's Blues' and 'Waiting for the Rain.'" *Critique* 36 (Spring, 1995): 195-209. Examines how art and history are related in "Sonny's Blues." Discusses the story as one in which a young musician replays tribal history in music. Argues that the story represents how African American writers try to reconstruct an invalidated tradition.

Toni Cade Bambara

Born: New York, New York; March 25, 1939
Died: Philadelphia, Pennsylvania; December 9, 1995

Principal short fiction • *Gorilla, My Love*, 1972; *The Sea Birds Are Still Alive: Collected Stories*, 1977; *Raymond's Run: Stories for Young Adults*, 1989.

Other literary forms • Before Toni Cade Bambara published her first collection of stories, *Gorilla, My Love* (1972), she edited two anthologies, *The Black Woman* (1970) and *Tales and Stories for Black Folks* (1971), under the name Toni Cade. Her 1980 novel, *The Salt Eaters*, was well received and won many awards. She was also an active screenwriter whose credits included Louis Massiah's *The Bombing of Osage Avenue* (1986), about the bombing of the Movement (MOVE) Organization's headquarters in Philadelphia, and Massiah's *W. E. B. Du Bois: A Biography in Four Voices* (1995). Her friend and editor, Toni Morrison, edited a collection of her previously uncollected stories and essays in 1996 called *Deep Sightings and Rescue Missions: Fiction, Essays, and Conversations*, and her final novel, *Those Bones Are Not My Child*, was published in 1999.

Achievements • *The Salt Eaters* won numerous awards, including the American Book Award, the Langston Hughes Society Award, and an award from the Zora Neale Hurston Society. Toni Cade Bambara's work on *The Bombing of Osage Avenue* led to an Academy Award for Best Documentary and awards from the Pennsylvania Association of Broadcasters and the Black Hall of Fame. Her other honors include the Peter Pauper Press Award (1958), the John Golden Award for Fiction from Queens College (1959), a Rutgers University research fellowship (1972), a Black Child Development Institute service award (1973), a Black Rose Award from *Encore* (1973), a Black Community Award from Livingston College, Rutgers University (1974), an award from the National Association of Negro Business and Professional Women's Club League, a George Washington Carver Distinguished African American Lecturer Award from Simpson College, *Ebony*'s Achievement in the Arts Award, and a Black Arts Award from the University of Missouri (1981), a Documentary Award from the National Black Programming Consortium (1986), and a nomination for the Black Caucus of the American Library Association Literary Award (1997).

Biography • Toni Cade Bambara was born Miltona Mirkin Cade in New York City in 1939 and grew up in Harlem, Bedford-Stuyvesant, and Queens, New York, and in Jersey City, New Jersey. She attended Queens College in New York and received a bachelor's degree in theater arts in 1959, the same year she published her first short story, "Sweet Town." From 1960 to 1965, she worked on a master's degree in American literature at City College of New York, while also working as a caseworker at the Department of Welfare, and later as program director of the Colony Settlement House. Starting in 1965, she taught at City College for four years before moving on to Livingston College at Rutgers University in 1969. She also taught at Emory University, Spelman College (where she was a writer-in-residence during the 1970's), and Atlanta University, at various times teaching writing, theater, and social work.

Bambara's publication of *The Black Woman*, an anthology of poetry, fiction, and nonfiction by established writers (such as Nikki Giovanni, Alice Walker, and Paule Marshall) and students demonstrated her commitment to both the women's movement and the Civil Rights campaign. By the time she had published her first collection of short stories, *Gorilla, My Love*, in 1972, she had adopted the last name of Bambara from a signature she found on a sketch pad in a trunk of her grandmother's things.

Bambara's belief in the connection between social activism and art was strengthened by a trip to Cuba in 1973, when she met with women's organizations there. The increased urgency of concern for social activism appears in her second collection of short stories, *The Sea Birds Are Still Alive*. After her first novel, *The Salt Eaters*, was published in 1980 and received numerous awards, she increasingly turned her attention to her work in the arts, becoming an important writer of independent films, though she never stopped working on fiction. She died of cancer on December 9, 1995.

Analysis • Toni Cade Bambara's short fiction is especially notable for its creativity with language and its ability to capture the poetry of black speech. In a conversation that was printed in her posthumous collection *Deep Sightings and Rescue Missions* as "How She Came by Her Name," she claimed that in the stories from *Gorilla, My Love* about childhood, she was trying to capture the voice of childhood, and she was surprised that readers received these efforts to use black dialect as a political act. Nonetheless, her writing (like her work as a teacher, social worker, and filmmaker) was always informed by her sense of social activism and social justice in the broadest sense. In her later work outside the field of short fiction (in films and in her last novel), she focused on the bombing of the black neighborhood in Philadelphia where the MOVE Organization was headquartered, the life of W. E. B. Du Bois, and the Atlanta child murders of the 1980's, all topics that were rife with political meaning.

Nonetheless, what enlivens her writing is her originality with language and a playful sense of form which aims more to share than to tell directly. Another essay from *Deep Sightings and Rescue Missions*, "The Education of a Storyteller" tells of Grandma Dorothy teaching her that she could not really know anything that she could not share with her girlfriends, and her stories seem to grow out of the central wish to share things with this target audience of black women peers. Her stories are usually digressive, seldom following a linear plot. Most of them are structured in an oral form that allows for meaningful side issues with the aim of bringing clear the central point to her audience. Though this technique can be daunting when used in the novel-length *The Salt Eaters*, it allows her to make her short stories into charming, witty, and lively artistic performances whose social messages emerge organically.

Gorilla, My Love • *Gorilla, My Love* was Toni Cade Bambara's first collection of her original work, and it remains her most popular book. The stories in it were written between 1959 and 1970, and as she explains in her essay, "How She Came by Her Name," she was trying to capture the language system in which people she knew lived and moved. She originally conceived it as a collection of the voices of young, bright, and tough girls of the city, but she did not want it to be packaged as a children's book, so she added some of the adult material to it. "My Man Bovane," for instance, features a matronly black woman seducing a blind man at a neighborhood political rally, while her children look on in disapproval. Similarly, among the fifteen stories (most of which are written in the first person) that make up this book is "Talkin Bout

Sonny," in which Betty and Delauney discuss their friend Sonny's recent breakdown and assault on his wife. Delauney claims he understands exactly how such a thing could happen, and it is left unclear how this unstable relationship between Betty and Delauney (who is married) will resolve itself.

Most of the stories, however, focus on young girls determined to make their place in the world and the neighborhood. "The Hammer Man," for instance, tells of a young girl who first hides from a mentally disturbed older boy she has humiliated in public but later futilely attempts to defend against two policemen who try to arrest him. The adult themes and the childhood themes come together best in "The Johnson Girls," in which a young girl listens in as a group of women try to console Inez, whose boyfriend has left with no promise of

Joyce Middler

return. As the young narrator listens in the hope that she will not have to endure "all this torture crap" when she becomes a woman, it becomes clear that the intimate conversation between women is a form of revitalization for Inez.

A delightful preface to *Gorilla, My Love* assures readers that the material in the book is entirely fictional, not at all autobiographical, but it is hard for a reader not to feel that the voices that populate the work speak for Bambara and the neighborhood of her youth.

"Gorilla, My Love" • The title story of Bambara's first book-length collection of her own work, "Gorilla, My Love" is also her most irresistible work. The narrator is a young girl named Hazel who has just learned that her "Hunca Bubba" is about to be married. She is clearly upset about both this news and the fact that he is now going by his full name, Jefferson Winston Vale. The story proceeds in anything but a linear manner, as Hazel sees a movie house in the background of Hunca Bubba's photos, and starts to tell about going to the movies on Easter with her brothers, Big Brood and Little Jason. When the movie turns out to be a film about Jesus instead of "Gorilla, My Love," as was advertised, Hazel gets angry and demands her money back, and not getting it, starts a fire in the lobby—"Cause if you say Gorilla My Love you supposed to mean it."

What is really on her mind is that when Hunca Bubba was baby-sitting her, he promised he was going to marry her when she grew up, and she believed him. Hazel's attempt to keep her dignity but make her feeling of betrayal known by confronting Hunca Bubba is at once both a surprise and a completely natural outgrowth of her character. Her grandfather's explanation, that it was Hunca Bubba who promised to marry her but it is Jefferson Winston Vale who is marrying someone else, is at once both compassionate and an example of the type of hypocrisy that Hazel associates with the adult world. The example she gives in her story about going to the movie makes it clear that she has always seen her family as better than most, but she sees hypocrisy as a universal adult epidemic.

"Raymond's Run" • "Raymond's Run," a short story that was also published as a children's book, is about the relationship between the narrator, Hazel (not the same girl from "Gorilla, My Love," but about the same age), her mentally disabled brother, Raymond, and another girl on the block, Gretchen. Hazel's reputation is as the fastest thing on two feet in the neighborhood, but coming up to the annual May Day run, she knows that her new rival, Gretchen, will challenge her and could win. Mr. Pearson, a teacher at the school, suggests it would be a nice gesture to the new girl, Gretchen, to let her win, which Hazel dismisses out of hand. Thinking about a Hansel and Gretel pageant in which she played a strawberry, Hazel thinks, "I am not a strawberry . . . I run. That is what I'm all about." As a runner, she has no intention of letting someone else win.

In fact, when the race is run, she does win, but it is very close, and for all her bravado, she is not sure who won until her name is announced. More important, she sees her brother Raymond running along with her on the other side of the fence, keeping his hands down in an awkward running posture that she accepts as all his own. In her excitement about her brother's accomplishment, she imagines that her rival Gretchen might want to help her train Raymond as a runner, and the two girls share a moment of genuine warmth.

The central point of the story is captured by Hazel when she says of the smile she shared with Gretchen that it was the type of smile girls can share only when they are not too busy being "flowers of fairies or strawberries instead of something honest and worthy of respect . . . you know . . . like being people." The honest competition that brought out their best efforts and enticed Raymond to join them in his way brought them all together as people, not as social competitors trying to outmaneuver one another but as allies.

"The Lesson" • "The Lesson" is a story about a child's first realization of the true depth of economic inequity in society. The main characters are Miss Moore, an educated black woman who has decided to take the responsibility for the education of neighborhood children upon herself, and Sylvia, the narrator, a young girl. Though it is summer, Miss Moore has organized an educational field trip. This annoys Sylvia and her friend, Sugar, but since their parents have all agreed to the trip, the children have little choice but to cooperate. The trip is actually an excursion to a high-priced department store, F. A. O. Schwartz.

The children look with astonishment at a toy clown that costs $35, a paperweight that sells for $480, and a toy sailboat that is priced at $1,195. The children are discouraged by the clear signs of economic inequality. When Miss Moore asks what they have learned from this trip, only Sugar will reply with what she knows Miss Moore wants them to say: "This is not much of a democracy." Sylvia feels betrayed but mostly because she sees that Sugar is playing up to Miss Moore, while Sylvia has been genuinely shaken by this trip. At the end, Sugar is plotting to split the money she knows Sylvia saved from the cab fare Miss Moore gave her, but Sylvia's response as Sugar runs ahead to their favorite ice cream shop, "ain't nobody gonna beat me at nothin'," indicates she has been shaken and is not planning to play the same old games. However, Sylvia cannot so easily slough it off.

"Medley" • The most popular story from *The Sea Birds Are Still Alive*, "Medley" is the story of Sweet Pea and Larry, a romantic couple who go through a poignant breakup in the course of the story. Though neither of them is a musician, both are music fans, and their showers together are erotic encounters in which they improvise songs together, pretending to be playing musical instruments with each other's body. Sweet Pea is a manicurist with her own shop, and her best customer is a gambler named Moody, who likes to keep his nails impeccable. Because he goes on a winning streak after she starts doing his nails, he offers to take her on a gambling trip as his personal manicurist, for which he pays her two thousand dollars. Sweet Pea takes the offer, though Larry objects, and when she gets back, he seems to have disappeared from her life. Nonetheless, she remembers their last night in the shower together, as they sang different tunes, keeping each other off balance, but harmonizing a medley together until the hot water ran out.

Though Sweet Pea is faced with the choice of losing two thousand dollars or her boyfriend and chooses the money, the story does not attempt to say that she made the wrong choice. Rather, it is a snapshot of the impermanence of shared lives in Sweet Pea's modern, urban environment. This transience is painful, but is also the basis for the enjoyment of life's beauty.

Thomas Cassidy

Other major works

ANTHOLOGIES: *The Black Woman: An Anthology*, 1970; *Tales and Stories for Black Folks*, 1971; *Southern Exposure*, 1976 (periodical; Bambara edited volume 3).

NOVELS: *The Salt Eaters*, 1980; *Those Bones Are Not My Child*, 1999.

MISCELLANEOUS: "What It Is I Think I'm Doing Anyhow," *The Writer on Her Work*, 1981 (Janet Sternburg, editor); *Deep Sightings and Rescue Missions: Fiction, Essays, and Conversations*, 1996.

SCREENPLAYS: *The Bombing of Osage Avenue*, 1986 (documentary); *W. E. B. Du Bois—A Biography in Four Voices*, 1995 (with Amiri Baraka, Wesley Brown, and Thulani Davis).

Bibliography

Alwes, Derek. "The Burden of Liberty: Choice in Toni Morrison's *Jazz* and Toni Cade Bambara's *The Salt Eaters*." *African American Review* 30, no. 3 (Fall, 1996): 353-365. In comparing the works of Morrison and Bambara, Alwes argues that while Morrison wants readers to participate in a choice, Bambara wants them to choose to participate. Bambara's message is that happiness is possible if people refuse to forget the past and continue to participate in the struggle.

Butler-Evans, Elliott. *Race, Gender, and Desire: Narrative Strategies in the Fiction of Toni Cade Bambara, Toni Morrison, Alice Walker*. Philadelphia: Temple University Press, 1989. The first book-length study to treat Bambara's fiction to any extent, this study uses narratology and feminism to explore Bambara's works.

Evans, Mari, ed. *Black Women Writers (1950-1980): A Critical Evaluation*. Garden City, N.Y.: Anchor Press/Doubleday, 1984. In the essay "Salvation Is the Issue," Bambara says that the elements of her own work that she deems most important are laughter, use of language, sense of community, and celebration.

Hargrove, Nancy. "Youth in Toni Cade Bambara's *Gorilla, My Love.*" In *Women Writers of the Contemporary South*, edited by Peggy Whitman Prenshaw. Jackson: University Press of Mississippi, 1984. Thorough examination of an important feature of Bambara's most successful collection of short fiction—namely, that most of the best stories center on young girls.

May, Charles E., ed. *Masterplots II: Short Story Series, Revised Edition.* 8 vols. Pasadena, Calif.: Salem Press, 2004. Designed for student use, this reference set contains articles providing detailed plot summaries and analyses of these four short stories by Bambara: "Gorilla, My Love" (vol. 3); "The Lesson" (vol. 4); "My Man Bovanne" (vol. 5); and "Raymond's Run" (vol. 6).

Vertreace, Martha M. *Toni Cade Bambara.* New York: Macmillan Library Reference, 1998. The first full-length work devoted to the entirety of Bambara's career. A part of the successful Twayne series of criticism, this will be quite helpful for students interested in Bambara's career.

Williamson, Judith Barton. "Toni Cade Bambara." In *Critical Survey of Long Fiction, Revised Edition*, edited by Carl Rollyson. Vol. 1. Pasadena, Calif.: Salem Press, 2000. Analysis of Bambara's longer fictional works that may offer insights into her short fiction.

Willis, Susan. "Problematizing the Individual: Toni Cade Bambara's Stories for the Revolution." In *Specifying: Black Women Writing the American Experience.* Madison: University of Wisconsin Press, 1987. Though largely centered on an analysis of *The Salt Eaters*, this essay also has clear and informative analysis of Bambara's most important short fiction.

Russell Banks

Born: Newton, Massachusetts; March 28, 1940

Principal short fiction • *Searching for Survivors*, 1975; *The New World*, 1978; *Trailerpark*, 1981; *Success Stories*, 1986; *The Angel on the Roof: The Stories of Russell Banks*, 2000.

Other literary forms • Russell Banks has published several collections of poetry and many novels. *Continental Drift* (1985) was a finalist for the Pulitzer Prize and *Affliction* (1989) was nominated for both the PEN/Faulkner Award for Fiction and the Irish International Prize. His other major works include the novels *Family Life* (1975), *Hamilton Stark* (1978), *The Sweet Hereafter* (1991), *Rule of the Bone* (1995), *Cloudsplitter* (1998), and *The Darling* (2004). His poems, stories, and essays have appeared in *The Boston Globe Magazine*, *Vanity Fair*, *The New York Times Book Review*, *Esquire*, and *Harper's*.

Achievements • Russell Banks has been awarded a Woodrow Wilson Foundation Award, a John Simon Guggenheim Memorial Fellowship, a National Endowment for the Arts grant, the Ingram Merril Award, the Fels Award, the John Dos Passos Award, the St. Lawrence Award for Fiction from St. Lawrence University and *Fiction International*, and the American Academy of Arts and Letters Award for work of distinction. His work has been anthologized in *Prize Stories: The O. Henry Awards* and *The Best American Short Stories*.

Biography • Russell Earl Banks was born in Newton, Massachusetts, on March 28, 1940, and raised in New Hampshire. The first in his family to attend college, Banks found the atmosphere at Colgate University incompatible with his working-class background and relinquished his scholarship after eight weeks. He headed for Florida, fully intending to align himself with rebel Cuban leader Fidel Castro, but, lacking enough incentive and money, worked at odd jobs until his career path became clear. He was at various times a plumber (like his father), a shoe salesman, a department store window dresser, and an editor.

In 1964 he enrolled at the University of North Carolina at Chapel Hill and graduated Phi Beta Kappa in 1967. His sense of political and social injustice became more finely honed in this city, which is touted as the most northern of the southern states, the most dramatic incident being the disruption of an integrated party by gun-wielding members of the local Ku Klux Klan.

A John Simon Guggenheim Memorial Foundation Fellowship in 1976 allowed him to move to Jamaica, where he immersed himself in the culture, trying to live as a native rather than as a tourist. The experience of living in an impoverished nation helped him professionally as well as personally and gave him a broad perspective on issues of race. Married four times and the father of four grown daughters, Banks has taught at major universities, including Columbia University, Sarah Lawrence College, New York University, and Princeton University. Critic Fred Pfeil called Banks the most important living white male American on the official literary map, a writer we, as readers *and* writers, can actually learn from, whose books help and urge us to change.

Analysis • Russell Banks's work is largely autobiographical, growing out of the chaos of his childhood: the shouting and hitting, physical and emotional abuse inflicted on the family by an alcoholic father, who abandoned them in 1953. Being forced at the age of twelve to assume the role of the man in the family and always living on the edge of poverty greatly influenced Banks's worldview and consequently his writing. Banks's struggle to understand the tight hold that the past has on the present and the future led him to create a world in which people come face to face with similar dilemmas. Banks's characters struggle to get out from under, to free themselves from the tethers of race, class, and gender. He writes of working people, those who by virtue of social status are always apart, marginalized, often desperate, inarticulate, silenced by circumstances. He aims to be their voice, to give expression to their pain, their aspirations, their angsts. Their emotional makeup can be as complex as those more favored by birth or power. In an interview in *The New York Times Book Review,* Banks noted that

> part of the challenge . . . is uncovering the resiliency of that kind of life, and part is in demonstrating that even the quietest lives can be as complex and rich, as joyous, conflicted and anguished, as other seemingly more dramatic lives.

Banks's main strength, besides his graceful style, keen powers of observation, intelligence, and humanity, is his ability to write feelingly of often unlovable people. He never condescends or belittles. He does not judge. He always attempts to show, rather than tell, why characters are as they are, and it is in the telling that Banks is able to understand himself and exorcise the devils of his own past. He did not necessarily set out on self-discovery, but learned, through writing, who he was and what he thought. He grew to understand himself through understanding the elements of his past that shaped him.

Banks is sometimes grouped with Raymond Carver, Richard Ford, and Andre Dubus as writers in a "Trailer-Park Fiction" genre, which, according to critic Denis M. Hennessy, examines

> American working-class people living their lives one step up from the lowest rung on the socioeconomic ladder and doing battle every day with the despair that comes from violence, alcohol, and self-destructive relationships.

Some of Banks's plots and themes are derivative, with heavy borrowings from Mark Twain and E. L. Doctorow, but his unique touch sets them apart. Banks is both a chronicler and a critic of contemporary society.

Influenced by James Baldwin, who said that the true story about race would have to be "written from the point of view of a member of a lynch mob," Banks attempts to elicit an understanding of the perpetrators as well as of the victims of crimes, cruelties, and injustices. He believes that understanding a situation depends on knowing how the players who created it were created themselves. His characters all search for transformation, for something that will redeem them, lift them above their present circumstances. Their searches lead them to greater desolation and very seldom to contentment. The lower echelon is forever pitted against and at the mercy of the middle class. Hennessy has called Banks's short fiction the "testing ground of his most innovative ideas and techniques." The major themes revolve around disharmony, both in the family and in society, and the eternal search for the lost family. Banks admits that much of his fiction centers on "Russell Banks searching for his father. . . . I spent a great deal of my youth running away from him and obsessively returning to him."

Searching for Survivors • Banks's first collection combines reality and fantasy, with the fourteen stories divided into three general groups: five moral and political parables, a trilogy of stories that feature Latin American revolutionary Che Guevara, and six substantially autobiographical tales set in New England. Banks's experiments with narrative style, structure, and point of view met with mixed response. He was credited for trying but faulted for lacking a unifying thread. Critic Robert Niemi says of the parables that if the

> theme . . . is the modern divorce between cognition and feeling [they] stylistically enact that schism with a vengeance . . . almost all [being] solemn in tone, and written in a detached, clinically descriptive style that tends toward the cryptic.

Each story ends on a note of either defeat or disillusionment. Survival is highly unlikely. The American Dream has failed.

The opening tale deals with a man driving along the Henry Hudson Parkway, thinking about his childhood friend's car, a Hudson, and about the explorer, who was set adrift in 1611 in the waters that eventually bore his name. The narrator imagines going to the shores of Hudson Bay to look for evidence of the explorer's fate. Therein is an attempt to understand the past. Banks often deals with

> the Old World and the early exploration of North America, and he shows the connections between those who set out from their comfortable but unjust homelands to settle the unknown, and modern Americans who have been shunted out of their safe cocoons of fixed values and family security into the relativistic reality of the latter half of the twentieth century.

In a story confirming Thomas Wolfe's thesis that one "can't go home again," a young man returns from adventures with guerrilla leader Che Guevara, only to find his hometown irrevocably changed and himself so different that no one recognizes him. In another story, "With Che at Kitty Hawk," a newly divorced woman and her two daughters visit the Wright Brothers Memorial. An almost-happy ending has the woman feeling somewhat liberated after being trapped in marriage, but that optimism is fleeting. In yet another, "Blizzard," Banks shifts the narrator, first having him be omniscient, then having him speak through a man who is losing touch with reality, succumbing to guilt and bleak wintry surroundings.

The New World • Banks's search for a comfortable voice caused him to continue to experiment with narrative voice, switching from first- to second-person, and sometimes third-, at times unsettling readers and critics who deemed his shifts haphazard rather than intentional. Never fully at ease with an omniscient, all-knowing narrator, yet not wanting his storyteller to be a character, an integral player, and hence subject to the vagaries of plot, Banks tries to approach his writing as the telling of a story to a partner, perhaps in a darkened room while lying comfortably in bed. He wants to share his story, yet not to tell it from a position of privilege. This approach gives readers the immediacy needed for involvement in the story, but, at the same time, enough detachment on the part of the narrator to trust him.

Banks called his second collection, which was far more positively received, "a carefully structured gathering of ten tales that dramatize and explore the process and progress of self-transcendence, tales that . . . embrace the spiritual limits and possibilities of life in the New World."

The collection is divided into two parts: "Renunciation" and "Transformation." The opening story, "The Custodian," deals with a forty-three-year-old man whose father's death finally frees him "to move to a new village . . . to drink and smoke and sing bawdy songs." As he is now also free to marry, he, "reasoning carefully . . . conclude[s] that he would have good luck in seeking a wife if he started with women who were already married." Fortuitously, he has many married male friends and thus begins his series of conquests. He proposes to a few likely prospects; they succumb; he changes his mind; they return to their husbands, never to know satisfaction again.

In another story, "The Conversion," a young boy is wracked by guilt at not being a good person, at engaging in excessive masturbation, always falling short of what he thought he should be. Alvin wants to change. He wants to be good, decent, and chaste. He fails miserably until one day he sees an angel in a parking lot and decides to become a preacher. His conversion, readers realize, is not so much religious as it is a hope to start anew. His new religious life starts as a dishwasher in a religious camp. Robert Niemi observes that, "much like Banks in his youth, Alvin is torn between the promise of upward mobility and loyalty to his father's proletarian ethos." Alvin's father suspects him of "selling out his working-class identity by associating himself with a bourgeois profession," reflecting Banks's own social background in which attempts to move upward were considered a criticism of what was left behind.

Historical figures are featured in some of the stories: Simón Bolívar, Jane Hogarth (wife of the eccentric painter William), Edgar Allan Poe, and others. In the Hogarth tale, "Indisposed," the wife is sadly used by the husband, who treats her as a sexual convenience and housekeeper. She is overwhelmed by the nothingness of her existence. She is fat and self-loathing until she experiences a sickbed transformation which allows her to move beyond "pitying [her large, slow] body to understanding it." She is then, according to Niemi, able to "inhabit her body fully and without shame, thus reclaiming herself." Then, when her husband is caught in the upstairs bed with the young domestic helper, Jane is able to exact swift punishment and completely change the tenor of the home. Niemi observes that Banks's history

> shades into fiction and fiction melds into history. [His] central theme, though, is the enduring human need to reinvent the self in order to escape or transcend the constrictions of one's actual circumstances. This means creating a "new world" out of the imagination, just as the "discovery" of the Americas opened up vast horizons for a culturally exhausted Old World Europe.

Banks believes that "the dream of a new life, the dream of starting over" is the quintessential American Dream, the ideological keystone of American civilization from its inception to the present day.

Trailerpark • In this collection, perhaps his most structurally satisfying, Russell Banks takes readers into the very heart of a community of people who, while not having lowered expectations, do have less grandiose or unrealistic ambitions than those in the mainstream. They go through life earning enough to meet basic needs, never going far beyond their environs. Some work full time, some seasonally; some leave for a while and then return. Most seem to find the day-to-day process of getting by nearly enough. Heartaches, anger, depression, and just plain weirdness are often eased with marijuana and alcohol.

This collection's twelve stories are interrelated because they all deal with the residents of the Granite State Trailerpark in Catamount, New Hampshire. They have little in common other than the circumstances of their housing. They are detached physically as well as emotionally, yet they do form a community with at least some common concerns. One of the residents notes that when you are "a long way from where you think you belong, you will attach yourself to people you would otherwise ignore or even dislike." Each story deals with one of the dozen or so denizens, all of whom are "generally alone in the world."

Trailer #1 is the heartbeat of the park, where French Canadian manager Marcelle Chagnon oversees operations. She lost a child when an unscrupulous doctor found her more interesting than her illness. Bank teller Leon LaRoche lives in #2 next to Bruce Severance, in #3, a college student who is an afficionado of homegrown cannabis. Divorcée Doreen Tiede and her five-year-old daughter are in #4 next to the burned remains of #5, where Ginnie and Claudel Bing lived until Ginnie left the stove burner on. Retired army captain Dewey Knox is in #6; Noni Hubner and her mother Nancy are in #7. Merl Ring, in #8, enjoys self-imposed isolation, eagerly awaiting the blasting winters when he can set up his equipment in the middle of frozen Skitters Lake and spend months of solitary ice fishing. The former resident of #9, Tom Smith, killed himself, and the place remains empty. The only black resident, Carol Constant, sometimes shares #10 with her brother Terry. Number 11 houses Flora Pease and more than 115 guinea pigs, which threaten to overtake the trailer and the whole park. The opening story, "The Guinea Pig Lady," introduces all the residents as they share their concerns about the situation. Most notable is the trailer and occupant not mentioned at all—#12, probably the narrator's place. Banks's park people have offbeat but understandable pathologies. Some are just achingly lonely. Critic Johnathan Yardley credits Banks with drawing together a "small but vibrant cast of characters, a human comedy in microcosm" made up of "utterly unconnected people [who] find themselves drawn together by the accident of living in the same place; the trailer park, grim and dreary as it may be, is a neighborhood."

Success Stories • This 1986 collection of twelve stories, six autobiographical, six parabolic, has more to do with failed attempts to change the course of lives than it does with acquisition of fame and fortune. The characters in the collection have been called "dreamers, nourished on giddy expectations, but disenfranchised by accidents of class, economy, looks or simple luck." They think that life holds all sorts of possibilities but learn quickly that fate has not cast a favorable eye on them. Banks sets out to show that success is more elusive for the disenfranchised.

Four stories revolve around Earl Painter, a young child in the story "Queen for a Day," who writes to the host of the popular television show of the same name numerous times hoping that his mother's plight will land her a place as a contestant. In subsequent stories, Earl attempts to come to grips with his parents and their lies and imaginings. His search for fulfillment leads him to Florida, where he experiences short-lived success. He toys with the idea of marrying into a new life but instead engages in adultery with a neighbor's wife, learning from her husband that he is just one of her many dalliances.

These stories are interspersed with ones that are either fabular or close to surreal.

Three deal with situations possibly slated to show a similarity between Third World exploitation and an American tendency to disenfranchise the working class. All deal with the terrible consequences of false promises of success.

One story, "Sarah Cole: A Type of Love Story," shows the impermeability of the walls separating the classes. The hero, exceptionally handsome, develops an unlikely relationship with his antithesis, an alarmingly ugly barroom pickup named Sarah. His initial curiosity about lovemaking with someone so badly put together turns into a kind of commitment but not one strong enough to be made public. The contrast in their appearances proves too great for him. He is indeed superficial and acts hatefully. Years later, the truth of his love dawns on him, but Sarah is long gone, and he is left with his shame.

Critic Trish Reeves notes in an interview that "the irony of finally becoming a literary success by writing about the failure of the American Dream was not lost on Banks." He said:

> I still view myself in the larger world the way I did when I was an adolescent. . . . [as a member of] a working class family: powerless people who look from below up. I'm unable to escape that—how one views oneself in the larger structure is determined at an extremely early age. The great delusion is that if you only can get success then you will shift your view of yourself . . . you will become a different person. That's the longing, for success is really not material goods, but in fact to become a whole new person.

Gay Annette Zieger

Other major works

ANTHOLOGY: *Brushes with Greatness: An Anthology of Chance Encounters with Greatness,* 1989 (with Michael Ondaatje and David Young).

NOVELS: *Family Life,* 1975 (revised, 1988); *Hamilton Stark,* 1978; *The Book of Jamaica,* 1980; *The Relation of My Imprisonment,* 1983; *Continental Drift,* 1985; *Affliction,* 1989; *The Sweet Hereafter,* 1991; *Rule of the Bone,* 1995; *Cloudsplitter,* 1998; *The Darling,* 2004.

NONFICTION: *The Autobiographical Eye,* 1982 (David Halpern, editor); *The Invisible Stranger: The Patten, Maine Photographs of Arturo Patten,* 1999.

POETRY: *Fifteen Poems,* 1967 (with William Matthews and Newton Smith); *30/6,* 1969; *Waiting to Freeze,* 1969; *Snow: Meditations of a Cautious Man in Winter,* 1974.

Bibliography

Chapman, Jeff, and Pamela S. Dean. *Contemporary Authors* 52 (1996). A short but information-packed study under the headings "Personal," "Career," "Memberships," "Awards and Honors," "Writings," and "Sidelights" (containing author quotes and discussions, mostly of longer fiction but also touching on *Trailerpark*), followed by an invaluable list of biographical and critical sources.

Contemporary Literary Criticism 37, 1986. Provides a good overview of Banks's life up to 1985 and gives a substantial sampling of literary criticism.

Contemporary Literary Criticism 72, 1992. Strong biographical overview of Banks's life and influences, followed by critical analyses of work published between 1986 and 1991. Included is a valuable interview conducted by writer Trish Reeves that provides a good understanding of the author. Top literary critics provide illuminating commentary.

Haley, Vanessa. "Russell Banks's Use of 'The Frog King' in 'Sarah Cole: A Type of Love Story.'" *Notes on Contemporary Literature* 27 (1997): 7-10. Proposes that the story from the Grimm brothers' folktale collection is a source for Banks's narrative.

May, Charles E., ed. *Masterplots II: Short Story Series, Revised Edition.* 8 vols. Pasadena, Calif.: Salem Press, 2004. Designed for student use, this reference set contains articles providing detailed plot summaries and analyses of these three short stories by Banks: "The Moor" (vol. 5), "Sarah Cole: A Type of Love Story" (vol. 6), and "The Visitor" (vol. 8).

Meanor, Patrick, ed. *American Short Story Writers Since World War II.* Vol. 130 in *Dictionary of Literary Biography.* Detroit: Gale Research, 1993. Good background material on Banks's life and the general content of his fiction with some discussion of thematic and narrative approaches.

Niemi, Robert. *Russell Banks.* Twayne's United States Authors series. New York: Twayne, 1997. Comprehensive biography that includes critical analyses of all his major literary works. It is rife with charming and telling details that convey the essence of the author, but it maintains the objectivity necessary to present a fair portrait.

_____. "Russell Banks." In *American Writers: A Collection of Literary Biographies, Supplement V—Russell Banks to Charles Wright,* edited by Jay Parini. New York: Scribner's, 2000. This accessible article summarizes and updates Niemi's book on Banks. The bibliography expands and updates the earlier one.

Somerson, Wendy. "Becoming Rasta: Recentering White Masculinity in the Era of Transnationalism." *Comparatist* 23 (1999): 128-140. Analyzes *Rule of the Bone*'s treatment of white masculinity and racial identity politics in an era when national boundaries are becoming more porous.

Donald Barthelme

Born: Philadelphia, Pennsylvania; April 7, 1931
Died: Houston, Texas; July 23, 1989

Principal short fiction • *Come Back, Dr. Caligari,* 1964; *Unspeakable Practices, Unnatural Acts,* 1968; *City Life,* 1970; *Sadness,* 1972; *Amateurs,* 1976; *Great Days,* 1979; *Sixty Stories,* 1981; *Overnight to Many Distant Cities,* 1983; *Forty Stories,* 1987.

Other literary forms • In addition to his one hundred and fifty or so short stories, Donald Barthelme published four novels, a children's volume that won a National Book Award, a number of film reviews and unsigned "Comment" pieces for *The New Yorker,* a small but interesting body of art criticism, and a handful of book reviews and literary essays, two of which deserve special notice: "After Joyce" and "Not Knowing."

Achievements • For nearly three decades, Donald Barthelme served as American literature's most imitated and imitative yet inimitable writer. One of a small but influential group of innovative American fictionists that included maximalists John Barth, Robert Coover, and Thomas Pynchon, Barthelme evidenced an even greater affinity to the international minimalists Samuel Beckett and Jorge Luis Borges. What distinguishes Barthelme's fiction is not only his unique "zero degree" writing style but also, thanks to his long association with the mass-circulation magazine *The New Yorker,* his reaching a larger and more diversified audience than most of the experimentalists, whose readership has chiefly been limited to the ranks of college professors and their students. For all the oddity of a fiction based largely upon "the odd linguistic trip, stutter, and fall" (*Snow White,* 1967), Barthelme may well come to be seen as the Anthony Trollope of his age. Although antirealistic in form, his fictions are in fact densely packed time capsules—not the "slices of life" of nineteenth century realists such as Émile Zola but "the thin edge of the wedge" of postmodernism's version of Charles Dickens's hard times and Charles Chaplin's modern ones.

For all their seeming sameness, Barthelme's stories cover a remarkable range of styles, subjects, linguistic idioms, and historical periods (often in the same work, sometimes in the same sentence). For all their referential density, Barthelme's stories do not attempt to reproduce mimetically external reality but instead offer a playful meditation on it (or alternately the materials for such a meditation). Such an art makes Barthelme in many respects the most representative American writer of the 1960's and of the two decades that followed: postmodern, postmodernist, post-Freudian, poststructuralist, postindustrial, even (to borrow Jerome Klinkowitz's apt term) postcontemporary.

Biography • Often praised and sometimes disparaged as one of *The New Yorker* writers, a narrative innovator, and a moral relativist whose only advice (John Gardner claimed) is that it is better to be disillusioned than deluded, Donald Barthelme was born in Philadelphia on April 7, 1931, and moved to Houston two years later. He grew up in Texas, attended Roman Catholic diocesan schools, and began his writing career as a journalist in Ernest Hemingway's footsteps. His father, an architect who favored the modernist style of Ludwig Mies Van Der Rohe and Le Corbusier, taught at the University of Houston and designed the family's house, which became as much an object of surprise and wonder on the flat Texas landscape as his son's oddly shaped fictions were to become on the equally flat narrative landscape of postwar American fiction. While majoring in journalism, Barthelme wrote for the university newspaper as well as the *Houston Post*. He was drafted in 1953 and arrived in Korea on the day the truce was signed—the kind of coincidence one comes to expect in Barthelme's stories of strange juxtapositions and incongruous couplings. After his military service, during which he also edited an Army newspaper, he returned to Houston, where he worked in the university's public relations department ("writing poppycock for the President," as he put it in one story), and where he founded *Forum*, a literary and intellectual quarterly that

Bill Wittliff

published early works by Walker Percy, William H. Gass, Alain Robbe-Grillet, Leslie Fiedler, and others.

Barthleme published his first story in 1961, the same year that he became director of the Contemporary Arts Museum of Houston. The following year, Thomas Hess and Harold Rosenberg offered him the position of managing editor of their new arts journal, *Location*. The journal was short-lived (only two issues ever appeared), but Barthelme's move to New York was not. Taking up residence in Greenwich Village, he published his first story in *The New Yorker* in 1963, his first collection of stories, *Come Back, Dr. Caligari*, in 1964, and his first novel, *Snow White* (among other things an updating of the Brothers Grimm fairy tale and the Walt Disney feature-length animated cartoon), in 1967. Although he left occasionally for brief periods abroad or to teach writing at Buffalo, Houston, and elsewhere, Barthelme spent the rest of his life chiefly in Greenwich Village, with his fourth wife, Marion Knox. He lived as a writer, registering and remaking the "exquisite mysterious muck" of contemporary urban American existence, as witnessed from his corner of the global (Greenwich) village.

Analysis • Donald Barthelme's fiction exhausts and ultimately defeats conventional approaches (including character, plot, setting, theme—"the enemies of the novel" as fellow writer John Hawkes once called them) and defeats, too, all attempts at generic classification. His stories are not conventional, nor are they Borgesian *ficciones* or Beckettian "texts for nothing." Thematic studies of his writing have proved utterly inadequate, yet purely formalist critiques have seemed almost as unsatisfying. To approach a Barthelme story, the reader must proceed circuitously via various, indeed at times simultaneous, extraliterary forms: collage, caricature, Calder mobile, action painting, jazz, atonality, the chance music of John Cage, architecture, information theory, magazine editing and layout, ventriloquism, even Legos (with all their permutational possibilities, in contrast with the High Moderns' love of cubist jigsaw puzzles). In Barthelme's case, comparisons with twentieth century painters and sculptors seem especially apropos: comical like Jean Dubuffet, whimsical and sad like Amedeo Modigliani, chaste like Piet Mondrian, attenuated like Alberto Giacometti, composite like Kurt Schwitters, improvisational like Jackson Pollock, fanciful like Marc Chagall and Paul Klee. Like theirs, his is an art of surfaces, dense rather than deep, textured rather than symbolic, an intersection of forces rather than a rendered meaning. Adjusting to the shift in perspective that reading Barthelme entails—and adjusting as well to Barthelme's (like the poet John Ashbery's) unwillingness to distinguish between foreground and background, message and noise—is difficult, sometimes impossible, and perhaps always fruitless.

However attenuated and elliptical the stories may be, they commit a kind of "sensory assault" on a frequently distracted reader who experiences immediate gratification in dealing with parts but epistemological frustration in considering the stories as wholes, a frustration which mirrors that of the characters. Not surprisingly, one finds Barthelme's characters and the fictions themselves engaged in a process of scaling back even as they and their readers yearn for that "more" to which Beckett's figures despairingly and clownishly give voice. Entering "the complicated city" and singing their "song of great expectations," they nevertheless—or also—discover that theirs is a world not of romantic possibilities (as in F. Scott Fitzgerald's fiction) but of postmodern permutations, a world of words and undecidability, where "our Song of Songs is the Uncertainty Principle" and where "double-mindedness makes for mixtures." These are stories that, like the red snow in Barthelme's favorite and most Borgesian work, "Paraguay," invite "contemplation" of a mystery that there is "no point solving—an ongoing low-grade mystery." Expressed despondently, the answer to the question, "Why do I live this way?"—or why does Barthelme write this way?—is, as the character Bishop says, "Best I can do." This, however, sums up only one side of Barthelme's double-mindedness; the other is the pleasure, however fleeting, to be taken "in the sweet of the here and the now."

"Me and Miss Mandible" • Originally published as "The Darling Duckling at School" in 1961, "Me and Miss Mandible" is one of Barthelme's earliest stories and one of his best. Written in the form of twenty-six journal entries (dated September 13 to December 9), the story evidences Barthelme's genius for rendering even the most fantastic, dreamlike events in the most matter-of-fact manner possible. The thirty-five-year-old narrator, Joseph, finds himself sitting in a too-small desk in Miss Mandible's classroom, having been declared "officially a child of eleven," either by mistake or, more likely, as punishment for having himself made a mistake in his former life as claims adjuster (a mistake for justice but against his company's interests). Having spent ten years "amid the debris of our civilization," he has come "to see the world as a vast junkyard" that includes the failure of his marriage and the absurdity of his military duty. At once a biblical Joseph in a foreign land and a Swiftian Gulliver among the Lilliputians, he will spend his time observing others and especially observing the widening gap between word and world, signifier and signified, the ideals expressed in teachers' manuals and the passions of a class of prepubescents fueled by film magazine stories about the Eddie Fisher/Debbie Reynolds/ Elizabeth Taylor love triangle. Unlike his biblical namesake, Joseph will fail at reeducation as he has failed at marriage and other forms of social adjustment, caught by a jealous classmate making love to the freakishly named Miss Mandible.

"A Shower of Gold" • The coming together of unlike possibilities and the seeming affirmation of failure (maladjustment) takes a slightly different and more varied form in "A Shower of Gold." The former claims adjuster, Joseph, becomes the impoverished artist, Peterson, who specializes in large junk sculptures that no one buys and that even his dealer will not display. Desperate for money, he volunteers to appear on *Who Am I?*, the odd offspring of the game show craze on American television and of existentialism transformed into pop culture commodity. (There is also a barber who doubles as an analyst and triples as the author of four books all titled *The Decision to Be*.) Peterson convinces the show's Miss Arbor that he is both interesting enough and sufficiently de trop to appear on *Who Am I?*, only to feel guilty about selling out for two hundred dollars. Watching the other panelists be subjected to a humiliating barrage of questions designed to expose their bad faith, Peterson, accepting his position as a minor artist, short-circuits the host's existential script by out-absurding the absurd (his mother, he says, was a royal virgin and his father, a shower of gold). Peterson's situation parallels Barthelme's, or indeed any American writing at a time when, as Philip Roth pointed out in 1961, American reality had begun to outstrip the writer's imagination, offering a steady diet of actual people and events far more fantastic than any that the writer could hope to offer. What, Roth wondered, was left for the writer to do? "A Shower of Gold" offers one possibility.

"The Indian Uprising" • "The Indian Uprising" and "The Balloon" represent another possibility, in which in two quite different ways Barthelme directs the reader away from story and toward the act of interpretation itself (interpretation as story). As Brian McHale and Ron Moshe have demonstrated, "The Indian Uprising" comprises three overlapping yet divergent and even internally inconsistent narratives: an attack by Comanche on an unidentified but clearly modern American city; the narrator's (one of the city's defender's) unsatisfying love life; and the conflict between modern and postmodern sensibilities manifesting itself in a variety of allusions to modernist texts, including T. S. Eliot's *The Waste Land* (1922). Near the end of his poem, Eliot writes, "These fragments I have shored against my ruins." "The Indian Uprising" presents a very different approach, transforming Eliot's shoring up of high culture into a "barricade" that recycles Eliot and Thomas Mann along with ashtrays, doors, bottles of Fad #6 sherry, "and other items." Behind Eliot's poem lies the possibility of psychic, spiritual, and sociocultural wholeness implied by Eliot's use of the "mythic method." Behind Barthelme's story one finds recycling rather than redemption and, instead of the mythic method, what Ronald Sukenick has called "the Mosaic Law," or "the law of mosaics, a way of dealing with parts in the absence of wholes." Short but beyond summary, filled with non sequiturs, ill-logic, self-doubts, and anti-explanations, "The Indian Uprising" rises against readers in their efforts to know it by reducing the story to some manageable whole. At once inviting and frustrating the reader's interpretive maneuvers, "The Indian Uprising" follows the "plan" outlined in "Paraguay" insofar as it proves "a way of allowing a very wide range of tendencies to interact."

Attacking and defending are two operant principles at play here, but just who is attacking and what is being defended are never made clear. Sides change, shapes shift in a story in which American Westerns, the Civil Rights movement, and American involvement in Vietnam all seem to have their parts to play, but never to the point where any one can be said to dominate the others. Small but indomitable, the story resists the linearity of an interpretive domino theory in favor of a semiotic quagmire (more evidence of Barthelme's interest in current affairs—Vietnam, in this case—and "mysterious muck"). In "The Indian Uprising," there is no final authority to come like the cavalry to the rescue and so no release from the anxiety evident in this and so many other Barthelme stories. Although there may be no permanent release, however, there is some temporary relief to be had in the "aesthetic excitement" of "the hard, brown, nutlike word" and in the fact that "Strings of language extend in every direction to bind the world into a rushing ribald whole."

"The Balloon" • "The Balloon" is a more compact exploration and a more relentless exploitation of interpretation as a semiotic process rather than a narrowly coded act. Covering only a few pages (or alternately an area forty-five city blocks long by up to six blocks wide), "The Balloon" is Barthelme's American tall-tale version of the short French film *The Red Balloon* and an *hommage* to Frederick Law Olmsted (who designed New York's Central Park) and environmental artist Cristo (one of his huge sculptural wrappings). Analogies such as these help readers situate themselves in relation to the inexplicable but unavoidable oddity of "The Balloon" in much the same way that the viewers in the story attempt to situate themselves in relation to the sudden appearance of a balloon which, even if it cannot be understood ("We had learned not to insist on meanings"), can at least be used (for graffiti, for example) and appreciated despite, or perhaps because of, its apparent uselessness. Ultimately the narrator will explain the balloon, thus adding his interpretive graffiti to its blank surface. The balloon, he says, was "a spontaneous autobiographical disclosure" occasioned by his lover's departure; when, after twenty-two days, she returns, he deflates the balloon, folds it, and ships it to West Virginia to be stored for future use. His explanation is doubly deflating, for while the balloon's "apparent purposelessness" may be vexing, in a world of "complex machinery," "specialized training," and pseudoscientific theories that make people marginal and passive, it has come to exist as the "prototype" or "rough draft" of the kind of solution to which people will increasingly turn, to what the Balloon Man calls his best balloon, the Balloon of Perhaps.

Until the narrator's closing comments, the balloon is not a scripted text but a blank page, not an object but an event, not a ready-made product, a prefab, but a performance that invites response and participation. It is a performance that the narrator's explanation concludes, assigning both an origin (cause) and destination (result, function, use, addressee). Yet even as the explanation brings a measure of relief, it also adds a new level of anxiety insofar as the reader perceives its inadequacy and feels perhaps a twinge of guilty pleasure over having made so much of so little. In a way, however, the balloon was always doomed to extinction, for it exists in a consumer culture in which even the most remarkable objects (including "The Balloon") quickly become all too familiar, and it exists too in a therapeutic society in thrall to the illusion of authoritative explanations.

"Robert Kennedy Saved from Drowning" • Appearing only two months before the real Robert F. Kennedy's assassination, "Robert Kennedy Saved from Drowning" explores epistemological uncertainty by exploiting the contemporary media's and its audience's claiming to know public figures, whether politicians or celebrities (a distinction that began to blur during the eponymous Kennedy years). The story exists at the intersection of two narrative styles. One is journalistic: twenty-four sections of what appear to be notes, each with its own subject heading and for the most part arranged in random order (the last section being a conspicuous exception) and presumably to be used in the writing of a profile or essay "about" Kennedy.

The second narrative style is Kafkaesque fantasy and is evoked solely by means of the reporter's use of journalistic shorthand, the initial "K," which "refers" to Kennedy but alludes to the main characters of the enigmatic (and unfinished) novels *Der Prozess* (1925; *The Trial*, 1937) and *Das Schloss* (1926; *The Castle*, 1930) and ultimately to their equally enigmatic author, Franz Kafka himself. The narrator of "See the Moon?" claims that fragments are the only forms he trusts; in "Robert Kennedy Saved from Drowning," fragments are the only forms the reader gets. The conflicting mass of seemingly raw material—quotes, impressions, even fragments of orders to waiters—saves Kennedy from drowning in a media-produced narcissistic image that turns even the most inane remarks into orphic sayings. Kennedy cannot drown; he can only float on the postmodern surface. Instead of the Kennedy image, Barthelme turns Kennedy into a series of images, the last being the most ludicrous and yet also the most revealing: Kennedy as Zorro, masked and floundering in the sea, his hat, cape, and sword safely on the beach. Saved from drowning (by the narrator), Kennedy is unmasked as a masked image, a free-floating signifier, a chameleon in superhero's clothing who proves most revealing when most chameleon-like, offering a summary of Georges Poulet's analysis of the eighteenth century writer Pierre Marivaux. Only here, at this third or even fourth remove, will many readers feel that they have gotten close to the "real" Kennedy:

> The Marivaudian being is, according to Poulet, a pastless, futureless man, born anew at every instant. The instants are points which organize themselves into a line, but what is important is the instant, not the line. The Marivaudian being has in a sense no history. Nothing follows from what has gone before. He is constantly surprised. He cannot predict his own reaction to events. He is constantly being *overtaken* by events. A condition of breathlessness and dazzlement surrounds him. In consequence he exists in a certain freshness which seems, if I may say so, very desirable. This freshness Poulet, quoting Marivaux, describes very well.

"Views of My Father Weeping" • "Views of My Father Weeping" combines epistemological uncertainty with typically postmodern problematizing of the relationship between past and present (hinted at in the above quotation). Several days after his father has died under the wheels of an aristocrat's carriage, the narrator sets out to investigate whether the death was accidental, as the police reported, or an example of the aristocracy's (and the police's) indifference to the poor. Spurred on less by a desire for truth and justice than a vague sense of filial obligation and even more by the slight possibility of financial gain, but fearful that he may be beaten for making inquiries, perhaps (like his father) even killed, the narrator-son proceeds, more hesitant than Hamlet. Hamlet had his father's ghost appear to remind him of his duty to avenge a murder most foul. Barthelme's story also has a ghost (of sorts), a weeping father who sits on his son's bed acting in decidedly untragic fashion like a spoiled, sulky child whose very identity as father the son quietly questions. Complicating matters still further, this father seems to appear in a second story within "Views of My Father Weeping," which takes place in a more contemporary and clearly, although fantastically, American setting. These important if often blurred differences aside, the two narrators suffer from the same twin diseases that are pandemic in Barthelme's fiction: abulia (loss of the ability to decide or act) and acedia (spiritual torpor). They certainly would benefit from a reading of a slightly later story, "A Manual for Sons," a self-contained part of Barthelme's second novel, *The Dead Father* (1975), which concludes with this advice:

> You must become your father, but a paler, weaker version of him. The enormities go with the job, but close study will allow you to perform the job less well than it previously has been done, thus moving toward a golden age of decency, quiet, and calmed fever. Your contribution will not be a small one, but "small" is one of the concepts that you should shoot for. . . . *Fatherhood can be, if not conquered, at least "turned down" in this generation*—by the combined efforts of all of us together.

The extreme brevity of his densely allusive and highly elliptical stories suggests that Barthelme sides with the smallness of sons in their comic struggle with their various fathers (biological, historical, cultural). Against the authoritative word of the All Father, Barthelme offers a range of ventriloquized voices. "Here I differ from Kierkegaard," says one of the characters in "The Leap." "Purity of heart is not," as Kierkegaard claimed, to will one thing; it is, rather, "to will several things, and not know which is the better, truer thing, and to worry about this forever."

Barthelme's own double-mindedness and preference for mixtures and the guilty pleasures of the son's uncertainty and anxiety of influence become especially apparent in his collages of verbal and visual materials in which he puts the magazine editor's skills—layout in particular—to the fiction writer's use in order to achieve for fiction the kind of "immediate impact" generally available only to those working in the visual arts.

"At The Tolstoy Museum" • "At the Tolstoy Museum," one of the best of these collages, literalizes, chiefly through visual means, the canonization of Leo Tolstoy as a metaphorical giant of literature, a cultural institution, an object of public veneration. Visitors to the "Tolstoy museum" must gaze at the prescribed distances and times and in the proper attitude of awe and submission.

Readers of "At the Tolstoy Museum" find all the rules broken, temporal and spatial boundaries transgressed, and distances subject to a new and fantastic geometry. Against the museum as a repository of cult(ural) memorabilia, the story serves a narrative riposte in the form of a study in perspective. Barthelme whittles Tolstoy down to manageable size by exaggerating his proportions (much as he does with another dead father in his second novel): the thirty thousand photographs, the 640,086 pages of the Jubilee edition of Tolstoy's works, the coat that measures at least twenty feet high, the head so large it has a hall of its own (closed Mondays, Barthelme parenthetically adds), even a page-long summary of one of Tolstoy's shortest stories, "The Three Hermits." There are also the two huge Soviet-style portraits on facing pages, identical in all but one feature: the tiny figure of Napoleon I (The Little Emperor), from Tolstoy's *Voyna i mir* (1865-1869; *War and Peace*, 1886), playing the part of viewer/reader. Best of all is Barthelme's rendering of The Anna-Vronsky Pavilion, devoted to the adulterous pair from *Anna Karenina* (1875-1877; English translation, 1886), a cutout of a nineteenth century man and woman superimposed on an early (and now adulterated) study in perspective dating from 1603. "At the Tolstoy Museum" does more than merely mix and match, cut and paste. It makes hilariously clear the artifice of art and of what the passive consumer of culture may naively assume is both natural and eternal.

"Sentence" • "Sentence" makes a similar point, but it does so by exploring the literal in a quite different way. As its title suggests, the story takes the form of a single sentence of approximately twenty-five hundred words and manages to combine the brevity, open-endedness, and formal innovation that together serve as the hallmarks of Barthelme's idiosyncratic art. The subject of "Sentence" is the sentence itself: its progress and process. Beginning with one of Barthelme's favorite words, "or" ("etc." and "amid" are others), it proceeds by means of accretion and ends (if a work without any terminal punctuation can be said to end) as much an "anxious object" as any of those works of modern art to which Harold Rosenberg applied that phrase. Even as it pursues its own meandering, self-regarding, seemingly nonreferential way down the page, "Sentence" remains mindful of its reader, no less susceptible to distraction than the sentence itself and lured on by whatever promise the sentence holds out yet also feeling threatened by the sentence's failure to play by the rules. As the narrator sums up, "Sentence" is "a man-made object, not the one we wanted of course, but still a construction of man, a structure to be treasured for its weakness, as opposed to the strength of stones."

Earlier in "Sentence," Barthelme alludes to the Rosetta Stone that Champollion used to decipher the ancient Egyptian hieroglyphs. Barthelme's fiction, although written in a familiar language, proves more resistant to decoding. Barthelme uses the past as he uses the present, but neither offers anything approaching an interpretive touchstone, only the raw material, the bits and bytes out of which he constructs his oddly shaped but nevertheless aesthetically crafted "archaeological slices."

"The Glass Mountain" • Built upon the cultural ruins of an ancient Norse tale entitled "The Princess and the Glass Hill," "The Glass Mountain" resembles "Sentence" and "The Balloon" more than it does its nominal source in that it, too, is largely about one's reading of it. "I was trying to climb the glass mountain," the narrator declares in the first of the story's one hundred numbered sections (most only one sentence long). Like the reader, the narrator is "new to the neighborhood," persistent, comically methodical, and methodologically absurd; the plumber's friends he uses to scale the glass mountain at the corner of Thirteenth Street and Eighth Avenue seem no less inappropriate than his by-the-book how-to approach drawn from medieval romance—or the reader's efforts to climb (surmount, master) Barthelme's see-through metafiction by means of equally outdated reading strategies. Once atop the glass mountain the narrator finds exactly what he hoped to, "a beautiful enchanted symbol" to disenchant. Once kissed (like the frog of fairy tales), the symbol proves disenchanting in a quite different sense of the word, changed "into only a beautiful princess" whom the narrator (now himself disenchanted) hurls down in disappointment. Having staked his life on the eternal symbol of medieval romance, the narrator finds the temporary and the merely human (princess) disappointing.

"The New Music" • Making a postmodern something, however small and self-consuming, out of the existential nothing became Barthelme's stock-in-trade, most noticeably in "Nothing: A Preliminary Account." His art of the nearly negligible works itself out comically but almost always against a sympathetic understanding for the permanence for which the climber in "The Glass Mountain" and the characters in so many of his other stories, "The New Music," for example, yearn. A fusion of two stories published earlier the same year, one with the same title, the other entitled "Momma," "The New Music" takes the dialogue form that Barthelme often used to new and dizzying heights of nearly musical abstraction, akin to what Philip Roth would accomplish more than a decade later in his novel, *Deception* (1990). The subject here is slight (even for Barthelme), as the story's two unidentified, no-longer-young speakers go through (or are put through) a number of routines analogous to vaudeville comedy and improvisational jazz. After a few opening bars, one speaker suggests that they go to Pool, "the city of new hope. One of those new towns. Where everyone would be happier." They then segue into an exchange on, or consideration of, the new music done as a version of the familiar song "Momma don' 'low." Among the many things that Momma (now dead) did not allow was the new music. "The new music burns things together, like a welder," or like the sculptor Peterson from "A Shower of Gold" or like Barthelme, who, along with his two speakers, understands that the new music always has been and always will be ever changing, ever ephemeral, ever new, and forever beyond Momma's prohibitions and the reader's explanations.

Robert A. Morace

Other major works

CHILDREN'S LITERATURE: *The Slightly Irregular Fire Engine: Or, The Hithering Thithering Djinn*, 1971.

NOVELS: *Snow White*, 1967; *The Dead Father*, 1975; *Paradise*, 1986; *The King*, 1990.

MISCELLANEOUS: *Guilty Pleasures*, 1974; *The Teachings of Don B.: Satires, Parodies, Fables, Illustrated Stories and Plays of Donald Barthelme*, 1992 (Kim Herzinger, editor); *Not-knowing: The Essays and Interviews of Donald Barthelme*, 1997 (Herzinger, editor).

Bibliography

Barthelme, Helen Moore. *Donald Barthelme: The Genesis of a Cool Sound.* College Station: Texas A&M University Press, 2001. The author, a senior lecturer of English at Texas A&M University, was married to Barthelme for a decade in the 1950's and 1960's. She traces his life from his childhood in Houston to his development as a writer.

Couturier, Maurice, and Regis Durand. *Donald Barthelme.* London: Methuen, 1982. This brief study focuses on the performance aspect of Barthelme's stories and considers them in relation to the multiplicity of varied responses that they elicit from readers. Readings are few in number but highly suggestive.

Hudgens, Michael Thomas. *Donald Barthelme, Postmodernist American Writer.* Lewiston, N.Y.: Edwin Mellen Press, 2001. This volume in the series Studies in American Literature examines Barthelme's novels *The Dead Father* and *Snow White* and his short story "Paraguay." Includes bibliographical references and an index.

Klinkowitz, Jerome. *Donald Barthelme: An Exhibition.* Durham, N.C.: Duke University Press, 1991. Klinkowitz is easily the best informed and most judicious scholar and critic of contemporary American fiction in general and Barthelme in particular. Building on his Barthelme chapter in *Literary Disruptions: The Making of a Post-Contemporary American Fiction* (2d ed., 1980), he emphasizes the ways in which Barthelme reinvented narrative in the postmodern age and places Barthelme's fiction in the larger aesthetic, cultural, and historical contexts. Perhaps the single most important study of Barthelme.

May, Charles E., ed. *Masterplots II: Short Story Series, Revised Edition.* 8 vols. Pasadena, Calif.: Salem Press, 2004. Designed for student use, this reference set contains articles providing detailed plot summaries and analyses of these twelve short stories by Barthelme: "The Balloon" (vol. 1), "Critique de la Vie Quotidienne" (vol. 2), "The Glass Mountain" (vol. 3), "The Indian Uprising" and "Lightning" (vol. 4), "Margins" (vol. 5), "Paraguay" and "See the Moon?" (vol. 6), "A Shower of Gold" and "Some of Us Had Been Threatening Our Friend Colby" (vol. 7), and "Views of My Father Weeping" and "Wrack" (vol. 8).

Molesworth, Charles. *Donald Barthelme's Fiction: The Ironist Saved from Drowning.* Columbia: University of Missouri Press, 1982. Objecting to those who emphasize the experimental nature of Barthelme's fiction, Molesworth views Barthelme as essentially a parodist and satirist whose ironic stance saves him from drowning in mere innovation.

Patteson, Richard, ed. *Critical Essays on Donald Barthelme.* New York: G. K. Hall, 1992. Collection of critical essays on Barthelme from book reviews and academic journals. Provides an overview of critical reaction to Barthelme in the introduction. Essays deal with Barthelme's use of language, his fragmentation of reality, his montage technique, and his place in the postmodernist tradition.

Roe, Barbara L. *Donald Barthelme: A Study of the Short Fiction.* New York: Twayne, 1992. Introduction to Barthelme's short stories, with discussion of the major stories arranged in chronological order. Also includes several interviews with Barthelme, as well as previously published essays by other critics.

Stengel, Wayne B. *The Shape of Art in the Stories of Donald Barthelme.* Baton Rouge: Louisiana State University Press, 1985. Discusses such themes as play, futility, stasis, affirmation, and education in four types of stories: identity stories, dialogue stories, social fabric stories, and art-object stories. Focuses on Barthelme's emphasis on art in his self-reflexive stories.

Waxman, Robert. "Apollo and Dionysus: Donald Barthelme's Dance of Life." *Studies in Short Fiction* 33 (Spring, 1996): 229-243. Examines how the interplay between the Apollonian search for order and the Dionysian longing for freedom from convention informs much of Barthelme's work and is often embodied in the metaphor of music.

Ann Beattie

Born: Washington, D.C.; September 8, 1947

Principal short fiction • *Distortions*, 1976; *Secrets and Surprises*, 1978; *Jacklighting*, 1981; *The Burning House*, 1982; *Where You'll Find Me, and Other Stories*, 1986; *The Best American Short Stories 1987*, 1987; *What Was Mine, and Other Stories*, 1991; *Park City: New and Selected Stories*, 1998; *Perfect Recall: New Stories*, 2001; *Follies and New Stories*, 2005.

Other literary forms • Although Ann Beattie's reputation rests primarily on her short stories, particularly those that first appeared in *The New Yorker*, she has also written several novels. The first, *Chilly Scenes of Winter* (1976), appeared simultaneously with *Distortions*, a rare occurrence in the publishing world, especially for a first-time author. Her second novel, *Falling in Place* (1980), is her most ambitious and her best. In *Love Always* (1985), she uses an approach that is closer to that of her short stories than in either of the previous novels. The subject matter is narrower, and the characters are more distanced from the narrative voice. *Picturing Will* followed in 1989. Eight years later, she published *My Life, Starring Dara Falcon* (1997), which was scorned as her weakest novel to date. *The Doctor's House* (2002) did not fare much better with the critics. In 1986 and 1987, Beattie worked on her first nonfiction project, the text to accompany a monograph containing twenty-six color plates of the paintings of Alex Katz.

Achievements • The author of ten collections of short stories through 2005, Ann Beattie has been called the most imitated short-story writer in the United States, an amazing claim for a woman whose publishing career did not begin until the early 1970's. Along with such writers as Raymond Carver, she is a premier practitioner of minimalism, the school of fiction-writing that John Barth has characterized as the "less is more" school. In 1977, she was named Briggs-Copeland Lecturer in English at Harvard, where she was apparently uncomfortable. She used a John Simon Guggenheim Memorial Foundation grant to leave Harvard and move back to Connecticut, where she had attended graduate school. In 1980, she received an award of excellence from the American Academy of Arts and Letters and a Distinguished Alumnae award from American University. In 1992, she was elected to the American Academy and Institute of Arts and Letters.

Biography • Born on September 8, 1947, Ann Beattie grew up with television, rock music, and all the other accoutrements of the baby boomers. The child of a retired Health, Education, and Welfare Department administrator, Beattie took a bachelor's degree in English at American University in 1969 and completed her master's degree at the University of Connecticut in 1970. She began, but did not complete, work on her doctorate. In 1972 she married David Gates, a writer for *Newsweek* and a singer, whom she later divorced. Together they had one son. Before her appointment at Harvard, Beattie taught at the University of Virginia in Charlottesville. After living in the Connecticut suburbs and in New York City, she returned to Charlottesville and the university in 1985. She appeared as a waitress in the film version of *Chilly Scenes of*

Winter and, after her divorce, was named one of the most eligible single women in America. In 1985, Beattie met painter Lincoln Perry, whom she later married. The couple lived for a time in Charlottesville. Later, Beattie and Perry settled in a turn-of-the-century farmhouse in York, Maine, one of America's oldest cities. Beattie has said that she does not go to book-publishing parties, does not know many writers, has an unlisted phone number, and shies away from writers' colonies.

Analysis • Ann Beattie has been called the spokesperson for a new lost generation, a sort of Ernest Hemingway for those who came of age during the 1960's and 1970's. Many of her themes and much about her style support the assertion that she, like Hemingway, voices a pervasive and universal feeling of despair and alienation, a lament for lost values and lost chances for constructive action. Yet to limit one's understanding of Beattie's work to this narrow interpretation is a mistake.

Beattie shares much with writers such as Jane Austen, who ironically portrayed the manners and social customs of her era, and with psychological realists such as Henry James, who delved into the meanings behind the subtle nuances of character and conflict. Her primary themes are loneliness and friendship, family life, love and death, materialism, art, and, for want of a better term, the contemporary scene. Her short fiction tends to be spare and straightforward. Her vocabulary and her sentence structure are quite accessible, or minimalist, to use a more literary label. Even when the stories contain symbols, their use is most often direct and self-reflexive.

Beattie's combination of subject matter and style leads to a rather flat rendering of the world, and she is sometimes criticized for that flatness. Because her narrators usually maintain a significant distance from the stories and their characters, critics and readers sometimes assume that Beattie is advocating such remove and reserve as the most feasible posture in contemporary life. Even her most ironic characters and narrative voices, however, experience a profound longing for a different world. Despite the ennui that dominates the texture of their lives, Beattie's characters hold on to the hope of renewal and redemption, often with great fierceness, even though the fierceness frequently suggests that these people are clutching at hope so hard that they are white-knuckling their way through life. If members of the generation about which she writes are indeed lost, they have not accepted their condition, even though they recognize it. They are still searching for the way out, for a place in which to find themselves or to be found.

"Dwarf House" • "Dwarf House," the first story in *Distortions*, establishes an interest in the grotesque, the bizarre, and the slightly askew that surfaces several times in this first of Beattie's collections. The main characters of the story are James and MacDonald, brothers who struggle to find understanding and respect for each other and to deal with their possessive and intrusive mother. Because James, the older of the two, is a dwarf, Beattie immediately plays upon the collection's title and places the story beyond the plane of realism.

The irony of the story develops as the reader realizes that MacDonald's supposedly normal life is as distorted as the life of his sibling. When MacDonald goes to visit James in the dwarf house where he lives, along with several other dwarfs and one giant, he finds himself repulsed by the foreign environment. Yet, when he gets home, he cannot face his own "normal" world without his martinis. He is as alienated and isolated at home and at work as he would be if he were a dwarf. Beattie uses the ludicrous, the exaggerated scenario of James's life, complete with his wedding to a fellow

Sigrid Estrada

dwarf, conducted by a hippie minister and culminating in the releasing of a caged parrot, as a symbol of hope and the new freedom of married life, to bring into focus the less obvious distortions of regular American life.

MacDonald is typical of many Beattie characters. He is relatively young—in his late twenties—and well educated. He works, but his work provides little challenge or stimulation. He has enough money to live as he wants, but he struggles to define what it is he does want. His wife is his equal—young, well educated, hip—but they have less than nothing to talk about.

MacDonald wants to make his brother's life more normal—that is, get him out of the dwarf house, the one place where James has ever been happy, and back into their mother's home, where James and MacDonald will both be miserable. MacDonald is motivated not by malice toward James but by an overdeveloped sense of guilt and responsibility toward his mother, a trait he shares with many of Beattie's young male characters. By the story's end, the reader cannot say who is better off: James, whose life is distorted but productive and satisfying to him, or MacDonald, who has everything a man could want but still lacks an understanding of what it is he should do with what he has.

"The Lifeguard" • In "The Lifeguard," the final story in *Distortions*, Beattie portrays the offbeat and grotesque elements that permeate the collection, in a sharply realistic setting where their humor and irony disappear. The impact of these elements is, then, all the more forceful for the reader's sense of sudden dislocation. Without warning, the book becomes too real for comfort, and at the same time it continues to use shades of the unreal to make its point.

"The Lifeguard" tells the story of the Warner family and their summer vacation. The mother, Toby, finds herself fantasizing about the young college student who is the lifeguard on the beach. Yet when her children Penelope and Andrew die in a boat deliberately set afire by their playmate Duncan Collins, the inappropriateness and incapacity of the lifeguard and of her infatuation are too vividly brought home to Toby. The monstrousness of Duncan Collins's action is but another kind of distortion; there are no simple lives in a distorted world.

"A Vintage Thunderbird" • If *Distortions* emphasizes the outward manifestations of the disordered contemporary world, *Secrets and Surprises*, the second collection, turns inward, as its title suggests. "A Vintage Thunderbird" features a woman who comes to New York to have an abortion against the wishes of her husband. The friends to whom she turns, Karen and Nick, have their own problems in love. By mirroring the sense of loss that follows the abortion with the sense of loss felt by Karen and Nick when she sells the vintage car of the title, Beattie addresses the connection between spiritual and emotional needs and material needs.

Very few of the people in Beattie's fiction suffer for want of material goods; almost all suffer from lack of spiritual and emotional fulfillment. The interesting aspect of this dichotomy is that the characters do not, as a rule, actively pursue material well-being. Their money is often inherited, as are their houses and many of their other possessions. The main character in "Shifting," for example, inherits an old Volvo from an uncle to whom she was never very close. The money earned by these characters is almost always earned halfheartedly, without conspicuous ambition or enthusiasm. These are not yuppies who have substituted acquisition for all human emotion; they are people who, by accident of birth or circumstance, have not had to acquire material wealth; for whatever reason, wealth comes to them.

What does not come is peace, satisfaction, and contentment. When a material object does provide emotional pleasure, as the Thunderbird does for Karen and Nick, Beattie's characters tend to confuse the emotion with the symbol and to conclude, erroneously, that ridding themselves of the object will also rid them of the gnawing doubts that seem to accompany contentment and satisfaction. It is sometimes as frightening, Beattie seems to suggest, to be attached to things as to people.

"The Cinderella Waltz" • In *The Burning House*, Beattie's third collection, she turns to the darker, more richly textured veins of her standard subject matter to produce stories that are less humorous but more humane, less ironic but wiser than those in the earlier collections. Infidelity, divorce, love gone bad—all standard Beattie themes—are connected to parenthood and its attendant responsibilities, to homosexuality, to death, and to birth defects. The affairs and the abortions that were entered into, if not concluded, with a "me-generation" bravado suddenly collide with more traditional values and goals.

Many of Beattie's characters, both married and single, have lovers. In fact, having a lover or having had one at some time during a marriage is almost standard. In "The Cinderella Waltz," Beattie adds a further complication to the de rigueur extramarital affair by making the husband's lover a male. Yet, in much the same way that she makes the unusual work in a story such as "Dwarf House," Beattie manages to make this story more about the pain and suffering of the people involved than about the nontraditional quality of the love relationship.

The wife in "The Cinderella Waltz," left to understand what has happened to her marriage and to help her young daughter to reach her own understanding, finds herself drawn into a quiet, resigned acceptance of her husband's relationship with his lover. She laments the loss of innocence in the world, for her child and for them all, but she chooses to go forward with the two men as part of her life and the child's. She rejects—really never even considers—the negative, destructive responses that many women would have had.

"The Cinderella Waltz" ends with images of enormous fragility—glass elevators and glass slippers. Yet they are images that her characters embrace and cling to, recognizing that fragile hope is better than none. The cautious nature of such optimism is often mistaken for pessimism in Beattie's work, but her intention is clearly as affirmative as it is tentative.

"Winter: 1978" • Another story from *The Burning House*, "Winter: 1978," offers a glimpse of most of Beattie's concerns and techniques. An unusually long story for

Beattie, "Winter: 1978" features a selfish mother who is hosting a wake for her younger son, who has drowned in a midwinter boating accident. His death is mystifying, for there were life preservers floating easily within his reach, a fact that suggests the ultimate despair and surrender often present in Beattie's characters. An older son blames the mother for placing too much guilt and responsibility on the dead son, but he himself has done nothing to assume some of that burden. The older son's former wife, their child, his current girlfriend, and his best friend are all present at the wake. The best friend's girlfriend is alone back in California, having her uterus cauterized. His former wife seems inordinately grief-stricken, until it is revealed that the dead man was her lover. During the course of the wake, which lasts several days, she becomes the lover of her former husband's best friend.

This extremely baroque and convoluted situation contains much that is ironically humorous, but it also reflects deep pain on the part of all the characters, not only the pain of having lost a loved one but also the pain of reexamining their own lives and measuring them against the idea of death. That sort of existential questioning, rarely overt but frequently suggested, contributes to the idea of a lost generation brought to life on the pages of Beattie's fiction.

Yet Beattie rarely leaves her characters in perpetual existential angst, as is the case in a Hemingway story such as "A Clean, Well-Lighted Place," an embodiment of the existential despair and the longing for some minute, self-created order and refuge typical of the original literary lost generation. Instead, Beattie often opts for a neo-Romantic, minimalist version of hope and redemption, of continued searching as opposed to acquiescence.

"Winter: 1978" concludes with the absentee father, the surviving son, taking his own child upstairs for a bedtime story. The little boy, like the daughter in "The Cinderella Waltz," is far too wise to take comfort from the imaginary world of the story; he has been exposed to far too much of the confused adult world of his parents. On this occasion, however, he pretends to believe, and he encourages his father's tale about the evolution of deer. According to the story, deer have such sad eyes because they were once dinosaurs and cannot escape the sadness that comes with having once been something else.

This story serves as a metaphor for the melancholy cast of characters in this and Beattie's other collections of short fiction. Almost all of her characters have a Keatsian longing to connect with a better, more sublime existence that seems to be part of their generation's collective consciousness. Far too aware and too ironic to follow the feeling and thereby to transcend reality, they linger in their unsatisfactory lesser world and struggle to accommodate their longing to their reality.

"Snow" • More than her other collections, *Where You'll Find Me* displays Beattie's awareness of her own reputation as a writer. In particular, in a story called "Snow," she appears to write a definition of the kind of story her work has come to define. Fewer than three pages long, the story takes a single image, that of snow, and uses it not only as a symbol of the lost love the narrator is contemplating but also as a metaphor for storytelling as practiced by the author.

The remembered lover has explained to the narrator at one point that "any life will seem dramatic if you omit mention of most of it." The narrator then tells a story, actually one paragraph within this story, about her return to the place where the lovers had lived in order to be with a dying friend. She offers her story-within-a-story as an example of the way in which her lover said stories should be told.

The narrator goes on to say that such efforts are futile, bare bones without a pattern to establish meaning. For her, the single image, snow in this case, does more to evoke the experience of her life with the man than does the dramatized story with the details omitted. In the story's final paragraph, the narrator concludes that even the single image is too complex for complete comprehension. The mind itself, let alone the narratives it creates, is incapable of fully rendering human experience and emotion. The best a writer, a storyteller, can do is to present the essence of the experience in the concrete terms in which his or her consciousness has recorded it.

What the reader almost inevitably receives, then, is minimal, to return to John Barth's theory. It is equally important, however, that Barth argues that the minimal can be more than enough. The characters in this fourth collection are generally older and wiser than their predecessors. They have, as a rule, survived an enormous loss and are still hoping for a richer, more rewarding life, or at least one in which they feel less out of place and alone.

"Janus" • Andrea, the real-estate agent who is the main character of "Janus," is typical. Safely married to a husband who is interesting and financially secure, she is also successful in her career. The two of them take great pleasure in the things that they have accumulated. Yet Andrea takes most pleasure in a relatively inexpensive and quite ordinary-looking ceramic bowl, a gift from a former lover who asked her to change her life, to live with him.

Although she has long since turned him down, Andrea finds herself growing increasingly obsessed with the bowl. She begins to believe that all of her career success comes from the bowl's being precisely placed in the homes that she shows to her clients. A mystery to her, the bowl seems to be connected to the most real, the most private parts of herself. She loves the bowl as she loves nothing else. She fears for its safety. She is terrified at the thought that it might disappear. She has lost the chance that the lover represents, choosing instead stasis and comfort, remaining intransigent about honoring her previous commitments. Sometimes she goes into her living room late at night and sits alone contemplating the bowl. She thinks, "In its way, it was perfect; the world cut in half, deep and smoothly empty."

Such is the world that Beattie observes, but Beattie is, after all, an artist, not a real-estate agent. All that Andrea can do is contemplate. Beattie can fill the bowl, to use a metaphor, with whatever she chooses. She can capture, again and again, the story behind the "one small flash of blue, a vanishing point on the horizon," that Andrea can only watch disappear.

Barth's description of the impulse behind minimalism, the desire "to strip away the superfluous in order to reveal the necessary, the essential," is a fair assessment of Beattie's work. Yet it is equally important to recall what necessary and essential elements remain after the superfluous has been stripped away. They are love, friendship, family, children, music, and creativity. Beattie fills the bowl of her fiction with much the same fruits that other writers have used.

"Windy Day at the Reservoir" • In contrast to her earlier, so-called minimalist stories, Beattie's more recent short fictions seem to be moving more toward length and elaboration, making more use of novelistic techniques of character exploration and realistic detail. "Windy Day at the Reservoir," the longest story in her collection *What Was Mine*, focuses on two people who, while house-sitting for another couple, make a number of discoveries both about the homeowners and about themselves—for example, about the vacationing couple's impending breakup because of the wife's mastectomy and their own inability to have children. The point of view moves from the house-sitting husband, to the wife, to the mentally disabled son of the housekeeper, who walks into the reservoir and drowns. The final section focuses on the housekeeper, who provides a novelistic resolution to the two couples who have both broken up. Ending with a realistic resolution rather than a metaphoric embodiment of conflict, the story reflects Beattie's moving away from short-story techniques to novelistic devices.

"Going Home With Uccello" and **"Park City"** • A clear contrast between short-story and novelistic technique can be seen in the difference between two of the eight new stories in Beattie's collection of selected stories, *Park City*—"Going Home with Uccello" and the title story "Park City." In the former, a woman on a trip to Italy with her boyfriend has a realization about why he has taken her there when he flirts with a Frenchwoman about an Uccello painting. She understands that he has taken her to Italy not to persuade her to join him in London forever, but to persuade himself that he loves her so much that no other woman can come between them. The story ends in a typical Beattie ambiguity about whether the man in the story can commit himself to a relationship or whether he is continuing, as so many of Beattie's male characters do, to look for some ineffable dream.

In "Park City" the central character spends a week at a Utah ski resort during the off-season looking after her half-sister's daughter, Nell, who is three, and her half-sister's boyfriend's daughter, Lyric, who is fourteen. The story is filled with dialogue among the three female characters in which it seems increasingly clear that the woman is more naïve than the precocious fourteen-year-old. In one particular encounter, the girl spins out a long invented tale to a stranger about having had breast implants. The story ends when the central character tries to get on a ski lift with the child Nell and the two almost fall off. They are saved by a man who, significantly, tells her, "the one thing you've got to remember next time is to request a slow start."

In the twenty-odd years that Beattie has been publishing short stories, mostly in *The New Yorker*, her milieu and her method have changed little, which has led some to complain that she has nothing new to say about the era she has evoked so sharply. However, Beattie has said, "My test was not did I get it right about the sixties, but is it literature. I am not a sociologist."

Jane Hill
With updates by Melissa E. Barth and Charles E. May

Other major works

CHILDREN'S LITERATURE: *Goblin Tales*, 1975; *Spectacle*, 1985.

NOVELS: *Chilly Scenes of Winter*, 1976; *Falling in Place*, 1980; *Love Always*, 1985; *Picturing Will*, 1989; *Another You*, 1995; *My Life, Starring Dara Falcon*, 1997; *The Doctor's House*, 2002.

NONFICTION: *Alex Katz*, 1987.

Bibliography

Atwood, Margaret. "Stories from the American Front." *The New York Times Book Review*, September 26, 1982, 1, 34. Discusses *The Burning House* as it represents the loss of the American dream for the children of the 1960's. For Beattie, freedom equals the chance to take off, run away, split. Beattie's stories chronicle domesticity gone awry, where there are dangers and threats lurking beneath the surface of even the most mundane event. Observes that most of the stories in this collection concern couples in the process of separating.

Barth, John. "A Few Words About Minimalism." *The New York Times Book Review*, December 28, 1986, 1- 2, 25. Explores Beattie's spare style and considers her fiction as it represents a current stylistic trend in the American short story. Spends a considerable amount of space describing the origins of the contemporary minimalist movement in American short fiction. Sees this form as a nonverbal statement about theme: the spareness of life in America. Places Beattie's work among that of other minimalists, including Raymond Carver, Bobbie Ann Mason, James Robison, Mary Robison, and Tobias Wolff. Discusses Edgar Allan Poe as an early proponent of minimalism. Says that Beattie's fiction is clearly shaped by the events surrounding the Vietnam War. A helpful essay for gaining an understanding of Beattie as a minimalist.

Beattie, Ann. "An Interview with Ann Beattie." Interview by Steven R. Centola. *Contemporary Literature* 31 (Winter, 1990): 405-422. Contains a photograph of Beattie. This article is useful to the general reader, providing information about Beattie's biography. Beattie discusses herself as a feminist writer and talks about how she goes about creating credible male protagonists. Asserts that most of her fiction centers on exploring human relationships.

McKinstry, Susan Jaret. "The Speaking Silence of Ann Beattie's Voice." *Studies in Short Fiction* 24 (Spring, 1987): 111-117. Asserts that Beattie's female speakers puzzle readers because they tell two stories at once: an open story of the objective, detailed present juxtaposed against a closed story of the subjective past, which the speaker tries hard not to tell.

May, Charles E., ed. *Masterplots II: Short Story Series, Revised Edition.* 8 vols. Pasadena, Calif.: Salem Press, 2004. Designed for student use, this reference set contains articles providing detailed plot summaries and analyses of these ten short stories by Beattie: "The Big-Breasted Pilgrim" and "The Burning House" (vol. 1); "The Cinderella Waltz" (vol. 2); "Imagined Scenes," "In the White Night," "Jacklighting," and "Janus" (vol. 4); "Shifting" (vol. 6); "Snow" (vol. 7); and "Winter: 1978" (vol. 8).

Montresor, Jaye Berman, ed. *The Critical Response to Ann Beattie.* Westport, Conn.: Greenwood Press, 1993. Includes contemporary reaction to Beattie's novels and collections of short stories, as well as scholarly and academic analyses of her work by various critics.

Stein, Lorin. "Fiction in Review." *Yale Review* 85, no. 4 (1997): 156-165. After an excellent summary of Beattie's early fiction, the writer proceeds to analyze *My Life, Starring Dara Falcon*, which he thinks has been underrated by critics.

Wyatt, David. "Ann Beattie." *The Southern Review* 28, no. 1 (1992): 145-159. Presents evidence that in the mid-1980's there was a marked alteration in Beattie's fiction. Instead of withdrawing from life and its dangers, her characters chose to care about other people and to commit themselves to creativity. A perceptive and convincing analysis.

Saul Bellow

Born: Lachine, Quebec, Canada; June 10, 1915
Died: Brookline, Massachusetts; April 5, 2005

Principal short fiction • *Mosby's Memoirs, and Other Stories*, 1968; *Him with His Foot in His Mouth, and Other Stories*, 1984; *Something to Remember Me By: Three Tales*, 1991; *Collected Stories*, 2001.

Other literary forms • Saul Bellow is known primarily for his novels, which include *The Adventures of Augie March* (1953), *Herzog* (1964), *Mr. Sammler's Planet* (1970), and *Ravelstein* (2000). He also published plays, a book of nonfiction prose about a trip to Jerusalem, and a number of essays.

Achievements • Few would deny Saul Bellow's place in contemporary American literature. Any assessment of his contributions would have to account for his realistic yet inventive style, the rich Jewish heritage upon which he draws, the centrality of Chicago in his fictional world, the role of the intellectual, and a fundamental wit, rare in contemporary American fiction. In 1976, Bellow's achievement was internationally recognized when he was awarded the Pulitzer Prize and the Nobel Prize in Literature. He also won the 1988 National Medal of Arts and four National Book Awards—for *The Adventures of Augie March* in 1954, for *Herzog* in 1965, for *Mr. Sammler's Planet* (1970) in 1971, and for *The Bellarosa Connection* (1989) in 1990. In 1997, *The Actual* (1997) won the National Jewish Book Award, given by the Jewish Book Council.

Biography • Saul Bellow was born in Canada. After spending his first nine years in the Montreal area, he moved with his family to Chicago and graduated from high school there. He spent his first two years of college at the University of Chicago and the last two at Northwestern University, graduating in 1937. That same year he began a brief interlude of graduate work in anthropology at the University of Wisconsin. A few years later he started his writing career. He also taught at the University of Chicago from 1962 to 1993, moving to Boston University thereafter.

Married five times, Bellow had three sons by his first three wives. At the age of 84, he had a daughter by his fifth wife. After a long residence in Chicago, he relocated to Massachusetts in 1994. There he became a professor of literature at Boston University and became coeditor of a new literary journal, *The Republic of Letters*. His last novel, *Ravelstein*, published in 2000, may be seen as his literary farewell, as it voices his concern about the survival of the human spirit amid the luxurious entanglements of contemporary life. He died at his Brookline, Massachusetts, home in April, 2005, at the age of eighty-nine.

Analysis • Saul Bellow's stature in large measure owes something to the depths to which he plumbed the modern condition. He addressed the disorder of the modern age, with all its horror and darkness as well as its great hope. Though intensely identified with the United States, his heroes are preoccupied with dilemmas arising out of European intellectual and cultural history. Bellow's fictional world is at once cerebral and sensual. His concern is with the interconnections between art, politics, business, personal sexual proclivities and passions, the intellectual, and the making of culture in modern times. He is heady, like German writer Thomas Mann, revealing the limitations and powers of the self. Few contemporary American writers deal with such weighty issues as masterfully as did Bellow.

Bellow's honors and reputation document but do not explain his importance, although it will be more clearly seen in the future when some of the main tendencies of American fiction of his era have been fully developed. He is important because he both preserved and enhanced qualities that are present in the great fictional works of the eighteenth and nineteenth centuries, yet he fully participated in the tumult and uncertainty of the modern era. Though he often opposed the political left and espoused "tradi-

© The Nobel Foundation

tional" cultural positions, Bellow was not primarily a polemical writer. His main concern was not with maintaining social or cultural order but was more spiritual and philosophical in nature. In this, he differed from the group of "New York intellectuals" that centered in the 1940's and 1950's on the journal *Partisan Review.* Although Bellow was for a time friendly with members of this group he took pains to distance himself from it and to stress his essential independence of any creed or ideology, as his paramount concern was for the individual. This theme is especially prominent in his short fiction, whose smaller canvas gives heightened emphasis to Bellow's stress on the struggle of the individual for self-definition and development against the background of the sundry obstacles the world has in store.

Bellow's characters have selves and interact with a society and a culture that Bellow created in detail after careful observation. In some of his works, especially *Mr. Sammler's Planet,* Bellow's attitude toward that society and that culture borders on scorn, but his attitude has been earned, not merely stated in response to limitations on his own sensibility. The interaction between self and society in his work occurs against the backdrop of moral ideas. This is not to say that Bellow was didactic; rather, his work is infused with his sophisticated understanding of moral, social, and intellectual issues. In addition to preserving a rich but increasingly neglected tradition, Bellow enriched that tradition. After the exuberant opening words of *The Adventures of Augie March,* he also added new possibilities to the prose style of American fiction. In short, his work offers some of the benefits that readers in previous centuries sought in fiction—most notably, some ideas about how to be a person in the world—yet it also offers a technical brilliance that Bellow keeps in rein instead of letting it control his work.

Mosby's Memoirs, and Other Stories • The stories collected in *Mosby's Memoirs, and Other Stories* explore characteristic Bellow themes and clearly demonstrate the writer's moral and aesthetic vision. "Looking for Mr. Green" is set in Chicago during the Depression and recounts the efforts of a civil servant, George Grebe, to deliver relief checks to black residents of the south side. This is the stuff of social protest literature, and Bellow's story does dramatize the suffering that was endemic at that time, but it is much more than didactic. Bellow avoids a single-minded attack on economic injustice and the resulting inartistic story by, among other things, using a number of contrasts and ironies. For example, two scenes set on the streets and in the tenements of Chicago are separated by a scene at Grebe's office, and in that scene a philosophical discussion between Grebe and his boss, Raynor, is interrupted by a welfare mother's tirade. The basic situation of the story is ironic, because it seems odd that anyone would have trouble delivering checks to persons who desperately need them. These persons, however, are difficult to ferret out, and their neighbors will not reveal their whereabouts because they fear that Grebe is a bill collector, process-server, or other source of trouble, and because he is white. This irony vividly illustrates the degree to which the Depression exaggerated the instinct of self-preservation and widened the gulf between blacks and whites.

Grebe's name points out several of the contrasts in "Looking for Mr. Green." Grebes are birds known for their elaborate courtship dances, but George Grebe is a bachelor. More important for the story, grebes live in pairs rather than in flocks and remain in their own territories, but George, because of his job, is forced into society and into territory where he is an alien, not only because he is white but also because he is the son of the last English butler in Chicago and was a professor of classics. This is not to say that he is a stranger to trouble: He "had had more than an average seasoning in hardship." Despite his troubles, Grebe is shocked by suffering, distrust, and decrepit physical settings.

Oddly enough, these conditions are for him not only a moral problem but also an epistemological one. Raynor, his supervisor, brings up this problem by asserting that "nothing looks to be real, and everything stands for something else, and that thing for another thing." In contrast, Grebe later concludes that objects "stood for themselves by agreement, . . . and when the things collapsed the agreement became visible." The physical setting and the social and economic structure in this story are rapidly deteriorating, if not collapsing. Grebe complicates his analysis by asking "but what about need?," thereby suggesting that because of the Depression the agreement itself is collapsing and perhaps with it reality. Some of the persons he meets want to hasten that collapse. The welfare mother "expressed the war of flesh and blood, perhaps turned a little crazy and certainly ugly, on the place and condition," and another person advocates an alternate agreement, a plan whereby blacks would contribute a dollar apiece every month to produce black millionaires. Grebe's finding Mr. Green indicates that he can do something about this obscure world in which appearance and reality are mixed. Near the end of the story he asserts that it "was important that there was a real Mr. Green whom they could not keep him from reaching because he seemed to come as an emissary from hostile appearances."

"The Gonzaga Manuscripts" • "The Gonzaga Manuscripts" is a subtle story that traces changes in a young man, Clarence Feiler, and puts those changes in the context of important issues pertinent to the proper functions of literature and to its relation to everyday reality. Bellow carefully delineates the psychological state of Feiler, to whom literature makes an enormous difference, and shows the impingement upon him of Spanish society, which also was the environment of the writer about whom he cares passionately, Manuel Gonzaga. These themes are developed in the context of Feiler's search in Madrid and Seville for the unpublished manuscripts of poems written by Gonzaga. Feiler learns finally that the poems are lost forever, buried with Gonzaga's patron.

When Feiler arrives in Spain he is a confirmed Gonzagan, and while searching for the manuscripts he immerses himself in Spanish society and even in Gonzaga's former milieu. Bellow meticulously paints in the Spanish background by describing the cities, religious processions, political climate, and a representative group of Spaniards. As a result of his immersion Feiler begins virtually to relive Gonzaga's poems. For example, early in the story Feiler quotes part of a poem:

> I used to welcome all
> And now I fear all.
> If it rained it was comforting
> And if it shone, comforting,
> But now my very weight is dreadful.

The story ends thus: as "the train left the mountains, the heavens seemed to split. Rain began to fall, heavy and sudden, boiling on the wide plain. He knew what to expect from the redheaded Miss Walsh at dinner." That is, the rain is not comforting, and he fears that Miss Walsh will continue to torment him.

Feiler maintains his allegiance to Gonzaga, but there is considerable evidence in the story indicating that his allegiance is misplaced. For example, Gonzaga's friends are unimpressive. His best friend, del Nido, is a babbling mediocrity who sees little need for more poetry, and Gonzaga's patron has had the poems buried with her, thus denying them to the world. Another acquaintance misunderstands Feiler's search, thinking that he is after mining stock. One of Gonzaga's main beliefs is that one needs to take a dim view of human potential; he advocates being little more than a creature and avoiding the loss of everything by not trying to become everything. Even though Feiler himself has few aspirations besides finding the lost poems, he ends in despair. In fact, Gonzaga resembles the writers whom Bellow castigates in "Some Notes on Recent American Fiction" because of their minimal conception of human potential and their concomitant solicitousness for their own sensibility. Bellow's essay is a defense of a view of literature that Feiler unflatteringly contrasts to Gonzaga's.

"Mosby's Memoirs" • "Mosby's Memoirs" was published in 1968, two years before *Mr. Sammler's Planet,* and, like that novel, is a study in world weariness. Mosby is writing his memoirs in Oaxaca, Mexico, where the fecund land and the earthy existence of the people contrast to his own dryness. His mind ranges back through his life, particularly to recall two friends: Ruskin, a poet who has a theoretical bent of mind, and Lustgarden, who alternates between endlessly elaborated Marxism and piratical capitalism. At the end of the story Mosby is in a tomb that, along with his inability to get enough air to breathe, suggests that he is moribund. Although *Mr. Sammler's Planet* depicts a sympathetic character fending off as best he can the horrors of contemporary life, "Mosby's Memoirs" shows the danger of rejecting one's era.

Mosby's critique is conservative: He had worked for Hearst, had shaken Franco's hand, had agreed with Burnham's emphasis on managing, even to the point of admiring Nazi Germany's skill at it. Partly because Lustgarden's Marxism is not made to appear attractive either, Mosby's politics are not as unattractive as his attitude toward other persons. He is intolerant and is characterized by "acid elegance, logical tightness, factual punctiliousness, and merciless laceration in debate." Even more damaging to him is a scene at a concert in which he is described as "stone-hearted Mosby, making fun of flesh and blood, of those little humanities with their short inventories of bad and good." His attitude is also obvious in his treatment of Lustgarden in his memoirs. Rather than using his friend's disastrous attempts to make money as a political parable or as an occasion to demonstrate pity, Mosby plans to use them for comic relief, in the process eschewing his "factual punctiliousness" in order to make Lustgarden more laughable.

Him with His Foot in His Mouth, and Other Stories • The stories brought together in *Him with His Foot in His Mouth, and Other Stories* can be divided into two types: The title story and *What Kind of Day Did You Have?* (both novella-length pieces) feature powerful, aging Jewish intellectuals trying to come to grips with the course their lives have taken and bridge the world of ideas with the sensate, real world around them. The other three stories in the volume—"Zetland: By a Character Witness," "A Silver Dish," and "Cousins"—are cut from the same fabric as "Looking for Mr. Green." They vividly, almost nostalgically, evoke a past, between the wars and after, and portray the assimilation of Jews in the United States. What is impressive in all of these stories is the wide historical swath they cut; Bellow's concern here, as elsewhere, is no less than the human condition in the twentieth century.

Herschel Shawmut, the narrator of *Him with His Foot in His Mouth*, a man in his sixties, is a successful Jewish musicologist. His story, a sort of confession, is addressed to a "Miss Rose" whom he evidently mortally offended with an inadvertent verbal barb years ago. Shawmut confesses to other slips of the tongue as well. As he writes about all the incidents, revealing a certain pattern of personality, he attributes them simply to fate. His confession also reveals that he has been swindled by his own brother Philip, a materialist living a sumptuous bourgeois life in Texas. Philip persuades his naïve brother to hand over all of his hard-earned money (made from his musicological ventures) and form a partnership in a company rife with fraud and other illegal activities. After Philip's untimely death, Shawmut, hounded by creditors, seeks exile. He is, in the end, living a lonely life in Canada. Through his confessions, Shawmut seems to find some kind of order and the satisfaction of having articulated the nature of his fate, for better or worse.

Victor Wulpy, the older Jewish intellectual in *What Kind of Day Did You Have?* is a charismatic figure who sweeps a much younger Katrina Goliger, mother of two, off her feet. On the day in question, Wulpy calls Katrina to ask her to come to Buffalo and fly back to Chicago with him for a speaking engagement. Not daring to question this cultural giant, she takes off immediately, cancelling an appointment with a psychiatrist for an evaluation of her psychiatric condition in a fierce battle with her former husband for custody of her children. In the climactic scene of the story, the small Cessna plane they are in seems, in the thick of a winter storm, to be in a fatal dive toward Lake Michigan. In the face of possible death Katrina wants him to say he loves her, but he refuses. "If we don't love each other," she then wonders aloud, "What are we doing? How did we get here?" In the end, Wulpy makes his speaking engagement and Trina makes it home, to find her children gone. Soon they return, escorted by Krieggstein, a police officer and a suitor waiting for the passing of the Wulpy phase.

"A Silver Dish" and "Cousins" • Bellow's Jewish wit, evident in all these stories, sparkles in "A Silver Dish" and "Cousins," both cleverly conceived. In "A Silver Dish," a sixty-year-old Woody Selbst mourns his father's death and recalls an incident in his youth. Woody's mother and father had split up, leaving Woody's upbringing in the hands of his mother and a Protestant evangelical minister. Woody's father, "Pop," returns one day to ask his son a favor. Would he introduce his father to a certain wealthy Protestant, Mrs. Skoglund, who had made money in the dairy business? Woody reluctantly agrees and takes his father to the woman's home. While she and her suspicious maid leave the room to pray and decide whether or not to comply with Pop's request for money, Pop steals a silver dish from a locked cabinet. Woody and his father get into a scuffle, and his father promises to put the dish back if Mrs. Skoglund coughs up the money. She does, but Pop, unbeknownst to his son, keeps the dish. When the dish is missed, Woody gets the blame and falls from grace in the eyes of the evangelical crowd—which is exactly the effect his father desired.

In "Cousins," the narrator, Ijah Brodsky, an international banker, tells the story of his contact with three cousins. The first, Tanky Metzger, is connected to mobs and wants Ijah to use his influence with a certain judge and gain a lighter sentence. The second cousin is Mordecai, or "Cousin Motty," whom Ijah goes to visit in the hospital after he has been hurt in an automobile crash. Cousin Motty has letters to deliver to Ijah from another cousin, Scholem Stavis. The intellectual in the family, Stavis has ended up, however, driving a cab. All through the narrative are reminiscences, a calling up of the past, a restitching of old relationships. Ijah's existence seems somehow to be tied to, and defined by, his connection to these cousins.

The Actual • *The Actual,* a short, self-contained novella, has many of the traits and characteristics associated with Bellow's earlier work. In fact, for these reasons it is an excellent introduction to Bellow's fictional world. Yet, strikingly for a work published in its author's eighty-second year, it also breaks new ground for Bellow. The hero of *The Actual* is a man named Harry Trellman, who is at the time of the action semiretired and living in Chicago. Trellman has always been perceived by those he encounters as a bit different from everybody else, standing out from the rest of the crowd. Trellman worked as a businessman in Asia and later served as an adviser to Siggy Adletsky, a tycoon and racketeer who controls a huge financial empire and who is now ninety-two years old. Adletsky finds Trellman valuable because of his wide-ranging knowledge. This is a situation often found in Bellow's work: the alliance between the shady millionaire and the intellectual.

As a teenager, Trellman had been in love with Amy Wustrin, who had eventually chosen as her second husband Trellman's best friend in high school, Jay Wustrin. Throughout the years, Harry Trellman had kept firm to the inner image of Amy in his mind even as he went through his varied career and activities. After Jay Wustrin dies prematurely, he is buried in the cemetery plot originally reserved for Amy's father, who had sold it to him years earlier. Now Amy wants to remove Jay's body to the burial plot of his own family so that her father, who is still alive at an advanced age, can eventually be buried there. In a limousine provided by Adletsky, Amy and Trellman disinter and rebury the body. Moved by this scene of death and renewal, Trellman confesses to Amy that he has always loved her, that he has what he terms an "actual affinity" for her (hence the title of the story). He then asks her to marry him.

This declaration of love is striking as Trellman, for most of his life, has remained uncommitted and rather inscrutable, not exposing his inner secrets to others. Harry's privacy is contrasted with the willful self-exposure of men such as Jay Wustrin, who love making a spectacle of themselves. This dichotomy between the public and private man is mirrored by the tensions in Trellman's relationship with Adletsky, who is concerned only with money and profit-making, yet needs the intellectual-minded, knowledgeable Trellman in order to succeed; equally, Trellman becomes dependent on the financial largesse of Adletsky. Trellman stands slightly outside the world's network of relationships yet cannot do entirely without them.

In most of his fictions, Bellow's male protagonists tend to have troubled relationships with women and are often suffering in the aftermath of divorce. The serenity of Trellman's love for Amy stands in vivid contrast especially to earlier short fictions of Bellow's such as *What Kind of Day Did You Have?* and sounds a note of romantic celebration that is basically unprecedented in Bellow's work.

John Stark
With updates by Allen Hibbard,
Nicholas Birns, and the Editors

Other major works

PLAYS: *The Wrecker*, pb. 1954; *The Last Analysis*, pr. 1964; *Under the Weather*, pr. 1966 (also known as *The Bellow Plays*; includes *Out from Under*, *A Wen*, and *Orange Soufflé*).

ANTHOLOGY: *Great Jewish Short Stories*, 1963

NOVELS: *Dangling Man*, 1944; *The Victim*, 1947; *The Adventures of Augie March*, 1953; *Seize the Day*, 1956; *Henderson the Rain King*, 1959; *Herzog*, 1964; *Mr. Sammler's Planet*, 1970; *Humboldt's Gift*, 1975; *The Dean's December*, 1982; *More Die of Heartbreak*, 1987; *A Theft*, 1989; *The Bellarosa Connection*, 1989; *The Actual*, 1997 (novella); *Ravelstein*, 2000; *Novels, 1944-1953*, 2003 (includes *Dangling Man*, *The Victim*, and *The Adventures of Augie March*).

NONFICTION: *To Jerusalem and Back: A Personal Account*, 1976; *Conversations with Saul Bellow*, 1994 (Gloria L. Cronin and Ben Siegel, editors); *It All Adds Up: From the Dim Past to the Uncertain Future*, 1994.

Bibliography

American Studies International 35 (February, 1997). A special issue on Bellow, in which a number of distinguished contributors discuss the importance of Bellow's work as a symbol of the civilization of the United States. The issue contains tributes, critiques, and analyses of Bellow's thought and art.

Atlas, James. *Bellow*. New York: Random House, 2000. Full and accessible biography, written with the cooperation of its subject. Bibliography.

Bellow, Saul. "Moving Quickly: An Interview with Saul Bellow." *Salmagundi* (Spring/Summer, 1995): 32-53. In this special section, Bellow discusses the relationship between authors and characters, John Updike, intellectuals, gender differences, Sigmund Freud, and kitsch versus avant-garde art.

Bloom, Harold, ed. *Saul Bellow.* New York: Chelsea House, 1986. This volume, with an introduction by Bloom, is an omnibus of reviews and essays on Bellow. Collected here are comments on Bellow by writers such as Robert Penn Warren, Malcolm Bradbury, Tony Tanner, Richard Chase, and Cynthia Ozick. Gives the reader a good sense of early critical responses to Bellow.

Boyers, Robert. "Captains of Intellect." *Salmagundi* (Spring/Summer, 1995): 100-108. Part of a special section on Bellow. A discussion of characters in stories from the collection *Him with His Foot in His Mouth, and Other Stories* as captains of intellect who pronounce authoritatively on issues of the modern. Discusses Bellow as an intellectual leader with a multifaceted perspective.

Cronin, Gloria L., and L. H. Goldman, eds. *Saul Bellow in the 1980's: A Collection of Critical Essays.* East Lansing: Michigan State University Press, 1989. This anthology brings together a sampling of a wave of criticism that focuses variously on Bellow's women, his debts to Judaism, connections to theories of history, and modernism.

Freedman, William. "Hanging for Pleasure and Profit: Truth as Necessary Illusion in Bellow's Fiction." *Papers on Language and Literature* 35 (Winter, 1999): 3-27. Argues that Bellow's realism is a search for truth, not the discovery of it. Discusses how Bellow deals with the question of whether a man is isolated or a member of a human community. Contends that for Bellow the value of literature is the ceaseless search for truth in a world that promises truth but seldom provides it.

The Georgia Review 49 (Spring, 1995). A special issue on Bellow in which a number of contributors discuss his life and art, his contribution to American thought and culture, and the wide range of his works.

May, Charles E., ed. *Masterplots II: Short Story Series, Revised Edition.* 8 vols. Pasadena, Calif.: Salem Press, 2004. Designed for student use, this reference set contains articles providing detailed plot summaries and analyses of these six short stories by Bellow: "A Father-to-Be" and "The Gonzaga Manuscripts" (vol. 3), "Leaving the Yellow House" (vol. 4), "Looking for Mr. Green" and "Mosby's Memoirs" (vol. 5), and "A Silver Dish" (vol. 7).

Pifer, Ellen. *Saul Bellow Against the Grain.* Philadelphia: University of Pennsylvania Press, 1990. In a study that deals comprehensively with the writings, Pifer's central observation is that Bellow's heroes are divided against themselves and conduct an inner strife that dooms and paralyzes them. Their struggle, like Bellow's, is a search for language to articulate the modern condition.

Ambrose Bierce

Born: Horse Cave Creek, Ohio; June 24, 1842
Died: Mexico(?); January, 1914(?)

Principal short fiction • *Cobwebs: Being the Fables of Zambri the Parse*, 1884; *Tales of Soldiers and Civilians*, 1891 (also known as *In the Midst of Life*, 1898); *Can Such Things Be?*, 1893; *Fantastic Fables*, 1899; *The Cynic's Word Book*, 1906; *My Favourite Murder*, 1916; *Ghost and Horror Stories of Ambrose Bierce*, 1964; *The Collected Fables of Ambrose Bierce*, 2000 (S. T. Joshi, editor).

Other literary forms • As a lifelong journalist and commentator, Ambrose Bierce wrote prodigiously. He was fond of vitriolic epigrams and sketches, together with miscellaneous works of literary criticism, epigrams, and both prose and verse aphorisms. His most famous work is almost certainly *The Devil's Dictionary* (1906), a collection of typically ironic and cynical definitions, such as that for a *bore*: "A person who talks when you wish him to listen." Many of Bierce's nonfiction writings have been published posthumously. These include *Shadows of Blue and Gray: The Civil War Writings of Ambrose Bierce* (2002) and *The Fall of the Republic, and Other Political Satires* (2000). Bierce also published several volumes of verse during his lifetime, and a collected edition of his poetry was published in 1995.

Achievements • For many years, Ambrose Bierce was labeled a misanthrope or pessimist, and his dark short stories of murder and violence were understood as the work of a man who, obsessed with the idea of death, showed himself incapable of compassion. A less moralistic and biographical reevaluation of Bierce's work, however, reveals his intellectual fascination with the effect of the supernatural on the human imagination. Many of his morally outrageous stories are tall tales, which certainly cannot be taken at face value. Their black humor, combined with the coolly understated voices of their criminal or psychopathic narrators, reflects a society gone to seed and pokes fun at the murderous dangers of American life in the West during the Gilded Age.

Biography • Ambrose Gwinett Bierce was brought up on the farm in Horse Cave Creek, Ohio, where he was born in 1842. Although information about his early life is sparse, the evidence of his stories and the fact that he quarreled with and repudiated his large family with the exception of one brother indicate an unhappy childhood and an abnormal hatred of parental figures. His only formal education consisted of one year at a military academy. He fought with the Indiana infantry in the American Civil War (1861-1865), was wounded at the battle of Kennesaw Mountain, and ended the conflict as a brevet major. After the war, he settled in California, where, following a brief stint as a watchman at the San Francisco mint, he drifted into literary work. He wrote for the San Francisco *Argonaut* and *News Letter* and published his first story, "The Haunted Valley" (1871), in the *Overland Monthly*. He married and, on money received as a gift from his father-in-law, traveled abroad to England in 1872, returning to California in 1876 because of bad health. Upon his return he again became associated with the *Argonaut*. From 1879 to 1881 he took part in the Black Hills gold rush, returning in 1881 to San Francisco, having found no success as a miner. There he began, in association with the San Francisco *Wasp*, his famous column "The Prattler," transferred to William Randolph Hearst's San Francisco *Examiner* upon the *Wasp*'s failure, and continued at the *Examiner* until 1896, when Hearst sent him to Washington as a correspondent for the New York *American*. Much of Bierce's subsequently collected work appeared first in "The Prattler." Divorced in 1904, Bierce resigned from the Hearst organization in 1909 and, in a final quixotic gesture, disappeared into Mexico in the thick of the Mexican Revolution. He was never heard from again.

Analysis • Perhaps the most rewarding way to approach Ambrose Bierce's writing is to note that it was in many respects the product of two intertwined biographical factors, inseparable for purposes of analysis. The first of these reflects Bierce's thorny and irascible personality which made him, on the one hand, quarrel with practically everyone he ever knew, and on the other, follow romantic and often impossible causes, the last of which led to his death. The second reflects his lifelong employment as a journalist, more specifically as a writer of short columns, generally aphoristic in nature, for various newspapers. The interaction of these two often contradictory strands explains, as well as any single factor can, both the strengths and weaknesses of Bierce's writing.

Philosophically, Bierce's work is almost completely uncompromising in its iconoclasm; his view of existence is despairing, revealing only the bitterness of life within a totally fallen world promising neither present happiness nor future redemption. This "bitterness," which almost every critic has remarked in Bierce's work, is not completely fortunate. It can, and in Bierce's case often does, lead to that kind of adolescent cynicism which delights in discovering clouds in every silver lining. Too many of the insights which once seemed sterling are now fairly obviously only tinfoil. The definition of "economy" in *The Devil's Dictionary* (1906) is a case in point: "Purchasing the barrel of whiskey that you do not need for the price of the cow that you cannot afford"—an arresting idea, certainly, succinctly expressed, but by no means a profound one. In fact, it is precisely the kind of item one would expect to find on the editorial page of the morning newspaper and perhaps remember long enough to repeat at the office. Indeed, this particular aphorism did first appear in a newspaper, with most of the other contents of *The Devil's Dictionary* and, predictably, did not really survive the transformation into book form. *The Devil's Dictionary*, like much of Bierce's work, is now much more generally read about than actually read.

"An Occurrence at Owl Creek Bridge" • At its best, however, Bierce's cynicism is transformed into often-passionate statements of the tragedy of existence in a world in which present joys are unreal and future hopes vain, as a glance at one of Bierce's best-known stories, "An Occurrence at Owl Creek Bridge," will show.

This story, for all its apparent simplicity, has attracted uniform critical admiration and has been complimented not only by being extensively anthologized but also by having been made into an award-winning film. Purporting to be an incident from the American Civil War, the story opens with the execution by hanging of a Confederate civilian. His name, Peyton Farquhar, is revealed later, as is his apparent crime: He was apprehended by Union soldiers in an attempt to destroy the railroad bridge at Owl Creek, from which he is about to be hanged. The hangman's rope breaks, however, sending Farquhar into the current below. He frees his bound hands and, by swimming, manages to escape both the fire of the Union riflemen who have been assembled to witness the execution and, more miraculously, the fire of their cannon. Reaching shore, Farquhar sets out for home along an unfamiliar road, and after a night-long journey in a semidelirious condition arrives at his plantation some thirty miles away. His wife greets him at the entrance, but as he reaches to clasp her in his arms he suffers what is apparently a stroke and loses his senses. He has not, it develops, suffered a stroke; the last sentence of the story tells us what has really happened. The rope had not broken at all: "Peyton Farquhar was dead; his body, with a broken neck, swung gently from side to side beneath the timbers of the Owl Creek bridge."

"An Occurrence at Owl Creek Bridge" sounds, in summary, contrived. What is it, after all, more than a tired descant on the familiar theme of the dying man whose life passes before his eyes, coupled with the familiar trick of the unexpected happy ending put in negative terms? The answer, from the perspective of one who has read the story rather than its summary, is that it is much more. For one thing, the careful reader is not left totally unprepared for the final revelation; he has been alerted to the fact that something may be amiss by Bierce's remark that Farquhar had, before his apparent death, fixed "his last thoughts upon his wife and children." Moreover, Farquhar's journey home is described in terms which become constantly less real. The unreality of the details of his homeward journey not only expresses Farquhar's growing estrangement from the world of reality, his "doom," perhaps, or—for those more at home in modern Freudianism—his "death wish," but also subtly indicates that what *seems* to be happening in the story may not in fact actually *be* happening, at least in the real world. In any event, Bierce's point is clear and reinforced within the story by a consistent movement in grammatical usage from the actual, "he was still sinking" (speaking of Farquhar's fall from the bridge into the water), toward the hypothetical, such as "doubtless," the word Bierce uses to describe Farquhar's apparent return to his plantation.

What, then, makes this story more than the predictable reverse of the typical tricky story with the illogical happy ending? The difference is to be found simply in Bierce's uncompromisingly negative view of the world. The reader begins in a world where everyone is symbolically sentenced to death, from which his or her reprieve is only temporary, and the reader wanders with him through a field of illusions which become more attractive as they escape the confines of reality. The reader ends, reaching for a beauty and love which was sought but which was unobtainable, dead under Owl Creek Bridge. The symbolism of Owl Creek is not gratuitous: Wise old owls discover that every road leads only to death.

"Chickamauga" • The master image of "An Occurrence at Owl Creek Bridge" of a delusory journey leading to an ultimately horrible and horrifying revelation is central to many of Bierce's stories, one more of which is worth brief mention here. "Chickamauga," not as well known as the former story, is equally chilling and equally cunning in its artistry. It tells of a nameless young boy, "aged about six years," who with toy sword in hand wanders away from his home one day into the adjacent woods, where he successfully plays soldier until, unexpectedly frightened by a rabbit, he runs away and becomes lost. He falls asleep, and when he awakens it is nearly dusk. Still lost, his directionless night journey through the forest brings him upon a column of retreating soldiers, all horribly wounded and unable to walk, who are trying to withdraw from a battle (presumably the 1863 Battle of Chickamauga in the American Civil War, although this is never specifically stated) which has been fought in the neighborhood and of which the child, whom we later discover to be both deaf and mute, has been unaware. In a ghastly parody of military splendor, the child takes command of these horribly wounded soldiers and leads them on, waving his wooden sword. As the ghastly cavalcade limps forward, the wood mysteriously begins to brighten. The brightness is not the sun, however, but the light from a burning house, and when the little boy sees the blazing dwelling he deserts his troops and, fascinated by the flames, approaches the conflagration. Suddenly he recognizes the house as his own, and at its doorway he finds the corpse of his mother.

Again, the magic of this story vanishes in paraphrase, in which the masterfully controlled feeling of horror almost inevitably sounds contrived, the revelation slick rather than profound. The compelling quality of "Chickamauga" is largely a function of Bierce's style, which at once conceals and reveals what is going on. The story of a small boy who wanders off into the woods with a toy sword and who is frightened by a rabbit scarcely seems to be the kind of fictional world in which such uncompromising horrors should logically take place. Yet on a symbolic level, the story has a curiously compelling logic. The first reading of the tale leaves one with a slightly false impression of its meaning. The story does not tell us, as it seems to, and as so many fairy tales do, that it is better not to leave home and venture into the wild wood; the story's meaning is darker than this. In the world of "Chickamauga," safety is to be found neither at home nor abroad. By wandering away into the woods the boy perhaps escaped the fate of those who remained at home, and yet his symbolic journey has only brought him back to a world where death is everywhere supreme. To emphasize this point more strongly, in 1898 Bierce retitled the book of short stories in which both the above tales appeared *In the Midst of Life*. Readers are expected to complete the quotation themselves: " . . . we are in death."

Although most of Bierce's stories which are widely remembered today deal with military themes, many of his other stories are quite frankly supernatural. By and large these supernatural stories seem less likely to survive than his military ones, if only because Bierce has less sense for the implicit thematic structure of supernatural tales than he does for macabre stories about the military. His ghost stories are avowedly "shockers," without the psychological depth to be found in the works of true masters of the supernatural. They do not have the profundity, for example, of Mary Shelley's *Frankenstein* (1818) or Bram Stoker's *Dracula* (1897). Nevertheless, the best of them do have a certain compelling quality simply because of the bizarre nature of the revelation of what lies at the heart of the supernatural event which Bierce relates.

"The Damned Thing" • "The Damned Thing" offers a convenient case in point. This is, quite simply, the story of a man who is hunted down and finally killed by some kind of animal, apparently a wildcat. The reader never knows precisely what kind of animal it is, however, since it has one peculiar quality: It is invisible. The story is told with the last scene first. This last scene, entitled "One Does Not Always Eat What Is on the Table," takes place at the coroner's inquest over the body of one Hugh Morgan, who has met a violent death. His friend, William Harker, explains how Morgan had acted inexplicably on a hunting trip, apparently falling into a fit. The coroner's jury agrees, at least to an extent. Their ungrammatical verdict is "We, the jury, do find that the remains come to their death at the hands of a mountain lion, but some of us thinks, all the same, they had fits." In the closing scene of the story, Morgan's diary is introduced as explanation, and in it we read of his growing awareness that he is being stalked by some kind of invisible animal. A pseudoscientific rationale is given for this invisibility. The animal is "actinic," at least according to Morgan. "Actinic" colors, we are informed, are colors that exist at either end of the spectrum and that cannot be perceived by the human eye. We have, in other words, either an infrared or an ultraviolet mountain lion. Neither choice is particularly satisfactory, and the difficulty with our willing suspension of disbelief in the tale is indicated by precisely this: The science is bad, and yet it pretends not to be. The notion of an ultraviolet mountain lion is basically more silly than chilling, and since the story has no fiber to it other than the revelation of what the mountain lion actually consists of, we cannot take it seriously. In fact, the reader feels vaguely victimized and resentful, as though having been set up as the butt of some kind of pointless joke.

Yet even in this story, relatively unsuccessful as it is, we see at work the underlying preoccupations which make some of Bierce's other stories unforgettable. The attempt in a Bierce story is always to shock someone by removing him from a commonplace world and placing him—like the little boy in "Chickamauga"—in another world whose laws are recognizable, though strange. The logic of a Bierce story is often very like the logic of a nightmare, in which the reader is placed in the position of the dreamer. When trapped in a nightmare, the reader feels the presence of a certain inexorable logic, even though one may not, at the moment, be able to define exactly how that logic operates or of what precisely it consists. It is the feeling for the presence of this hostile and malevolent order which gives the best of Bierce's stories their perennial fascination.

James K. Folsom
With updates by R. C. Lutz

Other major works

MISCELLANEOUS: *The Collected Works of Ambrose Bierce*, 1909-1912; *Shadows of Blue and Gray: The Civil War Writings of Ambrose Bierce*, 2002 (Brian M. Thomsen, editor).

NONFICTION: *Nuggets and Dust Panned in California*, 1873; *The Fiend's Delight*, 1873; *Cobwebs from an Empty Skull*, 1874; *The Dance of Death*, 1877; *The Dance of Life: An Answer to the Dance of Death*, 1877 (with Mrs. J. Milton Bowers); *The Devil's Dictionary*, 1906; *The Shadow on the Dial, and Other Essays*, 1909; *Write It Right: A Little Blacklist of Literary Faults*, 1909; *The Letters of Ambrose Bierce*, 1922; *Twenty-one Letters of Ambrose Bierce*, 1922; *Selections from Prattle*, 1936; *Ambrose Bierce on Richard Realf by* Wm. McDevitt, 1948; *A Sole Survivor: Bits of Autobiography*, 1998 (S. T. Joshi and David E. Schultz, editors); *The Fall of the Republic, and Other Political Satires*, 2000 (Joshi and Schultz, editors); *A Much Misunderstood Man: Selected Letters of Ambrose Bierce*, 2003 (Joshi and Schultz, editors).

POETRY: *Vision of Doom*, 1890; *Black Beetles in Amber*, 1892; *How Blind Is He?*, 1896; *Shapes of Clay*, 1903; *Poems of Ambrose Bierce*, 1995.

TRANSLATION: *The Monk and the Hangman's Daughter*, 1892 (with Gustav Adolph Danziger; of Richard Voss's novel).

Bibliography

Butterfield, Herbie. "'Our Bedfellow Death': The Short Stories of Ambrose Bierce." In *The Nineteenth Century American Short Story*, edited by A. Robert Lee. Totowa, N.J.: Barnes & Noble Books, 1985. Brief, general introduction to the themes and techniques of some of Bierce's most representative short stories.

Conlogue, William. "A Haunting Memory: Ambrose Bierce and the Ravine of the Dead." *Studies in Short Fiction* 28 (Winter, 1991): 21-29. Discusses Bierce's symbolic use of the topographical feature of the ravine as a major symbol of death in five stories, including "Killed at Resaca," "Coulter's Notch," and "The Coup de Grâce." Shows how the ravine symbolizes the grave, the underworld, and lost love for Bierce, all derived from his Civil War memories and the death of his first love.

Davidson, Cathy N. *The Experimental Fictions of Ambrose Bierce: Structuring the Ineffable.* Lincoln: University of Nebraska Press, 1984. Discusses how Bierce intentionally blurs distinctions between such categories as knowledge, emotion, language, and behavior. Examines how Bierce blurs distinctions between external reality and imaginative reality in many of his most important short stories.

_____, ed. *Critical Essays on Ambrose Bierce.* Boston: G. K. Hall, 1982. Comprehensive compilation of thirty essays and reviews of Bierce's work, this collection is an essential tool for any serious study of Bierce. Davidson's introduction locates the essays in relation to the ongoing process of reevaluating Bierce's work, and her thoroughly researched bibliography contains more than eighty further critical references.

Fatout, Paul. *Ambrose Bierce: The Devil's Lexicographer.* Norman: University of Oklahoma Press, 1951. Fatout's impressive collation of painstakingly researched biographical data represents an important landmark in the scholarly study of Bierce's life. Supplemented by illustrations and a bibliography.

Gale, Robert L. *An Ambrose Bierce Companion.* New York: Greenwood Press, 2001. Comprehensive guide to the life and writings of the American satirist.

Grenander, Mary Elizabeth. *Ambrose Bierce.* New York: Twayne, 1971. This volume is well researched, balanced, and readable, and it is perhaps the single most accessible study of Bierce's work and life. Contains a valuable, annotated bibliography and a list of primary sources.

Hoppenstand, Gary. "Ambrose Bierce and the Transformation of the Gothic Tale in the Nineteenth-Century American Periodical." In *Periodical Literature in Nineteenth-Century America,* edited by Kenneth M. Price and Susan Belasco Smith. Charlottesville: University Press of Virginia, 1995. Examines Bierce's relationship to the San Francisco periodicals, focusing on the influence he had in bringing the gothic tale into the twentieth century; discusses themes and conventions in "The Damned Thing" and "Moxon's Master."

May, Charles E., ed. *Masterplots II: Short Story Series, Revised Edition.* 8 vols. Pasadena, Calif.: Salem Press, 2004. Designed for student use, this reference set contains articles providing detailed plot summaries and analyses of these five short stories by Bierce: "Chickamauga" (vol. 1), "The Coup de Grâce" (vol. 2), "Killed at Resaca" (vol. 4), and "An Occurrence at Owl Creek Bridge" and "One of the Missing" (vol. 5).

Morris, Roy, Jr. *Ambrose Bierce: Alone in Bad Company.* New York: Crown, 1996. Compelling, if somewhat slight, biography of one of American's most eccentric yet quotable authors.

Giovanni Boccaccio

Born: Florence or Certaldo (now in Italy); June or July, 1313
Died: Certaldo (now in Italy); December 21, 1375

Principal short fiction • *Decameron: O, Prencipe Galetto*, 1349-1351 (*The Decameron*, 1620).

Other literary forms • Although Giovanni Boccaccio's greatest work is the masterfully framed collection of one hundred Italian short stories known as *The Decameron*, he also left a large and significant corpus of poetry. His earliest poetry, written in Naples, is in Italian and includes the *Rime* (c. 1330-1340; poems), which comprises more than one hundred lyrics, mostly sonnets and not all of sure attribution. These short poems are largely dedicated to the poet's beloved Fiammetta, who is identified in some of Boccaccio's pseudoautobiographical writings as Maria d'Aquino; supposedly, she was the illegitimate daughter of King Robert of Naples, but more probably she was the invention of the poet. Similarly, the longer poem *La caccia di Diana* (c. 1334; Diana's hunt), *Il filostrato* (c. 1335; *The Filostrato*, 1873), *Il filocolo* (c. 1336; *Labor of Love*, 1566), and *Teseida* (1340-1341; *The Book of Theseus*, 1974) are all poems ostensibly inspired by Boccaccio's ardor for Fiammetta, whose name means "little flame." Other poems that were composed in the 1340's also treat the formidable power of love and include the *Commedia delle ninfe*, entitled *Il ninfale d'Ameto* by fifteenth century copyists (1341-1342; the comedy of the nymphs of Florence), *L'amorosa visione* (1342-1343; English translation, 1986), *Elegia di Madonna Fiammetta* (1343-1344; *Amorous Fiammetta*, 1587), and *Il ninfale fiesolano* (1344-1346; *The Nymph of Fiesole*, 1597).

Achievements • Giovanni Boccaccio created many literary firsts in Italian letters. He is often credited, for example, with the first Italian hunting poem (*La caccia di Diana*), the first Italian verse romance by a nonminstrel (*The Filostrato*), the first Italian prose romance (*Labor of Love*), and the first Italian idyll (*The Nymph of Fiesole*). Many scholars also regard Boccaccio as the greatest narrator Europe has produced. Such high esteem for the Tuscan author assuredly arises from his masterpiece, *The Decameron*, which has provided a model or source material for many notable European and English authors, from Marguerite de Navarre and Lope de Vega Carpio to Gotthold Ephraim Lessing and Alfred, Lord Tennyson. Even if Boccaccio had never composed his magnum opus, however, he would still enjoy significant acclaim in European literary history for his presumedly minor writings. For example, many consider his *Amorous Fiammetta* to be the first modern (that is, postclassical) psychological novel. Certainly his *Il ninfale d'Ameto* anticipates Renaissance bucolic literature. Contemporary medieval authors also looked to Boccaccio for inspiration. In *The Filostrato*, Geoffrey Chaucer found ample material for his *Troilus and Criseyde* (1382), and in *The Book of Theseus* Chaucer discovered the source for "The Knight's Tale." Boccaccio's encyclopedic works in Latin resulted in his being regarded as one of the most prominent Trecento humanists. Indeed, it was as a Latin humanist, rather than as a raconteur of vernacular tales, that Boccaccio was primarily remembered during the first century following his demise.

Biography • The exact place and date of the birth of Giovanni Boccaccio are not known. Until the first half of the twentieth century, it was believed that he was born in Paris of a noble Frenchwoman; scholars now regard that story as another one of the author's fictional tales. Most likely, he was born in Florence or Certaldo, Italy, in June or July, 1313, the natural son of Boccaccio di Chellino and an unidentified Tuscan woman. His father, an agent for a powerful Florentine banking family (the Bardi), recognized Giovanni early as his son; the boy, as a result, passed both his infancy and his childhood in his father's house. Boccaccio's teacher in his youth was Giovanni Mazzuoli da Strada, undoubtedly an admirer Dante Alighieri, whose *La divina commedia* (c. 1320; *The Divine Comedy*, 1802) greatly influenced Boccaccio's own writings.

In his early teens, sometime between 1325 and 1328, Boccaccio was sent to Naples to learn the merchant trade and banking business as an apprentice to the Neapolitan branch of the Bardi Company. The Bardi family, as the financiers of King Robert of Anjou, exerted a powerful influence at the Angevin court in Naples. The experiences Boccaccio enjoyed with the Neapolitan aristocracy and with the breathtaking countryside and beautiful sea are reflected in many of his early poems. During his sojourn in Naples, Boccaccio also studied canon law, between 1330 or 1331 and 1334. While studying business and law, however, he anxiously sought cultural experiences to broaden his awareness of belles lettres. Largely self-taught in literary matters, he soon began to study the writings of his somewhat older contemporary, Francesco Petrarca, known as Petrarch. Later, the two men became friends and met on a number of occasions (1350 in Florence, 1351 in Padua, 1359 in Milano, 1363 in Venice, and 1368 in Padua again).

Boccaccio left Naples and returned to Florence between 1340 and 1341 because of a financial crisis in the Bardi empire. Although Boccaccio rued having to leave Naples, so often associated in his imagination and writings with love and adventure and poetry, his highly bourgeois Florentine experience added an important and desirable dimension of realism to his work. Little is documented about Boccaccio's life between 1340 and 1348, although it is known (from one of Petrarch's letters) that he was in Ravenna between 1345 and 1346 and that he sent a letter from Forlì in 1347. He was back in Florence in 1348, where he witnessed at first hand the horrible ravages of the Black Death, or bubonic plague. Between 1349 and 1351, he gave final form to *The Decameron*, which takes as it *mise en scène* Florence and the Tuscan countryside during the plague of 1348.

After his father's death in 1349, Boccaccio assumed many more familial responsibilities and financial burdens. As his fame as an author and scholar burgeoned, his fellow Florentines began to honor him with various ambassadorial duties, starting with his 1350 assignment as ambassador to the lords of Romagna. Such posts, however, did little to alleviate the financial difficulties caused by the collapse of the Bardi Company. Boccaccio longed to return to the pleasant life he had known in Naples, but visits there in 1355 and again in 1362 and 1370 to 1371 were extremely disappointing. Between 1360 and 1362, he studied Greek, the first among the literati of his time to do so seriously; from that time until his death, his home became the center for Italian humanism. Sometime around 1361 or 1362, he left Florence to take up residence in the family home in Certaldo, where he died, on December 21, 1375, the year after the death of his friend and fellow humanist, Petrarch.

Analysis • Giovanni Boccaccio's short fiction, one hundred *novelle*, or tales, is collectively and contemporaneously his longest work of fiction, known as *The Decameron*.

That fact must be kept foremost in mind in any serious analysis of the tales. In other words, Boccaccio's individual short stories are best understood when examined as part of a much larger work of fiction which has an elaborate *cornice*, or frame, striking symmetry, and selective and oft-repeated themes.

The word *decameron*, Greek for "ten days," refers to the number of days Boccaccio's fictional characters (three young men and seven young women) dedicate to swapping tales with one another in the tranquil Tuscan countryside away from the plague-infested city of Florence. The work's subtitle, "Prencipe Galeotto" (Prince Galahalt), refers to the panderer Galahalt, who brought Guinevere and Lancelot together, and emphasizes that Boccaccio's book—dedicated to women—is written, not unlike many of his early poems, in the service of love. As the narration of the first day begins, three men—Panfilo ("all love"), Filostrato ("overcome by love"), and Dioneo ("the lascivious"), alluding to the love goddess Venus, daughter of Dione—come by chance one Tuesday upon seven women, who are between the ages of eighteen and twenty-eight, in the Church of Santa Maria Novella. The year is 1348, and the Black Death is the macabre background for what happens in the course of the telling of the tales. The seven women—Pampinea ("the vigorous"), Fiammetta (whose name echoes that of Boccaccio's beloved), Filomena ("lover of song"), Emilia ("the flatterer"), Lauretta (in homage to Petrarch's beloved Laura), Neifile ("new in love"), and Elissa (another name for Vergil's tragic heroine Dido)—anxiously wish to remove themselves from the diseased and strife-torn city and repair to the healthful and peaceful countryside. The young men agree to accompany the ladies, and the following day (a Wednesday) the group leaves for a villa in nearby and idyllic Fiesole. Better to enjoy what is essentially a fortnight's holiday, Pampinea suggests that they tell stories in the late afternoon when

it is too hot to play or go on walks. It is decided that one of them will be chosen as king or queen for each day, and the chosen person will select a theme for the stories to be told on that day. Only Dioneo, who tells the last tale each day, has the liberty of ignoring the general theme if he so desires. They then proceed to tell ten stories per day over a two-week period, refraining from tale-telling on Fridays and Saturdays out of reverence for Christ's crucifixion and in order to prepare properly for the Sabbath. On a Wednesday, the day following the last day of telling tales and exactly two weeks from the day the group left Florence, they return to their respective homes.

The emphasis on order

and propriety, the presentation of the countryside as a *locus amoenus*, the repetition of the number ten (considered a symbol of perfection in the Middle Ages), and even the total number of tales (one hundred, equal to the number of cantos in Dante's *The Divine Comedy*) are all aspects of the work which contrast sharply with the disorder, impropriety, and lack of harmony which characterized Florence during the 1348 plague. The author graphically depicts, in the opening pages of the book, examples of the social chaos caused by the plethora of plague-induced deaths. The pleasant pastime of telling tales in the shade of trees and the skillful ordering of the stories serve, in other words, as an obvious antidote or salutary response to the breakdown of society which resulted from the deadly pestilence which swept Italy and much of Europe in the mid-fourteenth century. Further supporting the notion that *The Decameron* presents an ordered universe as an alternative to the chaos and anarchy created by the plague is Boccaccio's insistence that his storytellers, though they may occasionally tell ribald tales, are uniformly chaste and proper in their behavior toward one another.

Boccaccio's Themes • The stories told on each of the ten days that make up *The Decameron* explore a predetermined subject or theme. On the first day, everyone is free to choose a topic—one is the character "Abraam giudeo" ("Abraham the Jew"). On the second day, the stories treat those, such as the subject of "Andreuccio da Perugia" ("Andreuccio of Perugia"), who realize unexpected happiness after serious misfortune. Then, on the third day, the stories discuss people who have accomplished difficult goals or who have repossessed something once lost, among which is the tale "Alibech" ("Alibech and Rustico"). The next day, the narrators tell love stories which end unhappily (see "Tancredi, Prenze di Salerno" and its English translation). On the fifth day, they tell love stories which depict misfortune but end felicitously (see "Nastagio degli Onesti" and the English translation). The stories told on the sixth day deal with the role of intelligence in helping one avoid problems—one of the most famous among these is "Cisti fornaio" ("Cisti the Baker"). On the seventh day, the stories relate tricks which wives play on husbands (see "Petronella mette un so amante in un doglio," or "Petronella and the Barrel"), and on the eighth day, the stories recount tricks men and women play on each other, as in "Calandrino" ("Calandrino and the Heliotrope"). On the ninth day, once again everyone is free to choose a topic (one is described in "Le vasi una badessa in fretta ed al buio per trovare una sua monaca a lei accusata" and its translation, "The Abbess and the Nun"). Finally, on the tenth day, the narrators tell of men and women who have performed magnanimous deeds and acquired renown in so doing (see "Il Marchese di Saluzzo," or "The Marchese di Saluzzo and Griselda").

In addition to the pronounced framing technique created by the introductions to the various days and by the themes themselves, there seems to be a degree of subtle thematic framing within the stories themselves from first to last. The first story of the first day, "Ser Cepparello," tells how a most wicked man—clearly a *figura diaboli*, or type of the devil—deceived a friar with a false confession and came to be reputed a saint. On one hand, the tale ridicules gullible priests and credulous common folk, but on the other hand, it presents the undeniable power of human cunning. The tenth story of the tenth day recounts the story of how the Marquis of Saluzzo marries the peasant Griselda and subjects her to inhuman trials to ascertain her devotion; for example, he pretends to have their two children killed. His cruelty is ostensibly designed to test her love or respect for him; her extraordinary patience in responding

to his bestiality assuredly makes of her a *figura Christi,* or type of Christ. From the co-
medic devil figure of Cepparello to the tragic Christ figure of Griselda there appears
to be in *The Decameron* a revelation of the breadth of the human condition and the
wide-ranging possibilities of human experience. Nevertheless, Boccaccio explores a
variation on at least one of two themes in almost all of his stories: the power of human
intelligence (for good or bad) and the effect of love or human passion (for the well-
being or detriment of those involved). At times, these themes are intermingled, as in
so many of the stories of the seventh day having to do with the ingenious tricks wives
play on their (usually cuckolded) spouses.

Boccaccio's Settings • Often when treating the advantages of human wit, Boccaccio
provides a Florentine or Tuscan setting to his story. For example, in the sixth day,
"Cisti the Baker" is set in Florence and illustrates the rise and power of the hardwork-
ing and hard-thinking merchant class Boccaccio knew so well in his hometown. Similarly, "Guido Cavalcanti," told on the same day, has Florence as its setting and reveals
the barbed wit of one of the city's native sons. There are also tales told of Florentines
who are dull-witted; examples would include the various eighth- and ninth-day stories about the simple-minded painter Calandrino, who is constantly being tricked by
his supposed friends Bruno and Buffalmacco. Those who outsmart him, however, are
fellow Florentines. By contrast, many of the highly adventurous tales are set in cities far away from Florence, often in exotic locations. Not surprisingly, Naples figures prominently in perhaps the most notable of the adventure tales—that is,
"Andreuccio of Perugia," the story of a provincial young man who goes to a big city
(Naples) to buy horses and ends up suffering a series of misfortunes only to return
home with a ruby of great value. In the tale, Naples symbolizes adventure and daring
and is undoubtedly meant to recall the city of the author's youth.

Boccaccio's Love Tales • Boccaccio's love tales repeatedly, though not exclusively,
present realistic women in place of the idealized and angelic women Dante was wont
to exalt. In stories scattered throughout *The Decameron,* but especially in those of
the third and fifth day, the physical and pleasurable union of man and woman is
portrayed as the healthy and correct goal of human love. Although some interpret
such unabashed celebration of humankind's sexuality as a sure indication that *The
Decameron* is a Renaissance work, it should be remembered that approximately 90
percent of Boccaccio's tales derive from medieval sources. G. H. McWilliam, in the
introduction to his excellent English translation of *The Decameron,* reviews with insight the problem of how to classify the book with regard to historical period. He
points out that the harsh judgment leveled against friars and monks, whether they
are philanderers or simoniacs, has numerous precedents in the literature of the Middle Ages, including Dante's thoroughly medieval *The Divine Comedy.*

This is not to say, however, that *The Decameron* does not look to the future, for it
most certainly does. For one thing, when Boccaccio attacks the superstitious religious beliefs and corrupt ecclesiastical practices of his times, he does so with more
severity than did his predecessors; for another, he presents the centrality of sexuality
to the human condition without recourse to sermons or condemnations of the same.
In both ways, he draws closer to the spirit of a new age and distances himself from
the Middle Ages. His overriding purpose in the tales, however, is to illuminate the
spectrum of humankind's experiences and to point, in a world accustomed to
pain and disease, a way to happiness and health. Boccaccio's medium is always the

well-worded and exquisitely framed story; his best medicine, more often than not, is laughter or the praise of life.

Madison V. Sowell
With updates by Victor A. Santi

Other major works

NONFICTION: *Genealogia deorum gentilium*, c. 1350-1375; *Trattatello in laude di Dante*, 1351, 1360, 1373 (*Life of Dante*, 1898); *Corbaccio*, c. 1355 (*The Corbaccio*, 1975); *De casibus virorum illustrium*, 1355-1374 (*The Fall of Princes*, 1431-1438); *De montibus, silvis, fontibus lacubus, fluminubus, stagnis seu paludibus, et de nominbus maris*, c. 1355-1374; *De mulieribus claris*, c. 1361-1375 (*Concerning Famous Women*, 1943); *Esposizioni sopra la Commedia di Dante*, 1373-1374.

POETRY: *Rime*, c. 1330-1340; *La caccia di Diana*, c. 1334; *Il filostrato*, c. 1335 (*The Filostrato*, 1873); *Il filocolo*, c. 1336 (*Labor of Love*, 1566); *Teseida*, 1340-1341 (*The Book of Theseus*, 1974); *Il ninfale d'Ameto*, 1341-1342 (also known as *Commedia delle ninfe*); *L'amorosa visione*, 1342-1343 (English translation, 1986); *Elegia di Madonna Fiammetta*, 1343-1344 (*Amorous Fiammetta*, 1587, better known as *The Elegy of Lady Fiammetta*); *Il ninfale fiesolano*, 1344-1346 (*The Nymph of Fiesole*, 1597); *Buccolicum carmen*, c. 1351-1366 (*Boccaccio's Olympia*, 1913).

Bibliography

Bergin, Thomas G. *Boccaccio*. New York: Viking Press, 1981. Excellent general introduction to Boccaccio. It begins with a historical background to Florentine life in the fourteenth century and proceeds to delineate the life of the author with emphasis on the major influences on his work. The early works are analyzed individually for their own merit and for their relationship to *The Decameron*. Contains lengthy but lucid discussion of *The Decameron* followed by notes and a useful list of works.

Branca, Vittore. *Boccaccio: The Man and His Works*. Translated by Richard Monges. New York: New York University Press, 1976. The definitive biography of Boccaccio by an eminent scholar in the field of medieval literature.

Caporello-Szykman, C. *The Boccaccian Novella: The Creation and Waning of a Genre*. New York: Peter Lang, 1990. Defines the novella as a form that existed only between Boccaccio and Cervantes. Discusses generic characteristics of the *Decameron*, Boccacio's narrative theory, and the novella's place within the oral tradition.

Edwards, Robert R. *Chaucer and Boccaccio: Antiquity and Modernity*. New York: Palgrave, 2002. Examines the influence of Boccaccio on Chaucer.

Forni, Pier Massimo. *Adventures in Speech: Rhetoric and Narration in Boccaccio's "Decameron."* Philadelphia: University of Pennsylvania Press, 1996. Examines Boccaccio's style in his seminal work. Includes bibliographical references and an index.

Hollander, Robert. *Boccaccio's Two Venuses*. New York: Columbia University Press, 1977. Thorough analysis of all Boccaccio's works except *The Decameron*. The author contrasts classical and Christian influences in Boccaccio's work and concludes that, although the latter predominates in the later works, even in the earlier prose the classical Venus is tempered by the use of irony.

Moe, Nelson. "Not a Love Story: Sexual Aggression, Law and Order in *Decameron* X 4." *Romanic Review* 86 (November, 1995): 623-638. Discusses the fourth tale of

the tenth day as a reworking of an earlier Boccaccio treatment; examines his refor-
mulation of the social significance of sexual transgression that is at the center of
both versions of the tale.

Stierle, Karlheinz. "Three Moments in the Crisis of Exemplarity: Boccaccio-Petrarch,
Montaigne, and Cervantes." *Journal of the History of Ideas* 59 (October, 1998): 581-
595. Discusses Boccaccio's response to the exemplum as a form of narration that
presumes more similarity in human behavior than diversity; analyzes Boccaccio's
turn from exemplum to novella as a shift that indicates a crisis of exemplarity.

Wright, Herbert G. *Boccaccio in England, from Chaucer to Tennyson.* London: Athlone
Press, 1957. Analysis of the influence of Boccaccio on well-known authors such as
Geoffrey Chaucer, William Shakespeare, and Alfred, Lord Tennyson, with an es-
pecially lengthy and perspicacious discussion of the presence of Boccaccio in *The
Canterbury Tales.*

Jorge Luis Borges

Born: Buenos Aires, Argentina; August 24, 1899
Died: Geneva, Switzerland; June 14, 1986

Principal short fiction • *Historia universal de la infamia,* 1935 (*A Universal History of Infamy,* 1972); *El jardín de senderos que se bifurcan,* 1941; *Seis problemas para don Isidro Parodi,* 1942 (with Adolfo Bioy Casares, under joint pseudonym H. Bustos Domecq; *Six Problems for Don Isidro Parodi,* 1981); *Ficciones, 1935-1944,* 1944 (English translation, 1962); *Dos fantasías memorables,* 1946 (with Bioy Casares, under joint pseudonym Domecq); *El Aleph,* 1949, 1952 (translated in *The Aleph, and Other Stories, 1933-1969,* 1970); *La muerte y la brújula,* 1951; *La hermana de Eloísa,* 1955 (with Luisa Mercedes Levinson); *Cuentos,* 1958; *Crónicas de Bustos Domecq,* 1967 (with Bioy Casares; *Chronicles of Bustos Domecq,* 1976); *El informe de Brodie,* 1970 (*Doctor Brodie's Report,* 1972); *El matrero,* 1970; *El congreso,* 1971 (*The Congress,* 1974); *El libro de arena,* 1975 (*The Book of Sand,* 1977); *Narraciones,* 1980.

Other literary forms • Though most famous for his work in short fiction, Jorge Luis Borges also holds a significant place in Latino literature for his work in poetry and the essay. In fact, Borges would be considered a major writer in Latino letters for his work in these two genres (the vast majority of which was produced before the Argentine writer branched into short fiction) even had he never written a single short story. Borges's early poetry (that for which he earned his reputation as a poet) is of the ultraist school, an avant-grade brand of poetry influenced by expressionism and Dadaism and intended by its Latino practitioners as a reaction to Latino modernism. Borges's essays, as readers familiar with his fiction might expect, are imaginative and witty and usually deal with topics in literature or philosophy. Interestingly, because of the writer's playful imagination, many of his essays read more like fiction than essay, while, because of his propensity both for toying with philosophical concepts and for fusing the fictitious and the real, much of his fiction reads more like essay than fiction. It seems only fitting, however, that for a writer for whom the line between fiction and reality is almost nonexistent the line between fiction and essay should be almost nonexistent as well.

Achievements • It is virtually impossible to overstate the importance of Jorge Luis Borges within the context of Latino fiction, for he is, quite simply, the single most important writer of short fiction in the history of Latino literature. This is true not only because of his stories themselves, and chiefly those published in *Ficciones, 1935-1944* and *El Aleph,* but also, just as important, because of how his stories contributed to the evolution of Latino fiction, both short and long, in the latter half of the twentieth century.

Borges was the founder of Latino literature's "new narrative," the type of narrative practiced by the likes of Julio Cortázar, Gabriel García Márquez, Carlos Fuentes, Mario Vargas Llosa, and others. Latino fiction prior to Borges was chiefly concerned with painting a realistic and detailed picture of external Latino reality. His imaginative *ficciones* (or fictions) almost single-handedly changed this, teaching Latino writers to be creative, to use their imagination, to treat fiction as fiction, to allow the fictional world to be just that: fictional. Borges's works also taught Latino writers to deal with universal themes and to write for an intellectual reader. Without Borges, not only would the literary world be without some superb stories, but also Latino narrative in the second half of the twentieth century would have been radically different from what it evolved to be.

Biography • Jorge Luis Borges was born on August 24, 1899, in Buenos Aires, Argentina, the first of two children born to Jorge Guillermo Borges and Leonor Acevedo de Borges. (His sister, Norah, was born in 1901.) Borges's ancestors included prominent Argentine military and historical figures on both sides of his family and an English grandmother on his father's.

"Georgie," as Borges's family called him, began reading very early, first in English, then in Spanish. Tutored first by his English grandmother and later by a private governess, and with access to his father's library (which contained numerous volumes in English), young Borges devoured a wide range of writings, among them those of Robert Louis Stevenson, Rudyard Kipling, and Mark Twain, as well as works of mythology, novels of chivalry, *The Thousand and One Nights* (c. 1450), and Miguel de Cervantes' *Don Quixote de la Mancha* (1605, 1615).

Borges finally entered school at the age of nine, and at the age of thirteen he published his first story, a dramatic sketch entitled "El rey de la selva" (the king of the jungle), about his favorite animal, the tiger. Borges and his family traveled to Europe in 1914. World War I broke out while they were visiting Geneva, Switzerland, and they remained there until 1918. During his time in Geneva, Borges began to take an interest in French poetry, particularly that of Victor Hugo and Charles Baudelaire, as well as the poetry of Heinrich Heine and the German expressionists. He also began to read the works of Walt Whitman, Arthur Schopenhauer, and G. K. Chesterton, and he maintained his literary connection to his native Argentina by reading *gauchesca* (gaucho) poetry.

In 1919 Borges and his family moved to Spain, living for various lengths of time in Barcelona, Majorca, Seville, and Madrid. While in Spain, Borges associated with a group of ultraist poets and published some poetry in an ultraist magazine. In 1921, Borges and his family returned to Buenos Aires. His return to his native city after a seven-year absence inspired him to write his first volume of poetry, entitled *Fervor de Buenos Aires* (fervor of Buenos Aires) and published in 1923. During this same period (in 1922), he collaborated on a "billboard review" entitled *Prisma* (prism) and edited the manifesto "Ultraísmo" (ultraism), published in the magazine *Nosotros* (us). He also helped found a short-lived magazine entitled *Proa* (prow). Following a second trip with his family to Europe (1923-1924), Borges continued to write poetry during the 1920's, but he began to branch out into the essay genre as well, publishing three collections of essays during this period: *Inquisiciones* (inquisitions) in 1925, *El tamaño de mi esperanza* (the size of my hope) in 1926, and *El idioma de los argentinos* (the language of the Argentines) in 1928. One of his collections of poetry, *Cuaderno San Martín* (San Martín notebook), won for him second prize in the Municipal Literature Competition in 1929. The prize carried an award of three thousand pesos, which Borges used to buy an edition of the *Encyclopædia Britannica*.

Borges continued writing both poetry and essays in the 1930's, but this decade would also bring his first (though unconventional) steps into fiction. He began contributing to the magazine *Sur* (south) in 1931 (through which he met his friend and future literary collaborator Adolfo Bioy Casares); later, in 1933, he became the director of *Crítica* (criticism), a Saturday literary supplement for a Buenos Aires newspaper. As a contributor to the supplement, Borges began to rewrite stories that he took from various sources, adding his own personal touches and reworking them as he saw fit. He finally wrote, under a pen name, a wholly original piece entitled "Hombres de las orillas" (men from the outskirts), which appeared on September 16, 1933, in the supplement. This story and his other *Crítica* pieces were well received and published together in 1935 in a volume entitled *Historia universal de la infamia*.

Borges's foray into fiction writing continued to follow an unconventional path when in 1936 he began writing a book-review page for the magazine *El Hogar* (the

© *Washington Post,* reprinted by permission of the D.C. Public Library

home). Each entry carried a brief biography of the author whose work was being reviewed. Once again, Borges could not leave well enough alone. To the author's true biographical facts, Borges began to add his own "facts," even including apocryphal anecdotes from the author's life and supplementing the author's bibliography with false titles. This mix of fact and fiction, with no regard or concern for which was which, would come to be one of the trademarks of Borges's fiction.

Borges took a job as an assistant librarian in a suburban Buenos Aires library in 1937, a position whose work load and setting afforded the writer ample time and resources to read and write. In December of 1938, however, the Argentine writer suffered a near-fatal accident, slipping on a staircase and striking his head while returning to his apartment. The resulting head injury developed into septicemia, and Borges was hospitalized for more than two weeks. While still recovering in early 1939, Borges decided that he would abandon poetry and the essay (though he would later return to these genres) and dedicate his literary efforts to short fiction. Though it is somewhat unclear as to precisely why he made this decision (there are various accounts), it is speculated by some (and Borges's own comments have supported such speculation) that he did so because after his head injury he was not sure that he could write poetry and essays of the quality for which he had been known before the accident. Short stories, for which he was virtually unknown at this point, would not allow anyone to compare an old Borges with a new, and potentially inferior, Borges. Again, this is only one suggestion as to why the Argentine writer made the decision he did; what is most important, however, is that he made it, and this decision, and the accident that seems to have caused it, would change the face of Latino fiction of the twentieth century.

Almost immediately, Borges began to produce a series of short stories that would make him the most important writer in Latino fiction and that would eventually make him famous. The first of these stories was "Pierre Menard, autor del *Quijote*" ("Pierre Menard, Author of the *Quixote*"), which appeared in *Sur* in May of 1939. This story was followed in 1940 by "Tlön, Uqbar, Orbis Tertius" ("Tlön, Uqbar, Orbis Tertius") and the collection *El jardín de senderos que se bifurcan* (the garden of forking paths) in 1941. Six stories were added to the eight collected in *El jardín de senderos que se bifurcan*, and a new collection, entitled *Ficciones, 1935-1944*, one of the most important collections of short fiction in Latino literature, appeared in 1944. Another landmark collection, *El Aleph*, followed in 1949.

During this time, the height of his literary career up to this point, Borges, who was anti-Peronist, fell into disfavor with the government of Argentine president Juan Perón. He was dismissed from his position at the library in 1944 and appointed inspector of poultry and eggs in the municipal market. He resigned, but he did return to public service in 1955 when, following the fall of Perón, he was named the director of the National Library. Ironically, in the same year, he lost his sight, which had been declining for several years.

Despite the loss of his sight, Borges continued to write (through dictation), though less than before. At the same time, his two collections of stories from the 1940's had made him a household name among Latino literati. Worldwide recognition came in 1961, when he shared the Formentor Prize (worth ten thousand dollars) with Samuel Beckett. The fame that this award brought Borges changed his life. That fall, he traveled to the United States to lecture at the University of Texas, and between 1961 and his death in 1986, he would make numerous trips to the United States and elsewhere teaching and speaking at colleges and universities, attending literary conferences on his works, collecting literary awards, and otherwise serving as an international ambassador for Latino literature.

Borges married for the first time (at the age of sixty-eight) in 1967, the same year that he accepted an invitation to teach at Harvard University as a Charles Eliot Norton lecturer. The marriage dissolved in 1970, with Borges, according to one popular anecdote, leaving the home he shared with his wife and taking only his prized *Encyclopædia Britannica* with him. Perón returned to the Argentine presidency in 1973, and Borges resigned as director of the National Library. His mother died at the age of ninety-nine in 1975.

Borges continued to write during the 1970's and until his death, working in short fiction, poetry, and the essay (having returned to these last two genres in the 1950's). The bulk of his fame, however, and particularly that specifically related to short fiction, had come from his two collections of stories from the 1940's. He was nominated repeatedly for the Nobel Prize in Literature but never won it. In 1986, he married his companion María Kodama and shortly thereafter died of cancer of the liver on June 14, 1986, in Geneva, Switzerland.

Analysis • Jorge Luis Borges may be, quite simply, the single most important writer of short fiction in the history of Latino literature. The stories he published in his collections *Ficciones, 1935-1944* and *El Aleph*, particularly the former, not only gave Latino (and world) literature a body of remarkable stories but also opened the door to a whole new type of fiction that would be practiced by the likes of the above-mentioned Julio Cortázar, Gabriel García Márquez, Carlos Fuentes, and Mario Vargas Llosa, and that, in the hands of these writers and others like them, would put Latino fiction on the world literary map in the 1960's.

Prior to Borges, and particularly between 1920 and 1940, Latino fiction, as stated previously, was concerned chiefly with painting a realistic and detailed picture of external Latino reality. Description frequently ruled over action, environment over character, and types over individuals. Social message, also, was often more important to the writer than was narrative artistry. Latino fiction after Borges (that is, after his landmark collections of stories of the 1940's) was decidedly different in that it was no longer documentary in nature, turned its focus toward the inner workings of its fully individualized human characters, presented various interpretations of reality, expressed universal as well as regional and national themes, invited reader participation, and emphasized the importance of artistic—and frequently unconventional—presentation of the story, particularly with respect to narrative voice, language, structure (and the closely related element of time), and characterization. This "new narrative," as it came to be called, would have been impossible without Borges's tradition-breaking fiction.

This is not to say that Borges's stories fully embody each of the characteristics of the Latino "new narrative" listed above. Ironically, they do not. For example, Borges's characters are often far more archetypal than individual, his presentation tends to be for the most part quite traditional, and reader participation (at least as compared to that required in the works of other "new narrativists") is frequently not a factor. The major contributions that Borges made to Latino narrative through his stories lie, first, in his use of imagination, second, in his focus on universal themes common to all human beings, and third, in the intellectual aspect of his works.

During the 1940's, Borges, unlike most who were writing so-called Latino fiction, treated fiction as fiction. Rather than use fiction to document everyday reality, Borges used it to invent new realities, to toy with philosophical concepts, and in the process to create truly fictional worlds, governed by their own rules. He also chose to write chiefly about universal human beings rather than exclusively about Latinos. His characters are, for example, European, or Chinese, frequently of no discernible nationality, and only occasionally Latino. In most cases, even when a character's nationality is revealed, it is of no real importance, particularly with respect to theme. Almost all Borges's characters are important not because of the country from which they come but because they are human beings, faced not with situations and conflicts particular to their nationality but with situations and conflicts common to all human beings.

Finally, unlike his predecessors and many of his contemporaries, Borges did not aim his fiction at the masses. He wrote instead, it seems, more for himself, and, by extension, for the intellectual reader. These three aspects of his fiction—treating fiction as fiction, placing universal characters in universal conflicts, and writing for a more intellectual audience—stand as the Argentine writer's three most important contributions to Latino fiction in the latter half of the twentieth century, and to one degree or another, virtually every one of the Latino "new narrativists," from Cortázar to García Márquez, followed Borges's lead in these areas.

Borges's stories are more aptly called "fictions" than "stories," for while all fit emphatically into the first category, since they contain fictitious elements, many do not fit nearly so well into a traditional definition of the second, since they read more like essays than stories. His fictions are sophisticated, compact, even mathematically precise narratives that range in type from what might be called the "traditional" short story (a rarity) to fictionalized essay (neither pure story nor pure essay but instead a unique mix of the two, complete, oddly enough, with both fictitious characters and footnotes, both fictitious and factual) to detective story or spy thriller (though always with an unmistakably Borgesian touch) to fictional illustration of a philosophical concept (this last type being, perhaps, most common). Regardless of the specific category into which each story might fall, almost all, to one degree or another, touch on either what Borges viewed as the labyrinthine nature of the universe, irony (particularly with respect to human destiny), the concept of time, the hubris of those who believe they know all there is to know, or any combination of these elements. Most of Borges's fame as a writer of fiction and virtually all of his considerable influence on Latino "new narrative" are derived from his two masterpiece collections, *Ficciones, 1935-1944* and *El Aleph*. Of these two, the first stands out as the more important and may be the single most important collection of short fiction in the history of Latino literature.

Ficciones, 1935-1944 contains fourteen stories (seventeen for editions published after 1956). Seven of the fourteen were written between 1939 and 1941 and, along with an eighth story, were originally collected in *El jardín de senderos que se bifurcan* (the garden of forking paths). The other six stories were added in 1944. Virtually every story in this collection has become a Latino classic, and together they reveal the variety of Borges's themes and story types.

"Death and the Compass" • "*La muerte y la brújula*" ("Death and the Compass") is one of the most popular of the stories found in *Ficciones, 1935-1944*. In it, detective Erik Lönnrot is faced with the task of solving three apparent murders that have taken place exactly one month apart at locations that form a geographical equilateral triangle. The overly rational Lönnrot, through elaborate reasoning, divines when and where the next murder is to take place. He goes there to prevent the murder and to capture the murderer, only to find himself captured, having been lured to the scene by his archenemy, Red Scharlach, so that he, Lönnrot, can be killed.

This story is a perfect example of Borges's ability to take a standard subgenre, in this case the detective story, and give it his own personal signature, as the story is replete with Borgesian trademarks. The most prominent of these concerns irony and hubris. Following the first murder and published reports of Lönnrot's line of investigation, Scharlach, who has sworn to kill Lönnrot, constructs the remainder of the murder scenario, knowing that Lönnrot will not rest until he deciphers the apparent patterns and then—believing he knows, by virtue of his reasoning, all there is to know—will blindly show up at the right spot at the right time for Scharlach to capture and kill him. Ironically, Lönnrot's intelligence and his reliance (or over-reliance) on reasoning, accompanied in no small measure by his self-assurance and intellectual vanity, which blind him to any potential danger, bring him to his death. Other trademark Borgesian elements in the story include the totally non-Latino content (from characters to setting), numerous references to Jews and things Jewish (a talmudic congress, rabbis, and Cabalistic studies, to name only a few), and an intellectual content and ambience throughout not typical of the traditional detective story. (Lönnrot figures out, for example, that the four points that indicate the four apparent murders—there are really only three—correspond to the Tetragrammaton, the four Hebrew letters that make up "the ineffable name of God.")

"The Garden of Forking Paths" • "The Garden of Forking Paths" is another story from *Ficciones, 1935-1944* which in the most general sense (but only in the most general sense) fits comfortably into a traditional category, that of spy thriller, but like "Death and the Compass," in Borges's hands it is anything but a story typical of its particular subgenre. In this story, Dr. Yu Tsun (once again, a non-Latino character), a Chinese professor of English, working in England (a non-Latino setting as well) as a spy for the Germans during World War I, has been captured and now dictates his story. Yu tells of how he had needed to transmit vital information to the Germans concerning the name of the town in which the British were massing artillery in preparation for an attack. Yu's superior, however, had been captured, thus severing Yu's normal lines of communication.

Identified as a spy and pursued by the British, Yu tells how he had selected, from the phone directory, the only man he believed could help him communicate his message, one Stephen Albert (though the reader at this point is not aware of exactly how Albert could be of help to Yu). Yu tells of how he traveled to Albert's house, hotly pursued by a British agent. Yu had never met Albert, but Albert mistook him for someone else and invited Yu into the house. The two talked for a hour about Chinese astrologer and writer Ts'ui Pêen (who happened to be one of Yu's ancestors) and Ts'ui's labyrinthine book *The Garden of Forking Paths* (which, given its content, gives Borges's story a story-within-a-story element) as Yu stalled for time for the British agent to catch up with him. Yu says that as the agent approached the house, Yu killed Albert and then allowed himself to be captured by the agent. The final paragraph of the story reveals that Yu had chosen to kill Albert and then be arrested so that news of the incident would appear in the newspaper. He knew that his German colleagues would read the small news item and would divine Yu's intended message: that the British had been massing artillery near the French town of Albert—thus Yu's reason for having chosen Stephen Albert.

"The Circular Ruins" • "Las ruinas circulares" ("The Circular Ruins") is one of a number of examples in *Ficciones, 1935-1944* of Borges's frequent practice of using a story to illustrate (or at least toy with) philosophical concepts, in this particular case, most notably, the Gnostic concept of one creator behind another creator. In this story, a mysterious man travels to an equally mysterious place with the intention of creating another person by dreaming him. The man experiences great difficulty in this at first, but eventually he is successful. The man instructs his creation and then sends him off. Before he does, however, the man erases his creation's knowledge of how he came to be, for the man does not wish him to know that he exists only as the dream of another. Soon after the man's creation has left, fire breaks out and surrounds the man. He prepares for death, but as the flames begin to engulf him, he cannot feel them. He realizes then that he, too, ironically, is but an illusion, not real at all but simply the dream of another.

"Pierre Menard, Author of the *Quixote*" • "*Pierre Menard, autor del Quijot*" ("*Pierre Menard, Author of the Quixote*"), also from *Ficciones, 1935-1944*, is one of Borges's most famous stories that may be classified as a fictionalized essay, for it is clearly not a story: a fiction, yes, but a story (at least by any traditional definition of the term), no. In it, a pompous first-person narrator, a literary critic, in what is presented as an essay of literary criticism, tells of the writer Pierre Menard (fictional in the real world but completely real in Borges's fictive universe). After considerable discussion of Menard's bibliography (complete with titles and publication dates, all fictional but with titles of real literary journals—once again, an example of Borges's practice of fusing the fictive and the real), as well as other facts about the author, the critic discusses Menard's attempt to compose a contemporary version of Cervantes' *Don Quixote de la Mancha*. Menard accomplishes this not by writing a new *Don Quixote de la Mancha* but simply by copying Cervantes' original text word for word. The critic even examines identical passages from the two versions and declares that Menard's version, though identical to Cervantes', is actually richer. The critic pursues the reasons and ramifications of this fact further. The result is, among other things, a tongue-in-cheek send-up of scholars and literary critics and the snobbish and often ridiculous criticism that they publish.

"The South" • Finally, "El Sur" ("The South"), from *Ficciones, 1935-1944* as well, is a classic Borges story that demonstrates the author's ability to mix reality (at best a relative term in Borges's world and in Latino "new narrative" as a whole) with fantasy and, more important, to show that the line between the two is not only very subtle but also of no real importance, for fantasy is just as much a part of the universe as so-called reality. This story, which Borges once said he considered his best, concerns Johannes Dahlmann, a librarian in Buenos Aires. Dahlmann, the reader is told, has several heroic, military ancestors, and though he himself is a city-dwelling intellectual, he prefers to identify himself with his more romantic ancestors. In that spirit, Dahlmann even maintains a family ranch in the "South" (capitalized here and roughly the Argentine equivalent, in history and image, to North America's "Old West"). He is, however, an absentee landowner, spending all of his time in Buenos Aires, keeping the ranch only to maintain a connection, although a chiefly symbolic one, with his family's more exciting past. Entering his apartment one night, Dahlmann accidentally runs into a doorway (an accident very similar to that which Borges suffered in 1938). The resulting head injury develops into septicemia (as was the case with Borges as well), and he is sent off to a sanatorium. Finally, he recovers well enough to travel, at his doctor's suggestion, to his ranch in the South to convalesce. His train trip to the South is vague to him at best, as he slips in and out of sleep. Unfamiliar with the region, he disembarks one stop too early and waits in a general store for transportation. While there, he is harassed by a group of ruffians. He accepts the challenge of one among them, and as the story ends, he is about to step outside for a knife fight he knows he cannot win.

If that were all there were to "The South," the story would be interesting, perhaps, but certainly nothing spectacular, and it would probably fit fairly comfortably into the type of Latino narrative popular before Borges. There is more, however, and it is this "more" that places the story firmly within the parameters of Latino "new narrative." The story is, in fact, the literary equivalent of an optical illusion. For those who can perceive only one angle, the story is essentially that described above. For those who can make out the other angle, however, the story is completely different. There are numerous subtle though undeniably present hints throughout the second half of the story, after Dahlmann supposedly leaves the sanatorium, that suggest that the protagonist does not step out to fight at the end of the story. In fact, he never even leaves the sanatorium at all but instead dies there. His trip to the South, his encounter with the ruffians, and his acceptance of their challenge, which will lead to certain death, are all nothing but a dream, dreamt, it seems, in the sanatorium, for death in a knife fight is the death that he, Dahlmann—the librarian who likes to identify himself with his heroic and romantic ancestors—would have preferred compared to that of the sanatorium. This added dimension as well as the rather subtle manner in which it is suggested (an attentive reader is required) separates both the story and its author from the type of fiction and fiction writer that characterized Latino fiction before Borges. It is this type of added dimension that makes Borges's fiction "new" and makes him a truly fascinating writer to read.

Borges continued to write short fiction after *Ficciones, 1935-1944* and *El Aleph*, but the stories produced during this period never approached the popularity among readers nor the acclaim among critics associated with the two earlier collections. This is attributable in part to the fact that most of the stories the Argentine writer published in the 1960's, as well as the 1970's and 1980's, lack much of what makes Borges Borges. Most are decidedly more realistic, often more Argentine in focus, and in general less complex—all in all, less Borgesian and, according to critics, less impressive. Some of this, particularly the change in complexity, has been explained as attributable to the fact that because of his loss of sight, Borges turned to dictation, which made reediting and polishing more difficult. Regardless of the reason, most of Borges's fiction after his two landmark collections of the 1940's has been largely ignored.

Keith H. Brower

Other major works

NOVEL: *Un modelo para la muerte*, 1946 (with Adolfo Bioy Casares, under joint pseudonym B. Suárez Lynch).

SCREENPLAYS: *"Los orilleros" y "El paraíso de los creyentes,"* 1955 (with Bioy Casares); *Les Autres*, 1974 (with Bioy Casares and Hugo Santiago).

POETRY: *Fervor de Buenos Aires*, 1923, 1969; *Luna de enfrente*, 1925; *Cuaderno San Martín*, 1929; *Poemas, 1923-1943*, 1943; *Poemas, 1923-1953*, 1954; *Obra poética, 1923-1958*, 1958; *Obra poética, 1923-1964*, 1964; *Seis poemas escandinavos*, 1966; *Siete poemas*, 1967; *El otro, el mismo*, 1969; *Elogio de la sombra*, 1969 (*In Praise of Darkness*, 1974); *El oro de los tigres*, 1972 (translated in *The Gold of Tigers: Selected Later Poems*, 1977); *La rosa profunda*, 1975 (translated in *The Gold of Tigers*); *La moneda de hierro*, 1976; *Historia de la noche*, 1977; *La cifra*, 1981; *Los conjurados*, 1985; *Selected Poems*, 1999.

NONFICTION: *Inquisiciones*, 1925; *El tamaño de mi esperanza*, 1926; *El idioma de los argentinos*, 1928; *Evaristo Carriego*, 1930 (English translation, 1984); *Figari*, 1930; *Discusión*, 1932; *Las Kennigar*, 1933; *Historia de la eternidad*, 1936; *Nueva refutación del tiempo*, 1947; *Aspectos de la literatura gauchesca*, 1950; *Antiguas literaturas germánicas*, 1951 (with Delia Ingenieros; revised as *Literaturas germánicas medievales*, 1966, with Maria Esther Vásquez); *Otras Inquisiciones*, 1952 (*Other Inquisitions*, 1964); *El "Martin Fierro,"* 1953 (with Margarita Guerrero); *Leopoldo Lugones*, 1955 (with Betina Edelberg); *Manual de zoología fantástica*, 1957 (with Guerrero; *The Imaginary Zoo*, 1969; revised as *El libro de los seres imaginarios*, 1967, *The Book of Imaginary Beings*, 1969); *La poesía gauchesca*, 1960; *Introducción a la literatura norteamericana*, 1967 (with Esther Zemborain de Torres; *An Introduction to American Literature*, 1971); *Prólogos*, 1975; *Cosmogonías*, 1976; *Libro de sueños*, 1976; *Qué es el budismo?*, 1976 (with Alicia Jurado); Siete noches, 1980 (*Seven Nights*, 1984); *Nueve ensayos dantescos*, 1982; *The Total Library: Non-fiction, 1922-1986*, 2001 (Eliot Weinberger, editor); *This Craft of Verse*, 2000.

MISCELLANEOUS: *Obras completas*, 1953-1967 (10 volumes); *Antología personal*, 1961 (*A Personal Anthology*, 1967); *Labyrinths: Selected Stories, and Other Writings*, 1962, 1964;

Nueva antología personal, 1968; *Selected Poems, 1923-1967,* 1972 (also includes prose); *Adrogue,* 1977; *Obras completas en colaboración,* 1979 (with others); *Borges: A Reader,* 1981; *Atlas,* 1984 (with María Kodama; English translation, 1985).

TRANSLATIONS: *Orlando,* 1937 (of Virginia Woolf's novel); *La metamórfosis,* 1938 (of Franz Kafka's novel *Die Verwandlung*); *Un bárbaro en Asia,* 1941 (of Henri Michaux's travel notes); *Bartleby, el escribiente,* 1943 (of Herman Melville's novella *Bartleby the Scrivener*); *Los mejores cuentos policiales,* 1943 (with Bioy Casares; of detective stories by various authors); *Los mejores cuentos policiales, segunda serie,* 1951 (with Bioy Casares; of detective stories by various authors); *Cuentos breves y extraordinarios,* 1955, 1973 (with Bioy Casares; of short stories by various authors; *Extraordinary Tales,* 1973); *Las palmeras salvajes,* 1956 (of William Faulkner's novel *The Wild Palms*); *Hojas de hierba,* 1969 (of Walt Whitman's *Leaves of Grass*).

ANTHOLOGIES: *Antología clásica de la literatura argentina,* 1937; *Antología de la literatura fantástica,* 1940 (with Adolfo Bioy Casares and Silvia Ocampo); *Antología poética argentina,* 1941 (with Bioy Casares and Ocampo); *El compadrito: Su destino, sus barrios, su música,* 1945, 1968 (with Silvina Bullrich); *Poesía gauchesca,* 1955 (with Bioy Casares; 2 volumes); *Libro del cielo y del infierno,* 1960, 1975 (with Bioy Casares); *Versos,* 1972 (by Evaristo Carriego); *Antología poética,* 1982 (by Leopoldo Lugones); *Antología poética,* 1982 (by Franciso de Quevedo); *El amigo de la muerte,* 1984 (by Pedro Antonio de Alarcón).

Bibliography

Aizenberg, Edna, ed. *Borges and His Successors.* Columbia: University of Missouri Press, 1990. Collection of essays by various critics on Borges's relationship to such writers as Italo Calvino and Umberto Eco, his influence on such writers as Peter Carey and Salvador Elizondo, and his similarity to such thinkers as Michel Foucault, Paul de Man, and Jacques Derrida.

Bell-Villada, Gene H. *Borges and His Fiction: A Guide to His Mind and Art.* Chapel Hill: University of North Carolina Press, 1981. Excellent introduction to Borges and his works for North American readers. In lengthy sections entitled "Borges's Worlds," "Borges's Fiction," and "Borges's Place in Literature," Bell-Villada provides detailed and very readable commentary concerning Borges's background, his many stories, and his career, all the while downplaying the Argentine writer's role as a philosopher and intellectual and emphasizing his role as a storyteller. A superb study.

McMurray, George R. *Jorge Luis Borges.* New York: Frederick Ungar, 1980. Intended by the author as "an attempt to decipher the formal and thematic aspects of a synthetic universe that rivals reality in its almost overwhelming complexity," namely Borges's universe. A very good and well-organized study of Borges's dominant themes and narrative devices, with many specific references to the Argentine author's stories. Includes an informative introduction on Borges's life and a conclusion that coherently brings together the diverse elements discussed in the book.

May, Charles E., ed. *Masterplots II: Short Story Series, Revised Edition.* 8 vols. Pasadena, Calif.: Salem Press, 2004. Designed for student use, this reference set contains articles providing detailed plot summaries and analyses of these thirteen short stories by Borges: "The Aleph" (vol. 1); "The Circular Ruins" (vol. 2); "Funes, the Memorious," "The Garden of Forking Paths," and "The Gospel According to Mark" (vol. 3); "The Library of Babel" (vol. 4); "The Lottery in Babylon" (vol. 5); "Pierre Menard, Author of the *Quixote*," "The Secret Miracle," and "The Shape of the Sword" (vol. 6); and "The South," "Theme of the Traitor and the Hero," and "Tlön, Uqbar, Orbis Tertius" (vol. 7).

Nuñez-Faraco, Humberto. "In Search of *The Aleph*: Memory, Truth, and Falsehood in Borges's Poetics." *The Modern Language Review* 92 (July, 1997): 613-629. Discusses autobiographical allusions, literary references to Dante, and cultural reality in the story "El Aleph." Argues that Borges's story uses cunning and deception to bring about its psychological and intellectual effect.

Rodríguez Monegal, Emir. *Jorge Luis Borges: A Literary Biography.* New York: E. P. Dutton, 1978. This nearly definitive biography of Borges was written by one of the Argentine writer's (and contemporary Latin American literature's) most prominent critics. Particularly interesting for its constant blending of facts about Borges's life and literary text by him concerning or related to the events or personalities discussed. Detailed, lengthy, and highly informative. Very useful for anyone seeking a better understanding of Borges the writer.

Soud, Stephen E. "Borges the Golem-Maker: Intimations of 'Presence' in 'The Circular Ruins.'" *MLN* 110 (September, 1995): 739-754. Argues that Borges uses the legend of the golem to establish authorial presence in the story. Argues that Borges did not seek to deconstruct literature but to re-sacralize it and to salvage the power of the logos, the Divine Word.

Stabb, Martin S. *Borges Revisited.* Boston: Twayne, 1991. Update of Stabb's *Jorge Luis Borges*, published in 1970. Though Borges's early works, including those from the 1940's and 1950's, are discussed and analyzed here, emphasis is on Borges's post-1970 writings, how the "canonical" (to use Stabb's term) Borges compares to the later Borges, and "a fresh assessment of the Argentine master's position as a major Western literary presence." An excellent study, particularly used in tandem with Stabb's earlier book on Borges.

Williamson, Edwin. *Borges: A Life.* New York: Viking Press, 2004. Drawing on interviews and extensive research, the most comprehensive and well-reviewed Borges biography.

Wreen, Michael J. "Don Quixote Rides Again." *Romanic Review* 86 (January, 1995): 141-163. Argues that Pierre Menard is not the new Cervantes in Borges's story "Pierre Menard, Author of the Quixote," but rather the new Quixote. Asserts that in the story Borges pokes fun at himself and that a proper interpretation of the story requires readers to understand that Menard's Quixote is simply Cervantes' Quixote, although Menard thinks it is a new and important work.

Zubizarreta, Armando F. "'Borges and I,' a Narrative Sleight of Hand." *Studies in 20th Century Literature* 22 (Summer, 1998): 371-381. Argues that the two characters in the sketch are involved in the implementation of vengeance. Argues that the character Borges, driven by a compulsive pattern of stealing, unsuspectingly takes over the "I" character's grievances against him through his own writing.

Elizabeth Bowen

Born: Dublin, Ireland; June 7, 1899
Died: London, England; February 22, 1973

Principal short fiction • *Encounters*, 1923; *Ann Lee's, and Other Stories*, 1926; *Joining Charles*, 1929; *The Cat Jumps, and Other Stories*, 1934; *Look at All Those Roses*, 1941; *The Demon Lover*, 1945 (pb. in U.S. as *Ivy Gripped the Steps, and Other Stories*, 1946); *The Early Stories*, 1951; *Stories by Elizabeth Bowen*, 1959; *A Day in the Dark, and Other Stories*, 1965; *Elizabeth Bowen's Irish Stories*, 1978; *The Collected Stories of Elizabeth Bowen*, 1980.

Other literary forms • Elizabeth Bowen is as well known for her ten novels as she is for her short-story collections. She also wrote books of history, travel, literary essays, personal impressions, a play, and a children's book.

Achievements • Elizabeth Bowen's career is distinguished by achievements on two separate, though related, fronts. On the one hand, she was among the best-known and accomplished British women novelists of her generation, a generation which, in the period between the wars, did much to consolidate the distinctive existence of women's fiction. Bowen's work in this area is noteworthy for its psychological acuity, sense of atmosphere, and impassioned fastidiousness of style.

As an Anglo-Irish writer, on the other hand, she maintained more self-consciously than most of her predecessors an understanding of her class's destiny. Themes that are prevalent throughout her work—loss of innocence, decline of fortune, impoverishment of the will—gain an additional haunting quality from her sensitivity to the Irish context. Her awareness of the apparent historical irrelevance of the Anglo-Irish also gives her short stories in particular an important cultural resonance.

Biography • Elizabeth Dorothea Cole Bowen received her formal education at Downe House in Kent and at the London County Council School of Art. In 1923 she married Alan Charles Cameron and lived with him in Northampton and Old Headington, Oxford. In 1935 she and her husband moved to Regent's Park, London, where Bowen became a member of the Bloomsbury group. During World War II she stayed in London, where she worked for the Ministry of Information and as an air-raid warden. In 1948 she was made a Commander of the British Empire. She was awarded an honorary Doctor of Letters by Trinity College, Dublin, in 1949. After the death of her husband in 1952, Bowen returned to live at Bowen's Court in Ireland, her family estate. In 1957 she was awarded an honorary Doctor of Letters by the University of Oxford. In 1960 she sold Bowen's Court and returned to Old Headington, Oxford. After a final trip to Ireland, Elizabeth Bowen died in London on February 22, 1973.

Analysis • Elizabeth Bowen's stories are set in the first half of the twentieth century in England and Ireland. Often the action takes place against a background of war. Taken together, her stories provide a chronicle of the social, political, and psychic life of England from the beginning of the century through World War II. Her characters are mainly drawn from the middle class, although upper- and lower-class characters appear as well. Although Bowen's protagonist is usually a woman, men also play important roles. By selecting significant detail and by utilizing mythic parallels, Bowen constructs stories whose settings, actions, and characters are simultaneously realistic and symbolic.

Bowen's characters exist in a world which has lost contact with meaning; traditional forms and ideas have lost meaning and vitality. Both identity and a sense of belonging are lost; "Who am I?" and "Where am I?" are typical questions asked by Bowen protagonists. Some characters merely go through the motions and rituals of daily life, experiencing pattern without meaning. Others have a vague consciousness that something is wrong; unfulfilled, they suffer from boredom, apathy, and confusion. Sometimes, such characters are driven to seek alternatives in their lives.

"Summer Night" • In "Summer Night," while the Major, an example of the first type of character, goes about his evening routine, shutting up the house for the night, his wife, Emma, pretending to visit friends, leaves her traditional family for an assignation with Robinson, a man she hardly knows. He represents another type: the man who adapts to meaninglessness by utilizing power amorally to manipulate and control. Emma is disillusioned in her search for vitality and love when she discovers that Robinson wants sex and nothing else. Other characters, such as Justin, are fully conscious of the situation; they know that they "don't live" and conceive the need for a "new form" but are impotent to break through to achieve one.

Although Bowen's stories focus on those characters who seek meaning or who are in the process of breaking through, they also represent a final type—one whose thinking and feeling are unified and in harmony with existence. An example from

"Summer Night" is Justin's deaf sister, Queenie. While Robinson is left alone in his house, while Emma leans drunk and crying against a telegraph pole, and while Justin goes to mail an angry letter to Robinson, Queenie lies in bed remembering a time when she sat with a young man beside the lake below the ruin of the castle now on Robinson's land: "While her hand brushed the ferns in the cracks of the stone seat emanations of kindness passed from him to her. The subtle deaf girl had made the transposition of this nothing or everything into an everything." Queenie imagines: "Tonight it was Robinson who, guided by Queenie down leaf tunnels, took the place on the stone seat by the lake." It is Queenie's memory and imagination that creates, at least for

Library of Congress

herself, a world of love, unrealized, but realizable, by the others. Memory recalls the lost estate of human beings, represented here by the castle, its grounds, and its garden, as well as man's lost identity. Queenie *is* a queen. All human beings are rightfully queens and kings in Bowen's fiction. Queenie's memory reaches back to the archetypal roots of being, in harmony with life; her imagination projects this condition in the here and now and as a possibility for the future. Queenie's thinking is the true thinking Justin calls for, thinking that breaks through to a "new form," which is composed of archetypal truth transformed to suit the conditions of modern life. Throughout Bowen's fiction this kind of thought takes the form of fantasy, hallucination, and dream. Bowen's fiction itself, the expression of *her* imagination, also exemplifies this thinking.

"Her Table Spread" • Toward the end of "Summer Night" it occurs to Justin that possibly Emma should have come to him rather than Robinson. In "Her Table Spread" Bowen brings together two characters much like Emma and Justin. Valeria Cuff, heir and owner of a castle in Ireland, situated on an estuary where English ships are allowed to anchor, invites Mr. Alban, a cynical and disillusioned young man from London, to a dinner party. These characters represent opposites which concern Bowen throughout her fiction: male and female, darkness and light, thought and feeling, physical and spiritual, rational and irrational. The separation or conflict of these opposites creates a world of war; their unification creates a world of love.

Valeria's orientation is romantic, "irrational," and optimistic: "Her mind was made up: she was a princess." She invites Alban to her castle, "excited" at the thought of marrying him. Alban is realistic, rational, and pessimistic: "He had failed to love. . . . He knew some spring had dried up at the root of the world." Alban is disconcerted by Valeria's erratic, impulsive behavior and by her apparent vulgarity. He has heard "she was abnormal—at twenty-five, of statuesque development, still detained in childhood." Ironically, as Alban realizes "his presence must constitute an occasion," he is "put out of" Valeria's mind when a destroyer anchors in the estuary. Valeria believes it is the same destroyer that had anchored there the previous spring at Easter when two officers, Mr. Graves and Mr. Garrett, came ashore and were entertained by friends. Valeria's expectation that the officers will come to dinner initially separates her from Alban. When the officers fail to arrive, she runs outside to signal them with a lantern. Old Mr. Rossiter, uncle to Mrs. Treye, Valeria's aunt, leads Alban to the boathouse to prevent Valeria from rowing out to the destroyer. When a bat flies against Alban's ear, he flees, and, ascending the steps back toward the castle, he hears Valeria sobbing in the dark. When he calls to her, expressing concern and sympathy, she mistakes him for Mr. Garrett. Her fantasy of love is realized as she and Alban stand together, unified in a field of light shining from the castle.

Symbolic details and analogies with pagan and Christian myth universalize the meaning of the story. Alban is associated with the destroyer, with Graves and Garrett, and with their emblems, statues of Mars and Mercury. Like the destroyer, Alban is "fixed in the dark rain, by an indifferent shore." The officers represent aspects of Alban. The name Graves suggests death; and the statue associated with Graves is Mars, god of war. Garrett is a pun on *garret*, which derives from a word meaning to defend or protect. Garrett's statue is Mercury, a god associated by the Romans with peace. Alban's link with the destroyer, with death and war, threatens the destruction of Valeria's dreams of love and peace. The Garrett aspect of Alban, however, linked with protection and peace, offers the possibility of the realization of Valeria's dreams.

Valeria is associated with two symbolic items. Among the gifts she has to offer is a leopard skin, suggesting the animal and the sensual, and a statue of Venus, goddess of love. Valeria thus offers love in both its physical and spiritual aspects. Contained in her fantasies is the expectation that love will put an end to war. She thinks: "Invasions from the water would henceforth be social, perhaps amorous," and she imagines marrying Garrett and inviting "all the Navy up the estuary" for tea: "The Navy would be unable to tear itself away." As Valeria attempts to signal the destroyer with the lantern, she thinks that Graves and Garrett will have to fight for her; instead, the battle takes place within Alban.

The pagan symbolism in "Her Table Spread" is overlain and transformed by Christian symbolism. Valeria's castle and its grounds, like the ruins of the castle in "Summer Night," represent a lost Eden. Valeria *is* an heir and a princess; she is an incarnation of Eve seeking her rightful role and place in a paradise of love and peace. Symbolically, she calls to Adam (Alban) to reclaim *his* inheritance—to join her in re-creating the garden. The way is expressed in Bowen's use of the second major Christian myth. Alban must undergo the experience of Christ, the second Adam, to redeem his "fallen" self; he must reject temptation and undergo crucifixion—sacrifice his ego. The trip to the boathouse is Alban's descent into hell. There he is tempted by Old Mr. Rossiter, the Devil. Rossiter offers Alban whiskey, which he refuses, and tempts him with Valeria: "She's a girl you could shape. She's got a nice income." Alban's rejection of this temptation, his refusal to *listen* to the Devil, is signified by his flight from the boathouse when a bat flies against his ear.

As Alban ascends the steps, he recognizes where he is: "Hell." This recognition is the precondition for discovering where he belongs. At this point he undergoes a symbolic crucifixion. Hearing Valeria "sobbing" in "absolute desperation," Alban clings "to a creaking tree." The sympathy Alban feels for Valeria signifies the death of Graves within him and the resurrection of Garrett. Valeria has also experienced crucifixion. Graves and Garrett have not arrived, and her lantern has gone out; she, too, is in hell. Humbled and in darkness, the two meet. Alban speaks with tenderness: "Quietly, my dear girl." Valeria speaks with concern. "Don't you remember the way?" The year before the destroyer had anchored "at Easter." Now Valeria is present at and participates in resurrection: "*Mr. Garrett has landed.*" She laughs "like a princess, and magnificently justified." Standing with Valeria in the glow of light from the castle, observed by the two female guests, Alban experiences love: "Such a strong tenderness reached him that, standing there in full manhood, he was for a moment not exiled. For the moment, without moving or speaking, he stood, in the dark, in a flame, as though all three said: 'My darling.'"

"The Demon Lover" • A world of love is achieved, if only momentarily, in "Her Table Spread." In "The Demon Lover" Bowen creates a story of love denied or repressed, and its power transformed into the demonic. The stories complement each other. The first takes place at a castle in Ireland in the spring and recalls the previous Easter; the second is set in an abandoned London flat in autumn during the bombing of London in World War II and recalls a previous autumn during World War I. The action of "Her Table Spread" concludes with the coming of night. The protagonists of the first story are a young woman in search of love and a young man associated with war; those of the second are a forty-year-old married woman who has denied love and her fiancé of twenty years before, a solider lost in action during World War I. Both female characters are "abnormal": Valeria of "Her Table Spread" caught up in fantasy, Kathleen of "The Demon Lover" subject to hallucination. Bowen utilizes elements of the Eden myth to universalize the meaning of both stories.

In "The Demon Lover" Mrs. Kathleen Drover returns to her abandoned London flat to pick up some things she had left behind when her family moved to the country to escape the bombing. In the dark flat where everything is covered with a dustlike film, she opens a door, and reflected light reveals an unstamped letter recently placed on a hall table. Since the caretaker is away and the house has been locked, there is no logical explanation for the appearance of the letter. Unnerved, Mrs. Drover takes it upstairs to her bedroom, where she reads it. The letter reminds her that today is the anniversary of the day years before when she made a promise of fidelity to a young soldier on leave from France during World War I—and that they had agreed to meet on this day "at an hour arranged." Although her "fiancé was reported missing, presumed killed," he has apparently survived and awaits the meeting. When Kathleen hears the church clock strike six, she becomes terrified but maintains enough control to gather the items she came for and to formulate a plan to leave the house, hire a taxi, and bring the driver back with her to pick up the bundles. Meanwhile, in the basement "a door or window was being opened by someone who chose this moment to leave the house."

This statement provides a realistic solution to the problem of the letter's appearance, but a psychological interpretation offers an alternative conclusion. The London flat symbolizes Kathleen's life as Mrs. Drover, and the shock of finding the letter reveals to Kathleen the meaninglessness of this life and the falseness of her identity as Mrs. Drover. By marrying Drover, Kathleen has been "unfaithful" not only to the soldier but also to herself. It is this self which emerges as a result of the "crisis"—actually the crisis of World War II—and which has unconsciously motivated Mrs. Drover's return to the house. The fact that the letter is signed K., Kathleen's initial, suggests that she wrote the letter, which is a sign of the reemergence of her lost self. The house represents not only Kathleen's life as Mrs. Drover but also the repressed-Kathleen aspect of her identity. The person in the basement who leaves the house at the same moment Mrs. Drover lets herself out the front door is a projection of this repressed self, the self Mrs. Drover now unknowingly goes to face.

Overlying the psychological meaning of the story are two additional levels of meaning, one allegorical, the other archetypal. The young Kathleen represents England, defended and protected by the soldier, who represents the generation of those who fought for the country during the first war. Kathleen's loveless and meaningless marriage to Drover represents England's betrayal of the values the war was fought to defend—a betrayal which has contributed to the creation of World War II. The letter writer asserts: "In view of the fact that nothing has changed, I shall rely upon you to keep your promise." Because Kathleen and England have betrayed themselves, because love has failed, war continues, and both the individual and the country must suffer destructive consequences.

On the archetypal level, Kathleen and the soldier are incarnations of Eve and Adam, although the soldier is an Adam transformed by war into a devil who coerces Eve to "fall," forces her to make the "sinister truth." The soldier's uniform is the sign of his transformation. His true nature, his Adamic self, is covered and denied by the clothes of war. Kathleen is unable to touch the true self of the soldier, and he is unable to reach out to her. The scene takes place at night in a garden beneath a tree. Intimidated by not being kissed, Kathleen imagines "spectral glitters in the place" of the soldier's eyes. To "verify his presence," she puts out a hand, which he takes and presses "painfully, onto one of the breast buttons of his uniform." In this way he forces her to make a vow of fidelity—a pact with the Devil. He says, "I shall be with you . . . sooner or later. You won't forget that. You need do nothing but wait." Kathleen suffers the fate of Eve, feels that unnatural promise drive down between her and the rest of all humankind. When the soldier, her "fiancé," is reported "missing, presumed killed," she experiences "a complete dislocation from everything."

Compelled now to confront her fate, she gets into a taxi, which seems to be awaiting her. When the driver turns in the direction of her house without being told where to drive, Kathleen leans "forward to scratch at the glass panel that divided the driver's head from her own . . . driver and passenger, not six inches between them, remained for an eternity eye to eye." Reunited with her demon lover, Kathleen screams "freely" as the taxi accelerates "without mercy" into the "hinterland of deserted streets." The failure of love condemns Kathleen—and by implication humankind—to insanity and damnation in the modern wasteland.

In spite of the pessimistic conclusion of "The Demon Lover," Bowen's short fiction is ultimately affirmative. In a 1970 *McCall's* essay she lamented that many people, especially the young, are "adrift, psychologically . . . homeless, lost in a void." She expresses her desire to "do something that would arrest the drift, fill up the vacuum, convey the sense that there is, after all, SOMETHING. . . . (For I know that there is.)" Bowen's fiction conveys the existence of this something, which some would call God, others simply the source of being. Whatever it is called, it exists within each individual and in the natural world. Its primary nature is love, expressed in acts of kindness, sympathy, understanding, and tolerance. It is the potential for unity among people and harmony with the world. This potential is mirrored in the unity and harmony of Bowen's stories. The lyric descriptive passages, the coherence of matter and form, the intense visual images, and the emotional force of her stories demonstrate Bowen's mastery of the short-story form. Her stories deserve to be recognized as among the best written in the twentieth century.

James L. Green
With updates by George O'Brien

Other major works

CHILDREN'S LITERATURE: *The Good Tiger,* 1965.

PLAY: *Castle Anna,* pr. 1948 (with John Perry).

NOVELS: *The Hotel,* 1927; *The Last September,* 1929; *Friends and Relations,* 1931; *To the North,* 1932; *The House in Paris,* 1935; *The Death of the Heart,* 1938; *The Heat of the Day,* 1949; *A World of Love,* 1955; *The Little Girls,* 1964; *Eva Trout,* 1968.

NONFICTION: *Bowen's Court,* 1942; *Seven Winters,* 1942; *English Novelists,* 1946; *Collected Impressions,* 1950; *The Shelbourne: A Center of Dublin Life for More than a Century,* 1951; *A Time in Rome,* 1960; *Afterthought: Pieces About Writing,* 1962; *Pictures and Conversations,* 1975; *The Mulberry Tree: Writings of Elizabeth Bowen,* 1986.

Bibliography

Austin, Allan E. *Elizabeth Bowen.* Rev. ed. New York: Twayne, 1989. Austin contends Bowen's better stories investigate psychological states that are more unusual than those in her novels. He calls "The Demon Lover" a ghost story that builds up and culminates like an Alfred Hitchcock movie.

Bloom, Harold, ed. *Elizabeth Bowen: Modern Critical Views*. New York: Chelsea House, 1987. Collection of eleven essays, surveying the range of Bowen criticism. Excerpts from the main book-length critical works on Bowen are included. The volume also contains some comparatively inaccessible articles on Bowen's short fiction, and essays on her work by the poets Mona Van Duyn and Alfred Corn. Supplemented by an extensive bibliography.

Craig, Patricia. *Elizabeth Bowen*. Harmondsworth, Middlesex, England: Penguin Books, 1986. Short biographical study. Indebted to Victoria Glendinning's work, though drawing on later research, particularly on Bowen's Irish connections. The work also contains perceptive readings of Bowen's stories and novels. Includes a useful chronology.

Hoogland, Renée C. *Elizabeth Bowen: A Reputation in Writing*. New York: New York University Press, 1994. Another good source. From the series The Cutting Edge: Lesbian Life and Literature.

Jarrett, Mary. "Ambiguous Ghosts: The Short Stories of Elizabeth Bowen." *Journal of the Short Story in English*, no. 8 (Spring, 1987): 71-79. A discussion of the themes of alienation, imprisonment, loss of identity, and the conflict of fiction and reality in Bowen's stories, focusing primarily on the so-called ghost stories.

Lassner, Phyllis. *Elizabeth Bowen: A Study of the Short Fiction*. New York: Twayne, 1991. Introduction to Bowen's short fiction focusing on its unique characteristics. Deals with the basic conflicts in the stories between the present and the past, often embodied in female ghosts and ancestral homes. Interprets many of her stories in terms of women's struggle with a patriarchal society that stands in the way of their pursuit of a creative life. Includes essays on short fiction by Bowen and discussions of her stories by William Trevor and Eudora Welty.

May, Charles E., ed. *Masterplots II: Short Story Series, Revised Edition*. 8 vols. Pasadena, Calif.: Salem Press, 2004. Designed for student use, this reference set contains articles providing detailed plot summaries and analyses of these eight short stories by Bowen: "The Demon Lover" (vol. 2); "The Happy Autumn Fields" and "Her Table Spread" (vol. 3); "Ivy Gripped the Steps" (vol. 4); "Mysterious Kôr" (vol. 5); "A Queer Heart" (vol. 6); and "Summer Night" and "Tears, Idle Tears" (vol. 7).

Partridge, A. C. "Language and Identity in the Shorter Fiction of Elizabeth Bowen." In *Irish Writers and Society at Large*, edited by Masaru Sekine. Totowa, N.J.: Barnes & Noble Books, 1985. Overview of Bowen's short stories that focuses on her impressionism, her economy, and her Jamesian approach to narrative. Illustrates that style is Bowen's overriding preoccupation.

Rubens, Robert. "Elizabeth Bowen: A Woman of Wisdom." *Contemporary Review* 268 (June, 1996): 304-307. Examines the complex style of Bowen's work as a reflection of her personality and background; discusses her romanticism and her rejection of the dehumanization of the twentieth century.

Walshe, Eibhear, ed. *Elizabeth Bowen Remembered*. Dublin: Four Courts Press, 1998. Brief biography that includes helpful bibliographical references.

Kay Boyle

Born: St. Paul, Minnesota; February 19, 1902
Died: Mill Valley, California; December 27, 1992

Principal short fiction • *Short Stories*, 1929; *Wedding Day, and Other Stories*, 1930; *The First Lover, and Other Stories*, 1933; *The White Horses of Vienna, and Other Stories*, 1936; *The Crazy Hunter, and Other Stories*, 1940; *Thirty Stories*, 1946; *The Smoking Mountain: Stories of Postwar Germany*, 1951; *Nothing Ever Breaks Except the Heart*, 1966; *Fifty Stories*, 1980; *Life Being the Best, and Other Stories*, 1988.

Other literary forms • In addition to her short stories, Kay Boyle published several novels, volumes of poetry, children's books, essay collections, and a book of memoirs. *Breaking the Silence: Why a Mother Tells Her Son About the Nazi Era* (1962) is her personal account, written for adolescents, of Europe during the Nazi regime. Boyle also ghostwrote, translated, and edited many other books. Hundreds of her stories, poems, and articles have appeared in periodicals ranging from the "little magazines" published in Paris in the 1920's to *The Saturday Evening Post* and *The New Yorker*, for which she was a correspondent from 1946 to 1953.

Achievements • Both prolific and versatile, Kay Boyle has been respected during her long career for her exquisite technical style and her ardent political activism. She was very much a part of the expatriate group of writers living in Paris in the 1920's, and her work appeared in the avant-garde magazines alongside that of James Joyce, Gertrude Stein, Ernest Hemingway, and others. Her work is in many ways typical of the period, stylistically terse, carefully crafted, displaying keen psychological insight through the use of stream of consciousness and complex interior monologues. That her work was highly regarded is evidenced by her many awards: two John Simon Guggenheim Memorial Foundation Fellowships; O. Henry Awards in both 1935 and 1961; an honorary doctorate from Columbia College, Chicago; and membership in the National Institute of Arts and Letters. She taught at San Francisco State University and Eastern Washington University.

Biography • Born into an affluent family in St. Paul, Minnesota, in 1902, Kay Boyle moved and traveled frequently and extensively with her family during her childhood. After studying architecture for two years in Cincinnati, Boyle married Robert Brault, whose family never accepted her or the marriage. What was to have been a summer trip to France in 1923 became an eighteen-year expatriation, during which Boyle continued to write poetry and fiction. Boyle left her husband to live with editor Ernest Walsh until his death from tuberculosis in 1926. Boyle later returned to Brault with Walsh's child. They divorced in 1932, when she married Laurence Vail, a fellow American expatriate. After her marriage to Vail also ended in divorce, Boyle married Joseph von Franckenstein, an Austrian baron who had been forced out of his homeland during the Nazi invasion. She lived much of the time in Europe and was a correspondent for *The New Yorker*. She returned to the United States in 1953; Franckenstein died in 1963. Boyle taught at San Francisco State University from 1963 to 1979 and

at Eastern Washington University in 1982. Her arrest and imprisonment following an anti-Vietnam War demonstration is the basis of her novel *The Underground Woman* (1975). She would remain actively involved in movements protesting social injustices and violations of human rights.

Analysis • In a 1963 article Kay Boyle defines what she saw as the role of the serious writer: to be "the spokesman for those who remain inarticulate . . . an aeolian harp whose sensitive strings respond to the whispers of the concerned people of his time." The short-story writer, she believed, is "a moralist in the highest sense of the word"; the role of the short-story writer has always been "to speak briefly and clearly of the dignity and integrity of [the] individual." Perhaps it is through this definition that the reader may distinguish the central threads that run through the variegated fabric of Boyle's fiction and bind it into a single piece.

During the 1920's, when the young expatriate artists she knew in Paris were struggling to cast off the yokes of literary convention, Boyle championed the bold and experimental in language, and her own early stories are intensely individual explorations of private experiences. Yet when the pressures of the social world came to bear so heavily on private lives in the twentieth century that they could not be ignored, Boyle began to expand the scope of her vision and vibrate to the note of the *new* times to affirm on a broader scale the same basic values—the "dignity and integrity" of the individual. Beginning in the 1930's, her subject matter encompassed the rise of Nazism, the French resistance, the Allied occupation of postwar Germany, and the civil rights and anti-Vietnam War movements in the United States, yet she never lost sight of the individual dramas acted out against these panoramic backdrops.

In the same article Boyle also quotes Albert Camus's statement that "a man's work is nothing but a long journey to recover through the detours of art, the two or three simple and great images which first gained access to his heart." In Boyle's journey of more than fifty years, a few central themes remained constant: a belief in the absolute essentiality of love to human well-being—whether on a personal or a global level; an awareness of the many obstacles to its attainment; and a tragic sense of loss when it fails and the gulfs between human beings stand unbridged.

"Wedding Day" • "Wedding Day," the title story of her first widely circulated volume of short stories, published in 1930, is typical of her early works. It is an intense exploration of a unique private experience written in an experimental style. The action is primarily psychological, and outward events are described as they reflect states of consciousness. Yet it is representative of Boyle's best work for decades to come, both in its central concern with the failure of love and in its bold use of language.

"The red carpet that was to spurt like a hemorrhage from pillar to post was stacked in the corner," the story begins. From the first sentence the reader senses that things are out of joint. The wedding cake is ignored as it is carried into the pantry "with its beard lying white as hoarfrost on its bosom." "This was the last lunch," Boyle writes, and the brother and sister "came in with their buttonholes drooping with violets and sat sadly down, sat down to eat." To the funereal atmosphere of this wedding day, Boyle injects tension and bitterness. The son and mother argue as to whether the daughter will be given the family's prized copper saucepans, and he mocks the decorum his mother cherishes when he commands her not to cry, pointing his finger directly at her nose "so that when she looked at him with dignity her eyes wavered and crossed" and "she sat looking proudly at him, erect as a needle staring through its one open eye." As the mother and son bicker over who wanted the wedding in the first place, the bride-to-be is conspicuously silent. Finally, as the son snatches away each slice of roast beef his mother carves until she whimpers her fear of getting none herself, he and his sister burst into laughter. He tosses his napkin over the chandelier, and she follows him out of the room, leaving their mother alone "praying that this occasion at least pass off with dignity, with her heart not in her mouth but beating away in peace in its own bosom."

With the tension between children and mother clearly delineated and the exclusive camaraderie between brother and sister suggested, Boyle shifts both mood and scene and describes in almost incantatory prose the pair's idyllic jaunt through the spring afternoon in the hours remaining before the wedding:

> The sun was an imposition, an imposition, for they were another race stamping an easy trail through the wilderness of Paris, possessed of the same people, but of themselves like another race. No one else could by lifting of the head only be starting life over again, and it was a wonder the whole city of Paris did not hold its breath for them, for if anyone could have begun a new race, it was these two.

The incestuous overtones are strong. "It isn't too late yet, you know," the brother repeatedly insists as they stride through the streets, take a train into the *bois*, and row to the middle of a pond. "Over them was the sky set like a tomb," and as tears flow down their cheeks, the slow rain begins to fall. There is perfect correspondence between landscape and emotion, external objects mirroring the characters' internal states. The rain underscores the pair's frustration and despair as they realize the intensity of their love and the impossibility of its fulfillment:

> Everywhere, everywhere there were other countries to go to. And how were they to get from the boat with the chains that were on them, how uproot the willowing trees from their hearts, how strike the irons of spring that shackled them? What shame and shame that scorched a burning pathway to their dressing rooms! Their hearts were mourning for every Paris night and its half-hours before lunch when two straws crossed on the round table top on the marble anywhere meant I had a drink here and went on.

The inevitable wedding itself forms the final segment of the story, and the lyrical spell binding the pair is broken the instant they set foot in the house again to find their mother "tying white satin bows under the chins of the potted plants." The boy kicks down the hall the silver tray that will collect the guests' calling cards, and his mother is wearily certain "that this outburst presaged a thousand mishaps that were yet to come." The irony of the story lies not only in the reversal of expectations the title may have aroused in the reader but also in the discrepancy between different characters' perceptions of the same situation. The self-pitying matron worries only about the thousand little mishaps possible when a major disaster—the wedding itself—is imminent; but the guests arrive "in peace" and the brother delivers his sister to the altar. Boyle captures magnificently the enormous gulf between the placid surface appearance and the tumultuous inner reality of the situation as she takes the reader inside the bride's consciousness:

> This was the end, the end, they thought. She turned her face to her brother and suddenly their hearts fled together and sobbed like ringdoves in their bosoms. This was the end, the end, the end, this was the end.
>
> Down the room their feet fled in various ways, seeking an escape. To the edge of the carpet fled her feet, returned and followed reluctantly upon her brother's heels. Every piped note of the organ insisted that she go on. It isn't too late, he said. Too late, too late. The ring was given, the book was closed. The desolate, the barren sky continued to fling down dripping handfuls of fresh rain.

The mindless repetition of the phrase "the end" and the blind panic of the bride's imaginary flight have an intense psychological authenticity, and the recurrence of the brother's phrase "It isn't too late" and its perversion in "Too late, too late," along with the continuing rain, are evidence of the skill with which Boyle has woven motifs into the fabric of her story.

"Wedding Day" ends with dancing, but in an ironic counterpoint to the flight she had imagined at the altar, the bride's feet "were fleeing in a hundred ways throughout the rooms, fluttering from the punch bowl to her bedroom and back again." Through repetition and transformation of the image, Boyle underscores the fact that her path is now circumscribed. While the brother, limbered by the punch, dances about scattering calling cards, the mother, "in triumph on the arm of the General, danced lightly by" rejoicing that "no glass had yet been broken." "What a real success, what a *real* success," is her only thought as her feet float "over the oriental prayer rugs, through the Persian forests of hemp, away and away" in another absurdly circumscribed "escape" that is yet another mockery of the escape to "other countries" that the pair had dreamed of that afternoon on the lake.

Ironies and incongruities are hallmarks of Kay Boyle's fiction. For Boyle, reality depends on perception, and the fact that different perceptions of the same situation result in disparate and often conflicting "realities" creates a disturbing world in which individuals badly in need of contact and connection collide and bounce off one another like atoms. In "Wedding Day" Boyle juxtaposes a *real* loss of love with the surface gaiety of a wedding that celebrates no love at all, but which the mother terms "a *real* success." She exposes the painful isolation of each individual and the tragedy that the only remedy—a bonding through love—is so often thwarted or destroyed.

The barriers to love are many, both natural and man-made. In some of Boyle's stories those who would love are severed by death. Sometimes, as in the case of the brother and sister in "Wedding Day," love's fulfillment is simply made impossible by the facts of life in this imperfect world, and although readers can mourn for what has been lost, they can hardly argue about the obstacle itself—the incest taboo is nearly universal. Yet in many of her works Boyle presents a more assailable villain. In "Wedding Day" she treats unsympathetically the mother, who stands for all the petty proprieties that so often separate people. Boyle finds many barriers to human contact to be as arbitrary and immoral as the social conventions which cause Huck Finn's "conscience" to torment him as he helps his friend Jim to escape slavery, and in her fiction she quietly unleashes her fury against them. An obstacle she attacks repeatedly is a narrow-mindedness which blinds individuals to the inherent dignity and integrity of others, an egotism which in the plural becomes bigotry and chauvinism.

"The White Horses of Vienna" • While Boyle and her family were living in Austria in the 1930's, she was an eyewitness as the social world began to impose itself on private lives, and she began to widen the scope of her artistic vision; yet her "political" stories have as their central concern the ways in which external events affect the individual. In one of her best-known stories, "The White Horses of Vienna," which won the O. Henry Award for best story of 1935, Boyle exposes the artificial barricades to human understanding and connection. The story explores the relationship between a Tyrolean doctor, who has injured his leg coming down the mountain after lighting a swastika fire in rebellion against the current government, and Dr. Heine, the young assistant sent from Vienna to take over his patients while he recovers. The Tyrolean doctor and his wife see immediately that Dr. Heine is a Jew.

The Tyrolean doctor is a clean-living, respected man. He had been a prisoner of war in Siberia and had studied abroad, but the many places in which he had been "had never left an evil mark." Boyle writes: "His face was as strong as rock, but it had seen so much of suffering that it had the look of being scarred, it seemed to be split in two, with one side of it given to resolve and the other to compassion." In his personal dealings it is the compassionate side that dominates. When his wife asks in a desperate whisper what they will do with "*him*," the Tyrolean doctor replies simply that they will send for his bag at the station and give him some *Apfelsaft* if he is thirsty. "It's harder on him than us," he tells her. Neither has the wife's own humanity been extinguished entirely by institutionalized bigotry, for when Dr. Heine's coat catches fire from a sterilizing lamp on the table, she wraps a piece of rug around him immediately and holds him tightly to smother the flames. Almost instinctively, she offers to try patching the burned-out place, but then she suddenly bites her lip and stands back "as if she had remembered the evil thing that stood between them."

The situation of the Tyrolean doctor, described as a "great, golden, wounded bird," is counterpointed in a story Dr. Heine tells at dinner one evening about the famous Lipizzaner horses of the Spanish Riding School in Vienna, still royal, "without any royalty left to bow their heads to, still shouldering into the arena with spirits a man would give his soul for, bending their knees in homage to the empty, canopied loge where royalty no longer sat." He tells of a particular horse that the government, badly in need of money, had sold to an Indian maharaja. When the time had come for the horse to be taken away, a wound was discovered cut in his leg. After it had healed and it was again time for the horse to leave, another wound was found on its other leg. Finally the horse's blood was so poisoned that it had to be destroyed. No one knew who had caused the wounds until the horse's devoted little groom committed suicide that same day. When the after-dinner conversation is interrupted by the knocking of Heimwehr troops at the door, "men brought in from other parts of the country, billeted there to subdue the native people," the identification between the doctor and the steed is underscored. He cannot guide the troops up the mountain in search of those who have lit that evening's swastika fires because of his wounded leg.

Dr. Heine is relieved that the rest of the evening will be spent with family and friends watching one of the Tyrolean doctor's locally renowned marionette shows. After staring out the window at the burning swastikas, the "marvelously living flowers of fire springing out of the arid darkness," the "inexplicable signals given from one mountain to another in some secret gathering of power that cast him and his people out, forever out upon the waters of despair," Dr. Heine turns back, suddenly angry, and proclaims that the whole country is being ruined by politics, that it is impossible to have friends or even casual conversations on any other basis these days. "You're much wiser to make your puppets, *Herr Doktor*," he says.

Even the marionette show is political. The characters are a clown who explains he is carrying artificial flowers because he is on his way to his own funeral and wants them to be fresh when he gets there, and a handsome grasshopper, "a great, gleaming beauty" who prances about the stage with delicacy and wit to the music of Mozart. "It's really marvellous! He's as graceful as the white horses at Vienna, *Herr Doktor*," Dr. Heine calls out in delight. As the conversation continues between the clown, called "Chancellor," and the grasshopper addressed as "The Leader," Dr. Heine is not laughing so loudly. The Chancellor has a "ludicrous faith in the power of the Church" to support him; the Leader proclaims that the cities are full of churches, but "the country is full of God." The Leader speaks with "a wild and stirring power that sent the cold of wonder up and down one's spine," and he seems "ready to waltz away at any moment with the power of stallion life that was leaping in his limbs." As the Chancellor proclaims, "I believe in the independence of the individual," he promptly trips over his own sword and falls flat among the daisies.

At the story's conclusion, Dr. Heine is standing alone on the cold mountainside, longing to be "indoors, with the warmth of his own people, and the intellect speaking." When he sees "a small necklace of men coming to him" up the mountain, the lights they bear "coming like little beacons of hope carried to him," Dr. Heine thinks,

> Come to me . . . come to me. I am a young man alone on a mountain. I am a young man alone, as my race is alone, lost here amongst them all.

Yet ironically, what Dr. Heine views as "beacons of hope" are carried by the Heimwehr troops, the Tyrolean doctor's enemies. As in "Wedding Day," Boyle presents a single situation and plays off the characters' reactions to it against one another to illustrate the gaps between individuals and the relativity of truth and reality in the world.

Because his personal loyalties transcend his politics, Dr. Heine rushes to warn the family of the Heimwehr's approach. When the troops arrive they announce that the Austrian chancellor, Dollfuss, had been assassinated in Vienna that afternoon. They have come to arrest the doctor, whose rebel sympathies are known. "Ah, politics, politics again!" cries Dr. Heine, wringing his hands "like a woman about to cry." He runs outdoors and takes the doctor's hand as he is being carried away on a stretcher, asking what he can do to help. "You can throw me peaches and chocolate from the street," replies the Tyrolean doctor, smiling, "his cheeks scarred with the marks of laughter in the light from the hurricane lamps that the men were carrying down." His wife is not a good shot, he adds, and he missed all the oranges she had thrown him after the February slaughter. At this image of the Tyrolean doctor caged like an animal but still noble, with his spirit still unbroken, Dr. Heine is left "thinking in anguish of the snow-white horses, the Lipizzaners, the relics of pride, the still unbroken vestiges of beauty bending their knees to the empty loge of royalty where there was no royalty any more."

In "The White Horses of Vienna," Boyle expresses hope, if not faith, that even in the face of divisive social forces, the basic connections of compassion between individuals might survive. In a work that is a testament to her humanity, she presents the Tyrolean doctor's plight with such sensitivity that readers, like the Jewish assistant, are forced to view with understanding and empathy this proud man's search for a cause that will redeem the dignity and honor of his wounded people while at the same time abhorring the cause itself. Boyle sees and presents in all its human complexity what at first glance seems a black-and-white political issue. Boyle, however, was no Pollyanna. As the social conflict that motivates this story snowballed into world war and mass genocide, she saw with a cold, realistic eye how little survived of the goodwill among human beings she had hoped for. In many of her stories written in the 1940's and up to her death, she examined unflinchingly and sometimes bitterly the individual tragedies played out in the shadow of the global one.

"Winter Night" • In "Winter Night," published in 1946, she draws a delicate portrait of a little girl named Felicia and a woman sent by a "sitting parent" agency to spend the evening with her in a New York apartment. The woman, in her strange accent, tells Felicia that today is an anniversary, that three years ago that night she had begun to care for another little girl who also studied ballet and whose mother, like Felicia's, had had to go away. The difference was that the other girl's mother had been sent away on a train car in which there were no seats, and she never came back, but she was able to write a short letter on a smuggled scrap of paper and slip it through the cracks on the floor of the moving train in the hope that some kind stranger would send it to its destination. The woman can only comfort herself with the thought that "They must be quietly asleep somewhere, and not crying all night because they are hungry and because they are cold."

"There is a time of apprehension which begins with the beginning of darkness, and to which only the speech of love can lend security," the story begins, as Boyle describes the dying light of a January afternoon in New York City. Felicia and the "sitting parent," both left alone, have found that security in each other. When, after midnight, Felicia's mother tiptoes in the front door, slipping the three blue foxskins from her shoulder and dropping the velvet bag on a chair, she hears only the sound of breathing in the dark living room, and no one speaks to her in greeting as she crosses to the bedroom: "And then, as startling as a slap across her delicately tinted face, she saw the woman lying sleeping on the divan, and Felicia, in her school dress still, asleep within the woman's arms." The story is not baldly didactic, but Boyle *is* moralizing. By juxtaposing the cases of the two little girls left alone by their mothers and cared for by a stranger, she shows that the failure of love is a tragic loss on an individual as well as on a global scale. Again, personal concerns merge with political and social ones, and readers find the failure of love on any level to be the fundamental tragedy of life.

Some of the stories Boyle wrote about the war and its aftermath were less subtle, "artistic" explorations of individual struggles than they were frankly moralistic adventure stories written for commercial magazines, and they were more popular with the public than with the critics. Yet one of her finest works was also a product of her war experiences. *The Smoking Mountain: Stories of Postwar Germany* (1951) consists of eleven stories, several originally published by *The New Yorker,* which had employed

Boyle as a correspondent for the express purpose of sending "fiction out of Germany." It is prefaced by a seventy-seven-page nonfiction account of a de-Nazification trial Boyle witnessed in Frankfurt in 1948, which reveals her immense skill as a reporter as well. The book presents a painful vision. Any hope that a renewed understanding among peoples might result from the catastrophic "lesson" of the war is dashed, for the point of many of the stories and certainly of the introduction is how little difference the war has made in the fundamental attitudes of the defeated but silently defiant Germans who can still say of 1943 and 1944—"the years when the gas chambers burned the brightest. . . .Those were the good years for everyone."

In 1929, Boyle, with poet Hart Crane, Vail, and others, signed Eugene Jolas's manifesto, "Revolution of the Word," condemning literary pretentiousness and outdated literary conventions. The goal, then, was to make literature at once fresh and experimental and at the same time accessible to the reader. Boyle would remain politically involved and productive as a writer, publishing collections of poetry, short stories, and essays in the 1980's. She would continue in her work to test the individual against events of historical significance, such as the threat of Nazism or the war in Vietnam. Although critics have accused her later works of selling out to popular taste, and her style of losing its innovative edge, Boyle remained steadfast in defining her artistic purpose as a moral responsibility to defend the integrity of the individual and human rights. To do so, Boyle argued, she must be accessible to the public.

Sandra Whipple Spanier
With updates by Lou Thompson

Other major works

CHILDREN'S LITERATURE: *The Youngest Camel*, 1939, 1959; *Pinky, the Cat Who Liked to Sleep*, 1966; *Pinky in Persia*, 1968.

ANTHOLOGIES: *365 Days*, 1936 (with others); *The Autobiography of Emanuel Carnevali*, 1967; *Enough of Dying! An Anthology of Peace Writings*, 1972 (with Justine van Gundy).

NOVELS: *Process*, wr. c. 1925, pb. 2001 (Sandra Spanier, editor); *Plagued by the Nightingale*, 1931; *Year Before Last*, 1932; *Gentlemen, I Address You Privately*, 1933; *My Next Bride*, 1934; *Death of a Man*, 1936; *Monday Night*, 1938; *Primer for Combat*, 1942; *Avalanche*, 1944; *A Frenchman Must Die*, 1946; *1939*, 1948; *His Human Majesty*, 1949; *The Seagull on the Step*, 1955; *Three Short Novels*, 1958; *Generation Without Farewell*, 1960; *The Underground Woman*, 1975.

NONFICTION: *Breaking the Silence: Why a Mother Tells Her Son About the Nazi Era*, 1962; *Being Geniuses Together, 1920-1930*, 1968 (with Robert McAlmon); *The Long Walk at San Francisco State, and Other Essays*, 1970; *Words That Must Somehow Be Said: The Selected Essays of Kay Boyle, 1927-1984*, 1985.

POETRY: *A Glad Day*, 1938; *American Citizen Naturalized in Leadville, Colorado*, 1944; *Collected Poems*, 1962; *Testament for My Students, and Other Poems*, 1970; *This Is Not a Letter, and Other Poems*, 1985; *Collected Poems of Kay Boyle*, 1991.

Bibliography

Bell, Elizabeth S. *Kay Boyle: A Study of the Short Fiction*. New York: Twayne, 1992. Excellent introduction to Boyle's short stories. Includes bibliographical references and an index.

Carpenter, Richard C. "Kay Boyle." *English Journal* 42 (November, 1953): 425-430.

This essay provides a helpful and general look at Boyle's early novels and short fiction.

_____. "Kay Boyle: The Figure in the Carpet." *Critique: Studies in Modern Fiction* 7 (Winter, 1964-1965): 65-78. Carpenter rejects the common complaint that Boyle is a mere "stylist," discussing her thematic depth, particularly in "The Bridegroom's Body" and "The Crazy Hunter."

Elkins, Marilyn, ed. *Critical Essays on Kay Boyle.* New York: G. K. Hall, 1997. Collection of reviews and critical essays on Boyle's work by various critics, reviewers, and commentators.

Hollenberg, Donna. "Abortion, Identity Formation, and the Expatriate Woman Writer: H. D. and Kay Boyle in the Twenties." *Twentieth Century Literature* 40 (Winter, 1994): 499-517. Discusses the theme of self-loss through the roles of marriage and motherhood in Boyle's early works. Shows how expatriation allowed some psychic space to explore the effect of gender roles on her aspirations. Discusses the effect of inadequate maternal role models her identity as an artist.

May, Charles E., ed. *Masterplots II: Short Story Series, Revised Edition.* 8 vols. Pasadena, Calif.: Salem Press, 2004. Designed for student use, this reference set contains articles providing detailed plot summaries and analyses of these four short stories by Boyle: "Astronomer's Wife" (vol. 1), "Summer Evening" (vol. 7), and "The White Horses of Vienna" and "Winter Night" (vol. 8).

Mellen, Joan. *Kay Boyle: Author of Herself.* New York: Farrar, Straus and Giroux, 1994. Drawing on personal conversations with Boyle and her family, Mellen discusses the autobiographical nature of Boyle's writing and lays bare much of Boyle's own mythologizing of her life in her autobiographical writing.

Porter, Katherine Anne. "Kay Boyle: Example to the Young." In *The Critic as Artist: Essays on Books, 1920-1970,* edited by Gilbert A. Harrison. New York: Liveright, 1972. This essay examines Boyle as she fits in the literary movement of her time. Focuses on some of her stories, as well as on the novel *Plagued by the Nightingale.*

Spanier, Sandra Whipple. *Kay Boyle: Artist and Activist.* Carbondale: Southern Illinois University Press, 1986. Heavily annotated, thorough, and the first critical biography and major work on Boyle. Supplemented by select but extensive primary and secondary bibliographies. Illustrated.

Twentieth-Century Literature 34 (Fall, 1988). A special issue on Kay Boyle, with personal reminiscences by Malcolm Cowley, Jessica Mitford, Howard Nemerov, and Studs Terkel, among others. Also contains several critical essays on Boyle's work.

T. Coraghessan Boyle

Born: Peekskill, New York; December 2, 1948

Principal short fiction • *Descent of Man*, 1979; *Greasy Lake, and Other Stories*, 1985; *If the River Was Whiskey*, 1989; *Without a Hero*, 1994; *T. C. Boyle Stories: The Collected Stories of T. Coraghessan Boyle*, 1998; *After the Plague: Stories*, 2001; *Tooth and Claw*, 2005; *The Human Fly, and Other Stories*, 2005.

Other literary forms • T. Coraghessan Boyle is primarily a writer of prose fiction who has divided his energy roughly equally between short stories and novels. His novels explore many of the same subjects and themes as his short fiction and have received both popular attention and critical praise. He published his first novel, *Water Music*, in 1981, followed by two more during the 1980's, four during the 1990's, and three during the first years of the twenty-first century: *Drop City* (2003), *The Inner Circle* (2004), and *Talk Talke* (2006). His 1993 novel, *The Road to Wellville*, was made into a motion picture in 1994.

Achievements • T. Coraghessan Boyle received a National Endowment for the Arts Fellowship in 1977. *Descent of Man*, his first collection of stories, won the St. Lawrence Award for Short Fiction. His novel *Water Music* (1981) received the Aga Khan Award, and another novel, *World's End* (1987), was awarded the PEN/Faulkner Award for Fiction. Boyle also received O. Henry Awards for "Sinking House" (1988), "The Ape Lady in Retirement" (1989), "The Underground Gardens" (1999), "The Love of My Life" (2001), and "Swept Away" (2003). *T. C. Boyle Stories: The Collected Stories of T. Coraghessan Boyle* (1998) won the Bernard Malamud Prize in Short Fiction from the PEN/Faulkner Foundation. In 2003, he was a National Book Award finalist for *Drop City*. In 2004, "Tooth and Claw" was a Best American Stories selection.

Biography • Born into a lower-middle-class family in Peekskill, New York, in 1948, Thomas John Boyle was a rebellious youth who performed in a rock-and-roll band, committed acts of vandalism, and drank heavily. He did not get along with his father, a school-bus driver who died of alcoholism at the age of fifty-four, in 1972. Boyle's mother, a secretary, was also an alcoholic and died of liver failure. Assuming the name T. Coraghessan Boyle at the State University of New York at Potsdam, he studied saxophone and clarinet until he realized that he lacked the necessary discipline for music. He then drifted into literature. After college, to avoid military service during the Vietnam War, he taught English for two years at his alma mater, Lakeland High School, in Shrub Oak, New York, while indulging in heroin on weekends.

In 1972, Boyle entered the creative writing program at the University of Iowa, where he studied under Vance Bourjaily, John Cheever, and John Irving, earning a doctorate in 1977, with a short-story collection, later published as *Descent of Man*, serving as his dissertation. Such academic achievement is ironic for someone placed in a class for slow learners in the second grade. Boyle became a teacher at the University of Southern California, where he founded an undergraduate creative writing program, and settled in Woodland Hills with his wife, Karen Kvashay, and their children, Kerrie, Milo, and Spencer. One of the most public and flamboyant writers of his time, Boyle delighted in performing public and recorded readings.

Analysis • During a time when the majority of serious American writers have been concerned with the minutiae of everyday life, T. Coraghessan Boyle has stood out by exploring a wide range of subjects, locales, periods, and strata of society. Distinctive as a stylist, storyteller, and satirist, Boyle enthusiastically encompasses numerous literary conventions into his fiction, turning them into something fresh and often humorous. He examines both the detritus and the silliness of the world, exulting in its absurdities.

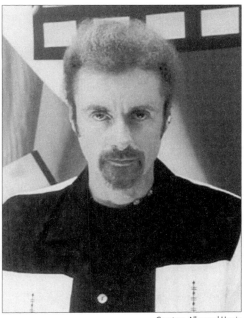

Courtesy, Allen and Unwin

Boyle's short fiction is most notable for its extraordinary range of subjects, which include a chimpanzee who has translated works by Charles Darwin, Friedrich Wilhelm Nietzsche, and Noam Chomsky into Yerkish; the final performance of blues musician Robert Johnson; the importation of starlings into the United States; an attempt to improve the public image of the Ayatollah Ruhollah Khomeini; and a statue of the Virgin Mary that re-creates a man's sins for all the world to see. Boyle's stories delve into such topics as violence, sexuality, paranoia, guilt, and the clichés of popular culture. Although some of his stories are realistic, most exaggerate the world's absurdities for comic effect. His tone is predominantly satirical but rarely angry.

"Bloodfall" • "Bloodfall" depicts the effects of an apparently endless rainfall of blood on seven young adults who live together. Although they smoke marijuana, burn incense, and listen to thunderously loud rock and roll, they are not hippies but well-to-do materialists who use electric toothbrushes and drive BMWs. They sleep together in a bed that they appropriately think of as "the nest," since they have attempted to withdraw from the often disconcerting realities of the outside world, seeking comfortable refuge in their home.

The inexplicable rain of blood cuts them off completely from the rest of the world by knocking out their telephone and television. They cannot drive to get food since they cannot see through a blood-smeared windshield. Their response to this terrifying situation is to ignore it: "Isabelle said it would be better if we all went to bed. She expressed a hope that after a long nap things would somehow come to their senses." The blood begins to stain everything about their antiseptic existence: their white clothing when they venture outside, their white carpet when the flood begins to seep under their door. They are confident that the bloodfall will stop, since logic demands that it will, and it does. Since such an event is illogical to begin with, however,

"Bloodfall" ends with the start of a new downpour, this time consisting of "heavy, feculent, and wet" fecal matter.

Boyle often satirizes modern human beings' feeble efforts to protect themselves from outside forces, as in "Peace of Mind," an attack on home security systems, but the image of the blood invading the white world of these smug materialists is his strongest statement on this theme. Boyle's vividly contrasting images of red and white and his telling accumulation of the trite details of the lives of contemporary American consumers contribute to the story's effectiveness. As throughout his fiction, Boyle borrows from the conventions of popular culture, in this case horror fiction and films, to create a compelling vision of modern alienation.

"The Big Garage" • "The Big Garage" is a frightening but comic horror story. When the Audi belonging to B. breaks down, a tow truck mysteriously appears and takes it to Tegeler's Big Garage, an enormous service center in the middle of nowhere. Because it is late at night and no mechanics are available, B. is forced to sleep on a cot in a storage closet where other customers are also waiting for their vehicles to be repaired. B. discovers that he must go through a complicated maze to the appointment office and fill out a seven-page application for an appointment to have his car serviced. Fed up with this nonsense, B. confronts a team of German mechanics who taunt him and throw him down a chute into the car wash, where he is washed and waxed. After trying and failing to escape by hitchhiking, B. gives in and goes across the street to Tegeler's Big Lot, where the owner of the Big Garage sells his broken customers Tegelers, his own inferior make.

B. is caught up in a bureaucratic nightmare out of a Franz Kafka novel, such as *Der Prozess* (1925; *The Trial*, 1937). Boyle takes a familiar situation and exaggerates it to show how everyday life can become an impersonal, nerve-racking, humiliating experience. He makes a serious statement about alienation and the often vicious insensitivity of a consumer culture while also having fun through slapstick and literary parody.

"The Overcoat II" • Boyle combines homage to a favorite work of literature with political satire in "The Overcoat II," an updating of Nikolai Gogol's "Shinel" (1839; in *The Overcoat, and Other Stories*, 1923) to the Moscow of the 1980's. Akaky Akakievich Bashmachkin, a devoted clerk in the Soviet bureaucracy, has no interests outside his work, no time for anything but waiting in endless queues for scarce goods. Yet the only blemish on his party-line life is the cheap, tattered overcoat he has bought because a central department store clerk, attacking the quality of Soviet-made products, tried to sell him a black-market overcoat.

Akaky is ridiculed by his unpatriotic coworkers because he appears to use the coat to give himself the aura of a Marxist saint. Old Studniuk, one of the fourteen residents who share his apartment, tells Akaky he must use the black market to get everything he can: "There ain't no comrade commissioner going to come round and give it to you." Akaky sells his television set and exhausts his savings to spend three months' salary on a camel's hair overcoat with a fox collar. His fellow clerks are impressed, and one, Mishkin, invites Akaky to his home. After leaving Mishkin's house, where he had one of the best times of his life, he is beaten and his coat stolen. The police recover the coat but keep it and fine Akaky for receiving stolen goods. Feeling betrayed by all he has believed in, Akaky develops pneumonia, dies, and is soon forgotten. The police inspector who has interrogated him wears the coat proudly.

Like "Ike and Nina," in which President Dwight D. Eisenhower and Premier Nikita S. Khrushchev's wife have an affair in 1959, "The Overcoat II" satirizes Soviet life. Gogol's Akaky dies from the despair of losing his beloved coat, Boyle's from losing his belief in the Soviet system, something even more irreplaceable. Gogol ends his story with Akaky's ghost seeking revenge against those who have wronged him, Boyle's with an enemy profiting from the clerk's naïve belief in a system that exploits him. The happiness that Akaky experiences at Mishkin's party must be short-lived, for in Boyle's paranoid universe, some unexpected, uncontrollable force is out to get the individual. Only those as cynical as the society in which they live can survive.

"Two Ships" • The uncontrollable force confronting the protagonist of "Two Ships" is his childhood best friend. The teenage Jack and Casper are rebels together, assaulting symbols of wealth and religion. They run away from home, but Jack gives up two weeks before Casper. During this experience, Jack recognizes the streak of madness in his friend and is both repelled by and attracted to it: "He was serious, he was committed, his was the rapture of saints and martyrs, both feet over the line." Casper's passion leads him to convert fervently to Marxism. When he is drafted during the Vietnam War, he deserts the Army.

Jack does not see Casper for several years after he goes into the Army, but he receives several packages containing lengthy, incoherent poems expressing Casper's political views. Jack then goes to law school, marries, and settles down. After he receives a telephone call from Casper asking him to stick up for his friend, Jack tells an agent at the Federal Bureau of Investigation (FBI) that Casper is "seriously impaired." Following eleven months in a mental institution, Casper returns to his hometown, and Jack is frightened. Casper finally visits him but terrifies Jack even further by saying little. Jack begins packing.

More than guilt about betraying his friend to the FBI, Jack experiences shame over how their lives have diverged: "I'd become what we'd reacted against together, what he'd devoted his mad, misguided life to subverting." Jack is disturbed by Casper's reminding him how he has failed himself through his willingness to play society's game by its rules, his becoming a corporate attorney who defends polluters, his lack of passion for and commitment to anything but his family, and his failure to accept any responsibility for the state of the world. "Two Ships" effectively blends such major Boyle subjects as paranoia, friendship, and betrayal. His characters are constantly betraying one another and themselves.

"The Hector Quesadilla Story" • Although generally satirical and often condemnatory, Boyle's fiction is not always cynical and unforgiving. "The Hector Quesadilla Story," one of the best baseball stories ever written, demonstrates the possibility of getting a chance to overcome failure. The title character plays for the Los Angeles Dodgers but only pinch-hits, because he is too old, too fat, and too slow to perform well in the field. (Boyle has loosely based this character on Manny Mota, the legendary pinch hitter for the Dodgers in the 1970's.) A grandfather whose official baseball age is several years short of actuality, Hector lives only to eat the spicy Mexican food that he passionately loves and to play the game that he loves even more. He keeps telling his wife he will play one more season but secretly has no intention of quitting. Meanwhile, he waits patiently at the end of the bench to prove himself again, to come alive in the only way he knows how.

Hector is convinced that something special will happen during a game with the

Atlanta Braves, whom the Dodgers are battling for first place, because it falls on his birthday. With the score tied in the ninth inning, he is denied his "moment of catharsis," his chance to win the game. As the contest drags on into extra innings, the manager refuses to let him bat because the Dodgers have run out of players and Hector would have to play in the field if the score remained tied. With his team trailing by one run in the bottom of the thirty-first inning in the longest game in major league history, Hector finally gets his chance but is foolishly thrown out trying to stretch a double into a triple. When the next batter hits a home run, Hector is forced to pitch for the first time because no one else is available. All seems lost when the Braves score four runs off him in the next inning, but Hector redeems himself with a bases-loaded home run to tie the score once again. The game then "goes on forever."

"The Hector Quesadilla Story" works on two levels. On one, it is about the most magical quality of baseball: "How can he get old?" Hector asks himself. "The grass is always green, the lights always shining, no clocks or periods or halves or quarters, no punch-in and punch-out: this is the game that never ends." Without the restraints of time seen in such games as football and basketball, a baseball game could theoretically last forever. On the second level, the story deals with how the individual feels the limitations that time imposes upon him and how he fights against them. Hector tries to ignore what his body, his family, and common sense tell him. Because a baseball game can go on forever, so can he. He appropriates the magic of the game for himself: "it's a game of infinite surprises." Boyle makes baseball a metaphor for life itself.

"Sorry Fugu" • The tone of most of Boyle's stories is primarily comic, and in one of the best, "Sorry Fugu," he also displays the gentler side of his satire. Albert D'Angelo, owner and chef of D'Angelo's, wants his new restaurant to be both good and successful. He wants it to meet the challenge of Willa Frank, the restaurant critic who always gives negative reviews, even to those places that Albert reveres. He fears and longs for the day when she and her companion, known only as "the Palate," will enter his establishment. Luckily, Albert knows when the great moment has arrived, since one of his employees knows Willa and her boyfriend, Jock McNamee. Unfortunately, she has come on one of those nights when all goes wrong, and Albert knows he has failed on the first of her three visits. They arrive the second time with an older couple. Albert is prepared this time, only to see each of them pass the dishes to Jock, who is not interested in any of them.

Albert understands what to do on the third visit after his employee tells him that what Jock really likes is the "shanty Irish" food his mother used to make. Albert then ignores what the couple orders and serves the Palate peas, boiled potatoes, a slab of cheap, overcooked meat, and catsup. When the outraged Willa charges into the kitchen, Albert seduces her with squid rings in aioli sauce, lobster tortellini, *taglierini alla pizzaiola*, Russian *coulibiac* of salmon, and fugu, a Japanese blowfish. Willa confesses that she relies on Jock's crude judgment, since at least he is consistent in disliking everything, and that she is afraid to risk a positive review.

Although other American writers of Boyle's generation fill their fiction with brand names and trendy antiques as a means of delineating their characters, Boyle uses food to explore their social status and individuality. What is most important about "Sorry Fugu," however, is its depiction of the roles of the critic and the artist. Boyle satirizes the superficiality of many critics through Willa's uncertainty about her tastes and dishonesty in relying on Jock's lack of taste. Albert is an artist in the care he takes in creating his dishes: "Albert put his soul into each dish, arranged and garnished the plates with all the patient care and shimmering inspiration of a Toulouse-Lautrec bent over a canvas." Boyle takes the same care as a stylist, as when Albert contemplates Willa's name: "It was a bony name, scant and lean, stripped of sensuality, the antithesis of the round, full-bodied Leonora. It spoke of a knotty Puritan toughness, a denying of the flesh, no compromise in the face of temptation." Since Boyle has said in interviews that he wants to be both popular and critically praised, Albert appears to be a self-portrait of an artist who needs to be judged by the highest standards.

Without a Hero • Boyle continued his eclectic exploration of the absurdities of the world in his short-story collection *Without a Hero*. "Filthy with Things" tells the humorous yet oddly disturbing story of a married couple suffocating in a world of suburban materialism that has advanced so far beyond their control that they must hire an organizing specialist to kick them out of their own house and take possession of their belongings. As the narrator watches the workers sort through and catalog everything he owns, he feels "as if he doesn't exist, as if he's already become an irrelevance in the face of the terrible weight of his possessions," or, more broadly, of a late twentieth century American culture in which materiality often defines the person.

One of the most prominent of Boyle's many recurring obsessions is his interest in the influence that animals have on human behavior, and vice versa. The narrator of "Carnal Knowledge" gets involved with a group of animal-rights activists when he falls in love with Alena, a militant vegetarian whose crippled dog urinates on him at the beach. After quitting his job to take part in antifur demonstrations in Beverly Hills, the narrator is coerced into taking part in a plot to "liberate" thousands of turkeys from a poultry farm a few weeks before Thanksgiving. The raid does more harm than good, however, when large numbers of turkeys wander onto a fog-enshrouded freeway and cause a truck to jackknife. After being spurned by Alena, who travels north with another man to defend grizzly bears, the protagonist drives by the accident scene, where the road is "coated in feathers, turkey feathers" and where there is "a red pulp ground into the surface of road." He promptly returns to eating the Big Macs that he has been subconsciously craving for days. Beneath the humor of such stories lies a message to which Boyle often returns: The universe is an ambiguous, unpredictable place, and each person must find his or her own solitary way to negotiate its absurdities.

T. C. Boyle Stories • *T. C. Boyle Stories: The Collected Stories of T. Coraghessan Boyle* is a 691-page volume which includes all the tales from the author's previous short-story collections, plus four stories previously unpublished in book form and three previously unpublished anywhere, an impressive sixty-eight over a twenty-five-year period. Although reading a complete collection of an author's work often means plowing through the mediocre to get to the good (and this book is no exception), one benefit is the opportunity to see the development of the writer over time. In Boyle's case, there is a clear tendency for early stories to be driven more by premise than by character. In stories such as "Bloodfall," characterization tends to be subordinate to the idea. In subsequent stories, Boyle began demonstrating a willingness to invest more time and effort into exploring the multiple dimensions of his characters, and by the 1980's, a clear preference for dwelling on the subtleties of the human condition had emerged.

In the midst of this development, several common threads tie most, if not all, of Boyle's stories together, most notably his use of humor of all types—parody, slapstick, satire, wit, and irony—and his dedication to keen observation rendered through bold, colorful language. This latter quality, which seems to be missing from a large portion of contemporary American fiction, is a clear reflection of Boyle's belief that it is possible for fiction to possess the same vitality as rock-and-roll music.

Michael Adams
With updates by Douglas Long and the Editors

Other major works

ANTHOLOGY: *Doubletakes: Pairs of Contemporary Short Stories,* 2003.

NOVELS: *Water Music,* 1981; *Budding Prospects: A Pastoral,* 1984; *World's End,* 1987; *East Is East,* 1990; *The Road to Wellville,* 1993; *The Tortilla Curtain,* 1995; *Riven Rock,* 1998; *A Friend of the Earth,* 2000; *Drop City,* 2003; *The Inner Circle,* 2004; *Talk Talke,* 2006.

Bibliography

Boyle, T. Coraghessan. "A Punk's Past Recaptured." Interview by Anthony DeCurtis. *Rolling Stone,* January 14, 1988, 54-57. In his most revealing interview, Boyle talks about his drug use, the importance of understanding history, and the autobiographical element in his fiction. He expresses the desire to be like Kurt Vonnegut, in showing that literature can be both serious and entertaining, and like John Updike, in constantly changing his approach to fiction and improving as an artist.

_____. "Rolling Boyle." Interview by Tad Friend. *The New York Times Magazine,* December 9, 1990, 50, 64, 66, 68. Boyle portrays himself as a missionary for literature who promotes himself to ensure that he is read. He comments on the new maturity and reality in some of his fiction but admits that the absurd and bizarre are more natural for him. Boyle also expresses pessimism about the future of the human race.

Chase, Brennan. "Like, Chill!" *Los Angeles* 38 (April, 1993): 80-82. A biographical sketch, focusing on Boyle's successful literary career and celebrity status in Hollywood. Boyle maintains that he is an academic whose purpose is to write.

Hume, Kathryn. *American Dream, American Nightmare: Fiction Since 1960.* Urbana: University of Illinois Press, 2000. Boyle's work is discussed in an extensive study of the tension between utopian and dystopian tendencies in late twentieth century American fiction.

May, Charles E., ed. *Masterplots II: Short Story Series, Revised Edition.* 8 vols. Pasadena, Calif.: Salem Press, 2004. Designed for student use, this reference set contains articles providing detailed plot summaries and analyses of these four short stories by Boyle: "Greasy Lake" and "The Hector Quesadilla Story" (vol. 3), "If the River Was Whiskey" (vol. 4), and "The Overcoat II" (vol. 6).

Pope, Dan. "A Different Kind of Post-Modernism." *Gettysburg Review* 3 (Autumn, 1990): 658-669. A discussion of Boyle's collection *If the River Was Whiskey,* along with a collection of short fiction by Rick DeMarinis and Paul West, as typifying the work of a new generation of writers who look beyond "the age of innocent realism."

Shelden, Michael. "T. Coraghessan Boyle: The Art of Fiction CLXI." *Paris Review* 155 (Summer, 2000): 100-126. General appreciation of Boyle's writings.

Spencer, Russ. "The Jester Who Hath No King." *Book*, December, 1998-January, 1999, 38-43. Day-in-the-life type feature based on a visit to Boyle's home, with Boyle—described as "the Bacchus of American letters"—assessing his career and personal philosophies following the publication of *Riven Rock* and *T. C. Boyle Stories.*

Vaid, Krishna Baldev. "Franz Kafka Writes to T. Coraghessan Boyle." *Michigan Quarterly Review* 35 (Summer, 1996): 533-549. As if writing a letter from Franz Kafka, Vaid discusses the work of Boyle, investigates the similarity between the two writers, and argues that the reader could grow as tired of Kafka's logic as of Boyle's broad panoramas.

Ray Bradbury

Born: Waukegan, Illinois; August 22, 1920

Principal short fiction • *Dark Carnival*, 1947; *The Martian Chronicles*, 1950; *The Illustrated Man*, 1951; *The Golden Apples of the Sun*, 1953; *The October Country*, 1955; *A Medicine for Melancholy*, 1959; *Twice Twenty-two*, 1959; *The Machineries of Joy*, 1964; *Autumn People*, 1965; *Vintage Bradbury*, 1965; *Tomorrow Midnight*, 1966; *I Sing the Body Electric!*, 1969; *Long After Midnight*, 1976; *"The Last Circus," and "The Electrocution,"* 1980; *The Stories of Ray Bradbury*, 1980; *Dinosaur Tales*, 1983; *A Memory of Murder*, 1984; *The Toynbee Convector*, 1988; *Quicker than the Eye*, 1996; *Driving Blind*, 1997; *One More for the Road: A New Short Story Collection*, 2002; *Bradbury Stories: One Hundred of His Most Celebrated Tales*, 2003; *The Best of Ray Bradbury: The Graphic Novel*, 2003; *The Cat's Pajamas*, 2004.

Other literary forms • Although Ray Bradbury has described himself as essentially a short-story writer, his contributions to a wide variety of other genres have been substantial. Indeed, he has intentionally sought to compose successfully in virtually every literary form. His best-known novels are *Fahrenheit 451* (1953), *Dandelion Wine* (1957), and *Something Wicked This Way Comes* (1962), the last being his personal favorite from among all his works. After publishing *Green Shadows, White Whale* in 1992, Bradbury concentrated mostly on shorter forms. However, after reaching the age of eighty, he returned to the longer form with *From the Dust Returned: A Family Remembrance* in 2001, *Let's All Kill Constance* in 2003, and *Farewell Summer* in 2006.

Among Bradbury's screenplays, the most successful have been *Moby Dick* (1956), written in collaboration with filmmaker John Huston, and *Icarus Montgolfier Wright* (1961) with George C. Johnson, which was nominated for an Academy Award. Bradbury had his stage plays produced in Los Angeles and New York City, and several of them have been published, representative samples of which are *The Anthem Sprinters and Other Antics* (1963) and *The Pedestrian* (1966). He also wrote many plays for radio and television. Some of the most important of the several volumes of poetry that he published were collected in *The Complete Poems of Ray Bradbury* (1982). Five more volumes of poems followed later, including *I Live By the Invisible: New and Selected Poems* (2002).

Bradbury has also written books for children and adolescents, including *Ahmed and the Oblivion Machines: A Fable* (1998); compiled anthologies of fantasy and science-fiction stories, such as *The Circus of Dr. Lao, and Other Improbable Stories* (1956); and published nonfiction works dealing with his interests in creativity and the future, such as *Yestermorrow: Obvious Answers to Impossible Futures* (1991) and *Bradbury Speaks: Too Soon from the Cave, Too Far from the Stars* (2005).

Achievements • Despite the fact that Bradbury was once named the best-known American science-fiction writer in a poll, his actual literary accomplishments are based on work whose vast variety and deeply humanistic themes transcend science fiction as it is commonly understood. His many stories, from gothic horror to social criticism, from playful fantasies to nostalgic accounts of midwestern American life, have been anthologized in several hundred collections, in English as well as many foreign languages, and several of the stories that he published early in his career now occupy a distinguished niche in twentieth century American literature.

Some of his early tales were recognized with O. Henry Prizes in 1947 and 1948, and in 1949 he was voted Best Author by the National Fantasy Fan Federation. Bradbury's "Sun and Shadow" won the Benjamin Franklin Magazine Award as the best story of 1953-1954, and in 1954 he received a National Institute of Arts and Letters Award in Literature. His novel *Fahrenheit 451* won a gold medal from the Commonwealth Club of California, and his book *Switch on the Night* (1955) was honored with a Boy's Club of America Junior Book Award in 1956. He received the Mrs. Ann Radcliffe Award of the Count Dracula Society in 1965 and 1971, the Writers' Guild of America West Valentine Davies Award in 1974, and the World Fantasy Award for Life Achievement in 1977. Whittier College gave him an honorary doctor of literature degree in 1979. PEN, an international writers' organization of poets, playwrights, editors, essayists, and novelists, gave Bradbury its Body of Work Award in 1985. In 1988 Bradbury won the Nebula Award, and in 1995 he was named Los Angeles Citizen of the Year. In 2002, he was honored with a star on the Hollywood Walk of Fame, and in 2004, he received the National Medal of the Arts.

Thomas Victor

Biography • Ray Douglas Bradbury often makes use of his own life in his writings, and he insisted that he had total recall of the myriad experiences of his life through his photographic—some would say eidetic—memory: He stated that he always had vivid recollections of the day of his birth, August 22, 1920, in Waukegan, Illinois. Leonard Spaulding Bradbury, his father, was a lineman with the Bureau of Power and Light (his distant ancestor Mary Bradbury was among those tried for witchcraft in Salem, Massachusetts); Esther Marie (née Moberg) Bradbury, his mother, had emigrated from Sweden to the United States when she was very young. A child with an exceptionally lively imagination, Ray Bradbury amused himself with his fantasies but experienced anguish from his nightmares. His mother took him to his first film, *The Hunchback of Notre Dame* (1923), when he was three years old, and he was both frightened and entranced by Lon Chaney's performance. This experience originated his lifelong love affair with motion pictures, and he wrote that he could remember the scenes and plots of all the films that he ever saw.

As he grew up, Bradbury passed through a series of passions that included circuses, dinosaurs, and Mars (the latter via the writings of Edgar Rice Burroughs). Neva Bradbury, an aunt, assisted his maturation as a person and writer by introducing him to the joys of fairy tales, L. Frank Baum's Oz books, live theater, and the stories of Edgar Allan Poe. In Bradbury's own view, the most important event in his childhood occurred in 1932 when a carnival came to town. He attended the performance of a magician, Mr. Electrico, whose spellbinding act involved electrifying himself to such an extent that sparks jumped between his teeth and every white hair on his head stood erect. Bradbury and the magician became friends, and their walks and talks along the Lake Michigan shore behind the carnival so energized his imagination that he began to compose stories for several hours a day. One of his first efforts was a sequel to a Martian novel of Burroughs.

During the Depression, Bradbury's father had difficulty finding work, and in 1932 the family moved to Arizona, where they had previously spent some time in the mid-1920's. Still in search of steady work, his father moved the family to Los Angeles, which was where Ray Bradbury attended high school and which became his permanent home. His formal education ended with his graduation from Los Angeles High School, but his education as a writer continued through his extensive reading and his participation in theater groups (one of which was sponsored by the actor Laraine Day). To support his writing, he worked as a newsboy in downtown Los Angeles for several years.

During World War II, Bradbury's poor eyesight prevented him from serving in the Army, but this disappointment gave him the freedom to pursue his career as a writer, and he began to publish his stories in such pulp magazines as *Weird Tales* and Hugo Gernsback's *Amazing Stories*. The high quality of Bradbury's stories was quickly recognized, and he was able to get his new stories published in such mass-circulation magazines as *Collier's, The Saturday Evening Post, Harper's Magazine,* and *Mademoiselle.* Because of his success as a writer, he had the financial security to marry Marguerite Susan McClure in 1947 (they had met when she, a book clerk, had waited on him). The marriage produced four daughters.

By the early 1950's, Bradbury, now recognized as an accomplished science-fiction and fantasy writer, began his involvement with Hollywood through an original screenplay that would eventually be released as *It Came from Outer Space* (1952). During the mid-1950's, he traveled to Ireland in connection with a screenplay of *Moby Dick* that he wrote with John Huston (he later drew on his experiences with the Irish for several stories and plays that took his work in a new direction). Upon his return to the United States, Bradbury composed a large number of television scripts for such shows as *Alfred Hitchcock Presents, Suspense,* and *The Twilight Zone.*

During the late 1950's and early 1960's, Bradbury moved away from science fiction, and his stories and novels increasingly focused on humanistic themes and his midwestern childhood. During the late 1960's and throughout the 1970's and 1980's, Bradbury's output of short and long fiction decreased, and his ideas found outlets in such literary forms as poems, plays, and essays. He also participated in a number of projects, such as "A Journey Through United States History," the exhibit that occupied the upper floor of the United States Pavilion for the New York World's Fair in 1964. Because of this display's success, the Walt Disney organization hired him to help develop the exhibit Spaceship Earth for the Epcot Center at Disney World in Florida. He continued to diversify his activities during the 1980's by collaborating on projects to turn his novel *Fahrenheit 451* into an opera and his novel *Dandelion Wine* into a musical. During the late 1980's and early 1990's, he returned to some of the subjects and themes that had earlier established his reputation with the publication of short-story collections *The Toynbee Convector, Quicker than the Eye*, and *Driving Blind*, and the novels *A Graveyard for Lunatics: Another Tale of Two Cities* (1990) and *Green Shadows, White Whale* (1992).

Analysis • Ray Bradbury once said that he had not so much thought his way through life as he had done things and discovered what those things meant and who he was after the doing. This metamorphosis of experience under the aegis of memory also characterizes many of his stories, which are often transmogrifications of his personal experiences. He therefore used his stories as ways of hiding and finding himself, a self whose constant changes interested, amused, and sometimes frightened him. He believed that human beings are composed of time, and in many of his science-fiction stories, a frequent theme is the dialectic between the past and the future. For example, in several of his Martian stories, the invaders of the Red Planet have to come to terms with their transformation into Martians, since survival in an alien world necessitates the invader's union with the invaded. Aggression and submission might represent the initial dialectic, but survival or death becomes the most determinative.

Even in stories where Bradbury's characters and settings seem ordinary, this theme of metamorphosis is nevertheless present, because these stories often show ordinary people being transformed by extraordinary, sometimes bizarre situations. Sometimes Bradbury's purpose is to point out the enlightening power of the abnormal; sometimes he wants to reveal the limitations of the everyday and ordinary. His best works are often wrenching indictments of the dangers of unrestrained scientific and technical progress, though his work also encourages the hope that humanity will deal creatively with the new worlds it seems driven to make. His characters are changed by their experiences, particularly when they encounter great evil beneath the surface of seemingly normal life, but in other stories Bradbury gives the reader a window through which to see the positive meaning of life (these stories, usually sentimental, are life-affirming, permitting readers to believe that human dreams can be fulfilled). By helping readers to imagine the unimaginable, he helps them to think about the unthinkable. He speaks of his tales as "idea fiction," and he prefers to call himself a Magical Realist. He casts magic spells through his poetic words and highly imaginative visions, and because of this aura of enchantment, some critics have seen his chief subject as childhood or the child hidden in the adult unconscious.

A danger exists, however, in treating Bradbury as a writer of fantasy suitable only for adolescents. This may be true for some of his works, but many of his stories exhibit emotional depths and logical complexities that call for a sophisticated dialectic between the adult and his buried childhood. The difference between fantasy and reality is not strongly developed in the child, whose experience of the world is minimal. Bradbury often plays with this tension between fantasy and reality in dealing with his principal themes—the power of the past, the freedom of the present, and the temptations and traps of the future. In the world of Bradbury's stories, fantasy becomes essential for a person existing in an increasingly technological era or with experiences that, like an iceberg, are nine-tenths buried below the surface. In these cases, the abilities to fantasize various alternatives or futures, and to choose the best among them, become necessary for survival.

Because of Bradbury's woefully inadequate knowledge of science and the lack of verisimilitude in the technological gadgetry of his science-fiction stories, many aficionados of the genre do not consider him a genuine science-fiction writer. He agrees. His science-fiction settings are backgrounds for characters with social, religious, and moral dilemmas. Like fellow science-fiction writer Isaac Asimov, Bradbury believes that science fiction's value lies in helping human beings to visualize and solve future problems before they actually occur, but unlike Asimov, he has a deep suspicion of the machine and a great faith in the human heart's capacity to perceive, do good, and create beauty. Because of this attitude, many critics view Bradbury as essentially a romantic. Since F. L. Lucas once counted 11,396 definitions of "romanticism," however, perhaps Bradbury's brand of romanticism should be more fully articulated. He has expressed an attraction for spontaneity of thought and action, and he actively cultivates his own unconscious. He believes deeply in the power of the imagination, and he accepts Blaise Pascal's sentiment that the heart has reasons about which the reason knows nothing.

In making an assessment of Bradbury's contribution to modern American literature, one must come to terms with the role he played in popularizing science fiction and making it critically respectable. Bradbury himself once stated that, for him, science fiction is "the most important literature in the history of the world," since it tells the story of "civilization birthing itself." He has also said that he considers himself not a science-fiction writer but an "idea writer," someone who loves ideas and enjoys playing with them. Many of his science-fiction critics would concur in this characterization, since they have had problems categorizing this man who knows so little about science as a traditional science-fiction writer. When asked whether the Mariner mission's revelations about the inhospitability of Mars to humankind had invalidated his stories about the planet, Bradbury responded that these discoveries in no way affected them, because he had been composing poetic myths, not scientific forecasts.

In addition to their lack of scientific verisimilitude, his stories have other weaknesses. Few of his characters are memorable, and most are simply vehicles for his ideas. He has said frankly that he devises characters to personify his ideas and that all of his characters—youths, astronauts, and grotesques—are, in some way, variations on himself. Other critics have noticed failures in Bradbury's imaginative powers, particularly in his later stories. The settings and images that seemed fresh when first used in the early stories became stale as they continued to be used in the later ones. Thomas M. Disch complained that Bradbury's sentimental attachments to his past themes "have made him nearly oblivious to new data from any source."

Despite these criticisms, Bradbury's stories possess great strengths. If his characters are made negligible by the burden of the ideas that they are forced to carry, these same ideas can open readers to his enchanting sense of wonder. These readers can be inspired by his enthusiasm for new experiences and new worlds. They may also be uplifted by the underlying optimism present even in his most pessimistic work and come to share his belief that human beings will overcome materialism, avarice, and obsession with power to achieve the expansion of what is best in the human spirit that has been his principal theme.

Dark Carnival • Many of these characteristics, along with Bradbury's penchant for the grotesque and macabre, can be seen in his first collection of stories, *Dark Carnival*. August Derleth, a Wisconsin writer who had established Arkham House to publish stories of fantasy and horror for a limited audience, had read Bradbury's stories in the pulp magazine *Weird Tales*, recognized their quality, and suggested that

Bradbury collect them in a book. *Dark Carnival* was very successful with its specialized market, and its three thousand copies were quickly sold and soon become collectors' items. The book's title was aptly chosen, since the stories often deal with the dark and strange. Several stories make use, although in highly altered forms, of emotions and events in Bradbury's own life. For example, "The Small Assassin" depicts an infant, terrified at finding himself in a hostile world, taking revenge on his parents. Bradbury uses this metamorphosis of a supposedly innocent newborn into an assassin to explore some of the feelings he had as a very young child.

Death is a motif that appears often in these tales, but unlike Poe, whom he admired, Bradbury uses the morbid not for its macabre fascination, as Poe did, but to shift readers onto a different level from which they can see reality in a new and enlightening way. In most of these tales, more happens in the imaginations of Bradbury's characters than happens in their lives. He has the ability to reach down into the labyrinthine unconscious of his characters and pull out odd desires, strange dreams, and horrendous fears. For example, in "The Next in Line," a story that grew out of his own experience on a trip to Guanajuato, northwest of Mexico City, a young American wife is simultaneously frightened and fascinated by the rows of propped-up mummified bodies in a Guanajuato catacomb. After her traumatic ordeal, she finds herself increasingly immobilized by her alienation from the death-haunted Mexican society and by her fear that her own body is a potential mummy.

Another story, "Skeleton," has a similar theme. A man is obsessed by the horrible bones that he carries within him, but when a strange creature crawls down his throat and consumes the bones that were the source of his obsession, he is transformed into a human jellyfish. These and other fantasies and horrors serve as exorcisms through which the devils of one's unconscious are expelled. The best of these stories leave the reader cleansed and transformed, with an expanded consciousness and control of the fears that can make people prisoners of their own hidden emotions.

The Martian Chronicles • Some critics see the twenty-six stories collected in *The Martian Chronicles* as the beginning of the most prolific and productive phase of Bradbury's career. Like *Dark Carnival*, this collection resulted from the suggestion of an editor, but in this case Bradbury added passages to link together his stories about Mars. These bridge passages help to interrelate the stories, but they do not make them into a unified novel. This places *The Martian Chronicles* into a peculiar literary category—less than a novel but more than a collection of short stories. Despite difficulties in categorizing this book, it is commonly recognized as Bradbury's most outstanding work. When it was first published, it was widely reviewed and read by people who did not ordinarily read science fiction. The poet Christopher Isherwood, for example, praised the book for its poetic language and its penetrating analysis of human beings forced to function on the frontier of an alien world. Within twenty years of its publication, *The Martian Chronicles* sold more than three million copies and was translated into more than thirty languages.

The Martian Chronicles is not totally unrelated to *Dark Carnival*, since Bradbury's Mars is a fantasy world, a creation not of a highly trained scientific imagination but of a mythmaker and an explorer of the unconscious. Within the time frame of 1999 to 2026, Bradbury orders his stories to give the reader a sense of the coherent evolution of the settling of Mars by Earthlings. The early stories deal with the difficulties the emigrants from Earth have in establishing successful colonies on Mars. The fifteen stories of the middle section explore the rise and fall of these colonies. The stories in the final section are concerned with the possible renovation of the human race on Mars after an annihilative nuclear war on Earth.

In several of the stories in *The Martian Chronicles*, Bradbury is once again fascinated by the subject of death. Earthlings who make the mistake of trying to duplicate Earth's culture on Mars meet difficulties and death. This theme is particularly clear in "The Third Expedition," a story that was originally titled "Mars Is Heaven" and that deeply impressed the critic and writer Jorge Luis Borges. In "The Third Expedition," Captain John Black and his crew constitute a third attempt by Earthlings to create a successful settlement on Mars, this time in a town that bears a striking resemblance to traditional midwestern American towns of the 1920's. It turns out that the Martians have deceived the Earthlings by using telepathic powers to manufacture this counterfeit town in their receptive imaginations. Captain Black and his crew have such a deep desire to believe in what they think they see that they delude themselves into seeing what the Martians want them to see. This mass hypnosis produced by the Martians capitalizes on the crew's self-delusion and on its members' need to re-create their past. When each Earthling is securely locked within what he believes is his home, he is murdered by the Martians. Trapped by their past and unable to resist, they are destroyed. Illusion and reality, time and identity, change and stability are the themes that intertwine in Bradbury's treatment of this story (one can understand why Borges liked it so much, since his own work dwells on the theme of the Other as an inextricable element in one's own identity).

The Illustrated Man • Soon after *The Martian Chronicles* appeared, Bradbury published another book of interlinked stories, *The Illustrated Man*. Most of its eighteen stories had been published in various magazines between 1947 and 1951, but some had been written specifically for this book. The framing device, which is neither as consistent nor as unifying as the bridge passages in *The Martian Chronicles*, derives from tattoos that completely cover the skin of a running character. The tattoos, however, do not grow out of the personality of this character, as would be expected for a real tattooed man whose likes and dislikes would be represented in the permanent images he chooses to decorate his body. Instead, each tattoo embodies a Bradburian idea that comes alive in a particular story.

The otherwise unrelated stories fall into several categories—tales of robots and space travel as well as stories of Mexicans and Martians. Four of the stories are set on Bradbury's Mars, and two of these are closely related to *The Martian Chronicles*. Some of the stories have themes related to those initially developed in *Dark Carnival*. For example, like "The Small Assassin," "The Veldt" concerns the revenge of children against their parents, this time in a futuristic setting. The children, who are obsessed with a room-filling television device that can depict scenes with three-dimensional realism, choose to watch an African veldt inhabited by lions gorging themselves on carcasses. The parents, who try to get their children to control their television addiction, end up as food for the lions. In this story, Bradbury makes use of a favorite theme—the blurred distinction between illusion and reality. Other stories in *The Illustrated Man* are animated by such social concerns as racism and with ethical and religious dilemmas derived from modern science and technology. For example, "The Fire Balloons" focuses on a religious missionary's discovery that the only surviving Martians have metamorphosed from human forms to floating balls of blue flame (reminiscent of the fire balloons in Earth's Fourth of July celebrations). After undergoing this transformation, these Martian flames are no longer capable of sin. Bradbury implies that a new planet means a new theology, the Fall is reversible, and a state of innocence can be regained.

The Golden Apples of the Sun • Bradbury's fourth collection, *The Golden Apples of the Sun*, used neither linking passages nor a frame narrative to interrelate the twenty-two stories. Instead, this book initiated the Bradburian potpourri of stories that would characterize most of his later collections: nostalgic, satiric, and humorous stories whose settings could be Mars, Mexico, or the Midwest and whose genre could be fantasy, science fiction, crime, or horror. He would use this variety of approach, setting, and genre to cast a revelatory light on aspects of modern life that conventional fiction was avoiding. Although the critical reception of *The Golden Apples of the Sun* was largely favorable, some critics found several of the stories disappointing and noted a falling-off from the high level of quality of *The Martian Chronicles* and *The Illustrated Man*. Despite the divided opinions, general agreement existed on the success of several of the stories, for example, "Sun and Shadow," which was set in Mexico and which won both praise and awards. Another story, "The Fog Horn," became the basis of a film, *The Beast from Twenty Thousand Fathoms* (1953). It is about a lonely dinosaur which is attracted by the sound of a foghorn, interpreting it as the mating call of a potential companion (he dies of a broken heart when he swims to shore and discovers his error). The story "A Sound of Thunder" develops a favorite Bradburian theme of the profound effect of the past on the future. It depicts what happens when a time traveler steps on a butterfly in the past and inadvertently changes the future (this will remind modern readers of the "butterfly effect" in chaos theory, in which the beating of a butterfly's wings in a Brazilian rain forest may cause a tornado in Kansas via a long chain of cause and effect).

The October Country • *The October Country*, a collection that has as its core the stories of *Dark Carnival* along with four new stories, appeared appropriately in October of 1955. Bradbury described the country of the title as a place "whose people are autumn people, thinking only autumn thoughts" and whose steps "at night on the empty walks sound like rain." In the light of the earlier success of *Dark Carnival*, it is surprising that several critics were not as kind to this collection as they had been to Bradbury's earlier ones. For example, Carlos Baker, Ernest Hemingway's biographer, predicted in his review that the only route that Bradbury's writings could follow if he continued in the direction that he had chosen was down. Some critics did see him trying, in this and later collections, to develop new subjects, themes, and approaches. For them, his imagination was still nimble, his mind adventurous, and his heart sensitive. They also noticed his increased emphasis on social issues and his desire to treat the joyous side of human nature. For most critics, however, Bradbury's later collections of stories were repetitive mixes of ideas, themes, and treatments that he had used many times before.

A Medicine for Melancholy • The problems sensed by Bradbury's critics can be seen in the collection of twenty-two stories titled *A Medicine for Melancholy*. In addition to the expected stories of fantasy and science fiction, *A Medicine for Melancholy* includes tales from the lives of the Irish, Mexicans, and Mexican Americans. The title story explores the awakening womanhood of an eighteenth century London girl who is cured of melancholia by the visit of what she interprets as Saint Bosco but who is in reality a dustman. Two of the stories in this collection, "Icarus Montgolfier Wright" and "In a Season of Calm Weather," led to films, and others, "A Fever Dream" for example, are reminiscent of films. In "A Fever Dream," aliens invade Earth not externally but by taking over the minds and hearts of their Earth victims (the film analogue is the 1956 *The Invasion of the Body Snatchers*). Derivative, too, seems the story "All Summer in a Day," about a group of children on cloud-enshrouded Venus who get to see the sun only once every seven years (the analogue here is Isaac Asimov's classic story "Nightfall").

The Machineries of Joy • During the 1960's and 1970's, Bradbury's career entered a new phase characterized by a decreasing output of short stories and novels and an increasing output of plays and poetry. When he did bring out short-story collections, the majority of critics saw little suggesting artistic growth, though a minority actually preferred his new stories, interpreting them as examples of a mature writer whose stories had acquired humanity, depth, and polish. These latter critics are also the ones who were not attracted to his tales about corpses, vampires, and cemeteries and who preferred his new optimism and his emphasis on civil rights, religion, and morality. Many of the stories in *The Machineries of Joy* provide good examples of these new tendencies. There are still stories characteristic of the old Bradbury—a science-fiction tale in which the explorers of a new planet find themselves possessed by a resident intelligence, and a horror story in which raising giant mushrooms gets out of hand. Many of the stories, however, contain the epiphanic appearance of human warmth in unexpected situations. For example, in "Almost the End of the World," when sunspots destroy television reception, a world addicted to this opiate of the mind and heart is forced to rediscover the forgotten joys of interpersonal communication.

I Sing the Body Electric! • Bradbury's next collection, *I Sing the Body Electric!* also met with a mixed critical response. Academic critics and readers who had formed their taste for Bradbury on his early works found this potpourri of seventeen stories pretentious and a decline from his best science-fiction, fantasy, and horror stories. Some stories are slight—indeed, little more than anecdotes: In "The Women," for example, a man experiences the sea as a woman and his wife as her rival. On the other hand, some critics found Bradbury's new stories enthralling and insightful, with the unexpected—a robot Abraham Lincoln, Ernest Hemingway's spirit, and an automated Martian city—confronting the reader at every turn of the page. The stories of *I Sing the Body Electric!* certainly contain some of Bradbury's favorite themes—the dialectic between past and future, reality and illusion. For example, the title story concerns a robot grandmother ideally programmed to meet the needs of the children of a recently motherless family. This electrical grandmother embodies the past (she has all the sentiment humans conventionally associate with this figure) and the future (she is a rechargeable AC-DC Mark V model and can never die). Another story that deals with the presentness of the past is "Night Call, Collect." In this tale, an old man alone on a deserted Mars receives a telephone call from himself when he was much younger (he has forgotten that he devised this plan many years earlier in order to assuage the loneliness of his old age). His young self battles with his old self, and as the old man dies, past, present, and future commingle in an odd but somehow enlightening amalgam.

Long After Midnight • *Long After Midnight* contains twenty-two stories, several of which had been written in the late 1940's and early 1950's but never previously anthologized. Some critics found the new stories aimless, uninspired, and self-indulgent, but others thought that many of them were poignant, sensitive, and touching. These latter critics thought that several of these stories represented Bradbury's new grasp of the power of love to overcome evil and to make permanent valued moments from the past. A few of the stories broke new ground in terms of subject matter: "The Better Part of Wisdom" is a compassionate and restrained treatment of homosexuality, and "Have I Got a Chocolate Bar for You!" deals gracefully with a relationship between a priest and a penitent.

The Stories of Ray Bradbury • In 1980, Bradbury selected one hundred stories from three decades of his work in *The Stories of Ray Bradbury*. Many reviewers treated this book's publication as an opportunity to analyze Bradbury's lifetime achievement as a short-story writer. Some found much to praise, comparing his body of work to Edgar Allan Poe's, O. Henry's, and Guy de Maupassant's. Thomas M. Disch, however, in an influential essay in *The New York Times Book Review*, denigrated Bradbury's stories as "schmaltzy" and "more often meretricious than not." Unlike those critics who praised Bradbury's early work and saw a decline in the quality of his later stories, Disch stated that early and late are "meaningless distinctions" in Bradbury's output. He criticized Bradbury condescendingly as a child manqué, attributing his success to the fact that "like Peter Pan, he won't grow up."

The Toynbee Convector • To those who thought that Bradbury was using *The Stories of Ray Bradbury* to bid farewell to the form that had been his home for most of his life as a writer, another collection, *The Toynbee Convector*, showed that they were mistaken. As with his other late collections, this, too, contained the familiar blend of science fiction and gothic horror as well as sentimental tales of Ireland and Middle America, but it broke little new ground.

Quicker than the Eye • Most of the twenty-one stories in *Quicker than the Eye* are loaded with symbols and metaphors about look-alikes, death, doors that open to the unknown, revelations from the unconscious mind, and psychic connections to the past and future. Magicians always fascinated Bradbury. They pretend to do something, the audience blinks, and "quicker than the eye, silks fall out of a hat." Bradbury performs magic with words, and stories "fall out" of his imagination.

In "Quicker than the Eye," the narrator and his wife watch a magician saw a woman in half and make her disappear. Men in the audience laugh. Then, Miss Quick, a pickpocket, nimbly removes wallets and other personal items from ten unsuspecting male volunteers. Miss Quick particularly humiliates one volunteer, who looks exactly like the narrator, by stripping him "quicker than the eye." The angry narrator identifies with his "double's" vulnerability, but his wife laughs.

Several stories have themes of revenge and death. In "The Electrocution," carnival worker Johnny straps Electra in the Death Chair, blindfolds her, and pulls the switch. Blue flames shoot from her body, and, with a sword, she touches and "connects" with a fascinated youth in the crowd. After Electra and her lover meet secretly, Johnny, in a jealous rage, beats him up. The next time he "electrocutes" Electra, he turns up the voltage and says, "You're dead!" She replies, "Yes, I am."

Some doors that open to the unknown are better left closed. The title "Dorian in

Excelsus" is wordplay on the liturgical phrase *Gloria in excelsis* and refers to Oscar Wilde's *The Picture of Dorian Gray* (1890 serial, 1891 expanded). A handsome youth invites the aging, dissipated narrator to become a Friend of Dorian at a spa. Behind golden doors, the narrator discovers how Friends of Dorian shed age and become physically beautiful. To regain youth, he must wrestle in Dorian's gym with hundreds of lustful men. Dorian is a "gelatinous, undulant jellyfish, the sponge of men's depravity and guilt, a pustule, bacteria, priapic jelly." He lives by breathing the sweaty stench of human passion and sin. The horrified narrator refuses Dorian's offer and scratches him with a fingernail. Dorian screams as noxious gases escape, and he and his Friends die.

Psychic connections to the past and future are recurring themes in *Quicker than the Eye*. The title character in "That Woman on the Lawn" awakens a teenage boy with her crying. Her picture is in his family album. He directs her to an address down the street, and they agree to meet in three years; he is her future baby.

Robert J. Paradowski
With updates by Martha E. Rhynes

Other major works

CHILDREN'S LITERATURE: *Switch on the Night*, 1955; *R Is for Rocket*, 1962; *S Is for Space*, 1966; *The Halloween Tree*, 1972; *Fever Dream*, 1987; *Ahmed and the Oblivion Machines: A Fable*, 1998.

PLAYS: *The Anthem Sprinters and Other Antics*, pb. 1963; *The World of Ray Bradbury: Three Fables of the Future*, pr. 1964; *The Day It Rained Forever*, pb. 1966; *The Pedestrian*, pb. 1966; *Dandelion Wine*, pr. 1967 (adaptation of his novel); *Madrigals for the Space Age*, pb. 1972; *The Wonderful Ice Cream Suit, and Other Plays*, pb. 1972; *Pillar of Fire, and Other Plays for Today, Tomorrow, and Beyond Tomorrow*, pb. 1975; *That Ghost, That Bride of Time: Excerpts from a Play-in-Progress*, pb. 1976; *The Martian Chronicles*, pr. 1977; *Fahrenheit 451*, pr. 1979 (musical); *A Device Out of Time*, pb. 1986; *On Stage: A Chrestomathy of His Plays*, pb. 1991.

ANTHOLOGIES: *Timeless Stories for Today and Tomorrow*, 1952; *The Circus of Dr. Lao, and Other Improbable Stories*, 1956.

NOVELS: *Fahrenheit 451*, 1953; *Dandelion Wine*, 1957; *Something Wicked This Way Comes*, 1962; *Death Is a Lonely Business*, 1985; *A Graveyard for Lunatics: Another Tale of Two Cities*, 1990; *Green Shadows, White Whale*, 1992; *From the Dust Returned: A Family Remembrance*, 2001; *Let's All Kill Constance*, 2003; *Farewell Summer*, 2006.

NONFICTION: *Teacher's Guide to Science Fiction*, 1968 (with Lewy Olfson); *"Zen and the Art of Writing" and "The Joy of Writing": Two Essays*, 1973; *Mars and the Mind of Man*, 1973; *The Mummies of Guanajuato*, 1978; *The Art of the Playboy*, 1985; *Zen in the Art of Writing: Essays on Creativity*, 1989; *Yestermorrow: Obvious Answers to Impossible Futures*, 1991; *Bradbury Speaks: Too Soon from the Cave, Too Far from the Stars*, 2005.

POETRY: *Old Ahab's Friend, and Friend to Noah, Speaks His Piece: A Celebration*, 1971; *When Elephants Last in the Dooryard Bloomed: Celebrations for Almost Any Day in the Year*, 1973; *Where Robot Mice and Robot Men Run Round in Robot Towns: New Poems, Both Light and Dark*, 1977; *The Bike Repairman*, 1978; *Twin Hieroglyphs That Swim the River Dust*, 1978; *The Aqueduct*, 1979; *The Haunted Computer and the Android Pope*, 1981; *The Complete Poems of Ray Bradbury*, 1982; *Forever and the Earth*, 1984; *Death Has Lost Its Charm for Me*, 1987; *Dogs Think That Every Day Is Christmas*, 1997; *With Cat for Comforter*, 1997 (with Loise Max); *I Live By the Invisible: New and Selected Poems*, 2002.

SCREENPLAYS: *It Came from Outer Space*, 1952 (with David Schwartz); *Moby Dick*, 1956 (with John Huston); *Icarus Montgolfier Wright*, 1961 (with George C. Johnson); *The Picasso Summer*, 1969 (with Ed Weinberger).

Bibliography

Bloom, Harold, ed. *Ray Bradbury*. New York: Chelsea House, 2001. Critical essays cover the major themes in Bradbury's works, looking at, among other topics, his Martian stories, his participation in the gothic tradition, the role of children in his work, and his use of myth.

Badbury, Ray. "The Ray Bradbury Chronicles." Interview by J. Stephen Bolhafner. *St. Louis Post-Dispatch*, December 1, 1996. Interview with Bradbury on the occasion of the publication of his collection of short stories *Quicker than the Eye*. Bradbury reminisces about the beginnings of his career, talks about getting over his fear of flying, and discusses *The Martian Chronicles* as fantasy, mythology, and Magical Realism.

_____. "Sci-fi for Your D: Drive." *Newsweek* 126 (November 13, 1995): 89. In this interview-story, Bradbury discusses why he is putting his most widely acclaimed short-story collection, *The Martian Chronicles*, on CD-ROM. Bradbury also discusses the role of imagination in technology, the space program, and his favorite literary figures.

Eller, Jonathan R., and William F. Touponce. *Ray Bradbury: The Life of Fiction*. Kent, Ohio: Kent State University Press, 2004. First full biography of Bradbury.

Greenberg, Martin Henry, and Joseph D. Olander, eds. *Ray Bradbury*. New York: Taplinger, 1980. This anthology of Bradbury criticism is part of the Writers of the Twenty-first Century series. Some of the articles defend Bradbury against the charge that he is not really a science-fiction writer but an opponent of science and technology; other articles defend him against the charge that he is mawkish. Includes an extensive Bradbury bibliography compiled by Marshall B. Tymn and an index.

May, Charles E., ed. *Masterplots II: Short Story Series, Revised Edition*. 8 vols. Pasadena, Calif.: Salem Press, 2004. Designed for student use, this reference set contains articles providing detailed plot summaries and analyses of these four short stories by Bradbury: "The April Witch" (vol. 1), "I See You Never" (vol. 4), "There Will Come Soft Rains" (vol. 7), and "The Veldt" (vol. 8).

Mogen, David. *Ray Bradbury*. Boston: Twayne, 1986. This brief introduction to Bradbury's career centers on analyses of the literary influences that shaped the development of his style and the themes whose successful embodiment in his short stories and novels shaped his reputation. The detailed notes at the end of the book contain many useful references. Bibliography and index.

Reid, Robin Ann. *Ray Bradbury: A Critical Companion*. Westport, Conn.: Greenwood Press, 2000. Part of the publisher's series of reference books on popular contemporary writers for students, this volume provides detailed plot summaries and analyses of Bradbury's fictional works, along with character portraits, a biography of Bradbury and an extensive bibliography.

Touponce, William F. *Naming the Unnameable: Ray Bradbury and the Fantastic After Freud*. Mercer Island, Wash.: Starmont House, 1997. Touponce finds the psychoanalytic ideas of Sigmund Freud and Carl Jung helpful in plumbing the effectiveness of much of Bradbury's work (though in a letter to the author, Bradbury himself denies any direct influence, since he has "read little Freud or Jung").

Nevertheless, Touponce believes that Bradbury has written stories of a modern consciousness that often forgets its debt to the unconscious.

Weist, Jerry, and Donn Albright. *Bradbury, an Illustrated Life: A Journey to Far Metaphor.* New York: William Morrow, 2002. "Visual biography" of Bradbury made up mostly of images from pulps, films, television, and other mass media that both influenced Bradbury and have been influenced by him. An innovative approach to understanding a writer who transcends the printed page.

Weller, Sam. *The Bradbury Chronicles.* New York: William Morrow, 2005. This authorized biography, was written with access to Bradbury and his personal papers and correspondence. Not a critical work, but rather an admiring portrait of the writer.

Morley Callaghan

Born: Toronto, Ontario, Canada; February 22, 1903
Died: Toronto, Ontario, Canada; August 25, 1990

Principal short fiction • *A Native Argosy*, 1929; *Now That April's Here, and Other Stories*, 1936; *Morley Callaghan's Stories*, 1959; *The Lost and Found Stories of Morley Callaghan*, 1985.

Other literary forms • Although Morley Callaghan was a masterful short-story writer, he also won recognition for his many novels, the most highly regarded being *Such Is My Beloved* (1934), *More Joy in Heaven* (1937), *The Loved and the Lost* (1951), and *Close to the Sun Again* (1977). He is also the author of a novella (*No Man's Meat*), a children's book (*Luke Baldwin's Vow*, 1948), and three plays (*To Tell the Truth*, pr. 1949; *Turn Home Again*, pr. 1940; and *Season of the Witch*, pb. 1976). He recorded some of his stories for children, and others, such as *Luke Baldwin's Vow*, have been filmed. Starting his career as a journalist, Callaghan contributed articles and essays to newspapers and journals throughout his life. His nonfiction works include the text for a book of John de Visser's photographs, entitled *Winter* (1974), and *That Summer in Paris: Memories of Tangled Friendships with Hemingway, Fitzgerald, and Some Others* (1963), an entertaining account of the heady days in Paris in 1929, when he socialized with Ernest Hemingway, F. Scott Fitzgerald, James Joyce, and other writers. Throughout his life, Callaghan continued to make significant contributions to Canadian cultural life as a book reviewer and essayist as well as a novelist.

Achievements • During the 1920's, Morley Callaghan's stories impressed Ernest Hemingway, who introduced them to Ezra Pound. Pound subsequently printed them in his magazine, *The Exile*. The stories also impressed F. Scott Fitzgerald, who presented them to Maxwell Perkins, his editor at Scribner's. Perkins later published Callaghan's stories as well as some of his novels. Although considered a highly promising writer in the 1920's and 1930's, Callaghan neither developed a large audience nor achieved the type of reputation that his works warrant. Edmund Wilson commented that Callaghan was "perhaps the most unjustly neglected novelist in the English-speaking world." Even so, Callaghan was the recipient of several awards: Canada's Governor General's Literary Award (1951), the Gold Medal of the Royal Society of Canada (1958), the Lorne Pierce Medal (1960), the Canada Council Molson Prize (1970), the Royal Bank of Canada Award (1970), and the Companion of the Order of Canada (1982). He was also nominated for a Nobel Prize. His fiction is praised for its direct, unornamented prose, though later criticism has suggested that his writing is wooden, with technical weaknesses. His fiction is also valued for its sympathetic portrayal of ordinary people and for its honest treatment of the problems of contemporary life. Callaghan's lifelong exploration of the conflict between spirituality and human weakness and alienation has illuminated the best of his writing.

Callaghan held a doctorate in literature from the University of Western Ontario (1965), a law degree from the University of Toronto (1966), and a doctorate in litera-

John Martin

ture from the University of Windsor (1973). In 1989, the city of Toronto awarded him a Lifetime Achievement Award.

Biography • Born in Toronto, Canada, on September 22, 1903, Edward Morley Callaghan was reared by Roman Catholic parents of Irish descent. He grew up interested in sports, especially boxing and baseball, but at a young age he also displayed a talent for writing, selling at the age of seventeen his first article, a description of Yonge and Alberta streets in Toronto, to the *Star Weekly* for twelve dollars. In 1921, he entered St. Michael's College of the University of Toronto, and during the summers and part-time during the school year, he was a reporter for the Toronto *Daily Star*, the same newspaper that employed Ernest Hemingway, who encouraged him in his attempts at fiction writing. Callaghan received his bachelor's degree in 1925, and enrolled in Osgoode Hall Law School in Toronto. He continued to write short stories, mailing them to Hemingway, who was then in Paris. Some of these stories, through Hemingway's assistance, appeared in various magazines, such as *This Quarter, Transition,* and *The Exile.* In 1928, the year that Callaghan finished law school and was admitted to the Ontario bar, Maxwell Perkins, of Scribner's, published several of his stories in *Scribner's Magazine* and agreed to print his first novel, *Strange Fugitive* (1928), as well as a collection of short stories, *A Native Argosy.* Forsaking law, Callaghan decided to be a writer. After marrying Loretto Florence Dee in 1929, he traveled to Paris, where he met with Hemingway and became acquainted with F. Scott Fitzgerald and James Joyce. He later recorded this volatile period in *That Summer in Paris.*

Leaving Paris in the autumn, Callaghan returned to Toronto, which became his home except for occasional stays in Pennsylvania and New York, where he socialized with Sherwood Anderson, Thomas Wolfe, James T. Farrell, Sinclair Lewis, and other writers. During this early period, from 1928 to 1937, he published a novel or a collection of short stories almost yearly. From 1937 to 1948, he neglected his fiction and devoted his time to radio programming and writing essays. It has been suggested that the events of that time—the rise of Nazism, the Spanish Civil War (1936-1939), the purges of Joseph Stalin, and World War II—contributed to his lack of interest in fiction. In 1948, he resumed writing novels and short stories, which appeared regularly in leading magazines. In his later years he devoted his energy to novels and nonfiction works. He also gained public recognition and respect in Canada as a radio broadcast personality and commentator on Canadian cultural life. Callaghan died on August 25, 1990, in Toronto.

Analysis • Over his long career, Morley Callaghan published more than one hundred short stories, in such magazines as *The New Yorker, Scribner's Magazine*, and numerous other magazines. Many of these have been collected in his four volumes of short stories.

Although there are variations and exceptions, Callaghan's stories generally have recognizable characteristics. Foremost of these is the style: Most noticeably in the early works, Callaghan employs short declarative sentences, colloquial dialogue, and plain, unadorned language. As he remarked in *That Summer in Paris*, he attempts to "tell the truth cleanly." This sparse, economical, straightforward style has been compared with Hemingway's. Perhaps Callaghan was influenced by Hemingway (he admired and respected the older author), but it is likely that Callaghan's work on a newspaper shaped his writing, just as Hemingway's style was honed by his years of reporting.

Like a journalist, Callaghan presented the events in his stories objectively, neither condemning nor praising his character. By precisely recording his observations, Callaghan allows his readers to form their own judgments. He strives "to strip the language, and make the style, the method, all the psychological ramifications, the ambience of the relationships, all the one thing, so the reader couldn't make separations. Cézanne's apples. The appleness of the apples. Yet just apples." In other words, he endeavored to capture the essence of the moment.

Although Callaghan's stories are often set in Canada, he should not be classified as a regional writer. His appeal ranges beyond the borders of his country. The themes he treats are universal and are not limited to Canadian issues; in fact, he has been criticized for not addressing Canadian problems more forcefully. Many of his stories examine human relationships, and they therefore revolve around psychological issues rather than physical actions. They depict the ordinary person and his or her desire for happiness. This desire is often frustrated by environmental forces such as unemployment and injustice and by internal drives such as fear and sex. In the early stories, the characters, inarticulate and of less than normal intelligence, are on the edge of society: the poor, the disabled, the criminal, and the insane. The characters in Callaghan's later stories are more likely to be educated, but they still struggle in their quest for a better life. All Callaghan's characters reflect his concerns as a Roman Catholic, and a certain pessimism underlies their portrayals. Rarely in Callaghan's characters are innate spirituality and nobility of character allowed to triumph over the more ignoble of human instincts and behavior.

In 1928, Scribner's published Callaghan's first novel, *Strange Fugitive*, and followed this a year later with *A Native Argosy*, a collection of short fiction containing fourteen stories and two novellas. These stories are some of the most naturalistic produced by Callaghan, and the characters, themes, and style resemble that found in work by other naturalistic writers, such as Stephen Crane, Theodore Dreiser, and Frank Norris. Influenced by Charles Darwin, Karl Marx, and Sigmund Freud, these authors applied the principles of scientific determinism to their fiction. Humans are viewed as animals trapped in a constant struggle to survive. They are limited by forces that are beyond their control and even beyond their understanding. Callaghan, like the other naturalistic writers, presents the material in an objective and documentary manner, eschewing moral judgments and optimistic endings.

"A Country Passion" • "A Country Passion," originally printed in *Transition*, portrays an inarticulate character who is ultimately destroyed by a combination of his instincts and society's strictures. Jim Cline loves Ettie Corley, a mentally disabled girl twenty-nine years his junior, who will soon be sent to an asylum. He wants to marry the sixteen-year-old girl, but the minister forbids it because Jim has been in jail, as the reader learns later, for stealing chickens and for fighting. Although unable to marry, Jim nevertheless "had come to an agreement with her any way," and now he faces a charge of seduction which carries a life sentence. Jim's interest in Ettie is more than sexual. Out of concern for her, Jim has bought coal and food for Ettie's family in the winter and clothes for her. She needs him; as the minister comments, "she's had the worst home in town and something should have been done about it long ago." Nevertheless, the culture will not accept their union. After being arrested, Jim escapes from jail, harboring the vague notion that "if he could get out he could explain his idea to everybody and get people behind him," his problem would be solved. Unable to concentrate, he cannot formulate his idea. He is caught and will presumably spend the rest of his life in jail, while Ettie will spend hers in an institution. Though Jim and Ettie struggle to attain happiness, they cannot overcome the forces that oppose them. The depressing outcome is relieved partly by their achieving, even for a brief moment, a sharing of their affection.

"Amuck in the Bush" • The naturalistic tone is found throughout the collection. In "Amuck in the Bush," Gus Rapp is portrayed as an animal, controlled by his instincts. Fired from his lumberyard job, he seeks revenge by attacking the boss's wife and five-year-old daughter. The attack is savage, and only because of his own awkwardness does he not kill them. After the attack, he appears as a mute and uncomprehending animal as he crashes through the forest. Eventually, he is drawn back to the town, where he is captured and roped to a lamppost.

"A Wedding Dress" and "An Escapade" • Many of the characters in *A Native Argosy* are dissatisfied and troubled by vague, unarticulated desires. In "A Wedding Dress," Lena Schwartz has waited fifteen years to marry. Finally, when her fiancé has a good job, the wedding is scheduled. She longs for a dress that will show her to her advantage and make her desirable to her future husband. Unaware of her own actions, she steals an expensive dress from a store. Regretting the deed, she nevertheless tries on the fancy but ill-fitting dress. Still wearing it, she is arrested. Her fiancé bails her out and takes her into his custody. In "An Escapade," a middle-aged woman is lonely and repressed. Because of the titillating gossip of her bridge-club friends, Rose Carew misses the service at her Catholic church in order to attend another service being held in a theater. During the service, she is sexually attracted to the man next to her. She does not, however, recognize the emotion; she only knows that she is uncomfortable. She hurriedly leaves, goes to her Catholic church, and prays until she recovers her equanimity. Both of these characters yearn for a change in their lives, but they cannot articulate their desires and are unable to initiate actions that might bring about the desired results.

"A Predicament" • Throughout Callaghan's work appear stories that contain characters, settings, and conflicts that are familiar to Catholics. In "A Predicament," a young priest hearing confessions must deal with a drunk who has wandered into the confessional booth. The man, thinking that he is on a streetcar, waits for his stop. The priest, ignoring him, hears confessions from the other booth, but it soon becomes apparent that the man will not go away and will probably cause a disturbance. The priest, young and somewhat insecure, is afraid of any embarrassment. To resolve the issue, the priest slips into the role of a streetcar conductor and announces to the man, "Step lively there; this is King and Young. Do you want to go past your stop?" The drunk quietly leaves. The priest is at first satisfied with his solution, but then his dishonesty bothers him. Earlier, he had chided a woman for telling lies, instructing her that lies lead to worse sins. Unsure of his position, he thinks that he should seek the bishop's advice but then decides to wait until he can consider his actions more closely. Thus, he postpones what might be a soul-searching encounter. Callaghan, gently and with humor, has shown that priests are no strangers to human weaknesses.

In His Own Country • In *A Native Argosy*, Callaghan included two novellas. One of these, *In His Own Country*, presents a man who attempts to find a synthesis between religion and science. Although Bill Lawson dreams of becoming a latter-day St. Thomas Aquinas, he is unsuited for the project because of his overwhelming ignorance. Indeed, the task throws him into a catatonic state. Flora, his wife, is concerned first with the income that the project might generate, then with his neglect of her, and finally with his well-being: He does not eat, shave, or take care of his clothes. She longs for the days when they would enjoy the evenings together. Eventually, he quits his job because the small hypocrisies associated with newspaper work taint him, or so he reasons, and render him unsuitable for his grand task. He grows increasingly bewildered as he tries to summarize what is known about geology, chemistry, and the other sciences. At one point, he argues that he can reduce all life to a simple chemical formula. He even converts to Catholicism in order to understand religion better. Finally, returning from a long walk, he discovers his wife with an old beau and dashes out of the house. Flora searches for him, but failing to find him, she retreats to her father's farm, a three-hour walk from town. Later, Bill is found incoherent on a bench. At first not expected to live, he is force-fed by his mother, and eventually Flora returns to care for him. The town treats Bill as a marvel and admires him for the philosophical thoughts they assume that he is thinking. The ending is ambiguous. Is Bill a prophet, a saint, or a madman?

Flora as the point-of-view character is well chosen. Limited in intelligence, she makes no attempt to comprehend Bill's thoughts, which ultimately drive him to insanity. The sparse, economical prose style matches the limited perceptions of Flora. Bill and Flora belong to the roster of marginal characters in *A Native Argosy* who lack control over their own lives.

Now That April's Here, and Other Stories • Callaghan's second collection of short stories, *Now That April's Here, and Other Stories*, contains thirty-five stories that were published in magazines from 1929 to 1935. This later work shows the influence of Christian humanism, a belief in a Christian interpretation of the world coupled with a focus on humans' happiness and an emphasis on the realization of their potential. In 1933, Callaghan spent many hours with Jacques Maritain, the French theologican and philosopher, who was then a visiting scholar at the University of Toronto. Maritain is credited with developing Christian existential thought as a response to Jean-Paul Sartre's essentially atheistic existentialism. His influence led Callaghan to moderate the strongly pessimistic tone of his fiction.

Less naturalistic in tone than the earlier tales, these stories present characters who, while they still cannot greatly alter the courses of their lives, can occasionally achieve a measure of peace, contentment, and dignity. Unlike the inarticulate characters of the previous volume, these later characters are more intelligent. Matching this change in the characterization, Callaghan's style is more complex; the sentences are longer and of greater variety as opposed to the pared-down style of the earlier volume. Yet while the style is more mature and the stories more optimistic, there is less variety than in the earlier volume. The stories presented in this collection for the most part follow a set pattern. The equilibrium of the opening is interrupted by a crisis; after the crisis is met, an equilibrium is again established, but some insight is achieved, all within the span of a few hours.

"The Blue Kimono" • Many of the selections in *Now That April's Here, and Other Stories* depict the struggles of young lovers to overcome the effects of the Depression. In "The Blue Kimono," George and his wife, Marthe, had come to the city for better opportunities, but since they have arrived in the city, their situation has worsened. Frustrated, George blames his wife for his unemployment. One night, he awakens and discovers Marthe tending their son. The woman is frightened, but George is too frustrated to notice his wife's concern; all he sees is her tattered blue kimono. He had bought it when they were first married, and now it seems to mock his attempts to secure a job. Gradually, his wife communicates her fears to him; the boy's symptoms resemble those of infantile paralysis. Immediately, the husband forgets his problems and tries to entertain the little boy. When the boy finally responds to the aspirin, the couple, who have weathered the crisis, are drawn closer. The wife thinks that she can mend the kimono so that it would not appear so ragged. Through their love for each other and for their son, the two have, for a moment, eliminated the tension caused by their poverty. In "The Blue Kimono" as in "A Wedding Dress," Callaghan uses clothing symbolically. These items suggest a happier moment and reveal the discrepancy between the characters' dreams and the reality that makes those dreams unattainable.

"A Sick Call" • In this story Callaghan utilizes a situation that is familiar to Catholics. In "A Sick Call," Father Macdowell, an elderly priest, who is often chosen to hear confessions because nothing shocks him, is called to the bedside of a sick woman. Even though she has left the Church, she, afraid of dying, wants to be absolved of her sins. Her husband, John, however, who rejects all religion, opposes the priest's visit. John is afraid that she will draw close to the Church and thereby reject him, thus destroying the love they share. Yet the priest's advanced age, his gentleness, and his selective deafness secure for him a place at the side of the woman's bed. In order to hear her confession, Father Macdowell requests that John leave, but John refuses. Father Macdowell seemingly accepts defeat and in preparation for departing asks the husband for a glass of water. As John complies, the priest quickly hears the woman's confession and grants absolution. John, returning as the priest is making the sign of the Cross, knows that he has been tricked.

The priest leaves with a sense of satisfaction, yet gradually he grows concerned that he came between the wife and her husband. The priest recognizes John's love for her and remarks on the beauty of such strong love, but then he dismisses it, calling it pagan. He begins to doubt his convictions, however, and allows that perhaps the pagan love is valid. In "A Sick Call," Callaghan has again presented a priest with human failings; Father Macdowell relies on subterfuge in order to hear a confession. Yet the story is more than a character study of a priest; it is a discussion of what is sacred, and the answer is left ambiguous. Callaghan implies that sacredness is not the sole property of religion.

Morley Callaghan's Stories • After a ten-year hiatus in writing fiction, Callaghan resumed writing novels and short stories in the late 1940's. In 1959, he published his third collection of short stories, *Morley Callaghan's Stories*. For this, he selected his favorite stories from 1926 to 1953. Twelve had appeared earlier in *A Native Argosy*, thirty-two in *Now That April's Here, and Other Stories*; the remaining thirteen, previously uncollected, had been written between 1936 and 1953. Callaghan in the prologue writes of the stories, "These are the ones that touch times and moods and people I like to remember now. Looking back on them I can see that I have been concerned with the problems of many kinds of people but I have neglected the very, very rich." These stories, as well as those in the other collections, show a sympathy for beleaguered ordinary human beings and an understanding of their problems.

"The Cheat's Remorse" • In "The Cheat's Remorse" (reprinted in the 1938 edition of Edward O'Brien's *Best Short Stories*), Callaghan focuses on people who have been adversely affected by the Depression. Phil, out of work, is drinking coffee in a diner. Although he has a possibility of a job, he needs a clean shirt before he can go for the interview. Yet his shirts are at the laundry, and he lacks the money to get them. At the diner, he notices a wealthy drunk drop a dollar when he pays the bill for a sandwich he did not even eat. Phil waits until the man leaves. As he stoops to pick up the money, however, a young woman places her foot on it. She, too, has been waiting for the drunk to leave, and she, too, needs the money. Phil offers to flip a coin to resolve the issue. The woman loses. Having used his trick coin, Phil cheated her. Yet immediately he regrets it, tries to give her the dollar, and even confesses his guilt, but she refuses. She argues perceptively that a single dollar could not begin to alleviate her problems but it might make some difference to him. He feels so bad that at the conclusion he is eyeing a tavern, planning to assuage his guilt with alcohol.

The characters are affected by economic forces over which they have little or no control. Thus the story has some affinities with the earlier naturalistic tales from *A Native Argosy*. In "The Cheat's Remorse," both the best and the worst are depicted. Phil, selfishly, willingly cheats the woman, but the woman, ignoring her need, offers to help Phil. So even though she is affected by the same forces, she maintains her humanity and dignity.

"A Cap for Steve" • Callaghan effectively wrote stories from the point of view of characters who are limited in intelligence, and he was just as effectively able to employ a child's point of view. In "A Cap for Steve," Steve, a painfully shy young boy, is obsessed with baseball. His father belittles the sport, however, not realizing that baseball is Steve's only pleasure. Grudgingly, his father takes him to a baseball game during which Steve acquires the cap of one of the star players. The cap changes Steve into a leader. Yet he loses the cap and becomes despondent. Later he discovers another boy, a lawyer's son, wearing his cap, and he and his father call on the boy's father. The difference between the two families is apparent immediately. Steve's family is barely surviving, while the other boy's is wealthy. Since the lawyer's son bought the cap from another, the lawyer offers to sell it to Steve for the price he paid, five dollars. Even though five dollars represents a sacrifice for Steve and his father, they agree. Then the lawyer offers to buy back the cap because his son values it. At twenty dollars, Steve's father agrees. Stunned, Steve will not walk with his father on the return home. Steve's father realizes that he does not know his son and resolves to be more of a father. The boy accepts his father's apology and is willing to forget the cap as "the price

[he] was willing to pay to be able to count on his father's admiration and approval."

Although the story is set in the Depression and illustrates class differences, the focus is on the father-and-son relationship. The father does not accept his son until he comes close to losing his love, but the boy is willing to forgive his father's indifference for the chance at a closer relationship. The emphasis is on the love that can survive under adverse conditions.

The Lost and Found Stories of Morley Callaghan • In 1985, Callaghan published a fourth volume of collected stories, *The Lost and Found Stories of Morley Callaghan*. The twenty-six stories in this volume were originally published in leading magazines in the 1930's, 1940's, and 1950's. During the preparation of *Morley Callaghan's Stories*, they had been overlooked, and in 1984, they were "found." The stories are similar in tone, style, and theme to the work that appears in the other collections.

In Callaghan, the inarticulate and the forgotten—the rural and urban poor, the insane, and the mentally weak—have found a voice. Throughout his career, in a straightforward narrative style, he told their story. Although Callaghan might not have received the recognition he deserves, he nevertheless should be studied. As one reviewer has written, Callaghan "sits across the path of Canadian literature like an old Labrador, you're not sure how to approach him, but you can't ignore him."

Barbara Wiedemann
With updates by Jill Rollins

Other major works

CHILDREN'S LITERATURE: *Luke Baldwin's Vow*, 1948.

PLAYS: *Turn Home Again*, pr. 1940 (also known as *Going Home*); *To Tell the Truth*, pr. 1949; *Season of the Witch*, pb. 1976.

NOVELS: *Strange Fugitive*, 1928; *It's Never Over*, 1930; *No Man's Meat*, 1931 (novella); *A Broken Journey*, 1932; *Such Is My Beloved*, 1934; *They Shall Inherit the Earth*, 1935; *More Joy in Heaven*, 1937; *The Varsity Story*, 1948; *The Loved and the Lost*, 1951; *The Many Coloured Coat*, 1960; *A Passion in Rome*, 1961; *A Fine and Private Place*, 1975; *Season of the Witch*, 1976; *Close to the Sun Again*, 1977; *"No Man's Meat," and "The Enchanted Pimp,"* 1978; *A Time for Judas*, 1983; *Our Lady of the Snows*, 1985; *A Wild Old Man on the Road*, 1988.

NONFICTION: *That Summer in Paris: Memories of Tangled Friendships with Hemingway, Fitzgerald, and Some Others*, 1963; *Winter*, 1974.

Bibliography

Boire, Gary A. *Morley Callaghan: Literary Anarchist*. Toronto: ECW Press, 1994. Very good biography of Callaghan. Includes bibliographical references.

Cude, Wilfred. "Morley Callaghan's Practical Monsters: Downhill from Where and When?" In *Modern Times*. Vol. 3 in *The Canadian Novel*, edited by John Moss. Toronto: NC Press, 1982. This florid essay treats the darker side of Callaghan's vision through a discussion of characterization in several of his short stories and in some of his novels.

Gadpaille, Michelle. *The Canadian Short Story*. Toronto: Oxford University Press, 1988. Includes a brief discussion of Callaghan's short-story writing career, commenting on his working-class characters, the simplicity of his style, and his contribution to the development of the modern Canadian short story.

Kendle, Judith. "Morley Callaghan: An Annotated Bibliography." In *The Annotated Bibliography of Canada's Major Authors*, edited by Robert Lecker and Jack David. Vol. 5. Toronto: ECW Press, 1984. Contains the most exhaustive listing of primary sources and secondary sources for Callaghan's work up to 1984 that a student is likely to need. The categories cover the spectrum from books and articles to interviews to audiovisual material. A helpful "Index to Critics Listed in the Bibliography" is also included.

May, Charles E., ed. *Masterplots II: Short Story Series, Revised Edition.* 8 vols. Pasadena, Calif.: Salem Press, 2004. Designed for student use, this reference set contains articles providing detailed plot summaries and analyses of these five short stories by Callaghan: "All the Years of Her Life" and "A Cap for Steve" (vol. 1), "The Faithful Wife" (vol. 3), "Now That April's Here" (vol. 5), and "A Sick Call" (vol. 7).

Morley, Patricia. *Morley Callaghan.* Toronto: McClelland and Stewart, 1978. This study considers Callaghan's fiction to the mid-1970's, including thorough, useful analysis of his short fiction.

Stuewe, Paul. "The Case of Morley Callaghan." In *Clearing the Ground: English-Canadian Fiction After "Survival."* Toronto: Proper Tales Press, 1984. In this chapter, Stuewe takes Callaghan to task for sloppy writing and his critics to task for concentrating on Callaghan's thematic concerns to the exclusion of his technical flaws. Stuewe's own writing and tone are lively and incisive.

Tracey, Grant. "One Great Way to Read Short Stories: Studying Character Deflection in Morley Callaghan's 'All the Years of Her Life.'" In *Short Stories in the Classroom*, edited by Carole L. Hamilton and Peter Kratzke. Urbana, Ill.: National Council of Teachers of English, 1999. Analysis of the story through the perspective of how events affect and change a single character.

Woodcock, George. "Possessing the Land: Notes on Canadian Fiction." In *The Canadian Imagination: Dimensions of a Literary Culture*, edited by David Staines. Cambridge, Mass.: Harvard University Press, 1977. Callaghan's fiction is discussed in the context of Canadian fiction and its development and direction since the nineteenth century. The student is provided with a valuable overview that underscores the significance of Callaghan's contribution to Canadian literature.

Truman Capote

Born: New Orleans, Louisiana; September 30, 1924
Died: Los Angeles, California; August 25, 1984

Principal short fiction • *A Tree of Night, and Other Stories*, 1949; *Breakfast at Tiffany's: A Short Novel and Three Stories*, 1958; *One Christmas*, 1983; *I Remember Grandpa: A Story*, 1986; *The Complete Collected Stories of Truman Capote*, 2004.

Other literary forms • In addition to stories and short novels, Truman Capote wrote travel sketches and various kinds of nonfiction, much of which has been collected, along with some of Capote's short stories and novellas, in *A Capote Reader* (1987). The volume *Local Color* (1950), on the other hand, is a collection solely of travel essays. Capote also did some screenwriting, including critically well-received scripts for *Beat the Devil* (1954) and *The Innocents* (1961), an adaptation of the Henry James story *The Turn of the Screw* (1898), and an adaptation of *Breakfast at Tiffany's*, which became a well-known film in 1961.

In Cold Blood (1966), probably his most famous work, is a "nonfiction novel," a documented re-creation of the murder of a family in Kansas. The novel was both a critical and a popular success, and the television film version won an Emmy Award in 1967. Capote's last work, another nonfiction novel, *Answered Prayers: The Unfinished Novel* (1986), set off a social scandal with its gossipy revelations. Capote finished his writing career in ignominy.

In 2004, the handwritten manuscript of a novel that Capote had composed when he was only nineteen turned up in a Sotheby's auction. The following year, that book was published as *Summer Crossing*. The brief story is about a young woman left on her own in a Manhattan penthouse, as the rest of her family are traveling abroad. Though immature and often confused, the book shows many signs of Capote's later strengths as a writer.

Achievements • The best of Truman Capote's writing is regarded as elegant prose, noted for its lucidity, although at its worst it became an example of vain excess and gossip. Yet Capote was one of the United States' leading post-World War II writers. He pioneered the genre of the "nonfiction novel" with *In Cold Blood* and gained renown for his short stories and novellas. His story "Miriam" won the O. Henry Memorial Award in 1943, and "Shut a Final Door" won the same prize in 1946. Although much of his work has been both critically and popularly praised, Capote was rarely formally recognized during his writing career.

Biography • Because his parents were divorced when he was four years old, Truman Capote was reared by aunts and cousins in a small town in Alabama. At the age of seventeen, he moved to New York City and worked his way up from mailroom clerk to feature writer for *The New Yorker*. Capote's early promise seemed fulfilled with the success of *In Cold Blood*, and he spent many years traveling around the world as a celebrated author. He became the pet celebrity for a number of high-society women, most notably Barbara "Babe" Paley and Lee Bouvier Radziwill, sister of Jacqueline Kennedy

Onassis. His charmed life seemed to fade, however, under the pressure of trying to produce another successful novel. During the 1970's and early 1980's, Capote's health was ruined by alcoholism and drug dependency.

The downslide began in 1975, however, when *Esquire* magazine published Capote's story "La Côte Basque: 1965." The story was a thinly veiled exposé of the scandals of the rich and famous, and its targets did not appreciate the publicity. Capote's friends immediately ostracized him, and he became persona non grata in many of the places he had previously frequented. Depressed by the reaction that his story generated, Capote became reclusive. His work deteriorated even more, and he did not produce anything to rival his earlier writing before he died at the home of his longtime friend Joanne Carson in 1984.

Library of Congress

Analysis • Truman Capote's stories are best known for their mysterious, dreamlike occurrences. As his protagonists try to go about their ordinary business, they meet with unexpected obstacles—usually in the form of haunting, enigmatic strangers. Corresponding to some childhood memory or to someone the protagonist once knew, these people take on huge proportions and cause major changes in the character's life. The central figures of these stories are usually people who have left their hometowns, who travel, or who live alone, for they seem most vulnerable to chance encounters. Their isolation gives them the time, and their loneliness gives them the motivation to see these experiences through to their conclusions—and often with great risk.

Capote was a careful craftsman. His words are meticulously chosen for their evocative power, and, at their best, they create highly charged images and symbols. His descriptions of the seasons or weather further heighten the effects he wants to create. Snow, rain, dusk, and sunlight serve to separate the particular setting from a larger landscape, thus reinforcing the self-reflexive nature of his stories. Attics, kitchens, one-room walk-ups, and isolated apartments are typical settings that also provide sequestered settings. The atmosphere, location, characters, and events present a touching but often chilling and ominous beauty. The combination of reality and dream also produces an eerie beauty.

"A Tree of Night" • In "A Tree of Night," one of his finest stories, Kay is a young, attractive student returning to college after the funeral of an uncle. It is late on a winter night, bare and icy, when she boards the train from the deserted platform. Taking the only available seat, she sits opposite an odd-looking couple. The woman is in her fifties, with a huge head and a dwarfish body, while the man is mute, with marblelike eyes and an expressionless face. Although Kay is initially polite, she hopes to be left alone, but the woman wants company and conversation. Kay tries to remain distant, but the woman and man are persistent and aggressive. Without any warning, the man reaches toward Kay and strokes her cheek. Her reaction is immediate but confused: She is repelled by the boldness of the gesture while, at the same time, she is touched by the delicacy.

From this point on, Kay seems to view the man and woman as harbingers of danger. Capote's style remains realistic and his tone objective, but the couple behave as though they are part of Kay's nightmare. The woman talks endlessly, always wanting a response from her listener. She forces Kay to drink liquor with her and even grabs her wrist. As in a nightmare, Kay wants to scream and awaken the other passengers, but no sounds come out. Trying to escape from the woman's irritating voice, Kay has a reverie as she stares into the void face of the man, and suddenly his face and her uncle's dead face blend. She sees, or imagines that she sees, a shared secret and a stillness. This association of the stranger with someone from her past is deadly, preparing the reader for the end of the story.

By degrees, the man assumes control over Kay. He takes from his pocket a peach seed and fondles it gently. The woman insists that he only wants Kay to purchase it as a good-luck charm, but Kay is frightened, interpreting his action as some kind of warning. Trying to avoid the man, she leaves her seat for the observation platform and fresh air, but soon she senses someone beside her and knows that it must be the man. Now, without the distracting annoyance of the woman, Kay understands why she finds him so threatening. Unable to speak or to hear, he is like her uncle, dead, and the dead can haunt. She further recognizes him as a figure from her childhood dreams, the boogeyman, the "wizard-man," the mysterious personage that could bring alive "terrors that once, long ago, had hovered above her like haunted limbs on a tree of night." Kay's submission is unquestionable, but precisely what she submits to is left ambiguous. Together, she and the man return to their seats, and she gives him money for the peach seed. Then the woman takes possession of Kay's whole purse and, although Kay wants to shout, she does not. Finally the woman takes Kay's raincoat and pulls it "like a shroud" over her head. No longer struggling, Kay sinks into a strange passivity.

"A Tree of Night" raises many questions but provides few answers. The characters are realistically presented, but eccentric, to say the least. Kay is not wholly convincing, yet is still three-dimensional. It is rather the events themselves that appear unlikely and nightmarish, but since Capote delights in paradox, his story cannot be classified as either pure dream or simple reality. Why does Kay not protest? To what extent do she and the mute actually communicate? Is the submission of the young girl carefully planned by the couple? Are the two travelers real passengers who want to do her harm, or can they be projections from Kay's psyche? Or are they merely two unique strangers to whom Kay attributes much more power than they really have? These ambiguities are the source of both the story's weaknesses and its strengths; they enrich the encounter and abstract it, but they also leave the reader feeling baffled. Nevertheless, Capote seems to imply that human beings are extremely vulnerable to destructive instincts. Perhaps beginning with a memory or fear from deep within the psyche, one projects it and expands it until it acquires a frightening degree of reality. In fact, it may become a deadly kind of reality. Kay essentially wills herself first into isolation from other passengers and finally into submission. She returns from the observation platform accompanied by the stranger. She chooses neither to change her seat nor to scream. Eventually, she chooses not to struggle. Human beings are delicate creatures, and the power of the "wizard-man" is enough to cause Kay to sink into nightmarish and unnecessary helplessness.

"Master Misery" • The mysterious realm of dream can invade the workaday world and then consume it. This is precisely what happens in "Master Misery" when Sylvia leaves her hometown of Easton to stay with married friends who live in New York City. Soon she becomes frustrated with her daily routine and her "namby-pamby, bootsytotsy" friends. Hoping to earn money to find her own apartment, Sylvia overhears a conversation in the Automat. As unlikely as it sounds, a certain Mr. Revercomb purchases dreams. Intrigued, Sylvia visits his Fifth Avenue brownstone and discovers that Mr. Revercomb does indeed purchase dreams for cash. As she continues to visit his office, events take an unfortunate turn. The more Sylvia sees him, the more he seems eccentric, even unnatural. One time as she whispers her dream, Mr. Revercomb bends forward to brush her ear with his lips, apparently in a sexual approach.

Sylvia becomes so obsessed with selling her dreams that everything else in her life loses significance. She cuts off communication with her married friends, quits her office job, and rents a dingy studio apartment. Her only friend is Oreilly, a former clown whom she meets in Mr. Revercomb's waiting room. They have much in common, for Oreilly used to sell his dreams also, but now Mr. Revercomb has no use for them. Although he spends most of his time drunk, Oreilly has the foresight to warn his new companion against the man he calls the Master of Misery, who is so adept at convincing people that parting with a dream is worth five dollars. He explains to Sylvia that she must not lose her independence or her private world of memory and dream, and he compares Mr. Revercomb with the demon of childhood nightmare, the ominous figure who haunted the trees, chimneys, attics, and graveyards of make-believe. Like the mute in "A Tree of Night," Revercomb is "a thief and a threat," for after he appropriates one's dreams, it is a short passage to one's subconscious and one's soul.

Sylvia's life contracts to unhappy proportions. She moves from Revercomb's waiting room back to Oreilly, her waiting companion, who commiserates with her shrinking self before consuming the liquor she buys with her dream-money. He does, however, advise her to ask Revercomb for her dreams back, provided that she gradually returns the money over a period of time. Sylvia agrees, for her life has become miserable and isolated, but this is a Faustian story, and what was spent cannot be retrieved. Revercomb informs Sylvia that under no circumstances would he return what she has sold and, besides, he has already used them up. Walking home in the falling snow, Sylvia acknowledges that she is no longer her own master and has no individuality; soon she will not have even Oreilly, who will go his own way. Thinking she used Revercomb, it turns out that he has used her, and now they are inseparable—until he discards her as he did Oreilly. The story concludes as Sylvia overhears footsteps following behind. There are two boys, who have followed her from the park and continue to do so. Sylvia is frightened, but like Kay in "A Tree of Night," she becomes passive and submissive, for there is "nothing left to steal."

As in much of Capote's short fiction, the individual tacitly gives a stranger enormous power. Once Sylvia abdicates full responsibility for herself and enters Revercomb's world, she becomes vulnerable and he becomes omniscient. Gradually she is emptied of friends, an orderly routine, ambition, desire, and, finally, of self-possession. The reader can never be sure who Revercomb is or what he does with dreams, but Sylvia, not the Master of Misery, is the focus of interest. She allows him to create her misery, leaving her with no one, not even her former self.

Capote's early work especially makes use of the gothic tradition, but because the details remain realistic and controlled, the mysterious elements are subtle and therefore even more insidious. The "wizard-man" is Capote's archetype—the mute in "A Tree of Night," Mr. Revercomb in "Master Misery," the young girl in "Miriam," Mr. Destronelli in "The Headless Hawk." This figure transforms the actual world of the protagonist, usually in undesirable and irreversible ways. Whether the encounter with this stranger is a final retreat into narcissism or a submission to a purely external presence may not be clarified, but the fragility of the human psyche is all too clear.

Miriam Fuchs
With updates by Jo-Ellen Lipman Boon and the Editors

Other major works

PLAYS: *The Grass Harp: A Play*, pr., pb. 1952 (adaptation of his novel); *House of Flowers*, pr. 1954 (with Harold Arlen).

NOVELS: *Summer Crossing*, wr. 1943, pb. 2005; *Other Voices, Other Rooms*, 1948; *The Grass Harp*, 1951; *A Christmas Memory*, 1956 (serial); *In Cold Blood*, 1966; *The Thanksgiving Visitor*, 1967 (serial); *Answered Prayers: The Unfinished Novel*, 1986.

MISCELLANEOUS: *Selected Writings*, 1963; *Trilogy: An Experiment in Multimedia*, 1969 (with Eleanor Perry and Frank Perry); *Music for Chameleons*, 1980; *A Capote Reader*, 1987; *Too Brief a Treat: The Letters of Truman Capote*, 2004 (edited by Gerald Clarke).

NONFICTION: *Local Color*, 1950; *The Muses Are Heard*, 1956; *Observations*, 1959 (with Richard Avedon); *The Dogs Bark: Public People and Private Places*, 1973.

SCREENPLAYS: *Beat the Devil*, 1954 (with John Huston); *The Innocents*, 1961.

Bibliography

Brinnin, John Malcolm. *Truman Capote: Dear Heart, Old Buddy.* Rev. ed. New York: Delacorte Press, 1986. Chronicles Capote's life from before the success of *In Cold Blood* to his ruin from alcoholism and drugs. Most useful is the insight into the literary circles in which Capote moved. Includes an index.

Clarke, Gerald. *Capote: A Biography.* New York: Simon & Schuster, 1988. Arguably the definitive biographical work on Capote, this lengthy text covers all the ups and downs of his career. Contains copious references and an index.

Garson, Helen S. *Truman Capote: A Study of the Short Fiction.* New York: Twayne, 1992. Divided into three sections: a critical analysis of the short fiction, an exploration of Capote's biography and his "inventing a self," and a selection of essays by Capote's most important critics. Also includes a chronology and bibliography.

Grobel, Lawrence. *Conversations with Capote.* New York: New American Library, 1985. This biography uses interview material to flesh out its information. Grobel covers Capote's life from childhood to his fall from society's grace and his subsequent death. In chapter 4, entitled "Writing," Capote discusses his writing career and the authors who he believed had the greatest influence on him. Includes a brief primary bibliography that lists films that Capote scripted and an index.

Hardwick, Elizabeth. "Tru Confessions." *The New York Review of Books* 45 (January 15, 1998): 4-5. Discusses George Plimpton's recording the remarks of those who came into contact with Capote's journey to literary fame; notes that Plimpton arranges these voices to produce the effect of the unrehearsed, companionable exchange at a cocktail party; argues that the method and result suit their subject, given that Capote, when not writing, was partying, forever receiving and producing banter.

Inge, M. Thomas, ed. *Truman Capote: Conversations.* Jackson: University Press of Mississippi, 1987. This book is a collection of interviews with Capote done by interviewers who range from Gloria Steinem to George Plimpton to Capote himself, in a section called "Self-Portrait." The index allows the reader to find specific references to individual short stories.

Long, Robert Emmet. "Truman Capote." In *Critical Survey of Long Fiction, Revised Edition,* edited by Carl Rollyson. Vol. 2. Pasadena, Calif.: Salem Press, 2000. Analysis of Capote's longer fictional works that may offer insights into his short fiction.

May, Charles E., ed. *Masterplots II: Short Story Series, Revised Edition.* 8 vols. Pasadena, Calif.: Salem Press, 2004. Designed for student use, this reference set contains articles providing detailed plot summaries and analyses of these six short stories by Capote: "Children on Their Birthdays" and "A Christmas Memory" (vol. 2); "The Headless Hawk" (vol. 3); "Miriam" and "My Side of the Matter" (vol. 5); and "A Tree of Night" (vol. 7).

Plimpton, George. *Truman Capote: In Which Various Friends, Enemies, Acquaintances, and Detractors Recall His Turbulent Career.* New York: Doubleday, 1997. This biography based on interviews provides dramatic, primary information, but it also must be checked against the more reliable biography by Gerald Clarke. Includes biographies of contributors and a chronology.

Windham, Donald. *Lost Friendships: A Memoir of Truman Capote, Tennessee Williams, and Others.* New York: William Morrow, 1987. A friend of the major literary lights of the 1950's and 1960's, as well as a novelist himself, Windham dedicates the first half of *Lost Friendships* to his relationship with Capote and its subsequent decline. No reference material is included.

Raymond Carver

Born: Clatskanie, Oregon; May 25, 1938
Died: Port Angeles, Washington; August 2, 1988

Principal short fiction • *Put Yourself in My Shoes*, 1974; *Will You Please Be Quiet, Please?*, 1976; *Furious Seasons, and Other Stories*, 1977; *What We Talk About When We Talk About Love*, 1981; *Cathedral*, 1983; *Elephant, and Other Stories*, 1988; *Where I'm Calling From*, 1988; *Short Cuts: Selected Stories*, 1993.

Other literary forms • Raymond Carver distinguished himself as a short-story writer and poet, and he wrote in both forms until his death. His poetry has been published in the following collections: *Near Klamath* (1968), *Winter Insomnia* (1970), *At Night the Salmon Move* (1976), *Two Poems* (1982), *Fires: Essays, Poems, Stories* (1983), *If It Please You* (1984), *This Water* (1985), *Where Water Comes Together with Other Water* (1985), *Ultramarine* (1986), and *A New Path to the Waterfall* (1989).

Achievements • Raymond Carver's greatest achievement was overcoming his economically and culturally disadvantaged background to become an author of world renown. He made the short story a workable literary form; since Carver, short-story collections have again become a marketable commodity in the book trade. Both as a model and as a teacher, he had such an influence on younger fiction writers that author Jay McInerney could truthfully say (alluding to a famous statement that Fyodor Dostoevski made about Nikolai Gogol) that there is hardly a single American short-story writer younger than Carver who did not "come out of Carver's overcoat."

With only a bachelor's degree and mediocre grades, Carver was invited to teach at distinguished universities and became a professor of English at Syracuse University in 1980. He received many honors during his lifetime, including a Strauss Living Award, which guaranteed him an annual stipend of thirty-five thousand dollars and enabled him to devote all his time to writing during the last years of his life. Just before his death, he received a doctorate of letters from the University of Hartford.

Biography • Raymond Carver grew up in a sparsely populated corner of the Pacific Northwest. This rustic environment had an indelible effect upon his character and writing. Like Ernest Hemingway, one of the writers who influenced him, he loved the purity and freedom of the American wilderness, and he also respected the simplicity, honesty, and directness of the men and women who earned meager and precarious livelihoods in that primitive setting. He married young and had two children to support by the time he was twenty. He had wanted to be a writer from the time he was in the third grade, but the responsibilities of parenthood made it extremely difficult for him to find time to write. His limited education forced him to take menial jobs for which he was temperamentally unsuited. He was unable to consider tackling anything as ambitious as a full-length novel, so he spent his odd free hours writing short stories and poetry. He managed to get some of his work published in little magazines, but these publications paid little or nothing for his work, so he was haunted by financial problems for much of his life.

One of the most important influences in Carver's life was John Gardner (1933-1982), who taught creative writing at California State University at Chico and said, "You cannot be a great writer unless you feel greatly." The idealistic Gardner introduced his students to the literary magazines that represented the cutting edge in contemporary American fiction and poetry, and he urged them to write honestly about what they knew, as opposed to turning out formula fiction in an attempt to make money. This is exactly what Carver did, and, ironically, he found that the hardships and distractions that were preventing him from writing were the very things that provided him with material to write about. This may account for the characteristic stoical humor to be found in many of his stories.

© Marion Ettlinger

Another profound influence in his life was alcohol. One of Carver's distinguishing traits as a writer is his astonishing candor, and anyone who reads a dozen of his short stories will get a good idea of what his life was like for nearly two decades. His drinking caused serious domestic and financial problems, which led to feelings of guilt and more drinking. Amazingly, his strong constitution and unwavering motivation enabled him to continue producing stories and poems.

With the publication of *What We Talk About When We Talk About Love* in 1981, Carver achieved critical and popular fame. His financial problems were ameliorated because he was receiving valuable grants and teaching assignments and was also selling his work to high-paying, slick magazines such as *Esquire, Harper's Bazaar, Playgirl,* and *The New Yorker.* Collections of his short stories sold well. He was earning money teaching creative writing courses and appearing as a featured attraction at many workshops and seminars.

By the late 1970's, Carver had separated from his first wife and was living with the poet and teacher Tess Gallagher. She helped him cope with his drinking problem and provided a much-needed stabilizing influence. Carver, always a heavy cigarette smoker, died of lung cancer in 1988. By that time, his works had been published all over the world in more than twenty languages.

Analysis • Nearly everything written about Raymond Carver begins with two observations: He is a minimalist, and he writes about working-class people. Even when the critic is sympathetic, this dual categorization tends to stigmatize Carver as a minor artist writing little stories about little people. Although it is true that most of Carver's characters belong to the working class, their problems are universal. Carver writes about divorce, infidelity, spiritual alienation, alcoholism, bankruptcy, rootlessness, and existential dread; none of these afflictions is peculiar to the working class, and in fact, all were once more common to members of the higher social classes.

Carver was a minimalist by preference and by necessity. His lifelong experience had been with working-class people. It would have been inappropriate to write about simple people in an ornate style, and, furthermore, his limited education would have made it impossible for him to do so effectively. The spare, objective style that he admired in some of Hemingway's short stories, such as "The Killers" and "Hills Like White Elephants," was perfectly suited to Carver's needs.

The advantage and appeal of minimalism in literature is that it draws readers into the story by forcing them to conceptualize missing details. One drawback is that it allows insecure writers to imply that they know more than they know and mean more than they are actually saying. This was true of the early stories that Carver collected in *Will You Please Be Quiet, Please?* A good example of Carver's strengths and weaknesses is a short story in that volume titled "Fat."

"Fat" • As the title suggests, "Fat" is about a fat man. It is little more than a character sketch; nothing happens in the story. Throughout his career, Carver based stories and poems on people or incidents that he observed or scraps of conversation that he overheard; these things seemed to serve as living metaphors or symbols with broader implications. Carver frames his story by setting it in a restaurant and by describing the fat man from the point of view of a waitress. She says that she has never seen such a fat person in her life and is somewhat awestruck by his appearance, by his gracious manners, and by the amount of food that he can consume at one sitting. After she goes home at night, she is still thinking about him. She says that she herself feels "terrifically fat"; she feels depressed, and finally ends by saying, "My life is going to change. I feel it."

The reader can feel it too but might be hard pressed to say what "it" is. The story leaves a strong impression but an ambiguous one. No two readers would agree on what the story means, if anything. It demonstrates Carver's talent for characterization through dialogue and action, which was his greatest asset. Both the waitress and her fat customer come alive as people, partially through the deliberate contrast between them. His treatment of the humble, kindly waitress demonstrates his sensitivity to the feelings of women. His former wife, Maryann Carver, said of him, "Ray loved and understood women, and women loved him."

"Fat" also shows Carver's unique sense of humor, which was another trait that set him apart from other writers. Carver was so constituted that he could not help seeing the humorous side of the tragic or the grotesque. His early, experimental short stories most closely resemble the early short stories of William Saroyan reprinted in *The Daring Young Man on the Flying Trapeze, and Other Stories* (1934) and subsequent collections of his stories that appeared in the 1930's. Saroyan is perhaps best remembered for his novel *The Human Comedy* (1943), and it might be said that the human comedy was Carver's theme and thesis throughout his career. Like the early stories of Saroyan, Carver's stories are the tentative vignettes of a novice who knows very well that he wants to be a writer but still does not know exactly what he wants to say.

"Neighbors" • *Will You Please Be Quiet, Please?* includes the tragicomic "Neighbors," the first of Carver's stories to appear in a slick magazine with a large circulation. Gordon Lish, editor of the men's magazine *Esquire*, recognized Carver's talent early but did not immediately accept any of his submissions. Lish's welcome encourage-

ment, painful rejections, and eventual acceptance represented major influences in
Carver's career. "Neighbors" deals with ordinary people but has a surrealistic humor,
which was to become a Carver trademark.

Bill and Arlene Miller, a couple in their thirties, have agreed to feed their neighbors' cat and water the plants while they are away. The Stones' apartment holds a
mysterious fascination, and they both find excuses to enter it more often than necessary. Bill helps himself to the Chivas Regal, eats food out of their refrigerator, and
goes through their closets and dresser drawers. He tries on some of Jim Stone's
clothes and lies on their bed masturbating. Then he goes so far as to try on Harriet
Stone's brassiere and panties and then a skirt and blouse. Bill's wife also disappears
into the neighbors' apartment on her own mysterious errands. They fantasize that
they have assumed the identities of their neighbors, whom they regard as happier
people leading fuller lives. The shared guilty adventure arouses both Bill and Arlene
sexually, and they have better lovemaking than they have experienced in a long
while. Then disaster strikes: Arlene discovers that she has inadvertently locked the
Stones' key inside the apartment. The cat may starve; the plants may wither; the
Stones may find evidence that they have been rummaging through their possessions.
The story ends with the frightened Millers clinging to each other outside their lost
garden of Eden.

This early story displays some of Carver's strengths: his sense of humor, his powers
of description, and his ability to characterize people through what they do and say. It
also has the two main qualities that editors look for: timeliness and universality. It is
therefore easy to understand why Lish bought this piece after rejecting so many others. "Neighbors" portrays the alienated condition of many contemporary Americans
of all social classes.

"Neighbors," however, has certain characteristics that have allowed hostile critics
to damn Carver's stories as "vignettes," "anecdotes," "sketches," and "slices-of-life."
For one thing, readers realize that the terror they briefly share with the Millers is unnecessary: They can go to the building manager for a passkey or call a locksmith. It is
hard to understand how two people who are so bold about violating their neighbors'
apartment should suddenly feel so helpless in the face of an everyday mishap. The
point of the story is blunted by the unsatisfactory ending.

What We Talk About When We Talk About Love • The publication of the collection titled *What We Talk About When We Talk About Love* made Carver famous. These short,
rather ambiguous stories also got him permanently saddled with the term "minimalist." Carver never accepted that label and claimed that he did not even understand
what it meant. He had a healthy mistrust of critics who attempted to categorize writers with such epithets: It was as if he sensed their antagonism and felt that they themselves were trying to "minimize" him as an author. A friend of Carver said that he
thought a minimalist was a "taker-out" rather than a "putter-in." In that sense, Carver
was a minimalist. It was his practice to go over and over his stories trying to delete all
superfluous words and even superfluous punctuation marks. He said that he knew he
was finished with a story when he found himself putting back punctuation marks that
he had previously deleted. It would be more accurate to call Carver a perfectionist
than a minimalist.

"Why Don't You Dance?" • One of the best short stories reprinted in *What We Talk
About When We Talk About Love* is "Why Don't You Dance?" It is one of the most repre-

sentative, the most "Carveresque" of all Carver's short stories. A man who is never given a name has placed all of his furniture and personal possessions outside on the front lawn and has whimsically arranged them as if they were still indoors. He has run an extension cord from the house and hooked up lamps, a television, and a record player. He is sitting outside drinking whiskey, totally indifferent to the amazement and curiosity of his neighbors. One feels as if the worst is over for him: He is the survivor of some great catastrophe, like a marooned sailor who has managed to salvage some flotsam and jetsam.

A young couple, referred to throughout the story as "the boy" and "the girl," drive by and assume that the man is holding a yard sale. They stop and inquire about prices. The man offers them drinks. The boy and girl get into a party spirit. They put old records on the turntable and start dancing in the driveway. The man is eager to get rid of his possessions and accepts whatever they are willing to offer. He even makes them presents of things that they do not really want. Weeks later, the girl is still talking about the man, but she cannot find the words to express what she really feels about the incident. Perhaps she and her young friends will understand the incident much better after they have worked and worried and bickered and moved from one place to another for ten or twenty years.

"Why Don't You Dance?" is a humorous treatment of a serious subject, in characteristic Carver fashion. The man's tragedy is never spelled out, but the reader can piece the story together quite easily from the clues. Evidently there has been a divorce or separation. Evidently there were financial problems, which are so often associated with divorce, and the man has been evicted. Judging from the fact that he is doing so much drinking, alcoholism is either the cause or the effect of his other problems. The man has given up all hope and now sees hope only in other people, represented by this young couple just starting out in life and trying to collect a few pieces of furniture for their rented apartment.

Divorce, infidelity, domestic strife, financial worry, bankruptcy, alcoholism, rootlessness, consumerism as a substitute for intimacy, and disillusionment with the American Dream are common themes throughout Carver's stories. The symbol of a man sitting outside on his front lawn drinking whiskey, with all of his worldly possessions placed around him but soon to be scattered to the four winds, is a striking symbol of modern human beings. It is easy to acquire possessions but nearly impossible to keep a real home.

Carver did not actually witness such an event but had a similar episode described to him by a friend and eventually used it in this story. A glance at the titles of some of Carver's stories shows his penchant for finding in his mundane environment external symbols of subjective states: "Fat," "Gazebo," "Vitamins," "Feathers," "Cathedral," "Boxes," "Menudo." The same tendency is even more striking in the titles of his poems, for example, "The Car," "Jean's TV," "NyQuil," "My Dad's Wallet," "The Phone Booth," "Heels."

In his famous essay "The Philosophy of Composition," Edgar Allan Poe wrote that he wanted an image that would be "emblematical of Mournful and Never-ending Remembrance," so he created his famous raven perched on the bust of Pallas Athena and croaking the refrain "nevermore." To highlight the difference in Carver's method, Carver might have seen a real raven perched on a real statue, and it would have suggested mournful and never-ending remembrance. This kind of "reverse symbolism" seems characteristic of modern American minimalists in general, and Carver's influence on their movement is paramount.

Poe states that he originally thought of using a parrot in his famous poem but rejected that notion because it did not seem sufficiently poetic and might have produced a comical effect; if Carver had been faced with such a choice, he probably would have chosen the parrot. What distinguishes Carver from most minimalists is a sense of humor that is impervious to catastrophe: Like the man on the front lawn, Carver had been so far down that everyplace else looked better. He would have concurred heartily with William Shakespeare's often-quoted lines in *As You Like It* (pr. c. 1599-1600):

> Sweet are the uses of adversity,
> Which, like a toad, ugly and venomous,
> Wears yet a precious jewel in his head

On a different level, "Why Don't You Dance?" reflects Carver's maturation as a person and an author. The responsibilities of parenthood as well as the experience of teaching young students were bringing home to him the fact that his personal problems could hold instructional utility for others. As a teacher of creative writing, placed more and more in the limelight, interacting with writers, editors, professors, and interviewers, he was being forced to formulate his own artistic credo. The older man in the story sees himself in his young yard-sale customers and wants to help them along in life; this is evidently a reflection of the author's own attitude. Consequently, the story itself is not merely an autobiographical protest or lament like some of Carver's earlier works but is designed to deliver a message—perhaps a warning—for the profit of others. The melancholy wisdom of Carver's protagonist reflects Carver's own mellowing as he began to appreciate the universally tragic nature of human existence.

"Where I'm Calling From" • "Where I'm Calling From" is a great American short story. It originally appeared in the prestigious *The New Yorker,* was reprinted in the collection titled *Cathedral,* and appears once again as the title story in the best and most comprehensive collection of Carver's stories, *Where I'm Calling From.* The story is narrated by an alcoholic staying at a "drying-out facility," an unpretentious boardinghouse where plain meals are served family style and there is nothing to do but read, watch television, or talk. The bucolic atmosphere is strongly reminiscent of the training-camp scenes in one of Hemingway's most brilliant short stories, "Fifty Grand."

The narrator in Carver's story tells about his drinking problems and interweaves his own biography with that of a friend he has made at the drying-out facility, a man he refers to as J. P. The only thing unusual about their stories is that J. P. is a chimney sweep and is married to a chimney sweep. Both J. P. and the narrator ruined their marriages through their compulsive drinking and are now terrified that they will be unable to control their craving once they get out of the facility. They have made vows of abstinence often enough before and have not kept them. They have dried out before and gone right back to the bottle.

Carver manages to convey all the feelings of guilt, remorse, terror, and helplessness experienced by people who are in the ultimate stages of alcoholism. It is noteworthy that, whereas his alcoholic protagonists of earlier stories were often isolated individuals, the protagonist-narrator of "Where I'm Calling From" not only is actively seeking help but also is surrounded by others with the same problem. This feature indicates that Carver had come to realize that the way to give his stories the point or meaning that they had previously often lacked was to suggest the existence of large-scale social problems of which his characters are victims. He had made what author Joan Didion called "the quantum leap" of realizing that his personal problems were actually social problems. The curse of alcoholism affects all social classes; even people who never touch a drop of alcohol can have their lives ruined by it.

"The Bridle" • "The Bridle" first appeared in *The New Yorker* and was reprinted in *Cathedral.* It is an example of Carver's mature period, a highly artistic story fraught with social significance. The story is told from the point of view of one of Carver's faux-naïf narrators. Readers immediately feel that they know this good-natured soul, a woman named Marge who manages an apartment building in Arizona and "does hair" as a sideline. She tells about one of the many families who stayed a short while and then moved on as tumbleweeds being blown across the desert. Although Carver typically writes about Northern California and the Pacific Northwest, this part of Arizona is also "Carver Country," a world of freeways, fast-food restaurants, Laundromats, mindless television entertainment, and transient living accommodations, a homogenized world of strangers with minimum-wage jobs and tabloid mentalities.

Mr. Holits pays the rent in cash every month, suggesting that he recently went bankrupt and has neither a bank account nor credit cards. Carver, like minimalists in general, loves such subtle clues. Mrs. Holits confides to Marge that they had owned a farm in Minnesota. Her husband, who "knows everything there is about horses," still keeps one of his bridles, evidently symbolizing his hope that he may escape from "Carver Country." Mrs. Holits proves more adaptable: She gets a job as a waitress, a favorite occupation among Carver characters. Her husband, however, cannot adjust to the service industry jobs, which are all that are available to a man his age with his limited experience. He handles the money, the two boys are his sons by a former marriage, and he has been accustomed to making the decisions, yet he finds that his wife is taking over the family leadership in this brave new postindustrial world.

Like many other Carver male characters, Holits becomes a heavy drinker. He eventually injures himself while trying to show off his strength at the swimming pool. One day the Holitses, with their young sons, pack and drive off down the long, straight highway without a word of explanation. When Marge trudges upstairs to clean the empty apartment, she finds that Holits has left his bridle behind.

The naïve narrator does not understand the significance of the bridle, but the reader feels its poignancy as a symbol. The bridle is one of those useless objects that everyone carts around and is reluctant to part with because it represents a memory, a hope, or a dream. It is an especially appropriate symbol because it is so utterly out of place in one of those two-story, frame-stucco, look-alike apartment buildings that disfigure the landscape and are the dominant features of "Carver Country." Gigantic economic forces beyond the comprehension of the narrator have driven this farm family from their home and turned them into the modern equivalent of the Joad family in John Steinbeck's classic novel *The Grapes of Wrath* (1939).

There is, however, a big difference between Carver and Steinbeck. Steinbeck believed in and prescribed the panacea of socialism; Carver has no prescriptions to offer. He seems to have no faith either in politicians or in preachers. His characters are more likely to go to church to play bingo than to say prayers or sing hymns. Like many of his contemporary minimalists, he seems to have gone beyond alienation, beyond existentialism, beyond despair. God is dead; so what else is new?

Carver's working-class characters are far more complicated than Steinbeck's Joad family. Americans have become more sophisticated as a result of the influence of radio, motion pictures, television, the Internet, more abundant educational opportunities, improved automobiles and highways, cheap air transportation, alcohol and drugs, more leisure time, and the fact that their work is less enervating because of the proliferation of labor-saving machinery. Many Americans have also lost their religious faith, their work ethic, their class consciousness, their family loyalty, their integrity, and their dreams. Steinbeck saw it happening and showed how the Joad family was splitting apart after being uprooted from the soil; Carver's people are the Joad family a half-century down the road. Oddly enough, Carver's mature stories do not seem nihilistic or despairing because they contain the redeeming qualities of humor, compassion, and honesty.

"Boxes" • *Where I'm Calling From* is the most useful volume of Carver's short stories because it contains some of the best stories that had been printed in earlier books plus a generous selection of his later and best efforts. One of the new stories reprinted in *Where I'm Calling From* is "Boxes," which first appeared in *The New Yorker.* When Carver's stories began to be regularly accepted by *The New Yorker,* it was an indication that he had found the style of self-expression that he had been searching for since the beginning of his career. It was also a sign that his themes were evoking sympathetic chords in the hearts and minds of *The New Yorker*s' middle and upper-class readership, the people at whom that magazine's sophisticated advertisements for diamonds, furs, highrise condominiums, and luxury vacation cruises are aimed.

"Boxes" is written in Carver's characteristic tragicomic tone. It is a story in which the faux-naïf narrator, a favorite with Carver, complains about the eccentric behavior of his widowed mother who, for one specious reason or another, is always changing her place of residence. She moves so frequently that she usually seems to have the bulk of her worldly possessions packed in boxes scattered about on the floor. One of her complaints is about the attitude of her landlord, whom she calls "King Larry." Larry Hadlock is a widower and a relatively affluent property owner. It is evident through Carver's unerring dialogue that what she is really bitter about is Larry's indifference to her own fading charms. In the end, she returns to California but telephones to complain about the traffic, the faulty air-conditioning unit in her apartment, and the indifference of management. Her son vaguely understands that what his mother really wants, though she may not realize it herself, is love and a real home and that she can never have these things again in her lifetime no matter where she moves.

What makes the story significant is its universality: It reflects the macrocosm in a microcosm. In "Boxes," the problem touched on is not only the rootlessness and anonymity of modern life but also the plight of millions of aging people, who are considered by some to be useless in their old age and a burden to their children. It was typical of Carver to find a metaphor for this important social phenomenon in a bunch of cardboard boxes.

Carver uses working-class people as his models, but he is not writing solely about the working class. It is simply the fact that all Americans can see themselves in his little, inarticulate, bewildered characters that makes Carver an important writer in the dominant tradition of American realism, a worthy successor to Mark Twain, Stephen Crane, Sherwood Anderson, Theodore Dreiser, Willa Cather, John Steinbeck, and William Faulkner, all of whom wrote about humble people. Someday it may be generally appreciated that, despite the odds against him and despite the antipathy of certain mandarins, Raymond Carver managed to become the most important American fiction writer in the second half of the twentieth century.

Bill Delaney

Other major works
ANTHOLOGY: *American Short Story Masterpieces*, 1987 (with Tom Jenks).

MISCELLANEOUS: *Fires: Essays, Poems, Stories*, 1983; *No Heroics, Please: Uncollected Writings*, 1991 (revised and expanded as *Call If You Need Me: The Uncollected Fiction and Other Prose*, 2001).

POETRY: *Near Klamath*, 1968; *Winter Insomnia*, 1970; *At Night the Salmon Move*, 1976; *Two Poems*, 1982; *If It Please You*, 1984; *This Water*, 1985; *Where Water Comes Together with Other Water*, 1985; *Ultramarine*, 1986; *A New Path to the Waterfall*, 1989; *All of Us: The Collected Poems*, 1996.

SCREENPLAY: *Dostoevsky*, 1985.

Bibliography
Bugeja, Michael. "Tarnish and Silver: An Analysis of Carver's Cathedral." *South Dakota Review* 24, no. 3 (1986): 73-87. Discusses the revision of an early Carver story, "The Bath," which was reprinted in *Cathedral* as "A Small Good Thing." The changes made throughout the story, and especially the somewhat more positive resolution, reflect Carver's evolution as a writer.

Campbell, Ewing. *Raymond Carver: A Study of the Short Fiction*. New York: Twayne, 1992. Introduction to Carver's stories that focuses on such issues as myth and archetype, otherness, and the grotesque. Discusses the difference between "early" and "late" versions of the same story, such as "So Much Water Close to Home" and "The Bath" and "A Small Good Thing." Includes Carver's own comments on his writing as well as articles by other critics who challenge the label of minimalist for Carver.

Carver, Raymond. "A Storyteller's Shoptalk." *The New York Times Book Review*, February 15, 1981, 9. In this interesting article, Carver describes his artistic credo, evaluates the work of some of his contemporaries, and offers excellent advice to aspiring young writers. The article reveals his perfectionism and dedication to his craft.

Gentry, Marshall Bruce, and William L. Stull, eds. *Conversations with Raymond Carver*. Jackson: University Press of Mississippi, 1990. Wide-ranging collection of interviews covering Carver's career from the early 1980's until just before his death.

Halpert, Sam. *Raymond Carver: An Oral Biography*. Iowa City: University of Iowa Press, 1995. Expanded edition of a collection of conversations originally published in 1991 as *When We Talk About Raymond Carver*. Includes contributions from Carver's first wife, his daughter, an early writing instructor, and some of his lifetime friends.

_____, ed. *When We Talk About Raymond Carver*. Layton, Utah: Gibbs Smith, 1991. Collection of transcripts of interviews with ten writers who knew Carver on a personal basis, including a fascinating interview with Carver's first wife, Maryann, who provides a fresh perspective on the incidents on which many of Carver's stories were based.

Kesset, Kirk. *The Stories of Raymond Carver*. Athens: Ohio University Press, 1995. Intelligent discussion of Carver's stories, focusing on Carver's development of his own moral center.

May, Charles E., ed. *Masterplots II: Short Story Series, Revised Edition.* 8 vols. Pasadena, Calif.: Salem Press, 2004. Designed for student use, this reference set contains articles providing detailed plot summaries and analyses of these nine short stories by Carver: "Careful" and "Cathedral" (vol. 1); "Errand" (vol. 2); "Neighbors" (vol. 5); "A Small, Good Thing" and "So Much Water So Close to Home" (vol. 7); and "What We Talk About When We Talk About Love," "Why Don't You Dance?," and "Will You Please Be Quiet, Please?" (vol. 8).

Nesset, Kirk. *The Stories of Raymond Carver: A Critical Study.* Athens: Ohio University Press, 1995. The first book-length study of Carver's work, Nesset calls the book "a preliminary exploration." Includes an extensive bibliography.

Powell, Jon. "The Stories of Raymond Carver: The Menace of Perpetual Uncertainty." *Studies in Short Fiction* 31 (Fall, 1994): 647-656. Discusses the sense of menace Carver creates by leaving out or only providing clues to central aspects of his stories. Argues that this technique forces both the characters and the readers to try to understand the clues.

Runyon, Randolph Paul. *Reading Raymond Carver.* Syracuse, N.Y.: Syracuse University Press, 1992. Analyzes Carver's stories as "intratextual" and argues that they should be read in relationship to one another. Claims that in *Will You Please Be Quiet, Please?* and *Cathedral* each story is linked to the immediately preceding story and the one after it.

Scofield, Martin. "Story and History in Raymond Carver." *Critique* 40 (Spring, 1999): 266-280. Shows how three late Carver stories—"Intimacy," "Blackbird Pie," and "Elephant"—embody a new experimental technique for integrating fiction and autobiographical or historical events.

Willa Cather

Born: Back Creek Valley, near Gore, Virginia; December 7, 1873
Died: New York, New York; April 24, 1947

Principal short fiction • *The Troll Garden*, 1905; "Paul's Case," 1905; *Youth and the Bright Medusa*, 1920; *Obscure Destinies*, 1932; *The Old Beauty and Others*, 1948; *Willa Cather's Collected Short Fiction: 1892-1912*, 1965; *Uncle Valentine, and Other Stories: Willa Cather's Collected Short Fiction, 1915-1929*, 1973.

Other literary forms • Willa Cather is best known as a novelist, but she wrote prolifically in other forms, especially as a young woman; she had been publishing short stories for more than twenty years before she published her first novel. Although her fame rests largely on her twelve novels and a few short stories, she has a collection of poetry, several collections of essays, and hundreds of newspaper columns and magazine pieces to her credit. Only one of her books, *A Lost Lady* (1923), was filmed in Hollywood; after that one experience, Cather would not allow any of her work to be filmed again.

Achievements • Willa Cather was one of America's first modern writers to make the prairie immigrant experience an important and continuing subject for high-quality fiction. Although her setting is often the American western frontier, she masterfully locates the universal through the specific, and her literary reputation transcends the limitations of regional or gender affiliation. In her exploration of the human spirit, Cather characteristically defends artistic values in an increasingly materialistic world, and she is known for her graceful rendering of place and character.

Praised in the 1920's as one of the most successful novelists of her time, Cather was sometimes criticized in the next decade for neglecting contemporary social issues. Later, however, and especially since her death, she was recognized as a great artist and one of the most important American writers of the twentieth century. In 1923, she was awarded the Pulitzer Prize for the novel *One of Ours* (1922). She also received the Howells Medal for fiction from the Academy of the National Institute of Arts and Letters in 1930, the Prix Fémina Américain for *Shadows on the Rock* (1931) in 1933, and the gold medal from the National Institute of Arts and Letters in 1944. With time, interest in Cather's fiction continued to increase, rather than diminish, and she enjoys appreciative audiences abroad as well as in her own country.

Biography • Willa Sibert Cather moved with her family from Virginia to Nebraska when she was only nine years old, a move that was to influence her mind and art throughout her life. As a student at the University of Nebraska, she wrote for various college magazines; she also became a regular contributor to the *Nebraska State Journal*, publishing book, theater, and concert reviews, as well as commentary on the passing scene. Even after she moved to Pittsburgh to take an editorial job, she continued to send columns home to the *Nebraska State Journal*. Later she also began contributing to the Lincoln *Courier*. She taught English in Pittsburgh, Pennsylvania (an experience that became the source for one of her most famous short stories, "Paul's Case"), and then moved to New York to take a position with *McClure's Magazine.* After the publication of her first novel, *Alexander's Bridge*, in 1912, she left *McClure's Magazine*, financially able to devote her full time to her creative work. Over the next three decades, she published successfully and to critical acclaim.

Analysis • Willa Cather was always conscious of a double urge in herself, toward art and toward the land. As long as her parents were living, she found herself torn between the western prairie and the cultural centers of the East and Europe. That basic polarity appears again and again in her stories, some of which deal with the artist's struggle against debilitating influences, and some with both the pleasant and the difficult aspects of the prairie experience. Perhaps only in her work did Cather achieve a comfortable reconciliation of these polarities, by making the prairie experience the subject of her art.

All of Cather's work is consistently value-centered. She believed in characters who are good, artists who are true to their callings, people who can appreciate and use what is valuable from the past, and individuals who have a special relationship with the land. Her chief agony lay in what she saw as a general sellout to materialism—in the realm of art, in the prairie and desert, in the small town, in the city.

The struggle of the artist to maintain integrity against an unsympathetic environment and the forces of an exploitative materialism is explored in three stories that are particularly important in the Cather canon. Two of them, "The Sculptor's Funeral" and "Paul's Case," have been widely anthologized and are well known. The third, "Uncle Valentine," is an important later story.

"The Sculptor's Funeral" • "The Sculptor's Funeral" is about the return in death of a world-renowned sculptor to the pinched little prairie town from which he somehow miraculously sprang. Harvey Merrick's body arrives by train in the dead of winter, accompanied by one of his former students. There to meet the coffin are several prominent townsmen, among them a brusque, red-bearded lawyer named Jim Laird. Only he can appreciate the magnitude of Harvey Merrick's achievement. The watchers around the body chuckle and snort over poor Harvey's uselessness as a farmhand, over his inability to "make it" in the only things that count for them—money-making ventures in Sand City. Jim Laird, in a storm of self-hatred for having become the scheming lawyer these harpies wanted him to be, enters the room and blasts them mercilessly. He reminds the town elders of the young men they have ruined by drumming "nothing but money and knavery into their ears from the time they wore knickerbockers." They hated Harvey, Laird says, because he left them and rose above them, achieving in a world they were not fit to enter. He reminds them that Harvey "wouldn't have given one sunset over your marshes" for all of their material properties and possessions. Laird is too drunk the next day to attend the funeral, and it is learned that he dies some years later from a cold he caught while "driving across the Colorado mountains to defend one of Phelps's sons who had got into trouble there by cutting government timber."

Harvey Merrick is not the tragic figure of the story, for he, thanks to a timid father who sensed something special about this one son, managed to escape destruction. He became the artist he was destined to be, in spite of his unlikely beginnings. The money-grubbing first citizens of Sand City can wag their tongues feebly over his corpse, but they cannot touch him or detract from his accomplishment. If there is a tragic element in the story, it is the life of Jim Laird. Like Harvey, he went away

Edward Steichen/Courtesy, George Bush
Presidential Library and Museum

to school full of idealistic fire; like Harvey, he wanted to be a great man and make the hometown people proud of him. Instead, he says, "I came back here to practice, and I found you didn't in the least want me to be a great man. You wanted me to be a shrewd lawyer." He became that shrewd lawyer and lost his soul in the process. The dead artist, imposing and serene in his coffin, serves as a perfect foil for Jim Laird, and the story stands as one of Cather's most powerful treatments of the conflict between artistic ideals and materialistic value systems.

"Paul's Case" • "Paul's Case" presents a somewhat different view of that conflict. Paul, a high school youngster, is not a practicing artist, but he has an artistic temperament. He loves to hang around art galleries and concert halls and theaters, talking with the performers and basking in their reflected glory. It is glitter, excitement, and escape from the dripping taps in his home on Pittsburgh's Cordelia Street that Paul craves. A hopeless "case," Paul is finally taken out of high school by his widowed father because his mind is never on his studies. Forced from his usher's job at the concert hall and forbidden to associate with the actors at the theater, he loses the only things he had lived for and cared about. When he is denied those vital outlets for his aesthetic needs and sent to do dull work for a dull company, he carries out a desperate plan. One evening, instead of depositing his firm's receipts in the bank, he catches a train for New York. With swift determination, he buys elegant clothes and installs himself in a luxurious hotel suite, there to live for a few brief days the life he had always felt himself suited for. Those days are lovely and perfect, but the inevitable reckoning draws near: He learns from a newspaper that his father is en route to New York to retrieve him. Very deliberately Paul plots his course, even buying carnations for his buttonhole. Traveling to the outskirts of town, he walks to an embankment above the Pennsylvania tracks. There he carefully buries the carnations in the snow, and when the appropriate moment comes, he leaps into the path of an oncoming train.

A sensitive youngster with limited opportunity, Paul is not an artist in the usual sense. His distinction is that he responds to art, almost any art, with an unusual fervor. To him, anything associated with the world of art is beautiful and inspiring, while anything associated with lower-middle-class America is ugly and common. He is wrong about both worlds. With eyes only for the artificial surface glitter that spangles the world of art, he never sees the realities of hard work and struggle that define the life of every artist. Clearly, Cordelia Street is not as bad as Paul imagines it to be; it is, in fact, a moderately nice neighborhood where working people live and rear their families. Cordelia Street, however, has inadvertently taught him that money is the answer to all desires, that it can buy all the trappings that grace the world of art. Cordelia Street's legendary heroes are the Kings of Wall Street.

In spite of his blindness, Paul captures the reader's sympathies because he feels trapped in an aesthetic wasteland to which he cannot and will not return; the reader realizes at the end that perhaps Paul's only escape lies in his final choice. The Waldorf, after all, provided temporary breathing space at best. His only real home is, as Cather tells us, in the "immense design of things."

"Uncle Valentine" • Valentine Ramsay, the title character in "Uncle Valentine," is like Paul in many ways: He is sensitive, charming, flighty, unpredictable, temperamental, and intolerant of commonness. Unlike Paul, however, Valentine is a true artist, a gifted composer; it is not the artificial shell of art that he values, but the very heart of it. After several years abroad, he decides to return to Greenacre, his family home in the lush Pennsylvania countryside. He feels that perhaps at Greenacre he can shut out the world and find the peace he needs to write music.

Ramsay and the neighbors next door, with whom he shares a special affection, both artistic and social, have a magnificent year together, a "golden year." They roam the fields and woods, they share music, and they increase in aesthetic understanding. Casting a tragic shadow over this happy group, however, is the figure of Valentine's uncle, who haunts the premises like a grieving ghost. A child prodigy, he had left home to pursue his art, but for reasons never disclosed, he gave up his music and returned, burying himself in the ashes of his ruined life.

As a young man, Valentine had made a bad marriage to a rich woman whose materialistic coarseness became a constant affront to him; her very presence beside him in a concert hall was enough to shatter his nerves and obliterate the music he came to hear. Valentine has escaped from her, but she is destined to destroy his peace once again. He and his neighbors discover that she has purchased the large piece of property next to theirs, the property they had loved and tramped through for endless days. She intends to move in soon, bringing her fortune, her brash assertiveness, and Valentine's only son. She, along with the encroaching factory smoke downriver, spells the end of the blessed life the little group of art fanciers has known at Greenacre. Valentine is forced to flee again, and the reader learns that he is killed while crossing a street in France.

Cather's message is clear. The important things in life—art and the sharing of its pleasures, friendships, a feeling for land and place, a reverence for the past—are too often destroyed in the name of progress. When economic concerns are given top priority, whether on the prairie or in Pennsylvania, the human spirit suffers. Happily, in a much-loved story called "Neighbor Rosicky," Cather affirms that material temptations can be successfully resisted. Valentine is defeated, but Rosicky and his values prevail.

"Neighbor Rosicky" • Anton Rosicky, recognizable as another rendering of Ántonia's husband in Cather's best-known novel, *My Ántonia* (1918), has instinctively established a value system that puts life and the land above every narrow-minded material concern. For example, when his entire corn crop is destroyed in the searing heat one July day, he organizes a little picnic so that the family can enjoy the few things they have left. Instead of despairing with his neighbors, Rosicky plays with his children. It is no surprise that he and his wife, Mary, agree without discussion as to what things they can let go. They refuse to skim the cream off their milk and sell it for butter because Mary would "rather put some colour into my children's faces than put money into the bank." Doctor Ed, who detects serious heart trouble in Rosicky, observes that "people as generous and warm-hearted and affectionate as the Rosickys never got ahead much; maybe you couldn't enjoy your life and put it into the bank, too."

"Neighbor Rosicky" is one of Cather's finest tributes to life on the Nebraska prairie, to a value system that grows out of human caring and love for the land. Rosicky had lived in cities for many years, had known hard times and good times there, but it occurred to him one lonely day in the city that he had to get to the land. He realized that "the trouble with big cities" was that "they built you in from the earth itself, cemented you away from any contact with the ground," so he made his decision and went West.

The only thing that disturbs his sleep now is the discontentment of his oldest son. Rudolph is married to a town girl, Polly, and he wants to leave the farm and seek work in the city. Rosicky understands Rudolph's restlessness and Polly's lonesomeness and looks for every opportunity to help the young couple find some recreation time in town. In spite of his efforts, however, Polly continues to dislike farm life and to find the Rosickys strange and "foreign." Then one day Rosicky suffers a heart attack near Rudolph's place. No one is there to care for him but Polly, and that day something lovely happens between the two of them: She has a revelation of his goodness that is "like an awakening to her." His warm brown hand somehow brings "her to herself," teaches her more about life than she has ever known before, offers her "some direct and untranslatable message." With this revelation comes the assurance that at last all will be well with Rudolph and Polly. They will remain on the land and Rosicky's spirit will abide with them, for Polly has caught the old man's vision. It is fitting that Rosicky's death a few months later is calmly accepted as a natural thing, and that he is buried in the earth he loved. That way there will be no strangeness, no jarring separation.

Rosicky is Cather's embodiment of all that is finest in the human character. He had been a city man, a lover of opera and the other cultural advantages of city life, but he found his peace in the simple life of a Nebraska farm. By contrast, Harvey Merrick, the sculptor, had been a country boy, a lover of the prairie landscape, but he found his peace in the art capitals of the world. Nevertheless, Merrick and Rosicky would have understood each other perfectly. One's talent lay in molding clay, the other's in molding lives.

Cather is sometimes accused of nostalgia, of denying the present and yearning for the past. What seems clear in her work, however, is not that she wants to live in the past but that she deplores a total rejection of the values of the past. She fears a materialistic takeover of the human heart, or a shriveled view of human life. She is convinced that the desire for money and the things money can buy corrupts character, cheapens life, destroys the landscape, and enervates art. In her exploration of the conflicts engendered by a destructive materialism, in her celebration of art and the land, Willa Cather's devotion to an enduring system that spans time and space to embrace the good, the beautiful, and the true is made evident.

Marilyn Arnold
With updates by Jean C. Fulton

Other major works

NOVELS: *Alexander's Bridge*, 1912; *O Pioneers!*, 1913; *The Song of the Lark*, 1915; *My Ántonia*, 1918; *One of Ours*, 1922; *A Lost Lady*, 1923; *The Professor's House*, 1925; *My Mortal Enemy*, 1926; *Death Comes for the Archbishop*, 1927; *Shadows on the Rock*, 1931; *Lucy Gayheart*, 1935; *Sapphira and the Slave Girl*, 1940.

MISCELLANEOUS: *Writings from Willa Cather's Campus Years*, 1950.

NONFICTION: *Not Under Forty*, 1936; *Willa Cather on Writing*, 1949; *Willa Cather in Europe*, 1956; *The Kingdom of Art: Willa Cather's First Principles and Critical Statements, 1893-1896*, 1966; *The World and the Parish: Willa Cather's Articles and Reviews, 1893-1902*, 1970 (2 volumes).

POETRY: *April Twilights*, 1903.

Bibliography

Arnold, Marilyn. *Willa Cather's Short Fiction*. Athens: Ohio University Press, 1984. In this indexed volume, Arnold discusses all Cather's known short fiction chronologically. The detailed investigations will be helpful both for readers new to Cather's stories and those who are more familiar with them. Discussions of stories which have received little critical attention are especially useful. Includes a selected bibliography.

Gerber, Philip L. *Willa Cather*. Rev. ed. New York: Twayne, 1995. In this revised edition, Gerber focuses more on Cather's short fiction than in the first edition, as well as on the resurgence of criticism of her work. Discusses the major themes of the experience of the artist and life in rural Nebraska in major Cather short stories.

Harris, Jeane. "Aspects of Athene in Willa Cather's Short Fiction." *Studies in Short Fiction* 28 (Spring, 1991): 177-182. Discusses Cather's conflict between her gender and her inherited male aesthetic principles and how this is reflected in some of her early short stories by "manly" female characters modeled after the Greek goddess Athene. Maintains that Cather's androgynous female characters represent her dissatisfaction with traditional notions of femininity and masculinity.

Lindermann, Marilee. *The Cambridge Companion to Willa Cather*. New York: Cambridge University Press, 2005. Thirteen essays examining Cather's most noted novels and short stories.

May, Charles E., ed. *Masterplots II: Short Story Series, Revised Edition*. 8 vols. Pasadena, Calif.: Salem Press, 2004. Designed for student use, this reference set contains articles providing detailed plot summaries and analyses of these four short stories by Cather: "Coming, Aphrodite" (vol. 2); "Neighbor Rosicky" (vol. 5); "Paul's Case" (vol. 6); and "The Sculptor's Funeral" (vol. 6).

Meyering, Sheryl L. *A Reader's Guide to the Short Stories of Willa Cather*. New York: G. K. Hall, 1994. Discusses individual Cather stories, focusing on publishing history, circumstances of composition, sources, influence, relationship to other Cather works, and interpretations and criticism. Deals with her debt to Henry James, the influence of her sexual orientation on her fiction, and the influence of Sarah Orne Jewett.

Murphy, John J., ed. *Critical Essays on Willa Cather*. Boston: G. K. Hall, 1984. Among the thirty-five essays in this substantial collection are reprinted reviews and articles by Eudora Welty, Katherine Anne Porter, Leon Edel, Blanche H. Gelfant, and Bernice Slote. It also includes original essays by David Stouck, James Leslie Woodress, Paul Cameau, and John J. Murphy. The introduction offers a history of Cather scholarship.

Robinson, Phyllis C. *Willa: The Life of Willa Cather.* Garden City, N.Y.: Doubleday, 1983. Popular biography, with good material on Cather's family and friends. It contains some biographical analyses of Cather's major works.

Skaggs, Merrill Maguire, ed. *Willa Cather's New York: New Essays on Cather in the City.* Madison, N.J.: Fairleigh Dickinson University Press, 2001. Collection of twenty essays focusing on Cather's urban fiction and her work for *McClure's.*

Wasserman, Loretta. *Willa Cather: A Study of the Short Fiction.* Boston: Twayne, 1991. Focuses on selected short stories that the author feels are the most challenging and lend themselves to different critical approaches. Includes interviews with Cather, one of Cather's essays on the craft of writing, samples of current criticism, a chronology, and a select bibliography.

Geoffrey Chaucer

Born: London(?), England; c. 1343
Died: London, England; October 25(?), 1400

Principal short fiction • *Book of the Duchess,* c. 1370; *Romaunt of the Rose,* c. 1370 (translation, possibly not by Chaucer); *House of Fame,* 1372-1380; *The Legend of St. Cecilia,* 1372-1380 (later used as "The Second Nun's Tale"); *Tragedies of Fortune,* 1372-1380 (later used as "The Monk's Tale"); *Anelida and Arcite,* c. 1380; *Palamon and Ersyte,* 1380-1386 (later used as "The Knight's Tale"); *Parlement of Foules,* 1380; *The Legend of Good Women,* 1380-1386; *Troilus and Criseyde,* 1382; *The Canterbury Tales,* 1387-1400.

Other literary forms • In addition to the works listed above, Geoffrey Chaucer composed *Boece* (c. 1380), a translation of Boethius's *The Consolation of Philosophy* (523), which Boethius wrote while in prison. Chaucer also wrote an astrological study, *A Treatise on the Astrolabe* (1387-1392), and a miscellaneous volume entitled *Works* (1957).

Achievements • Geoffrey Chaucer is generally agreed to be the most important writer in English literature before William Shakespeare. Recognized internationally in his own time as the greatest of English poets and dubbed "the father of English poetry" by John Dryden as early as 1700, his central position in the development of English literature and even of the English language is perhaps more secure today than it has ever been. One of the keys to Chaucer's continued critical success is the scope and diversity of his work, which extends from romance to tragedy, from sermon to dream vision, from pious saints' lives to bawdy fabliaux. Readers from every century have found something new in Chaucer and learned something about themselves.

Biography • Household records seem to indicate that as a boy, Geoffrey Chaucer served as a page for the countess of Ulster, wife of Edward III's son Lionel, Duke of Clarence. Chaucer undoubtedly learned French and Latin as a youth, to which languages he later added Italian. Well versed in both science and pseudoscience, Chaucer was familiar with physics, medicine, astronomy, and alchemy. Spending most of his life in government service, he made many trips abroad on diplomatic missions and served at home in such important capacities as comptroller of customs for the Port of London, justice of the peace for the county of Kent, and clerk of the King's Works, a position that made him responsible for the maintenance of certain public structures. He married Philippa de Roet, probably in 1367, and he may have had two daughters and two sons, although there is speculation concerning the paternity of some of those children believed to have been Chaucer's. Since Chaucer's career was his service to the monarchy, his poetry was evidently an avocation which did not afford him a living.

Analysis • Geoffrey Chaucer's best-known works are *Troilus and Criseyde* and the unfinished *The Canterbury Tales,* with the *Book of the Duchess,* the *Hous of Fame,* the *Parlement of Foules,* and *The Legend of Good Women* positioned in the second rank. In addition to these works and to *Boece* (c. 1380; translation of Boethius's *The Consolation of*

Philosophy, c. 523-524) and the *Romaunt of the Rose*, there exist a number of shorter and lesser-known poems, some of which merit brief attention.

These lesser-known poems demonstrate Chaucer's abilities in diverse but typically medieval forms. Perhaps the earliest extant example of Chaucer's work is "An ABC to the Virgin"; this poem, primarily a translation from a thirteenth century French source, is a traditional series of prayers in praise of Mary, the stanzas of which are arranged in alphabetical order according to the first letter of each stanza. Another traditional form Chaucer used is the "complaint," or formal lament. "A Complaint to His Lady" is significant in literary history as the first appearance in English of Dante's terza rima, and "The Complaint unto Pity" is one of the earliest examples of rime royal; this latter poem contains an unusual analogy which represents the personified Pity as being buried in a heart. "The Complaint of Mars" illustrates Chaucer's individuality in treating traditional themes and conventions; although the poem purports to be a Valentine poem, and akin to an aubade, its ironic examination of love's intrinsic variability seems to make it an anti-Valentine poem. Chaucer similarly plays with theme and form in *To Rosemounde*, a ballade in which the conventions of courtly love are exaggerated to the point of grotesquerie; the narrator says, for example, that he is as immersed in love as a fish smothered in pickle sauce. Finally, Chaucer's poem "Gentilesse" is worthy of note for its presentation of a theme, developed in "The Wife of Bath's Tale" and in "The Clerk's Tale," which posits that "gentilesse" depends not on inheritance or social position but on character. In sum, these poems, for most of which dates of composition cannot be assigned, represent a variety of themes and forms with which Chaucer may have been experimenting; they indicate not only his solid grounding in poetic conventions but also his innovative spirit in using new forms and ideas and in treating old forms and ideas in new ways.

Book of the Duchess • Of those poems in the second rank, the *Book of the Duchess* was probably the earliest written and is believed to have been composed as a *consolation* or commemoration of the death of Blanche, Duchess of Lancaster and wife of John of Gaunt, with whom Chaucer was associated. The poem uses the technique of the dream vision and the device of the fictional narrator as two means of objectifying the subject matter, of presenting the consolation at a remove from the narrator and in the person of the bereaved knight himself. The poem thus seems to imply that true consolation can come only from within; the narrator's human sympathy and nature's reassurance can assist in the necessary process of acceptance of and recovery from the loss of a loved one, but that movement from the stasis of deprivation to the action of catharsis and healing can occur only within the mourner's own breast.

The poem is told by a lovesick narrator who battles his insomnia by reading the story of Ceyx and Alcyone. Finally falling asleep, he dreams that he awakens in the morning to the sounds of the hunt and, following a dog, comes upon a distinguished young knight dressed in black who laments his lost love. In response to the dreamer's naïve and persistent questions, the knight is eventually prodded into telling of his loss; he describes his lady in love-filled superlatives, reveals that her outer beauty was symbolic of her inner nobility, and acknowledges the great happiness they enjoyed in their mutual love. At the end of this lengthy discourse, when the narrator inquires as to the lady's whereabouts, the knight states simply that she is dead, to which the narrator replies, "Be God, hyt ys routhe!"

The poem thus blends the mythological world, the natural world, and the realm of human sympathy to create a context within which the mourner can come to accept his loss. The dreamer's lovesickness causes him to have a natural affinity with the knight, and, by posing as stupid, naïve, and slow-witted, the dreamer obliges the knight to speak and to admit his loss, a reality he must acknowledge if he is to move beyond the paralysis caused by his grief to a position where he is accessible to the consolation that can restore him. This restoration is in part accomplished by the dreamer's "naïve" questions, which encourage the knight to remember the joys he experienced with his lady and the love that they shared. The knight is then able to be consoled and comforted by the corrective and curative powers of his own memories.

Library of Congress

The poem thus offers a psychologically realistic and sophisticated presentation of the grief process, a process in which the dreamer-narrator plays a crucial role, since it is the dreamer who, through his seemingly obtuse questioning, propels the knight out of the stasis to which his grief has made him succumb; the cathartic act of speaking to the dreamer about his lost love renders the knight open to the healing powers available in human sympathy and the natural world. The poem, even as it is elegiac in its tribute to the lost lover, is in the genre of the *consolatio* as it records the knight's conversion from unconsolable grief to quiet acceptance and assuagement. In establishing the persona of the apparently naïve and bumbling narrator, Chaucer initiates a tradition which not only has come to be recognized as typical of his works but also has been used repeatedly throughout literature. Probably the earliest English writer to use such a narrative device, Chaucer thereby discovered the rich possibilities for structural irony implicit in the distance between the author and his naïve narrator.

Hous of Fame • In contrast to the well-executed whole that is the *Book of the Duchess*, the *Hous of Fame*, believed to have been composed between 1372 and 1380, is an unfinished work; its true nature and Chaucer's intent in the poem continue to elude critics. Beyond the problems posed by any unfinished work is the question of this particular poem's unity, since the connections between the three parts of the poem which Chaucer actually finished are tenuous. In the first book of the poem, the narrator dreams of the Temple of Venus, where he learns of Dido and Aeneas. The second book, detailing the narrator's journey, in the talons of a golden eagle, to the House of Fame, and the contrast between the eagle's chatty friendliness and volubility and the obviously terrified narrator's monosyllabic responses as they swoop through the air, provides much amusement. The third book, describing the House of Fame and its presiding goddess, demonstrates the total irrationality of fame, which the goddess awards according to caprice rather than merit. After visiting the House of Rumor, the narrator notices everyone running to see a man of great authority, at which point the poem breaks off.

Critical opinion differs considerably as to the poem's meaning. Some believe it attempts to assess the worth of fame or perhaps even the life of the poet, in view of the mutability of human existence; others believe the poem intends to consider the validity of recorded history as opposed to true experience; yet other critics believe the poem attempts to ascertain the nature of poetry and its relationship to love. Although scholars have certainly not as yet settled on the poem's meaning, there is agreement that the flight of the eagle and the narrator in book 2 is one of literature's most finely comic passages. Beyond this, it is perhaps wisest to view the poem as an experiment with various themes which even Chaucer himself was apparently disinterested in unifying.

Parlement of Foules • In contrast to the *Hous of Fame*, the *Parlement of Foules*, composed around 1380, is a finely crafted and complete work in which Chaucer combines several popular conventions, such as the dream vision, the parliament of beasts, and the *demande d'amour* to demonstrate three particular manifestations of love: divine love, erotic love, and procreative love, or natural love. The fictional narrator is here a person who lacks love, who knows of it only through books, and whose very dreams even prove emotionally unsatisfying. The narrator recounts his reading of Scipio Africanus the Younger, who dreamed that his ancestor came to him, told him of divine justice and the life hereafter, and urged him to work to the common profit. Having learned of the nature of divine love, the narrator dreams that Scipio comes to him as he sleeps to take him to a park where there are two gardens, one the garden of Venus and the other the garden of Nature. The garden of Venus is clearly the place of erotic or carnal love; it is located away from the sun and consequently is dark, and it has an illicit and corrupt atmosphere. In addition to such figures as Cupid, Lust, Courtesy, and Jealousy, the narrator sees Venus herself, reclining half-naked in an atmosphere that is close and oppressive.

In contrast, the garden of Nature is in sunlight; it is Valentine's Day, and the birds have congregated to choose their mates. In addition to the natural surroundings, the presence of Nature herself, presiding over the debate, helps to create an atmosphere of fertility and creativity. The choice of mates is, however, impeded by a quarrel among three male eagles who love a formel. Each eagle has a different claim to press: The first asserts that he has loved her long in silence, the second stresses the length of his devotion, and the third emphasizes his devotion's intensity, pointing out that it is the quality rather than the length of love that matters. Since the lower orders of birds cannot choose mates until the eagles have settled their quarrel, the lesser birds enter the debate, aligning themselves variously either for or against the issues of courtly love which are involved. When the various birds' contributions deteriorate into invective without any positive result, Nature intervenes to settle the matter, but the formel insists upon making her own choice in her own time, that is, at the end of a year. The other birds, their mates chosen, sing a joyful song which ends the dream vision. When the narrator awakes he continues to read, hoping to dream better.

The poem, then, presents love in its divine, erotic, and procreative forms. Although the narrator sees these various manifestations of love, he is unable to experience them since all are unavailable to him. He is, in some ways, thus akin to the eagles and in contrast to the lower orders of birds who obviously fare well, since at the end of the parliament they are paired with their mates and blissfully depart. The eagles and the formel, however, because of the formel's need to deliberate upon and choose among her courtly lovers, are in a kind of emotional limbo for a year; in effect, they are all denied for a relatively long period love's natural expression. Thus, even as the system of courtliness raises and ennobles love, the system also provides an impediment to the ultimate realization of love in mating. Although there seems to be a movement in the debate from the artificiality of courtly love to the naturalness of pairing off, this movement does not affect the eagles, who remain constrained, in large part because of their commitment to the courtly code. The poem examines, then, not merely the various faces of love but the nature of courtly love in particular and its seemingly undesirable effects upon its adherents.

The Legend of Good Women • Like the *Hous of Fame*, the *The Legend of Good Women* is unfinished; although the poem was intended to contain a prologue and a series of nineteen or twenty stories telling of true women and false men, the extant material consists of two versions of the prologue and only nine legends. The poem purports to be a penance for the poet's offenses against the God of Love in writing of the false Criseyde and in translating the antifeminine *Romaunt of the Rose*.

In the prologues, Chaucer uses the techniques of the dream vision and the court of love to establish a context for his series of tales, which are much akin to saints' lives. In fact, the poem seems to parody the idea of a religion of love; the poet, although he worships the daisy as the God of Love's symbol, commits by his work heresy against the deity and must therefore repent and do penance by writing of women who were saints and martyrs in love's service. The two prologues differ in the degree to which they use Christian conventions to describe the conduct of love; the "G" prologue, believed to be later than the "F" prologue, has lessened the strength of the analogy to Christian worship. The legends, however, are very much in the hagiographic tradition, even to the extent of canonizing women not customarily regarded as "good," such as Cleopatra and Medea. Evidently wearying of his task, however, Chaucer did not complete the poem, perhaps because of the boredom inherent in the limited perspective.

Troilus and Criseyde • Of Chaucer's completed work, *Troilus and Criseyde* is without question his supreme accomplishment. Justly considered by many to be the first psychological novel, the poem places against the epic background of the Trojan War the tragedy and the romance of Troilus, son of Priam, and Criseyde, daughter of Calchas the soothsayer. Entwined with their lives is that of Pandarus, friend of Troilus and uncle of Criseyde, who brings the lovers together and who, in consequence, earns lasting disapprobation as the first panderer. In analyzing the conjunction of these three characters' lives, the poem considers the relationship of the individual to the society in which the individual lives and examines the extent to which events in one's life are influenced by external circumstances and by internal character. At a deeper level, the poem assesses the ultimate worth of human life, human love, and human values. Yet the poem does not permit reductive or simplistic interpretation; its many thematic strands and its ambiguities of characterization and narrative voice combine to present a multidimensional poem which defies definitive analysis.

The poem's thematic complexity depends upon a relatively simple plot. When callow Troilus is stricken with love for Criseyde, he follows all the courtly rules: He suffers physically, loves her from a distance, and rises to great heights of heroism on the battlefield so as to be worthy of her. When Troilus admits to Pandarus that his misery can only be cured by Criseyde's love, Pandarus is only too happy to exercise his influence over his niece. By means of a subtle mix of avuncular affection, psychological manipulation, and veiled threats, Pandarus leads Criseyde to fall in love with Troilus. The climax of Pandarus's machinations occurs when he arranges for Troilus and Criseyde to consummate their love affair, ostensibly against the stated will of Criseyde and in spite of Troilus's extremely enfeebled condition. Until this point the poem, reflecting largely the conventions of *fabliau*, has been in the control of Pandarus; he generates the action and manipulates the characters much as a rather bawdy and perhaps slightly prurient stage manager. With the love scene, however, the poem's form shifts from that of *fabliau* to that of romance; Pandarus becomes a minor figure, and the love between Troilus and Criseyde achieves much greater spiritual significance than either had anticipated.

Although the tenets of courtly love demand that the lovers keep their affair secret, they enjoy for three years a satisfying and enriching relationship which serves greatly to ennoble Troilus; the poem's shape then shifts again, this time from romance to tragedy. Calchas, having foreseen the Trojan defeat and having therefore defected to the Greeks, requests that a captured Trojan be exchanged for his daughter. The distraught lovers discover that the constraints placed upon them by their commitments to various standards and codes of behavior combine with the constraints imposed upon them by society to preclude their preventing the exchange, but Criseyde promises within ten days to steal away from the Greek camp and return to Troilus. Once in the Greek camp, however, Criseyde finds it difficult to escape; moreover, believing that the Greek Diomede has fallen in love with her, she decides to remain in the Greek encampment until the grief-stricken Troilus eventually has to admit that she has, indeed, betrayed him.

At the end of the poem, having been killed by Achilles, Troilus gazes from the eighth sphere upon the fullness of the universe and laughs at those mortals who indulge in earthly endeavor. In his bitter wisdom he condemns all things of the earth, particularly earthly love, which is so inadequate in comparison with heavenly love. This section of the poem, erroneously called by some "the epilogue," has been viewed as Chaucer's retraction of his poem and a nullification of what has gone before. Chaucer's poetic vision, however, is much more complex than this interpretation supposes; throughout the poem he has been preparing the reader to accept several paradoxes. One is that even as human beings must celebrate and strive for secular love, which is the nearest thing they have to divine love, they must nevertheless and simultaneously concentrate on the hereafter, since secular love and human connections are, indeed, vastly inferior to divine love. A second paradox is that humans should affirm the worth of human life and human values while at the same time recognizing their mutability and their inferiority to Christian values. The poem also presents courtly love as a paradox since, on one hand, it is the system that inspires Troilus to strive for and achieve a vastly ennobled character even though, on the other, the system is proven unworthy of his devotion. Criseyde is similarly paradoxical in that the narrator portrays her as deserving of Troilus's love, even though she proves faithless to him.

These paradoxes are presented against a classical background which contributes to the poet's juxtaposition of several oppositions. The world of the classical epic provides the setting for a medieval courtly romance so that, although the characters exist in a pagan environment, they are viewed from the Christian medieval perspective which informs the poem. The poem's epic setting and its romance form, then, like its pagan plot and its Christian point of view, seem thus to be temporally misaligned; this misalignment does not, however, lead to dissonance but instead contributes to the poem's thematic ambiguity.

The characters also contribute significantly to the poem's ambiguity. Criseyde, particularly, resists classification and categorization. The ambivalent narrator encourages the reader to see Criseyde in a variety of contradictory postures: as a victim, but also as a survivor, one who takes the main chance; as a weak and socially vulnerable person, but also as a woman who is self-confident and strong; as an idealistic and romantic lover, but also as a careful pragmatist; as a greatly self-deceived character, but also as a self-aware character who at times admits painful truths about herself.

Also ambiguous, but to a lesser degree, is Pandarus, whose characterization vacillates between that of the icily unsentimental cynic and that of the sensitive human being who bemoans his failures to achieve happiness in love and who worries about what history will do to his reputation. He seems to see courtly love as a game and to disbelieve in the total melding of two lives, but he betrays his own sentimentality when he indicates that he longs to find such love for himself.

Although his mentor seems not to take courtly love seriously, to Troilus it is the center of his life, his very reality. His virtue lies in large part in his absolute commitment to courtly ideals and to Criseyde. The solidity of that commitment, however, prevents Troilus from taking any active steps to stop the exchange, since such action would reveal their love affair, soil Criseyde's reputation, and violate the courtly love code. In this sense, Troilus is trapped by his own nobility and by his idealism, so that his course of action is restrained not only by external forces but also by his own character.

In fact, the poem seems to show that both Troilus and Criseyde are ultimately responsible for what happens to them; the role of fate in their lives is relatively insignificant because their very characters are their fate. As Troilus is governed by his dedication to heroic and courtly ideals, Criseyde is governed by the fact that she is "slydynge of corage." It is her nature to take the easiest way, and because of her nature she is untrue to Troilus.

From the poet's point of view, however, Criseyde's faithlessness does not invalidate for Troilus the experience of her love. Because of his own limited perspective, Troilus is himself unable to assess the worth of his life, his love affair, and the values to which he subscribed; the parameters of his vision permit him to see only the inadequacy and imperfection of earthly experience in comparison with the experience of the divine. The poet's perspective, however, is the one that informs the poem, and that perspective is broader, clearer, and more complex, capable of encompassing the poem's various paradoxes and oppositions. In consequence, even though Troilus at the end discounts his earthly experience, the poem has proven its worth to an incontrovertible degree; human life, even though inferior to the afterlife, nevertheless affords the opportunity for experiences which, paradoxically, can transcend their earthly limitations. Ultimately, then, the poem affirms the worth of human life, human love, and human idealism.

The Canterbury Tales • Although Chaucer never completed *The Canterbury Tales*, it is his most important work and the one for which he is best known. In its conceptual richness, in its grace and precision of execution, and in its broad presentation of humanity, *The Canterbury Tales* is unequaled. The poem occupied Chaucer for the last one and a half decades of his life, although several of the stories date from an earlier period; it was not until sometime in the middle 1380's, when he conceived the idea of using a framing device within which his stories could be placed, that the work began to assume shape. That shape is the form of a springtime pilgrimage to Canterbury to see the shrine of Thomas à Becket. The fictional party consists of some thirty pilgrims, along with the narrator and the host from the Tabard Inn; each pilgrim was to tell two stories en route to Canterbury and two on the return trip, making an approximate total of 120 tales. There are extant, however, only the prologue and twenty-four tales, not all of which are completed; moreover, the sources of these extant tales (more than eighty manuscript fragments) contain considerable textual variations and arrange the tales in many differing orders. Thus, it is impossible for critics to determine the order which Chaucer envisioned for the tales.

The notion of using the pilgrimage as a framing device was a stroke of narrative brilliance, since the device provides infinite possibilities for dramatic action while it simultaneously unifies a collection of widely disparate stories. In response to the host's request for stories of "mirth" or "doctryne," the pilgrims present an eclectic collection of tales, including romances, fabliaux, beast-fables, saints' lives, tragedies, sermons, and exempla. The frame of the pilgrimage also permits the poet to represent a cross section of society, since the members of the party range across the social spectrum from the aristocratic knight to the bourgeois guild members to the honest plowman. Moreover, since the tales are connected by passages of dialogue among the pilgrims as they ride along on their journey, the pilgrimage frame also permits the characters of the storytellers to be developed and additional dramatic action to occur from the pilgrims' interaction. These "links" between the tales thus serve to define a constant fictional world, the pilgrimage, which is in juxtaposition to and seemingly in control of the multiple fictional worlds created in the tales themselves; the fictional world of the pilgrims on their pilgrimage thereby acquires a heightened degree of verisimilitude, especially because the pilgrims' interchanges with one another often help to place them at various recognizable points on the road to Canterbury.

The pilgrimage frame also permits the creation of an exquisitely ironic tension between the fictional narrator and the poet himself. The narrator is Chaucer's usual persona, naïve, rather thick-witted, and easily and wrongly impressed by outward show. This narrator's gullible responses to the various pilgrims are contrasted to the attitude of the poet himself; such use of the fictional narrator permits the poet not only to present two points of view on any and all action but also to play upon the tension deriving from the collision of those two perspectives. The device of the pilgrimage frame, in sum, allows the poet virtually unlimited freedom in regard to form, content, and tone.

The context of the pilgrimage is established in the poem's prologue, which begins by indicating that concerns both sacred and secular prompt people to go on pilgrimage. Those people are described in a formal series of portraits which reveals that the group is truly composed of "sondry folk" and is a veritable cross section of medieval society. Yet the skill of the poet is evident in the fact that even as the pilgrims are "types"—that is, they are representative of a body of others like themselves—they are also individuals who are distinguished not simply by the realistic details describing their external appearances but more crucially by the sharply searching analysis that penetrates their external façades to expose the actualities of character that lie beneath.

"The Knight's Tale" • The tales begin with a group that has come to be seen as Chaucer's variations on the theme of the love-triangle and which consists of "The Knight's Tale," "The Miller's Tale," and "The Reeve's Tale." Like *Troilus and Criseyde,* "The Knight's Tale" superimposes a romance against the background of the classical world as it tells of Palamon and Arcite, knights of Thebes who are captured by Theseus during his battle with Creon and sentenced to life imprisonment in Athens. While imprisoned they fall in love with Emily, over whom they quarrel; since Palamon, who saw and loved her first, thought she was a goddess, Arcite, who saw her second but who loved her as a woman, insists that his is the better claim. Several years later, Arcite having been freed and Palamon having escaped from prison, the knights meet and again quarrel, agreeing to settle the matter with a duel. When Theseus comes upon them he stops the duel and decrees that they must instead meet a year later with their troops to decide the matter in a tournament.

For this tournament Theseus erects a magnificent stadium with temples to Venus, Mars, and Diana. When the stadium is completed and the time for the tournament has arrived, the three members of the love-triangle pray for the assistance of their particular gods: Palamon asks Venus for Emily or for death; Arcite asks Mars for victory; and Emily asks Diana to permit her to remain a virgin or, failing that, to be wedded to the one who most loves her. These various petitions cause a quarrel between Venus and Mars which Saturn resolves by announcing that Palamon shall have his lady even though Mars assists Arcite to victory. Arcite, in consequence, wins the tournament, but in the midst of his victory parade, his horse rears, and he is mortally injured. From his deathbed Arcite summons both Palamon and Emily and commends them to each other, but they continue to grieve during the next several years. Finally, Theseus summons Palamon and Emily to him and tells them that since grief should end and life go on, they are to marry and thus make joy from sorrows.

The poem's plot, then, concerns the resolution of the love-triangle typical of romance. This plot, however, is in the service of a more serious conflict, that between order and chaos. Theseus serves as the civilizing instrument, the means by which order is imposed on the anarchy of human passion. In actuality, by assuming control over the hostility between Palamon and Arcite, Theseus reshapes their primitive emotional conflict into a clearly defined ritual; by distancing it as well in time and space, Theseus forces that conflict into a shape and an expression that is socially acceptable and which poses no threat to the culture's peaceful continuance. Theseus thus makes order and art out of raw emotion and violent instincts.

"The Miller's Tale" • The love conflict which in "The Knight's Tale" serves to develop this cosmic theme is in "The Miller's Tale" acted out on the smaller scale and in the more limited space of the sheerly natural world and thus serves no such serious or noble end. Again there is a triangle, but the romantic discord among the aristocratic Palamon, Arcite, and Emily becomes in "The Miller's Tale" the bawdy comedy of the fabliau as it arises from the interaction of the young clerk Nicholas and the effeminate dandy Absolon, both of whom desire Alison, the young wife of John, an old and jealous carpenter. At the same time that the amorous Absolon serenades her nightly and sends her gifts in an effort to win her, Alison agrees to give her love to Nicholas as soon as he can create the opportunity. In fact, however, no elaborate stratagem is needed to make possible the encounter Alison and Nicholas both desire. Since Alison's husband is away all day working, and since Nicholas, as a student who boards with the couple, is at home with Alison all day, there really are no obstacles preventing the lovers from acting on their passions immediately. Alison's insistence, then, that Nicholas devise a plan whereby they can give rein to their passions, reflects an important stylistic and thematic connection between the tale and "The Knight's Tale."

In "The Knight's Tale," Theseus controls the passions of Palamon and Arcite by postponing their encounter and dictating its arena; the distancing in time and space results in a civilized, restrained expression of their passions. In "The Miller's Tale," by contrast, the distancing Alison demands parodies the conventions of romance and courtly love. This distance in actuality simply ennobles base instincts, for Alison and Nicholas inhabit not a courtly world but a natural one, and their intellectual, spiritual, and romantic pretensions constitute only a thin veneer covering their healthy animalism. By using distance as a means of ennobling base instincts, "The Miller's Tale" parodies not only the world and the theme of "The Knight's Tale" but also its poetic treatment.

Nicholas's seduction plan plays upon both the strengths and the weaknesses of the carpenter's character. Telling John that another flood is coming, Nicholas convinces the carpenter that he must hang three barrels from the rafters in which Nicholas, John, and Alison can remain until the waters rise; then they will cut themselves free to float away. The carpenter's pretensions to spiritual and theological superiority cause him to accept this prophecy unquestioningly, but at the same time his genuine love for his wife causes his first reaction to be fear for her life. When all three on the appointed night have ostensibly entered their barrels, Nicholas and Alison sneak down to spend a night in amorous play.

At this point the plot is entered by Absolon, who comes to Alison's window to serenade her; pleading for a kiss, he finds himself presented with Alison's backside. Bent then on avenging his misdirected kiss, he brings a hot colter and asks for another kiss; presented this time with the backside of Nicholas, Absolon smacks it smartly with the red-hot colter, causing Nicholas to cry out "Water!" which in turn causes the carpenter to cut the rope on his barrel and crash to the ground, injuring both his person and his dignity. Whereas in "The Knight's Tale" the three major characters ultimately obtain what they desire most—Arcite, victory; Palamon, Emily; and Emily, the man who loves her most—"The Miller's Tale" reverses this idea; John, the jealous carpenter, is cuckolded and humiliated in front of the entire town, the fastidious Absolon has kissed Alison's "nether ye," and Nicholas has lost a hand's-breadth of skin from his backside. Only Alison remains unscathed, but then, she must spend her life being married to John.

The poem thus parodies the romance tradition, the idealistic notion that civilized or courtly processes can elevate and ennoble fundamental human passions. Even as it transfers various themes, mechanisms, and perspectives from "The Knight's Tale," "The Miller's Tale" transforms these and reflects them negatively. The generic differences between the two poems, however, demand that content and tone differ. "The Knight's Tale," combining epic and romance, deals seriously with serious considerations, whereas "The Miller's Tale," by virtue of its being a fabliau, has as one of its purposes the humorous depiction of human shortcomings.

"The Reeve's Tale" • "The Knight's Tale" and "The Miller's Tale" are different tales that have structural similarities; "The Reeve's Tale," which completes the poem's first thematic grouping, shares with "The Miller's Tale" the fabliau form, but the two differ considerably in tone. The Reeve's story results from his outrage at the Miller's story, which has belittled carpenters; in angry retaliation the Reeve relates the popular fabliau concerning the two students who, cheated by a dishonest miller, exact revenge by sleeping with both his wife and his daughter. The plot, which hangs in part upon the device of the misplaced cradle, has as its end the unsophisticated students' triumph over the social-climbing miller. The tone of "The Reeve's Tale," therefore, is bitter and vindictive, told, the Reeve acknowledges, solely to repay the Miller.

Chaucer uses the romance and the fabliau, the two forms with which he begins his series of tales, again and again in the course of the poem. Other romances are the unfinished "The Squire's Tale," which has an Asian setting; "The Man of Law's Tale," which blends romance and a saint's life in the story of the unfortunate Constance; and "The Wife of Bath's Tale," "The Clerk's Tale," and "The Franklin's Tale," which will be discussed together as "the marriage group." The genre of the fabliau is also further represented in "The Shipman's Tale" of the debt repaid by the adulterous monk to his lender's wife, and in "The Friar's Tale" and "The Summoner's Tale," stories that are attacks on each other's professions and which are told to be mutually insulting.

Chaucer's Use of Saints' Lives • Another popular genre Chaucer employs in his collection is that of the saints' lives, a type used in "The Second Nun's Tale" of St. Cecilia and in "The Prioress's Tale" of the martyred Christian boy slain by Jews. Although both tales conventionally concern "miracles of the Virgin," the tale of the Prioress is of particular interest because of the nature of the storyteller. Although she is supposed to be a spiritual being, a guardian of other spiritual beings, she is described in the same manner as the heroine of a courtly romance; moreover, although her description points to sensitivity and charity, her moral sensibility is clearly faulty. She worries over a little mouse but tells a violent tale of religious intolerance. Moreover, the ironies implicit in the engraving on her brooch—"Amor vincit omnia"—are extensive, as are the ironies deriving from the conflicting perspectives of the narrator, who naïvely admires her for all the wrong reasons, and the poet, who clearly sees her as possessed of many shortcomings.

"The Nun's Priest's Tale" • Another popular genre in the Middle Ages was the beast-fable, a form that Chaucer uses brilliantly in "The Nun's Priest's Tale." The story concerns Chauntecleer and Pertelote, a cock and hen owned by a poor widow. When Chauntecleer one night dreams of a fox, he and Pertelote have an extended discussion on the validity of dreams. Believing that dreams are caused by bile or overeating, Pertelote advises the use of a laxative; Chauntecleer, however, holding a different opinion, tells a story wherein a dream is proven prophetic. At this point the fox appears, whom the Nun's Priest likens to such other traitors as Simon and Judas Iscariot. Even as he insists that his antifeminine statements are not his own but the cock's, the Nun's Priest clearly believes that woman's counsel often brings misfortune and points with relish to the fox's sudden appearance as proof of this belief.

The encounter between the fox and the cock reveals the weaknesses of both. Relying hugely on flattery, the fox persuades Chauntecleer to relax his guard, close his eyes, and stretch his neck, providing the perfect opportunity to seize Chauntecleer and race off. As the widow and her household set chase, Chauntecleer advises the fox to tell the pursuers to turn back because he will soon be eating Chauntecleer in spite of them; when the fox opens his mouth to do this, Chauntecleer escapes. Although the fox tries to persuade Chauntecleer to come down out of the tree, Chauntecleer wisely declares that he will not again be fooled by flattery and that no one should prosper who closes his eyes when he should watch. The fox, as one might expect, disagrees, declaring that no one should prosper who talks when he should hold his peace.

The poem thus uses the beast-fable's technique of personifying animals to the end of revealing human truths; it also uses the conventions and the rhetoric of epic and courtly romance to talk about the lives of chickens, thus creating a parody of the epic form and a burlesque of the courtly attitude. The poem is also, to a degree, homiletic in treating the dangers inherent in succumbing to flattery; each character suffers as a result of this weakness, the cock by having foolishly permitted himself to be captured, and the fox by having gullibly permitted himself to be hoodwinked by one pretending affinity.

"The Wife of Bath's Tale" • Having begun the discussion of *The Canterbury Tales* with an analysis of the group of tales concerned with the love-triangle, it seems fitting to end the discussion with an analysis of those tales referred to as "the marriage group." "The Wife of Bath's Tale," "The Clerk's Tale," "The Merchant's Tale," and "The Franklin's Tale" bring to that group several perspectives on women and the relation between the sexes. The Wife of Bath, in complete opposition to the traditional view of women, presents one extreme point of view that advocates sensuality and female authority. An excellent example of what she advocates, the wife is strong and lusty and insists on dominance in her marriages. In her lengthy prologue to her story she takes issue with patristic doctrine concerning chastity and female inferiority and uses scriptural allusions to buttress her opinions. Her prologue thus provides a defense of women and of sensuality.

The Wife of Bath's tale, an exemplum illustrating the argument contained in her prologue, concerns a knight who must, in order to save his life, find out what women desire most. Despairing over his inability to get a consensus of opinion, he one day comes upon a "loathly lady" who offers to give him the answer if he in turn will do what she requests. Gratefully agreeing, he learns that women most want "sovereyne-tee" and "maistrie" over their husbands; he is less pleased, however, to learn that her request is that he marry her. Having kept his promise, the knight on their wedding night is understandably distant from his new wife; when pressed for an explanation, he notes that she is ugly, old, and lowly born. She in turn explains that nobility comes not from wealth or birth, that poverty is virtuous, and that her age and ugliness ensure her chastity. She gives the knight a choice: He can have her ugly and old but faithful, or young and pretty but untrue. The knight chooses, however, to transfer this decision and consequently the control of the marriage to her, whereupon she announces that she will be not only young and pretty but also faithful, thus illustrating the good that comes when women are in control.

"The Clerk's Tale" • The Wife's tale, and the wife herself, with her heretical opinions concerning marriage and sexual relations, outrage the Clerk, who tells a tale to counter the Wife's; his tale reinforces the doctrine that male dominance on earth conforms to the order of the divine hierarchy. His story treats the patient Griselda, who promises her husband, Walter, to do everything he wishes and never to complain or in any way indicate disagreement. When a daughter is born to them, Walter, who is an Italian marquis, tells Griselda that since the people are complaining about her low birth, he must have the child killed, to which Griselda meekly agrees; Walter, however, sends the child secretly to a relative to be reared. When a son is born, Walter again does the same thing, again to test her obedience, and again Griselda is perfectly submissive. Twelve years later Walter secretly sends for the two children and tells Griselda that since he is divorcing her in order to marry someone else, she must return to her father. Moreover, he insists that she return to her father just as she had left him, that is, naked, since Walter had provided her with clothes. Griselda, with great dignity, requests at least a shift as recompense for the virginity which she had brought to him but which she cannot take away with her. When asked later to come and make arrangements for Walter's new bride, Griselda cheerfully complies, although she does, at this point, give some indication of the great price she has paid for her obedience and her faithfulness to her vow; she asks Walter not to torment his new wife as he tormented her, the bride-to-be having been tenderly reared and therefore not so well able to withstand such adversity. Walter, finally satisfied as to Griselda's steadfastness, restores her as his wife and reunites her with her children. The Clerk concludes by noting that it is hard to find women like Griselda nowadays.

The tale is one with which critics have long grappled, since it presents seemingly insurmountable interpretive problems. The story can hardly be taken as realistic, even though the Clerk, through his efforts to give Walter psychological motivation, attempts to provide verisimilitude. Although the poem may be intended as allegory, to illustrate that one must be content in adversity, it seems also to have a tropological level of meaning, to illustrate the proper attitude for wives. The narrator's own uncertainty as to whether he tells a tale of real people, a saint's life, or an allegory, contributes to the difficulty one has in assessing the poem's nature and purpose. It is obvious, though, that the Clerk's intended corrective to "The Wife of Bath's Tale" is perfectly accomplished through his tale of the impossibly patient Griselda.

"The Merchant's Tale" • At the end of his tale the Clerk appears to switch directions; he advises that no husband should try what Walter did, and that furthermore wives should be fierce to their husbands, should provoke their jealousy, and should make them weep and wail. The Merchant picks up this notion and echoes the line in the first sentence of his own remarks, which are intended to counter the Clerk's presentation of the saintly wife. The Merchant's own unhappy marriage experience adds a painfully personal coloration to his tale of the old husband and the young wife.

The Merchant's story of May, Januarie, and the pear tree is well known in the history of the fabliau. Immediately after wedding the sixty-year-old Januarie, whose lovemaking she considers not "worth a bene," May meets and falls in love with Damian, who loves her in return. When Januarie becomes temporarily blind, the lovers plot to consummate their love in the pear tree above Januarie's head. Pluto and Proserpina, debating how men and women betray each other, decide to restore Januarie's sight but to give May a facile tongue. Consequently, when Januarie's sight returns and he sees May and Damian making love in the pear tree, May explains that her struggling in a tree with a man was an effort to restore his sight, which is obviously as yet imperfect. Placated, Januarie accepts her explanation, and they are reconciled.

The three tales thus present varying views of woman as lascivious termagant, as obedient saint, and as clever deceiver; marriage, accordingly, is seen as a struggle for power and freedom between combatants who are natural adversaries. It remains for Chaucer in "The Franklin's Tale" to attempt a more balanced view, to try to achieve a reconciliation of the oppositions posed in the tales of the Wife of Bath, the Clerk, and the Merchant.

"The Franklin's Tale" • "The Franklin's Tale" is a particular kind of romance called a Breton lai, which conventionally is concentrated, imaginative, and exaggeratedly romantic. Although the tale is interesting in its depiction of an integrity which rests upon absolute commitment to the pledged word, the intricacies of the poem's moral issues are ultimately resolved, in a rather disappointing fashion, by something akin to a deus ex machina. The tale, nevertheless, has been seen traditionally to function as the reconciliation of the marriage group because of the more balanced relationship portrayed between Arveragus, a knight, and Dorigen, his wife. The couple agree that he will show no sovereignty except for that semblance of it which may be necessary for his dignity, and that their effort will be for freedom, harmony, and mutual respect in marriage, rather than for mastery. In this regard, they represent an ideal example of marriage which is totally antithetical to those of the preceding marriage tales; in Dorigen and Arveragus, Chaucer seems to be exploring the possibility that chivalric ideals and middle-class virtues can be compatible in marriage. Whether the poet really believes this is possible, however, is placed in question by the tale's romance form and by its contrived ending.

While Arveragus is away on knightly endeavors, Dorigen mourns and grieves, worrying particularly about the black rocks that make the coastline hazardous. When Aurelius, who has loved her long, pleads for her attentions, she explains that she will never be unfaithful to her husband but adds, in jest, that if he will remove the rocks she will love him. Two years after Arveragus has come home, Aurelius, made ill by his long-frustrated passion, finds a magician who, for a large fee, creates the illusion that the rocks have vanished. Asked then to fulfill her end of the bargain, the horrified Dorigen contemplates suicide to avoid this dishonor, but her miserably unhappy husband, declaring that "Trouthe is the hyeste thyng that man may kepe," sends Dorigen to fulfill her promise. Pitying them, Aurelius releases her from her promise and is in turn released from his debt by the magician; the tale ends by asking who was the most generous.

Although Dorigen and Arveragus have a marriage based on respect, honesty, and love, and although they share a moral sensibility and agree on the importance of honor to them individually and to their marriage, the artificial resolution of the plot by totally unexpected elements—the decisions of both Aurelius and the magician not to press their just claims—would seem to suggest that the poet himself dared not treat in a realistic fashion the unpleasant and probably disastrous results of the plot which he had created. In effect, he established an ideal marriage situation, set up a test of that marriage's strength, but then decided not to go through with the test. In placing his attempted solution of the marriage problem in the form of a Breton lai, in failing to pursue to the end the very questions he himself raises, and in providing a typical romance ending, the poet seems to indicate that any real solution to the problems pertaining to women and to marriage are not going to be so easily attained.

The Canterbury Tales, then, represents one of the earliest collections of short stories of almost every conceivable type. In addition to being a generic compendium, the poem is also a compendium of characters, since the pilgrims who tell the stories and the people who inhabit the stories together constitute the widest possible representation of character types. In framing his collection of tales with the pilgrimage, Chaucer permitted himself an eclecticism in form, content, and treatment which was unprecedented in English literature. There are those who would eagerly affirm that the grace of vision which permeates *The Canterbury*

Tales makes the work not only one which was unprecedented but also one which has not since been equaled.

Evelyn Newlyn
With updates by William Nelles

Other major works

MISCELLANEOUS: *Works*, 1957 (second edition; F. N. Robinson, editor).

NONFICTION: *Boece*, c. 1380 (translation of Boethius' *The Consolation of Philosophy*); *A Treatise on the Astrolabe*, 1387-1392.

Bibliography

Borroff, Marie. *Traditions and Renewals: Chaucer, the Gawain-Poet, and Beyond*. New Haven, Conn.: Yale University Press, 2003. Collection of essays that provide a fresh and different analysis of Chaucer's work.

Brewer, Derek. *A New Introduction to Chaucer*. New York: Longman, 1998. Written by an expert in the field, this volume provides ample biographical and historical material for anyone who is unfamiliar with Chaucer's life and work. Includes a thorough bibliography and index.

Brown, Peter, ed. *A Companion to Chaucer*. Malden, Mass.: Blackwell, 2000. Part of the *Blackwell Companions to Literature and Culture* series, offers broad and detailed essays by scholars of Chaucer and his era.

Condren, Edward I. *Chaucer and the Energy of Creation: The Design and the Organization of "The Canterbury Tales."* Gainesville: University Press of Florida, 1999. Examines the motives behind Chaucer's layout of the stories.

Gittes, Katherine S. *Framing the Canterbury Tales: Chaucer and the Medieval Frame Narrative Tradition*. Westport, Conn.: Greenwood Press, 1991. Analyzes the influence of the Asian frame narrative tradition on *The Canterbury Tales*; argues that what was once taken for incompleteness is the result of the influence of Eastern modes of narrative structure.

Narkiss, Doron. "The Fox, the Cock, and the Priest: Chaucer's Escape from Fable." *The Chaucer Review* 32 (1997): 46-63. Examines Chaucer's reworking of Aesop's fable in "The Nun's Priest's Tale." Argues that Chaucer moves the fable away from the realm of learning and wisdom to mockery and a way of reading that in "The Nun's Priest's Tale" fable is extended by characterization and action. Claims that Chaucer's use of the fable suggests doubling, repetition, and substitutions.

Percival, Florence. *Chaucer's Legendary Good Women*. New York: Cambridge University Press, 1998. Suitable for introductory students yet containing challenging insights for scholars. Percival attempts to provide a comprehensive interpretation of the puzzling Legend of Good Women without ignoring any of the contradictory views that it contains about women.

Rossignol, Rosalyn. *Chaucer A to Z: The Essential Reference to His Life and Works*. New York: Facts on File, 1999. Indispensable guide for the student of Chaucer.

West, Richard. *Chaucer 1340-1400: The Life and Times of the First English Poet*. New York: Carroll & Graf, 2000. Discussion of the history surrounding Chaucer's achievements and the events of his life. Chapters take up such matters as the Black Death's impact on the anti-Semitism evident in "The Prioress's Tale" and the impact of the great English Peasants' Revolt of 1381 on Chaucer's worldview.

John Cheever

Born: Quincy, Massachusetts; May 27, 1912
Died: Ossining, New York; June 18, 1982

Principal short fiction • *The Way Some People Live*, 1943; *The Enormous Radio, and Other Stories*, 1953; "The Country Husband," 1954; *The Housebreaker of Shady Hill, and Other Stories*, 1958; *Some People, Places, and Things That Will Not Appear in My Next Novel*, 1961; *The Brigadier and the Golf Widow*, 1964; *The World of Apples*, 1973; *The Stories of John Cheever*, 1978; *Thirteen Uncollected Stories*, 1994.

Other literary forms • Believing that "fiction is our most intimate and acute means of communication, at a profound level, about our deepest apprehensions and intuitions on the meaning of life and death," John Cheever devoted himself to the writing of stories and novels. Although he kept voluminous journals, he wrote only a handful of essays and even fewer reviews, and only one television screenplay, *The Shady Hill Kidnapping*, which aired January 12, 1982, on the Public Broadcasting Service. A number of Cheever's works have also been adapted by other writers, including several early short stories such as "The Town House" (play, 1948), "The Swimmer" (film, 1968), "Goodbye, My Brother" as *Children* (play, 1976), and "O Youth and Beauty," "The Five-Forty-Eight," and "The Sorrows of Gin" (teleplays, 1979). Benjamin Cheever has edited selections of his father's correspondence, *The Letters of John Cheever* (1988), and journals, *The Journals of John Cheever* (1991).

Achievements • A major twentieth century novelist, John Cheever has achieved even greater fame as a short-story writer. He published his first story, "Expelled," in *The New Republic* when he was only eighteen. Reviewers of his first collection, *The Way Some People Live*, judged Cheever to be a promising young writer. Numerous awards and honors followed: two John Simon Guggenheim Memorial Foundation grants (1951, 1961), a Benjamin Franklin award for "The Five-Forty-Eight" (1955), an O. Henry Award for "The Country Husband" (1956), election to the National Institute of Arts and Letters in 1957, elevation to the American Academy in 1973, a National Book Award in 1958 for *The Wapshot Chronicle* (1957), the Howells Medal in 1965 for *The Wapshot Scandal* (1964), cover stories in *Time* (1964) and *Newsweek* (1977), the Edward MacDowell Medal in 1979, a Pulitzer Prize and a National Book Critics Circle award (both in 1978), an American Book Award (1979) for *The Stories of John Cheever*, and the National Medal for Literature (1982). Cheever's achievements, however, cannot be measured only in terms of the awards and honors that he has received (including the honorary doctorate bestowed on this high school dropout), for his most significant accomplishment was to create, with the publication of *The Stories of John Cheever*, a resurgence of interest in, and a new respect for, the short story on the part of public and publishers alike.

Biography • The loss of his father's job in 1930, followed by the loss of the family home and the strained marital situation caused, John Cheever believed, by his mother's growing financial and emotional dependence, all had a lifelong effect on

Cheever. When he was expelled from Thayer Academy at the age of seventeen, Cheever was already committed to a writing career. His career, however, would do little to assuage his sense of emotional and economic insecurity. Although he liked to claim that "fiction is not crypto-autobiography," from the beginning, his stories were drawn from his personal experiences. They have even followed him geographically: from New England, to New York City, through his military service, to the suburbs (first Scarborough, then Ossining), with side trips to Italy (1956-1957), the Soviet Union (on three government-sponsored trips), and Sing Sing prison, where he taught writing (1971-1972). The stories have, more importantly, followed Cheever over hazardous emotional terrain, transforming personal obsessions into published fictions: alcoholism, bisexuality, self-doubts, strained marital relations, and the sense of "otherness." The stories also evidence the longing for stability and home that manifested itself in three of the most enduring relationships of his fifty-year career: with the Yaddo writers' colony in Saratoga Springs, New York (beginning in 1934); with *The New Yorker* (which began publishing his work in 1935); and with his wife Mary Winternitz Cheever (whom he met in 1939 and married two years later, and with whom he bickered over the next forty years).

Cheever did not become free of his various fears and dependencies—including his nearly suicidal addiction to alcohol—until the mid-1970's. After undergoing treatment for alcoholism at Smithers Rehabilitation Center, he transformed what might well have become his darkest novel into his most affirmative. *Falconer* (1977) was both a critical and a commercial success. Like its main character, Cheever seemed for the first time in his life free, willing at least to begin talking about the private life that he had so successfully guarded, even mythified before, when he had played the part of country squire. The triumph was, however, short-lived. After two neurological seizures in 1980, a kidney operation and the discovery of cancer in 1981, and, shortly after the publication of his fifth novel, the aptly and perhaps whimsically titled *Oh What a Paradise It Seems* (1982), he died on June 18, 1982.

Analysis • John Cheever has been called both "the Chekhov of the exurbs" and "Ovid in Ossining"—which suggests both the variety and the complexity of the man and his fiction. Accused by some of being a literary lightweight—a writer merely of short stories and an apologist for middle-class life—he has been more often, and more justly, praised as a master chronicler of a way of life that he both celebrates and satirizes in stories that seem at once conventional and innovative, realistic and fantastic. His stories read effortlessly, yet their seeming simplicity masks a complexity that deserves and repays close attention. The line "The light from the cottage, shining into the fog, gave the illusion of substance, and it seems as if I might stumble on a beam of light," for example, only appears simple and straightforward. It begins with a conventional image, light penetrating darkness, thus illuminating the way to truth, but the next five words undermine the "illusion" first by calling attention to it, then by paradoxically literalizing the metaphor, making this substantive light a stumbling block rather than a source of spiritual or philosophical truth.

"A Miscellany of Characters That Will Not Appear in My Next Novel" • Nothing in Cheever's fiction of stark contrasts—light and dark, male and female, city and country—ever exists independent of its opposite. His stories proceed incrementally and contrapuntally, at times in curiously indirect ways. In "A Miscellany of Characters That Will Not Appear in My Next Novel," for example, Cheever's narrator

© Nancy Crampton

banishes seven kinds of characters and situations from his fiction, including alcoholics, homosexuals, and "scornful descriptions of American landscapes." However, not only did his next novel, as well as much of the rest of his fiction, include all three, but also the very act of listing them in this "miscellany" confirms their power, giving them a prominence that far outweighs their hypothetical banishment from any later work. This play of voices and positions within individual works also exists between stories.

The same narrative situations will appear in various Cheever stories, handled comically in some, tragically in others. In effect, the stories offer a series of brilliant variations on a number of basic, almost obsessive themes, of which the most general and the most recurrent as well as the most important is the essential conflict between his characters' spiritual longings and social and psychological (especially sexual) nature. "What I wanted to do," one of his narrator-protagonists says, is "to grant my dreams, in so incoherent a world, their legitimacy," "to celebrate," as another claims, "a world that lies spread out around us like a bewildering and stupendous dream." Their longings are tempered not only by the incoherence of their world but also by a doubt concerning whether what they long for actually exists or is rather only an illusion conjured out of nothing more substantial than their own ardent hopes for something or some place or someone other than who, what, and where they currently are. Even when expressed in the most ludicrous terms possible, the characters' longings seem just as profound as they are ridiculous, as in the case of "Artemis the Honest Well Digger" searching "for a girl as pure and fresh as the girl on the oleomargarine package." The line seems both to affirm and to qualify the yearning of a character who may confuse kitsch with Kant, advertising copy with lyrical longings, but who nevertheless seems as much a holy fool as a deluded consumer.

Whether treated comically or tragically, Cheever's characters share a number of traits. Most are male, married, and white-collar workers. All—despite their Sutton Place apartments or, more often, comfortable homes in affluent Westchester communities—feel confused, dispossessed, lost; they all seem to be what the characters in Cheever's Italian stories actually are: expatriates and exiles. Physical ailments are rare, emotional ones epidemic. Instead of disease, there is the "dis-ease" of "spiritual nomadism." They are as restless as any of Cheever's most wayward plots and in need of "building a bridge" between the events of their lives as well as between those lives and their longings.

Trapped in routines as restricting as any prison cell and often in marriages that seem little more than sexual battlefields, where even the hair curlers appear "bellicose," Cheever's characters appear poised between escaping into the past in a futile effort to repeat what they believe they have lost and aspiring to a lyrical future that can be affirmed, even "sung," though never quite attained. Even the latter can be dangerous. "Dominated by anticipation" (a number of Cheever's characters hope excessively), they are locked in a state of perpetual adolescence, unwilling to grow up, take responsibility, and face death in any form. Although their world may lie spread out like a bewildering and stupendous dream, they find it nevertheless confining, inhospitable, even haunted by fears of emotional and economic insecurity and a sense of personal inadequacy and inconsequentiality, their sole inheritance, it seems, from the many fathers who figure so prominently in the stories, often by virtue of their absence from the lives of their now-middle-aged sons. Adrift in an incoherent world and alone in the midst of suburbs zoned for felicity, they suffer frequent blows to their already fragile sense of self-esteem, seeing through yet wanting the protection of the veneer of social decorum and ceremoniousness that is the outward and visible sign of American middle-class aspiration and which Cheever's characters do not so much court as covet.

"The Enormous Radio" • The thinness of the veneer of social decorum is especially apparent in "The Enormous Radio," a work that shows little trace of the Ernest Hemingway style that marks many of Cheever's earlier stories. The story begins realistically enough. Jim and Irene Westcott, in their mid-thirties, are an average couple in all respects but one: their above-average interest in classical music (and, one assumes, in the harmony and decorum that such music represents). When their old radio breaks down, Jim generously buys an expensive new one to which Irene takes an instant dislike. Like their interest in music, which they indulge as if a secret but harmless vice, this small disruption in their harmonious married life seems a minor affair, at least at first. The radio, however, appearing "like an aggressive intruder," shedding a "malevolent green light," and possessing a "mistaken sensitivity to discord," soon becomes a divisive, even diabolical presence, but the evil in this story, as in Nathaniel Hawthorne's "Young Goodman Brown," to which it has often been compared, comes from within the characters, not from without (the radio). When the radio begins to broadcast the Westcotts' neighbors' quarrels, lusts, fears, and crimes, Irene becomes dismayed, perversely entertained, and finally apprehensive; if she can eavesdrop on her neighbors' most intimate conversations, she thinks that perhaps they can listen in on hers. Hearing their tales of woe, she demands that her husband affirm their happiness. Far from easing her apprehensiveness, his words only exacerbate it as he first voices his own previously well-guarded frustrations over money, job prospects, and growing old, and as he eventually exposes his wife's own evil nature. As frustration explodes into accusation, the illusion of marital happiness that the Westcotts had so carefully cultivated shatters. As with so many Cheever stories, "The Enormous Radio" has its origin in biographical fact: While writing in the basement of a Sutton Place apartment house, Cheever would hear the elevator going up and down and would imagine that the wires could carry his neighbors' conversations down to him.

"Goodbye, My Brother" • "Goodbye, My Brother" derives from another and far more pervasive biographical fact, Cheever's relationship with his elder brother, Fred, the father figure to whom he developed too close an attachment. Fred turned to business and for a time supported Cheever's writing but, like Cheever, eventually became an alcoholic. Beginning with "The Brothers" and culminating in the fratricide in *Falconer,* relations between brothers figure nearly as prominently in Cheever's fiction as those between spouses. Just as stories such as "The Enormous Radio" are not simply about marital spats, "Goodbye, My Brother" is not just about sibling rivalry. Just as the relationship between Irene and the malevolent radio is actually about a condition within the marriage and more especially within Irene herself, the external relationship between the story's narrator and his brother Lawrence is actually about the narrator's own Dr. Jekyll and Mr. Hyde personality—in psychological terms, a matter of split personality and projection.

Lawrence's narrator objectifies Lawrence's own frustrations, self-loathing, and fears. Lawrence and the narrator are two of the Pommeroys who have gathered on Laud's Head in August for their annual family vacation. Like his sister, just back after her divorce, and their widowed mother, who drinks too much while trying to keep up the family's upper-crust pretensions, the narrator needs these few weeks of respite from the grind of his dead-end teaching job. Together they swim, play cards and tennis, drink, and go to costume dances, where in an almost Jungian freak of chance, all the men come dressed as football players and all the women as brides, as eloquent a statement of the sadness of their blighted but still aspiring lives as one can imagine. Lawrence partakes in none of it. A lawyer moving from one city and job to another, he is the only family member with prospects and the only one unable to enjoy or even tolerate the illusion of happiness that the family seeks to maintain. He is also the only one willing, indeed eager, to detect the flaws and fakery in the Pommeroys' summer home, its protective sea wall, and its equally protective forms of play.

Gloomy and morose as well as critical, Lawrence is, to borrow the title of another Cheever story, the worm in the Pommeroy apple. He is the messenger bearing the bad news, whom the narrator nearly kills with a blow to the head as the two walk along the beach. He strikes not only to free himself from his brother's morbid presence but also to extirpate the Lawrence side of his own divided self: Cain and Abel, murderer and good Samaritan. Once Lawrence and his sickly looking wife and daughter leave, the narrator turns to the purifying water and the triumphant vision of his mythically named wife and sister, Helen and Diana, rising naked from the sea. The story closes on a lyrically charged note that seems both to affirm all that the Pommeroys have sought and, by virtue of the degree of lyrical intensity, to accentuate the gap between that vision and Lawrence's more factual and pessimistic point of view.

"O Youth and Beauty" • "O Youth and Beauty" makes explicit what virtually all Cheever's stories imply, the end of youth's promise, of that hopeful vision that the ending of "Goodbye, My Brother" sought to affirm. Thus it seems ironically apt that "O Youth and Beauty" should begin with a long (two-hundred-word) Whitmanesque sentence, which, in addition to setting the scene and establishing the narrative situation, subtly evokes that Transcendental vision that Walt Whitman both espoused and, in his distinctive poetic style, sought to embody. Beginning "At the tag end of nearly every long, large Saturday night party in the suburb of Shady Hill," it proceeds through a series of long anaphoric subordinate clauses beginning with the word "when" and ending with "then Trace Bearden would begin to chide Cash Bentley about his age and thinning hair." The reader is thus introduced to what, for the partygoers, has already become something of a suburban ritual: the perfectly named

Cash Bentley's hurdling of the furniture as a way of warding off death and reliving the athletic triumphs of the youth that he refuses to relinquish. When Cash, now forty, breaks his leg, the intimations of mortality begin to multiply in his morbid mind. Although he may run his race alone, and although the Lawrentian gloominess that comes in the wake of the accident may make him increasingly isolated from his neighbors and friends, Cash is not at all unique, and his fears are extreme but nevertheless representative of a fear that pervades the entire community and that evidences itself in his wife's trying to appear younger and slimmer than she is and her "cutting out of the current copy of *Life* those scenes of mayhem, disaster, and violent death that she felt might corrupt her children." It is rather ironic that a moment later she should accidentally kill her husband in their own living room with the starter's pistol, as he attempts to recapture the past glories of all those other late Saturday night races against time and self in an attempt always, already doomed, to recapture the past glories of his days as a young track star. The track is in fact an apt symbol for Cash's circular life, in which, instead of progress, one finds only the horror of Nietzschean eternal recurrence.

"The Five-Forty-Eight" • Upon first reading, "The Five-Forty-Eight" seems to have little in common with the blackly humorous "O Youth and Beauty." A disturbed woman, Miss Dent, follows Blake, whose secretary she had been for three weeks and whose lover she was for one night, some six months earlier. She trails him from his office building to his commuter train. Threatening to shoot him, she gets off at his stop and forces him to kneel and rub his face in the dirt for having seduced and abandoned her. One of Cheever's least likable characters, Blake gets what he deserves. Having chosen Miss Dent as he has chosen his other women (including, it seems, his wife) "for their lack of self-esteem," he not only had her fired the day after they made love but also took the afternoon off. Miss Dent fares considerably better, for in choosing not to kill Blake she discovers "some kindness, some saneness" in herself that she believes she can put to use. Blake too undergoes a change insofar as he experiences regret for the first time and comes to understand his own vulnerability, which he has heretofore managed to safeguard by means of his "protective" routines and scrupulous observance of Shady Hill's sumptuary laws. Whether these changes will be lasting remains unclear; he is last seen picking himself up, cleaning himself off, and walking home, alone.

"The Housebreaker of Shady Hill" • "The Five-Forty-Eight" is quite literally one of Cheever's darkest stories; only the dimmest of lights and the faintest of hopes shine at its end. Although it too ends at night, "The Housebreaker of Shady Hill" is one of Cheever's brightest and most cheerful works, full of the spiritual phototropism so important in *Falconer*, the novel that *Newsweek* hailed as "Cheever's Triumph." The housebreaker is thirty-six-year-old Johnny Hake, kindly and comical, who suddenly finds himself out of work, at risk of losing his house, his circle of friends, and the last shreds of his self-esteem. Desperate for cash, he steals nine hundred dollars from a neighbor, a theft that transforms his vision of the world. Suddenly, he begins to see evil everywhere and evidence that everyone can see him for what he now is. The "moral bottom" drops out of his world but in decidedly comic fashion: Even a birthday gift from his children—an extension ladder—becomes an acknowledgment of his wrongdoing (and nearly cause for divorce). Chance, however, saves Johnny. Walking to his next victim's house, he feels a few drops of rain fall on his head and awakens from his ludicrous nightmare, his vision of the world restored. Opting for life's simple pleasures (he is after all still unemployed), he returns home and has a pleasant dream in which he is seventeen years old. Johnny cannot get his youth back, but he does get his job back (and he does return the money he has stolen). The happy endings proliferate as the story slips the yoke of realism and romps in the magical realm of pure fairy tale, where, as Cheever puts it far more sardonically in his third novel, *Bullet Park* (1969), everything is "wonderful wonderful wonderful wonderful."

"The Country Husband" • Comic exaggeration and hyperbolically happy endings characterize many of the stories of the late 1950's and early 1960's. In "The House-breaker of Shady Hill," it is losing his job that starts Johnny Hake on his comical crime spree; in "The Country Husband," it is nearly losing his life that sends Francis Weed on an ever more absurdly comical quest for love and understanding. Weed has his brush with death when his plane is forced to make an emergency landing in a field outside Philadelphia. The danger over, his vulnerability (like Blake's) and mortality (like Cash Bentley's) established, the real damage begins when Weed can find no one to lend a sympathetic ear—not his friend, Trace Bearden, on the commuter train, not even his wife, Julia (too busy putting dinner on the table), or his children (the youngest are fighting and the oldest is reading *True Romance*). With his very own True Adventure still untold, Weed goes outside, where he hears a neighbor playing "Moonlight Sonata," rubato, "like an outpouring of tearful petulance, lonesomeness, and self-pity—of everything it was Beethoven's greatness not to know," and everything it will now be Weed's comic misfortune to experience as he embarks upon his own True Romance with the rather unromantically named Anne Murchison, his children's new teenage babysitter.

Playing the part of a lovesick adolescent, the middle-aged Weed acts out his midlife crisis and in doing so jeopardizes his family's social standing and his marriage. The consequences are potentially serious, as are the various characters' fears and troubles (Anne's alcoholic father, Julia's "natural fear of chaos and loneliness," which leads to her obsessive partygoing). What is humorous is Cheever's handling of these fears in a story in which solecisms are slapstick, downfalls are pratfalls, and pariahs turn out to be weeds in Cheever's suburban Garden of Eden. When Francis finally decides to overcome his Emersonian self-reliance, to confide in and seek the help of a psychiatrist (who will do what neither friends nor family have thus far been willing to do—that is, listen), the first words Weed tearfully blurts out are, "I'm in love, Dr. Harzog." Since "The Country Husband" is a comedy, Weed is cured of his "dis-ease" and able to channel his desires into more socially acceptable ways (conjugal love and, humorously enough, woodworking). The story ends with a typically Cheeveresque affirmation of Fitzgerald-like romantic possibilities, no less apparent in Shady Hill than in *The Great Gatsby*'s (1925) West Egg. It is an affirmation, however, tempered once again by the tenuousness of the characters' situation in a "village that hangs, morally and economically, from a thread."

"The Death of Justina" • The thread will break—although still comically—in "The Death of Justina." Here, the focus is double, on the parallel plights of the authorial narrator, a fiction writer, and the protagonist-narrator of the story that he writes (like "The Housebreaker of Shady Hill," in oral style), also a writer (of advertising copy). Briefly stated, their shared predicament is this: how (for the one) to write about and (for the other) to live in a world that seems to grow increasingly chaotic and prepos-terous. As the authorial narrator explains, "Fiction is art and art is the triumph over chaos (no less) and we can accomplish this only by the most vigilant exercise of choice, but in a world that changes more swiftly than we can perceive there is always the danger that our powers of selection will be mistaken and that the vision we serve will come to nothing."

The authorial narrator then offers a man named Moses' account of the death of his wife's cousin Justina as "one example of chaos." Ordered by his doctor to stop smoking and drinking and by his boss to write copy for a product called Elixircol (something of a cross between Geritol and the Fountain of Youth), Moses suddenly finds himself at a complete loss when he tries to arrange for Justina's funeral, for Justina has died in his house, and his house is an area of Proxmire Manor not zoned for death. No doctor will issue a death certificate, and the mayor refuses to sign an ex-emption until a quorum of the village council is available, but when Moses threatens to bury Justina in his yard, the mayor relents. Victorious but still shaken, Moses that night has a strange dream set in a vast supermarket where the shoppers stock their carts with unlabeled, shapeless packages, which are then, much to their shame, torn open at the checkout counters by brutish men who first ridicule the selections and then push the shoppers out the doors into what sounds much like Dante's inferno. The scene is amusing but, like the ludicrously comical scenes in Franz Kafka's works, also unsettling. The story does not affirm the shoppers any more than it does the vil-lage council that drew up the zoning laws, but it does understand what compels them even as it sympathetically satirizes the inadequacy of their means. As Moses points out, "How can a people who do not mean to understand death hope to understand love, and who will sound the alarm?"

"The Brigadier and the Golf Widow" • "The Brigadier and the Golf Widow" makes a similar point in a similar way. Here too, the authorial narrator is perplexed, won-dering what the nineteenth century writers Charles Dickens, Anton Chekhov, Nikolai Gogol, and William Makepeace Thackeray would have made of a fallout shel-ter (bizarrely decorated and disguised with gnomes, plaster ducks, and a birdbath). He also understands, however, that fallout shelters are as much a part of his mid-twentieth century landscape as are trees and shrubbery. The shelter in question be-longs to Charlie Pastern, the country club general who spends his time calling loudly for nuclear attacks on any and all of his nation's enemies. His world begins to unravel when, by chance, he begins an affair with a neighbor whose own fears and insecurity lead her first to promiscuity and then to demanding the key to the Pasterns' shelter (a key that the local bishop also covets). Apparently the last words of "The Death of Justina," taken verbatim from the Twenty-third Psalm, about walking through the shadow of the valley of death and fearing no evil, no longer apply.

For all the good cheer, hearty advice, biblical quotations, comical predicaments, and lyrical affirmations, there lies at the center of Cheever's fiction the fear of insuf-ficiency and inadequacy—of shelters that will not protect, marriages that will not en-dure, jobs that will be lost, threads that will not hold.

"The Swimmer" • The fact that the thread does not hold in "The Swimmer," Cheever's most painstakingly crafted and horrific work, is especially odd, for the story begins as comedy, a lighthearted satire, involving a group of suburban couples sitting around the Westerhazys' pool on a beautiful midsummer Sunday afternoon talking about what and how much they drank the night before. Suddenly Neddy Merrill, yet another of Cheever's middle-aged but youthfully named protagonists, decides to swim home pool to pool. More than a prank, it is for him a celebration of the fineness of the day, a voyage of discovery, a testament to life's romantic possibilities. Neddy's swim will cover eight miles, sixteen pools, in only ten pages (as printed in *The Stories of John Cheever*).

Although he encounters some delays and obstacles—drinks graciously offered and politely, even ceremoniously, drunk, a thorny hedge to be gotten over, gravel underfoot—Neddy completes nearly half the journey in only two pages (pages 3-4; pages 1-2 are purely preparatory). The story and its reader move as confidently and rapidly as Neddy, but then there are a few interruptions: a brief rain shower that forces Neddy to seek shelter, a dry pool at one house, and a for-sale sign inexplicably posted at another. Midway through both journey and story, the point of view suddenly and briefly veers away from Neddy, who now looks pitifully exposed and foolishly stranded as he attempts to cross a divided highway. His strength and confidence ebbing, he seems unprepared for whatever lies ahead yet unable to turn back. Like the reader, he is unsure when his little joke turned so deadly serious. At the one public pool on his itinerary, he is assaulted by crowds, shrill sounds, and harsh odors.

After being very nearly stalled for two pages, the pace quickens ever so slightly but only to leave Neddy still weaker and more disoriented. Each "breach in the succession" exposes Neddy's inability to bridge the widening gap between his vision of the world and his actual place in it. He is painfully rebuffed by those he had previously been powerful enough to mistreat—a former mistress, a socially inferior couple whose invitations he and his wife routinely discarded. The apparent cause of Neddy's downfall begins to become clear to the reader only as it begins to become clear to Neddy—a sudden and major financial reversal—but Neddy's situation cannot be attributed to merely economic factors, nor is it susceptible to purely rational analysis. Somewhere along Neddy's and the reader's way, everything has changed: The passing of hours becomes the passage of whole seasons, perhaps even years, as realism gives way to fantasy, humor to horror as the swimmer sees his whole life pass before him in a sea of repressed memories. Somehow Neddy has woken into his own worst dream. Looking into his empty house, he comes face to face with the insecurity that nearly all Cheever's characters fear and the inadequacy that they all feel.

The stories (and novels) that Cheever wrote during the last two decades of his life grew increasingly and innovatively disparate in structure. "The Jewels of the Cabots," for example, or "The President of the Argentine" matches the intensifying disunity of the author's personal life. Against this narrative waywardness, however, Cheever continued to offer and even to extend an affirmation of the world and his protagonists' place in it in a lyrically charged prose at once serene and expansive ("The World of Apples," *Falconer*). In other words, he continued to do during these last two decades what he had been doing so well for the previous three: writing a fiction of celebration and incoherence.

Robert A. Morace

Other major works

NOVELS: *The Wapshot Chronicle*, 1957; *The Wapshot Scandal*, 1964; *Bullet Park*, 1969; *Falconer*, 1977; *Oh, What a Paradise It Seems*, 1982.

NONFICTION: *The Letters of John Cheever,* 1988 (Benjamin Cheever, editor); *The Journals of John Cheever,* 1991; *Glad Tidings, a Friendship in Letters: The Correspondence of John Cheever and John D. Weaver, 1945-1982,* 1993.

TELEPLAY: *The Shady Hill Kidnapping,* 1982.

Bibliography

Bosha, Francis J., ed. *The Critical Response to John Cheever.* Westport, Conn.: Greenwood Press, 1994. Collection of reviews and critical essays on Cheever's novels and short-story collections by various commentators and critics.

Cheever, Susan. *Home Before Dark.* Boston: Houghton Mifflin, 1984. This memoir by Cheever's daughter is especially important for fleshing out his troubled early years and providing an insider's look at his marital and other personal difficulties (alcoholism, illnesses, sexual desires). Suffers from lack of documentation and indexing. More valuable as a synthesis of previously published material than as a daughter's intimate revelations.

Collins, Robert G., ed. *Critical Essays on John Cheever.* Boston: G. K. Hall, 1982. Reprints an excellent sampling of reviews, interviews, and early criticism (including many dubbed "new" that are in fact only slightly reworked older pieces). Of the truly new items, three deserve special mention: Collins's biocritical introduction, Dennis Coale's bibliographical supplement, and particularly Samuel Coale's "Cheever and Hawthorne: The American Romancer's Art," arguably one of the most important critical essays on Cheever.

Dessner, Lawrence Jay. "Gender and Structure in John Cheever's 'The Country Husband.'" *Studies in Short Fiction* 31 (Winter, 1994): 57-68. Argues that the story is structured as a comedy with a farcical narrow escape and a tension between the domestic and the wild; contends the plot pattern dissolves pain into laughter.

Donaldson, Scott. *John Cheever: A Biography.* New York: Random House, 1988. Scrupulously researched, interestingly written, and judiciously argued, Donaldson's biography presents Cheever as both author and private man. Donaldson fleshes out most of the previously unknown areas in Cheever's biography and dispels many of the biographical myths that Cheever himself encouraged. The account is sympathetic yet objective.

Hipkiss, Robert. "'The Country Husband': A Model Cheever Achievement." *Studies in Short Fiction* 27 (Fall, 1990): 577-585. Analyzes the story as a prose poem filled with imagery of war, myth, music, and nature. Argues that the elaborate image pattern makes one realize how rooted in the American value system the protagonist's final fate really is.

May, Charles E., ed. *Masterplots II: Short Story Series, Revised Edition.* 8 vols. Pasadena, Calif.: Salem Press, 2004. Designed for student use, this reference set contains articles providing detailed plot summaries and analyses of these ten short stories by Cheever: "The Angel of the Bridge" and "The Brigadier and the Golf Widow" (vol. 1); "The Country Husband" and "The Enormous Radio" (vol. 2); "The Five-Forty-Eight" and "Goodbye, My Brother" (vol. 3); "The Housebreaker of Shady Hill" (vol. 4); "Metamorphoses" (vol. 5); "The Swimmer" (vol. 7); and "The World of Apples" (vol. 8).

Meanor, Patrick. *John Cheever Revisited.* New York: Twayne, 1995. The first book-length study of Cheever to make use of his journals and letters published in the late 1980's and early 1990's. Focuses on how Cheever created a mythopoeic world in his novels and stories. Includes two chapters on his short stories, with detailed analyses of stories in *The Enormous Radio, and Other Stories* and *The Brigadier and the Golf Widow.*

O'Hara, James E. *John Cheever: A Study of the Short Fiction.* Boston: Twayne, 1989. In addition to reprinting five important reviews and critical essays and providing a detailed chronology and annotated selected bibliography, this volume offers a 120-page analysis of Cheever as a writer of short stories that goes well beyond the introductory level. O'Hara's discussion of the early unanthologized stories is especially noteworthy.

Waldeland, Lynne. *John Cheever.* Boston: Twayne, 1979. This volume in Twayne's United States Authors series is introductory in nature. Although it lacks the thematic coherence of other works, it has great breadth and evidences an awareness of previous critical commentary.

Anton Chekhov

Born: Taganrog, Russia; January 29, 1860
Died: Badenweiler, Germany; July 15, 1904

Principal short fiction • *Skazki Melpomeny*, 1884; *Pystrye rasskazy*, 1886; *Nevinnye rechi*, 1887; *V sumerkakh*, 1887; *Rasskazy*, 1888; *The Tales of Tchehov*, 1916-1922 (13 volumes); *The Undiscovered Chekhov: Forty-three New Stories*, 1999 (revised and expanded, 2001).

Other literary forms • Anton Chekhov's literary reputation rests as much on his drama as on his stories and sketches, despite the fact that he was a far more prolific writer of fiction, having written only seventeen plays but almost six hundred stories. *Chayka* (1896, rev. 1898; *The Seagull*, 1909), *Dyadya Vanya* (1897; *Uncle Vanya*, 1914), *Tri sestry* (1901; *The Three Sisters*, 1920), and *Vishnyovy sad* (1904; *The Cherry Orchard*, 1908), Chekhov's chief dramatic works, are universally considered classics of modern theater. Chekhov was also an indefatigable correspondent, and his letters, along with his diaries and notebooks, form an important segment of his writing. He also wrote numerous journal articles and one long work, *Ostrov Sakhalin* (serialized in 1893 and 1894), a scholarly exposé of an island penal colony that Chekhov visited in 1890.

Achievements • In his lifetime, Anton Chekhov gained considerable critical acclaim. In 1888, he won the Pushkin Prize for his fiction, and in 1900, he was selected to honorary membership in the Russian Academy of Sciences for both his fiction and his drama.

Chekhov's fiction departs from the formulaic, heavily plotted story to mirror Russian life authentically, concentrating on characters in very ordinary circumstances that often seem devoid of conflict. A realist, Chekhov treads a fine line between detachment and a whimsical but sympathetic concern for his subjects. In his mature work, he is perhaps the most genial of Russian masters, compassionate and forgiving, seldom strident or doctrinaire. Equally important, that mature work reflects very careful artistry, worthy of study for its technique alone.

Biography • Anton Pavlovich Chekhov, the third of six Chekhov children, was born on January 29, 1860, in Taganrog, a provincial city in southern Russia. His father, Pavel Egorovich Chekhov, son of a serf, ran a meager grocery store, which young Anton often tended in his neglectful father's absence. A religious fanatic and stern disciplinarian, Pavel gave his children frequent beatings and forced them to spend long hours in various devotional activities. For Anton, who did not share his father's zeal, it was a depressing, gloomy childhood.

Although the family was poor and Pavel's marginal business was slowly failing, Anton was able to get some schooling, first at a Greek parochial school, then at the boys' gymnasium, or high school. In 1875, after a bout with acute peritonitis, young Chekhov decided to become a physician. His future brightened when, in 1876, his father, trying to evade his creditors, secretly moved the family to Moscow, leaving Anton to finish school.

In 1879, Anton moved to Moscow, entered the medical school of the University of

Library of Congress

Moscow, and almost immediately began publishing stories in various magazines and newspapers. A very prolific apprentice, by 1884, when he graduated from medical school, he had published his first collection of short fiction. By 1886, Chekhov had begun his long association and friendship with A. S. Suvorin, the owner of an influential conservative newspaper to which Chekhov contributed dozens of pieces. Recognized as a significant new author, Chekhov devoted more time to writing and less and less to his medical practice, which, in time, he would abandon altogether.

Chekhov's greatly improved finances allowed him to buy a better Moscow house and gave him time to travel, which he frequently did, despite ill health. In 1887, he journeyed to the Don Steppe, and two years later crossed Asia to visit the Russian penal colony on Sakhalin Island. The next year he traveled to Europe with Suvorin. In 1892, Chekhov purchased Melikhovo, an estate outside Moscow. It became a gathering place for family, relatives, and associates. There, too, Chekhov practiced medicine, more as a human service to poor villagers than as a necessary source of income.

In 1896, Chekhov had his first theatrical success with *The Seagull*, although the reaction of the opening-night audience greatly distressed the author. Suffering from tuberculosis, by the mid-1890's he began coughing up blood, and in 1897 he had to be hospitalized. In 1898, Chekhov began his propitious association with the newly formed Moscow Art Theater and its great director, Konstantin Stanislavski. He also met Olga Leonardovna Knipper, a young actor. Despite his ill health and his frequent sojourns to Yalta, they carried on a love affair and were married in 1901.

The last six years of Chekhov's life, from 1898 to 1904, brought him as much recognition as a dramatist as his earlier career had brought him as a writer of fiction. *Uncle Vanya*, *The Three Sisters*, and *The Cherry Orchard*, his last significant work, were all major successes. In 1904, in one last attempt to stay the course of his disease, Chekhov and his wife went to Germany, where, at Badenweiler, he died on July 15.

Analysis • Anton Chekhov published his earliest stories and sketches in various popular magazines under pseudonyms, the most often used being "Antosha Chekhonte." As that pen name hints, he was at first an unassuming and relatively compliant "hack," willing to dash off careless pieces fashioned for the popular reader. Most are light, topical studies of social types, often running fewer than a thousand words. Many are mere sketches or extended jokes, often banal or cynical. Some are farces, built on caricatures. Others are brief parodies of popular genres, including the romantic novel. Few display much originality in subject. Still, in their technique, economy of expression, and themes, the early pieces prefigure some of Chekhov's most mature work. In them, Chekhov experimented with point of view and most particularly the use of irony as a fictional device. He also established his preference for an almost scientific objectivity in his depiction of character and events, an insistence that, in the course of his career, he would have to defend against his detractors.

Chekhov's penchant for irony is exemplified in his very first published story, "Pis'mo k uchenomu sosedu" ("A Letter to a Learned Neighbor"), which appeared in 1880. The letter writer, Vladimirovich, is a pompous, officious oaf who makes pretentious statements about science and knowledge with inane blunders in syntax, spelling, and diction, inadvertently revealing his boorish stupidity while trying to ingratiate himself with his erudite neighbor.

As does this sketch, many of Chekhov's first pieces lampoon types found in Russian society, favorite satirical targets being functionaries in the czarist bureaucracy and their obsequious regard for their superiors. One sketch, "Smert' chinovnika" ("The Death of a Government Clerk"), deals with a civil servant named Chervyakov who accidentally sneezes on a general and is mortified because he is unable to obtain the man's pardon. After repeated rebukes, he resigns himself to defeat, lies down, and dies. His sense of self-worth is so intricately bound up in his subservient role that, unpardoned, he has no reason to continue living.

In another story, "Khameleon" ("The Chameleon"), Ochumelov, a police officer, vacillates between placing blame on a dog or the man whom the dog has bitten until it can be confirmed that the dog does or does not belong to a certain General Zhigalov. When it turns out that the dog belongs to the general's brother, the officer swears that he will get even with the dog's victim. Like so many other characters in Chekhov's fiction, Ochumelov is a bully to his subordinates but an officious toady to his betters.

Other stories, not built on irony or a momentous event in the central character's life, are virtually plotless fragments. Some chronicle the numbing effects of living by social codes and mores rather than from authentic inner convictions, while others record human expectations frustrated by a sobering and often grim reality. In several stories, Chekhov deals with childhood innocence encountering or narrowly evading an adult world that is sordid, deceitful, or perverse. For example, in "V more" ("At Sea"), a man decides to provide a sex education for his son by having him observe a newly married couple and a third man through a bulkhead peephole. Presumably to satisfy his own puerile interest, the father peeps first and is so mortified by what he sees that he does not allow his son to look at all.

Sometimes severely restricted by magazine requirements, Chekhov learned to be direct and sparse in statement. Many of his early stories have little or no exposition at all. The main character's lineage, elaborate details of setting, authorial incursions—all disappear for economy's sake. In his precipitous openings, Chekhov often identifies a character by name, identifies his class or profession, and states his emotional condition, all in a single sentence. Others open with a snippet of conversation that has presumably been in progress for some time. When he does set a scene with description, Chekhov does so with quick, deft, impressionistic strokes, with only the barest of details.

Chekhov also learned the value of symbols as guides to inner character. In "Melyuzga," a pathetic clerk named Nevyrazimov is trying to write a flattering Easter letter to his superior, whom, in reality, he despises. Hoping for a raise, this miserable underling must grovel, which contributes to his self-loathing and self-pity. As he tries to form the ingratiating words, he spies a cockroach and takes pity on the insect because he deems its miserable existence worse than his own. After considering his own options, however, and growing more despondent, when he again spies the roach he squashes it with his palm, then burns it, an act which, as the last line divulges, makes him feel better. The destruction of the roach is a symbolic act. It seems gratuitous and pointless, but it reveals the dehumanizing effect that *chinopochitanie*, or "rank reverence," has on the clerk. In destroying the roach, Nevyrazimov is able to displace some of the self-loathing that accompanies his self-pity. His misery abates because he is able, for a moment, to play the bully.

Despite the limitations that popular writing imposed, between 1880 and 1885 there is an advance in Chekhov's work, born, perhaps, from a growing tolerance and sympathy for his fellow human beings. He gradually turned away from short, acrid farces toward more relaxed, psychologically probing studies of his characters and their ubiquitous misery and infrequent joy. In "Unter Prishibeev" ("Sergeant Prishibeev"), Chekhov again develops a character who is unable to adjust to change because his role in life has been too rigid and narrow. A subservient army bully, he is unable to mend his ways when returned to civilian life and torments his fellow townspeople through spying, intimidation, and physical abuse. His harsh discipline, sanctioned in the military, only lands him in jail, to his total astonishment.

By 1886, Chekhov had begun to receive encouragement from the Russian literati, notably Dmitrí Grigorovich, who, in an important unsolicited letter, warned Chekhov not to waste his talents on potboilers. The impact on Chekhov was momentous, for he had received the recognition that he desired. Thereafter, he worked to perfect his craft, to master the *literature nastroenija*, or "literature of mood," works in which a single, dominant mood is evoked and action is relatively insignificant.

This does not mean that all Chekhov's stories are plotless or lack conflict. "Khoristka" ("The Chorus Girl"), for example, is a dramatic piece in method akin to the author's curtain-raising farces based on confrontation and ironic turns. The singer, confronted by the wife of one of her admirers, an embezzler, gives the wife all of her valuables to redeem the philanderer's reputation. His wife's willingness to humble herself before a chorus girl regenerates the man's love and admiration for his spouse. He cruelly snubs the chorus girl and, in rank ingratitude, leaves her alone in abject misery.

Other stories using an ironic twist leave the principal character's fate to the reader's imagination. "Noch' pered sudom" ("The Night Before the Trial") is an example. The protagonist, who narrates the story, makes a ludicrous blunder. On the eve of his trial for bigamy, he poses as a doctor and writes a bogus prescription for a woman. He also accepts payment from her husband, only to discover at the start of his trial that the husband is his prosecutor. The story goes no further than the man's brief speculation on his approaching fate.

In yet another, more involved story, "Nishchii" ("The Beggar"), a lawyer, Skvortsov, is approached by a drunken and deceitful but resourceful beggar, Lushkov, whom he unmercifully scolds as a liar and a wastrel. He then sets Lushkov to work chopping wood, challenging him to earn his way through honest, hard work. Before long, Skvortsov persuades himself that he has the role of Lushkov's redeemer and manages to find him enough work doing odd jobs to earn a meager livelihood. Eventually, growing respectable and independent, Lushkov obtains decent work in a notary's office. Two years later, encountering Skvortsov outside a theater, Lushkov confides that it was indeed at Skvortsov's house that he was saved—not, however, by Skvortsov's scolding but by Skvortsov's cook, Olga, who took pity on Lushkov and always chopped the wood for him. It was Olga's nobility that prompted the beggar's reformation, not the pompous moral rectitude of the lawyer.

In 1887, when Chekhov took the time to visit the Don Steppe, he was established as one of Russia's premier writers of fiction. With the accolades, there almost inevitably came some negative criticism. A few of his contemporaries argued that Chekhov seemed to lack a social conscience, that he remained too detached and indifferent to humanity in a time of great unrest and need for reform. Chekhov never believed that his art should serve a bald polemical purpose, but he was sensitive to the unjust critical opinion that he lacked strong personal convictions. In much of his mature writing, Chekhov worked to dispel that misguided accusation.

For a time Chekhov came under the spell of Leo Tolstoy, his great contemporary, not so much for that moralist's religious fervor but for his doctrine of nonresistance to evil. That idea is fundamental to "The Meeting." In this tale, which in tone is similar to the didactic Russian folktales, a thief steals money from a peasant, who had collected it for refurbishing a church. The thief, baffled by the peasant's failure to resist, gradually repents and returns the money.

"The Steppe" • In 1888, Chekhov wrote and published "Step'" ("The Steppe"), inspired by his journey across the Don Steppe. The story, consisting of eight chapters, approaches the novella in scope and reflects the author's interest in trying a longer work, which Grigorovich had advised him to do. In method, the piece is similar to picaresque tales, in which episodes are like beads, linked only by a common string—the voyage or quest.

The main characters are a merchant, Kuznichov, his nine-year-old nephew, Egorushka, and a priest, Father Christopher, who set out to cross the steppe in a cart. The adults travel on business, to market wool, while Egorushka is off to school. The monotony of their journey is relieved by tidbits of conversation and brief encounters with secondary characters in unrelated episodes. Diversion for young Egorushka is provided by various denizens of the steppe. These minor characters, though delineated but briefly, are both picturesque and lifelike.

Some of the characters spin a particular tale of woe. For example, there is Solomon, brother to Moses, the Jewish owner of a posting house. Solomon, disgusted with human greed, has burned his patrimony and now wallows in self-destructive misery. Another miserable figure is Pantelei, an old peasant whose life has offered nothing but arduous work. He has nearly frozen to death several times on the beautiful but desolate steppe. Dymov, the cunning, mean-spirited peasant, is another wretch devoid of either grace or hope.

The story involves a realistic counterpart to the romantic quest, for the merchant and the priest, joined by the charming Countess Dranitskaya, seek the almost legendary figure, Varlamov. Thus, in a quiet, subdued way, the work has an epic cast to it. Its unity depends on imagery and thematic centrality of the impressions of Egorushka, whose youthful illusions play off against the sordid reality of the adult world. The journey to the school becomes for Egorushka a rite of passage, a familiar Chekhovian motif. At the end of the story, about to enter a strange house, the boy finally breaks into tears, feeling cut off from his past and apprehensive about his future.

"The Steppe" marks a tremendous advance over Chekhov's earliest works. Its impressionistic description of the landscape is often poetic, and though, like most of Chekhov's fiction, the work is open plotted, it is structurally tight and very compelling. The work's hypnotic attraction comes from its sparse, lyrical simplicity and timeless theme. It is the first of the author's flawless pieces.

"A Boring Story" • Another long work, "Skuchnaia istoriia" ("A Boring Story"), shifts Chekhov's character focus away from a youth first encountering misery in the world to an old man, Nikolai Stepanovich, who, near the end of life, finally begins to realize its stupefying emptiness. The professor is the narrator, although, when the story starts, it is presented in the third rather than the first person. It soon becomes apparent, however, that the voice is the professor's own. The story is actually a diary, unfolding in the present tense.

The reader learns that although Stepanovich enjoys an illustrious reputation in public, of which he is extremely proud, in private he is dull and emotionally handicapped. Having devoted his life to teaching medicine, the value of which he never questions, the professor has sacrificed love, compassion, and friendship. He has gradually alienated himself from family, colleagues, and students, as is shown by his repeated failures to relate to them in other than superficial, mechanical ways. He admits his inability to communicate to his wife or daughter, and although he claims to love his ward, Katya, whom his wife and daughter hate, even she finally realizes that he is an emotional cripple and deserts him to run off with another professor who has aroused some jealousy in Nikolai.

The professor, his life dedicated to academe, has become insensitive to such things as his daughter Liza's chagrin over her shabby coat or her feelings for Gnekker, her suitor, who, the professor suspects, is a fraud. Unable to understand his family's blindness to Gnekker, whom he perceives as a scavenging crab, Nikolai sets out to prove his assumption. He goes to Kharkov to investigate Gnekker's background and confirms his suspicions, only to discover that he is too late. In his absence, Liza and Gnekker have married.

Bordering on the tragic, "A Boring Story" presents a character who is unable to express what he feels. He confesses his dull nature, but, though honest with himself, he can confide in no one. Detached, he is able to penetrate the illusions of others, but his approach to life is so abstract and general as to hinder meaningful interpersonal relationships. Near the end of life, he is wiser but spiritually paralyzed by his conviction that he knows very little of human worth. One notes in "A Boring Story" Chekhov's fascination with the fact that conversation may not ensure communication, and his treatment of that reality becomes a signatory motif in Chekhov's later works, including his plays. Characters talk but do not listen, remaining in their own illusory worlds, which mere words will not let them share with others.

"The Duel" • "Duel" ("The Duel"), a long story, is representative of Chekhov's most mature work. Its focal concern is with self-deception and rationalization for one's failures. It pits two men against each other. The one, Laevsky, is a spineless, listless, and disillusioned intellectual who has miserably failed in life. The other, Von Koren, is an active, self-righteous zoologist who comes to despise the other man as a parasite.

In his early conversations with his friend Dr. Samoilenko, Laevsky reveals his tendency to place blame on civilization for human failings, a notion espoused by Jean-Jacques Rousseau and a host of other romantic thinkers. The doctor, whose mundane, pragmatic values simply deflect Laevsky's lament, cannot understand his friend's ennui and disenchantment with his mistress, Nadezhda Feydorovna. Laevsky perceives himself as a Hamlet figure, one who has been betrayed by Nadezhda, for whom he feels an increasing revulsion, which he masks with hypocritical sweetness. He envisions himself as being caught without purpose, vaguely believing that an escape to St. Petersburg without Nadezhda would provide a panacea for all of his ills.

Laevsky's antagonist, Von Koren, is next introduced. Von Koren is a brash, outspoken, vain man who believes that Laevsky is worthy only of drowning. He finds Laevsky depraved and genetically dangerous because he has remarkable success with women and might father more of his parasitical type. During their encounters, Von Koren is aggressive and takes every chance to bait Laevsky, who is afraid of him.

Laevsky's situation deteriorates when Nadezhda's husband dies, and she, guilt ridden, looks to him to save her. Laevsky wants only to escape, however, and he runs off to Samoilenko, begging the doctor for a loan so he might flee to St. Petersburg. After confessing his depravity, he swears that he will send for Nadezhda after he arrives in St. Petersburg, but in reality he has no intention of doing so.

Caught up in his own web of lies and half-truths, Laevsky must deal with those of Nadezhda, who is carrying on affairs with two other men and who has her own deceitful plans of escape. Convinced that Samoilenko has betrayed him through gossiping about him, Laevsky starts an argument with him in the presence of Von Koren, who supports the doctor. The heated exchange ends with a challenge to a duel, gleefully accepted by Von Koren. The night before the duel, Laevsky is extremely frightened. He is petrified by the prospect of imminent death, and his lies and deceit weigh upon him heavily. He passes through a spiritual crisis paralleled by a storm that finally subsides at dawn, just as Laevsky sets out for the dueling grounds.

The duel turns into a comic incident. The duelists are not sure of protocol, and before they even start they seem inept. As it turns out, Laevsky nobly discharges his pistol into the air, and Von Koren, intent on killing his opponent, only manages to graze his neck. The duel has a propitious effect on both men. Laevsky and Nadezhda are reconciled, and he gives up his foolish romantic illusions and begins to live a responsible life. He is also reconciled to Von Koren, who, in a departing confession, admits that a scientific view of things cannot account for all life's uncertainties. There is, at the end, a momentary meeting of the two men's minds.

"The Duel" is representative of a group of quasi-polemical pieces that Chekhov wrote between 1889 and 1896, including "Gusev" ("Gusev"), "Palata No. 6" ("Ward Number Six"), and "Moia zhizn" ("My Life"). All have parallel conflicts in which antagonists are spokespersons for opposing ideologies, neither of which is capable of providing humankind with a definitive epistemology or sufficient guide to living.

"Rothschild's Fiddle" • Other mature stories from the same period deal with the eroding effect of materialism on the human spirit. "Skripka Rotshil'da" ("Rothschild's Fiddle") is a prime example. In this work, Yakov Ivanov, nicknamed Bronze, a poor undertaker, is the protagonist. Yakov, who takes pride in his work, also plays the fiddle and thereby supplements his income from coffin-making.

For a time, Yakov plays at weddings with a Jewish orchestra, whose members, inexplicably, he comes to hate, especially Rothschild, a flutist who seems determined to play even the lightest of pieces plaintively. Because of his belligerent behavior, after a time the Jews hire Yakov only in emergencies. Never in a good temper, Yakov is obsessed with his financial losses and his bad luck. Tormented by these matters at night, he can find some respite only by striking a solitary string on his fiddle.

When his wife, Marfa, becomes ill, Yakov's main concern is what her death will cost him. She, in contrast, dies untroubled, finding in death a welcome release from the wretchedness that has been her lot married to Yakov. In her delirium, she does recall their child, who had died fifty years earlier, and a brief period of joy under a willow tree by the river, but Yakov can remember none of these things. Only when she is buried does Yakov experience depression, realizing that their marriage had been loveless.

Sometime later Yakov accidentally comes upon and recognizes the willow tree of which Marfa had spoken. He rests there, beset by visions and a sense of a wasted past, regretting his indifference to his wife and his cruelty to the Jew, Rothschild. Shortly after this epiphany, he grows sick and prepares to die. Waiting, he plays his fiddle mournfully, growing troubled by not being able to take his fiddle with him to the grave. At his final confession, he tells the priest to give the fiddle to Rothschild, in his first and only generous act. Ironically, the fiddle for Rothschild becomes a means of improving his material well-being.

As "Rothschild's Fiddle" illustrates, Chekhov continued his efforts to fathom the impoverished spirit of his fellow man, often with a sympathetic, kindly regard. Most of his last stories are written in that vein. Near the end of the 1890's, Chekhov gave increasing attention to his plays, which, combined with his ill health, reduced his fictional output. Still, between 1895 and his last fictional piece, "Nevesta" ("The Bride"), published in 1902, he wrote some pieces that rank among his masterpieces.

As in "Rothschild's Fiddle," Chekhov's concern with conflicting ideologies gives way to more fundamental questions about human beings' ability to transcend their own nature. He examines characters who suffer desperate unhappiness, anxiety, isolation, and despair, experienced mainly through the characters' inability either to give or to accept love. He also, however, concerns himself with its antithesis, the suffocating potential of too much love, which is the thematic focus of "Dushechka" ("The Darling").

"The Darling" • In this story, Olenka, the protagonist, is a woman who seems to have no character apart from her marital and maternal roles. She is otherwise a cipher who, between husbands, can only mourn, expressing her grief in folk laments. She has no important opinions of her own, only banal concerns with petty annoyances such as insects and hot weather. She comes to life only when she fulfills her role as wife and companion to her husband, whose opinions and business jargon she adopts as her own, which, to her third husband, is a source of great annoyance.

Ironically, alive and radiant in love, Olenka seems to suck the life out of those whom she adores. For example, her love seems to cause the demise of her first husband, Kukin, a wretched, self-pitying theater manager. Only in the case of her last love, that for her foster son, Sasha, in her maternal role, does Olenka develop opinions of her own. Her love, however, ever suffocating, instills rebellion in the boy and will clearly lead to Olenka's downfall.

"The Bride" • By implication, the comic, almost sardonic depiction of Olenka argues a case for the emancipation of women, a concern to which Chekhov returns in "Nevesta" ("The Bride"). This story deals with a young woman, Nadya, who attempts to find an identity independent of roles prescribed by traditional mores and the oppressive influence of her mother, Nina, and her grandmother.

Nadya, at the age of twenty-three, is something of a dreamer. As the story begins, she is vaguely discontent with her impending marriage to Andrew, son to a local canon of the same name. Her rebellion against her growing unhappiness is encouraged by Sasha, a distant relative who becomes her sympathetic confidant. He constantly advises Nadya to flee, to get an education and free herself from the dull, idle, and stultifying existence that the provincial town promises.

When Andrew takes Nadya on a tour of their future house, she is repulsed by his vision of their life together, finding him stupid and unimaginative. She confides in her mother, who offers no help at all, claiming that it is ordinary for young ladies to get cold feet as weddings draw near. Nadya then asks Sasha for help, which, with a ruse, he provides. He takes Nadya with him to Moscow and sends her on to St. Petersburg, where she begins her studies.

After some months, Nadya, very homesick, visits Sasha in Moscow. It is clear to her that Sasha, ill with tuberculosis, is now dying. She returns to her home to deal with her past but finds the atmosphere no less oppressive than before, except that her mother and grandmother now seem more pathetic than domineering. After a telegram comes announcing Sasha's death, she leaves again for St. Petersburg, resolved to find a new life severed completely from her old.

As well as any story, "The Bride" illustrates why Chekhov is seen as the chronicler of twilight Russia, a period of stagnation when the intelligentsia seemed powerless to effect reform and the leviathan bureaucracy and outmoded traditions benumbed the people and robbed the more sensitive of spirit and hope. Although the contemporary reader of Chekhov's fiction might find that pervasive, heavy atmosphere difficult to fathom, particularly in a comic perspective, no one can doubt Chekhov's mastery of mood.

With Guy de Maupassant in France, Chekhov is rightly credited with mastering the form, mood, and style of the type of short fiction that would be favored by serious English-language writers from Virginia Woolf and James Joyce onward. His impact on modern fiction is pervasive.

John W. Fiero

Other major works

PLAYS: *Platonov*, wr. 1878-1881, pb. 1923 (English translation, 1930); *Ivanov*, pr., pb. 1887 (revised, pr. 1889; English translation, 1912); *Medved*, pr., pb. 1888 (*A Bear*, 1909); *Leshy*, pr. 1889 (*The Wood Demon*, 1925); *Predlozheniye*, pb. 1889, pr. 1890 (*A Marriage Proposal*, 1914); *Svadba*, pb. 1889, pr. 1890 (*The Wedding*, 1916); *Yubiley*, pb. 1892 (*The Jubilee*, 1916); *Chayka*, pr. 1896 (revised pr. 1898, pb. 1904; *The Seagull*, 1909); *Dyadya Vanya*, pb. 1897, pr. 1899 (based on his play *The Wood Demon*; *Uncle Vanya*, 1914); *Tri sestry*, pr., pb. 1901 (revised pb. 1904; *The Three Sisters*, 1920); *Vishnyovy sad*, pr., pb. 1904 (*The Cherry Orchard*, 1908); *The Plays of Chekhov*, pb. 1923-1924 (2 volumes); *Nine Plays*, pb. 1959; *The Complete Plays*, pb. 2006 (Laurence Senelick, editor).

MISCELLANEOUS: *The Works of Anton Chekhov*, 1929; *Polnoye sobraniye sochineniy i pisem A. P. Chekhova*, 1944-1951 (20 volumes); *The Portable Chekhov*, 1947; *The Oxford Chekhov*, 1964-1980 (9 volumes).

NONFICTION: *Ostrov Sakhalin*, 1893-1894; *Letters on the Short Story, the Drama, and Other Literary Topics*, 1924; *The Selected Letters of Anton Chekhov*, 1955.

Bibliography

Bartlett, Rosamund *Chekhov: Scenes from a Life.* New York: Simon & Schuster, 2006. This biography takes a look not only at Chekhov's life but also at the geography and history of the Russian empire.

Bloom, Harold, ed. *Anton Chekhov.* Philadelphia: Chelsea House, 1999. Volume in the series Modern Critical Views. Includes bibliographical references, an index, and an introduction by Bloom.

Clyman, Toby, ed. *A Chekhov Companion.* Westport, Conn.: Greenwood Press, 1985. Collection of critical essays, especially commissioned for this volume, on all aspects of Chekhov's life, art, and career. Some of the most important critics of Chekhov's work are represented here in essays on his major themes, his dramatic technique, his narrative technique, and his influence on modern drama and on the modern short story.

Flath, Carol A. "The Limits to the Flesh: Searching for the Soul in Chekhov's 'A Boring Story.'" *Slavic and East European Journal* 41 (Summer, 1997): 271-286. Argues that "A Boring Story" affirms the value of art and offers comfort against the harshness of the truth about ordinary life and death.

Gottlieb, Vera, and Paul Allain, eds. *The Cambridge Companion to Chekhov.* New York: Cambridge University Press, 2000. Guide to the life and works of Chekhov.

Johnson, Ronald J. *Anton Chekhov: A Study of the Short Fiction.* New York: Twayne, 1993. Introduction to Chekhov's short stories, from his earliest journalistic sketches and ephemera to his influential stories "Gooseberries" and "Lady with a Dog." Discusses Chekhov's objective narrative stance, his social conscience, and his belief in the freedom of the individual. Includes excerpts from Chekhov's letters in which he talks about his fiction, as well as comments by other critics who discuss Chekhov's attitude toward religion and sexuality.

Lantz, K. A. *Anton Chekhov: A Reference Guide to Literature.* Boston: G. K. Hall, 1985. Lantz offers an indispensable tool for the researcher. The work provides a brief biography, a checklist of Chekhov's published works with both English and Russian titles, chronologically arranged, and a very useful annotated bibliography of criticism through 1983.

Malcolm, Janet. *Reading Chekhov: A Critical Journey.* New York: Random House, 2001. With Cheklov as a guide, Malcolm draws on her observations as a tourist/journalist to compose a melancholy portrait of post-Soviet Russia. Malcolm weaves her encounters with contemporary Russians with biographical and critical analyses of Chekhov and his writings.

Martin, David W. "Chekhov and the Modern Short Story in English." *Neophilologus* 71 (1987): 129-143. Martin surveys Chekhov's influence on various English-language writers, including Katherine Mansfield, Virginia Woolf, James Joyce, Sherwood Anderson, and Frank O'Connor. He compares selected works by Chekhov with pieces by those he has influenced and discusses those Chekhovian traits and practices revealed therein. He credits Chekhov with showing how effete or banal characters or circumstances can be enlivened with the dynamics of style. The article is a good departure point for further comparative study.

May, Charles E., ed. *Masterplots II: Short Story Series, Revised Edition.* 8 vols. Pasadena, Calif.: Salem Press, 2004. Designed for student use, this reference set contains articles providing detailed plot summaries and analyses of these eighteen short stories by Chekhov: "The Bet," "The Bishop," and "The Chemist's Wife" (vol. 1); "The Darling," "The Duel," "Easter Eve," and "Enemies" (vol. 2); "Gooseberries" and "Gusev" (vol. 3); "The Kiss" and "The Lady with the Dog" (vol. 4); "The Man in a Case" and "Misery" (vol. 5); "Rothschild's Fiddle" (vol. 6); "The Steppe: The Story of a Journey" and "A Trifling Occurrence" (vol. 7); and "Vanka" and "Ward No. 6" (vol. 8).

Prose, Francine. "Learning from Chekhov." *Western Humanities Review* 41 (1987): 1-14. Prose's article is an appreciative eulogy on the staying power of Chekhov's stories as models for writers. She notes that while Chekhov broke many established rules, his stress on objectivity and writing without judgment is of fundamental importance. The piece would be of most help to creative writers.

Charles Waddell Chesnutt

Born: Cleveland, Ohio; June 20, 1858
Died: Cleveland, Ohio; November 15, 1932

Principal short fiction • *The Conjure Woman*, 1899; *The Wife of His Youth, and Other Stories of the Color Line*, 1899.

Other literary forms • Charles Waddell Chesnutt achieved his literary reputation and stature as a short-story writer. His scholarly bent and indelible concern for human conditions in American society, however, occasionally moved him to experiment in other literary forms. Based on his study of race relations in the American South, he wrote the novel *The Marrow of Tradition* (1901). *The Colonel's Dream* followed in 1905. As a result of the critical acclaim for these novels and for his first, *The House Behind the Cedars* (1900), Chesnutt became known not only as a short-story writer but also as a first-rate novelist. However, most of his novels were not published until long after he died. These include *Mandy Oxendine*, written in 1897 and first publishied in 1997; *A Business Career*, written in 1898 and published in 2005; *Evelyn's Husband*, written in 1903 and published in 2005; and *The Quarry*, written in 1928 and published in 1999.

In 1885, Chesnutt published several poems in *The Cleveland Voice*. The acceptance of his essay "What Is a White Man?" by the *Independent* in May of 1889 began his career as an essayist. Illustrating his diverse talent still further and becoming an impassioned voice for human justice, he wrote essays for a major portion of his life. Collections of his essays were published in 1999 and 2001, and a volume of his letters appeared in 2002. Chesnutt also demonstrated his skill as a biographer when he prepared *The Life of Frederick Douglass* (1899) for the Beacon biography series.

Achievements • One of Chesnutt's most significant achievements was his own education. Self-taught in the higher principles of algebra, the intricate details of history, the linguistic dicta of Latin, and the tenets of natural philosophy, he crowned this series of intellectual achievements by passing the Ohio bar examination after teaching himself law for two years.

A man of outstanding social reputation, Chesnutt received an invitation to Mark Twain's seventieth birthday party, an invitation "extended to about one hundred and fifty of America's most distinguished writers of imaginative literature." The party was held on December 5, 1905, at Delmonico's restaurant in New York City. Chesnutt's greatest public honor was being chosen as the recipient of the Joel E. Springarn Medal, an award annually bestowed on an American citizen of African descent for distinguished service.

Biography • Charles Waddell Chesnutt was born in Cleveland, Ohio, on June 20, 1858. He attended Cleveland public schools and the Howard School in Fayetteville, North Carolina. Having distinguished himself academically early in his schooling, Chesnutt was taken into the tutelage of two established educators, Robert Harris of the Howard School and his brother, Cicero Harris, of Charlotte, North Carolina. He later succeeded Cicero Harris as principal of the school in Charlotte in 1877 and followed this venture with an appointment to the Normal School in Fayetteville to train teachers for colored schools.

On June 6, 1878, Chesnutt married Susan Perry. Shortly after his marriage, he began his training as a stenographer. Even at this time, however, his interest in writing competed for his energies. He spent his spare time writing essays, poems, short stories, and sketches. His public writing career began in December of 1885 with the printing of the story "Uncle Peter's House" in the *Cleveland News and Herald.* After several years passed "The Goophered Grapevine" was accepted by *The Atlantic Monthly* and published in 1888. Continuing his dual career as a man of letters and a businessman/attorney for more than a decade after his reception as a literary artist, Chesnutt decided, on September 30, 1899, to devote himself full-time to his literary career. From that moment on he enjoyed a full and productive career as a man of letters.

Cleveland Public Library

At the beginning of the twentieth century, Chesnutt became more politically active as a spokesman for racial justice. He toured the South and its educational institutions such as Tuskegee Institute and Atlanta University. He joined forces with black leaders such as Booker T. Washington and W. E. B. Du Bois. In May of 1909, he became a member of the National Negro Committee, which later became the National Association for the Advancement of Colored People (NAACP). The last two decades of Chesnutt's life were less active because his health began to fail him in 1919. He was, however, elected to the Cleveland Chamber of Commerce in 1912. Chesnutt continued to write until his death on November 15, 1932.

Analysis • The short fiction of Charles Waddell Chesnutt embraces traditions characteristic of both formal and folk art. Indeed, the elements of Chesnutt's narrative technique evolved in a fashion that conspicuously parallels the historical shaping of the formal short story itself. The typical Chesnutt narrative, like the classic short story, assumes its heritage from a rich oral tradition immersed in folkways, mannerisms, and beliefs. Holding true to the historical development of the short story as an artistic form, his early imaginative narratives were episodic in nature. The next stage of development in Chesnutt's short fiction was a parody of the fable form with a folkloric variation. Having become proficient at telling a story with a unified effect, Chesnutt achieved the symbolic resonance characteristic of the Romantic tale, yet his awareness of the plight of his people urged him toward an increasingly realistic depiction of social conditions. As a mature writer, Chesnutt achieved depth of characterization, distinguishable thematic features, and a rare skillfulness in creation of mood, while a shrewdly moralizing tone allowed him to achieve his dual goal as artist and social activist.

"The Goophered Grapevine" • Chesnutt's journal stories constituted the first phase of his writing career, but when *The Atlantic Monthly* published "The Goophered Grapevine" in 1888, the serious aspects of his artistic skill became apparent. "The Goophered Grapevine" belongs to a tradition in Chesnutt's writings which captures the fable form with a folkloric variation. These stories also unfold with a didactic strain which matures significantly in Chesnutt's later writings. To understand clearly the series of stories in *The Conjure Woman*, of which "The Goophered Grapevine" is one, the reader must comprehend the allegorical features in the principal narrative situation and the thematic intent of the mythic incidents from African American lore.

The Conjure Woman contains narratives revealed through the accounts of a northern white person's rendition of the tales of Uncle Julius, a former slave. This storytelling device lays the foundation for Chesnutt's sociological commentary. The real and perceived voices represent the perspectives he wishes to expose, those of the white capitalist and the impoverished, disadvantaged African American. The primary persona is that of the capitalist, while the perceived voice is that of the struggling poor. Chesnutt skillfully melds the two perspectives.

Chesnutt's two volumes of short stories contain pieces that are unified in theme, tone, and mood. Each volume also contains a piece that might be considered the lead story. In *The Conjure Woman*, the preeminent story is "The Goophered Grapevine." This story embodies the overriding thematic intent of the narratives in this collection. Chesnutt points out the foibles of the capitalistic quest in the post-Civil War South, a venture pursued at the expense of the newly freed African American slave. He illustrates this point in "The Goophered Grapevine" by skillfully intertwining Aunt Peggy's gains as a result of her conjurations and Henry's destruction as a result of man's inhumanity to man. Chesnutt discloses his ultimate point when the plantation owner, McAdoo, is deceived by a Yankee horticulturist and his grape vineyard becomes totally unproductive.

Running episodes, such as Aunt Peggy's conjurations to keep the field hands from consuming the grape crop and the seasonal benefit McAdoo gains from selling Henry, serve to illustrate the interplay between a monied white capitalist and his less privileged black human resources. McAdoo used Aunt Peggy to deny his field laborers any benefit from the land they worked, and he sold Henry every spring to increase his cash flow and prepare for the next gardening season.

The central metaphor in "The Goophered Grapevine" is the bewitched vineyard. To illustrate and condemn man's inhumanity to man, Chesnutt contrasts the black conjure woman's protection of the grape vineyard with the white Yankee's destruction of it. McAdoo's exploitation of Henry serves to justify McAdoo's ultimate ruin. Through allegory, Chesnutt is able to draw attention to the immorality of capitalistic gain through a sacrifice of basic humanity to other people.

"Po' Sandy" • Following the theme of inhumanity established in "The Goophered Grapevine," "Po' Sandy" highlights the abuse of a former slave laborer. Accordingly, a situation with a folkloric variation is used to convey this message. Sandy, Master

Marabo's field hand, is shifted from relative to relative at various points during the year to perform various duties. During the course of these transactions, he is separated from his second common-law wife, Tenie. (His first wife has been sent to work at a distant plantation.) Tenie is a conjurer. She transforms Sandy into a tree, and she changes him back to his original state periodically so that they can be together. With Sandy's apparent disappearance, Master Marabo decides to send Tenie away to nurse his ailing daughter-in-law. There is therefore no one left to watch Sandy, the tree. The dehumanizing effects of industrialization creep into the story line at this point. The "tree" is to be used as lumber for a kitchen at the Marabo home. Tenie returns just in time to try to stop this transformation at the lumber mill, but she is deemed "mad."

Sandy's spirit thereafter haunts the Marabo kitchen, and no one wants to work there. The complaints are so extensive that the kitchen is dismantled and the lumber donated toward the building of a school. This structure is then haunted, too. The point is that industrialization and economic gain diminish essential human concerns and can lead to destruction. The destruction of Sandy's marital relationships in order to increase his usefulness as a field worker justifies this defiant spirit. In his depiction of Sandy as a tree, Chesnutt illustrates an enslaved spirit desperately seeking freedom.

"The Conjurer's Revenge" • "The Conjurer's Revenge," also contained in *The Conjure Woman*, illustrates Chesnutt's mastery of the exemplum. The allegory in this work conveys a strong message, and Chesnutt's evolving skill in characterization becomes apparent. The characters' actions, rather than the situation, contain the didactic message of the story. Some qualities of the fable unfold as the various dimensions of characters are portrayed. Consequently, "The Conjurer's Revenge" is a good example of Chesnutt's short imaginative sketch. These qualities are also most characteristic of Chesnutt's early short fiction.

"The Conjurer's Revenge" begins when Primus, a field hand, discovers the conjure man's hog alone in a bush one evening. Concerned for the hog and not knowing to whom the animal belongs, Primus carries it to the plantation where he works. Unfortunately, the conjurer identifies Primus as a thief and transforms Primus into a mule. Chesnutt uses this transformation to reveal Primus's personality. As a mule, Primus displays jealousy when other men show attraction to his woman, Sally. The mule's reaction is one of shocking violence in instances when Sally is approached by other men. The mule has a tremendous appetite for food and drink, an apparent compensation for his unhappiness. Laying the foundation for his exemplum, Chesnutt brings these human foibles to the forefront and illustrates the consequences of even the mildest appearance of dishonesty.

The conjurer's character is also developed more fully as the story progresses. After attending a religious revival, he becomes ill, confesses his act of vengeance, and repents. During the conjurer's metamorphosis, Chesnutt captures the remorse, grief, and forgiveness in this character. He also reveals the benefits of human compassion and concern for other human beings. A hardened heart undergoes reform and develops an ability to demonstrate sensitivity. Nevertheless, the conjurer suffers the consequences of his evil deed: He is mistakenly given poison by a companion, and he dies before he completely restores Primus's human features, a deed he undertakes after repenting. The conjurer dies prematurely, and Primus lives with a clubfoot for the rest of his life.

Features of Chesnutt's more mature writing emerge in the series of narratives that make up *The Wife of His Youth, and Other Stories of the Color Line.* The stories in this collection center on the identity crisis experienced by African Americans, portraying their true human qualities in the face of the grotesque distortions wrought by racism. In order to achieve his goal, Chesnutt abandons his earlier imaginative posture and embraces realism as a means to unfold his message. The dimensions of his characters are therefore appropriately self-revealing. The characters respond to the stresses and pressures in their external environment with genuine emotion; Mr. Ryder in "The Wife of His Youth" is no exception.

"The Wife of His Youth" • "The Wife of His Youth" follows the structural pattern that appears to typify the narratives in the collection. This pattern evolves in three phases: crisis, character response, and resolution. The crisis in "The Wife of His Youth" is Mr. Ryder's attempt to reconcile his new and old ways of life. He has moved North from a southern plantation and entered black middle-class society. Adapting to the customs, traditions, and mores of this stratum of society is a stressful challenge for Mr. Ryder. Tensions exist between his old life and his new life. He fears being unable to appear as if he belongs to this "blue vein" society and exposing his lowly background. This probable eventuality is his constant preoccupation.

The "blue veins" were primarily lighter-skinned blacks who were better educated and more advantaged than their darker counterparts. Relishing their perceived superiority, they segregated themselves from their brothers and sisters. It is within this web of social clamoring and essential self-denial that Mr. Ryder finds himself. The inherent contradictions of this lifestyle present a crisis for him, although a resolution is attained during the course of the narrative.

Mr. Ryder's efforts to fit into this society are thwarted when his slave wife appears at his doorstep on the day before a major social event that he has planned. He is about to introduce the Blue Vein Society to a widow, Mrs. Dixon, upon whom he has set his affections. The appearance of Liza Jane, his slave wife, forces Mr. Ryder to confront his new life. This situation also allows Chesnutt to assume his typically moralizing tone. Mr. Ryder moves from self-denial to self-pride as he decides to present Liza Jane to his society friends instead of Mrs. Dixon. The narrative ends on a note of personal triumph for Mr. Ryder as he proudly introduces the wife of his youth to society.

"The Passing of Grandison" • Chesnutt does not totally relinquish his allegiance to the use of myth in *The Wife of His Youth, and Other Stories of the Color Line.* The myth of the ascent journey, or the quest for freedom, is evident in several stories in the collection, among them "The Passing of Grandison" and "Wellington's Wives." Following the structured pattern of crisis, character response, and resolution, "The Passing of Grandison" is a commentary on the newly emerging moral values of the postbellum South. Colonel Owens, a plantation owner, has a son, Dick, who is in love with a belle named Charity Lomax. Charity's human values reflect the principles of human equality and freedom, and the challenge that she presents to Dick Owens becomes the crisis of the narrative.

Dick is scheduled to take a trip North, and his father insists on his being escorted by one of the servants. Grandison is selected to accompany his young master. Charity Lomax challenges Dick to find a way to entice Grandison to remain in the North and receive his well-deserved liberation. Charity's request conflicts with the values held by Dick and Grandison. Dick believes that slave/master relationships are essential to the survival of the South. Grandison holds that servants should be unequivocally loyal to their masters.

In spite of Dick's attempts to connect Grandison unobtrusively with the abolitionist movement in the North, the former slave remains loyal to Dick. Grandison's steadfastness perplexes Dick because his proposed marriage to Charity is at risk if he does not succeed in freeing Grandison. After a series of faulty attempts, Dick succeeds in losing Grandison. Dick then returns home alone and triumphant. Grandison ultimately returns to the plantation. He had previously proven himself so trustworthy that goodwill toward him is restored. To make the characterization of Grandison realistic, however, Chesnutt must have him pursue his freedom.

In a surprise ending typical of Chesnutt, Grandison plans the escape of all of his relatives who remain on the plantation. They succeed, and in the last scene of the narrative, Colonel Owens spots them from a distance on a boat journeying to a new destination. "The Passing of Grandison" successfully achieves the social and artistic goals of *The Wife of His Youth, and Other Stories of the Color Line.* Chesnutt creates characters with convincing human qualities and captures their responses to the stresses and pressures of their environment. While so doing, he advocates the quest for human freedom.

"Uncle Wellington's Wives" • "Uncle Wellington's Wives" contains several of the thematic dimensions mentioned above. The story concerns the self-identity of the African American and the freedom quest. Wellington Braboy, a light-skinned "mulatto" is determined to move North and seek his freedom. His crisis is the result of a lack of resources, primarily financial, to achieve his goal.

Braboy is portrayed as having a distorted view of loyalty and commitment. He justifies stealing money from his slave wife's life savings by saying that, as her husband, he is entitled to the money. On the other hand, he denies his responsibility to his slave wife once he reaches the North. In order to marry a white woman he denies the legality of a slave marriage.

Chesnutt takes Braboy on a journey of purgation and catharsis as he moves toward resolution. After being subjected to much ridicule and humiliation as a result of his mixed marriage, Braboy must honestly confront himself and come to terms with his true identity. Abandoned by his wife for her former white husband, Braboy returns to the South. This journey is also a symbolic return to himself; his temporary escape from himself has failed.

Milly, Braboy's first wife, does not deny her love for him, in spite of his previous actions. Milly receives and accepts him with a forgiving spirit. Chesnutt capitalizes on the contrast between Braboy's African and Anglo wives. The African wife loves him unconditionally because she has the capacity to know and understand him, regardless of his foibles. Braboy's Anglo wife was frustrated by what she considered to be irreparable inadequacies in his character and abandoned him.

"Cicely's Dream" • In his character development, Chesnutt repeatedly sought to dispel some of the stereotypical thinking about African Americans. An example of his success in this effort is found in "Cicely's Dream," set in the period of Reconstruction. Cicely Green is depicted as a young woman of considerable ambition. Like most African Americans, she has had very little education and is apparently limited in her capacity to achieve. She does have, however, many dreams.

Cicely's crisis begins when she discovers a wounded man on her way home one day. The man is delirious and has no recollection of who he is. Cicely and her grand-mother care for the man until his physical health is restored, but he is still mentally distraught. The tenderness and sensitivity displayed by Cicely keep the stranger rea-sonably content. Over a period of time, they become close and eventually pledge their love to each other. Chesnutt portrays a caring, giving relationship between the two lovers, one which is not complicated by any caste system which would destroy love through separation of the lovers. This relationship, therefore, provides a poignant contrast to the relationships among blacks during the days of slavery, and Chesnutt thereby exposes an unexplored dimension of the African American.

Typically, however, there is a surprise ending: Martha Chandler, an African Ameri-can teacher, enters the picture. She teaches Cicely and other black youths for one school term. During the final program of the term, the teacher reveals her story of lost love. Her lover had been killed in the Civil War. Cicely's lover's memory is jolted by the teacher's story, and he proves to be the teacher's long-lost love. The happy re-union is a celebration of purely committed love. Again, Chesnutt examines qualities in African Americans which had largely been ignored. He emphasizes the innate hu-manity of the African American in a natural and realistic way, combining great artis-tic skill with a forceful moral vision.

Patricia A. R. Williams
With updates by Earl Paulus Murphy

Other major works

NOVELS: *Mandy Oxendine*, wr. 1897, pb. 1997; *A Business Career*, wr. 1898, pb. 2005 (Matthew Wilson and Marjan van Schaik, editors); *The House Behind the Cedars*, 1900; *The Marrow of Tradition*, 1901; *Evelyn's Husband*, wr. 1903, pb. 2005 (Matthew Wilson and Marjan van Schaik, editors); *The Colonel's Dream*, 1905; *Paul Marchand, F.M.C.*, wr. 1921, pb. 1998; *The Quarry*, wr. 1928, pb. 1999.

NONFICTION: *The Life of Frederick Douglass*, 1899; *The Journals of Charles W. Chesnutt*, 1993; *"To Be an Author": The Letters of Charles W. Chesnutt, 1889-1905*, 1997; *Charles W. Chesnutt: Essays and Speeches*, 1999; *Selected Writings*, 2001 (SallyAnn H. Ferguson, edi-tor); *An Exemplary Citizen: Letters of Charles W. Chesnutt, 1906-1932*, 2002.

Bibliography

Delma, P. Jay. "The Mask as Theme and Structure: Charles W. Chesnutt's 'The Sher-iff's Children' and 'The Passing of Grandison.'" *American Literature* 51 (1979): 364-375. Argues that the story exploits the theme of the mask: the need to hide one's true personality and racial identity from self and others. Delma argues that be-cause Chesnutt uses the mask theme, the story is not a run-of-the-mill treatment of the long-lost-son plot.

Duncan, Charles. *The Absent Man: The Narrative Craft of Charles W. Chesnutt*. Athens: Ohio University Press, 1998. This informative volume includes bibliographical references and an index.

Filetti, Jean. "The Goophered Grapevine." *Explicator* 48 (Spring, 1990): 201-203. Dis-cusses the use of master-slave relationships within the context of storytelling and explains how Chesnutt's "The Goophered Grapevine" relates to this tradition. In-dicates that one of Chesnutt's concerns was inhumanity among people, but the story is told from a humorous perspective with the newly freed slave outwitting the white capitalist.

McElrath, Joseph R., Jr., ed. *Critical Essays on Charles W. Chesnutt.* New York: G. K. Hall, 1999. Includes bibliographical references and an index.

McFatter, Susan. "From Revenge to Resolution: The (R)evolution of Female Characters in Chesnutt's Fiction." *CLA Journal* 42 (December, 1998): 194-211. Discusses female revenge in Chesnutt's fiction. Argues that his women use intelligence and instinct for survival to manipulate their repressive environments.

May, Charles E., ed. *Masterplots II: Short Story Series, Revised Edition.* 8 vols. Pasadena, Calif.: Salem Press, 2004. Designed for student use, this reference set contains articles providing detailed plot summaries and analyses of these four short stories by Chesnutt: "The Goophered Grapevine" (vol. 3), "The Passing of Grandison" and "The Sheriff's Children" (vol. 6), and "The Wife of His Youth" (vol. 8).

Render, Sylvia. *The Short Fiction of Charles Chesnutt.* Washington, D.C.: Howard University Press, 1974. Discusses the collected short fiction of Chesnutt and indicates that it came out of the storytelling tradition of African Americans and was written within the conventions of local humor that were popular at the time.

Sollers, Werner. "Thematics Today." In *Thematics Reconsidered: Essays in Honor of Horst S. Daemmrich,* edited by Frank Trommler. Amsterdam: Rodopi, 1995. Detailed discussion of the themes in "The Wife of His Youth." Argues that contemporary thematic readings that stress race and gender are less likely to identify other themes such as marriage, fidelity, and age difference. Suggests that Chesnutt's special way of treating the race and age themes needs more attention.

Wonham, Henry B. *Charles W. Chesnutt: A Study of the Short Fiction.* New York: Twayne, 1998. Includes bibliographical references and an index.

G. K. Chesterton

Born: London, England; May 29, 1874
Died: Beaconsfield, Buckinghamshire, England; June 14, 1936

Principal short fiction • *The Tremendous Adventures of Major Brown*, 1903; *The Club of Queer Trades*, 1905; *The Perishing of the Pendragons*, 1914; *The Man Who Knew Too Much, and Other Stories*, 1922; *Tales of the Long Bow*, 1925; *Stories*, 1928; *The Sword of Wood*, 1928; *The Moderate Murder and the Honest Quack*, 1929; *The Poet and the Lunatics: Episodes in the Life of Gabriel Gale*, 1929; *Four Faultless Felons*, 1930; *The Ecstatic Thief*, 1930; *The Paradoxes of Mr. Pond*, 1936; *The Vampire of the Village*, 1947.

Other literary forms • One of the most prolific and versatile writers of his time, G. K. Chesterton published books in almost every genre. From 1901 until his death in 1936, he worked as a journalist in London. He was a prolific essayist and literary critic, and his 1909 book on his close friend George Bernard Shaw is still held in the highest esteem. He wrote several volumes of poetry, foremost of which was his 1911 *The Ballad of the White Horse*. After his conversion to Roman Catholicism in 1922, he became a fervent but tactful apologist for his new faith. His 1925 book *The Everlasting Man* and his 1933 study on Saint Thomas Aquinas reveal the depth of his insights into the essential beliefs of Catholicism. His *Autobiography* was published posthumously in late 1936.

Chesterton published more than a dozen novels during his lifetime, ranging from *The Napoleon of Notting Hill* in 1904 to *The Scandal of Father Brown* in 1935. His *The Vampire of the Village* was published eleven years after his death, in 1947. In 2001, *Basil Howe: A Story of Young Love*, a novel he had written in 1894, when he was only twenty, was published for the first time.

Achievements • Chesterton was a man of letters in the finest sense of the term. He expressed effectively and eloquently his ideas on a wide variety of literary, social, and religious topics. He was a master of paradox and always encouraged his readers to reflect on the subtle differences between appearance and reality. Reading his well-crafted short stories is a stimulating aesthetic experience because he makes readers think about the moral implications of what they are reading.

Although his critical writings on literature and religion reveal the depth of his intellect, Chesterton's major achievement was in the field of detective fiction. Between 1911 and 1935, he published five volumes of short stories in which his amateur sleuth is a Catholic priest named Father Brown. Unlike such famous fictional detectives as Arthur Conan Doyle's Sherlock Holmes and Edgar Allan Poe's Auguste Dupin, Father Brown relied not on deductive reasoning but rather on intuition in order to solve perplexing crimes. Father Brown made judicious use of his theological training in order to recognize the specious reasoning of criminals and to lead them to confess their guilt. His Father Brown stories explored moral and theological topics not previously treated in detective fiction.

Biography • Gilbert Keith Chesterton was born on May 29, 1874, in London. He was the second of three children born to Edward and Marie Louise Chesterton. Edward

Chesterton was a real estate agent. Gilbert's older sister, Beatrice, died at the age of eight, in 1877, and two years later his brother, Cecil, was born. Everything seems to indicate that Edward and Marie Louise were loving parents.

In 1982, Gilbert graduated from St. Paul's School in London. For the next three years, he studied at London's Slade Art School, but he finally realized that he would never develop into a truly creative artist. From 1895 until 1900, he worked for a publishing firm. From 1901 until his death, in 1936, he served as a journalist and editor for various London newspapers and magazines.

In 1901, he married Frances Blogg. Gilbert and Frances had no children. Theirs was a good marriage, each helping the other. Frances survived her husband by two years. During the first decade of the twentieth century, Chesterton met the writers Hilaire Belloc and Shaw, who became his lifelong friends. Although Belloc and Shaw seemed to have little in common because Belloc was an apologist for Catholicism and Shaw was an agnostic, Chesterton liked them both very much. Several times, Belloc organized lively but good-natured debates in which Shaw and Chesterton discussed religion and politics. Throughout his adult life, Chesterton supported the Liberal Party in Great Britain, but gradually he became disillusioned with the leadership of the Liberal prime minister David Lloyd George. After the coalition government run by Lloyd George fell apart in 1922, Chesterton lost much interest in politics. During the last fourteen years of his life, his major interests were literature and religion.

Before World War I began, Chesterton was already a well-known English writer, but he had not yet explored profound philosophical and religious themes. Two unexpected events forced Chesterton to think about his mortality and the reasons for his existence. In late 1914, he fell into a coma, which lasted four months. The cause of this coma was never fully explained to the public. After his recovery, he was a changed man. His view of the world became very serious. Then, less than one month after the end of World War I, Chesterton suffered a terrible personal loss when his only brother, Cecil, died from nephritis in a military hospital in France.

After's Cecil's death, Chesterton felt a void in his life. His friend Father John O'Connor, who was the apparent inspiration for Father Brown, spoke to him at length about Catholicism, and Chesterton became a Catholic on July 30, 1922. Four years later, his wife, Frances, joined him in the Catholic Church. The last decade of his life was a very productive period. He continued to write his Father Brown stories, but he also found much pleasure in writing and giving speeches on religious topics. Although firmly convinced that Catholicism was essential for his own spiritual growth and salvation, he was always tolerant and respectful of friends such as H. G. Wells and Shaw, who did not share his religious beliefs. Soon after he had completed his *Autobiography* in early 1936, he developed serious heart problems. He died at his home in Beaconsfield, England, on June 14, 1936, at the age of sixty-two.

Analysis • Before he began writing his Father Brown stories, G. K. Chesterton had already published one book of detective fiction. In *The Man Who Was Thursday*, Chesterton created a detective named Gabriel Syme, who infiltrates an anarchist group in which each of the seven members is named for a different day of the week. Syme replaces the man who had been Thursday. At first, this group seems strange to Syme because he does not understand what the anarchists wish to accomplish. This paradox is resolved when Chesterton explains that all seven "anarchists" are, in fact, detectives assigned separately to investigate this nonexistent threat to society. Although *The Man Who Was Thursday* does demonstrate Chesterton's ability to think

Library of Congress

clearly in order to resolve a problem, the solution to this paradox is so preposterous that many readers have wondered why Chesterton wrote this book, whose ending is so odd. It is hardly credible that all seven members of a secret organization could be police officers. Critics have not been sure how they should interpret this work. Chesterton's own brother, Cecil, thought that it expressed an excessively optimistic view of the world, but other reviewers criticized *The Man Who Was Thursday* for its pessimism.

In his Father Brown stories, this problem of perspective does not exist because it is the levelheaded Father Brown who always explains the true significance of scenes and events that had mystified readers and other characters as well. The other characters, be they detectives, criminals, suspects, or acquaintances of the victim, always come to the conclusion that Father Brown has correctly solved the case.

"The Secret of Father Brown" • In his 1927 short story "The Secret of Father Brown," Chesterton describes the two basic premises of his detective. First, Father Brown is very suspicious of any suspect who ues specious reasoning or expresses insincere religious beliefs. Father Brown senses intuitively that a character who reasons incorrectly might well be a criminal. Second, Father Brown strives to "get inside" the mind of "the murderer" so completely that he is "thinking his thoughts, wrestling with his passions." Father Brown needs to understand what drives the guilty party to commit a specific crime before he can determine who the criminal is and how the crime was committed.

Most critics believe that the best Father Brown stories are those that were published in Chesterton's 1911 volume *The Innocence of Father Brown*. Although his later Father Brown stories should not be neglected, his very early stories are ingenious and have remained popular with generations of readers. Several stories in *The Innocence of Father Brown* illustrate nicely how Father Brown intuitively and correctly solves crimes.

"The Blue Cross" • In "The Blue Cross," Aristide Valentin (the head of the Paris police) is sent to London to arrest a notorious thief named Flambeau, who is a master of disguises. Valentin knows that Flambeau is well over six feet tall, but he does not know how Flambeau is dressed. As Valentin is walking through London, his attraction is suddenly drawn to two Catholic priests. One is short and the other is tall. The short priest acts strangely so that he would attract attention. He deliberately throws soup on a wall in a restaurant, upsets the apples outside of a grocery store, and breaks a window in another restaurant. This odd behavior disturbs the merchants, who consequently ask police officers to follow the priests, who are walking toward the Hampstead Heath. Readers soon learn that the short priest wants to be followed for his own protection. Just as the tall priest, who is, in fact, Flambeau, orders Father Brown, the short priest, to turn over a sapphire cross that he was carrying to a church in Hampstead, Father Brown tells him that "two strong policemen" and Valentin are waiting behind a tree in order to arrest Flambeau. The astonished Flambeau asks Father Brown how he knew that he was not a real priest. Readers learn that Father Brown's suspicion began when, earlier in the story, the tall priest affirmed that only "modern infidels appeal to reason," whereas true Catholics have no use for it. Father Brown tells Flambeau: "You attacked reason. It's bad theology." His intuition told him that his tall companion could not have been a priest, and he was right.

Father Brown is not merely an amateur detective. He is above all a priest whose primary responsibility is to serve as a spiritual guide to upright people and sinners alike. Although he brought about Flambeau's arrest, Flambeau soon turned away from a life of crime. After his release from prison, he became a private detective, and his closest friend became Father Brown. This transformation can be attributed only to the religious teaching that Flambeau received from his spiritual mentor, Father Brown.

"The Eye of Apollo" • The tenth story in *The Innocence of Father Brown* is entitled "The Eye of Apollo." At the beginning of this short story, Flambeau has just opened his detective agency in a new building located near Westminster Abbey. The other tenants in the building are a religious charlatan named Kalon, who claims to be "the New Priest of Apollo," and two sisters, who are typists. Flambeau and Father Brown instinctively distrust Kalon, who has installed a huge eye of Apollo outside his office. Pauline Stacey, the elder of the two sisters, is attracted to Kalon, whom Joan Stacey dislikes intensely. One afternoon, Pauline falls down an elevator shaft and dies. Flambeau concludes hastily that this was an accident, but Father Brown wants to examine her death more thoroughly. He and Flambeau decide to talk with Kalon before the police officers arrive. Kalon presents the preposterous argument that his "religion" favors life, whereas Christianity is concerned only with death. Father Brown becomes more and more convinced that Kalon is a murderer. To the astonishment of Flambeau, Father Brown proves that Pauline "was murdered while she was alone." Pauline was blind, and Kalon knew it. As Kalon was waiting in the elevator, he called Pauline, but suddenly he moved the elevator, and the blind Pauline fell into the open shaft. Flambeau wonders, however, why Kalon killed her. Readers learn that Pauline had told Kalon that she was going to change her will and leave her fortune of five hundred thousand pounds to him. Kalon did not realize, however, that her pen had run out of ink before she could finish writing her will. When he first hears Kalon speak, Father Brown knows instantly that this hypocrite is a criminal. At the end of the story, he tells Flambeau: "I tell you I knew he [Kalon] had done it even before I knew what he had done." Once again Father Brown's intuition is perfectly correct.

"The Secret Garden" • Father Brown has the special ability to recognize the true meaning of seemingly insignificant clues, which other characters see but overlook. In *The Innocence of Father Brown*, there are two other stories, "The Secret Garden" and "The Hammer of God," that illustrate the effectiveness of Father Brown's powers of intuition and that also contain rather unexpected endings. Just as they are in "The Blue Cross," Valentin and Father Brown are major characters in "The Secret Garden." As the head of the Paris police, Valentin has been so successful in arresting criminals that many men whom he sent to prison have threatened to kill him as soon as they regain their freedom. For his own protection, Valentin has very high walls built around his garden, with the only access to it being through his house. His servants guard the entrance to his house at all times. One evening, Valentin holds a reception, which is attended by Father Brown, a medical doctor, an American philanthropist named Julius Brayne, Commandant O'Brien from the French Foreign Legion, Lord and Lady Galloway, and their adult daughter Lady Margaret. Father Brown learns that Valentin is especially suspicious of all organized religions, especially Catholicism, and Julius Brayne likes to contribute huge sums of money to various religions. During the party, a body with a severed head is found in the garden. All the guests are mystified because the head found next to the body does not belong to any of Valentin's servants or to any of the guests.

After much reflection on this apparent paradox, Father Brown proves that the head and the body belong to different men. The body was that of Julius Brayne, and the head belonged to a murderer named Louis Becker, whom the French police had guillotined earlier that day in the presence of Valentin, who had obtained permission to bring Becker's head back to his house. Valentin killed Brayne because of a rumor that Brayne was about to become a Catholic and donate millions to his new church. His hatred for Christianity drove Valentin mad. Father Brown explains calmly that Valentin "would do anything, *anything*, to break what he calls the superstition of the Cross. He has fought for it and starved for it, and now he has murdered for it." Valentin's butler Ivan could not accept this explanation, but as they all went to question Valentin in his study, they found him "dead in his chair." He had committed suicide by taking an overdose of pills. The ending of this short story is surprising because readers of detective fiction do not suspect that a police commissioner can also be a murderer.

"The Hammer of God" • In "The Hammer of God," readers are surprised to learn from Father Brown that the murderer is not a violent madman but rather a very respected member of the community. The Reverend Wilfred Bohun could no longer stand the scandalous behavior of his alcoholic brother Norman, who blasphemed God and humiliated the Reverend Bohun in the eyes of his parishioners. Chesterton states that Wilfred and Norman Bohun belong to an old noble family whose descendants are now mostly "drunkards and dandy degenerates." Rumor has it that there has been "a whisper of insanity" in the Bohun family. Although Father Brown empathizes with the Reverend Bohun, he nevertheless believes that he should express Christian charity toward his brother. When the body of Norman Bohun is found outside his brother's church, Father Brown begins to examine the case. Father Brown finally comes to the conclusion that the Reverend Bohun killed his brother by dropping a hammer on him from the church tower. The murderer tried to frame the village idiot because he knew that the courts would never hold an idiot responsible for murder. At the end of this story, the Reverend Bohun and Father Brown have a long conversation, and Father Brown dissuades the Reverend Bohun from committing suicide because "that door leads to hell." He persuades him instead to confess his sin to God and admit his guilt to the police. In prison, the Reverend Bohun, like Flambeau, may find salvation. In both "The Blue Cross" and "The Hammer of God," Father Brown hates the crime but loves the sinner. Readers are left with the definite impression that Father Brown is absolutely essential for the spiritual growth and eventual salvation of Flambeau and the Reverend Bohun.

Several critics have remarked that the character of Father Brown did not change much in the four volumes of detective fiction that Chesterton wrote after *The Innocence of Father Brown*. This stability represents, however, strength and not weakness. It would have been inappropriate for a member of the clergy to have stopped caring about the spiritual life of others. Father Brown knows that evil exists in the world, but he also believes that even sinners and murderers can be reformed in this life and saved in the next. Father Brown is a fascinating fictional detective who uses his own religious beliefs in order to solve crimes and express profound insights into the dignity of every person.

Edmund J. Campion
With updates by the Editors

Other major works

PLAYS: *Magic: A Fantastic Comedy*, pr. 1913; *The Judgment of Dr. Johnson*, pb. 1927; *The Surprise*, pb. 1952.

ANTHOLOGIES: *Thackeray*, 1909; *Samuel Johnson*, 1911 (with Alice Meynell); *Essays by Divers Hands*, 1926.

NOVELS: *Basil Howe: A Story of Young Love*, wr. 1894, pb. 2001; *The Napoleon of Notting Hill*, 1904; *The Man Who Was Thursday: A Nightmare*, 1908; *The Ball and the Cross*, 1909; *The Innocence of Father Brown*, 1911; *Manalive*, 1912; *The Flying Inn*, 1914; *The Wisdom of Father Brown*, 1914; *The Incredulity of Father Brown*, 1926; *The Return of Don Quixote*, 1926; *The Secret of Father Brown*, 1927; *The Floating Admiral*, 1931 (with others); *The Scandal of Father Brown*, 1935; *The Vampire of the Village*, 1947.

MISCELLANEOUS: *Stories, Essays, and Poems*, 1935; *The Coloured Lands*, 1938; *The Collected Works of G. K. Chesterton*, 1986-1999 (35 volumes); *The Truest Fairy Tale: An Anthology of the Religious Writings of G. K. Chesteron*, 2007 (Kevin L. Morris, editor).

NONFICTION: *The Defendant*, 1901; *Robert Louis Stevenson*, 1902 (with W. Robertson Nicoll); *Thomas Carlyle*, 1902; *Twelve Types*, 1902 (revised as *Varied Types*, 1903, and also known as *Simplicity and Tolstoy*); *Charles Dickens*, 1903 (with F. G. Kitton); *Leo Tolstoy*, 1903 (with G. H. Perris and Edward Garnett); *Robert Browning*, 1903; *Tennyson*, 1903 (with Richard Garnett); *Thackeray*, 1903 (with Lewis Melville); *G. F. Watts*, 1904; *Heretics*, 1905; *Charles Dickens: A Critical Study*, 1906; *All Things Considered*, 1908; *Orthodoxy*, 1908; *George Bernard Shaw*, 1909 (revised edition, 1935); *Tremendous Trifles*, 1909; *Alarms and Discursions*, 1910; *The Ultimate Lie*, 1910; *What's Wrong with the World*, 1910; *William Blake*, 1910; *A Defence of Nonsense, and Other Essays*, 1911; *Appreciations and Criticisms of the Works of Charles Dickens*, 1911; *The Future of Religion: Mr. G. K. Chesterton's Reply to Mr. Bernard Shaw*, 1911; *A Miscellany of Men*, 1912; *The Conversion of an Anarchist*, 1912; *The Victorian Age in Literature*, 1913; *Thoughts from Chesterton*, 1913; *London*, 1914 (with Alvin Langdon Coburn); *Prussian Versus Belgian Culture*, 1914; *The Barbarism of Berlin*, 1914; *Letters to an Old Garibaldian*, 1915; *The Crimes of England*, 1915; *The So-Called Belgian Bargain*, 1915; *A Shilling for My Thoughts*, 1916; *Divorce Versus Democracy*, 1916; *Temperance and the Great Alliance*, 1916; *A Short History of England*, 1917; *Lord Kitchener*, 1917; *Utopia of Usurers, and Other Essays*, 1917; *How to Help Annexation*, 1918; *Charles Dickens Fifty Years After*, 1920; *Irish Impressions*, 1920; *The New Jerusalem*, 1920; *The Superstition of Divorce*, 1920; *The Uses of Diversity*, 1920; *Eugenics and Other Evils*, 1922; *What I Saw in America*, 1922; *Fancies Versus Fads*, 1923; *St. Francis of Assisi*, 1923; *The End of the Roman Road: A Pageant of Wayfarers*, 1924; *The Superstitions of the Sceptic*, 1924; *The Everlasting Man*, 1925; *William Cobbett*, 1925; *A Gleaming Cohort, Being from the Words of G. K. Chesterton*, 1926; *The Catholic Church and Conversion*, 1926; *The Outline of Sanity*, 1926; *Culture and the Coming Peril*, 1927; *Robert Louis Stevenson*, 1927; *Social Reform Versus Birth Control*, 1927; *Do We Agree? A Debate*, 1928 (with George Bernard Shaw); *Generally Speaking*, 1928 (essays); *G. K. C. as M. C., Being a Collection of Thirty-seven Introductions*, 1929; *The Thing*, 1929; *At the Sign of the World's End*, 1930; *Come to Think of It*, 1930; *The Resurrection of Rome*, 1930; *The Turkey and the Turk*, 1930; *All Is Grist*, 1931; *Is There a Return to Religion?*, 1931 (with E. Haldeman-Julius); *Chaucer*, 1932; *Christendom in Dublin*, 1932; *Sidelights on New London and Newer York, and Other Essays*, 1932; *All I Survey*, 1933; *G. K. Chesterton*, 1933 (also known as *Running After One's Hat, and Other Whimsies*); *St. Thomas Aquinas*, 1933; *Avowals and Denials*, 1934; *Explaining the English*, 1935; *The Well and the Shallows*, 1935; *As I Was Saying*, 1936; *Autobiography*, 1936; *The Man Who Was Chesterton*, 1937; *The End of the Armistice*, 1940; *The Common Man*, 1950; *The Glass Walking-Stick, and Other Essays from the "Illustrated London News,"* 1905-1936, 1955; *Lunacy and Letters*, 1958; *Where All Roads Lead*, 1961; *The Man Who Was Orthodox: A Selection from the Uncollected Writings of G. K. Chesterton*, 1963; *The Spice of Life, and Other Essays*, 1964; *Chesterton on Shakespeare*, 1971.

POETRY: *Greybeards at Play: Literature and Art for Old Gentlemen—Rhymes and Sketches*, 1900; *The Wild Knight, and Other Poems*, 1900 (revised, 1914); *The Ballad of the White Horse*, 1911; *A Poem*, 1915; *Poems*, 1915; *Wine, Water, and Song*, 1915; *Old King Cole*, 1920; *The Ballad of St. Barbara, and Other Verses*, 1922; *Poems*, 1925; *The Queen of Seven Swords*, 1926; *Gloria in Profundis*, 1927; *Ubi Ecclesia*, 1929; *The Grave of Arthur*, 1930.

Bibliography

Clipper, Lawrence J. *G. K. Chesterton*. New York: Twayne, 1974. In this useful introduction to the works of Chesterton, Clipper does a fine job of describing the recurring themes in Chesterton's fictional and nonfictional writings. He analyzes very well Chesterton's poetry and literary criticism. Contains an excellent annotated bibliography.

Conlon, D. J., ed. *Chesterton: A Half Century of Views*. New York: Oxford University Press, 1987. Contains numerous short essays on Chesterton published during the first fifty years after his death. The wide diversity of positive critical reactions shows that not only his popular fiction but also his writings on literature and religion continue to fascinate readers.

Crowe, Marian E. "G. K. Chesterton and the Orthodox Romance of Pride and Prejudice." *Renascence* 49 (Spring, 1997): 209-221. Argues that Chesterton used the word "romance" to refer to three different concepts: erotic love, adventure stories, and orthodox faith.

Fagerberg, David W. *The Size of Chesterton's Catholicism*. Notre Dame, Ind.: University of Notre Dame Press, 1998. Analyzes Chesterton's apologetic works for the Catholic Church.

Horst, Mark. "Sin, Psychopathology, and Father Brown." *The Christian Century* 104 (January 21, 1987): 46-47. Compares Chesterton's detective Father Brown to Will Graham, a character in Michael Mann's film *Manhunt*. Argues that although both sleuths use introspection to pursue criminals, when Father Brown looks within himself, he sees sin, a universal reality, whereas when Will Graham looks within, he sees psychopathology, an aberration.

May, Charles E., ed. *Masterplots II: Short Story Series, Revised Edition*. 8 vols. Pasadena, Calif.: Salem Press, 2004. Designed for student use, this reference set contains articles providing detailed plot summaries and analyses of these three short stories by

Chesterton: "The Blue Cross" (vol. 1), "The Hammer of God" (vol. 3), and "The Invisible Man" (vol. 4).

Pearce, Joseph. *Wisdom and Innocence: A Life of G. K. Chesterton.* San Francisco: Ignatius Press, 1996. Scholarly and well-written biography of Chesterton. Contains many quotes from his works and good analysis of them, as well as useful data on his family and friends.

Schwartz, Adam. "G. K. C.'s Methodical Madness: Sanity and Social Control in Chesterton." *Renascence* 49 (Fall, 1996): 23-40. Part of a special issue on G. K. Chesterton. Argues that his view shifts from focus on mental condition of an individual to the way societies define sanity and make "insanity" a means of bourgeois class control.

Tadie, Andrew A., and Michael H. Macdonald, eds. *Permanent Things: Toward the Recovery of a More Human Scale at the End of the Twentieth Century.* Grand Rapids, Mich.: William B. Eerdmans, 1995. This volume includes a fairly thorough discussion of Chesterton's writing, along with works of T. S. Eliot and C. S. Lewis, looking primarily at its ethical and religious components.

Wills, Garry. *Chesterton.* New York: Doubleday, 2001. This biography is a revised edition of *Chesterton, Man and Mask* (1961).

Kate Chopin

Born: St. Louis, Missouri; February 8, 1851
Died: St. Louis, Missouri; August 22, 1904

Principal short fiction • *Bayou Folk*, 1894; *A Night in Acadie*, 1897.

Other literary forms • In addition to the short stories which brought her some fame as a writer during her own lifetime, Kate Chopin published two novels, *At Fault* (1890) and *The Awakening* (1899), the latter of which was either ignored or condemned because of its theme of adultery and frank depiction of a woman's sexual urges. Chopin also wrote a few reviews and casual essays and a number of undistinguished poems.

Achievements • Kate Chopin's short stories, published in contemporary popular magazines, won her fame as a local colorist with a good ear for dialect and as a writer concerned with women's issues (sexuality, equality, independence). After the publication of *The Awakening* in 1899, however, her popularity waned, in part because of the furor over the open treatment of adultery and sex in the novel. She wrote few stories after 1900, and her work was largely neglected until the rediscovery of *The Awakening* by feminist critics. Criticism of that novel and new biographies have spurred a new interest in her Creole short stories, which have been analyzed in detail in terms of their regionalism and their treatment of gender. Influenced by Guy de Maupassant, she herself did not exert any literary influence on later short-story writers, at least not until after the rediscovery of *The Awakening*.

Biography • Kate Chopin was born Katherine O'Flaherty in St. Louis, Missouri, in 1851. Her mother's family was Creole, descended from French settlers, and her father, a successful merchant, was an Irish immigrant. She was educated at the Academy of the Sacred Heart in St. Louis beginning in 1860, five years after her father's accidental death, and graduated in 1868. In 1870, she married Oscar Chopin, who took her to live in Louisiana, first in New Orleans and later in Natchitoches Parish, the setting for many of her stories. In 1882, Oscar died of swamp fever; Kate Chopin managed her husband's properties for a year and in 1884 returned to St. Louis. The next year her mother died, and in 1888 Chopin began writing out of a need for personal expression and to help support her family financially. Her stories appeared regularly in popular periodicals, and she published a novel, *At Fault*, in 1890. *Bayou Folk*, a collection of stories and sketches, appeared in 1894, the year her widely anthologized "The Story of an Hour" was written. *A Night in Acadie* followed, and she was identified as one of four outstanding literary figures in St. Louis by the *Star-Times*. Her celebrated novel, *The Awakening*, received hostile reviews that upset her, though reports about the book being banned were greatly exaggerated. She did, however, write relatively little after this controversy and died five years later in St. Louis, where she was attending the world's fair.

Analysis • Until the 1970's, Kate Chopin was known best literarily, if at all, as a "local colorist," primarily for her tales of life in New Orleans and rural Louisiana. Chopin manages in these stories (about two-thirds of her total output) to bring to life subtly the settings and personalities of her characters, usually Creoles (descendants of the original French settlers of Louisiana) or Cajuns (or Acadians, the French colonists who were exiled to Louisiana following the British conquest of Nova Scotia). What makes Chopin especially important for modern readers, however, is her insight into human characters and relationships in the context of their societies whether Creole, Cajun, or Anglo-Saxon—and into the social, emotional, and sexual roles of women within those societies.

Chopin's desire and hope for female independence can be seen in two of her earliest stories, "Wiser Than a God" and "A Point at Issue!" (both 1889). In the first story, the heroine Paula Von Stoltz rejects an offer of marriage in order to

Missouri Historical Society

begin a successful career as a concert pianist because music is the true sole passion of her life; it is an act that anticipates the actions of Edna Pontellier in *The Awakening*. In the second story, Eleanor Gail and Charles Faraday enter into a marriage based on reason and equality and pursue their individual careers in separate places. This arrangement works very well for some time, but finally each of the two succumbs to jealousy; in spite of this blemish in their relationship, Chopin's humorous tone manages to poke fun at traditional attitudes toward marriage as well.

"The Story of an Hour" • This questioning though humorous attitude is strongly evident in one of Chopin's most anthologized and best-known tales, "The Story of an Hour" (1894). Mrs. Mallard, a woman suffering from a heart condition, is told that her husband has been killed in a train accident. She is at first deeply sorrowful but soon realizes that even though she had loved and will mourn her husband, his death has set her free: "There would be no powerful will bending hers in that blind persistence with which men and women believe they have a right to impose a private will upon a fellow-creature." As Mrs. Mallard descends the stairs, however, the front door is opened by her husband, who had never been on the train. This time her heart gives out, and the cause ironically is given by the doctors as "the joy that kills."

"La Belle Zoraïde" • It is in her Louisiana stories, however, that Chopin's sympathy for female and indeed human longings emerges most fully, subtly blended with a distinct and evocative sense of locale and folkways. "La Belle Zoraïde" (1893) is presented in the form of a folktale being told by a black servant, Manna-Loulou, to her mistress, Madame Delisle (these two characters also are central to the story "A Lady of Bayou St. John," 1893). The tale itself is the story of a black slave, Zoraïde, who is forbidden by her mistress to marry another slave with whom she has fallen in love because his skin is too black and her mistress intends her for another, more "gentlemanly" servant. In spite of this, and although the slave she loves is sold away, she bears his child and refuses marriage to the other slave. Her mistress falsely tells Zoraïde that her child has been born dead, and the slave descends into madness. Even when her real daughter is finally brought back to her, Zoraïde rejects her, preferring to cling to the bundle of rags that she has fashioned as a surrogate baby. From then on,

> She was never known again as la belle Zoraïde, but ever after as Zoraïde la folle, whom no one ever wanted to marry. . . . She lived to be an old woman, whom some people pitied and others laughed at—always clasping her bundle of rags—her 'piti.'

The indirect narration of this story prevents it from slipping into the melodramatic or the maudlin. Chopin's ending, presenting the conversation of Manna-Loulou and Madame Delisle in the Creole dialect, pointedly avoids a concluding moral judgment, an avoidance typical of Chopin's stories. Instead, readers are brought back to the frame for the tale and concentrated upon the charm of the Creole dialect even while they retain pity and sympathy for Zoraïde.

"Désirée's Baby" • In spite of their southern locale, Chopin's stories rarely deal with racial relations between whites and blacks. One important exception is "Désirée's Baby" (1892). Désirée Valmondé, who was originally a foundling, marries Armand Aubigny, a plantation owner who is proud of his aristocratic heritage but very much in love with Désirée. He is at first delighted when she bears him a son, but soon begins to grow cold and distant. Désirée, puzzled at first, soon realizes with horror that her child has Negro blood. Armand, whose love for Désirée has been killed by "the unconscious injury she had brought upon his home and his name," turns her out of the house, and she disappears with her child into the bayou, never to be seen again. Later, in a surprise ending reminiscent of Maupassant, Armand is having all reminders of Désirée burned when he discovers a letter from his mother to his father which reveals that his mother had had Negro blood. In this story one sees the continuation of Chopin's most central theme, the evil that follows when one human being gains power over another and attempts to make that person conform to preset standards or expectations.

As suggested earlier, Chopin finds that power of one person over another is often manifested in the institution of marriage. Yet, as even her earliest stories suggest, she does not always find that marriage necessarily requires that a wife be dominated by her husband, and she demonstrates that both men and women are capable of emotional and spiritual growth.

"Athénaïse" • The possibility for growth is perhaps best seen in the story "Athénaïse" (1895). Athénaïse, an emotionally immature young woman, has married the planter Cazeau, but has found that she is not ready for marriage. She runs back to her family, explaining that she does not hate Cazeau himself:

> It's jus' being married that I detes' an' despise. . . . I can't stan' to live with a man; to have him always there; his coats and pantaloons hanging in my room; his ugly bare feet—washing them in my tub, befo' my very eyes, ugh!

When Cazeau arrives to bring her back, however, she finds that she has to go with him. As the couple rides home, they pass an oak tree which Cazeau recalls was where his father had once apprehended a runaway slave: "The whole impression was for some reason hideous, and to dispel it Cazeau spurred his horse to a swift gallop."

Despite Cazeau's attempt to make up and live with Athénaïse at least as friends, she remains bitter and unhappy and finally runs away again, aided by her romantic and rather foolish brother Montéclin. Cazeau, a sensitive and proud man, refuses to go after her again as though she too were a runaway slave: "For the companionship of no woman on earth would he again undergo the humiliating sensation of baseness that had overtaken him in passing the old oak-tree in the fallow meadow."

Athénaïse takes refuge in a boarding house in New Orleans where she becomes friendly with Mr. Gouvernail, a newspaper editor. Gouvernail hopes to make Athénaïse his lover, but he refrains from forcing himself on her: "When the time came that she wanted him . . . he felt he would have a right to her. So long as she did not want him, he had no right to her,—no more than her husband had." Gouvernail, though, never gets his chance; Athénaïse has previously been described as someone who does not yet know her own mind, and such knowledge will not come through rational analysis but "as the song to the bird, the perfume and color to the flower." This knowledge does come to her when she discovers that she is pregnant. As she thinks of Cazeau, "the first purely sensuous tremor of her life swept over her. . . . Her whole passionate nature was aroused as if by a miracle." Thus, Athénaïse returns to reconciliation and happiness with her husband.

Chopin's story illustrates that happiness in a relationship can come only with maturity and with mutual respect. Cazeau realizes that he cannot force his wife to love him, and Athénaïse finally knows what she wants when she awakens to an awareness of her own sexuality. If Cazeau has to learn to restrain himself, though, Mr. Gouvernail learns the need to take more initiative as well; not having declared his love for Athénaïse, he suffers when she goes back home. The tone of the entire story is subtly balanced between poignancy and humor, allowing one to see the characters' flaws while remaining sympathetic with each of them.

The importance of physical passion and of sexual self-awareness which can be found in "Athénaïse" can also be found in many of Chopin's stories and is one of the characteristics that make her writing so far ahead of its time. It is this theme that, as the title suggests, is central to her novel *The Awakening* and which was partly responsible for the scandal which that novel provoked. Chopin's insistence not merely on the fact of women's sexual desires but also on the propriety and healthiness of those desires in some ways anticipates the writings of D. H. Lawrence, but without Lawrence's insistence on the importance of male dominance.

"The Storm" • Sexual fulfillment outside of marriage without moral judgments can be found in "The Storm," written in 1898, just before *The Awakening*, but not published until 1969. The story concerns four characters from an earlier tale, "At the 'Cadian Ball" (1892). In that earlier story, a young woman, Clarisse, rides out in the night to the 'Cadian Ball to declare her love for the planter Alcée Laballière. Alcée is at the ball with an old girlfriend of his, Calixta, a woman of Spanish descent. Clarisse claims Alcée, and Calixta agrees to marry Bobinôt, a man who has been in love with her for some time.

"The Storm" is set several years later. Calixta and Bobinôt have had a child, and Alcée and Clarisse have been happily married. One day, while Bobinôt and his son are out on an errand, a huge storm breaks out. Alcée takes refuge at Calixta's house, and the old passion between the two is rekindled; as the storm breaks about them in mounting intensity, the two make love, Calixta's body "knowing for the first time its birthright." Although the storm mirrors the physical passion of the couple, neither it nor the passion itself is destructive. Where one would expect some retribution for this infidelity in a story, the results are only beneficial: Calixta, physically fulfilled, happily welcomes back her returning husband and son; Alcée writes to Clarisse, off visiting relatives, that he does not need her back right away; and Clarisse, enjoying "the first free breath since her marriage," is content to stay where she is for the time. Chopin's ending seems audacious: "So the storm passed and every one was happy."

Although written about a century ago, Chopin's stories seem very modern in many ways. Her concern with women's place in society and in marriage, her refusal to mix guilt with sexuality, and her narrative stance of sympathetic detachment make her as relevant to modern readers as her marked ability to convey character and setting simply yet completely. In the little more than a decade in which she produced most of her work, her command of her art grew ever stronger, as did her willingness to deal with controversial subjects. It is unfortunate that this career was cut so short by the reaction to *The Awakening* and her early death; but it is fortunate that Chopin left the writing that she did and that it has been preserved.

Donald F. Larsson
With updates by Thomas L. Erskine

Other major works
NOVELS: *At Fault*, 1890; *The Awakening*, 1899.
MISCELLANEOUS: *The Complete Works of Kate Chopin*, 1969 (2 volumes; Per Seyersted, editor).
NONFICTION: *Kate Chopin's Private Papers*, 1998.

Bibliography
Bonner, Thomas, Jr. *The Kate Chopin Companion.* New York: Greenwood Press, 1988. Guide, arranged alphabetically, to the more than nine hundred characters and over two hundred places that affected the course of Chopin's stories. Also includes a selection of her translations of pieces by Guy de Maupassant and one by Adrien Vely. Contains interesting period maps and a useful bibliographical essay.
Boren, Lynda S., and Sara de Saussure Davis, eds. *Kate Chopin Reconsidered: Beyond the Bayou.* Baton Rouge: Louisiana State University Press, 1992. Although most of these essays focus on *The Awakening*, several discuss such stories as "Charlie," "After the Winter," and "At Cheniere Caminada." Other essays compare Chopin with playwright Henrik Ibsen in terms of domestic confinement and discuss her work from a Marxist point of view.
Brown, Pearl L. "Awakened Men in Kate Chopin's Creole Stories." *ATQ*, n.s. 13, no. 1 (March, 1999). Argues that in Chopin's Creole stories, in intimate moments women discover inner selves buried beneath socially imposed ones and men discover subjective selves buried beneath public personas.
Erickson, Jon. "Fairytale Features in Kate Chopin's 'Désirée's Baby': A Case Study in Genre Cross-Reference." In *Modes of Narrative*, edited by Reingard M. Nischik and Barbara Korte. Würzburg: Königshausen and Neumann, 1990. Shows how Chopin's story conflicts with the expectations set up by the fairy-tale genre on which it is based; for example, the prince turns out to be the villain. Argues that the ending

of the story is justified, for in the fairy tale the mystery of origin must be solved and the villain must be punished.

Koloski, Bernard. *Kate Chopin: A Study of the Short Fiction.* New York: Twayne, 1996. Discusses Chopin's short stories in the context of her bilingual and bicultural imagination; provides readings of her most important stories, examines her three volumes of stories, and comments on her children's stories. Also includes excerpts from Chopin's literary criticism and brief discussions by other critics of her most familiar stories.

May, Charles E., ed. *Masterplots II: Short Story Series, Revised Edition.* 8 vols. Pasadena, Calif.: Salem Press, 2004. Designed for student use, this reference set contains articles providing detailed plot summaries and analyses of these five short stories by Chopin: "La Belle Zoraïde" (vol. 1), "Désirée's Baby" (vol. 2), "Madame Célestin's Divorce" (vol. 5), and "The Storm" and "The Story of an Hour" (vol. 7).

Petry, Alice Hall, ed. *Critical Essays on Kate Chopin.* New York: G. K. Hall, 1996. Comprehensive collection of essays on Chopin. This volume reprints early evaluations of the author's life and works as well as more modern scholarly analyses. In addition to a substantial introduction by the editor, it also includes seven original essays by such notable scholars as Linda Wagner-Martin and Heather Kirk Thomas.

Seyersted, Per. *Kate Chopin: A Critical Biography.* Baton Rouge: Louisiana State University Press, 1980. Seyersted's biography, besides providing invaluable information about the New Orleans of the 1870's, examines Chopin's life, views, and work. Provides lengthy discussions not only of *The Awakening* but also of her many short stories. Seyersted sees her as a transitional literary figure, a link between George Sand and Simone de Beauvoir.

Toth, Emily. *Kate Chopin.* New York: William Morrow, 1990. Toth's thoroughly documented, exhaustive work is the definitive Chopin biography. She covers not only Chopin's life but also her literary works and discusses many of the short stories in considerable detail. Toth updates Per Seyersted's bibliography of Chopin's work, supplies a helpful chronology of her life, and discusses the alleged banning of *The Awakening.* The starting point for Chopin research.

_____. *Unveiling Kate Chopin.* Jackson: University Press of Mississippi, 1999. Using newly discovered manuscripts, letters, and diaries of Chopin, Toth examines the source of Chopin's ambition and passion for her art, arguing that she worked much harder at her craft than previously thought.

Sandra Cisneros

Born: Chicago, Illinois; December 20, 1954

Principal short fiction • *The House on Mango Street*, 1984; *Woman Hollering Creek, and Other Stories*, 1991.

Other literary forms • Sandra Cisneros is known for her poetry as well as her short fiction. She has published several collections of poems, including *Bad Boys* (1980), *My Wicked, Wicked Ways* (1987), and *Loose Woman* (1994); much of her poetry remains uncollected and unpublished, according to the author's wishes. She has also published a series of essays explaining her own creative processes as a writer in *The Americas Review*. In addition, she published *Hairs = Pelitos* (1984), a children's book illustrated by Terry Ybanez which expands on the chapter "Hairs" in *The House on Mango Street*. In 2002, Cisneros published her second novel, *Caramelo*, which is about a multi-generation Mexican American family making a pilgrimage from Chicago to Mexico City.

Achievements • Together with authors such as Ana Castillo, Denise Chávez, and Alma Villanueva, Sandra Cisneros is one of the literary voices that emerged in the 1980's and was responsible for securing for Chicana fiction a place in mainstream American literature. Her collection of short stories *Woman Hollering Creek, and Other Stories* was the first work by and about Chicanas—Mexican American women—to receive a contract with a major publishing house (Random House). Cisneros was awarded the Before Columbus American Book Award and the PEN Center West Award for her first collection of short fiction, *The House on Mango Street*. She is a two-time recipient of a National Endowment for the Arts Fellowship for Creative Writers for her poetry and fiction. In 1985, Cisneros received a Dobie-Paisano Fellowship. She was granted a MacArthur Fellowship in 1995.

Biography • Sandra Cisneros was born in 1954 into a working-class family in Chicago, Illinois. With a Mexican American mother, a Mexican father, and six brothers, she described her circumstances as being similar to having seven fathers. Because of close familial and cultural ties with Mexico, the Cisneros family moved back and forth between a series of cramped apartments in Chicago and the paternal grandmother's home in Mexico City. The concept of home or the lack of one would later weigh heavily in Cisneros's writing. The combination of an uprooted lifestyle and an ever-changing circle of friends, schools, and neighborhoods, as well as the isolation that resulted from her brothers' unwillingness to let a girl join in their play, led Cisneros to turn inward to a life of books. That time spent alone allowed an observant, creative voice to take root in the author.

Cisneros considered her career as a professional writer to have begun in 1974—the year in which she enrolled in a writing class as a junior at Loyola University of Chicago, where she would later receive her bachelor of arts degree in English. It was her tenure at the University of Iowa's Writers' Workshop, from which she took a master of fine arts degree, however, that proved an invaluable aid in the formation of her own literary voice. During a discussion of Gaston Bachelard's *La Bétique de l'espace* (1957; *The Poetics of Space*, 1964), in which her classmates spoke of the house as a literary symbol complete with attics, stairways, and cellars of imagination and childhood, Cisneros realized that her experience was different from that of her college classmates. Her background was that of a multiethnic, working-class neighborhood complete with drunken bums, families sleeping on crowded floors, and rats. She ceased trying to make her style fit that of the perfect, white, and mostly male image that was foreign to her and, instead, undertook writing about that to which her classmates could not relate but was familiar to her.

Cisneros has used her education to foster change within the Chicano community. She taught high school dropouts for three years in a Chicano barrio. She has also worked as an administrative assistant at Loyola University, where she was involved in the recruitment of minority and disadvantaged students. In 1984, she was the literature director of the Guadalupe Cultural Arts Center of San Antonio, the city which she made her home. Cisneros served as writer-in-residence at the Michael Karolyi Artists Foundation in Vence, France, the University of Michigan in Ann Arbor, the University of California at Irvine, and the University of New Mexico in Albuquerque.

Analysis • Sandra Cisneros said that she writes about the memories that will not let her sleep at night—about the stories that are waiting to be told. Drawing on the memories of her childhood and her cultural identity—the run-down, crowded apartment, the double-edged sword of being American yet not being considered American, the sight of women in her community closed in behind apartment windows—Cisneros's fiction avoids any romantic clichés of life in the barrio. Despite the sobering themes upon which Cisneros touches—poverty, sexism, and racism—she tells her stories with a voice that is at the same time strong, playful, and deceptively simple. Cisneros's distinctive style is marked by the grace with which Spanish words and phrases are woven into her stories. Central to her stories is a preoccupation with the house, the community, and the condition of women. Her images are vivid and lyrical. She acknowledges that she was influenced in style by the mix of poetry and fiction in Jorge Luis Borges's *El hacedor* (1960; *Dreamtigers*, 1964). Indeed, while Cisneros herself classifies her fiction as stories that read like poems, critics have not reached an agreement, labeling her works *The House on Mango Street* and *Woman Hollering Creek, and Other Stories* alternatively as novels, short-story collections, series of vignettes, and prose poems.

The House on Mango Street • The series of sketches in *The House on Mango Street* offers a bittersweet view of life in a Chicago barrio. Readers follow the young adolescent narrator Esperanza—whose name (as explained in the story "My Name") means "hope" in Spanish and also implies too many letters, sadness, and waiting—as she makes the discoveries associated with maturing. She introduces the reader to her neighbors and her neighborhood, making them as familiar to the reader as they are to her. In the title story, Esperanza explains how her family came to live on Mango Street. The family had hoped that the house on Mango Street would be like the ones they had always dreamed of—with real stairs and several bathrooms and a great big yard with trees and grass.

Esperanza sadly explains, however, that their house does not fulfill this wish at all. She is ashamed of her red brick house, as she has been of all of her family's previous dwellings. She succinctly describes the embarrassment that she experienced when the family was living on Loomis and she had to show her apartment to a nun from

© Rubén Guzmán

her school. She pointed to the family's third-floor flat, located above a boarded-up laundry, and suffered the blow of the nun's disbelieving response, *"there?"* From that moment, Esperanza knew that she had to have a house—one that she could show with pride to people as if it were a reflection of herself. She was sure the family would have such a house soon. Yet the house on Mango Street is not that house.

"Bums in the Attic" • Because Esperanza remarks that she wants a house "all my own. With my porch and my pillow, my pretty purple petunias. My books and my stories," Cisneros has been read as creating a grasping and selfish protagonist. Yet the section titled "Bums in the Attic" dispels this notion of untoward individualism. In this sketch—which resembles one of Cisneros's favorite children's stories, Virginia Lee Burton's *The Little House* (1978), in which the owners of a house on a country hill promise the house never to sell it—Esperanza speculates about the grand home on a hill that she will have someday. As much as she wants to leave Mango Street, however, she stresses that even in her country home she will not forget from where she came. She will not make her house a secured palace that locks out the world; she will instead offer her attic to the homeless so that they too will have a home.

"Those Who Don't" • In "Those Who Don't," the young Esperanza discusses in a matter-of-fact tone the concept of being the "other" in society. She knows that people who happen into her neighborhood think that her community is dangerous, but she knows her neighbors by name and knows their backgrounds. Among her Latino friends she feels safe. Yet Esperanza can understand the stranger's apprehension, for when she and her family venture out of the security of their neighborhood, their bodies get tense and their eyes look straight ahead.

"Alicia Who Sees Mice" • Cisneros's concern for the place women hold in Latino society is evident in the powerful story "Alicia Who Sees Mice." Alicia, Esperanza's friend, must rise early every morning "with the tortilla star" and the mice in the kitchen to make her father's lunch-box tortillas. Alicia's mother has died, and, Esperanza remarks, young Alicia has inherited her mother's duty as the family caregiver along with her "rolling pin and sleepiness." Alicia has dreams of escaping this life of confinement and sacrifice, however, with a university education. She studies hard all night with the mice that her father says do not exist. With its precise imagery, "Alicia Who Sees Mice" is at once a criticism of patriarchal oppression of women and a beacon for those women who would struggle to break away from that oppression.

"Minerva Writes Poems" • The theme of education and writing as a means whereby women can escape from the barrio is also found in "Minerva Writes Poems." Minerva is only a bit older than Esperanza, "but already she has two kids and a husband who left . . . and keeps leaving." Minerva's husband reappears sporadically, but their reunion usually ends in violence and abuse. Minerva cries every day over her bad situation and writes poems at night. In an act of artistic and sisterly solidarity, she and Esperanza read their poems to each other, yet at this point, Esperanza feels helpless, unable to stop the beatings. In her reply, "There is nothing *I* can do," there is a sense that Esperanza is inciting Minerva to take action for herself as well as implying that society itself must change its attitudes.

"Edna's Ruthie" • This sisterly support for fulfillment through learning is echoed in "Edna's Ruthie." The title character is a talented but damaged woman who returns to her mother's home when she can no longer care for herself. Her own fondness for books—for hearing and telling a good story—inspires Esperanza in her own creative endeavors. Ruthie is moved to tears by Esperanza's recitation of children's stories, a response that conveys to the young girl the power of the word.

"Red Clowns" • Esperanza's passage into adulthood is not without setbacks. In "Red Clowns," she goes to the amusement park with her friend Sally. When the sexually precocious Sally abandons Esperanza to slip away with a boy, Esperanza is molested and possibly raped by an older boy who tells her, "I love you Spanish girl, I love you." She is angry and sad and confused over the loss of her innocence. She cannot understand why everyone told her that sex would be so wonderful when, in fact, she found nothing pleasant about the perpetrator's dirty fingernails and sour breath. She wants to forget that degrading experience; she does not want to speak its horror. She yells at her friend Sally for leaving her, but she also directs her anger at a society that is partner to such an awful lie.

"The Three Sisters" • The fundamental conflict that besets Esperanza is resolved in "The Three Sisters." Although Esperanza has repeatedly voiced her desire to escape the barrio and its double bind of racism and sexism which snares many women, she nevertheless loves her community and cannot come to terms with deserting it. Then three wise, eccentric, and decidedly feminist sisters settle the issue. Young Esperanza is strong, talented, and destined to "go very far," they tell her. Their encouraging words sanction her flight, yet the sisters remind her as well of the need for loyalty:

> When you leave you must remember to come back for the others. A circle, understand? You will always be Esperanza. You will always be Mango Street. You can't erase what you know. You can't forget who you are.

Young Esperanza can finally look to a life beyond the confines of her repressive environment.

Woman Hollering Creek, and Other Stories • Likewise, *Woman Hollering Creek, and Other Stories* offers a glimpse into the lives of Chicanas who must confront daily the triple bind of not being considered Mexican, not being considered American, and not being male. Cisneros said that while the pieces of *Woman Hollering Creek, and Other Stories* function individually, there is a single, unifying thread of vision and experience that runs throughout the collection of twenty-two narratives. Although the names of the narrators change with each work, each narrator retains a strong, determined, rebellious voice.

"Eleven" • In "Eleven," eleven-year-old Rachel's birthday prompts her to consider what it means to grow older. The wisdom of her eleven years has taught her that the years "underneath" the birthday, like the rings inside a tree trunk, make one a certain age. When people want to cry, she reasons, it is the part of them that is three that brings on tears; when they are scared, it is the part in them that is five that registers fear. For this reason, Rachel explains, she was not able to act eleven years old today in school when her teacher wrongly accused her of forgetting an ugly red sweater that had been in the coatroom for a month. All the years were welling up inside her, preventing Rachel from telling everyone that it was not her sweater. Instead, she was silent. She tries to be happy and remember that today she is eleven and that her mother will have a cake for her when she goes home. The part of Rachel that is three, however, comes out in front of the class instead. She wishes she were anything but eleven.

"One Holy Night" • The narrator of the chilling "One Holy Night" is an adolescent girl who sells fruits and vegetables from her grandmother's pushcart. She meets a wanderer named Chaq who tells her that he is a descendant of a long line of Mayan kings. Intrigued by his story, the young woman begins to follow Chaq to his little room behind an automobile garage after she has sold each day's produce. Chaq spins mystic tales of the past and future greatness of his family's lineage as he entices the girl into her first sexual experience. She returns home to her grandmother and uncle a changed woman, barely able to contain her excitement. The young woman's secret, however, is soon discovered: She is pregnant. The family, in total disgrace, attempts to locate Chaq, who has since left town. Her uncle writes a letter in hope of finding the man who could correct his niece's ruined life. A response arrives from Chaq's sister. She explains that her brother's name is actually Chato, which means "fat-face"; he is thirty-seven, not at all Mayan, and not at all royal. The girl's family sends her to Mexico to give birth and to avoid disgrace. It is later learned that Chato has been captured and charged with the deaths of eleven women. The girl appears unfazed by the news, however, and continues to plan her dreams of children. She becomes indifferent to love.

"Never Marry a Mexican" • The title "Never Marry a Mexican" sums up the advice that the protagonist Clemencia was told as a young girl by her Chicana mother who regretted marrying a Mexican. Her mother's words ultimately consign Clemencia to cultural and social marginality. Clemencia scorns the working-class Latino men in her life and refuses to consider any of them as potential husbands. However, ironically, the white men whom she favors follow the same advice her mother has instilled in her: They will become sexually involved with a Chicana, but they will not marry outside of their own race.

Caught uncomfortably between cultures, Clemencia attempts to make the most of her difficult status. She prides herself on remaining unattached, a seductress who beds white, married men while their wives are in the throes of childbirth. Yet her pain and loneliness are palpable. She nurses affection for one white married lover for eighteen years, eventually gaining revenge on him by entering into a sexual relationship with his son. For Clemencia, the unhealthy relationship yields and yet perverts what she ostensibly disavows: marriage and motherhood. Sexual intercourse with the young man, she believes, links her to his father and mother's marital relations, of which he is the product, and her lover's relative youth allows her to "mother" him.

"Woman Hollering Creek" • The collection's title story is one of its strongest. It is a story of Cleófilas, a woman reared in a small town in Mexico not far from the Texas border. Cleófilas dreams of the romance and passion of the soap operas that she watches at her girlfriend's house. She believes her fantasy is realized when she meets Juan Pedro, a Texan who wants to marry her right away, "without a long engagement since he can't take off too much time from work." Cleófilas is whisked away across the border to Seguin, Texas, a town like so many others, with nothing of interest to walk to, "built so that you have to depend on husbands."

Life on "the other side" is, at first, a blessing for Cleófilas. Texas is the land of Laundromats and dream homes. Running behind their new house is a creek that all call Woman Hollering. Cleófilas wonders if the odd name is connected to tales of La Llorona, the tragic mythical figure known to wail after drowning her children. Her enthusiasm for her new life ends quickly, however, with a slap to her face by Juan Pedro. That slap will start a long line of abuse and cause Cleófilas to think flatly, "This is the man I have waited my whole life for." Although she had always promised herself that she would not allow any man to hit her, Cleófilas, isolated at home, not allowed to correspond with her family, hindered by not knowing English, and afraid of Juan Pedro's rage, stays with him. When she begins to suspect that Juan Pedro is unfaithful, she thinks about returning to her native town but fears disgrace and does not act. Cleófilas had always thought that her life would be like a soap opera, "only now the episodes got sadder and sadder. And there were no commercials in between for comic relief." She becomes pregnant with their second child but is almost too afraid to ask Juan Pedro to take her to the clinic for prenatal care. Once at the clinic, Cleófilas breaks down and tells her plight to a sympathetic doctor who arranges a ride for her and her son to the bus station in San Antonio. The morning of their escape, Cleófilas is tense and frightened. As they pass over Woman Hollering Creek in a pickup truck, their spirited female driver lets out a Tarzan-like yell that startles her two passengers. On her way back to her father's home, Cleófilas catches a glimpse of what it is to be an autonomous woman.

Mary F. Yudin
With updates by Theresa Kanoza and the Editors

Other major works
CHILDREN'S LITERATURE: *Hairs = Pelitos*, 1984.
NOVEL: *Caramelo*, 2002.
MISCELLANEOUS: *Vintage Cisneros*, 2004.
POETRY: *Bad Boys*, 1980; *The Rodrigo Poems*, 1985; *My Wicked, Wicked Ways*, 1987; *Loose Woman*, 1994.

Bibliography
Brady, Mary Pat. "The Contrapuntal Geographies of *Woman Hollering Creek, and Other*

Stories." *American Literature* 71 (March, 1999): 117-150. Shows how Cisneros's narrative techniques challenge various spatial representations and lay bare hidden stories. Claims that Cisneros explores the various subtleties of violence of changing spatial relations.

Cisneros, Sandra. "On the Solitary Fate of Being Mexican, Female, Wicked, and Thirty-three: An Interview with Writer Sandra Cisneros." Interview by Pilar E. Rodríguez Aranda. *The Americas Review* 18, no. 1 (1990): 64-80. In an enlightening interview, Cisneros discusses her identity as a Chicana, her development as a writer, and her use of poetry and modern myth in her fiction. The interview focuses on the collections *My Wicked, Wicked Ways* and *The House on Mango Street.*

_____. "Sandra Cisneros: Conveying the Riches of the Latin American Culture Is the Author's Literary Goal." Interview by Jim Sagel. *Publishers Weekly* 238 (March 29, 1991): 74-75. In this informative interview, Cisneros speaks about the influence that her childhood had on her writing. The interview touches upon the personal side of the writer and includes a brief description of the genesis of the collection *Woman Hollering Creek, and Other Stories.*

Griffin, Susan E. "Resistance and Reinvention in Sandra Cisneros' *Woman Hollering Creek.*" In *Ethnicity and the American Short Story*, edited by Julie Brown. New York: Garland, 1997. Discusses the role that Mexican popular culture and traditional Mexican narratives play in limiting women's sense of identity. Focuses primarily on the negative effects of popular romances in Mexico and televised soap operas.

May, Charles E., ed. *Masterplots II: Short Story Series, Revised Edition.* 8 vols. Pasadena, Calif.: Salem Press, 2004. Designed for student use, this reference set contains articles providing detailed plot summaries and analyses of these three short stories by Cisneros: "Geraldo No Last Name" (vol. 3), "One Holy Night" (vol. 5), and "Woman Hollering Creek" (vol. 8).

Mullen, Harryette. "'A Silence Between Us Like a Language': The Untranslatability of Experience in Sandra Cisneros's *Woman Hollering Creek.*" *MELUS* 21 (Summer, 1996): 3-20. Argues that Spanish as a code comprehensible to an inside group and as a repressed language subordinate to English are central issues in *Woman Hollering Creek.*

Sanborn, Geoffrey. "Keeping Her Distance: Cisneros, Dickinson, and the Politics of Private Enjoyment." *Publications of the Modern Language Association* 116, no. 5 (2001): 1334-1348. Analyzes Cisneros's use of a poem by Emily Dickinson in *The House on Mango Street* as a means of evoking the pleasures of withdrawal from face-to-face sociality.

Thompson, Jeff. "'What Is Called Heaven?' Identity in Sandra Cisneros's *Woman Hollering Creek.*" *Studies in Short Fiction* 31 (Summer, 1994): 415-424. States that the overall theme of the stories is the vulnerability of the female narrators. The vignettes should be read as symptomatic of a social structure that allows little cultural movement and little possibility for the creation of an identity outside the boundaries of the barrio.

Wyatt, Jean. "On Not Being *La Malinche*: Border Negotiations of Gender in Sandra Cisneros's 'Never Marry a Mexican' and 'Woman Hollering Creek.'" *Tulsa Studies in Women's Literature* 14 (Fall, 1995): 243-271. Discusses how the stories describe the difficulties of living on the border between Anglo-American and Mexican cultures and how the female protagonists of the stories struggle with sexuality and motherhood as icons that limit their identity.

Walter Van Tilburg Clark

Born: East Orland, Maine; August 3, 1909
Died: Reno, Nevada; November 10, 1971

Principal short fiction • *The Watchful Gods, and Other Stories*, 1950.

Other literary forms • In addition to his short stories, Walter Van Tilburg Clark wrote three novels—*The Ox-Bow Incident* (1940), *The City of Trembling Leaves* (1945), and *The Track of the Cat* (1949). The first and last of these were made into motion pictures. *Tim Hazard* (1951) is the enlarged version of *The City of Trembling Leaves*. Clark also produced an early book of poems, *Ten Women in Gale's House and Shorter Poems* (1932).

Achievements • Although Walter Van Tilburg Clark is known primarily for his novels, his one volume of stories, as well as his uncollected short stories, have established him as a fine writer of short stories. In fact, his "The Wind and the Snow of Winter" received the O. Henry Award in 1945. In their Western settings, their ambiguous depiction of the American Dream, their concern about personal identity and oneness with nature, and their essentially tragic vision, the short stories are of a piece with his three novels. Unlike some "Western" writers, Clark used his landscape as both subject and backdrop for his own philosophical themes. Less concerned with characters—one story virtually omits them, concentrating instead on animals as "characters"—than with ideas, Clark used his characters, many of whom seem stereotypical, to embody and actualize his notions about the possibility of defining self and position in the cosmos.

Biography • Walter Van Tilburg Clark was born on August 3, 1909, in East Orland, Maine, the first child of Walter Ernest and Euphemia Abrams Clark. In 1917, his father, a distinguished economics professor, became president of the University of Nevada at Reno. Therefore, the family had to move when Clark was only eight. In Reno, Clark attended public schools and later received his bachelor's and master's degrees in English from the University of Nevada. Clark married Barbara Morse in 1933, and they became the parents of two children, Barbara Ann and Robert Morse. The couple settled in Cazenovia, New York, where Clark began a career in high school and college teaching as well as creative writing. In the next several years, Clark continued writing and taught at several schools, including the University of Montana, Reed College, and the University of Nevada, where he resigned after protesting the autocratic tendencies of the administration. He eventually returned there, however, to teach creative writing. Clark was also director of creative writing at San Francisco State College from 1956 to 1962. He died of cancer on November 10, 1971, at the age of sixty-two.

Analysis • Walter Van Tilburg Clark once wrote that the primary impulse of the arts has been religious and ritualistic—with the central hope of "propitiating or enlisting Nature, the Gods, God, or whatever name one wishes to give the encompassing and still mysterious whole." Certainly Clark's fiction attests to such a view. In a world in which thought is often confused and fragmented, he advocates for humanity a stance of intellectual honesty, an acceptance of instinctive values, and a belief in love. The key is human experience. As Max Westbrook so aptly put it in his study of Clark, "Clark's literary credo, then, is based on the capacity of the unconscious mind to discover and to give shape to objective knowledge about the human experience."

"The Buck in the Hills" • "The Buck in the Hills" may be Clark's clearest reflection in his stories of the literary credo mentioned above. Writing more or less in the terse, almost brittle, style of Ernest Hemingway, Clark opens the story with vividly descriptive passages of mountain scenery. The narrator, whose name the reader never learns, has returned to this setting after five years. It is really more than a return for him; it is a pilgrimage to a sacred place. Like Hemingway's heroes, he feels a deep need to replenish his spirit, to reattach himself to things solid and lasting. The clear sky, the strong mountains, and the cold wind all serve as a natural backdrop for the spiritual ritual of his pilgrimage. As he climbs toward the peak of a mountain, he recalls with pleasure an earlier climb with a dark girl "who knew all the flowers, and who, when I bet her she couldn't find more than thirty kinds, found more than fifty." On that day, as on this, the narrator felt a clear sense of the majesty of the mountains and the "big arch of the world we looked at," and he recalls spending two hours another time watching a hawk, "feeling myself lift magnificently when he swooped up toward me on the current up the col, and then balanced and turned above."

When he returns to his campsite by a shallow snow-water lake, he swims, naked, and as he floats in this cleansing ritual, looking up at the first stars showing above the ridge, he sings out "an operatic sounding something." At this point, just when his spiritual rejuvenation is nearly complete, the ritual is broken by the appearance of Tom Williams, one of the two men whom he had accompanied on this trip to the mountains. The plan had been for Williams and the other man, Chet McKenny, to spend a few days hunting, leaving the narrator alone. As he watches Williams approach, the narrator unhappily expects to see McKenny also, a man he dislikes not because of his stupidity but because of something deeper than that. Williams, however, is alone.

After a while Williams tells the narrator of the experience he has just had with McKenny, whom he calls a "first-rate bastard." During their hunt McKenny had purposely shot a deer in the leg so that he could herd it back to their camp rather than carry it. When they arrived at the camp, he slit the deer's throat, saying, "I never take more than one shot." Sickened by this brutal act, Williams drove off in his car, leaving McKenny to get out of the mountains as best he could. After Williams's story, both men agree that McKenny deserves to be left behind for what he did. In another cleansing ritual, they both take a swim, becoming cheerful later as they sit by their fire drinking beer. The next morning, however, it is snowing, and as they silently head back down the mountain, the narrator feels that there is "something listening behind each tree and rock we passed, and something waiting among the taller trees down slope, blue through the falling snow. They wouldn't stop us, but they didn't like us either. The snow was their ally."

Thus there are two contrasting moods in "The Buck in the Hills": that of harmony and that of dissonance. At the beginning of the story, the narrator has succeeded after five years in reestablishing a right relationship with nature and thus with himself, but at the end, this relationship has been destroyed by the cruel actions of McKenny. The narrator's ritual of acceptance of the primordial in human beings has been overshadowed by McKenny's ritual of acceptance that human beings are somehow above nature. Ernest Hemingway's belief that morality is what one feels good after is in one sense reversed here to the idea that immorality is what one feels bad after; certainly the narrator and Williams, on their way down the mountain, feel bad. Human beings and nature in a right relationship is not a mere romantic notion to Clark. It is reality—indeed, perhaps humankinds only reality.

"The Portable Phonograph" • In "The Portable Phonograph" Clark ventures, if not into science fiction, at least into a kind of speculative fiction as he sets his story in a world of the future, one marked by the "toothed impress of great tanks" and the "scars of gigantic bombs." It seems a world devoid of human existence; the only visible life is a flock of wild geese flying south to escape the cold of winter. Above the frozen creek in a cave dug into the bank, however, there is human life: four men—survivors of some undescribed Armageddon—huddle before a

Library of Congress

smoldering peat fire in an image of primitive existence. Clark provides little background of these four almost grotesque men. One, the reader learns, is a doctor, probably of philosophy rather than of medicine. One is a young musician, quite ill with a cough. The other two are middle-aged. All are obviously intelligent. The cave belongs to the doctor, whose name is Jenkins, and he has invited the others to hear him read from one of his four books—the Bible, *Moby Dick*, *The Divine Comedy*, and the works of William Shakespeare. In selfish satisfaction he explains that when he saw what was happening to the world, "I told myself, 'It is the end. I cannot take much; I will take these.'" His justification is his love for the books and his belief that they represent the "soul of what was good in us here."

When Jenkins finishes his reading from *The Tempest*, the others wait expectantly, and the former finally says grudgingly, "You wish to hear the phonograph." This is obviously the moment for which they have been waiting. Jenkins tenderly and almost lovingly brings out his portable phonograph and places it on the dirt-packed floor where the firelight will fall on it. He comments that he has been using thorns as needles, but that in deference to the musician, he will use one of the three steel needles that he has left. Since Jenkins will play only one record a week, there is some discussion as to what they will hear. The musician selects a Claude Debussy nocturne, and as Jenkins places the record on the phonograph, the others all rise to their knees "in an attitude of worship."

As the piercing and singularly sweet sounds of the nocturne flood the cave, the men are captivated. In all but the musician there occur "sequences of tragically heightened recollection"; the musician, clenching the fingers of one hand over his teeth, hears only the music. At the conclusion of the piece, the three guests leave—the musician by himself, the other two together. Jenkins peers anxiously after them, waiting. When he hears the cough of the musician some distance off, he drops his canvas door and hurries to hide his phonograph in a deep hole in the cave wall. Sealing up the hole, he prays and then gets under the covers of his grass bed, feeling with his hand the "comfortable piece of lead pipe."

Structurally a very simple story, "The Portable Phonograph" is rich in its implications. In a devastated world four men represent what Jenkins refers to as "the doddering remnant of a race of mechanical fools." The books that he has saved symbolize the beauty of humanity's artistic creativity as opposed to the destructiveness of its mechanical creativity. Again, Clark portrays two sides of human nature, that which aspires to the heights of human spiritual and moral vision and that which drives humankind on to its own destruction. The cruel and bitter irony is that essentially humankind imagination is at once its glory and its undoing. As the men kneel in expectation before the mechanical wonder of the phonograph, they worship it as a symbol of human ingenuity. The music that comes from the record provides for at least three of the men a temporary escape from their grim reality. Thus, humanity's drive for mechanical accomplishment—the same drive that has destroyed a world—now has also preserved the beauty of its musical accomplishment. This may well be what the musician understands as he lets his head "fall back in agony" while listening to the music. Human beings are forever blessed to create and doomed to destroy. That is why the piece of lead pipe is such a protective comfort to Jenkins as he closes "his smoke-smarting eyes." In order to protect what is left of art, he must rely on the very methods that have brought about its demise.

"The Indian Well" • In his excellent novel *The Track of the Cat*, Clark takes the reader into the realm of human unconscious as Curt Bridges, the protagonist, is driven to his own death while tracking both a real and an imagined cougar. In the short story "The Indian Well," set in the desert in 1940, Jim Suttler also seeks to kill a cougar, and although the mythological and psychological implications are not developed as fully as they are in the novel, the story is still powerful in its total effect. In what must be one of the best word pictures of the desert and the creatures that inhabit it, Clark devotes a half-dozen pages to the stark drama of life and death that takes place around a desert well; rattlesnakes, road runners, jackrabbits, hawks, lizards, coyotes, and a cow and her calf all play parts.

The story's only character is Jim Suttler, a grizzled old prospector who, with his mule Jenny, still seeks gold in abandoned and long-forgotten mines. Suttler is a man well-attuned to life in the desert wilderness. Armed with a rifle, an old six-shooter, and primitive mining tools, he is not merely a stereotyped prospector; his red beard and shoulder-length red hair might lead some to see in him a resemblance to Christ, but Suttler is unlike Christ in several ways. Early in the story, Suttler and Jenny arrive at Indian Well. The history of Indian Well is recorded on the walls of the rundown cabin nearby; names and dates go back to the previous century. All had used the well, and all had given vent to some expression, ranging from "God guide us" to "Giv it back to the injuns" to a more familiar libel: "Fifty miles from water, a hundred miles from wood, a million miles from God, and three feet from hell." Before Suttler leaves, he too will leave a message.

Finding some traces of gold in an abandoned mine near the well, Suttler decides to stay for a while to see if he can make it pay off. It is a comfortable time, and both he and Jenny regain some of the weight lost during their recent travels. Two events, however, change the idyllic mood of their stay. The first occurs when Suttler kills a range calf that, along with its mother, has strayed close to the well. Although he has some qualms about killing the calf, Suttler, enjoying the sensation of Providence, soon puts them out of his mind. Next, a cougar kills Jenny. This event inflames Suttler with the desire for revenge—even if "it takes a year"—so throughout the winter he sits up nights waiting for the cat to return. When he eventually kills it, he skins it and, uncovering Jenny's grave, places the skin over her carcass. His revenge complete, he cleanses himself at the well and leaves as a "starved but revived and volatile spirit." Thus, one more passerby has contributed to the history of Indian Well, and the life around the well goes on.

The basic element in "The Indian Well" is the ironic contrast between the beginning and the ending of the story, just as it is in "The Buck in the Hills." When they come upon Indian Well, Suttler and Jenny enter into a natural world that has its own ordered life and death, and they blend easily into it. Suttler appears to be a man at one with nature, yet at the end of the story, the death that he has inflicted upon the cougar stands as something apart from the ordered world of the well. It is a death that was motivated by the desire for revenge, a very human emotion. The reader might be suspicious when Suttler kills the calf, but he justifies such a killing on the basis of the meat that the calf provides. Killing the cougar, on the other hand, cannot be justified in any external way. The deep satisfaction that it brings to Suttler stands in opposition to any right relationship between human beings and nature; it is solely a part of Suttler's inner self. When the deed is done, Suttler can blend back into the natural world around him. For that one winter, however, as he lies in wait for the cougar, he exhibits humankind's all-too-common flaw of putting itself above the natural world. Still, because he knows what he has done and, moreover, accepts it, he is able once more to establish his relationship with the cosmic forces.

"Hook" • In a very real sense, this establishing of a relationship with the cosmic forces is the goal of many of Clark's characters. Caught in the ambiguities of good and evil, of morality and immorality, they struggle to maintain a faith in humanity and to bring moral law into accordance with natural law, for only in that way can human beings be saved from their own destructive tendencies. Some critics, such as Chester Eisinger, see Clark as being rather pessimistic regarding the success of such a human attempt at unity and attribute to him a desire to retreat from other human beings. If this view is correct, then perhaps the story "Hook" is the best expression of what Clark wants to say. The main character in this story is a hawk which fulfills itself in flight, in battle, and in sex, until it is killed by a dog. The hawk's life is a cycle of instinct, and it can easily enough be seen as an antihuman symbol. If Eisinger's view is wrong however, then it is possible to see Clark as a writer who seeks not a retreat from other human beings but an explanation of humanity. For, like the hawks that appear so often in Clark's stories, human beings are also a part of nature and because he is, it is possible to see his task as one of defining himself in the context of the natural order of things. Whatever the outcome, Clark's characters do make the attempt.

Wilton Eckley
With updates by Thomas L. Erskine

Other major works

NOVELS: *The Ox-Bow Incident,* 1940; *The City of Trembling Leaves,* 1945; *The Track of the Cat,* 1949; *Tim Hazard,* 1951.

NONFICTION: *The Journals of Alfred Doten, 1849-1903,* 1973 (3 volumes).
POETRY: *Ten Women in Gale's House and Shorter Poems,* 1932.

Bibliography

Court, Franklin E. "Clark's 'The Wind and the Snow of Winter' and Celtic Oisin." *Studies in Short Fiction* 33 (Spring, 1996): 219-228. Examines the mythic pattern of Clark's most famous story against the background of the Celtic legend of wandering Oisin.

Eisinger, Chester E. *Fiction of the Forties.* Chicago: University of Chicago Press, 1963. Eisinger regards Clark's short stories as similar in theme (search for identity, desire to merge with nature, and rejection by nature) to the novels. Although several short stories are mentioned in passing, Eisinger includes lengthy analyses of "The Buck in the Hills," "Hook," and "The Watchful Gods."

Kich, Martin. *Western American Novelists.* Vol. 1. New York: Garland, 1995. After a brief account of Clark's career, Kich provides an extensive, annotated bibliography, providing detailed commentary on reviews of virtually every significant prose fiction. Kich also annotates reference works with entries on Clark and books with chapters on his fiction.

Laird, Charlton, ed. *Walter Van Tilburg Clark: Critiques.* Reno: University of Nevada Press, 1983. Collection of eighteen pieces, some by Clark himself, on Clark's life, his major published work, and his literary craftsmanship. The book is most valuable for the essays on "The Watchful Gods" and "The Pretender," essays that portray Clark as a reviser/craftsman, and for the autobiographical information and the detailed chronology provided by his son.

Lee, L. L. *Walter Van Tilburg Clark.* Boise, Ida.: Boise State College Press, 1973. Lee devotes a separate chapter to the short stories, which he believes repeat the themes of the novels but with greater clarity and insight. "The Portable Phonograph" and "The Watchful Gods" are discussed in some detail. Supplemented by a helpful bibliography.

May, Charles E., ed. *Masterplots II: Short Story Series, Revised Edition.* 8 vols. Pasadena, Calif.: Salem Press, 2004. Designed for student use, this reference set contains articles providing detailed plot summaries and analyses of these three short stories by Clark: "Hook" (vol. 3), "The Portable Phonograph" (vol. 6), and "The Wind and the Snow of Winter" (vol. 8).

Ronald, Ann. "Walter Van Tilburg Clark's Brave Bird, 'Hook.'" *Studies in Short Fiction* 25 (Fall, 1988): 433-439. Discusses the complex irony of the story, arguing that critics have wrongfully ignored it as a simple fable or animal tale for children.

Westbrook, Max. *Walter Van Tilburg Clark.* New York: Twayne, 1969. Westbrook's book remains the best overall assessment of Clark's literary work; in addition to a chronology of Clark's life, a biographical chapter, and a select bibliography, Westbrook includes a chapter on Clark's novella, *The Watchful Gods, and Other Stories,* and several paragraph-length discussions of Clark's best short stories.

_____. "Walter Van Tilburg Clark and the American Dream." In *A Literary History of the American West,* edited by J. Golden Taylor. Fort Worth: Texas Christian University Press, 1987. Westbrook blends biography with criticism as he analyzes Clark's fiction and defines Clark's place in literary history. Using characters from stories and novels, Westbrook depicts the Clark "hero" as an idealistic dreamer incapable of practical action. As a result, the American dream, or its nightmarish counterpart, becomes a real concern for Clark.

Arthur C. Clarke

Born: Minehead, Somerset, England; December 16, 1917

Principal short fiction • *Expedition to Earth*, 1953; *Reach for Tomorrow*, 1956; *Tales from the White Hart*, 1957; *The Other Side of the Sky*, 1958; *Tales of Ten Worlds*, 1962; *The Nine Billion Names of God*, 1967; *Of Time and Stars: The Worlds of Arthur C. Clarke*, 1972; *The Wind from the Sun*, 1972; *The Best of Arthur C. Clarke, 1937-1971*, 1973; *The Sentinel: Masterworks of Science Fiction and Fantasy*, 1983; *Dilemmas: The Secret*, 1989; *Tales from Planet Earth*, 1989; *More than One Universe: The Collected Stories of Arthur C. Clarke*, 1991; *The Collected Stories of Arthur C. Clarke*, 2000.

Other literary forms • Arthur C. Clarke is best known for novels that chronicle near-future space and sea exploration or suggest transcendence of human form and limitations. He published an autobiographical novel based on his experience with radar in World War II, and he adapted several of his stories for film: *2001: A Space Odyssey* (1968) for Stanley Kubrick, *2010: Odyssey Two* (1982), and *Cradle* (1988). In 1997, he published *3001: The Final Odyssey*. Among his most important and best-known novels are *Against the Fall of Night*, 1953 (revised as *The City and the Stars*, 1956), *Childhood's End* (1953), *Rendezvous with Rama* (1973), *Imperial Earth* (1975), and *The Fountains of Paradise* (1979). Since the early 1990's, he has written most of his novels in collaboration with other authors, most notably Gentry Lee and Stephen Baxter. These later novels include *The Garden of Rama* (1991), *The Light of Other Days* (2000), *Time's Eye* (2004), and *Sunstorm* (2005).

Throughout his career, Clarke contributed numerous articles on science and speculation, edited various scientific and science-fiction magazines, and wrote more than twenty books of nonfiction, including *By Space Possessed* (1993) and *The Snows of Olympus: A Garden of Mars* (1994). In 2003, Clarke published *From Narnia to a Space Odyssey: The War of Ideas Between Arthur C. Clarke and C. S. Lewis*. Clarke recorded some of his fictional works, lectured widely on science, the sea, and futuristic technology, and authored a television series, *Arthur C. Clarke's World of Strange Powers*. His writing has appeared in popular magazines under the pseudonyms E. G. O'Brien and Charles Willis.

Achievements • Arthur C. Clarke has received numerous awards. The most representative include Hugo Awards for science fiction in 1956, 1974, and 1980; UNESCO's Kalinga Prize in 1961, for science writing; the Stuart Ballantine Gold Medal in 1963, for originating the concept of communications satellites; an Academy Award nomination in 1969 for best screenplay; Nebula Awards for science fiction in 1972, 1973, and 1980; a GALAXY Award for science fiction in 1979; and the Centennial Medal in 1984, for scientific achievements. Other distinguished honors include the prestigious Grand Master Award from the Science Fiction Writers of America in 1986, the Charles A. Lindbergh Award in 1987, and his election to the Society of Satellite Professions Hall of Fame in 1987 and to the Aerospace Hall of Fame in 1988. In 1989 Clarke became a Commander of the British Empire, and he received a knighthood for "services to literature" in 1998.

© *Washington Post,* reprinted by permission of the D.C. Public Library

Biography • Reared in the country, Arthur Charles Clarke worked as a government auditor (1936-1941) in London, where he became active in the British Interplanetary Society (eventually becoming chairman, 1946-1947, 1950-1952). A Royal Air Force instructor in the infant technology of radar during World War II, he published the first speculations on "stationary" communications satellites in 1945. After earning his bachelor's degree in physics and mathematics at King's College, London (1948), he became assistant editor of *Science Abstracts* (1949-1951) before turning to full-time writing. Introduced in 1953 to scuba diving, he moved to what was then Ceylon in 1956 and remained there for many years. Clarke married Marilyn Mayfield in 1954, but they were divorced in 1964.

Clarke has more than five hundred works attributed to him. He is known as one of the most influential writers in the science-fiction field, as well as a visionary seer on scientific speculation. Clarke was the first, for example, to propose the idea of communications satellites, in his article "Extraterrestrial Relays" in 1945. He is a mathematician and physicist as well as a novelist and commentator. His talent for peering into the future has involved him in advising governments on communication and on the human use of space. Clarke popularized his belief in the total exploration of space and the sea. He became chancellor of the University of Moratuwa in Sri Lanka and was founder of the Arthur C. Clarke Center for Advanced Technology.

Analysis • Exposed in his childhood to both the pulp magazines of Hugo Gernsback and the English literary tradition of fantasy and science fiction, Arthur C. Clarke sometimes forges an uneasy alliance between the two in his own stories. The matter-of-fact description of the marvelous of H. G. Wells, the poetic evocation of unknown places of Lord Dunsany, and the immense vistas of space and time of the philosopher Olaf Stapledon lie cheek-by-jowl with artificial suspense devices, awkward sentimentality, schoolboy silliness, and melodramatic manipulation of such hoary motifs as the "stranded astronaut" or the "end of the world" in his less distinguished fiction. At its best, however, Clarke's work shows glimpses of humanity's rise to interplanetary civilization or evokes the wonder, in suitably subdued tones, of confrontations with extraterrestrial intelligences.

Clarke's 1967 collection of his "favorites" represents many facets of his career, from the raconteur of tall tales and ghost stories to the fantasist, the sentimentalist, the realist, and the poet of wonder. Most of his best and best-known stories are included, from the haunting rite of passage of a young lunar exile getting his first glimpse of the unapproachably radioactive world of his ancestors ("'If I Forget Thee, Oh Earth . . . ,'") to such "alien fables" of technological complacency as "Superiority" and "Before Eden."

"Rescue Party" • Among them, "Rescue Party," his second professionally published story, looks forward to other tales of human progress and alien contact, but it is unusual in its strong story line and alien viewpoint. Although it makes one of his rare claims for human superiority, a fetish of *Astounding Science Fiction* editor John W. Campbell, Jr., the story's humor, style, and forecasts are vintage Clarke.

"Who was to blame?," it opens, setting the context of a paternalistic "Galactic Federation," sending a ship to rescue a few hundred survivors from Earth before its sun turns into a nova. With a million years between visits, the federation had been taken by surprise by humankind's rise to civilization in two-fifths of that time, signaled by radio waves detected two hundred light years away. With little more than four hours to go, the ship arrives at a deserted planet, sends out two search parties, and barely escapes the cataclysm, burning out its "main generators" in the effort. Directing its course to the receiving point of a communications array on Earth, the mile-long spaceship, now needing rescue itself, approaches rendezvous with an unexpected fleet of ships from the planet. Unprecedented in size, this fleet of "primitive" rockets demonstrates an acceleration of human technological development so astonishing that the captain, the tentacled Alveron, whose ancient people are "Lords of the Universe," teasingly suggests the vast federation beware of these upstarts. This "little joke" is followed by the narrator's quiet punch line: "Twenty years afterward, the remark didn't seem funny."

Humor of situation is evident throughout the story, from the concept of "administering" a galaxy to the discovery of the humans' "handicap" of bipedalism from an abandoned portrait of a city alderman. The incongruity of the rescuers' need for rescue is mirrored by the precision that allows the aliens an unflappable split-second escape but brings them there in the first place too late and with too little to do anything useful, then finds them baffled by relatively primitive communications devices and an automatic subway. Although the story creaks in places—contemporary theory says the sun cannot become a nova, vacuum tubes are outmoded, helicopters never did become the wave of the future—those details can be sacrificed for the sake of the fable. The primary forecasts of space travel and posturban civilization should not be discounted, at the risk of being as naïve and complacent as the aliens, without even their limited security in their own superiority.

More commonly, Clarke sees alien technology as older and better than humans', as in two stories in which *2001: A Space Odyssey* is rooted. In "Encounter at Dawn," ancient astronauts "in the last days of the Empire" give tools to primitives a hundred thousand years before Babylon.

"The Sentinel" • Even more understated, "The Sentinel" is allegedly told by an eyewitness who begins by directing the reader to locate on the Moon the Mare Crisium (Sea of Crises), where the discovery took place. Part of a large 1996 expedition, he recalls fixing breakfast when a glint of light in the mountains caught his eye; staring through a telescope so fascinated him that he burned the sausages. From such homey touches, he led the climb to "Wilson's Folly," a plateau artificially leveled for a twelve-foot crystal pyramid "machine." Its force field gave way, after twenty years of frustrated investigation, to an atomic assault which reduced the mystery to fragments. The rest of the story is speculation, successive stages of Wilson's inferences.

Not a relic of lunar civilization, the artifact, half the age of Earth, was left by visitors: Wilson imagines it saying "I'm a stranger here myself." After its destruction, he "guesses" it must have been a beacon; interrupting its signal has triggered a "fire alarm." Lacking explicit alien intent, the pyramid emblemizes the unknown. Although such a potentially multivalent symbol invites other interpretations, Wilson's is supported by *2001*, in which a *rectangular slab under* the lunar surface signals *after* being exposed to sunlight. The final savage attack on the pyramid also seems significant to the narrator, although the pyramid might have been programmed to self-destruct.

The quasi-religious awe, tinged with fear as well as positive expectation, with which Wilson awaits the aliens' return has echoes elsewhere in Clarke. This story, moreover, with its judgment of space travel as a first step toward an incalculable destiny, many readers see as an article of faith in a grand design of a creator god. Such a pattern may lie beneath some of his work, but Clarke has also taken pains to discourage conventional religious interpretations.

"The Nine Billion Names of God" • Clarke's work is dotted with attacks on religious or "mystical" belief and behavior, with one exception: the Scottish-born head of worldwide Buddhism in *The Deep Range* (1957), whose opposition to butchering whales is based partly on the conviction that aliens may judge humankind on its behavior toward its fellow creatures. Certainly the surprise ending of "The Nine Billion Names of God" is no proof of Clarke's sharing the faith of his Tibetan lamas. Although the story attacks the complacency of Western computer technicians whose efficiency speeds up the counting of all of God's names, the ending ("Overhead, without any fuss, the stars were going out") is that of a joke or a ghost story.

"The Star" • Rather than simply trivializing God, Clarke's award-winning short story "The Star" makes God destructive and merciless. A Jesuit astrophysicist, slightly defensive about being both a cleric and a scientist, the narrator is at the point of quiet desperation. Beginning "It is three thousand light-years to the Vatican," he finds no solace in the crucifix near his computer or the engraving of Loyola, whose order is not all that will end when an expedition makes public its findings.

In a retrospective narration that distances the action, the narrator recounts a ship's approach to the inappropriately named "Phoenix" Nebula, the debris of a supernova that destroyed an interplanetary civilization. Different from Wells's story of the same name, this cataclysm did not spare a people and let them find a sense of community. From their remains in a vault on the star's most distant planet, the crew finds evidence that this "disturbingly human" civilization was at its peak when it died. The narrator's colleagues see no room in nature for God's wrath or mercy, and the narrator denies his own right to judge God. He is troubled, however, by the date of the disruption; given its direction and distance, this must have been the "Star of Bethlehem," hanging low in the East before sunrise. Explicitly rejecting keeping the information secret or tampering with the data, he is troubled in his faith because he cannot refuse (or refute) the findings of science.

A masterpiece of compression, poetic in style, somber in tone, and totally devoid of action and dialogue (not even the two lines of "The Sentinel"), "The Star" does not even state its conclusion. The narrator must either conclude that his colleagues are right or accept a God who would destroy this culture to impress a few humans.

"A Meeting with Medusa" • Considerably at variance with these and most of Clarke's short fiction is "A Meeting with Medusa." Appearing four years after his retrospective collection, it is one of his longest stories not given book length, and a sharp improvement over most of his work in the 1960's. Allusive and subtly patterned, both a character study and a tale of adventure, it continues Clarke's interest in "first contact" and alien landscapes, but it also fictionalizes J. D. Bernal's suggestion in *The World, the Flesh, and the Devil* (1929) that space exploration is the proper province of a human mind in a posthuman body.

All but destroyed when a mismanaged robot camera platform sent his dirigible, the *Queen Elizabeth IV*, down in flames, Howard Falcon is restored to life as a cyborg, the physical form of which is not revealed until the last of eight chapters. Seven years later, stronger and more durable, he argues successfully to be sent on an expedition into the atmosphere of Jupiter. After an additional three years, the actual adventure takes place.

Almost a part of the "raft," *Kon-Tiki*, supported by a hot hydrogen balloon (with emergency ram-jet and rocket motors), the wingless Falcon is nevertheless at a disadvantage when it comes to making contact with native life forms. Expecting at most a kind of plankton, he comes upon creatures whose nearest Earth analogues, in miniature, are varieties of sea life. Manta rays a hundred yards across seem docile browsers of floating wax mountains until their natural enemies appear. Radio-sensitive jellyfish over a mile wide, they repel attacking mantas with electrical discharges that also function for communications. A dirigible pilot once again, Falcon has neither their maneuverability nor their familiarity with local conditions.

Wryly amused at his ambassadorial role, he is understandably reluctant to obey the "Prime Directive" requiring him to avoid attacking intelligent creatures, at the cost of his own life if need be. When tentacles descend around the *Kon-Tiki*, he descends still lower; when the "Medusa" begins to "pat" his craft tentatively with a single tentacle, he cuts loose with his auxiliary engines. The Great Red Spot, blizzards of wax, atmospheric maelstroms, and various other features of the "world of the gods" can wait until another time.

A hero who has reignited humankind's imagination, Falcon is slipping away from identity with the human race, one now discovers, along with the reader's first glimpse of his undercarriage, hydraulic lifts, balloon tires, and seven foot height, if not of his "leathery mask" (now seen in a different light). Like the panicky "superchimp" on the *Queen Elizabeth* whose face he used to see in dreams, he is "between two worlds," the biological and the mechanical. He represents at its extreme the "cosmic loneliness" of Clarke's heroes.

Falcon is at the center of the story, although the predominant interest may be more in what he sees than in what he does. Jupiter is the "hero," at least of the middle sections of the story, in which Clarke combines his undersea experience and astrophysical theory to draw plausible inferences about an unlikely place for "life as we know it." Although he is not an adequate "ambassador" to the Jovians—who could be?—because he is not quite human, Falcon is the best possible explorer. A "new breed," he is for some purposes "more than human," although one's bias toward the "handicap" of bipedalism may blind one to it. He is also one more piece of evidence that the "transcendence" of human limitations widespread in Clarke's fiction may be at best a mixed blessing. Suspenseful yet satiric, adventuresome yet calmly paced, "A Meeting with Medusa," in its poetic evocation of first contact and its sophisticated variations on transcendence and the "stranded astronaut," is a culmination of the shorter fiction that came before it.

"The Hammer of God" • Several years elapsed before Clarke agreed to write another short story, "The Hammer of God," for *Time* magazine's special issue *Beyond the Year 2000*, published in the fall of 1992. In this tale, Clarke wryly combines paradoxes to shape his whimsical yet ironic version of efforts to deflect an asteroid's possible collision with Earth.

Clarke combines extreme religious polarities; ancient mythological deities; futuristic technological, political, and economic achievements; and a cast characterized by their opposing actions and reactions: an eccentric politician, a sentimental captain, a very logical computer, an asteroid, and religious saboteurs. Facts about two previous asteroids serve to punctuate and divide the story into three parts. The first cataclysm sixty-five million years ago brought destruction to dinosaurs, plants, and other animals. In contrast, the second, in 1972, cut through Earth's atmosphere for two minutes, causing no damage. The third asteroid enters the solar system in 2212. Named Kali after the Hindu goddess of death and destruction, this traveler is the menace facing Captain Robert Singh, commander of the ship *Goliath*; his central computer, David; and his one-hundred-person team, Operation *ATLAS*. The captain's team wants to move a small chunk of the asteroid into a new path away from Earth.

Clarke envisions sophisticated technological and scientific advances. A neural-input cap, the "portable Brainman," fitting directly over a bald skull, allows the century-old Captain Singh to relive an experience from twenty years ago with his young son, Toby. The oil age ends with the advent of successful cold fusion. With lens-corrective laser shaping, eyeglasses are abolished, choices of skin coloring allow individuals to vary skin color as frequently as they change clothing, and scientific data from a radio beacon/measuring rod anchored within Kali supply David with facts to report on what the actual probability of impact would be.

Logical thinking is not characteristic for the captain of the *Goliath*. He focuses on whether his future friendships will be on Mars or the moon and speculates about how he can arrange that all the many decades of his life will be on Mars. His mind is not on ship business. Conversely, David's logical thoughts provide an alternative solution to the loss of hydrogen the ship experiences. With the remainder of the ship's own propellant, originally reserved to rendezvous with *Titan*, *Goliath* itself can push Kali into a new course that will bypass Earth. Unfortunately, no one explores Kali further before accepting David's maneuver.

This asteroid has a fatal hidden feature, a weak outer crust. When *Goliath* pushes with all its force against Kali, it breaks through this crust and is stuck. Despite all attempts to reverse and pull free, the effort is useless. Using the remainder of its fuel, the ship makes one final push on Kali, strong enough to slightly alter the asteroid's path and to permanently lock them into the asteroid's surface. Contrary to the ancient Hindu goddess Kali's almost endless blood sacrifices, this Kali's destructive sacrifices as she cuts through Earth's atmosphere for two minutes are trivial—only the ship's crew, ten thousand lives, and one trillion dollars in damages. With skilled understatement, numerous paradoxes, and wry humor, Clarke again demonstrates in "The Hammer of God" his ability to craft an entertaining tale about Earth's potential collision with a stray asteroid from outer space. As a poet of the infinite, whose fables judge humanity from an "alien" point of view, Clarke stands alone.

David N. Samuelson
With updates by Terry Theodore and the Editors

Other major works

CHILDREN'S LITERATURE: *Islands in the Sky*, 1952; *Dolphin Island*, 1963.

NOVELS: *Prelude to Space*, 1951; *The Sands of Mars*, 1951; *Against the Fall of Night*, 1953 (revised as *The City and the Stars*, 1956); *Childhood's End*, 1953; *Earthlight*, 1955; *The Deep Range*, 1957; *Across the Sea of Stars*, 1959; *A Fall of Moondust*, 1961; *From the Ocean, from the Stars*, 1962; *Glide Path*, 1963; *Prelude to Mars*, 1965; *"The Lion of Comarre," and "Against the Fall of Night,"* 1968; *2001: A Space Odyssey*, 1968; *Rendezvous with Rama*, 1973; *Imperial Earth*, 1975; *The Fountains of Paradise*, 1979; *2010: Odyssey Two*, 1982; *The Songs of Distant Earth*, 1986; *2061: Odyssey Three*, 1987; *Cradle*, 1988 (with Gentry Lee); *Rama II*, 1989 (with Lee); *Beyond the Fall of Night*, 1990 (with Gregory Benford); *The Ghost from the Grand Banks*, 1990; *The Garden of Rama*, 1991 (with Lee); *Rama Revealed*, 1993 (with Lee); *The Hammer of God*, 1993; *Richter 10*, 1996 (with Mike McQuay); *3001: The Final Odyssey*, 1997; *The Trigger*, 1999 (with Michael Kube-McDowell); *The Light of Other Days*, 2000 (with Stephen Baxter); *Time's Eye*, 2004 (with Baxter); *Sunstorm*, 2005 (with Baxter).

NONFICTION: *Interplanetary Flight*, 1950; *The Exploration of Space*, 1951 (revised, 1959); *Going into Space*, 1954; *The Exploration of the Moon*, 1954; *The Coast of Coral*, 1956; *The Making of a Moon*, 1957; *The Reefs of Taprobane*, 1957; *Voice Across the Sea*, 1958; *The Challenge of the Spaceship*, 1959; *The Challenge of the Sea*, 1960; *The First Five Fathoms*, 1960; *Indian Ocean Adventure*, 1961 (with Mike Wilson); *Profiles of the Future*, 1962; *Indian Ocean Treasure*, 1964 (with Wilson); *Man and Space*, 1964 (with others); *The Treasure of the Great Reef*, 1964; *Voices from the Sky*, 1965; *The Promise of Space*, 1968; *First on the Moon*, 1970 (with others); *Into Space*, 1971 (with Robert Silverberg); *Beyond Jupiter*, 1972 (with Chesley Bonestall); *Report on Planet Three*, 1972; *The Lost Worlds of 2001*, 1972; *The View from Serendip*, 1977 (autobiographical); *1984: Spring, a Choice of Futures*, 1984; *The Odyssey File*, 1985 (with Peter Hyams); *Arthur C. Clarke's July 20, 2019: Life in the Twenty-first Century*, 1986; *Astounding Days: A Science Fictional Autobiography*, 1989; *How the World Was One: Beyond the Global Village*, 1992; *By Space Possessed*, 1993; *The Snows of Olympus: A Garden on Mars*, 1994; *Greetings, Carbon-Based Bipeds! Collected Essays, 1934-1998*, 1999; *From Narnia to a Space Odyssey: The War of Ideas Between Arthur C. Clarke and C. S. Lewis*, 2003 (Ryder W. Miller, editor).

POETRY: *The Fantastic Muse*, 1992.

Bibliography

Clarke, Arthur C. *Astounding Days: A Science-Fictional Autobiography*. New York: Bantam Books, 1989. Although this volume is not really an autobiography, Clarke offers a brief memoir of his youth. He explains how writers and editors of *Astounding* magazine (later named *Analog*) first aroused his interest in science fiction and discusses his work on rocketry and radar.

_____. "An Odyssey of Sorts." Interview by Frederick V. Guterl. *Discover* 18 (May, 1997): 68-69. In this interview, Clarke discusses, among other subjects, the cold-fusion energy revolution and the evidence for life on Mars.

Dauer, Susan Jaye "The Star." In *Masterplots II: Short Story Series*, edited by Charles E. May. Rev. ed. Vol. 7. Pasadena, Calif.: Salem Press, 2004. Analysis of "The Star" with sections on themes and meaning and style and technique. Also includes a detailed synopsis of the story.

McAleer, Neil. *Arthur C. Clarke: The Authorized Biography*. Chicago: Contemporary Books, 1992. Definitive account of Clarke's career, written with Clarke's cooperation.

Meisenheimer, Donald K., Jr. "Machining the Man: From Neurasthenia to Psychasthenia in SF and the Genre Western." *Science-Fiction Studies* 24 (November, 1997): 441-458. Argues that although Clarke works within the tradition of Wellsian science fiction, he also makes heavy use of the genre-Western established by Owen Wister and Frederic Remington.

Olander, Joseph D., and Martin Harry Greenberg, eds. *Arthur C. Clarke*. New York: Taplinger, 1977. This collection of nine essays on Clarke examines his individual works and his science-fiction writings in general. The editors state that Clarke is a hard science-fiction author whose commitment is to the universe. Provides a good source of textual criticism. Supplemented by a select bibliography and a biographical note.

Rabkin, Eric S. *Arthur C. Clarke*. San Bernardino, Calif.: Borgo Press, 1980. Good short introduction to Clarke's important science-fiction work, with brief descriptions. Robkin has high praise for Clarke and considers him one of the best in the science-fiction genre. Complemented by a bio-critical introduction, an annotated bibliography, and a chronology.

Reid, Robin Anne. *Arthur C. Clarke*. Westport, Conn.: Greenwood Press, 1997. General introduction to Clarke's life and work, with a chapter on each of his nine novels.

Slusser, George Edgar. *The Space Odysseys of Arthur C. Clarke*. San Bernardino, Calif.: Borgo Press, 1978. Brief but provocative commentary on Clarke's fiction.

Virginia, Mary E. "The Sentinel." In *Masterplots II: Short Story Series*, edited by Charles E. May. Rev. ed. Vol. 6. Pasadena, Calif.: Salem Press, 2004. Student-friendly analysis of "The Sentinel" that covers the story's themes and style and includes a detailed synopsis.

Joseph Conrad

Born: Near Berdyczów, Podolia, Poland (now Berdychiv, Ukraine);
December 3, 1857
Died: Oswalds, Bishopsbourne, England; August 3, 1924

Principal short fiction • *Tales of Unrest*, 1898; *Youth: A Narrative, and Two Other Stories*, 1902; *Typhoon, and Other Stories*, 1903; *A Set of Six*, 1908; *'Twixt Land and Sea, Tales*, 1912; *Within the Tides*, 1915; *Tales of Hearsay*, 1925; *The Sisters*, 1928; *The Complete Short Stories of Joseph Conrad*, 1933.

Other literary forms • Joseph Conrad is best known for his powerful and psychologically penetrating novels, which, like his shorter fiction, are often set in exotic locales, frequently the Far East, at sea, or a combination of the two, as with his most famous novel, *Lord Jim: A Tale* (1900). Even when using a more conventional setting, such as London in *The Secret Agent: A Simple Tale* (1907), or Geneva, Switzerland, in *Under Western Eyes* (1911), Conrad maintains a sense of otherness because his characters live in a moral shadow world of revolutionaries and adventures.

In addition to three plays based on his stories, Conrad produced three volumes of autobiographical writings, which, however, often conceal more than they explain about his varied and often dramatic personal life. Following his death, several edited collections of Conrad's correspondence were published, and these letters offer some insight into his fiction.

Achievements • Joseph Conrad is one of the outstanding writers in English literature and, because of his background and achievements, occupies a unique position. To a great degree, Conrad was the creator of the psychological story and modern spy novel. Because of his genius and insight, Conrad transformed the typical setting of the adventure romance—the mysterious Far East, the shadowy underworld of the secret agent—into an acceptable setting for the serious writer and greatly expanded the range of English literature.

Conrad avoided direct narrative, presenting his plots as a tale told by someone who either recounted the events from memory or passed along a story heard from someone else. The narrator in a Conrad story also gives events obliquely, partially revealing them, speculating on their cause and possible meaning, and then adding new and often essential information, so that the reader must participate in interpreting the unfolding story.

Conrad used this method because he believed that it accurately reflected the manner in which people understand actions in real life but also employed it because of his characters, who cannot be understood quickly, for they are not simple persons. Complicated and often contradictory figures, their actions, like their personalities, must be apprehended gradually and from different angles.

A writer who did not learn English until his twenties, Conrad brought a sense of newness and scrupulous care to the language. He uses an extensive vocabulary, particularly in his descriptive passages of settings, internal as well as external. His style produces in the reader the moral and psychological equivalent to the emotions and inner

Library of Congress

struggles felt by the characters.

These qualities of plot, character, and style were recognized by the noted American critic H. L. Mencken when he wrote about Conrad that "[t]here was something almost suggesting the vastness of a natural phenomenon. He transcended all the rules."

Biography • Joseph Conrad had one of the most unusual lives of any major writer in English literature. He was born in Berdyczów, Poland, on December 3, 1857, and was christened Jósef Teodor Konrad Natęcz Korzeniowski. His father, Apollo Korzeniowski, was a Polish intellectual and writer whose works included original verse and translations of William Shakespeare. Apollo Korzeniowski was also a fervent Polish patriot, and his activities against Russian repression (Poland was at that time part of the Russian Empire) caused his arrest and exile in 1861. Apollo Korzeniowski, along with his wife, Ewelina Bobrowska, and his young son, Jósef, was sent to Vologda, a dismal town northeast of Moscow.

The climate was severe, and living conditions were harsh. Ewelina died in April, 1865, when young Jósef was only seven years old. A few years later, after Apollo had been released from exile because of ill health, he too died, and at the age of eleven, Jósef was placed in the care of his maternal uncle, a kindly man who provided for his education and supported him with funds for many years.

Because of these memories and his own intense patriotism, Jósef found life in occupied Poland unbearable, and, when doctors recommended a seaside environment for his own frail health, he left for Marseilles, France, in October, 1874. In Marseilles, he lived on funds from his uncle and engaged in a shadowy enterprise to smuggle weapons to royalist rebels in Spain. In 1877, Jósef and some companions bought a ship for that purpose, but their plot was betrayed, and their vessel, the *Tremolino*, was deliberately run aground to avoid capture. In the spring of the following year, having lost all of his money gambling at Monte Carlo, Jósef attempted suicide. The wound was minor, and within a month he was able to sign aboard his first English ship, the *Mavis*. On April 24, 1878, Jósef Korzeniowski, soon known as Joseph Conrad, became an English sailor; he would remain one for the next seventeen years, serving on eighteen different vessels but commanding only one, the *Otago*, in 1888.

During his voyages, Conrad traveled to the settings for his stories. In 1883, he was second mate onboard the *Palestine*, which caught fire and later sank, leaving the crew to survive in open boats until they reached land. In 1890, Conrad was in the Belgian Congo as part of a trading company, but within a year he left, his health seriously weakened by malaria and his psychological and moral sense severely shaken by the ruthless, amoral exploitation of the natives by Europeans who were avid for ivory.

By this time, Conrad had concluded that his seafaring career was unsuccessful, and he had already started work, in 1889, on his first novel, *Almayer's Folly* (1895), and achieved English citizenship in 1886. In January, 1894, Conrad ended his naval career, determined to become a writer. *Almayer's Folly* gained favorable critical notice, primarily for its exotic setting and characters. Conrad's next work, *An Outcast of the Islands* (1896), seemed to mark him as a talented but perhaps limited author of exotic romances. With the appearance of *The Nigger of the "Narcissus"* (1898), however, the literary world was forced to take note of a new and strikingly original talent.

Having dedicated himself to writing, Conrad settled at Pent Farm, in Kent, with his wife, Jessie George, whom he married on March 24, 1896. The Conrads had two sons, Alfred Borys, born in 1898, and John Alexander, born in 1906.

As an author, Conrad was critically acknowledged but was not very popular for many years. Even such powerful novels as *Lord Jim: A Tale* or *Nostromo: A Tale of the Seaboard* (1904) or *Under Western Eyes*, which have since been recognized as classics, had relatively modest sales. To supplement his income, Conrad wrote shorter fiction for popular magazines; these stories were collected in eight volumes during Conrad's lifetime. In 1913 came his first truly popular work, *Chance*. Having achieved financial stability, Conrad moved in 1919 to Oswalds, near Canterbury, where he spent the remaining years of his life. He was offered, but declined, a knighthood in 1924. That same year, after long bouts of frequent bad health, he died of a heart attack on August 3. He was buried at Canterbury.

Analysis • Throughout his career, Joseph Conrad returned to a constellation of central themes that were expressed through the actions of his characters and, more important, through those characters' reactions to events around them. These themes can best be considered when they are grouped into two generally opposing categories. A sense of personal, moral heroism and honor is contrasted to betrayal and guilt. Typically, a Conradian character will discover, in the crucible of a dangerous situation, that he does or does not live up to the inner standards he has hoped to maintain. This realization may not come immediately, and often the true meanings of a character's actions are revealed only long afterward, through a retelling of his story.

The second grouping contrasts illusion with reality. Illusion is often a belief in "progress" or some grand political scheme. It is unmasked by reality, which, in Conrad, almost inevitably assumes the form and tone of pessimistic irony. Through the device of a narrator recounting the story, the truth gradually emerges, revealing the tragic difference between what characters believe themselves and the world to be, and what they actually are.

"An Outpost of Progress" • The division between these two groupings is present even in Conrad's early story "An Outpost of Progress." Like many of his fictions, it is set in the tropics, specifically a desolate ivory trading station in the isolated reaches of the Congo. Two hapless Europeans, Kayerts and Carlier, arrive at the station, filled with dreams of riches and slogans of civilization. They quickly disintegrate, their original illusions giving way to true madness. Kayerts shoots his companion, then hangs himself from a cross in the station's unkempt graveyard. The outpost of progress has been overrun by the forces of savagery.

The story is fiercely ironic. Kayerts and Carlier are caricatures, the first fat, the second thin, both incredibly stupid. "Incapable of independent thought," as Conrad describes them, they are lost without society to dictate their thoughts and actions. Although they loudly repeat the hollow slogans of progress, the two white men are obviously greatly inferior to their native helper, who watches their decay with dark satisfaction. Using simple, unsympathetic characters and a violent, even melodramatic plot, Conrad presents his themes in the starkest possible fashion.

"The Lagoon" • In the story "The Lagoon," written at almost the same time as "An Outpost of Progress," Conrad handles the conflict between betrayal and guilt, on one hand, and guilt versus honor and heroism, on the other, with more subtlety. An unnamed white man spends the night in the house of Arsat, a young Malay, who is tending his dying wife. During the long tropical night, Arsat tells his friend the story of how he and his brother had fled with the woman from their local chief. The three had been pursued and, at the moment of their escape, Arsat's brother had fallen behind and cried out for help. Arsat had not responded, however, fleeing instead to safety with his lover. Now, when she is dead, he speaks of returning for revenge.

In a moment of crisis Arsat made a decision, and for years he has suffered the moral consequences of that action. Although Conrad refrains from judging his character, Arsat clearly believes that he has failed; his only hope is to perform some heroic action, such as seeking vengeance, that will restore his earlier sense of himself as an honorable, loyal person and brother. Implicit in the story, however, is the sense that Arsat cannot undo the past and that his hopes are only illusions. This sense is reinforced powerfully by Conrad's extensive descriptions of the Malaysian jungle, which seems to overwhelm the characters, rendering them incapable of action while mocking their vain hopes.

"Youth" • "Youth," Conrad's first indisputable masterpiece among his shorter fictions, introduces his famous narrator Marlow. In the story, Marlow, forty-two when he tells his tale, recounts events that happened twenty years before when he sailed on the *Judea*, laden with a cargo of coal for Bangkok. An ill-fated ship, the *Judea* is beset by an endless, almost comical series of calamities that climaxes when the coal catches fire and explodes, leaving the crew to reach land in open boats. The events are drawn largely from Conrad's own experiences as mate on the *Palestine* in 1881.

The contrasts between heroism and cowardice, between reality and illusion run throughout the story, but Conrad blends them in a fashion that reveals that the distinctions between them are not as simple as might be supposed. As Marlow recognizes, his earlier self was full of the illusions of youth, yet it was those very illusions that sustained him and allowed him to achieve the standards by which he wished to live and act. In that sense, illusion made heroism possible. Such a situation is obviously ironic, and throughout his story Marlow comments frequently on the tangled relationship between romanticism and practicality, illusion and reality. Unlike other Conrad tales, however, "Youth" does not treat this division with pessimism but with optimism, no doubt because it is a story of youth and because Marlow, for whatever reason, did uphold his personal standards of integrity and moral courage.

Heart of Darkness • *Heart of Darkness*, perhaps Conrad's most famous work, is a novella based on his experience as mate on the riverboat *Roi des Belges* in the Congo during 1890. In this story, Conrad once again uses Marlow as his main character and narrator, and the events are a literal and symbolic journey by Marlow into that "immense heart of darkness" that is both the African jungle and the human soul. A powerful, searing work, *Heart of Darkness* is one of the first masterpieces of symbolism in English literature and Conrad's most acutely penetrating psychological study.

The story itself is relatively simple. Marlow signs on with a Belgian company that exports ivory from the Congo; employed as a mate on the company's steamboat, he sails upriver to meet the renowned Kurtz, a trader who has become legendary for the success of his efforts and the force of his character. Marlow has heard, however, that Kurtz is more than an ivory trader and that he has evolved into a powerful force of civilization and progress. When Marlow arrives at Kurtz's station, he finds instead that the man has reverted to savagery, becoming a dreaded, almost supernatural figure to the natives. The site is ringed with posts decorated with human skulls, and Kurtz's presence casts an evil shadow over the African jungle. Marlow carries the sick, delirious Kurtz back down the river, but the man dies during the journey as the riverboat narrowly escapes an ambush by the terrified and outraged natives.

The impact of *Heart of Darkness* comes from the nearly devastating effects of what Marlow sees and experiences. A naïve young man in the earlier "Youth," Marlow is still relatively innocent at the start of *Heart of Darkness*. By the end of the story, that innocence has been forever shattered, a loss shared by the attentive reader. The world of the story grows increasingly corrupted and corrupting. The adventures Marlow undergoes become stranger, and the characters whom he meets are increasingly odd, starting with the greedy traders whom Marlow ironically describes as "pilgrims," to an eccentric Russian who wanders in dress clothes through the jungle, to Kurtz himself, that figure of ultimate madness. The native Africans, whether cruelly abused workers, actually slaves, of the trading company or savages in awe of Kurtz, retain a sort of primeval dignity, but they, too, are beyond Marlow's experience and initial comprehension. The Congo of *Heart of Darkness* is a strange and terrifying world, a place where the normal order of civilized life has become not only inverted but also perverted.

To render this complex and disturbing moral vision, Conrad uses an intricate framing structure for his narrative. The story opens with Marlow and four friends talking about their experiences. One of the listeners, who is never named, in turn conveys to the reader the story told by Marlow. This story-within-a-story shuttles back and forth, as Marlow recounts part of his tale, then comments upon it, and then often makes an additional reflection upon his own observations. In a sense, by retelling the events, Marlow comes to understand them, a process that is shared by the reader. Instead of interrupting the flow of the story, Marlow's remarks become an essential part of the plot, and often the reader does not fully understand what has happened until Marlow's explanations reveal the extent and significance of the action.

Heart of Darkness gains immensely through Conrad's use of symbolism, because much of the meaning of the story is too terrifying and bleak to be expressed in plain prose; the inhumanity and savagery of the European exploiters, Kurtz in particular, are expressed more powerfully through a symbolic, rather than overt, presentation. Throughout the narrative, clusters of images occur at significant points to underscore the meaning of events as Marlow comes to understand them. Opposites are frequent: Brightness is contrasted with gloom, the lush growth of the jungle is juxtaposed to the sterility of the white traders, and the luxuriant, even alarming life of the wild is always connected with death and decomposition. Running throughout the story are images and metaphors of madness, especially the insanity caused by isolation. The dominant symbol for the entire work is found in its title and final words: All creation is a vast "heart of darkness." Since its publication, *Heart of Darkness* has been recognized as a masterpiece of English literature, and readers have responded to the work on several different levels. An attack on imperialism, a parable of moral and ethical growth and decline, a psychological study—Heart of Darkness is all these things and something more.

"Typhoon" • With the writing of "Typhoon," Conrad suspended his customary moral and psychological complexities to present a fairly straightforward sea story. The *Nan-Shan*, a vessel filled with Chinese workers returning home from Malaysia, runs headlong into a ferocious typhoon. As the crew struggles above decks to save the ship, an equally dangerous furor erupts below, as the sea's violent motions scatter the passengers' baggage, mixing their hard-earned silver coins in total confusion. The Chinese begin a desperate combat among themselves, each man intent upon regaining his own money. Captain MacWhirr and his first mate, Jukes, must battle these two storms, either of which could wreck the ship.

Captain MacWhirr and Jukes are total opposites. MacWhirr is a stolid, perhaps stupid man, so devoid of imagination that he experiences little self-doubt and few terrors. Even the looming typhoon does not frighten him, since he has never experienced such a storm and cannot comprehend its dangers. Jukes, on the other hand, is a more typical Conradian character, sensitive, anxious to prove worthy of his own inner moral code, and acutely conscious of the dangers that the sea can pose. As with so many other figures in Conrad's fictions, Jukes seems to believe in a sense that these dangers are somehow meant for him personally, as a trial of his own character. MacWhirr suffers from no such beliefs, since they are beyond his comprehension.

With the onset of the typhoon, the seeming limitations of Captain MacWhirr become strengths, while Jukes's supposedly higher qualities might, if left unchecked, paralyze him at the critical moment. Ironically, MacWhirr is Jukes's salvation. Since the Captain lacks the imagination to realize that he should be afraid, he is therefore not afraid and continues in his plodding but effective fashion. Jukes, in order to live up to his moral code, has no choice but to follow, acting more bravely and coolly than his inner doubts might otherwise allow. Together, the two men lead the crew in heroic efforts that save the *Nan-Shan*.

The only complexity that Conrad employs in "Typhoon" is in his narrative structure. The story shifts from third person to passages of letters from Captain MacWhirr, Jukes, and the ship's engineer to their families. This second layer is overlain by a third, in which the letters are read, sometimes with commentary, by the families in England. Through this method, Conrad allows the major characters to present the story as they experience and perceive it and adds a further contrast between the men who actually endure the storm and those who only read about it, and so cannot fully grasp its strength and danger.

"The Duel" • "The Duel," sometimes titled "The Duellists," is the story of two officers in Napoleon Bonaparte's army, who wage their own private war for sixteen years, while about them all Europe is plunged into a larger, much more deadly combat. Conrad was an avid student of the Napoleonic period, and he based his story on an actual rivalry. More than the story of two men, "The Duel" is Conrad's reflections upon the Napoleonic age.

The two progatonists are Feraud from Gascony in southern France—a region noted for its hot-blooded, impetuous natives—and D'Hubert, a Picard, with the reserved nature characteristic of that northern region. Through an accidental incident, the two become engaged in an affair of honor that can be settled only by a duel. Once begun, the duel is protracted to farcical lengths, extending from Paris to Moscow, from the time of Napoleon's greatest triumphs to his final defeat at Waterloo. Finally, D'Hubert falls in love and marries, finding life more worthwhile than this questionable affair of honor. In the final encounter, he emerges victorious and spares Feraud's life on the promise that the combat will now, finally, end.

The tale is briskly and even comically rendered, with Conrad's typical ironies in this case turned positive. The darker aspects of his vision are reserved for his wider view of the Napoleonic age: What might be seen as humorous when only two men are involved becomes tragic almost beyond comprehension when entire nations are the duelists. Feraud and D'Hubert fight only each other in their affair, while Napoleon engaged all the countries of Europe. At the end of that wider struggle, Conrad implies, there was no happy resolution, only the desolation that follows the exhausted silence of the battlefield. This bleaker vision, however, is not allowed to overwhelm the essentially humorous basis of the story.

The title of the work may contain a clue to one of its themes, the typical Conrad subject of the "double," the other person who is so like the hero yet somehow different. During the interminable encounters, D'Hubert comes to believe that he is linked, in some mysterious and unbreakable fashion, to Feraud. They are "secret sharers," in one sense literally so, because they cannot reveal that their duel began over a trivial misunderstanding and was prolonged out of fear of embarrassment. They are also "secret sharers" in a wider sense, because their lives have fullest meaning only when joined together. In this way, the "duellists" are indeed "dual," and their relationship is not only one of combat but also, in fact, one of union.

"Gaspar Ruiz" • "Gaspar Ruiz" was based upon actual events in the Chilean revolution against Spain of the 1830's. The title character, an immensely strong but rather simpleminded peasant, joins the army of the rebels. Captured during battle, he is forced to join the Loyalist army and is then once again made a prisoner, this time by his former comrades. Condemned as a traitor, Gaspar Ruiz escapes and is sheltered by a Loyalist family whose daughter, Erminia, he later marries. A series of misadventures leads Gaspar to become a general in the Loyalist army, although his political sense is almost nonexistent and he wishes, as much as he can comprehend the matter, to be a Chilean patriot. When Erminia and her daughter are captured by the rebels and held in a mountain fort, Gaspar has a cannon strapped to his huge back so it can batter open the gate and free them. The desperate tactic works, but Gaspar is mortally wounded, and Erminia kills herself, dying with her husband.

The story is told in typical Conrad fashion—that is, long after the events have occurred and by two different narrators. One of them is General Santierra, who, as a lieutenant in the rebel army, knew Gaspar Ruiz and is now the guardian of Gaspar's grown daughter. The second narrator, who opens the story in the third person but who is revealed, at the close, to be a guest of General Santierra, answers questions that Santierra raises. This narrator explains that revolutions are a distillation of human experience and that they bring some human beings to fame who otherwise would be resigned to oblivion. In revolutions, genuine social ideals, such as freedom or equality, may be passionately held in the abstract but are ferociously violated in actuality, just as Gaspar Ruiz, a true if bewildered patriot, was condemned and made a traitor by circumstances and false accusations. In a sense, the unnamed guest is reinforcing a constant Conrad theme, the difference between reality and illusion.

"The Secret Sharer" • Probably Conrad's most famous short story, "The Secret Sharer" is a deceptively simple tale that carries such deep, perhaps unfathomable moral and psychological undertones that since its publication readers and critics have remained puzzled and fascinated by its elusive, evocative power. In the story, a young captain, new to his first command, is startled to discover a naked man swimming by his ship's side. Once aboard, the swimmer, named Leggatt, confesses that he is fleeing from his own ship, the *Sephora*, because he murdered a fellow sailor. The act was justified, as the young captain quickly realizes, for the *Sephora* was in danger of foundering during a violent storm, and the murdered man, by failing to obey Leggatt's orders, had placed the ship and its crew in immediate danger. Now, however, Leggatt is a hunted man. The captain hides Leggatt in his own cabin, keeping him safely out of sight until he can sail his ship close enough to an island to allow Leggatt to escape.

By pledging and then keeping his word to the mysterious Leggatt, the young captain upholds his own moral code, even though it runs counter to conventional law and morality. In doing so, he proves that he is capable of living up to that "ideal conception of one's personality every man sets up for himself secretly." The fact that morality is established and maintained secretly—in this case, literally so—is a Conradian irony and a central paradox of this tale. Adding to the reader's bewilderment is the fact that the young captain's "ideal conception" is nowhere presented explicitly. The reader is able to see the captain's code in action and perhaps assess its consequences but must deduce from these tantalizing clues what must constitute the standards that the young officer so earnestly desires to uphold.

The captain's code is indeed a puzzling one, for not only does it require him to be faithful to a murderer, but also it causes him to risk his own ship. To give Leggatt the best possible chance to swim to safety, the captain steers dangerously close to shore, risking running aground or perhaps breaking up on the shoals. Naturally, he cannot tell his crew why he orders this difficult, dangerous maneuver, so another secret is layered upon those already present. When the captain is successful in his plan, for the first time he feels a sense of unity and closeness with his vessel, a mystical—and again, secret—bond.

The meanings of "The Secret Sharer" are hidden in its deceptively straightforward narrative. The work is full of ambiguity and possible double meanings, all presented in brisk, even prosaic fashion. Even the title is multiple: Since Leggatt is unknown to anyone but the captain, his presence is indeed a secret, but he and the young commander also share common secrets, both Leggatt's presence and the "ideal conception of one's personality," which seems to be their joint moral code. Since these meanings are complementary, rather than contradictory, they add to the resonance of the story.

Other touches add to the story's depth. The young captain and Leggatt are so similar that they seem to be doubles, and Conrad obviously intends this identification to be as much moral as physical. Both men feel themselves to be outcasts, Leggatt actually so, because of his crime; the captain, psychologically, because of his newness to the ship and its crew. In one sense, Leggatt can be seen as an alter ego of the narrator, perhaps even a projection of his darker, maybe criminal, side. It may even be possible, as some critics have suggested, that Leggatt does not actually exist but is only a figment of the young captain's imagination.

Such an unusual, even implausible interpretation indicates the perplexity that "The Secret Sharer" elicits in readers and underscores why this story, so famous in itself, is also emblematic of all Conrad's fiction. Under the guise of a simple sea tale, he has gathered the themes that constantly flowed through his works: the ideal sense of self that must be tested and proved under difficult situations; the conflict between loyalty and betrayal, reality and illusion; and, above all, the innate need for human beings to preserve, even in trying circumstances and against conventional pressures, a moral code whose only reward is a secret that may, perhaps, never be shared.

Michael Witkoski

Other major works

PLAYS: *One Day More: A Play in One Act*, pr. 1905; *The Secret Agent: A Drama in Four Acts*, pb. 1921; *Laughing Anne: A Play*, pb. 1923.

NOVELS: *Almayer's Folly*, 1895; *An Outcast of the Islands*, 1896; *The Children of the Sea: A Tale of the Forecastle*, 1897 (republished as *The Nigger of the "Narcissus": A Tale of the Sea*, 1898); *Heart of Darkness*, 1899 (serial), 1902 (book); *Lord Jim*, 1900; *The Inheritors*, 1901 (with Ford Madox Ford); *Romance*, 1903 (with Ford); *Nostromo*, 1904; *The Secret Agent*, 1907; *The Nature of a Crime*, 1909 (serial), 1924 (book; with Ford); *Under Western Eyes*, 1911; *Chance*, 1913; *Victory*, 1915; *The Shadow-Line*, 1917; *The Arrow of Gold*, 1919; *The Rescue*, 1920; *The Rover*, 1923; *Suspense*, 1925 (incomplete).

NONFICTION: *The Mirror of the Sea*, 1906; *Some Reminiscences*, 1912 (pb. in U.S. as *A Personal Record*); *Notes on Life and Letters*, 1921; *Joseph Conrad's Diary of His Journey Up the Valley of the Congo in 1890*, 1926; *Last Essays*, 1926; *Joseph Conrad: Life and Letters*, 1927 (Gérard Jean-Aubry, editor); *Joseph Conrad's Letters to His Wife*, 1927; *Conrad to a Friend*, 1928 (Richard Curle, editor); *Letters from Joseph Conrad, 1895-1924*, 1928 (Edward Garnett, editor); *Lettres françaises de Joseph Conrad*, 1929 (Jean-Aubry, editor); *Letters of Joseph Conrad to Marguerite Doradowska*, 1940 (John A. Gee and Paul J. Sturm, editors); *The Collected Letters of Joseph Conrad*, 1983-2005 (7 volumes; Frederick R. Karl and Laurence Davies, editors).

Bibliography

Billy, Ted. *A Wilderness of Words: Closure and Disclosure in Conrad's Short Fiction.* Lubbock: Texas Tech University Press, 1997. In this study of Conrad's linguistic skepticism, Billy emphasizes endings in Conrad's short fiction and how they either harmonize or clash with other narrative elements in nineteen of Conrad's short novels and tales. Argues that Conrad presents knowledge of the world as fundamentally illusory.

Graver, Lawrence. *Conrad's Short Fiction.* Berkeley: University of California Press, 1969. This study of Conrad's stories is grouped chronologically and displays the linkages between the shorter fictions and individual stories, and between them as a group and the novels. Since it covers the lesser-known stories as well as the more famous ones, it is essential for placing Conrad's development of themes and styles within a larger artistic context.

Karl, Frederick R. *Joseph Conrad: The Three Lives.* New York: Farrar, Straus and Giroux, 1979. This book is, and will remain, the definitive Conrad biography, elucidating as it does Conrad's life in Poland, on the seas, and in England. The well-documented study is also replete with generously thorough analyses of Conrad's major works, as well as of his artistic development and political orientation. Karl tends at times to be stiltedly (and quite needlessly) insistent upon where and how his views differ from those of other interpreters of Conrad's life and work.

_____. *A Reader's Guide to Joseph Conrad.* Rev. ed. Syracuse, N.Y.: Syracuse University Press, 1997. Good handbook for students. Provides bibliographical references and an index.

Lewis, Pericles. "'His Sympathies Were in the Right Place': *Heart of Darkness* and the Discourse of National Character." *Nineteenth-Century Literature* 53 (September, 1998): 211-244. Shows how Conrad contributed to modernist literary technique by structuring conflict between the "ethical" and the "sociological" in Marlow's decision to align himself with Kurtz over the Company.

May, Charles E., ed. *Masterplots II: Short Story Series, Revised Edition.* 8 vols. Pasadena, Calif.: Salem Press, 2004. Designed for student use, this reference set contains articles providing detailed plot summaries and analyses of these eight short stories by Conrad: "Amy Foster" (vol. 1), "Il Conde" and "The Lagoon" (vol. 4), "An Outpost of Progress" and "The Secret Sharer" (vol. 6), "The Tale" (vol. 7), and "Typhoon" and "Youth" (vol. 8).

Meyers, Jeffrey. *Joseph Conrad: A Bibliography.* New York: Charles Scribner's Sons, 1991. Briskly moving, no-nonsense biography that surveys the key points and themes of the major works. Very good at placing Conrad within the social and intellectual milieu of his day and offering good insights from other literary figures, such as Ford Madox Ford, who significantly influenced Conrad's literary career.

Najder, Zdzislaw. *Joseph Conrad: A Chronicle.* Translated by Halina Carroll-Najder. Cambridge, England: Cambridge University Press, 1983. Thorough and sympathetic biography of Conrad written by a countryman. The volume stresses the influence of Conrad's Polish heritage on his personality and art. Najder draws many telling and intriguing parallels between Conrad's life and his writing.

Orr, Leonard, and Ted Billy, eds. *A Joseph Conrad Companion.* Westport, Conn.: Greenwood Press, 1999. Good manual, complete with bibliographical references and an index.

Stape, J. H. *The Cambridge Companion to Joseph Conrad.* Cambridge, England: Cambridge University Press, 1996. In this collection of essays on most of Conrad's major work by different critics, the most helpful for a study of his short fiction are the essays "Conradian Narrative" by Jakob Lothe, which surveys Conrad's narrative techniques and conventions, and "The Short Fiction" by Gail Fraser, which discusses Conrad's experimentation with short narrative.

Swisher, Clarice, ed. *Readings on Joseph Conrad.* San Diego, Calif.: Greenhaven Press, 1998. Contains essays by J. B. Priestley, Robert Penn Warren, and Richard Adams about many of Conrad's works.

Robert Coover

Born: Charles City, Iowa; February 4, 1932

Principal short fiction • *Pricksongs and Descants*, 1969; *The Water Pourer*, 1972 (a deleted chapter from *The Origin of the Brunists*); *Charlie in the House of Rue*, 1980; *The Convention*, 1981; *In Bed One Night and Other Brief Encounters*, 1983; *Aesop's Forest*, 1986; *A Night at the Movies: Or, You Must Remember This*, 1987; *The Grand Hotels (of Joseph Cornell)*, 2002 (vignettes); *A Child Again*, 2005.

Other literary forms • Besides the above-mentioned collections of short fiction and novellas and many uncollected short stories, Robert Coover's production includes the novels *The Origin of the Brunists* (1966), *The Universal Baseball Association, Inc., J. Henry Waugh, Prop.* (1968), *The Public Burning* (1977), *Gerald's Party* (1985), *Pinocchio in Venice* (1991), *John's Wife* (1996), *Ghost Town* (1998), and *The Adventures of Lucky Pierre: Directors' Cut* (2002); a collection of plays entitled *A Theological Position* (1972), which contains *The Kid, Love Scene, Rip Awake*, and the title play; the screenplay *After Lazarus* (1980); a play, *Bridge Hound* (1981); several poems, reviews, and translations published in journals; a screenplay/novella *Hair o' the Chine*; the film *On a Confrontation in Iowa City* (1969); and theater adaptations of "The Babysitter" and *Spanking the Maid*. Coover has also published a few essays on authors he admires, such as Samuel Beckett ("The Last Quixote," in *New American Review*, 1970) and Gabriel García Márquez ("The Master's Voice," in *New American Review*, 1977).

Achievements • Robert Coover is one of the authors regularly mentioned in relation to that slippery term "postmodernism." As a result of the iconoclastic and experimental nature of his fiction, Coover's work does not enjoy a widespread audience; his reputation among academics, however, is well established, and the reviews of his works have been consistently positive. Although in the beginning of his career he had to resort to teaching in order to support his family, he soon began to gain recognition, receiving several prizes and fellowships: a William Faulkner Award for Best First Novel (1966), a Rockefeller Foundation grant (1969), two John Simon Guggenheim Memorial Foundation Fellowships (1971, 1974), an Academy of Arts and Letters award (1975), a National Book Award nomination for *The Public Burning*, a National Endowment for the Humanities Award (1985), a Rea Award (1987) for *A Night at the Movies*, a Rhode Island Governor's Arts Award (1988), and Deutscher Akademischer Austauschdienst Fellowship (1990). The publisher Alfred A. Knopf's rejection of *The Public Burning* after initial acceptance brought some fame to Coover. Since the novel deals with the trials of Ethel and Julius Rosenberg and presents former president Richard M. Nixon as its central narrator, the publisher thought it would be too controversial. Eventually, *The Public Burning* was published by Viking Press and became a Book-of-the-Month Club selection. Critical studies about Coover started in the late 1970's. Still, in spite of the critical acclaim and the considerable amount of scholarship about his work, Coover's work remains relatively unknown to the public, and some of his early novels are now out of print.

Biography • Robert Lowell Coover was born in Charles City, Iowa. His family soon moved to Indiana and then to Herrin, Illinois. His father managed the local newspaper, the *Herrin Daily Journal*, which prompted Coover's interest in journalism. His college education began at Southern Illinois University (1949-1951), but he transferred to Indiana University, where he received a bachelor's degree in Slavic studies in 1953. After graduation, Coover was drafted and joined the United States Naval Reserve.

While in Spain, he met Maria del Pilar Sans-Mallafré, who became his wife on June 13, 1959. During these years, his interest in fiction began. His first published story, "Blackdamp," was the seed of his first novel, *The Origin of the Brunists*. He received a master's degree from the University of Chicago in 1965. During the following years, Coover and his family alternated stays in Europe with periods in the United States. The several awards he received during the 1970's made him financially secure and allowed him to continue writing.

Coover has held appointments at Bard College, the University of Iowa, Columbia University, Princeton University, the Virginia Military Institute, and he has been a distinguished professor at Brown University since 1979. He has also been writer-in-residence at Wisconsin State University. In spite of a large amount of time spent abroad (in Europe and in South America) and his outspoken need to take distance from his own country, Coover's production is very "American," since he often bases his fiction on American events, persons, and national myths. Coover often manipulates historical events for artistic purposes, but he has a solid knowledge of the facts.

During the late 1980's, Coover began teaching writing on computers. With the rise of the World Wide Web in the 1990's, he made significant progress in the use of hyperfiction. Hyperfiction, also referred to as hypertext fiction, tree fiction, nonlinear fiction, or electronic fiction, is fiction written with the capabilities of hypertext. Hyperfiction is truly nonlinear since it cannot be represented on a printed page. The reader takes an active role in hyperfiction, choosing which links to click on and which paths to follow. Thus, the narrative may be very different from one reading to the next, depending on the choices made by the reader. Readers can follow different characters, or points of view, or skip back and forth between different time zones. By clicking on an interesting name, place, event, or idea, the reader can be taken to a new page connected to that name, place, event, or idea.

Coover reads, writes, and reviews hyperfiction. He teaches hyperfiction workshops at Brown University. The Hypertext Hotel is a collaborative hyperfiction that grew out of Coover's workshops. During the 1990's, students, authors, and scholars have added to the fictional hotel text. Coover developed a course at Brown that introduces students to the possibilities of hyperfiction. He also been known to encourage the use of hyperfiction and the software that makes it possible. Coover is the author of the now classic "The End of the Book," an article in which he explains hyperfiction and his general optimism that it will someday replace books.

Analysis • Robert Coover's central concern is the human being's need for fiction. Because of the complexity of human existence, people are constantly inventing patterns that give them an illusion of order in a chaotic world. For Coover, any effort to explain the world involves some kind of fiction-making process. History, religion, culture, and scientific explanations are fictional at their core; they are invented narratives through which human beings try to explain the world to themselves. The problem, Coover would say, is that people tend to forget the fictional nature of the fictional systems they create and become trapped by them, making dogmas out of the fictions. The artist's function, then, is to reexamine these fictions, tear them down, and offer new perspectives on the same material, in order to make the reader aware of the arbitrariness of the construct.

Coover's fiction often has been labeled "metafiction"—that is, fiction about fiction—and indeed most of his works are comments on previously existing fictional constructs. If in his longer works he examines the bigger metaphoric narratives such as religion, history, or politics (that one of the theorists of postmodernism, Jean-François Lyotard, has called "metanarratives"), in his shorter works Coover turns to smaller constructs, usually literary fictions.

National Archives

In the prologue to the "Seven Exemplary Fictions" contained in *Pricksongs and Descants,* Coover addresses Miguel de Cervantes as follows:

> But, don Miguel, the optimism, the innocence, the aura of possibility you experienced have been largely drained away, and the universe is closing in on us again. Like you, we, too, seem to be standing at the end of one age and on the threshold of another.

Just as Cervantes stood at the end of a tradition and managed to open a door for a new type of fiction, modern authors confront a changing world in need of new fictional forms that can reflect this world's nature better. Just as Cervantes tried to stress the difference between romance and the real world through the mishaps of Don Quixote, Coover wants to stress the fictionality and arbitrariness of some fictions that hold a tight grip on the reader's consciousness. Like Cervantes, Coover wants to free readers from an uncritical acceptance of untrue or oversimplified ideas that limit and falsify their outlook on life. Fictions, Coover and Cervantes would say, are not there to provide an escape by creating fantasies for the reader. When they do so, Coover continues writing in his prologue, the artist "must conduct the reader to the real, away from mystification to clarification, away from magic to maturity, away from mystery to revelations."

This quotation, coming from an author whose work is usually considered "difficult," might seem somehow odd. How does Coover's fiction clarify, or what does it reveal? His work often presents constantly metamorphosing worlds, which mimic the state of constant change in the real world. Just as the world is continuously changing, Coover's fictions also refuse to present stable, easily describable characters or scenarios. Coover also calls attention to the fictionality of fiction by focusing on the process and the means of creation rather than on the product. As he states in the prologue, the novelist turns to the familiar material and "defamiliarizes" it in order to liberate readers' imagination from arbitrary constraints and in order to make them reevaluate their reactions to those constraints. These are the main strategies of Coover's two collections of stories, *Pricksongs and Descants* and *A Night at the Movies.*

Pricksongs and Descants • The title of the first collection refers to musical terms, variations played against a basic line (the basic line of the familiar narrative). As one character in one of the stories says, however, they are also "death-c— and prick-songs," which prepares the reader for the sometimes shocking motifs of death and sex scattered throughout the stories. In *Pricksongs and Descants*, Coover turns to the familiar material of folktales and biblical stories. Using this material offers him the possibility of manipulating the reader's expectations. One of the ways in which Coover forces the reader to look at familiar stories from new perspectives is by retelling them from an unfamiliar point of view. For example, the story "The Brother" is Coover's version of the biblical flood told from the point of view of Noah's brother, who, after helping Noah to build the ark, is left to drown. "J's Marriage" describes how Joseph tries to come to terms with his marriage to the Virgin Mary and his alternating moods of amazement, frustration, and desperation. Some of the stories of the same collection are based on traditional folktales: "The Door" evokes "Little Red Riding Hood," "The Gingerbread House," reminds one of "Hanzel and Gretel," "The Milkmaid of Samaniego" is based on the Spanish folktale of the same title; and *Hair o' the Chine*, a novella, mocks the tale of the "Three Little Pigs and the Wolf." Coover subverts, however, the original narratives by stressing the cruelty and the motifs of sex, violence, and death underlying most folktales. Revealing the darker side of familiar stories is in fact one of Coover's recurrent techniques.

In other stories of *Pricksongs and Descants*, Coover experiments with the formal aspects of fiction-making. He reminds the reader of the artificiality of fiction by presenting stories that are repertoires of narrative possibilities. Often, Coover juxtaposes several different beginnings, or potential stories, but leaves them undeveloped. He interweaves the different story lines, some of which are complementary and some of which might be contradictory, as is the case in "Quenby and Ola, Swede and Carl" and in "The Magic Poker." In the "Sentient Lens" section and in "Klee's Dead," Coover explores the possibilities and the limitations of the narrational voice: In the first set of stories, Coover denies the possibility of an objective narrative voice by portraying a camera that constantly interferes with the events of the story; in "Klee's Dead," the supposedly "omniscient" narrator is unable to explain the reasons for Paul Klee's suicide.

In most of the stories of *Pricksongs and Descants*, the figures are types described with a flaunted lack of depth of characterization, which prevents the reader from identifying with them in any possible way. This contributes to the critical distance that Coover thinks it is necessary to maintain toward fiction. As critic Cristina Bacchilega says in her article about Coover's use of the *Märchen* (folktales) in this collection, while "the *Märchen* is symbolic of development, of a passage from immaturity to maturity, Coover's fictions present rather static characters . . . the only dynamic process allowed is in the reader's new awareness of the world as a construct of fictions." The function of the artist in contemporary society is one of Coover's recurring concerns, which surfaces in "Panel Game," "Romance of Thin Man and Fat Lady," and "The Hat Act," all of which portray cruel and insatiable audiences who, in their thirst for entertainment, do not hesitate to exterminate the artists if their performance does not stand up to their expectations.

A Night at the Movies • In *A Night at the Movies,* Coover probes the nature of filmic fictions, which present a greater danger of being taken for "real" because of the immediacy of filmic images. Coover approaches film from three perspectives. In the stories "Shootout at Gentry's Junction," "Charlie in the House of Rue," "Gilda's Dream," and "You Must Remember This," Coover demythologizes specific films and offers his own version of the story, usually baring the ideology of the original version. In "After Lazarus" and "Inside the Frame," he explores the conventions through which these fictions create an illusion of an independent world on the screen. In "The Phantom of the Movie Palace" and "Intermission," he challenges the ontological status of reality and film by making the characters cross the boundaries that separate these two realms.

"Shootout at Gentry's Junction" is a parody of the ideology and of the form of the Western film *High Noon* (1952). Coover parodies the narrative line and the easy identification of good and evil typical of most Westerns. The film celebrates the code of honor and personal integrity typical of the Western hero; abandoned by everybody, the sheriff of the film, played by Gary Cooper, has to fight alone with the villain and his gang. In the story, however, the protagonist is a fastidious, neurotic sheriff who is obsessed with fulfilling the role imposed on him. The villain is Don Pedro, the Mexican bandit, whose major talent is expressing himself by expelling intestinal gas. As in the film, the narrative progresses toward the confrontation of the villain and the sheriff. The tight structure of the film, however, is disrupted in the story by giving both characters a different kind of discourse. The sheriff's discourse has a traditional narrative line. It is narrated in the past tense and refers to formulas taken directly from the visual tradition of the Western. The Mexican's discourse is in the present tense and in broken English, influenced by Spanish. Furthermore, Coover makes the Mexican ubiquitous. Readers never really know where he is—he seems everywhere at the same time, raping the schoolmarm at the local school, cheating at cards in the saloon, and burning papers at the sheriff's office. After shooting the sheriff, the Mexican sets the town on fire and rides into the sunset.

The irreverence of Coover's version of *Casablanca* (1942) is even greater. *Casablanca* has become the epitome of the romantic melodrama, drawing like the Western upon codes of honor and heroic behavior. In "You Must Remember This," Coover gives his version of what might have happened between frames. Quite literally, Rick and Ilsa fall between frames and make furious love several times. The love story becomes a pornographic movie. The disruption of the moral code of the film creates an avalanche of disruptions in other categories: Rick and Ilsa begin to sense that their senses of time and place are fading, and their identities become increasingly diffused. At the end of the story, the characters melt into nothingness after several desperate attempts to return to the mythic movie.

Other stories in the collection *A Night at the Movies* aim at exposing the artificiality of the technical conventions of film. Written in the form of a screenplay, "After Lazarus" parodies the notion of the camera as the ultimately objective narrator. In the story, the camera "hesitates," "pauses," "follows back at a discreet distance," and rapidly moves back when frightened. "Inside the Frame" refers in its very title to film-related terms. If films construct a narrative through the sum of frames that all have a reason and a function in the global construct of the story, this story presents several possible beginnings of stories in one single frame. In "Inside the Frame," the reader gets glimpses of what could be potential stories: a woman stepping off a bus, an Indian with a knife between his teeth, a man praying at a grave, a singing couple, a sleepwalker. There is no development, no explanation of the images. "Lap Dissolves" is a literary imitation of the film technique. The story fades from one film-related situation to the next, with the words giving the cues to the transformation of the scenario.

Coover disrupts the ontological boundaries between "reality" and fiction by making the protagonists of "The Phantom of the Movie Palace" and "Intermission" move between them. The mad projectionist of the first story lives in an abandoned movie palace and plays with the reels of film, constructing films by cutting and pasting images of other films. Somehow, his experiments go awry, and he becomes trapped in the fictions he has been creating. The girl of "Intermission" enters a film-related fantasy when the film in the story ends and she steps into the lobby of the movie theater to buy a snack. Outside the theater, she is thrown into a series of situations directly drawn from Hollywood films: She moves from a car race with gangsters, to a tent with Rudolph Valentino, to the sea surrounded by sharks. In what is supposed to be "reality," she becomes a dynamic individual, but back in the cinema she returns to the passivity that Hollywood fictions seem to invite.

Briar Rose • In *Briar Rose*, a novella and a retelling of the fable of Sleeping Beauty, Coover travels deeply into the dreams of the sleeping princess and into the forest of briars and brambles that plague the prince as he tries to rescue her. The story centers on the powers of the human imagination and escalates to an erotic pace as sex and storytelling fuse together. As the prince fights his way to the princess's bed chamber to awaken her from a deathly enchanted sleep, Coover involves the reader by dangling numerous interpretative possibilities just below the surface of this brief narrative.

Coover's genius is displayed in his use of words, drifting back and forth between reality and dreams. His speculations about what makes a prince forge through the briars and what a princess dreams about while magically asleep for one hundred years are thought-provoking, mysterious, compelling, and at times hilarious. As the tale unwinds, Coover exposes the masculine desire to prey on female beauty. In addition, he leads the reader to contemplate the necessity that women resist male yearnings that are projected onto them. The tale is a bit dull in places and lacks a definite ending with some culminating metaphor, but Coover constructs an intriguing story that is well known, turned in on itself, and explored to reveal different levels of human consciousness.

In his major collections of stories, Coover elaborates on his fundamental concern, namely the necessity for the individual to distinguish between reality and fiction and to be liberated from dogmatic thinking. In order to do so, Coover emphasizes the self-reflexive, antirealistic elements of his fiction. The result is original, highly engaging, and energetic stories that probe human beings' relationships to the myths that shape their lives.

Carlota Larrea
With updates by Alvin K. Benson

Other major works

PLAYS: *A Theological Position*, pb. 1972; *Love Scene*, pb. 1972; *Rip Awake*, pr. 1972; *The Kid*, pr., pb. 1972; *Bridge Hound*, pr. 1981.

NOVELS: *The Origin of the Brunists*, 1966; *The Universal Baseball Association, Inc., J. Henry Waugh, Prop.*, 1968; *Whatever Happened to Gloomy Gus of the Chicago Bears?*, 1975 (expanded, 1987); *The Public Burning*, 1977; *Hair o' the Chine*, 1979 (novella/screenplay); *A Political Fable*, 1980 (novella); *Spanking the Maid*, 1981 (novella); *Gerald's Party*, 1985; *Pinocchio in Venice*, 1991; *Briar Rose*, 1996 (novella); *John's Wife*, 1996; *Ghost Town*, 1998; *The Adventures of Lucky Pierre: Directors' Cut*, 2002.

SCREENPLAYS: *On a Confrontation in Iowa City*, 1969; *After Lazarus*, 1980.

Bibliography

Coover, Robert. "Interview." *Short Story*, n.s. 1 (Fall, 1993): 89-94. Coover comments on the difference between the short story and the novel, the writing of *Pricksongs and Descants*, his use of sexuality in his fiction, his iconoclastic streak, postmodernism, and his use of the short story to test narrative forms.

_____. Interview by Amanda Smith. *Publishers Weekly* 230 (December 26, 1986): 44-45. Coover discusses the motivations that lie behind his experimental fiction; states he believes that the artist finds his metaphors for the world in the most vulnerable areas of human outreach; he insists that he is in pursuit of the mainstream. What many people consider experimental, Coover argues, is actually traditional in the sense that it has gone back to old forms to find its new form.

Evenson, Brian K. *Understanding Robert Coover.* Columbia: University of South Carolina Press, 2003. Evenson explains the particularly dense style of Coover's metafiction (his writing about writing) in a comprehensive survey that is part of the Understanding Contemporary American Literature series. Evenson guides readers through Coover's postmodern fiction, which deals with myth- and storymaking and their power to shape collective, community action, which often turns violent.

Gordon, Lois. *Robert Coover: The Universal Fictionmaking Process.* Carbondale: Southern Illinois University Press, 1983. Like Richard Andersen's book, this volume provides a friendly introduction and overview of Coover's work, placing him in the context of metafictional or postmodernist literature. Notes, select bibliography, and index.

Kennedy, Thomas E. *Robert Coover: A Study of the Short Fiction.* New York: Twayne, 1992. Kennedy's study shows Coover's use of myth, fantasy, love, soap opera, slapstick comedy, parable, and daydream on the level of the short story, which he displays with extraordinary effect in his novels as well. Contains interviews with Coover and glosses on many of his critics.

Maltby, Paul. *Dissident Postmodernists: Barthelme, Coover, Pynchon.* Philadelphia: University of Pennsylvania Press, 1991. Comparative look at these three writers and their fictions. Includes a bibliography and an index.

May, Charles E., ed. *Masterplots II: Short Story Series, Revised Edition.* 8 vols. Pasadena, Calif.: Salem Press, 2004. Designed for student use, this reference set contains articles providing detailed plot summaries and analyses of these three short stories by Coover: "The Babysitter" and "The Brother" (vol. 1), and "A Pedestrian Accident" (vol. 6).

"The Pleasures of the (Hyper)text." *The New Yorker* 70 (June/July, 1994): 43-44. Discusses Coover's Hypertext Hotel, the United States' first online writing space dedicated to the computer-generated mode of literature known as hypertext; describes Coover's writing class at Brown University and its use of hypertext.

Pughe, Thomas. *Comic Sense: Reading Robert Coover, Stanley Elkin, Philip Roth.* Boston: Birkhäuser Verlag, 1994. Analyzes the humor in the writers' books. Includes bibliographical references and an index.

Scholes, Robert. "Metafiction." *The Iowa Review* 1, no. 3 (Fall, 1970): 100-115. Initially theoretical, then descriptive, this article discusses four major metafictional writers: Coover, William H. Gass, Donald Barthelme, and John Barth. Scholes categorizes the different types of metafictional writing and classifies Coover's *Pricksongs and Descants* as "structural" metafiction, since it is concerned with the order of fiction rather than with the conditions of being.

A. E. Coppard

Born: Folkestone, Kent, England; January 4, 1878
Died: London, England; January 13, 1957

Principal short fiction • *Adam and Eve and Pinch Me*, 1921; *Clorinda Walks in Heaven*, 1922; *The Black Dog*, 1923; *Fishmonger's Fiddle*, 1925; *The Field of Mustard*, 1926; *Count Stephan*, 1928; *Silver Circus*, 1928; *The Gollan*, 1929; *The Higgler*, 1930; *The Man from Kilsheelan*, 1930; *Easter Day*, 1931; *Nixey's Harlequin*, 1931; *The Hundredth Story of A. E. Coppard*, 1931; *Crotty Shinkwin, and the Beauty Spot*, 1932; *Dunky Fitlow*, 1933; *Ring the Bells of Heaven*, 1933; *Emergency Exit*, 1934; *Polly Oliver*, 1935; *Ninepenny Flute*, 1937; *These Hopes of Heaven*, 1937; *Tapster's Tapestry*, 1938; *You Never Know, Do You?*, 1939; *Ugly Anna, and Other Tales*, 1944; *Fearful Pleasures*, 1946; *Selected Tales from His Twelve Volumes Published Between the Wars*, 1946; *The Dark-Eyed Lady: Fourteen Tales*, 1947; *The Collected Tales of A. E. Coppard*, 1948; *Lucy in Her Pink Jacket*, 1954; *Simple Day*, 1978.

Other literary forms • A. E. Coppard published three slender volumes of poetry, *Hips and Haws* (1922), *Pelagea, and Other Poems* (1926), and *Cherry Ripe* (1935), and two collections, *Yokohama Garland* (1926) and *Collected Poems* (1928). In 1957, he published his autobiography, *It's Me, O Lord!*

Achievements • Though not widely known among general readers, Coppard has experienced a resurgence of popularity as a result of the adaptation of several of his stories for *Masterpiece Theatre* on public television. For both his mastery of the short-story form and his sensitive portrayal of English rural life, Coppard is an important figure in the development of the short story as a serious literary form. From a background of poverty and with no formal education, Coppard advanced through a number of clerical and accounting jobs in Oxford, reading and associating with the students there. Becoming increasingly active in political activities and writing for journals, Coppard eventually decided to write professionally. During the 1920's and 1930's, he was considered one of the foremost short-story writers in England. Coppard's stories are frequently compared to those of Anton Chekhov and Thomas Hardy, whose influence Coppard acknowledged, and also to those of his contemporaries H. E. Bates and D. H. Lawrence. Although his poetry has not generated much acclaim, Coppard's prose is eloquently lyrical, its evocation of mood and emotion particularly noteworthy.

Biography • Alfred Edgar Coppard's remarkable life contributed to his early success. To such an influential editor-writer as Ford Madox Ford, he was a rustic wise man or gypsy, a character out of one of his own dark country stories. Coppard was born into poverty and attended only four years of elementary school in Brighton. His father was a tailor, his mother a housemaid; when his father died young, Coppard had to help the family survive by taking a series of menial jobs. At the age of twenty-one, he became a clerk in an engineering firm in Brighton, where he remained for seven years, advancing to cashier. As a teenager and young man he walked the English countryside, absorbing its landscapes and the language of country folk he met in roadside taverns, a favorite setting for many of his later tales. He was a fine athlete and even supplemented his income as a successful professional sprinter. He married in 1906 and a year later took a better position as an accountant for an ironworks in Oxford, a position he held for twelve years.

During his years in Oxford Coppard read, often in the Bodleian, associated with students, heard and sometimes met such luminaries as Vachel Lindsay, Aldous Huxley, and William Butler Yeats, and, finally, began to write. He also became involved in Socialist politics and joined the Women's Social and Political Union. Finally, in 1919, having published seven or eight tales in journals such as the *Manchester Guardian* and a few poems in journals such as *The Egoist* (edited by T. S. Eliot), he decided to leave his position at the foundry and become a professional writer. On April 1, 1919, at the age of forty-one, he moved to a small cottage outside Oxford at Shepherd's Pit, where he lived alone in the woods, becoming aware of "the ignoring docility of the earth" and, finally, publishing his first collection of tales on the second anniversary (*Adam and Eve and Pinch Me*, 1921) of his new career. His first book was well received and thrust him into prominence as one of the leading English short-story writers. Over the next thirty years his production of tales, poems, and reviews was steady and of high quality. A second marriage, to Winifred May de Kok in 1931, endured, but his reputation as a short-story writer began to wane in the mid-1930's; his last collection of tales (1954) was not even reviewed by the *Times Literary Supplement*. *The Collected Tales*, however, was a clear success, and the autobiography he completed on the eve of his fatal illness in 1957 is a delight.

Analysis • The unique quality of A. E. Coppard's short fiction derives from his powers as a lyrical writer, his sympathetic understanding of the rural, lower-class folk who organically inhabit the English countryside so memorably evoked in his tales, and his "uncanny perception," as Frank O'Connor remarked, "of a woman's secretiveness and mystery." Coppard's earliest reviewers and critics emphasized the poetic quality of his tales. The title story from *The Field of Mustard* is one of the great stories in English, and it suggests the full range of Coppard's creative genius, including his lyric portrayal of the English countryside and its folk, especially its women, whose language and life-consciousness seem wedded to the landscape.

"The Field of Mustard" • Like other lyric short stories, "The Field of Mustard" is nearly plotless. It opens with the suggestion that everything has already happened to the main characters, "three sere disvirgined women from Pollock's Cross." What remains for Coppard is to evoke the quality of these lives and the countryside of which they are a part; the tale proceeds as a kind of lyric meditation on life and death in nature. The women have come to "the Black Wood" in order to gather "dead branches" from the living trees, and on their way home, two of them, Dinah Lock and Rose Olliver, become involved in an intimate conversation that reveals the hopelessness of their lives. Rose, wishing she had children but knowing she never will, cannot understand why Dinah is not happy with her four children. Dinah complains that "a family's a torment. I never wanted mine." Dinah's "corpulence dispossessed her of tragedy," and perhaps because she has had the burden as well as the fulfillment of motherhood, she expressed the bitterness of life in what serves almost as a refrain: "Oh God, cradle and grave is all for we." They are old but their hearts are young, and the truth of Dinah's complaint, "that's the cussedness of nature, it makes a mock of you," is reflected in the world around them: The depleted women are associated with the mustard field and the "sour scent rising faintly from its yellow blooms." Against this natural order, Dinah and Rose wish that "this world was all a garden"; but "the wind blew strongly athwart the yellow field, and the odour of mustard rushed upon the brooding women."

As Dinah and Rose continue their conversation, they complain of their feeble husbands and discover a mutual loss: Each had been a lover of Rufus Blackthorn, a local gamekeeper. He was "a pretty man," "handsome," "black as coal and bold as a fox"; and although "he was good to women," he was "a perfect devil," "deep as the sea." Gradually Coppard's pattern of imagery reveals the source of these women's loss to be the very wellspring of life—their love and sexual vitality. The suggestion is explicit in their lover's name, "Blackthorn," who had brought them most in life yet left them now with "old grief or new rancour." This grim reality is suggested earlier when the women meet an old man in the Black Wood; he shows them a timepiece given him by "a noble Christian man," but is met only with Dinah's profane taunt, "Ah! I suppose he slept wid Jesus?" Outraged, the old man calls Dinah "a great fat thing," shouts an obscenity, and leaving them, puts "his fingers to his nose." Dinah's bitter mockery of Christian love gradually merges with the sour scent of mustard and surfaces transformed in Rose's recollection of how Blackthorn once joked of having slept with a dead man. These women, gathered in "the Black Wood" to collect dead wood from the living trees, have in effect slept with death. The yellow mustard blooms quiver in the wind, yet they are sour. The same "wind hustled the two women close together," and they touch; but, bereft of their sexual vitality, they are left only with Dinah's earlier observation that "it's such a mercy to have a friend at all" and her repeated appeal, "I like you, Rose, I wish you was a man." The tale ends with the women "quiet and voiceless,"

> in fading light they came to their homes. But how windy, dispossessed, and ravaged roved the darkening world! Clouds were borne frantically across the heavens, as if in a rout of battle, and the lovely earth seemed to sigh in grief at some calamity all unknown to men.

Coppard's lyric tales celebrate the oral tradition. His stories are often tales of tales being told, perhaps in a country tavern (as in "Alas, Poor Bollington!"). In some tales an oral narrator addresses the reader directly, and in others the rural settings, the characters, and the events—often of love ending in violence—draw obviously upon the materials of traditional folk ballads. Coppard himself loved to sing ballads and Elizabethan folk songs, and the main characters in these stories are sometimes singers, or their tales are "balladed about." In many tales, Coppard used rhythmic language, poetically inverted constructions, and repeated expressions that function as refrains in ballads. The most explicit example of a tale intended to resound with balladic qualities is "A Broadsheet Ballad," a tale of two laborers waiting in a tavern for the rain to pass. They begin to talk of a local murder trial, and one is moved by the thought of a hanging: "Hanging's a dreadful thing," he exclaims; and at length, with "almost a sigh," he repeats. "Hanging's a dreadful thing." His sigh serves as the tale's refrain and causes his fellow to tell within the tale a longer tale of a love triangle that ended in a murder and an unjust hanging. Finally, the sigh-refrain and the strange narration coalesce in the laborer's language:

> Ah, when things make a turn against you it's as certain as twelve o'clock, when they take a turn; you get no more chance than a rabbit from a weasel. It's like dropping your matches into a stream, you needn't waste the bending of your back to pick them out—they're no good on, they'll never strike again.

Coppard's lyric mode is perfectly suited to his grand theme: the darkness of love, its fleeting loveliness and almost inevitable entanglements and treacheries. He writes of triangles, entrapping circumstances, and betrayals in which, as often as not, a lover betrays himself or herself out of foolishness, timidity, or blind adherence to custom. Some of his best tales, like "Dusky Ruth" and "The Higgler," dwell on the mysterious elusiveness of love, often as this involves an alluring but ungraspable woman. Men and women are drawn together by circumstances and deep undercurrents of un-articulated feeling but are separated before they consummate their love.

"The Higgler" • Because of its portrayal of unconsummated love, its treatment of the rural poor, and its poetic atmosphere that arises from the countryside itself, "The Higgler" (the first story in *The Collected Tales*) is fully characteristic of Coppard's best work. It is not simply a tale of unconsummated love, for its main character comes to absorb and reflect the eternal forces of conflict in nature. For Coppard this involves more than man's economic struggle to wrest his living from nature; it involves man's conflict with man in war, his conflict with his lover, his conflict with himself, and ulti-mately, with his own life source, the mother.

Harvey Witlow is the higgler, a man whose business it is to travel the countryside in a horse-drawn wagon, buying produce from small farms. The story opens with the higgler making his way across Shag Moor, a desolate place where "solitude . . . now . . . shivered and looked sinister." Witlow is shrewd and crafty, "but the season was back-ward, eggs were scarce, trade was bad"; and he stands to lose the meager business he has struggled to establish for himself since returning from the war, as well as his op-portunity to marry. "That's what war does for you," he says. "I was better off working for farmers; much; but it's no good chattering about it, it's the trick of life; when you get so far, then you can go and order your funeral." After this dismal beginning, Witlow is presented with an unexpected opportunity to improve his life in every way; but he is destined to outwit himself, as his name suggests, and to know more fully the "trick of life." As the tale develops, then, the reader watches him miss his opportunity and resume his descent into general desolation.

Witlow's chance comes when he stops at the farm of a Mrs. Sadgrove. Here the higgler finds plenty of produce as well as the intriguing possibility of a relation-ship with Mrs. Sadgrove's daughter, Mary, another of Coppard's alluring, secretive women. Mary's quiet beauty attracts Witlow, but he imagines her to be too "well-up" and "highly cultivated" for him. She shows no interest in him, so he is unprepared when, after several trips to the farm and an invitation to dinner, Mrs. Sadgrove tells him of her poor health and her desire that he should wed Mary and take over the farm. The higgler leaves bewildered. Here is his life's opportunity: The farm is pros-perous, and he is far more attracted to Mary than to Sophy, the poor girl he eventu-ally marries; besides, Mary will inherit five hundred pounds on her twenty-fifth birth-day. It is simply too good to believe, and after consulting with his mother about his opportunity, Witlow grows increasingly suspicious. The reader has already been told that "mothers are inscrutable beings to their sons, always"; and Witlow is confused by his mother's enthusiasm over his opportunity. Even the natural world somehow con-spires to frighten him: "Autumn was advancing, and the apples were down, the bracken dying, the furze out of bloom, and the farm on the moor looked more and more lonely. . . ."

So Witlow begins to avoid the Sadgrove farm and suddenly marries Sophy. Within months, his "affairs had again taken a rude turn. Marriage, alas, was not all it might be; his wife and his mother quarrelled unendingly," and his business fails badly. His only chance seems to be to return to the Sadgrove farm, where he might obtain a loan; but he does so reluctantly, for he knows Mrs. Sadgrove to be a hard woman. She exploits her help and "was reputed to be a 'grinder'"; and he has betrayed her confidence. In an increasingly dark atmosphere of loss, Witlow returns across Shag Moor to the Sadgrove farm, where Mary meets him with the news of her mother's death that day. Now a prolonged, eerie, and utterly powerful scene develops as the higgler agrees to help Mary prepare her mother's body, which lies alone upstairs in a state of rigor mortis. He sends Mary away and confronts the dead mother, whose stiff out-stretched arm had been impossible for Mary to manage.

Moments later, in their intimacy near the dead mother, Witlow blurts out, "Did you know as she once asked me to marry you?" Finally Mary reveals that her mother actually opposed the marriage: "The girl bowed her head, lovely in her grief and modesty. 'She was against it, but I made her ask you. . . . I was fond of you—then.'" To his distress and confusion, Mary insists that he leave at once, and he drives "away in deep darkness, the wind howling, his thoughts strange and bitter."

"Arabesque: The Mouse" • Coppard's vision of life caught in a struggle against it-self, of the violence in nature and its mockery of morality, of the deceit among hu-mans and of humans' denial of their true nature—all this is marvelously represented in one of his first and finest tales, "Arabesque: The Mouse." It is a psychological hor-ror story of a middle-aged man who sits alone one night reading Russian novels until he thinks he is mad. He is an idealist who was obsessed by the incompatibilities of property and virtue, justice and sin. He looks at a "print by Utamaro of a suckling child caressing its mother's breasts" and his mind drifts to recall his own mother and then a brief experience with a lover. These recollections merge in a compelling pat-tern of images that unite finally, and horribly, with an actual experience this night with a mouse. As a child horrified by the sight of some dead larks that had been in-tended for supper, he sought comfort from his mother and found her sitting by the fire with her bodice open, "squeezing her breasts; long thin streams of milk spurted into the fire with a little plunging noise." Telling him that she was weaning his little sister, she draws him to her breast and presses his face "against the delicate warmth of her bosom." She allows him to do it; "so he discovered the throb of the heart in his mother's breast. Wonderful it was for him to experience it, although she could not explain it to him." They feel his own beat, and his mother assures him his heart is "good if it beats truly. Let it always beat truly, Filip." The child kisses "her bosom in his ecstasy and whisper[s] soothingly: 'Little mother! little mother.'"

The boy forgets the horror of the dead larks bundled by their feet, but the next day his mother is run over by a heavy cart, and before she dies her mutilated hands are amputated. For years the image of his mother's bleeding stumps of arms had haunted his dreams. Into his mind, however, now floats the recollection of an experi-ence with a lovely country girl he had met and accompanied home. It was "dark, dark . . . , the night an obsidian net"; finally in their intimacy she had unbuttoned his coat, and with her hands on his breast asked, "Oh, how your heart beats! Does it beat truly?" In a "little fury of love" he cried "Little mother, little mother!" and confused the girl. At that moment footsteps and the clack of a bolt cause them to part forever.

The sound of the bolt hurls him into the present, where, frightened, he opens his cupboard to find a mouse sitting on its haunches before a snapped trap. "Its head was bowed, but its beadlike eyes were full of brightness, and it sat blinking, it did not flee." Then to his horror he sees that the trap had caught only the feet, "and the thing crouched there holding out its two bleeding stumps humanly, too stricken to stir." He throws the mouse from his window into the darkness, then sits stunned, "limp with pity too deep for tears" before running down into the street in a vain search for the "little philosopher." Later he drops the tiny feet into the fire, resets the trap, and carefully replaces it. "Arabesque: The Mouse" is a masterwork of interwoven imagery whose unity is caught in such details as the mother's heartbeat, the mother's milk streaming with a plunging noise into the fire, the mouse's eyes, and the "obsidian net" of night.

Coppard's characters are sometimes shattered by such thoughts and experiences, but the author never lost his own sense of the natural magnificence and fleeting loveliness in life. It is true that many of his late tales pursue in a more thoughtful and comic manner the natural and psychological forces in life that were simply, but organically and poetically, present in such earlier tales as "The Higgler"; that is, in some of his later stories the reader can too easily see him playing with thoughts about Alfred Adler, Sigmund Freud, and, repeatedly, Charles Darwin (whose prose he admired). Yet the last tale (the title story) of his final volume is one of his best. "Lucy in Her Pink Jacket" is almost a hymn to nature, a song of acceptance in which lovers meet accidentally in a magnificent mountain setting. Their lovemaking is beautiful, natural, and relaxed, and they accept the web of circumstances causing them to part. Coppard's description of his last parting character might serve as his reader's image of himself: "Stepping out into the bright eager morning it was not long before [he] was whistling softly as he went his way, a sort of thoughtful, plaintive, museful air."

Bert Bender
With updates by Lou Thompson

Other major works

CHILDREN'S LITERATURE: *Pink Furniture*, 1930.

NONFICTION: *Rummy: That Noble Game Expounded*, 1933; *It's Me, O Lord!*, 1957.

POETRY: *Hips and Haws*, 1922; *Pelagea, and Other Poems*, 1926; *Yokohama Garland*, 1926; *Collected Poems*, 1928; *Cherry Ripe*, 1935.

Bibliography

Allen, Walter. *The Short Story in English*. New York: Oxford University Press, 1981. Includes a brief analysis of Coppard's "The Higgler," suggesting that the story is as unpredictable as life itself, with nothing seemingly arranged or contrived by Coppard.

Bates, H. E. "Katherine Mansfield and A. E. Coppard." In *The Modern Short Story: A Critical Survey*. London: Evensford Productions, 1972. Coppard's contemporary and fellow author of short stories discusses Coppard's role in the development of the modern English short story. Bates discerns an unfortunate influence of Henry James on Coppard's work, which is remarkable in its Elizabethan lyricism and its homage to the oral tradition. Includes an index.

Beachcroft, T. O. *The Modest Art: A Survey of the Short Story in English*. New York: Oxford University Press, 1968. Discusses Coppard's two basic generic veins—the highly fantastic in such stories as "Adam and Eve and Pinch Me," and the naturalistic in stories such as "The Higgler" and "The Water Cress Girl."

Cowley, Malcolm. "Book Reviews: *Adam and Eve and Pinch Me*." *The Dial* 71, no. 1 (July,

1921): 93-95. Describes Coppard's careful workmanship, his skillful narration, and his artful blend of fantasy and realism. Cowley notes Coppard's emotional unity, his insight into characters, his animated landscapes, and his role in keeping the short-story form vital.

Ginden, James. "A. E. Coppard and H. E. Bates." In *The English Short Story, 1880-1945: A Critical History*, edited by Joseph M. Flora. Boston: Twayne, 1985. Compares Coppard's and H. E. Bates's treatment of rural life as well as their dedication to the short story as distinguished from other literary forms. Although both authors employed the techniques of the modern short story, Ginden does not consider them "modernists," arguing that their work lacks the reliance on symbol or metaphor and instead stresses anecdote and description.

Kalasky, Drew, ed. *Short Story Criticism: Excerpts from Criticism of the Works of Short Fiction Writers.* Vol. 21. Detroit: Gale Research, 1996. Thoughtful collection of criticism of works by Coppard, Jean Rhys, William Sansom, William Saroyan, Giovanni Verga, and others.

Lessing, Doris. Introduction to *Selected Stories by A. E. Coppard.* London: Jonathan Cape, 1972. Lessing attributes the general appeal of Coppard's fiction to his exceptional talent for storytelling. Coppard was an expert craftsman, but it is the authentic growth of characters and events that involves the reader.

May, Charles E., ed. *Masterplots II: Short Story Series, Revised Edition.* 8 vols. Pasadena, Calif.: Salem Press, 2004. Designed for student use, this reference set contains articles providing detailed plot summaries and analyses of these five short stories by Coppard: "Adam and Eve and Pinch Me" and "Arabesque—The Mouse" (vol. 1), "The Field of Mustard" and "The Higgler" (vol. 3), and "The Third Prize" (vol. 7).

O'Connor, Frank. *The Lonely Voice: A Study of the Short Story.* New York: World, 1962. O'Connor examines Coppard's themes of poverty, personal freedom, and women in the context of other modern short fiction by Irish, English, American, and Russian writers. The two great English storytellers, according to O'Connor, are Coppard and D. H. Lawrence. Though both authors had working-class backgrounds, Coppard is a more deliberate, self-conscious artist, and he betrays feelings of social inadequacy.

Schwartz, Jacob. *The Writings of Alfred Edward Coppard: A Bibliography.* 1931. Reprint. Folcroft, Pa.: Folcroft Library Editions, 1975. Features a biography by Schwartz and a foreword and notes by Coppard.

Julio Cortázar

Born: Brussels, Belgium; August 26, 1914
Died: Paris, France; February 12, 1984

Principal short fiction • *Bestiario*, 1951; *Final del juego*, 1956; *Las armas secretas*, 1959; *Historias de cronopios y de famas*, 1962 (*Cronopios and Famas*, 1969); *End of the Game, and Other Stories*, 1963 (also as *Blow-Up, and Other Stories*, 1967); *Todos los fuegos el fuego*, 1966 (*All Fires the Fire, and Other Stories*, 1973); "Octaedro," 1974 (included in *A Change of Light, and Other Stories*, 1980); "Alguien que anda por ahí y otros relatos," 1977 (included in *A Change of Light, and Other Stories*, 1980); *Un tal Lucas*, 1979 (*A Certain Lucas*, 1984); *Queremos tanto a Glenda y otros relatos*, 1980 (*We Love Glenda So Much, and Other Stories*, 1983); *Deshoras*, 1982.

Other literary forms • Julio Cortázar's literary career, which lasted almost forty years, includes—besides his short stories—novels, plays, poetry, translations, and essays of literary criticism. In his essay on short fiction entitled "Algunos aspectos del cuento" ("Some Aspects of the Short Story"), Cortázar studies the varying role of the reader with regard to different literary forms. Cortázar's first book, *Presencia* (1938), was a collection of poetry that he published under the pseudonym Julio Denís. He translated authors as diverse as Louisa May Alcott and Edgar Allan Poe into Spanish and considered French Symbolist poetry to be of enormous influence on his prose writing. He experimented with a form of collage in his later works of short fiction.

Achievements • An antirealist, Cortázar is often grouped with Gabriel García Márquez as one of the foremost proponents of the Magical Realism movement and, during his lifetime, one of the most articulate spokespersons on the subject of Latin American fiction.

Although Cortázar is most admired for his short stories (his short story "Las babas del diablo" was made into a classic film in 1966 called *Blow-Up* by director Michelangelo Antonioni), it was the publication of the novel *Rayuela* (1963; *Hopscotch*, 1966) that placed the author among the twentieth century's greatest writers. *The Times Literary Supplement* called *Hopscotch* the "first great novel of Spanish America."

Biography • Julio Cortázar was born in Brussels, Belgium, in 1914, during the German occupation. His Argentine parents were stationed there while his father was on the staff of a commercial mission. Cortázar's antecedents came from the Basque region of Spain, as well as France and Germany, and they had settled in Argentina. When Cortázar was four years old, his parents returned to Argentina, where he would grow up in Banfield, a suburb of Buenos Aires. His father abandoned the family, and he was reared by his mother and an aunt.

Cortázar attended the Escuela Norman Mariano Acosta in Buenos Aires and earned a degree as a public-school teacher in 1932. In 1937, he accepted a high school teaching post and shortly thereafter published *Presencia*, a collection of poems, under the pseudonym Julio Denís. In 1940, he published an essay on Arthur Rimbaud, under the same pseudonym, and began to teach a class on the French Symbolist movement at the University of Cuyo in Mendoza. In 1946, Jorge Luis Borges, at that time the editor of the literary journal *Anales de Buenos Aires*, published "Casa tomada" ("House Taken Over")—the first work that Julio Cortázar penned under his own name.

A writer with outspoken political beliefs, Cortázar was defiantly anti-Peronist. He was arrested and as a result was forced to relinquish his academic career in Argentina. Instead, however, he became a translator and, in 1951, went to Paris, where he soon established permanent residency. Much of his best short fiction, including "Bestiary" and "End of the Game," was published in the 1950's and reveals his experience as an expatriate—a Latin American living in Paris.

In Paris, Cortázar got a job as a translator for UNESCO, which he kept for the rest of his life despite his international success as an author. In 1953, he married Aurora Bernandez, with whom he translated Poe's prose works into Spanish, while they lived briefly in Rome. In 1963, he published *Hopscotch* and, after a visit to Cuba, became a powerful figure on both the literary and the political scenes. His audience grew wider during the 1960's and 1970's with the translation of *Rayuela* into dozens of languages and the appearance of the film *Blow-Up*. He also traveled extensively to such diverse places as Chile, New York, and Oklahoma to attend conferences, receive awards, and participate in political tribunals. In 1981, he finally became a French citizen. He died in Paris in February, 1984, of leukemia and heart disease. He is buried in the Montparnasse cemetery in Paris.

Analysis • Influenced by the European movements of nineteenth century Symbolism and twentieth century Surrealism, Julio Cortázar combines symbols, dreams, and the fantastic with what seems to be an ordinary, realistic situation in order to expose a different kind of reality that exists in the innermost heart and mind of modern human beings. Like Edgar Allan Poe, Cortázar is fascinated by terror. He uses human beings' worst nightmares to explore which fears control them and how phobias and dreams coexist with seemingly rational thought. Using symbols and metaphors for subconscious obsessions, Cortázar's short fictions, unlike those of the Surrealists, are carefully constructed. His journey into the irrational is not a free-flowing adventure; rather, it is a study of a particular corner of the mind that is common to all people.

"Bestiary" • "Bestiary," an early story published in 1951, contains many of the elements of poesy and mystery that are characteristic of the nineteenth century Symbolists so admired by Cortázar. The story is told by a child whose scope of understanding and point of view are limited, thereby leaving certain details vague and confusing. Isabel is sent to the country for the summer to stay in a home inhabited by another child, Nino, and three adults: Luis, Nino's father; Rema, who may or may not be Nino's mother, Luis' wife or sister, Nino's sister, or the housekeeper; and the Kid, who is not a kid but Luis' brother. The information given about the family is not specific in those terms, but it is quite specific in Isabel's feelings about each person. The overwhelming oddity about this summer home is that a tiger is allowed to roam freely about the house and grounds. The people are advised as to the location of the tiger each day, and they go about their business as usual by simply avoiding the room or part of the fields in which the tiger happens to be.

Life seems to be filled with very typical activities: Luis works in his study; the children gather an ant collection; and Rema supervises meals. Isabel is especially fond

Library of Congress

of Rema but not of the Kid. Events are relayed that expose Isabel's true feelings about the Kid and the kind of person she believes him to be. He is surly at the dinner table. Once, after Nino has hit a ball through the window leading to the Kid's room, the Kid hits Nino; the most disturbing moment, however, is a scene between Rema and the Kid during which Isabel acts as a voyeur, revealing some sort of sexual abuse on the part of the Kid toward Rema. Because of Isabel's admiration for Rema, she decides to take revenge on the Kid. The culmination of the story is that Isabel lies to the family about the whereabouts of the tiger, sending the Kid into the room where the animal is. Screams are heard, and it is clear that the Kid has been mauled to death. Isabel notices that Rema squeezes her hand with what the child believes to be gratitude.

Many critics have speculated about the meaning of the tiger. Cortázar, in true Symbolist fashion, has himself said that the reader receives a richer experience if no specific symbol is attributed to the animal in this story. As in the works of Poe, constant tension and terror pervade the work, and the tiger's meaning becomes a relative one—a personal nightmare for each character and each reader.

"Letter to a Young Lady in Paris" • "Letter to a Young Lady in Paris" begins on a charming note. It is a letter from a young man to his girlfriend, who is visiting Paris. She has asked him to move into her apartment, and, through very delicate language, he tries to convince her that he would disrupt her very orderly and truly elegant apartment. He succumbs to her wishes, however, and moves his belongings, but on the way up in the elevator he begins to feel sick. Panic ensues when he vomits a bunny rabbit, and, while living in the apartment, each wave of anxiety produces another. Soon, he is sequestering ten bunny rabbits in an armoire. The rabbits sleep in the daytime and are awakened at night; he manages to keep his secret from his girlfriend's nosy maid. The nocturnal insomnia and the constant production of bunny rabbits drive him to jump out the window along with the last one regurgitated. The charming letter is really a suicide note, and the seemingly eccentric but sweet story becomes a horrific account of phobia and insanity.

"Axolotl" • Cortázar seems particularly fascinated with the unusual placement of animals in these stories. In "Bestiary" and "Letter to a Young Lady in Paris," animals take over the lives of people. In another short story, "Axolotl," the man who visits the aquarium every day to see the axolotl swim becomes the axolotl. The narrative point of view switches back and forth between the man and the sea creature, telling the story from both points of view, but since there is no regular pattern or warning when the point of view changes, it is often difficult to determine inside whose skin readers are. The nightmare of being trapped inside the body of a beast is the human's experience, and the panic of being abandoned by the man is the axolotl's final cry. The only hope, as noted by the axolotl, is the creation of art where the writer can become another and communicate on behalf of all creatures—expressing the feelings of all creatures so that none may feel the terror of isolation and imprisonment.

"All Fires the Fire" • The shifting of narrative point of view as well as the alternation of time and place is a technique that Cortázar developed during his career as an author. A later story, "All Fires the Fire," revolves around two unhappy love triangles. One takes place in modern times and one during a gladiator fight in an ancient coliseum. Again, Cortázar uses animals to provide a menacing tone to what seem to be ordinary failures in romance. In both cases, raging blazes burn the lovers to death. No clear delineation is made when the story shifts scenes. The reader begins to sense these changes as the story unfolds; the scenes are different, but the tension never desists. The author creates deliberate ambiguity so that the reader, who is being intentionally confused by the author, nevertheless receives signals at the same time. Like the Symbolist writers whom he admired, Cortázar, in "All Fires the Fire," understands the power of the suggestive image and insists that readers use their own senses to feel the intensity of hate, lust, and love in both triangles. Through smell, sound, and sight, the reader gets two complete and distinct pictures that have similar endings. Like the Surrealist writers who unraveled the varying layers of the mind, Cortázar here projects two events that occur at two different times in two different places yet at the same moment in the reader's consciousness.

"Blow-Up" • Through fractured narration, Cortázar is able to examine how the mind can appropriate different personalities and points of view in this story, which he first published as "Las babas del diablo." The games of the mind are a constant theme in the works of Cortázar, and it is for that reason that a journey into his fictive world is an opportunity to explore the relationship between what seems to be real and what seems to be illogical. Cortázar confounds the reader's system of beliefs with his manipulation of discourse. He begins the story "Blow-Up," for example, by stating: "It'll never be known how this has to be told, in the first person or in the second, using the third person plural or continually inventing modes that will serve for nothing." He continues by telling readers how he writes—by typewriter—making them absolutely aware of the fact that they are going to enter the world of fiction. Although "Blow-Up" begins on this self-conscious trial, which seems to draw an obvious distinction between art and life, its actual theme is the interchangeability of the two. The narrator introduces the reader to the story's hero, a French-Chilean photographer named Robert Michel, and then becomes him. The story is narrated alternatively in first-person "I" and third-person "he" and becomes a collage of identities.

Out for a stroll on a pleasant November day, the photographer happens by chance upon a scene that disturbs him. Chance is an essential component of the world of magic, the fantastic and the illogical in Cortázar's short fiction. Chance rearranges preexisting order and creates a new future, past, and present for Cortázar's characters. The photographer/narrator witnesses a brief moment between a young man, a woman, and an older man sitting in a car—another love triangle with menacing undertones—and creates a history of what might have brought all three to the quai near the Seine. After the particular episode, he creates a future for them of what might happen to each of them afterward. Later, when he himself reflects on the episode, he studies his photographs as if the moments were frozen in time. Strangely, the more he studies his enlargements the more his memory alters. Because he creates a fiction about each of the people involved, the photo and his involvement in their little dramas become fiction as well, and he is not at all certain of what he has witnessed. The whole episode develops into a dream, a game of the mind.

The photographs that he had taken, which were supposed to reproduce reality with exactitude, become a collage of suggestions. Magnified, the photographs reveal even less about what he thought had occurred. The photographer believes that his camera is empowered with precision and with accuracy; he discovers, however, that the artwork has a life of its own that is constantly re-creating itself.

The search for truth in art is the pervading theme in Julio Cortázar's short fiction. He attempts to break with realist attitudes to force the reader to look beyond that which is ordinary and comfortable in order to explore the realms that seem, on the surface, incomprehensible and fearful. Cortázar believes that as human beings, people must recognize the inexplicable as just that and must admit that they do not have control over everything. The characters in "Bestiary" do not have control over the tiger. The young man in "Letter to a Young Lady in Paris" does not have control over the rabbits that he regurgitates. "All Fires the Fire" depicts the characters involved in passionate love triangles whose emotions are out of control. Finally, in "Blow-Up," the artist's work has a life of its own.

It was the Symbolist movement that gave Cortázar his stylistic signature and the Surrealists who divulged the irrational to later artists. Cortázar combined his appreciation for both movements and consolidated them with his own voice to create exciting and challenging short fiction.

Susan Nayel

Other major works

NOVELS: *Los premios*, 1960 (*The Winners*, 1965); *Rayuela*, 1963 (*Hopscotch*, 1966); *62: Modelo para armar*, 1968 (*62: A Model Kit*, 1972); *Libro de Manuel*, 1973 (*A Manual for Manuel*, 1978); *El examen*, wr. 1950, pb. 1986 (*Final Exam.*, 2000)

MISCELLANEOUS: *La vuelta al día en ochenta mundos*, 1967 (*Around the Day in Eighty Worlds*, 1986); *Último round*, 1969; *Divertimiento*, 1986.

NONFICTION: *Buenos Aires Buenos Aires*, 1968 (English translation, 1968); *Último round*, 1969; *Viaje alrededor de una mesa*, 1970; *Prosa del observatorio*, 1972 (with Antonio Galvez); *Fantomas contra los vampiros multinacionales: Una utopía realizable*, 1975; *Literatura en la revolución y revolución en la literatura*, 1976 (with Mario Vargas Llosa and Oscar Collazos); *Paris: The Essence of Image*, 1981; *Los autonautas de la cosmopista*, 1983; *Nicaragua tan violentamente dulce*, 1983 (*Nicaraguan Sketches*, 1989); *Cartas*, 2000 (3 volumes).

POETRY: *Presencia*, 1938 (as Julio Denís); *Los reyes*, 1949; *Pameos y meopas*, 1971; *Salvo el crepúsculo*, 1984.

TRANSLATIONS: *Robinson Crusoe,* 1945 (of Daniel Defoe's novel); *El inmoralista,* 1947 (of André Gide's *L'Immoraliste*); *El hombre que sabía demasiado,* c. 1948-1951 (of G. K. Chesterton's *The Man Who Knew Too Much*); *Vida y Cartas de John Keats,* c. 1948-1951 (of Lord Houghton's *Life and Letters of John Keats*); *Filosofía de la risa y del llanto,* 1950 (of Alfred Stern's *Philosophie du rire et des pleurs*); *La filosofía de Sartre y el psicoanálisis existentialista,* 1951 (of Stern's *Sartre, His Philosophy and Psychoanalysis*).

Bibliography

Alazraki, Jaime, and Ivan Ivask, eds. *The Final Island.* Norman: University of Oklahoma Press, 1978. Collection of essays, including two by Cortázar himself, about the role of magic or the marvelous as it works alongside what appears to be realism in Cortázar's fiction. Contains a chronology and an extensive bibliography that offers data on Cortázar's publications in several languages.

Alonso, Carlos J., ed. *Julio Cortázar: New Readings.* New York: Cambridge University Press, 1998. Part of the Cambridge Studies in Latin American and Iberian Literature series. Includes bibliographical references and an index.

Garfield, Evelyn Picon. *Julio Cortázar.* New York: Frederick Ungar, 1975. Garfield begins and ends her study with personal interviews that she obtained with Cortázar at his home in Provence, France. She studies the neurotic obsession of the characters in Cortázar's fiction and offers firsthand commentary by Cortázar on his methods of writing and his own experiences that helped create his work. Cortázar's philosophies, his preferences, and even his own personal nightmares are expounded upon, illuminating much of the symbolism found in his work. Chronology, analysis, complete bibliography, and index.

Guibert, Rita. *Seven Voices: Seven Latin American Writers Talk to Rita Guibert.* New York: Alfred A. Knopf, 1973. Includes an important interview with Cortázar, who discusses both his politics (his strenuous objection to U.S. interference in Latin America) and many of his fictional works.

Hernandez del Castillo, Ana. *Keats, Poe, and the Shaping of Cortázar's Mythopoesis.* Amsterdam: John Benjamins, 1981. Studies the influence of John Keats and Edgar Allan Poe on the work of Cortázar. The author states that of these two poets, whose works Cortázar translated, Poe had the greater influence on Cortázar. Studies the role of the archetypes in mythology and psychology and how they have been used in the works of all three writers. Contains an excellent index, which includes references that had an enormous impact on trends in the twentieth century.

May, Charles E., ed. *Masterplots II: Short Story Series, Revised Edition.* 8 vols. Pasadena, Calif.: Salem Press, 2004. Designed for student use, this reference set contains articles providing detailed plot summaries and analyses of these seven short stories by Cortázar: "Apocalypse at Solentiname," "Axolotl," and "Blow-Up" (vol. 1); "End of the Game" (vol. 2); "Instructions for John Howell" and "The Island at Noon" (vol. 4); and "The Southern Thruway" (vol. 7).

Peavler, Terry J. *Julio Cortázar.* Boston: Twayne, 1990. Peavler divides Cortázar's short fiction into four categories—the fantastic, the mysterious, the psychological, and the realistic—in order to show how Cortázar used these genres as games to study discourse. Includes a chronology and a through bibliography.

Stavans, Ilan. *Julio Cortázar: A Study of the Short Fiction.* New York: Twayne, 1996. See especially the chapters on the influence of Jorge Luis Borges on Cortázar's fiction, his use of the fantastic, and his reliance on popular culture. Stavans also has a section on Cortázar's role as writer and his interpretation of developments in Latin American literature. Includes chronology and bibliography.

Sugano, Marian Zwerling. "Beyond What Meets the Eye: The Photographic Analogy in Cortázar's Short Stories." *Style* 27 (Fall, 1993): 332-351. Summarizes and critiques Cortazar's analogy between the short story and photography in his essays, "Some Aspects of the Short Story" and "On the Short Story and Its Environs"; explains how Cortázar dramatizes the analogy in "Blow-Up" and "Apocalypse at Solentiname."

Yovanovich, Gordana. *Julio Cortázar's Character Mosaic: Reading the Longer Fiction.* Toronto: University of Toronto Press, 1991. Three chapters focus on Cortázar's four major novels and his fluctuating presentations of character as narrators, symbols, and other figures of language. Includes notes and bibliography.

Stephen Crane

Born: Newark, New Jersey; November 1, 1871
Died: Badenweiler, Germany; June 5, 1900

Principal short fiction • *The Little Regiment and Other Episodes of the American Civil War,* 1896; *The Open Boat, and Other Tales of Adventure,* 1898; *The Monster, and Other Stories,* 1899; *Whilomville Stories,* 1900; *Wounds in the Rain: War Stories,* 1900; *Last Words,* 1902.

Other literary forms • Stephen Crane began his brief writing life as a journalist, and he continued writing for newspapers, notably as a war correspondent, throughout his career, sometimes basing his short stories on events that he had first narrated in press reports. He also wrote raw-edged, realistic novels in which he employed journalistic techniques, most significantly in *Maggie: A Girl of the Streets* (1893) and *The Red Badge of Courage: An Episode of the American Civil War* (1895). By contrast, he composed wry, evocative, often cryptic poems, published in *The Black Riders and Other Lines* (1895) and *War Is Kind* (1899), that seemed to reveal the philosophy behind the world created in his fiction.

Achievements • Stephen Crane's fiction has proved hard to classify—not, however, because he defies categorization but because he worked in two nearly incompatible literary styles at once, while being a groundbreaker in both.

On one hand, he founded the American branch of literary naturalism (this style had originated in France) in his early novels. These works emphasized the sordid aspects of modern life, noted the overpowering shaping influence of environment on human destiny, and scandalously discounted the importance of morality as an effective factor touching on his characters' behavior. In this style, he was followed by writers such as Theodore Dreiser and Frank Norris.

On the other hand, in these same early novels he developed a descriptive style that made him a founder of American impressionism. Although the naturalist component of his writing stressed how subjectivity was dominated by social forces, the impressionist component, through coloristic effects and vivid metaphors, stressed the heightened perceptions of individual characters from whose perspectives the story was presented. The man closest to Crane in his own time in developing this impressionist style was Joseph Conrad, though, it will be recognized, this method of drawing from a character's viewpoint became a central tool of twentieth century literature and was prominently employed by authors such as William Faulkner, Virginia Woolf, and Henry James.

Crane took the unusual tack of both playing up his characters' points of view in presenting the world and downplaying the characters' abilities to influence that world. Although this combination of strategies could be made to work satisfactorily, later authors who have taken Crane's path have tended to develop only one of these strands. Moreover, many critics have found Crane's dual emphases to be jarring and incompletely thought through, particularly in his novels. In fact, many have believed that it is only in his short stories that he seemed thoroughly to blend the two manners.

Biography • To some degree, Stephen Crane's life followed a perverse pattern. He was acclaimed for the authenticity of his writings about events that he had never experienced and then spent the remainder of his few years experiencing the events that he had described in prose—often with disastrous consequences.

Born on November 1, 1871, in Newark, New Jersey, Crane was the last child in the large family of a Methodist minister, Jonathan Townley Crane. The family moved frequently from parish to parish and, in 1878, came to Port Jervis, New York, in forested Sullivan County, where Crane would set most of his early stories. Two years later, his father died, and his mother had to begin struggling to support the family, doing church work and writing for religious publications.

Crane determined to be a writer early in his life, and though he attended a few semesters at Lafayette College and then Syracuse University, his real interest in his college years was in soaking up the atmosphere of New York City lowlife and writing freelance articles for newspapers. In 1892, he completed his first novel, *Maggie: A Girl of the Streets*, the story of a young girl driven into streetwalking by a Bowery Romeo. This first novel was so shocking in tone and full of obscenity (in those days, this meant that it contained words such as "hell") that it was rejected by respectable publishers. Borrowing money, Crane printed the book himself, and though it went unread and unsold, it garnered the appreciation of two of the outstanding literary figures of the day, Hamlin Garland and William Dean Howells.

Crane's next book, *The Red Badge of Courage*, a novel about the Civil War (1861-1865), brought him universal acclaim and celebrity status. In the year of the book's publication, however, as if living out his fiction, he defended an unjustly accused prostitute against the corrupt New York City police, just as he had defended the poor prostitute Maggie in prose, and found undeserved blight attached to his name. From then on, life would be made difficult for him in New York City by the angered police force.

Crane more or less abandoned New York at this point, easily enough since the authority of his army novel had placed him in much demand as a war correspondent. Going to Florida to wait for a ship to Cuba, where a rebellion against the Spanish colonialists was taking place, Crane met Cora Taylor, the madame of a house of ill repute who was to become his common-law wife. The ill-fated ship that he eventually boarded sank, and Crane barely escaped with his life, though, on the positive side, he produced from the experience what many consider his greatest short story, "The Open Boat."

As if to show that he could describe real wars as well as he could imagine them, he began shuttling from battle to battle as a reporter, first going to the Greco-Turkish War and then back to view the Spanish-American War, ruining his health in the process. Between wars, he stayed in the manorial Brede Place in England, where he became acquainted with a number of other expatriates who lived in the area, including Joseph Conrad, Harold Frederic, and Henry James.

Crane's problems with the police and the irregularity of his liaison with Cora Taylor—she could not get a divorce from her long-estranged husband—would have made it difficult for Crane to live in his homeland, so in 1899, he settled at the manor for good. Sick and beset with financial woes brought on by extravagant living and an openhanded generosity to visitors, he wrote feverishly but unavailingly to clear his debts. He died the next year from tuberculosis, after having traveled to the Continent to seek a cure.

Analysis • Perhaps because his writing career was so short, critics have devoted much space to Stephen Crane's slight, decidedly apprentice series of sketches collectively entitled *The Sullivan County Tales*. One trait that the sketches do have in their favor is that they contain all the facets of style and theme that Crane was to utilize as his writing developed. The reader finds the overbearing power of the environment, the vivid descriptions, the premise that these descriptions reflect the heightened consciousness of a character or characters, and the idea that this very heightening involves a distortion of perception that needs to be overcome for the characters' adequate adjustment to, and comprehension of, reality. Also of significance is that these stories are generally concerned with the actions of four campers and hence reflect not only on individual psychology but also on the psychology of group dynamics. This was also to become a focus of Crane's writing.

Library of Congress

"Four Men in a Cave" • In one of the better pieces from this series, "Four Men in a Cave," a quartet of campers decides to explore a cave in order to have something to brag about when they return to the city. Their scarcely concealed fears about the expedition are rendered by Crane's enlivening of stalactites that jab down at them and stalagmites that shoot up at them from crevices. At the end of their path, they find a hermit who invites them to a game of poker, but their fear-stoked imaginations visualize the gamester as a ghoul or Aztec priest. Only later after escaping the cave, in a comic denouement, do they learn of the cave dweller's true identity, that of a mad farmer who took to solitude when he lost his land and wife through gambling. By this time, there seems to be little to brag about, since what has happened has exposed their cowardice and credulity.

The story provides an early example of the rough-and-ready combination of impressionist subjectivity, in how the descriptions in the piece are tinged by the campers' fears, and naturalist objectivity, in how the overwhelming environment of the cave, for part of the story, controls the men's action while dwarfing them. Further, the piece indicates the way, as Crane sees it, emotions can be constructed collectively, as when each camper tells the others how he has misidentified the hermit, adding to the growing hysteria.

"An Experiment in Misery" • In 1894, Crane published a maturer story, "An Experiment in Misery," in which he transposed the narrative of a cave journey into a serious study of urban social conditions. In the originally printed version of the piece, two middle-class men observe tramps and speculate about their motives and feelings. On impulse, the younger man decides to dress as a tramp in order to penetrate their secrets. (Such a tactic, of disguising oneself to uncover hidden areas of society, was a common practice of crusading reporters at that time.)

In the later, revised version of this story, the one that is more commonly known, Crane removed the beginning and ending that reveal the protagonist to be slumming; yet, though his social origins are obscured, the story still concerns a neophyte who knows nothing of the life of the underclass and who is being initiated into the ways of the Bowery slums. The high point of the tale, corresponding to the cave exploration, is the hero's entrance into an evil-smelling flophouse. He has trouble sleeping in the noisome room, for his keyed-up fancy sees morbid, highly romanticized symbols everywhere. He understands the shriek of a nightmare-tossed sleeper as a metaphoric protest of the downtrodden.

Awakening the next morning, the protagonist barely remarks on the stench, and this seems to indicate that, merely through familiarity, some of the falsely romantic pictures that he has entertained about the life of the city's poorest have begun to rub off. Exactly what positive things he has learned and of what value such learning will be to him are never clear and, indeed, as Crane grew, while his stories still turned on the loss of illusions, they began to lose the dogmatic assurance that such a change is necessarily for the good.

The last scene of the sketch, though, does make a more definite point, this one about the nature of groups. The hero has begun to associate with a fellow tramp called the assassin and now, after his initiatory night, seems both adjusted to his new station and accepted by the tramp world, at least insofar as the assassin is willing to regale him with his life story. By abandoning his preconceptions about poverty, the protagonist has quite seamlessly fitted himself into the alien milieu, yet this joining of one community has a negative side effect of distancing him from another. The last tableau has the assassin and the hero lounging on park benches as the morning rush-hour crowd streams by them. Here, soon after the hero has had the comfortable feeling of being accepted in one society, he has the poignant realization that, as a bum, he no longer belongs to the larger American working world. There is even a sly hint, given by the fact that the youth begins employing the same grandiose, romanticized terms in depicting his separation from the business world that he had earlier used to depict the flophouse, that he has embarked on a new course of building delusions. In other words, his loss of illusions about the reality of tramp life has been counteracted (as if a vacuum needed to be filled) by the imbibing of a new set of illusions about the vast gulf between the classes. Each community one may join seems to have its own supply of false perspectives.

"The Open Boat" • In 1897, after his near death at sea, Crane produced what most name his greatest short story and what some even rank as his supreme achievement, placing it above his novels. This is "The Open Boat." Again there are four men. They are in a small boat, a dinghy, escapees from a sunken vessel, desperately trying to row to shore in heavy seas.

The famed first sentence establishes both the parameters of the fictional world and a new chastening of Crane's style. It reads, "None of them knew the color of the sky." Literally, they are too intent on staying afloat to notice the heavens; figuratively, in this godless universe the men cannot look to the sky for help but must rely on their own muscles and wits, which, against the elements, are little enough. Furthermore, the opening's very dismissal of color descriptions, given that much of Crane's earlier work, such as *The Red Badge of Courage*, depends heavily on color imagery, can be seen as the author's pledge to restrain some of the flashiness of his style.

This restraint is evident not only in a more tempered use of language here but also in the nature of the protagonists' delusions. In works such as the slum experiment, the romanticized preconceptions that determine the protagonist's viewpoint can be seen as trivial products of a shallow culture—that is, as marginal concerns—whereas in the sea story, the men's illusions are necessities of life. The men in the boat want to believe that they must survive, since they have been fighting so hard. If they do not believe this, how can they continue rowing? The point is put wrenchingly at one moment when the men refuse to accept that they will drown, as it seems they will, in the breakers near the shore. Such illusions (about the meaningfulness of valor and effort) obviously have more universal relevance than others with which Crane has dealt, and that is why the story strikes so deep; the illusions also, ingeniously, tie in with readers' expectations. As much as readers begin to identify with the four men (and they are sympathetically portrayed), they will want them to survive and thus will be on the verge of agreeing to their illusions. Thus, Crane engineers a remarkable and subtle interlocking of readers' and characters' beliefs.

Furthermore, the functionality of the possibly delusive beliefs of the struggling men—that is, the fact that they need to believe that they will make it ashore to keep up the arduous fight for life—helps Crane to a fuller, more positive view of human community. The men in the cave were merely partners in error, but these toilers share a belief system that sustains them in their mutually supportive labor, which the characters themselves recognize as "a subtle brotherhood of men." The men's shared recognition of the supportive structure of human groups gives weight to the story's last phrase, which says, of the three survivors who have reached land, "and they felt that they could then be interpreters."

The story, written in the third person, is given largely from the viewpoint of one of the four, a newspaper correspondent. This is not evident at once, however, since the narrative begins by simply objectively reporting the details of the men's struggle to stay afloat and reproducing their laconic comments. In this way, the group is put first, and only later, when the correspondent's thoughts are revealed, does the reader learn of his centrality as the story begins to be slightly colored by his position. What the focus on his consciousness reveals, aiding Crane in deepening his presentation, is how the subtle brotherhood is felt individually.

After rowing near to the shore but not being able to attract anyone's attention, the crew settle down for a night at sea. While whoever is rowing stays awake, the others sleep like the dead they may soon become, and at this point, the story dwells more intently on the correspondent's outlook as he takes his turn at the oars. The newspaperman reconsiders the beliefs that have been keeping them afloat, seeing the weakness in them and accepting, now that he is alone, the possibility of an ironic death—that is, one coming in sight of shore after their courageous struggle. Yet his existential angst, an acknowledgment that there is no special heavenly providence, neither stops him from his muscle-torturing rowing nor diminishes his revived illusions on the morrow, when they again all breast the waves together.

If this line of reasoning shows him mentally divorcing himself from the collective ideology, another night thought implies that, in another direction, he is gaining a deeper sense of solidarity. He remembers a verse that he had learned in school about a legionnaire dying far from home with only a comrade to share his last moments.

The correspondent had thought little of the poem, both because he had never been in extremis (and so saw little to the pathos of the case) and, as Crane notes, had formerly looked cynically at his fellows (and so had found unpalatable or unbelievable the care of one soldier for another). A day's experience in the dinghy has made him keenly aware of the two aspects of experience that he had overlooked or undervalued, and thus has given him a clear understanding of the networks (those of democratic brotherhood) and circumstances (a no-holds-barred fight against an indifferent universe) that underlie the human social world. This understanding can be applied in many ways, not only toward a grasp of group interaction but also toward an interpretation of honest art.

Still, the most telling incident of his lonely watch is not so much any of his thoughts as an action. The boat, the correspondent finds, has become the magnet to a huge shark. Achingly, he wishes that one of his fellow sailors were awake to share his fidgety vigil; yet, he resists any impulse he has to rouse them or even to question aloud whether any of them is conscious for fear that he should waken a sleeper. Even if alone he cannot continue with the group illusion, he can, though alone, effortlessly maintain the group's implicit morality, which holds that each should uncomplainingly shoulder as much of the burden as possible, while never revealing irritation or fear. Much later, the newspaperman learns that another of the four, the captain, was awake and aware of the predator's presence during what had been taken to be the correspondent's moment of isolated anguish. The hidden coexistent alertness of the captain suggests the ongoing mutuality of the group that undergirds even seemingly isolated times of subjectivity.

To bring this story in line with the last one mentioned, it is worth noting that the small group in the boat is contrasted to a group on shore just as, in "An Experiment in Misery," the hoboes were contrasted to the society of the gainfully employed. When the rowers are near the coast on the first day, they vainly hope to attract the ministering attentions of people on land. They do attract their attention, but the people, tourists from a hotel, merrily wave at them, thinking that the men in the dinghy are fishermen. The heedlessness, inanity, and seeming stupidity of the group on shore compare unfavorably with the hard-won, brave alertness of the boatmen, pointing to the fact that the small group's ethical solidarity is not of a type with the weaker unity found in the larger society. The men's deep harmony rather—beautiful as it is—is something that can be found only in pockets. The depicting of the community on the land foreshadows elements of Crane's later, darker pictures of community, as in "The Blue Hotel," where what sustains a group is not a life-enhancing though flimsy hope but a tacitly accepted lie.

"The Bride Comes to Yellow Sky" • In the year that he wrote "The Open Boat" and the next year, Crane was to compose three other brilliant stories, two of which dealt with myths of the Old West. Both these Western tales were written in his mature, unadorned style, and both continued his focus on the belief systems of communities. What is new to them is a greater flexibility in the handling of plot. Previously, he had simply followed his characters through a continuous chronological sequence from start to finish; now, however, he began shifting between differently located character groups and jumping around in time.

In "The Bride Comes to Yellow Sky," the action begins on a train moving through Texas, carrying Yellow Sky's sheriff, Jack Potter, and his new wife back to town. Potter is apprehensive about his reception, since he has married out of town in a whirlwind courtship and none of the townspeople knows of his new status. The scene shifts to the interior of a Yellow Sky saloon, where the gathered, barricaded patrons have other things to be apprehensive about than Potter's marriage. Scratchy Wilson, the local ruffian, has gotten drunk and is shooting in the main street, while, as the bar's occupants admit, the only man able to cow him is the absent sheriff. Scratchy Wilson himself, as the reader learns in another scene shift, not aware of Potter's trip, is truculently looking for the sheriff so that they can engage in a showdown. In truth, the reader, knowing of Potter's imminence, will probably share Wilson's expectation of a gun battle, which is not an unreasonable forecast of the plot's unfolding. Yet, this expectation is founded on a deeper belief, that the West will always be an uncivilized place of outlaws and pistols. A chagrined Scratchy recognizes that this belief is invalid and that an era has passed when he finds that the sheriff has taken a wife. After meeting the couple, he holsters his guns and stalks off toward the horizon.

"The Blue Hotel" • A tragic variation on similar themes of violence and community beliefs appears in "The Blue Hotel," a story that a few critics rank in importance above "The Open Boat." The tale concerns a fatalistic traveler, the Swede, who stops for the night in a hotel in Nebraska. (This protagonist's name will be picked up by Ernest Hemingway, a Crane admirer, for an equally fatalistic character in his short-story masterpiece "The Killers.") Through the Swede's conversation with the hotel owner, Scully, and other stoppers, it appears that, based perhaps on an immersion in dime novels, the Swede thinks that this town—or, for that matter, any town in the West—is a hotbed of bloodshed and mayhem. After his fears seem to be allayed by the officious owner, who assures him that he is mistaken, the Swede overreacts by becoming boisterous and familiar. This mood of his eventually dissipates when, involved in a game of cards, he accuses the owner's son of cheating. The upshot is that the pair engage in a fistfight, which the Swede wins. He is now triumphant but can no longer find any welcome at the hotel; so he wanders off to a nearby saloon, in which his even more high-strung and aggressive demonstrations lead to his death at the hands of an icy but violent gambler he had been prodding to drink with him.

At this point, the story seems a grim meditation on the truth or falsity of myths. What seemed to be the manifestly absurd belief of the Swede has been proven partially true by his own death. Yet, it appears this truth would never have been exposed except for the Swede's own pushy production of the proper circumstances for Western violence to emerge. There is, however, another turn of the cards. A final scene is described in which, months later, two of the hotel's card players, witnesses of the dispute between the Swede and Scully's son, discuss events of that fateful evening. One of them, the easterner, claims that the whole group collected at the hotel that night is responsible for what led to the death since they all knew that the owner's son was cheating but did not back up the Swede when he accused the youth.

In one way, this final episode indicates that perhaps the Swede's suspicions were accurate in yet another sense; the whole town is made up, metaphorically, of killers in that the community is willing to sacrifice an outsider to maintain its own dubious harmony. From this angle, though, this Western town's particular violence merely crystallizes and externalizes any hypocritical town's underlying psychic economy. (Crane depicted this economy more explicitly in his novella *The Monster*.) In another way— and here the increasing complexity of Crane's thought on community is evident— even after the final episode, it still appears that the Swede's murder has some justification.

There are two points to be made in this connection. For one, throughout the story, Crane represents the frailty of human existence as it is established on the prairies in the depths of winter. The story begins by underlining the presumptuousness of Scully's hotel's bright blue color, not so much as it may be an affront to the other, staider buildings in town, but in its assertiveness against the grimness of the white wastes of nature surrounding and swamping the little burg. The insignificance of human beings measured against the universe is explicitly stated by Crane in an oft-quoted passage. He speaks of humans clinging to a "whirling, fire-smitten, icelocked, disease-stricken, space-lost bulb." He goes on to say that the "conceit of man" in striving to prevail in such conditions is "the very engine of life." It is true that they all killed the Swede in some sense, but the fragility of the human community, it may be surmised, demands that its members all practice respect and forbearance toward one another so that a common front can be presented against uncaring nature. If anyone consistently violates this unwritten code, as the Swede does, he must be eliminated for group self-preservation. It is significant in this light that the Swede, who demands a grudge match with the owner's son, would take the men away from the large, red-hot stove (symbol of the warmth of peaceful intercourse and home comfort) outside to fight in subzero weather. To restate this, for his own egotistical purposes, the Swede would drag everyone into a much greater exposure to a harsh environment than life in the community, were it running harmoniously, would ever make necessary.

The second point to be made is that Crane's portrait of the gambler, which interrupts the narrative at a high point and which, thus, seems at first sight a cumbersome miscalculation by the author, allows the reader a fuller understanding of the place of an outsider in this Western society. If readers were given only the Swede's treatment to go by, they would be forced to conclude that, whatever the necessity of the visitor's expulsion, this town has little tolerance for aberrant personalities. Yet, such a position has to be modified after Crane's presentation of the gambler, whose disreputable calling excludes him from the city's better social functions but whose behavior in other areas—he bows to the restrictions put on him with good grace and is a charitable family man who will not prey on the better citizens—conforms enough to standards to allow him to be generally accepted. Intervening at this point, Crane's portrayal of this second (relative) outsider is used to indicate that the community will permit in its midst a character who has not followed all of its rules, provided such a character does not, as the Swede does, insistently and continuously breach the accepted norms.

All this taken together does not, certainly, excuse a murder. What it does show is that Crane's understanding of how a community sustains itself has expanded beyond the understanding that he had at the time of the sea story. He indicates that the guiding principle of mutual support found in the dinghy has remained operative, even in a far less threatened situation, while adding that violations of this principle can lead to less happy consequences than might have been foreseen in the earlier story.

"Death and the Child" • Finally, in "Death and the Child," Crane produced an excellent story about war, the topic which had been both the most consistent and the least successful subject of his short pieces. The intertwined themes of the effect of illusions and the ways that an individual can be integrated into, or excluded from, a community, the most important themes of Crane's work, are again central. In this piece, the character who nurses illusions is Peza, a journalist who has decided to join the Greek side during the Greco-Turkish War, motivated by unrealistic ideas about the glories of classical Greece and the adventure of fighting. Once he reaches the battle lines, however, he finds it impossible to join the other combatants. He is displeased by the nonchalance of the troops, who refuse to strike heroic poses, but what actually ends up turning him away from solidarity is his realization that to become part of the group he must accept not only a largely humdrum life but also the possibility of a prosaic death. In other words, it is not coming down to earth with the common men that ultimately scares him but the understanding that he may have to come down under the earth (into a grave) with them.

The story exhibits what had become the traits of Crane's mature style. He writes with a terse, crisp, subdued prose that is occasionally shot through with startling or picturesque imagery, this imagery being the residue of his initial, more flowery style. Crane also exhibits a mastery of plotting. This is brought out by the careful joining of Peza's emotional states to his gyrations around the battle camp as well as by the story's final encounter, where Peza comes upon an abandoned child, who, too young to comprehend war, still has a clearer view of reality than the distraught journalist. This skill at plotting is not something that Crane possessed from the beginning, which brings up a last point.

It might be said that there is a chronological distinction between Crane's interests and his method of narration. Although his thematic concerns remained constant throughout his writing career, as he grew older his attention to how a community was created and sustained grew in weight. His ability to construct complex plots is one that he picked up during the course of his creative life. There are authors who advance little after their first books, but in Crane's case, it can definitely be said that there was a promise for the future that his short life never redeemed.

James Feast

Other major works

PLAYS: *The Blood of the Martyr,* wr. 1898?, pb. 1940; *The Ghost,* pr. 1899 (with Henry James; fragment).

NOVELS: *Maggie: A Girl of the Streets,* 1893; *The Red Badge of Courage: An Episode of the American Civil War,* 1895; *George's Mother,* 1896; *The Third Violet,* 1897; *The Monster,* 1898 (serial), 1899 (novella; pb. in *The Monster, and Other Stories*); *Active Service,* 1899; *The O'Ruddy: A Romance,* 1903 (with Robert Barr).

NONFICTION: *The Great Battles of the World,* 1901; *The War Dispatches of Stephen Crane,* 1964.

POETRY: *The Black Riders and Other Lines,* 1895; *A Souvenir and a Medley,* 1896; *War Is Kind,* 1899; *The University Press of Virginia Edition of the Works of Stephen Crane,* 1970 (volume 10).

Bibliography

Benfey, Christopher E. G. *The Double Life of Stephen Crane.* New York: Alfred A. Knopf, 1992. Narrative of Crane's life and literary work that argues that the writer attempted to live the life his works portrayed. Includes bibliography and index.

Berryman, John. *Stephen Crane: A Critical Biography.* Cooper Square Press, 2001. Reissue of the first major biography of the author, first published in 1950. Still valuable for its detail and insight.

Colvert, James B. *Stephen Crane.* New York: Harcourt Brace Jovanovich, 1984. This biography, aimed specifically at the nonspecialist, is highly readable and is enhanced by numerous illustrations. Its bibliography is limited but well selected. The author's research is impeccable.

_____. "Stephen Crane and Postmodern Theory." *American Literary Realism* 28 (Fall, 1995): 4-22. A survey of postmodern approaches to Crane's fiction. Summarizes the basic premises of postmodern interpretation, examining how these premises have been applied to such Crane stories as "The Open Boat," "The Upturned Face," and "Maggie"; balances such interpretive strategies against critics who affirm more traditional, humanistic approaches.

Halliburton, David. *The Color of the Sky: A Study of Stephen Crane.* New York: Cambridge University Press, 1989. Though somewhat thematically disorganized, the author's philosophical grounding and ability to look at Crane's works from unusual angles make for many provocative readings. In his discussion of "The Blue Hotel," for example, he finds much more aggression directed against the Swede than may at first appear, coming not only from seemingly benign characters but also from the layout of the town. Notes, index.

Knapp, Bettina L. *Stephen Crane.* New York: Frederick Ungar, 1987. Succinct introduction to Crane's life and career, with a separate chapter on his biography, several chapters on his fiction, and an extensive discussion of two poetry collections, *The Black Riders and Other Lines* and *War Is Kind.* Includes a detailed chronology, a bibliography of primary and secondary sources, and an index.

May, Charles E., ed. *Masterplots II: Short Story Series, Revised Edition.* 8 vols. Pasadena, Calif.: Salem Press, 2004. Designed for student use, this reference set contains articles providing detailed plot summaries and analyses of these eight short stories by Crane: "The Blue Hotel" and "The Bride Comes to Yellow Sky" (vol. 1), "Death and the Child" and "An Episode of War" (vol. 2), "An Experiment in Misery" (vol. 3), "The Monster" and "The Open Boat" (vol. 5), and "The Upturned Face" (vol. 8).

Metress, Christopher. "From Indifference to Anxiety: Knowledge and the Reader in 'The Open Boat.'" *Studies in Short Fiction* 28 (Winter, 1991): 47-53. Shows how the structure of "The Open Boat" (made up of four key moments) creates an epistemological dilemma for readers, moving them from a position of indifference to a state of epistemological anxiety. By suggesting that the survivors have become interpreters, Crane implies that one must get rid of indifference to the difficulty of gaining knowledge and embrace the inevitable anxiety of that failure.

Robertson, Michael. *Stephen Crane: Journalism and the Making of Modern American Literature.* New York: Columbia University Press, 1997. Argues that Crane's success inspired later journalists to think of their work as preparatory for writing fiction; claims the blurring of fact and fiction in newspapers during Crane's life suited his own narrative experiments.

Wertheim, Stanley. *A Stephen Crane Encyclopedia.* Westport, Conn.: Greenwood Press, 1997. Very thorough volume of Crane information. Includes bibliographical references and an index.

Wolford, Chester L., Jr. *Stephen Crane: A Study of the Short Fiction.* Boston: Twayne, 1989. This overly brief but useful look at Crane's short fiction provides Wolford's sensitive readings as well as commentary on the major points that have been raised in critical discussions of the Crane pieces. In describing "The Bride Comes to Yellow Sky," for example, Wolford explains his view of how the story fits into the archetypical patterns of the passing of the West narratives, while also exploring why other critics have seen Crane's story as a simple parody.

Walter de la Mare

Born: Charlton, Kent, England; April 25, 1873
Died: Twickenham, Middlesex, England; June 22, 1956

Principal short fiction • *Story and Rhyme: A Selection*, 1921; *The Riddle, and Other Stories*, 1923; *Ding Dong Bell*, 1924; *Broomsticks, and Other Tales*, 1925; *Miss Jemima*, 1925; *Readings*, 1925-1926 (2 volumes); *The Connoisseur, and Other Tales*, 1926; *Old Joe*, 1927; *Told Again: Traditional Tales*, 1927; *On the Edge*, 1930; *Seven Short Stories*, 1931; *The Lord Fish*, 1933; *The Nap, and Other Stories*, 1936; *The Wind Blows Over*, 1936; *Animal Stories*, 1939; *The Picnic*, 1941; *The Best Stories of Walter de la Mare*, 1942; *The Old Lion, and Other Stories*, 1942; *The Magic Jacket, and Other Stories*, 1943; *The Scarecrow, and Other Stories*, 1945; *The Dutch Cheese, and Other Stories*, 1946; *Collected Stories for Children*, 1947; *A Beginning, and Other Stories*, 1955; *Ghost Stories*, 1956; *Short Stories, 1927-1956*, 2001 (Giles de la Mare, editor).

Other literary forms • In addition to his numerous volumes of short fiction, Walter de la Mare published poetry, novels, anthologies of various kinds, collections of essays, one play, and scores of essays, reviews, and articles published separately. In the United States, de la Mare is better known as a children's writer than he is for the other genres in which he worked.

Achievements • Walter de la Mare's remarkable literary career spans more than five decades. The English novelist, poet, dramatist, short-story writer, critic, essayist, and anthropologist is best known today as a writer infused with a Romantic imagination. He has often been compared to William Blake and Thomas Hardy because of similarities in thematic development of mortality and visionary illumination. Often labeled as an escapist because of his retreat from reality, de la Mare touches on dreams, fantasy worlds, emotional states, and transcendent pursuits. Best known in the United States for his children's literature, he has produced numerous volumes of prose and verse in the genre. All his work is suffused by a childlike quality of imagination. De la Mare's writings have still not received the attention they deserve. He lived a quiet, uneventful life, always reluctant to impart information about himself. Throughout his life de la Mare wrote poetry. It is this work that represents his truest and most lasting literary achievement. In 1948, de la Mare received the Companion of Honour and in 1953, the Order of Merit. During the next three years he also received honorary degrees from five colleges, including Oxford and Cambridge.

Biography • Walter de la Mare was born on April 25, 1873, in Charlton, Kent, the son of well-to-do parents, James Edward de la Mare and Lucy Sophia Browning de la Mare. In her book *Walter de la Mare* (1966), Doris Ross McCrosson said that de la Mare's life "was singularly and refreshingly uneventful." De la Mare was educated at St. Paul's Cathedral Choir School in London, where he was the founder and editor of the school magazine, *The Choristers' Journal*. In 1890, at the age of seventeen, de la Mare began working as a bookkeeper at the Anglo-American Oil Company in London, a position he held for almost twenty years. While working as a bookkeeper, de la Mare began

Library of Congress

writing stories, essays, and poetry, many of which were published in various magazines. For a while, de la Mare wrote under the pseudonym "Walter Ramal." Soon after the publication of his first books, he was granted a civil list pension by the British government amounting to one hundred pounds a year. Thereafter, he devoted himself entirely to literature and writing. De la Mare died at home on June 22, 1956, at the age of eighty-three. He is buried at St. Paul's Cathedral.

Analysis • Walter de la Mare's stories take the form both of wish fulfillment and nightmare projections. Believing that the everyday world of mundane experience is a veil hiding a "real" world, de la Mare used dream forms as a means of piercing the veil as well as a means of suggesting that between dream and reality looms, as de la Mare said, "no impassable abyss." Because of their hallucinatory character, dreams merge with states of madness, travel to mysterious realms, childhood visions. The surfaces of de la Mare's stories belie an underlying reality; rendering the texture of everyday experience with exquisite detail, he built his surfaces with such lucidity that a reader is often surprised to find a horror beneath that which is apparently placid or a joy beneath that which is apparently mundane.

"The Riddle" • "The Riddle" starts like a fairy tale with such lightness and grace that one might expect a "happy ever after" ending. Soon, however, it becomes apparent that the quavering voice of the grandmother betokens something more than age, and the gifts she presents to her seven grandchildren become something more than sugar plums. Although it is never made explicit, one may assume that the grandchildren have come to live with their grandmother because of the death of their parents. The aged woman says to the children, "bring me smiling faces that call back to my mind my own son Harry." The children are told they may come in the presence of their grandmother twice a day—in the morning and in the evening. The rest of the time they have the run of the house with the exception of the large spare bedroom where there stands in a corner an old oak chest, older than the aged woman's own grandmother.

The chest represents death. It is later revealed to be decorated as a coffin, and it attracts the children one by one. Harry is first. Opening the chest, he finds something strangely seductive that reminds him of his mother, so he climbs in and the lid miraculously closes. When the other children tell their grandmother of Harry's disappearance, she responds, "Then he must be gone away for a time. . . . But remember, all of you, do not meddle with the oak chest."

Now it becomes apparent that the grandmother, herself so close to death that she seems more feeble every day, is also to be identified with the oak chest and that rather than a good fairy dispensing sugarplums she is a wicked witch seducing the children to their death. Ann is the last child to be called to the chest, and she walks as if in a dream and as if she were being guided by the hand. One paragraph more ends the story. With the children all gone, the grandmother enters the spare room, but her eyesight is too dim for her to see, and her mind is a tangled skein of memories which include memories of little children.

"The Orgy" • "The Orgy: An Idyll" seems an entirely different kind of story. Rather than being set in a house with myriad rooms suggesting something of the gothic, "The Orgy" is set mainly in a large and elegant department store in London; rather than beginning with a "once upon a time" element, it opens on a bright May morning, crisp, brisk, scintillating. Details of the great packed street down which Philip walks leave readers no doubt that here is the world of their own experience. Before the action is ended, however, it becomes clear that the story is an extravaganza. Philip is engaged in a buying orgy, charging everything that strikes his fancy to the account of his uncle who has just disinherited him, and the orgy is a fanciful idyll of the wish fulfillment variety. Philip's desire for revenge projected into bright, hallucinatory images is carried into action in exactly the way the uncle will understand—to the tune of "a couple of hundred thousand pounds," a considerable amount of money in 1931, the year the story was published.

"In the Forest" • "In the Forest" is a brilliant exercise in point of view restricted to the mind of a small boy in such a way that the childlike behavior and lack of perception characteristic of the very young take on the aura of nightmare. At no time does de la Mare vary the focus; no words are used that a child could not know; no insight is offered that a child could not understand. Although the child occasionally feels a twinge of guilt because he has not obeyed his mother, he is completely impervious to the horror of the action going on around him.

The story opens when the boy's father is leaving to go to war. The boy is half asleep and is moving in and out of consciousness. It is the advent of the fall of the year, and a storm has brought down leaves that are still green from the trees. Although the leaves are still green, it is getting cold. The boy asks his father to bring him a gun back from the war and notices without comment that his father, instead of leaving immediately, keeps coming back to say good-bye. Unaware of the anguish being suffered by his father and mother, the boy asks his mother if she is glad his father is going to the war. The mother does not answer, but the boy's simple statement makes the point. "But she was crying over the baby, so I went out into the forest till dinner."

Later the boy chops wood, an activity that causes him to be hot and excited, and then he brings the logs into the house. The wind is roaring as if it is angry, more leaves are falling, and the weather is cold and misty. The boy finds his mother asleep with the baby in her arms, and the baby, too, is asleep, although, as the boy notices, the baby scarcely seems to be breathing. The boy falls asleep by the warm hearth and stays there all night. In the morning he rushes out, glad that his father is gone, because now he can do just as he pleases. Visiting the snares, he finds a young rabbit caught by one leg and, imitating his father, kills the hare with a crack on the neck and carries it to the house by the hind legs. Later he wonders how "they would carry back" his father's body "if he was killed in the war."

Because the baby is crying, the boy chooses to spend his days in the forest until one day when he tells his mother he is going to "bring her some fish for dinner!" The dialogue that follows is the first that occurs in the story. The mother tells the boy that the baby is very ill and tries to get him to touch and hold his baby brother, asking: "Do you love it?" The boy shakes his head and persists: "I think I should *like* to go fishing mother . . . and I promise you shall have the biggest I catch." Then, denying the mother's plea that he go for the doctor, the boy runs out saying, "It's only crying."

The boy catches no fish and believes the fish would not bite because he has been wicked, so he goes home, and now for the first time he hears cannons on the other side of the forest. When he gets home, he finds his mother angry, calling him a coward, and the baby dead. The next day he consents to his mother's request that he go for the sexton, but as he is on his way he hears a rifle sound and "a scream like a rabbit," and he is frightened and runs home. Since his mother has already called him a coward, however, he lies to her, telling her the sexton was gone. Now the mother decides she must take the dead baby to the graveyard herself, and once again she addresses her son: "Won't you kiss your little brother, Robbie?"

Alone, the boy eats more than he should and builds the fire up so high that its noise drowns out any outside noises. Alone, he believes he is in a dream "that would never come to an end." He does not cry, but he feels angry at being left alone, and he is afraid. He also feels guilty about the amount of food he has consumed. He fears his mother's return and yet longs for her, feeling that he loves her and is sorry for his wickedness.

The next thing he knows, it is broad daylight. His mother has still not returned, but he hears a groan at the doorway. It is his father with a "small hole" at the back of his shoulder; dark, thick blood covers the withered leaves on which he lies. The boy tries to give his father water and tells him about the baby, "but he didn't show that he could hear anything." Then the boy hears his mother coming back and runs out to tell her "that it was father." The story ends as abruptly as it begins, but the point of view so neatly restricted and the image patterns masterfully arranged create the tenor and vehicle of an Everyman's Freudian nightmare. The subtly stated but powerfully conveyed theme delineates an Oedipal pattern that raises the story from an isolated and factual experience to an overwhelming and communal dream having mythic proportions.

"An Ideal Craftsman" • "An Ideal Craftsman" is just as powerful. Although the story makes use of a young boy as protagonist, point of view is different from that found in "In the Forest." This time de la Mare allows an omniscient narrator to move in and out of the consciousness of the two major characters. Once again, however, a horror is present, foreshadowed from the beginning of the story; once again the aura of dream is cast over the entire story; and once again death, this time murder, is the focal point of the story.

For a short-story writer of such consummate skill, de la Mare has attracted almost no critical attention, and what books have been written about him concentrate more on his other writings than on his pieces of short fiction. This lack of attention is a great pity. In her book *Walter de la Mare*, McCrosson devotes only one chapter of some twenty pages to de la Mare's short-story craft, but her summary of his achievement is accurate:

His preoccupation with good and evil puts him on a level with [Nathaniel] Hawthorne and [Joseph] Conrad; his mastery of suspense and terror is equal to [Edger Allen] Poe's; the subtlety of his characterizations occasionally rivals [Henry] James's. And the range of his portrayals is impressive: children, old maids, the demented, old idealists and young pessimists, artists, business men, dandys, young women in love—all of whom share in the mysterious and sometimes maddening business called living.

Mary Rohrberger
With updates by Terry Theodore

Other major works

PLAY: *Crossings: A Fairy Play*, pr. 1919.

ANTHOLOGIES: *Come Hither*, 1923; *The Shakespeare Songs*, 1929; *Christina Rossetti's Poems*, 1930; *Desert Islands and Robinson Crusoe*, 1930; *Stories from the Bible*, 1930; *Early One Morning in the Spring*, 1935; *Animal Stories*, 1939; *Behold, This Dreamer!*, 1939; *Love*, 1943.

NOVELS: *Henry Brocken*, 1904; *The Return*, 1910; *The Three Mulla-Mulgars*, 1910 (reprinted as *The Three Royal Monkeys: Or, The Three Mulla-Mulgars*, 1935); *Memoirs of a Midget*, 1921; *At First Sight: A Novel*, 1928.

NONFICTION: *Rupert Brooke and the Intellectual Imagination*, 1919; *The Printing of Poetry*, 1931; *Lewis Carroll*, 1932; *Poetry in Prose*, 1936; *Pleasures and Speculations*, 1940; *Chardin, J.B.S. 1699-1779*, 1948; *Private View*, 1953.

POETRY: *Songs of Childhood*, 1902; *Poems*, 1906; *A Child's Day: A Book of Rhymes*, 1912; *The Listeners, and Other Poems*, 1912; *Peacock Pie: A Book of Rhymes*, 1913; *The Sunken Garden, and Other Poems*, 1917; *Motley, and Other Poems*, 1918; *Flora: A Book of Drawings*, 1919; *Poems 1901 to 1918*, 1920; *Story and Rhyme*, 1921; *The Veil, and Other Poems*, 1921; *Down-Adown-Derry: A Book of Fairy Poems*, 1922; *Thus Her Tale*, 1923; *A Ballad of Christmas*, 1924; *Stuff and Nonsense and So On*, 1927; *Self to Self*, 1928; *The Snowdrop*, 1929; *News*, 1930; *Poems for Children*, 1930; *Lucy*, 1931; *Old Rhymes and New*, 1932; *The Fleeting, and Other Poems*, 1933; *Poems, 1919 to 1934*, 1935; *This Year, Next Year*, 1937; *Memory, and Other Poems*, 1938; *Haunted*, 1939; *Bells and Grass*, 1941; *Collected Poems*, 1941; *Collected Rhymes and Verses*, 1944; *The Burning-Glass, and Other Poems*, 1945; *The Traveller*, 1946; *Rhymes and Verses: Collected Poems for Young People*, 1947; *Inward Companion*, 1950; *Winged Chariot*, 1951; *O Lovely England, and Other Poems*, 1953; *The Complete Poems*, 1969.

Bibliography

Allen, Walter. *The Short Story in English.* New York: Oxford University Press, 1981. Argues that, as a short-story writer, de la Mare closely resembles Henry James in his supernatural stories, for his stories are rooted in mundane reality.

Beetz, Kirk H. "Walter de la Mare." In *Critical Survey of Long Fiction, Revised Edition*, edited by Carl Rollyson. Vol. 2. Pasadena, Calif.: Salem Press, 2000. Analysis of de la Mare's longer fictional works that may offer insights into his short fiction.

Benntinck, Anne. *Romantic Imagery in the Works of Walter de la Mare.* Lewiston, N.Y.: Edwin Mellen Press, 2001. Devotes one chapter apiece to each of seven major Romantic themes or leitmotifs in de la Mare's poetry. Includes bibliography, index of works, general index.

Manwaring, Randle. "Memories of Walter de la Mare." *Contemporary Review* 264 (March, 1994): 148-152. A reminiscence of a longtime acquaintance of de la Mare that comments on his style and his influence. Reflects de la Mare's childish delight in simple things that is so often reflected in his stories.

May, Charles E., ed. *Masterplots II: Short Story Series, Revised Edition.* 8 vols. Pasadena, Calif.: Salem Press, 2004. Designed for student use, this reference set contains articles providing detailed plot summaries and analyses of these four short stories by de la Mare: "A Recluse," "A Revenant," and "Seaton's Aunt" (vol. 6); and "The Trumpet" (vol. 7).

Perkins, David. "Craftsmen of the Beautiful and the Agreeable." In *A History of Modern Poetry.* Vol. 1. Cambridge, Mass.: Harvard University Press, 1976. Perkins emphasizes de la Mare's complicated relationship to the Romantics. Like them, he often wrote about the world as a dream. He was aware of the conventional nature of Romantic poetry, and often the poems are about conventions. Unlike certain Romantics, he does not portray evil as sublime. He is a master at interrogative conversation and anticipates the modernist stress on the accents of daily speech.

Sisson, C. H. *English Poetry, 1900-1950.* Manchester, England: Carcanet Press, 1981. Sisson mentions that de la Mare was the last of the Romantics. His poetry combines Romantic themes with the more personal themes of twentieth century verse. It is characterized by purity of language and hushed, intimate accents, and it succeeds in capturing the intimate rhythms of speech. De la Mare was at his best in a limited range of subjects. His finest work pictures life on the edge of a dream.

Wagenknecht, Edward. *Seven Masters of Supernatural Fiction.* New York: Greenwood Press, 1991. See the chapter on Walter de la Mare, which includes a brief biographical sketch and discusses his fiction in the context of the English literary tradition. Wagenknecht deals with both the short and the long fiction, providing a succinct overview of de la Mare's body of work in prose.

Whistler, Theresa. *Imagination of the Heart: The Life of Walter de la Mare.* London: Duckworth, 1993. Good biography of de la Mare. Includes bibliographical references and an index.

Isak Dinesen

Born: Rungsted, Denmark; April 17, 1885
Died: Rungsted, Denmark; September 7, 1962

Principal short fiction • *Seven Gothic Tales*, 1934; *Vinter-Eventyr*, 1942 (*Winter's Tales*, 1942); *Sidste Fortællinger*, 1957 (*Last Tales*, 1957); *Skæbne-Anekdoter*, 1958 (*Anecdotes of Destiny*, 1958); *Ehrengard*, 1963; *Efterladte Fortællinger*, 1975 (*Carnival: Entertainments and Posthumous Tales*, 1977).

Other literary forms • In addition to her numerous tales and stories, Isak Dinesen wrote many letters and essays. She is particularly well known, however, for her narrative *Den afrikanske Farm* (1937; *Out of Africa*, 1937), which tells of her years in Kenya (a sequel was published in 1960). After her death, two volumes of letters, written while in Africa, were published, as were her essays.

Achievements • Isak Dinesen has a special position in modern literature in that she is a major author in two languages. Although a native of Denmark, she wrote in both English and Danish, creating her tales as original works in both tongues. Popular with the critics as well as the general public, she was appointed an honorary member of the American Academy of Arts and Letters in 1957 and was repeatedly mentioned as a candidate for the Nobel Prize in Literature. Her initial success came in the English-speaking world. With time, however, she became successful also at home, where her magnetic personality and storytelling gifts gradually captivated the public. Aided by the medium of radio, she became a veritable cultural institution in Denmark. Since her death, her critical reputation has steadily grown both at home and abroad, and she has come to be considered a modern master of short fiction.

Biography • Isak Dinesen's life may be divided into three parts, namely her childhood and youth, her time in Africa, and her years as a recognized writer. Her parents came from very different social backgrounds. From her father, Wilhelm Dinesen, a landed proprietor, she inherited a love of adventure, nature, and storytelling. Her mother, in contrast, came from a bourgeois family of merchants and attempted to foster a sense of duty, obligation, and guilt in her three daughters. Karen Christenze (Isak is a pseudonym that she assumed at the beginning of her writing career) was her father's favorite daughter and thereby was able to avoid some of her mother's puritanical manacles. At the age of ten, however, her father's suicide turned her youth into a period of mostly joyless desperation. Early she began writing stories and short plays, for which she had been prepared by an unsystematic private education. She also studied art and traveled abroad with her mother, sisters, and aunt.

The second period in Dinesen's life began in 1914, when she married her first cousin, the Baron Bror Blixen-Finecke, and with him settled down to manage a coffee plantation outside Nairobi, in British East Africa. Her husband infected her with syphilis and proved himself a poor manager of the plantation; the couple was separated in 1921 and divorced four years later. Living in Kenya as the manager of a different, and larger, coffee farm, Dinesen cultivated a friendship with Denys Finch

Hatton, whom she had met in 1918. A confirmed bachelor, Finch Hatton had no desire to marry Dinesen, which grieved her. Dinesen's African life came to an end in 1931, when the coffee farm had to be sold and Finch Hatton died in the crash of his private plane.

Dinesen returned to Denmark in a state of abject poverty. Supported by her family and inspired by the success of a few stories, which years earlier had been published under the pen name Osceola, she set out to create a new life for herself as a writer. Other stories, written during her African sojourn, existed in draft form, and some of these gradually became perfected and included in *Seven Gothic Tales*, the English-language edition of which became both a critical and a popular success. Her autobiographical narrative *Out of Africa* established her as a major presence on the literary scene both in Denmark and in the English-language world, and subsequent books were also enthusiastically received. An indication of Dinesen's popularity in the United States is the fact that five of her titles were chosen as Book-of-the-Month Club selections. Living at her birthplace, Rungsted, north of Copenhagen, Denmark, she gathered her admirers around her and tended her literary reputation.

During most of her adult life, Dinesen was plagued by illness, which was exacerbated by much strenuous travel abroad and the entertainment of numerous guests at home. After a particularly taxing summer, she died at her home on September 7, 1962.

Analysis • Isak Dinesen reacted against the psychological and social realism of contemporary Danish literature and looked back to the Romantic storytellers for inspiration. Like them, she preferred the longer, drawn-out tale to the short story proper, and authorial narration, often with overtly present narrators, is a hallmark of her narratives. Her chosen form therefore often struck her contemporaries as old-fashioned. This was also the case with her thematic concerns, for her stories take place mostly in the century between 1770 and 1870 and express the ethos of a bygone age. She speaks in favor of such aristocratic values as duty, honor, and justice, but she also rejects the Christian dualistic worldview and questions the role of religion and the place of women in contemporary bourgeois society. Above all, however, the role of art in human life constitutes a central theme of her authorship. Through art, a unified vision is possible, and such a monistic perception of reality is, for Dinesen, a primary source of meaning in general and of comfort in difficult times.

"The Monkey" • "Aben" ("The Monkey"), a long story from *Seven Gothic Tales*, is a good example of Dinesen's "gothic" or fantastic narratives that also exhibits many of her thematic concerns. Its setting is a noble milieu in northern Germany in the 1830's; its theme is the nature of love. Boris, a young lieutenant in the Prussian Royal Guards, has become involved in a homosexual scandal in the capital and is seeking the aid of his maiden aunt, Cathinka, the Prioress of Cloister Seven, a convent for spinsters of noble blood. In order to escape dishonor and almost certain death, Boris has resolved to marry, thus hoping to lay to rest the rumors of his homosexual involvement with other members of his regiment. His aunt, who is well acquainted with the various noble families of the land, is being asked to select a suitable mate for him. The fantastic element of the story is found in the relationship between the Prioress and her little gray monkey, to which she has a mysterious bond and with which she, from time to time and in accordance with traditional Scandinavian folk belief in shape-shifting, exchanges her identity. The monkey is connected with the idea of love through the love goddess of an ancient Baltic people, the Wends. The goddess looks like a beautiful woman from the front and like a monkey from the back. Through this image, Dinesen argues against the Judeo-Christian distinction between the heteroerotic, which is acceptable to society, and the homoerotic, which is not. Speaking in favor of a monistic outlook on human sexuality, Dinesen, through the similarity between the Wendish love-goddess and the Janus face, problematizes the distinction between normal and abnormal sexuality. The text actually foregrounds the question of how it can be determined which side is the front and which is the back of the goddess, and the implied answer is that no such determination can be made on objective grounds.

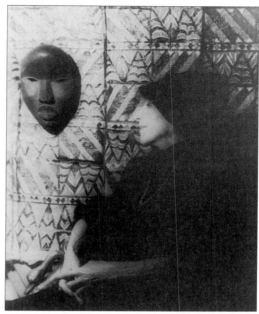

There is, nevertheless, a recognition on Dinesen's part that people have to live up to the expectations of their society if they are to get along in life. Boris has certain duties to his family, and, despite his sexual difference from the norm, he is obligated to repress his desires and to force himself to marry. The Prioress, who at this time and in a mysterious way is possessed by aspects of her monkey's personality, chooses as his bride the only daughter of a neighbor, a tall and strong young woman named Athena, whom Boris has known since childhood. Her father welcomes Boris as a suitor and says that he would delight in seeing the young man's features in the faces of his grandchildren. Athena rejects him, however, and states unequivocally that she will never marry; she will not, in other words, yield to her duty to her family. There is a strong implication in the text that Athena is as troubled by her gender role as Boris is by his.

Athena's rejection infuriates the Prioress, who arranges a supper of seduction during which Athena gets drunk. As the girl goes to her room, the Prioress gives Boris an aphrodisiac to help him complete his conquest, and he struggles with Athena, who knocks out two of his teeth. Boris interprets this as a symbolic castration and feels that he has been freed from his obligation to have a normal conjugal relationship with her, should they get married. She has won his battle with traditional sexuality for him, and he therefore triumphantly kisses her with his bloody mouth. The significance of this perverted and ironic image of defloration is not lost on Athena, who, in horror and disgust, loses consciousness. Boris does not touch her further.

The next morning, Athena is told by the Prioress that she is now most likely pregnant and that her only hope of avoiding dishonor is to marry Boris. Together, they then watch as the Prioress, who all along has been in the grip of the personality of the monkey, reasserts her own true self through an intense struggle with the little animal. This astonishing event affects Athena deeply, and she resigns herself to marrying Boris, with the proviso, however, that she is to have dominion in their relationship. Athena's and Boris's union is thus marked by the backside of the love goddess in several ways. Erotically, they are misfits in that they both look on heterosexuality with revulsion. Psychologically and emotionally, their union is a result of a power struggle, touched by the fantastic, rather than a consequence of the usual process of falling in love. Morally, their marriage represents a surrender to the expectations of their families, but it is unlikely that they will do their real duty and have children. Socially, their marriage will also be out of the ordinary, because, in opposition to the patriarchal norm of their time and place, the wife will rule the roost with the consent of her husband. Dinesen thus problematizes one of the fundamental oppositions of human life, namely that between male and female, and offers a critique of both sex roles and Christian dualism.

"The Young Man with the Carnation" • Although the stories in *Seven Gothic Tales* touch on the fantastic and frequently present challenges to the readers those of *Winter's Tales* are more traditional, and therefore also more accessible, narratives. Written during the German occupation of Denmark, they are tales for difficult times, in which the possibility of reconciliation and restoration is held dear.

"Den unge mand med nelliken" ("The Young Man with the Carnation"), which introduces the English-language edition of the collection, is a powerful expression of Dinesen's theory of art. Its protagonist, Charlie Despard, is a young English writer who, while born and reared in circumstances of great poverty, has transmuted the pain of his childhood experiences into his first novel, with which he has had tremendous success. Because of his newfound reputation as a writer, he has been able to marry a beautiful young woman from a family of means, and outwardly he has every reason to be happy, which indeed, for a time, he has been. As Dinesen indicates through his name, however, he is now in despair, for he has found that art has failed him. He has nothing more to say as a writer, while at the same time he feels that life holds no joys for him. His is not simply a bad case of writer's block, though, but a case of someone who, because of his erstwhile happiness, has lost his ability to create. The story tells about how Charlie comes to terms with his situation and regains his creativity.

While traveling on the Continent, Charlie and his wife have been separated for a few days but have planned to meet at a hotel in Amsterdam. Charlie arrives last and goes to his wife's room, where he finds her asleep with her door unlocked. Shortly after his arrival, someone else tries to open the door, and, when Charlie gets out of bed to investigate, he finds a young man who, wearing a carnation, is obviously on his way to a rendezvous. Charlie's first reaction is envy, for he believes the young man to have found the happiness which he, himself, is lacking. He then experiences a shock at his wife's infidelity, feels sorry for himself, writes her a brief note, and leaves in search of that happiness which he sensed in the face of the young man with the carnation.

During the next few hours, his mind is in turmoil, and he walks along the waterfront, contemplating his situation. He is then found by some sailors who believe him to be thinking of suicide and who therefore invite him to come with them to a tavern. The men spend the night telling one another stories, and Charlie's tales indicate that he now suffers from no loss of creativity; the experience of the night has given him the pain which is needed by the artist. His regained creativity gives him the strength to face his wife, and he returns to the hotel only to find that he, the previous night, had entered the wrong room. Dinesen's imagery shows that Charlie the fiction writer interprets his experience as a kind of resurrection, which is followed by a dialogue with God. Charlie is told by God that he had been created in order to write and that it is God who wants him to tell his stories and who therefore gave him the pain of the previous evening. He is promised, however, that God will not measure out any more distress to him than what is needed for his art. Charlie accepts the idea that pain is a necessary condition of creativity and realizes that it is the young man with the carnation who is to be pitied, rather than himself.

Dinesen's theory of art is thus basically a romantic one, in which the joys of life are viewed as inferior to art and therefore fundamentally incompatible with creative endeavor. The artist is required to sacrifice normal human happiness for the privilege of being able to commune with the divine, which is the essence of artistic creation.

"Sorrow-Acre" • Another significant aspect of "The Young Man with the Carnation" is the concept of duty, which manifests itself as Charlie's obligation to God to be a writer of stories. In "Sorg-agre" ("Sorrow-Acre"), the next story in *Winter's Tales*, duty is a central motif that contributes much to the story's theme. "Sorrow-Acre" tells about a young Dane named Adam who has spent several years in England, but who, at the beginning of the story, has just returned home to his ancestral estate only to find himself in conflict with his uncle, the ruler of the manor. Adam represents the beginnings of a new social order and serves as the embodiment of the ideas of the French Revolution (1789), while his uncle advocates a traditional, aristocratic view of life. The three intertwined plots of the story are played out against the backdrop of life on this semifeudal Danish country estate in the late eighteenth century.

The first plot concerns the uncle's dealings with Anne-Marie, the mother of a young man who has been accused of a crime. There is little proof in the case, and the uncle admits that he has no basis for making a judgment about the man's guilt or innocence. When Anne-Marie begs for the freedom of her son, however, he offers her a bargain: If she can cut a certain rye field in the course of one day, her son will receive his freedom. The outward drama of the story concerns Anne-Marie's superhuman attempt at harvesting the field, which is normally three days' work for a man. She succeeds but at the end dies from exhaustion.

The second plot line concerns the relationship between Adam and his uncle. Adam finds his uncle's action barbarous and threatens to leave because of his sense of outrage. The uncle defends himself by referring to the divine principle of arbitrary power, saying that because he is essentially like a god in his relationship to his serflike farm workers, his actions should not be questioned. Although the drama in the rye field may seem like a tragedy to most mortals, the unresolved question of the young man's innocence or guilt adds a divinely comic flavor to Anne-Marie's attempt to buy his freedom. A nobleman may approach the divine by accepting and appreciating the comic aspects of human life. The uncle would himself, he says, like nothing better than to be in a position where he might be able to buy himself a son at the cost of his own life, thus ensuring the succession of the family line. He has lost his only son and has recently, in his rather advanced age, married the young lady who was intended to be his son's bride.

The third strand of the plot involves the relationship between Adam and his uncle's young wife. It is very much against Adam's interests that his uncle should receive an heir, for if the uncle were to die childless, Adam would inherit the estate. It has been prophesied by a gypsy, however, that Adam's posterity is to possess the estate, and it is becoming clear to Adam that he has a duty to the family to give his uncle a legal heir. The young wife's attitude toward Adam would clearly facilitate such an unspoken arrangement.

All the main characters in this tale thus exemplify the principle of duty, particularly as it concerns the continuation of a family line. Adam recognizes that he has been brought back to Denmark by fate and that he must play his part in the drama of his family. He is reconciled to his uncle, who begs him to stay; the uncle surely knows that Adam is essential to the success of his project. The uncle's young wife knows that she has been brought into the family expressly for the purpose of providing an heir. Anne-Marie, whose death is a powerful reminder of a person's duty to his or her descendants, sets a powerful example of commitment to one's family.

"The Sailor-Boy's Tale" • Dinesen sees a connection between duty and the concept of justice, for it is a paramount duty of human beings to strive to be just. Her idea of justice is clearly expressed in "Skibsdrængens fortælling" ("The Sailor-Boy's Tale"), a rather simple story that is also found in *Winter's Tales*. Like "The Monkey," "The Sailor-Boy's Tale" presupposes that the reader is familiar with folk beliefs related to shape-shifting, the idea that a human being may temporarily take on the form of an animal. The story tells about a young sailor boy named Simon, who, during a storm in the Mediterranean, climbs the mainmast of his ship to free a peregrine falcon that has become caught in the rigging. Before Simon sets it free, the falcon pecks his thumb sufficiently hard to draw blood, and Simon retaliates by hitting it on the head. This incident proves to be significant to Dinesen's portrait of justice and its operation.

Two years later, Simon's ship has come to the herring markets in the town of Bodø in northern Norway, where Simon meets and falls in love with a young girl named Nora. One evening, when he is on his way to a meeting with the girl, he runs into an overly friendly Russian sailor, whose behavior has homosexual overtones. Simon, who does not want to be late for his meeting with the girl, stabs and kills the Russian, after which he is pursued by the dead man's shipmates. While he is hiding in the crowd at a dance, an old pagan Lapp woman named Sunniva shows up, says that Simon is her son, and tells him to come home with her. Sunniva wipes off his bloody knife on her skirt and, while hiding Simon when the Russian sailors come looking for him, cuts her thumb to explain the presence of blood. She then arranges for safe passage for him back to his ship, at which point she reveals that she is the falcon that Simon released during the storm in the Mediterranean. She has rescued him both because she likes him and because of her sense of justice, for he deserves to be paid back for helping her. To completely settle her accounts with him, she then boxes his ear in return for his blow to her head while she was in the shape of the falcon.

Sunniva also explains to Simon that she admires his devotion to the girl Nora and that the female residents of the earth hold together. Referring to men as their sons, she indicates that the world is really run by women, who are bound together with a matriarchal compact. Sunniva's pagan matriarchy gestures at Dinesen's questioning of both traditional sex roles and the Christian religion.

"The Heroine" • Dinesen's rather gentle critique of Christianity in "The Sailor-Boy's Tale" becomes relentlessly satirical in "Heloise" ("The Heroine"), in which she casts a woman stripper in the role of the Christian savior. A young Englishman named Frederick Lamond, together with a company of French travelers, is caught in a German border town at the time of the Franco-Prussian war. A student of religious philosophy, Frederick is at the time writing a treatise on the doctrine of the Atonement. When the German army marches into town, he and the other stranded travelers are accused of espionage. A famous messianic prophecy from the Book of Isaiah, which is quoted in Frederick's manuscript, is read as a code by the Germans and forms the main proof of their accusation.

One of the travelers is a woman named Heloise, whose rare beauty greatly impresses one of the German officers. Realizing that the accusation of espionage may not have much merit, he offers the travelers a bargain: If Heloise will appear before him in the nude, they will be permitted to continue to France; otherwise, they will be shot. Heloise turns to the company and leaves the decision in their hands, and they all vote to refuse the German's demand. The officer, who respects the courage of both Heloise and her companions, then decides to let them go after all, and he apologizes to Heloise, whom he terms a heroine, by sending her a big bouquet of roses.

Six years later, Frederick is in Paris to attend some lectures in his field. Entertained by a friend, he is taken to a music hall, where the most beautiful woman in Paris is appearing nude in a show. It turns out that the woman is Heloise, whom Frederick still remembers well. They meet and reminisce after the show, and Heloise explains what in her opinion was at stake in the dramatic incident six years earlier. It was not only the lives of the travelers, she says, which hung in the balance but also their ability to live with their consciences. It would have cost her very little to comply with the German's demand; for her, it would have been a professional matter, not one of conscience. The other travelers, however, would have never gotten over it if Heloise were to have bought their freedom at the cost of exposing her body. Frederick now understands that her heroism did not consist in standing up to the German officer's demands but in looking after the welfare of her companions' souls. Heloise, who through the imagery in the story has been carefully presented as a kind of Christ-figure, now appears, to both Frederick and the reader, as a full-blown savior.

Portraying a stripper as someone who saves people from guilt constitutes a truly ironic comment on traditional Christian religion. Casting a woman in such a position undercuts the traditional conception of women's roles as well. "The Heroine," through its overt questioning of central religious and social norms, therefore becomes one of Dinesen's most radical stories.

"Babette's Feast" • Heloise's parting comment to Frederick is that she wishes that he might have seen her perform six years earlier, when her beauty was at its fullest. Heloise has the temperament of an artist in that art, in her case the beauty of her body, gives meaning to her life. A similar commitment is held by the title character in "Babettes gæstebud" ("Babette's Feast") from *Anecdotes of Destiny*, who, like Heloise, is French. Babette is a famous Parisian chef who had to flee her country at the time of the Paris Commune. She finds her way to a small Norwegian fishing village, where she, for the next fourteen years, lives as a maid in the home of two spinsters. These two sisters are the daughters of a minister who founded a pietistic religious society and who, because of his asceticism, rejected his daughters' suitors. Years after his death, his daughters live solely for their father's memory and religious ideals.

Babette regularly plays the French lottery and chances to win ten thousand francs, which she wishes to spend on a French dinner at the centenary of the minister's birth. The various foreign dishes are disconcerting to the guests, who are all members of the minister's sect; only one of them, the former suitor of one of the daughters, is able to appreciate Babette's culinary artistry. When, at the end of the dinner, the two sisters learn that the utterly exhausted Babette has spent all her money on the project, they cannot understand her motivation, but Babette states that she has done it for her own sake: She is an artist who craves excellence in her field of endeavor.

Like Babette, Dinesen placed high demands on herself. She felt a strong sense of duty and loyalty to the artist within her, thus her tales are exquisitely crafted but not numerous. She relentlessly pursued her unitary vision, subtly criticizing those aspects of life that went against the grain of her thought, such as the dualism of received religion and traditional sex roles. Through her authorship she prepared a literary feast that continues to be enjoyed by numerous readers.

Jan Sjåvik

Other major works

NOVELS: *Gengældelsens Veje*, 1944 (as Pierre Andrézel; *The Angelic Avengers*, 1946).

NONFICTION: *Den afrikanske Farm*, 1937 (*Out of Africa*, 1937); *Skygger paa Græsset*, 1960 (*Shadows on the Grass*, 1960); *Essays*, 1965; *Breve fra Afrika, 1914-1931*, 1978 (*Letters from Africa, 1914-1931*, 1981); *Daguerreotypes, and Other Essays*, 1979; *Samlede Essays*, 1985.

Bibliography

Aiken, Susan Hardy. *Isak Dinesen and the Engendering of Narrative*. Chicago: University of Chicago Press, 1990. Offers thoughtful critical interpretation of Dinesen's works. Includes bibliographical references and an index.

Bassoff, Bruce. "Babette Can Cook: Life and Art in Three Stories by Isak Dinesen." *Studies in Short Fiction* 27 (Summer, 1990): 385-389. Discusses the plot elements of desire for transcendence, a fall caused by confrontation with the real world, and new knowledge or resignation in "The Ring," "The Diver," and "Babette's Feast."

Bjørnvig, Thorkild. *The Pact: My Friendship with Isak Dinesen*. Translated by Ingvar Schousboe and William Jay Smith. Baton Rouge: Louisiana State University Press, 1983. This short book offers Bjørnvig's account of his friendship with Dinesen, from their first meeting in 1948 to their definitive parting in 1954. Written by an accomplished poet, the volume is interesting in its own right as well as for the insight into Dinesen which it provides.

Donelson, Linda. *Out of Isak Dinesen in Africa: The Untold Story*. Iowa City, Iowa: Coulsong List, 1995. Good, updated biography of Dinesen. Includes bibliographical references and an index.

Henriksen, Aage. "The Empty Space Between Art and Church." In *Out of Denmark*, edited by Bodil Warmberg. Copenhagen: Danish Cultural Institute, 1985. Henriksen asserts that the underlying principle of all Dinesen's tales is the discovery that reality is transformed into a dream. Contends that Dinesen's stories are based on the complicated nature of human love.

Juhl, Marianne, and Bo Hakon Jørgensen. *Diana's Revenge: Two Lines in Isak Dinesen's Authorship*. Translated from the Danish by Anne Born. Odense, Denmark: Odense University Press, 1985. This volume contains two sophisticated scholarly and critical essays of considerable length. Juhl's contribution, "Sex and Consciousness," is informed by feminist theory. Jørgensen, in "The Ways of Art," discusses the relationship between Dinesen's sensuality and her art. Their book, which includes a good bibliography, is particularly strong in its discussion of Dinesen's use of classical symbols.

May, Charles E., ed. *Masterplots II: Short Story Series, Revised Edition.* 8 vols. Pasadena, Calif.: Salem Press, 2004. Designed for student use, this reference set contains articles providing detailed plot summaries and analyses of these eight short stories by Dinesen: "Babette's Feast," "The Blank Page," and "The Cardinal's First Tale" (vol. 1); "The Deluge at Norderney" (vol. 2); "The Monkey" (vol. 5); "The Sailor-Boy's Tale" (vol. 6); and "Sorrow-Acre" and "The Supper at Elsinore" (vol. 7).

Mullins, Maire. "Home, Community, and the Gift That Gives in Isak Dinesen's 'Babette's Feast.'" *Women's Studies* 23 (1994): 217-228. Argues that the meal Babette prepares is not a gift but a demonstration of her own aesthetic powers. Argues that Babette subverts the phallo-logocentric society in which she finds herself and transforms home and community through her presence.

Rashkin, Esther. "A Recipe for Mourning: Isak Dinesen's 'Babette's Feast.'" *Style* 29 (Fall, 1995): 356-374. Claims the story is a psychoanalytic reflection on the process involved in overcoming an inability to mourn, for which it writes a recipe for transcendence of that inability through the preparation and consumption of food.

Stambaugh, Sara. *The Witch and the Goddess in the Stories of Isak Dinesen: A Feminist Reading.* Ann Arbor, Mich.: UMI Research Press, 1988. Stambaugh offers a feminist-inspired examination of the portraits of women that are found in Dinesen's texts. The strength of her brief study is the recognition of the centrality of gender for an understanding of Dinesen's work; its weakness is its lack of theoretical sophistication. The book has a complete scholarly apparatus.

Fyodor Dostoevski

Born: Moscow, Russia; November 11, 1821
Died: St. Petersburg, Russia; February 9, 1881

Principal short fiction • *Sochineniya*, 1860 (2 volumes); *Polnoye sobraniye sochineniy*, 1865-1870 (4 volumes); *Povesti i rasskazy*, 1882; *The Gambler, and Other Stories*, 1914; *A Christmas Tree and a Wedding, and an Honest Thief*, 1917; *White Nights, and Other Stories*, 1918; *An Honest Thief, and Other Stories*, 1919; *The Short Novels of Dostoevsky*, 1945.

Other literary forms • In addition to short fiction, Fyodor Dostoevski wrote novels, nonfiction, criticism, and *Yevgeniya Grande* (1844), a translation of Honoré de Balzac's novel *Eugénie Grandet* (1833). In his own time, Dostoevski was exceptionally influential, especially through *Dnevnik pisatelya* (1876-1877, 1800-1881; *The Diary of a Writer*, 1949), a series of miscellaneous writings that he published occasionally in St. Petersburg. Dostoevski also wrote a series of essays on Russian literature, some feuilletons, and the well-known travelogue "Zimniye zametki o letnikh vpechatleniyakh" (1863; "Winter Notes on Summer Impressions," 1955). His most famous contribution in his own time was his speech in Alexander Pushkin's honor, given on the occasion of the dedication of a monument to Pushkin in 1880.

Achievements • In the world literature of the nineteenth century, Fyodor Dostoevski has few rivals. Some of his characters have penetrated literary consciousness and produced a new generation in the works of prominent twentieth century authors such as Jean-Paul Sartre and Jorge Luis Borges. He initiated psychological realism, inspiring both Friedrich Nietzsche and Sigmund Freud. His novels are read in translation in twenty-six languages. Dostoevski was originally suppressed in the Soviet Union, only to reemerge as even more influential in the second half of the twentieth century, finding a whole new generation of admirers in his transformed homeland. Even though his style is markedly nineteenth century, Dostoevski still seems quite modern even in the twenty-first century.

Biography • Fyodor Mikhailovich Dostoevski was born on November 11, 1821, in a small Moscow public hospital, where his father, Dr. Mikhail Andreevich Dostoevski, worked. He was the second son to the doctor and Marya Fyodorovna (née Nechaeva). One year after his mother's death, in 1837, Fyodor enrolled in the St. Petersburg Academy for Military Engineers. He completed his studies at the academy even after his father had died of a stroke in 1839, thanks to the inheritance of the Dostoevski estate.

Like so many writers' attempts, Dostoevski's first foray into the literary world was through translation—in his case, of Balzac's *Eugénie Grandet*, appearing in print in 1844. His first original work was a novel in letters, *Bednye lyudi* (1846; *Poor Folk*, 1887), which met with immediate success, creating quite a literary sensation even before its publication. The great critic Vissarion Belinsky hailed it with such enthusiasm that the novice writer was propelled into early fame.

Dostoevski followed this initial success with *Dvoynik* (1846; *The Double*, 1917). It was met more coolly, was considered an artistic failure, and was generally unpopular. The failure of *The Double*, as seen in the twenty-first century, is quite ironic, since it contains many of the thematic occupations that eventually made Dostoevski famous. His next novel, *Netochka Nezvanova* (1849; English translation, 1920), was fated never to be completed. Most novels then appeared in journals and were serialized; this was the case with all Dostoevski's novels. After the first three installments of *Netochka Nezvanova* appeared in 1849, Dostoevski was arrested for participating in a secret anticzarist society, the Petrashevsky Circle. He and thirty-two of his associates were arrested, imprisoned for eight months, and sentenced to death. At precisely the moment that his comrades were facing the firing squad, the sentence was commuted to hard labor. Dostoevski spent four years in hard labor at Omsk, followed by three years of exile from the capital.

Dostoevski married Marya Isaeva in 1857, while still in Siberia. He was beginning to suffer from epilepsy, however, and she was also sickly. They returned to St. Petersburg in 1859, and shortly thereafter his works began again to appear in print. Life, however, did not return to normal. In 1864, his brother died, leaving him a second family to support. His wife, too, died the same year. Strapped financially, Dostoevski accepted an advance payment, agreeing to deliver a novel to a publisher that same year—or else forfeit the profits from all his subsequent works. He succeeded in completing *Igrok* (1866; *The Gambler*, 1887), satisfying this publisher thanks to his stenographer, Anna Snitkina, whom he married in 1867. They left Russia for a few years, returning in 1871. The novels that he wrote while abroad established him as an important writer but not as a popular or successful one. In fact, during his life, he met with very little recognition.

The one shining exception to this neglect came at the dedication of a monument to Pushkin, in 1880. Thousands of people greeted his speech enthusiastically. He died only a few months later, in 1881, when an even larger crowd attended his funeral.

Analysis • Fyodor Dostoevski's works fall into two periods that coincide with the time before his imprisonment and following it. The seven-year hiatus in his creative output between 1849 and 1857 corresponds to the four years that he spent in prison and the three subsequent years during which he was banished in Siberia. The first period produced primarily shorter novels and short stories, many of which have never been translated into English; the latter period is represented more by the great novels, the epithet denoting both significance and size, as well as by *Dnevnik pisatelya*, 1876-1877, 1880-1881 (2 volumes, partial translation as *Pages from the Journal of an Author*, 1916; complete translation as *The Diary of a Writer*, 1949), which also contains several new short stories.

In Dostoevski's works, complex structures are created that introduce fundamentally antipodal constructs and that produce, among other effects, a mythologization of the antagonistic elements. Thus, the city, often the St. Petersburg of Dostoevski's present, contrasts with the countryside. The squalor of poverty permeates St. Petersburg with sounds and smells in Dickensian realistic fashion, as opposed to the quaint, provincial quiet of the country. Usually, problems or actual troublemakers come from the city, or, if one leaves the provinces for the city, one may become "infected" with urban discontent and return to plague the countryside. In another prevalent dichotomy, the "man of the forties" (that is, the optimistic believer in the Enlightenment) often clashes with the "man of the sixties" (that is, the atheistic or nihilistic revolutionary). This conflict often is positioned generationally, and it is seldom clear

Library of Congress

whether the representative of either generation should prevail.

Often throughout Dostoevski's works, men of a higher social class, although not necessarily a very high class, interact most significantly with women who are socially inferior, usually powerless or "compromised." The relationship takes on many different attitudes in the various works, but, in almost every case, the woman turns out to be of greater virtue or higher moral and spiritual constitution than the man who, nevertheless, from his privileged position in society, usually fares better than the woman.

Perhaps most important of all the themes in his work is the belief in God versus atheism. If there is no God, many of Dostoevski's characters realize, then either every human being is a God or every human being is nothing at all. This conflict can, and sometimes does, take place within a single person as well as between two characters. Atheism usually appears in its most extreme state—that is, in the belief that, since there is no God, the human being must be God. Although Dostoevski's proponents of atheism are strong-willed, disciplined, and morbidly dedicated, in Dostoevski's world they need to accept the existence of God as their only chance for peace or, in the final analysis, for existing in the world at all. Although free will is interpreted by these radical proponents as the ability to become gods, the submission to the will of the divine God is the only means toward happiness. Those who fail to redeem themselves through God either perish or are subject to enormous spiritual and psychological torment. Such conflict forms the crux of more than one novel in Dostoevski's latter period, and it will be the treatment of this element in Dostoevski's work that will earn for him recognition as the founder of existentialism in literature. Ironically from the point of view of Dostoevski's beliefs, it is his existential writings rather than his metaphysical ones that constitute his most profound influence on world literature in the twentieth century.

Most of Dostoevski's short stories are simpler works than the novels, both in terms of the psychology of the characters and in terms of structure.

"White Nights" • One of his best-known short stories, "Belye nochi" ("White Nights"), is subtitled "A Sentimental Story from the Diary of a Dreamer." The unnamed protagonist of this work meets a young woman, Nastenka, by chance one evening along the embankment. When they have the opportunity to speak to each other, they find that they have much in common: Neither of them is able to enjoy a life of his or her own, and both of them, because of varying circumstances, are confined to their own abodes, occupied most of the time in daydreaming. Nastenka is physically restrained by her grandmother by being pinned to her skirt; the male protagonist is confined by his abject poverty and the inertia of unsociability to his quarters, with the green wallpaper and the spiderwebs. At the end of the story, Nastenka, nevertheless, is able to escape her fate thanks to the offices of the young boarder, who has taken pity on her, but she has had to wait an entire year; it is precisely at the end of this year that she meets the protagonist, whom, she claims, she would certainly love, and does in fact love, but as she truly still loves the other, she must relinquish. Nastenka leaves, imploring the protagonist not to blame her, knowing that he cannot blame her because he loves her. The protagonist feels that, somehow, this "moment" that they have shared is enough love to sustain him for a lifetime of dreaming. This story, unusual in the works of Dostoevski, does not involve the motif of the abused young woman, and the rejected young man seems quite content with his fate. Unlike most of Dostoevski's women, Nastenka has succeeded in meeting an honorable man who seemingly keeps his word, making her a singular female in the works of Dostoevski.

"A Christmas Tree and a Wedding" • More in keeping with Dostoevski's image of the abused, victimized woman is the young girl in "Elka i svad'ba" ("A Christmas Tree and a Wedding"). The first-person narrator relates how he notices the indecent attention of a "great man" of society toward an eleven-year-old girl playing with dolls, who has been promised a huge dowry during one family's Christmas party. The "great man" is interested only in the fabulous dowry and bides his time. Five years later, the narrator notices a wedding taking place in the church and focuses on the face of the very young bride, "pale and melancholy," her eyes perhaps even red from "recent weeping" and her look of "childish innocence," where could be detected "something indescribably naive . . . mutely begging for mercy." He recognizes the young girl of a few years before and also the "great man," who is now the groom. The narrator concludes that it was a "good stroke of business." In this story, the theme of the helpless woman completely at the mercy of rapacious, evil men plays a major role, and the fate of the young girl in "A Christmas Tree and a Wedding," for all her money, bodes much worse than that of the impoverished Nastenka.

"The Dream of a Ridiculous Man" • Perhaps Dostoevski's best-known short story, "Son smeshnogo cheloveha" ("The Dream of a Ridiculous Man") presents more of the most typical Dostoevskian philosophy of any short story. In it, a petty clerk who has realized that he has no reason to live believes that he should commit suicide to put an end to his ridiculous existence. Just when he decides to do so, a young girl accosts him and seemingly tries to engage his assistance. He pushes her aside, but his action causes him great shame, and he feels deep pity for the young girl. The experience of these two emotions causes him to postpone his suicide, if only for a few hours. Meanwhile, he falls asleep, and in his dream he shoots himself. Then, after he is dead and buried, he is transported to an Earth-like planet inhabited by people who only love. Unfortunately, he corrupts the entire population, causing wars, antipathies, and alienation. Upon awakening, the man feels that he has undergone a revelation and must preach his new religion, trying to convince people that it is possible to live in harmony together and to love sincerely people other than oneself.

In "The Dream of a Ridiculous Man," many themes from Dostoevski's mature novels appear: whether one is a zero or a human, whether there is an afterlife, suffering as the only condition for the possibility of love, and suicide as a means of investing significance to human action, as well as many more. It is in the great novels that the complex world wherein the actions of all Dostoevski's creations take place, including the short works. To read a short story without a fundamental background in other seminal works—for example *Zapiski iz podpolya* (1864; *Notes from the Underground*, 1918)—would very likely lead to a trap that could trivialize what are, by themselves, minor works such as the short stories. If, however, the short stories are contextualized within the entire works of Dostoevski over both his major periods, they form several interesting transitional points between many of his philosophical designs.

The young girls, usually victimized by poverty and evil men, seem to be an outgrowth of an early novel, *Poor Folk*, and a continuing motif throughout the later period. Here, an orphan serf girl is pressured into a marriage that will doubtless cause her endless degradation and possibly physical harm. The paradoxical "spiteful man" of *Notes from the Underground* is the model of the "little clerk" who, nevertheless, has been influenced by German romantic philosophy and against logical positivism. His voice and "spite" reverberate almost palpably in the short stories as well as in the great novels. The theme of life as suffering and love or compassion as life's greatest suffering is developed throughout the great novels, which, when used as a backdrop for the short works, provides a glimpse into the motivations of many of the protagonists.

Dostoevski's short stories clearly have a place of their own in Russian literature. Together, they form a miniature portrait of the most compelling people in Dostoevski's world. Reading them, along with the longer works, gives the discriminating reader an insight into one of the most powerful and intricate minds of the nineteenth century.

Christine Tomei

Other major works

NOVELS: *Bednye lyudi*, 1846 (*Poor Folk*, 1887); *Dvoynik*, 1846 (*The Double*, 1917); *Netochka Nezvanova*, 1849 (English translation, 1920); *Unizhennye i oskorblyonnye*, 1861 (*Injury and Insult*, 1886; also known as *The Insulted and Injured*); *Zapiski iz myortvogo doma*, 1861-1862 (*Buried Alive: Or, Ten Years of Penal Servitude in Siberia*, 1881; better known as *The House of the Dead*); *Zapiski iz podpolya*, 1864 (*Letters from the Underworld*, 1913; better known as *Notes from the Underground*); *Igrok*, 1866 (*The Gambler*, 1887); *Prestupleniye i nakazaniye*, 1866 (*Crime and Punishment*, 1886); *Idiot*, 1868 (*The Idiot*, 1887); *Vechny muzh*, 1870 (*The Permanent Husband*, 1888; also known as *The Eternal Husband*); *Besy*, 1871-1872 (*The Possessed*, 1913; also known as *The Devils*); *Podrostok*, 1875 (*A Raw Youth*, 1916); *Bratya Karamazovy*, 1879-1880 (*The Brothers Karamazov*, 1912); *The Novels*, 1912 (12 volumes).

MISCELLANEOUS: *Polnoe sobranie sochinenii v tridtsati tomakh*, 1972-1990 (30 volumes).

NONFICTION: "Zimniye zametki o letnikh vpechatleniyakh," 1863 ("Winter Notes on Summer Impressions," 1955); *Dnevnik pisatelya*, 1876-1887, 1880-1881 (2 volumes; partial translation *Pages from the Journal of an Author*, 1916; complete translation *The Diary of a Writer*, 1949); *Pisma*, 1928-1959 (4 volumes); *Iz arkhiva F. M. Dostoyevskogo: "Idiot,"* 1931 (*The Notebooks for "The Idiot,"* 1967); *Iz arkhiva F. M. Dostoyevskogo: "Prestupleniye i nakazaniye,"* 1931 (*The Notebooks for "Crime and Punishment,"* 1967); *F. M. Dostoyevsky: Materialy i issledovaniya*, 1935 (*The Notebooks for "The Brothers Karamazov,"* 1971); *Zapisnyye tetradi F. M. Dostoyevskogo*, 1935 (*The Notebooks for "The Possessed,"* 1968); *Dostoevsky's Occasional Writings*, 1963; *F. M. Dostoyevsky v rabote nad romanom "Podrostok,"* 1965 (*The Notebooks for "A Raw Youth,"* 1969); *Neizdannyy Dostoyevsky: Zapisnyye knizhki i tetradi 1860-1881*, 1971 (3 volumes; *The Unpublished Dostoevsky: Diaries and Notebooks, 1860-1881*, 1973-1976); *F. M. Dostoyevsky ob iskusstve*, 1973; *Selected Letters of Fyodor Dostoyevsky*, 1987.

TRANSLATION: *Yevgeniya Grande*, 1844 (of Honoré de Balzac's novel *Eugénie Grandet*).

Bibliography

Adelman, Gary. *Retelling Dostoyesvky: Literary Responses and Other Observations.* Lewisburg, Pa.: Bucknell University Press, 2001. Study of the possible influence of Dostoevski on a number of authors from Joseph Conrad to Frank Herbert.

Bloom, Harold, ed. *Fyodor Dostoevsky.* New York: Chelsea House, 1989. Essays on all of Dostoevski's major novels as well as on his treatment of heroes and nihilism. Includes introduction, chronology, and bibliography.

Frank, Joseph. *Dostoevsky: The Seeds of Revolt, 1821-1849.* Princeton, N.J.: Princeton University Press, 1976. The first volume of Frank's monumental five-volume biography, the best available source on Dostoevski's life and art in English. Includes an appendix on neurologist Sigmund Freud's case history of Dostoevsky.

_____. *Dostoevsky: The Years of Ordeal, 1850-1859.* Princeton, N.J.: Princeton University Press, 1983. Reiterates Frank's effort to subordinate the writer's private life in favor of tracing his connection to the social-cultural history of his time.

_____. *Dostoevsky: The Stir of Liberation, 1860-1865.* Princeton, N.J.: Princeton University Press, 1986. Continues Frank's study.

_____. *Dostoevsky: The Miraculous Years, 1865-1871.* Princeton, N.J.: Princeton University Press, 1995. The fourth volume in Frank's series on the life and works of Dostoevksi. Includes an extended discussion of Dostoeski's novella *The Gambler* from an ethnic-psychological perspective as a commentary on the Russian national character and an extended discussion of the classical construction of the novella *The Eternal Husband*, which Frank sees as Dostoeski's most perfect shorter work.

_____. *Dostoevsky: The Mantle of the Prophet.* Princeton, N.J.: Princeton University Press, 2002. Volume 5, concluding Frank's biography.

Jackson, Robert Louis, ed. *Dialogues with Dostoevsky: The Overwhelming Questions.* Stanford, Calif.: Stanford University Press, 1993. Chapters on the writer's relationships with Ivan Turgenev, Leo Tolstoy, Anton Chekhov, Maxim Gorky, Nikolai Gogol, William Shakespeare, and Friedrich Nietzsche.

Kjetsaa, Geir. *Fyodor Dostoevsky: A Writer's Life.* Translated by Siri Hustvedt and David McDuff. New York: Viking Press, 1987. Thorough and compelling work on Dostoevski's life that seeks to shed light on the creation of Dostoevski's fiction, citing letters and notes as artistic points of departure for Dostoevski.

May, Charles E., ed. *Masterplots II: Short Story Series, Revised Edition.* 8 vols. Pasadena, Calif.: Salem Press, 2004. Designed for student use, this reference set contains articles providing detailed plot summaries and analyses of these seven short stories by Dostoevski: "Bobok" (vol. 1), "The Crocodile" and "The Dream of a Ridiculous Man" (vol. 2), "An Honest Thief" (vol. 3), "A Nasty Story" (vol. 5), "The Peasant Marey" (vol. 6), and "White Nights" (vol. 8).

Straus, Nina Pelikan. *Dostoevsky and the Woman Question: Rereadings at the End of a Century.* New York: St. Martin's Press, 1994. Although, like most books on Dostoevski, this study centers on the novels, it is helpful in understanding his work generally; it argues that Dostoevski's compulsion to depict men's cruelties to women is a constitutive part of his vision and his metaphysics. Claims that Dostoevski attacks masculine notions of autonomy and that his works evolve toward "the death of the patriarchy."

Sir Arthur Conan Doyle

Born: Edinburgh, Scotland; May 22, 1859
Died: Crowborough, East Sussex, England; July 7, 1930

Principal short fiction • *Mysteries and Adventures,* 1889 (also as *The Gully of Bluemansdyke, and Other Stories*); *The Captain of Polestar, and Other Tales,* 1890; *The Adventures of Sherlock Holmes,* 1892; *My Friend the Murderer, and Other Mysteries and Adventures,* 1893; *Round the Red Lamp: Being Fact and Fancies of Medical Life,* 1894; *The Great Keinplatz Experiment, and Other Stories,* 1894; *The Memoirs of Sherlock Holmes,* 1894; *The Exploits of Brigadier Gerard,* 1896; *The Man from Archangel, and Other Stories,* 1898; *The Green Flag, and Other Stories of War and Sport,* 1900; *The Adventures of Gerard,* 1903; *The Return of Sherlock Holmes,* 1905; *Round the Fire Stories,* 1908; *One Crowded Hour,* 1911; *The Last Galley: Impressions and Tales,* 1911; *His Last Bow,* 1917; *Danger!, and Other Stories,* 1918; *Tales of Terror and Mystery,* 1922 (also as *The Black Doctor, and Other Tales of Terror and Mystery*); *Tales of the Ring and Camp,* 1922 (also as *The Croxley Master, and Other Tales of the Ring and Camp*); *Tales of Twilight and the Unseen,* 1922 (also as *The Great Keinplatz Experiment, and Other Tales of Twilight and the Unseen*); *Three of Them,* 1923; *Last of the Legions, and Other Tales of Long Ago,* 1925; *The Dealings of Captain Sharkey, and Other Tales of Pirates,* 1925; *The Case-Book of Sherlock Holmes,* 1927; *The Maracot Deep, and Other Stories,* 1929; *The Final Adventures of Sherlock Holmes,* 1981 (revised and expanded 2001); *Uncollected Stories: The Unknown Conan Doyle,* 1982.

Other literary forms • Arthur Conan Doyle's more than one hundred published works include novels, autobiography, political treatises, plays adapted from his fiction, and works on spiritualism as well as his short stories, for which he is best known. His character Sherlock Holmes has been the subject of innumerable films, plays, and radio scripts and has become the archetype of the conventional detective hero.

Achievements • Although Doyle was not the first to write short stories featuring a detective with great analytical powers, and while he acknowledged his debt to such writers as Edgar Allan Poe and Émile Gaboriau, who had written tales of intelligent amateur detectives solving crimes through logical deduction, in Sherlock Holmes, Doyle created a character who has entered the popular imagination like no other. Sherlock Holmes is perhaps the most famous and popular character in detective fiction, if not in all modern fiction. Doyle's stories were a strong influence on writers such as Ellery Queen, Agatha Christie, John Dickson Carr, and the many others who create tightly constructed puzzles for their detectives to solve with clearly and closely reasoned analysis. Societies such as the Baker Street Irregulars have sprung up around the world to study Doyle's stories, and the name of Sherlock Holmes has become synonymous with deduction, while "Elementary, my dear Watson" is a catchphrase even among those who have never read the stories.

Biography • Arthur Conan Doyle was born in Scotland of devout Irish Catholic parents and educated by the Jesuits in England and Austria. He graduated from the medical school at the University of Edinburgh and first went to sea as a ship's surgeon on a

whaler to the Arctic, later on a West
African passenger liner. He opened
an office in Southsea, England, and
because of a dearth of patients, began
writing to fill his leisure time and to
supplement his income. He had previously published a few short stories
anonymously, and in 1887 completed
A Study in Scarlet, a novelette in
which Sherlock Holmes, as the central character, appears for the first
time. Urged on by his American editor, he wrote *The Sign of Four* (1890;
also pb. as *The Sign of the Four*) and
a series of Sherlock Holmes stories
which appeared in the *Strand Magazine*. The popularity of Holmes enabled Doyle to give up the practice of
medicine, but since the author desired to be known as a historical romancer, the character was "killed off"
in a struggle with his archenemy, Professor Moriarty, in the story "The Final Problem." Ten years later, yielding
to pressure from his publishers and
the public, he resurrected Holmes,

Courtesy, University of Texas at Austin

first in *The Hound of the Baskervilles* (1901-1902, serial; 1902, book) and later in another
series of Holmes short stories.

Doyle was knighted in 1902 for his political service and principally for his publications defending the conduct of the British in the South African (Boer) War. Having
left Roman Catholicism, he turned to spiritualism and devoted the rest of his life to
psychic research and propagandizing his beliefs.

Analysis • In spite of his desire to be acknowledged as a writer of "serious" literature,
Arthur Conan Doyle is destined to be remembered as the creator of a fictional character who has taken on a life separate from the literary works in which he appears.
Sherlock Holmes, as the prototype of almost all fictional detectives, has become a legend not only to his devotees but also to those who have not even read the works in
which he appears, the detective being immortalized by reputation and through the
media of movies, television, and radio.

Doyle claimed that the character of Sherlock Holmes was based on his memories
of Dr. Joseph Bell, a teacher of anatomy at the University of Edinburgh, whose diag-
nostic skills he had admired as a student of medicine. Bell, however, disclaimed the
honor and suggested that Doyle himself possessed the analytical acumen that more
closely resembled the skills of Sherlock Holmes. Regardless of the disclaimers and
acknowledgments, there is little doubt that Doyle owed a large debt to Edgar
Allan Poe and other predecessors in detective fiction, such as Émile Gaboriau and
François-Eugène Vidocq. Doyle records that he was familiar with *Mémoires* (1828-1829;
Memoirs of Vidocq, Principal Agent of the French Police, 1828-1829) and had read

Gaboriau's *Monsieur Lecoq* (1880). It is the influence of Poe, however, that is most in evidence in the character of Holmes and in many of his plots.

Poe's character of C. Auguste Dupin bears remarkable similarities to the Sherlock Holmes character. Both Holmes and Dupin, for example, are eccentrics; both are amateurs in the detective field; both have little regard for the official police; and both enter into investigations, not because of any overwhelming desire to bring a culprit to justice but out of the interest that the case generates and the challenge to their analytical minds. In addition, both have faithful companions who serve as the chroniclers of the exploits of their respective detective friends. Although Dupin's companion remains anonymous and the reader is unable to draw any conclusions about his personality, Dr. Watson, in contrast, takes on an identity (although always in a secondary role) of his own. The reader shares with Watson his astonishment at Holmes's abilities. In effect, Watson becomes a stand-in for the reader by asking the questions that need to be asked for a complete understanding of the situation.

Generally, the Sherlock Holmes stories follow a similar pattern: There is usually a scene at the Baker Street residence, at which time a visitor appears and tells his or her story. After Holmes makes some preliminary observations and speculates upon a possible solution to the puzzle, Holmes and Watson visit the scene of the crime. Holmes then solves the mystery and explains to Watson how he arrived at the solution. "The Adventure of the Speckled Band" follows this formula, and it is apparent that Poe's "The Murders in the Rue Morgue" had a direct influence on this "locked room" mystery. The murder, the locked room, and the animal killer are all variations on the ingredients in the first case in which C. Auguste Dupin appears. Even the reference to the orangutan on the grounds of the Manor House would appear to be an allusion to the murderer in Poe's story. The gothic romance influence is also apparent in this adventure of Sherlock Holmes: There is the mysterious atmosphere and the strange, looming manor house; and there is the endangered woman threatened by a male force. Changing the murderer from the ape of Poe's story to a serpent in Doyle's story suggests at least symbolically the metaphysical (or supernatural) struggle between the forces of good and evil.

Typically, this story as well as all the Holmes stories ends with the solution to the mystery. Sherlock Holmes acknowledges that, by driving the snake back into the room where Dr. Roylott, the murderer, is waiting, he is indirectly responsible for his death; yet he matter-of-factly states that it is not likely to weigh heavily on his conscience. The mystery has been solved; that has been the detective's only interest in the case. Because of this single-minded interest on the part of the detective, what happens to the criminal after discovery is no longer relevant. If the criminal is to stand trial, the story ends with the arrest and no more is heard of him. There are no trials, no dramatic courtroom scenes, and no reports of executions or prison sentences which had been popular in earlier detective stories and which were to regain immense popularity in the future.

Although the solution to the "ingenious puzzle" is the prime concern for the detective and certainly of interest to the reader, it is Sherlock Holmes's character with his multifaceted personality and his limitations which makes Doyle's stories about the detective's adventures so re-readable. Holmes, for example, is an accomplished musician, a composer as well as an instrumentalist; he is an expert in chemical research and has educated himself to be an authority on blood stains; he is the author of innumerable monographs on such esoteric subjects as different types of tobacco, bicycle tire impressions, and types of perfume; and he is an exceptional pugilist.

Sherlock Holmes's limitations, however, are what make him so attractive to the reader. He is sometimes frighteningly ignorant; for example, after Dr. Watson has explained the Copernican system to him, he responds: "Now that I know it. . . . I shall do my best to forget it"; he considers this information trivial, since it is not useful, and he feels that retaining it will crowd practical knowledge out of his mind. Holmes can also make erroneous judgments, and, perhaps most appealing of all, he can fail as a detective. It is this capacity for the detective to fail or to be outwitted that is perhaps Doyle's most significant contribution to the detective-fiction genre. Whereas Holmes's predecessors such as Lecoq and Dupin are presented as unerring in their conclusions and infallible in solving their cases, Doyle's hero demonstrates his fallibility early in his career.

"A Scandal in Bohemia" • It is in the first of the Sherlock Holmes short stories, "A Scandal in Bohemia," without doubt Doyle's version of Edgar Allan Poe's "The Purloined Letter," that this very human fallibility is revealed. Both stories deal with the need to recover items that are being used to blackmail a person of royal heritage. In both cases, attempts to find the items have failed and the detectives are called on for assistance; and, in both stories, a ruse is used to discover the whereabouts of the incriminating items.

Although the debt to Poe is large in this story, "A Scandal in Bohemia" also displays some significant departures that establish the work as Doyle's own, artistically. The scenes in the streets of London are conveyed with convincing detail to capture effectively "the spirit of the place" of Victorian England. The characters in Poe's Dupin stories are lightly drawn, and the central interest for these tales is not in the people but in what happens to them. Although the characters in Poe's stories talk about matters that are relevant only to the mystery at hand, the direct opposite is true in Doyle's story. The people in the Holmes story are interesting and full of dramatic movement, and Holmes's conversations with Watson and the others are filled with comments which are not related to the case.

In addition, Doyle introduces the device of disguises in "A Scandal in Bohemia." The king of Bohemia, wearing a small face mask to hide his identity, visits Holmes in his lodgings; his disguise, however, is immediately penetrated by the detective. Sherlock Holmes also assumes a disguise in the story that is so convincing and successful that even his close friend Dr. Watson is unable to recognize him. It is the skill of Irene Adler, Holmes's antagonist in the story, in assuming another identity that leads to the detective's being foiled. Holmes's failure in this story, however, in no way detracts from him. On the contrary, this failure and his others (such as in "The Yellow Face") serve to make him only more convincing and more three-dimensional as a human being than the always successful C. Auguste Dupin. Holmes loses no status through his errors; instead, he gains in the light of his past and future successes.

"The Red-Headed League" • Although there will always be disagreement among Sherlock Holmes aficionados about which of the many short stories is best, there is broad agreement that one of the best-constructed stories by Arthur Conan Doyle is the second short story in the first series, "The Red-Headed League." Doyle himself ranked the story very high when he was queried, and the Victorian reading public's response attested to its popularity. This story also introduces one of the recurring themes of the short stories: that of the doppelgänger, or double. The dual nature of the world and of personalities is developed in parallel manners throughout the unraveling of the mystery of Jabez Wilson's involvement with the Red-Headed League. The contemplative side of Holmes is repeatedly contrasted with his energized side, just as the orderliness of Victorian England is seen in stark relief against "the half that is evil." Repeatedly, when there is a lull in the chase or a mystery has been solved, Sherlock Holmes retreats to his contemplative side to forget at least temporarily "the miserable weather and the still more miserable ways of our fellowmen."

"The Red-Headed League" follows the traditional formula of a Sherlock Holmes story. Holmes is visited at his flat by Jabez Wilson, who relates his problem. Wilson, the owner of a small pawnshop, has been working for the Red-Headed League for eight weeks, until abruptly and under mysterious circumstances, the league has been dissolved. He qualified for the position because of his red hair, and his only duties were to remain in a room and copy the *Encyclopædia Britannica*. He has been able to perform these chores because his assistant, Vincent Spaulding, was willing to work in the pawnshop for half-wages. He has come to Sherlock Holmes because he does not want to lose such a position without a struggle.

Holmes and Watson visit the pawnshop, and Spaulding is recognized by the detective as being in reality John Clay, a master criminal and murderer. The detective is able to infer from the circumstances that the opposite of what is expected is true. He concludes that it is not the presence of Jabez Wilson in the room performing a meaningless "intellectual" task for the league that is important; rather, it is his absence from the pawnshop that gives his alter ego assistant the opportunity to perform the "physical" task of tunneling from the cellar into the nearby bank. Setting a trap, Holmes, Watson, and the police are able to capture Clay and his confederates in their criminal act.

The double theme of the story is also reinforced in Jabez Wilson's account of the applicants lining up to apply for the position with the Red-Headed League. He describes the crowd lining up on the stair; those in anticipation of employment ascending the stairs with hope; those who have been rejected descending in despair, forming a "double" stream. John Clay, Holmes's antagonist in this story, is the first in a long line of adversaries of the detective who serve in effect as doppelgängers of the sleuth. Clay has an aristocratic background and possesses royal blood. Holmes also has illustrious ancestors, being descended from country squires, and his grandmother is described as being "the sister of Vernet, the French artist." Clay is well educated and urbane, characteristics Holmes repeatedly shows throughout his adventures. Clay is described as being "cunning" in mind as well as skillful in his fingers, again a reflection of the detective's characteristics. Clay is also gracious in his defeat and expresses admiration for the ingenuity displayed by the victorious Holmes. He is truly a worthy adversary for the detective and the direct mirror image of Holmes.

"The Final Problem" • Other great master criminals and, in effect, doubles for the great detective are Colonel Sebastian Moran of "The Adventure of the Empty House," Van Bork of "His Last Bow," and, the most famous of them all, Professor Moriarty, who is described in "The Final Problem" as the "Napoleon of crime" and the "organizer of half that is evil and of nearly all that is undetected in this great city." In essence, "The Final Problem" is a departure from the formula that characterizes the previous twenty-two Holmesian short stories, basically because Doyle intended that this would be the final work in which his detective would appear. Tiring of his creation and motivated by the desire to pursue his other literary interests, he has Watson record the demise of his friend. The story has no ingenious puzzle for the detective to unravel but instead is a detailed account of Sherlock Holmes's confrontation with his nemesis. For years, Holmes, who could "see deeply into the manifold wickedness of the human heart" and who could "leave his body at will and place himself into the mind and soul" of others, had been unable to penetrate the veil that shrouded the power "which for ever stands in the way of the law, and throws its shield over the wrongdoer." In this manner, Doyle almost casually proposes a conspiracy theme in this story which, in the hands of other writers, becomes one of the overriding characteristics of the detective fiction and thriller genres.

It is the character of Professor Moriarty, however, which commands the interest of the reader, particularly when seen as a reflection of Holmes. Professor Moriarty's career, like Holmes's, "has been an extraordinary one. He is a man of good birth and excellent education, endowed by Nature with a phenomenal mathematical faculty. At the age of twenty-one he wrote a treatise upon the Binomial Theorem, which has had a European vogue." When the Professor visits Holmes at his flat, his physical appearance is described as "extremely tall and thin, his forehead domes out in a white curve, and his two eyes are deeply sunken in his head. He is clean shaven, pale, and ascetic looking." To Holmes, his appearance is quite familiar, even though he has never met the man before. It is entirely likely that Holmes's immediate recognition is intended to suggest that the detective, for the first time in his life, is viewing in the flesh the side of his nature that his great intellect has refused to allow him to acknowledge.

Even though Dr. Watson had made special efforts to characterize Holmes as being almost totally devoid of emotion in his previous chronicles of Holmes's adventures, there are many instances in which there are outbursts of extreme feelings on the part of the detective. Holmes fluctuates between ennui and expressions of delight. He is often impulsive and compassionate. He is patient and deferential to his female clients. He is moved to indignation and intends to exact a form of revenge in "The Five Orange Pips."

In this story, "The Final Problem," he shows a level of nervousness and caution which is almost akin to fear in response to the threat that the malevolent genius Moriarty poses toward his person. Professor Moriarty is too much like himself for the detective to remain scientifically detached. There is no doubt that Holmes is totally conscious of the significance of the parallels that exist between the two when the Professor states:

> It has been a duel between you and me, Mr. Holmes. You hope to place me in the dock. I tell you that I will never stand in the dock. You hope to beat me. I tell you that you will never beat me. If you are clever enough to bring destruction upon me, rest assured that I shall do as much to you.

Holmes, with Watson, flees this enemy whom he acknowledges as "being quite on the same intellectual plane" as himself. Then, at Reichenbach Falls, he is almost inevitably forced to come face-to-face once again with his other self. Sidney Paget, the illustrator of many of the original publications in the *Strand Magazine*, depicts the struggle between Holmes and Moriarty just before their dual plunge into the chasm as being entwined together.

Thus, the culmination of Holmes's illustrious career, as originally intended by Doyle, was brought about in an entirely satisfactory symbolic and literary manner. Holmes, who could idly concede, "I have always had an idea that I could have made a highly efficient criminal," and "Burglary was always an alternative profession had I cared to adopt it," had resisted those impulses. In "The Final Problem" he could say: "In over a thousand cases I am not aware that I have ever used my powers upon the wrong side." The detective, however, was keenly aware throughout this story that "if he could be assured that society was freed from Professor Moriarty he would cheerfully bring his own career to a conclusion." With the death of Moriarty, he achieves that end. Although "London is the sweeter for [my] presence," the destruction of the other side of his nature in Professor Moriarty makes it all the more so. The death of Sherlock Holmes along with his nemesis is comparable to self-destruction.

"The Adventure of the Empty House" • When Doyle "killed off" his detective hero, he was in no way prepared for the public reaction that followed. He resisted almost continuous pressure from his publishers and the public until 1902, when he finally relented and resurrected Holmes in *The Hound of the Baskervilles* and later in the story "The Adventure of the Empty House." In this story, a lieutenant of Professor Moriarty, Colonel Sebastian Moran, is the culprit and functions as the alter ego for Holmes. One of the more subtle acknowledgments of the double theme in this story is the use by Holmes of a wax model of himself to mislead his adversaries. Similar to "The Final Problem," the story of the return of Sherlock Holmes does not follow the usual formula for the previous works, but the rest in the series adheres rather closely. When the stories are read in sequence, however, one can understand why the mere presence of the detective, however contrived his survival, would be cause for rejoicing by his followers. Even a lapse of more than ten years since his last appearance (three years within the stories) has in no way diminished his skill or intellectual capacity. Sherlock Holmes remains all that he was before his showdown with Professor Moriarty. The dialogue between the characters is as crisp as ever; the scenes are portrayed as vividly as before; the careful construction of the plots and the unraveling of the mysteries are as provocative as ever; and the imagination of the author is very much in evidence. There is evidence, however, of Doyle's reluctance to take his hero as seriously as he had before.

"The Adventure of the Dancing Men" • The story "The Adventure of the Dancing Men," for example, is extremely contrived, almost totally dependent on cartoons as a cipher, and the reader is left with a feeling of dissatisfaction. The stories in the first series after the "death" of Sherlock Holmes are nevertheless of generally high quality and possess many memorable scenes which remain after the mysteries have been solved.

Later Holmes Stories • There is agreement that the quality of the Sherlock Holmes stories published in the two collections *His Last Bow* and *The Case-Book of Sherlock Holmes* is significantly diminished. Published in 1917 and 1927 respectively, the books demonstrate that Doyle was tired of his detective, as the works were written casually and almost impatiently. The onset of World War I in the title story of *His Last Bow* is pointed out by Jacques Barzun as being "perhaps symbolic of the end of a world of gaslight and order in which Holmes and Watson could function so predictably." The stories in *The Case-Book of Sherlock Holmes*, published only a few years before Doyle's death, possess some fine moments, but there is a singular failure on the part of the author to re-create the vividness of the Victorian world that had lifted the previous series of short stories out of the ordinary and enabled the reader to accept and admire so readily the reasoning powers of Sherlock Holmes.

Despite the uneven quality of these works, it is a tribute to Doyle's ability that Sherlock Holmes remains a memorable character. Although Watson informs the reader that Holmes's knowledge of formal philosophy is nil, he is a philosopher in his own way. Holmes has probed the most abstract of understandings—ranging from the motivation of humans to the nature of the universe—from the study of the physical world. He possesses a peculiar morality akin to the John Stuart Mill variety: Evil is doing harm to others. When he seeks justice, he almost inevitably finds it; justice in the social and structured sense. Holmes has little regard for the laws of human beings; he recognizes that they do not always serve the purposes of justice, so at times he rises above them and often ignores them. For him, the distinction between right and wrong is absolute and beyond debate. It was Doyle's skill in infusing such depth into his character that makes Holmes greater than Dupin and Lecoq.

Robert W. Millett
With updates by Karen M. Cleveland Marwick

Other major works

PLAYS: *Foreign Policy*, pr. 1893; *Jane Annie: Or, The Good Conduct Prize*, pr., pb. 1893 (with J. M. Barrie); *Waterloo*, pr. 1894 (also as *A Story of Waterloo*); *Halves*, pr. 1899; *Sherlock Holmes*, pr. 1899 (with William Gillette); *A Duet*, pb. 1903; *Brigadier Gerard*, pr. 1906; *The Fires of Fate*, pr. 1909; *The House of Temperley*, pr. 1909; *The Pot of Caviare*, pr. 1910; *The Speckled Band*, pr. 1910; *The Crown Diamond*, pr. 1921; *Exile: A Drama of Christmas Eve*, pb. 1925; *It's Time Something Happened*, pb. 1925.

EDITED TEXTS: *Dreamland and Ghostland*, 1886; *D. D. Home: His Life and Mission*, 1921 (by Mrs. Douglas Home); *The Spiritualist's Reader*, 1924.

NOVELS: *A Study in Scarlet*, 1887 (serial; 1888, book); *The Mystery of Cloomber*, 1888; *Micah Clarke*, 1889; *The Firm of Girdlestone*, 1889; *The Sign of Four*, 1890 (first pb. as *The Sign of the Four*); *Beyond the City*, 1891; *The Doings of Raffles Haw*, 1891; *The White Company*, 1891; *The Great Shadow*, 1892; *The Refugees*, 1893; *The Parasite*, 1894; *The Stark Munro Letters*, 1895; *The Surgeon of Gaster Fell*, 1895; *Rodney Stone*, 1896; *The Tragedy of the Koroska*, 1897 (also as *A Desert Drama*); *Uncle Bernac*, 1897; *A Duet, with an Occasional Chorus*, 1899 (revised 1910); *The Hound of the Baskervilles*, 1901-1902 (serial), 1902 (book); *Sir Nigel*, 1905-1906 (serial), 1906 (book); *The Lost World*, 1912; *The Poison Belt*, 1913; *The Valley of Fear*, 1914-1915 (serial), 1915 (book); *The Land of Mist*, 1926.

MISCELLANEOUS: *The Sir Arthur Conan Doyle Reader*, 2002.

NONFICTION: *The Great Boer War*, 1900; *The War in South Africa: Its Causes and Conduct*, 1902; *The Case of Mr. George Edalji*, 1907; *Through the Magic Door*, 1907; *The Crime of the Congo*, 1909; *The Case of Oscar Slater*, 1912; *Great Britain and the Next War*, 1914; *In Quest of Truth, Being a Correspondence Between Sir Arthur Conan Doyle and Captain H. Stansbury*, 1914; *To Arms!*, 1914; *The German War: Some Sidelights and Reflections*, 1915; *Western Wanderings*, 1915; *A Visit to Three Fronts*, 1916; *The British Campaign in France and Flanders*, 1916-1919 (6 volumes); *The Origin and Outbreak of the War*, 1916; *A Petition to the Prime Minister on Behalf of Roger Casement*, 1916(?); *The New Revelation*, 1918; *The Vital Message*, 1919; *A Debate on Spiritualism*, 1920 (with Joseph McCabe); *Our Reply to the Cleric*, 1920; *Spiritualism and Rationalism*, 1920; *Fairies Photographed*, 1921; *The Evidence for Fairies*, 1921; *The Wanderings of a Spiritualist*, 1921; *The Case for Spirit Photography*, 1922 (with others); *The Coming of the Fairies*, 1922; *Our American Adventure*, 1923; *Memories and Adventures*, 1924; *Our Second American Adventure*, 1924; *Psychic Experiences*, 1925; *The Early Christian Church and Modern Spiritualism*, 1925; *The History of*

Spiritualism, 1926 (2 volumes); *Pheneas Speaks: Direct Spirit Communications,* 1927; *A Word of Warning,* 1928; *What Does Spiritualism Actually Teach and Stand For?,* 1928; *An Open Letter to Those of My Generation,* 1929; *Our African Winter,* 1929; *The Roman Catholic Church: A Rejoinder,* 1929; *The Edge of the Unknown,* 1930; *Arthur Conan Doyle on Sherlock Holmes,* 1981; *Essays on Photography,* 1982; *Letters to the Press,* 1984.

POETRY: *Songs of Action,* 1898; *Songs of the Road,* 1911; *The Guards Came Through, and Other Poems,* 1919; *The Poems: Collected Edition,* 1922.

TRANSLATION: *The Mystery of Joan of Arc,* 1924 (Léon Denis).

Bibliography

Akinson, Michael. *The Secret Marriage of Sherlock Holmes and Other Eccentric Readings.* Ann Arbor: University of Michigan Press, 1996. Attempts to read Holmes's stories in the manner in which Holmes himself might read them. "The Adventure of the Speckled Band" is read in terms of the philosophy of Kundalini yoga; "A Scandal in Bohemia" is read in terms of its use of traditional romance motifs and its debt to Edgar Allan Poe; Jungian psychology is used to read *A Study in Scarlet*; and Derridian deconstruction is used to read "The Adventure of the Copper Breeches."

Barsham, Diana. *Arthur Conan Doyle and the Meaning of Masculinity.* Burlington, Vt.: Ashgate, 2000. Discussion of masculinity according to Doyle, delving into all Doyle's writings, including his war correspondence and travel writings.

Green, Richard Lancelyn. *A Bibliography of A. Conan Doyle.* New York: Oxford University Press, 1983. Provides a massive bibliography of all that Doyle wrote, including obscure short pieces. Illustrated and containing a seventy-five-page index, this book includes a list of more than one hundred books of biographical, bibliographical, and critical interest for the study of Doyle.

Hall, Jasmine Yong. "Ordering the Sensational: Sherlock Holmes and the Female Gothic." *Studies in Short Fiction* 28 (Summer, 1991): 295-304. Examines how gothic elements and female clients in a number of stories, including the well-known "The Speckled Band," establish the rational detective as a powerful, patriarchal hero. Argues that Holmes controls his female clients as much as the gothic villains in Doyle's stories.

Hodgson, John A., ed. *Sherlock Holmes: The Major Stories with Contemporary Critical Essays.* New York: St. Martin's Press, 1994. Includes nine essays on Holmes, from a variety of critical perspectives, including feminist, deconstruction, and discourse analysis approaches.

Jaffee, Jacqueline A. *Arthur Conan Doyle.* Boston: Twayne, 1987. Jaffee's solid work combines biography and a critical discussion of Doyle's stories and novels. Contains three chapters on the Sherlock Holmes stories, which closely examine the tales. Supplemented by an index, a bibliography of Doyle's work, and an annotated bibliography.

Jann, Rosemary. *The Adventures of Sherlock Holmes: Detecting Social Order.* New York: Twayne, 1995. Part of Twayne's Masterwork Series, this slim volume is divided into two parts, the first of which places the great detective in a literary and historical context, followed by Jann's own reading of Arthur Conan Doyle's Sherlockian approach to detective fiction. In addition to a selected bibliography, Jann's book includes a brief chronology of Doyle's life and work.

May, Charles E., ed. *Masterplots II: Short Story Series, Revised Edition.* 8 vols. Pasadena, Calif.: Salem Press, 2004. Designed for student use, this reference set contains articles providing detailed plot summaries and analyses of these five short stories by

Doyle: "The Adventure of the Dancing Men" and "The Adventure of the Speckled Band" (vol. 1), "The Greek Interpreter" (vol. 3), and "The Red-Headed League" and "A Scandal in and Bohemia" (vol. 6).

Orel, Harold, ed. *Critical Essays on Sir Arthur Conan Doyle.* New York: G. K. Hall, 1992. Including both evaluations by Doyle's contemporaries and later scholarship—some of it commissioned specifically for inclusion in this collection—*Critical Essays* is divided into three sections: "Sherlock Holmes," "Other Writings," and "Spiritualism." Harold Orel opens the collections with a lengthy and comprehensive essay, which is followed by a clever and classic meditation by Dorothy L. Sayers on "Dr. Watson's Christian Name." Also included are pieces by such literary lights as George Bernard Shaw, Max Beerbohm, and Heywood Broun.

Stashower, Daniel. *Teller of Tales: The Life of Arthur Conan Doyle.* New York: Henry Holt, 1999. Excellent biography of Doyle. Focuses less on the Holmes novels and more on the historical novels, personal crusades, and spiritualism.

Andre Dubus

Born: Lake Charles, Louisiana; August 11, 1936
Died: Haverhill, Massachusetts; February 24, 1999

Principal short fiction • *Separate Flights*, 1975; *Adultery and Other Choices*, 1977; *Finding a Girl in America*, 1980; *The Times Are Never So Bad*, 1983; *The Last Worthless Evening*, 1986; *Selected Stories*, 1988; *Dancing After Hours: Stories*, 1996; *In the Bedroom: Seven Stories*, 2002.

Other literary forms • Although Andre Dubus wrote an early novel, *The Lieutenant* (1967), which is highly regarded by some critics and readers, and a short novel, *Voices from the Moon* (1984), which has been printed separately, his most important contributions to literature are his shorter works. Besides his fiction, Dubus wrote two well-received books of autobiographical essays.

Achievements • Andre Dubus's literary career is notable in the way it stands outside the shifting fashions of the American literary scene. During the 1960's and 1970's, when the "postmodernism" of Donald Barthelme, John Barth, and Thomas Pynchon was creating a highly self-conscious, self-reflective literature that often used its own craft to explore itself, Dubus remained a committed realist, at his best when he used his craft to explore the lives of his characters. During the period when the so-called minimalist stories of writers such as Raymond Carver, Bobbie Ann Mason, and Lorrie Moore came into literary prominence, Dubus remained what might be called a "maximalist" writer, who seemed most at home in the form of the long story, or novella. In a period of shifting male and female definitions, Dubus wrote often about the waywardness of people who continue to define themselves by concepts of masculinity and femininity that the world around them no longer values. Not least of all, in an age of secular values, Dubus often looks to the Sacraments of the Roman Catholic Church to find deep values.

Biography • Andre Dubus was born in Lake Charles, Louisiana, on August 11, 1936, and attended the Christian Brothers Catholic School in Lafayette from 1944 until 1954, after which he enrolled in McNeese State University in Lake Charles. Upon graduating from college in 1958 with a bachelor's degree in English and journalism, he married Patricia Lowe and entered the Marine Corps with a commission as lieutenant. Over the next five years, four of the couple's children were born (Suzanne in 1958, Andre III in 1959, Jeb in 1960, and Nicole in 1963), and he was to rise to the rank of captain.

In 1963, he published his first story, "The Intruder," in *The Sewanee Review* and resigned his officer's commission to enter the master of fine arts program at the University of Iowa, the much respected Writers' Workshop program. Upon receiving his degree in 1965, he taught for one year as a lecturer at Nicholls State University in Louisiana, before accepting a position at Bradford College in Massachusetts in 1966, where he was to teach for the next fourteen years, until his retirement in 1984.

Dubus was married and divorced three times, and the pain of these broken marriages provided a source for much of his fiction. His first marriage, to Lowe in 1958, ended in divorce in 1970. His second marriage, to Tommie Gail Cotter in 1975, ended in divorce in 1977. His third marriage, to Peggy Rambach, also a writer, in 1979, produced two daughters, Cadence, born in 1982, and Madeline, born in 1987, but ended when his wife left in November, 1987, in the midst of family strain stemming from a 1986 automobile accident, which also cost Dubus a leg.

Many of Dubus's stories have been selected for the annual *The Best American Short Stories* and *Prize Stories: The O. Henry Awards* series. Among his national honors, he received a National Endowment for the Arts grant in 1985 and a John Simon Guggenheim Memorial Foundation Fellowship in 1986. Both of these honors came after his retirement from teaching in 1984. His plans to use the monetary freedom provided by these grants to spend more time writing were violently interrupted by an accident in which he had stopped to assist two distressed motorists, only to become the victim of another car. The pain of recovering from this accident, in which he saved a life but lost a leg, is chronicled in the title essay of his collection of essays *Broken Vessels*. On February 24, 1999, Dubus died in Haverhill, Massachusetts.

Analysis • Among American story writers of the twentieth century, the one to whom Andre Dubus is most often compared is Flannery O'Connor. Although Dubus's works are not generally marked by the wry, ironic wit that permeates O'Connor's work, both writers are marked by what Thomas E. Kennedy, among others, has called an "existential Christian" sensibility.

"If They Knew Yvonne" • An early Dubus story, "If They Knew Yvonne," first published in *The North American Review* in 1969 and collected both in *Separate Flights* and *Selected Stories*, displays this sensibility clearly. This story traces the development of a teenager, Harry Dugal, growing into manhood and caught between two powerful forces: his emerging sexuality and his need for the absolution and Communion provided by the Roman Catholic Church. Taught by the fathers at the Christian Brothers School to regard masturbation as "self-abuse" and a mortal sin, Harry, as he discovers his own inability to resist the urge to masturbate, goes to confession at every opportunity to confess his sins. Disgusted at his own weakness and at the sexual weakness that he discovers in his family around him, including his parents, whose store of condoms he discovers, and his sister Janet, who gets married while two months pregnant, the young Harry even considers emasculating himself at one point.

At the age of nineteen, however, he has his first sexual encounter with a woman his own age, Yvonne Millet, and discovers a type of sexuality that does not disgust him. When Yvonne implores him, "Love me, Harry, love me," he begins to perceive that this type of love is not the squalid lust that he had been warned to guard against but something else, something he is not sure the Catholic fathers at his school knew anything about. The story ends shortly after he has drifted apart from Yvonne and goes to confession again. After Harry has confessed his sexual affair, the priest quotes a line from St. John, in which Christ prays, "I do not pray that You take them out of the world but that You keep them from evil," a quote that delineates the story's Christian existentialist theme. Harry begins to understand that the higher good depends not on remaining pure and safe from the world but on being a responsible, conscientious member of the world.

In his full-length study, *Andre Dubus: A Study of the Short Fiction*, Thomas Kennedy points out that almost half of Dubus's first fifty stories deal with violent themes or subjects, but he further points out that violence is only secondary to the central theme, a symptom of the greater condition of "human isolation and disconnection in . . . modern America." This is not to say that Dubus in any way excuses violence, but rather that understanding how violence grows out of an acceptance of superficial values is an important source for his fiction.

"The Pretty Girl" • Dubus's novella "The Pretty Girl," collected in both *The Times Are Never So Bad* and *Selected Stories*, is one of his best extended examinations of this type of violence. One of the two point-of-view characters is Raymond Yarborough, who is presented as a wildly exploding tinderbox of violence. When the reader meets him, he is divorced from the other main character, Polly Comeau, but still obsessed by her. The reader learns early that Raymond has already raped her, though he considers that he was only "taking back my wife for a while." Before long, he beats up and severely injures a man whom he knows she has slept with and lights a fire around the house where Polly is staying, not to destroy anything but to terrorize her.

If Raymond is in many ways the antagonist in the story, he is also the most interesting character, and his former wife Polly is not presented in particularly sympathetic terms. A waitress by trade, Polly is in many ways best described in the terms of the story's title as a twenty-six-year-old "pretty girl" who has used her beauty to avoid fashioning an adult identity and instead has tended to drift from one sexual affair to another, even during the course of her marriage, without much sense of responsibility or consequences.

Polly is a loner almost as much as Raymond is. She shares a house with a male acquaintance but has no close friends either male or female. Her relationships with women tend to be competitive, and her friendships with men tend to be brief, quickly sacrificed to her love affairs. She is significantly alone when Raymond breaks into her house at the end of the story to confront her about why she left him and what she really wants. Though he is unarmed, Polly, who has been ill and alone for several days, uses a gun she bought for protection to kill him when he begins to take off his clothes. Both main characters are carefully constructed to be unlikable, though only Raymond is presented as truly repugnant. The success of the story is that it compels the reader nevertheless to want to understand each of them and to appreciate each character's struggle, while not inviting the reader to forget or overlook their immature self-obsession or moral rootlessness.

"Finding a Girl in America" • A number of Dubus's stories deal with recurring characters. Two stories of the three that deal with Hank Allison, a middle-aged, philandering college professor, show Dubus's art at both its best and its worst. "Finding a Girl in America" shows both the character Hank Allison and the writer Andre Dubus at their worst. In it, Hank is presented as a divorced college professor who has been having affairs with his female students. As the story opens, he has learned that a former lover had an abortion and feels cheated because he believes that had the baby been born, it would have filled the void left in his life by his daughter growing up; the point of view of the woman who would have had a baby she did not want fathered by a man she did not love is not seriously considered. The attention to detail, which in other stories creates a convincing illusion of reality, in this story seems tedious and self-indulgent. Dubus's insistence on finding moral frameworks to understand his characters, a tendency that in many stories uplifts his art, in this story misleads him.

Hank's life is so self-indulgent that it is hard for a reader to take him half as seriously as he takes himself.

"Adultery" • The earlier story, "Adultery," is by contrast one of the finest examples of Dubus's art. To be sure, Hank Allison is the same self-centered, self-justifying man that the reader meets in the later story (as well as in "We Don't Live Here Anymore"). "Adultery," however, is carefully constructed to consider not only marital fidelity but also spiritual fidelity.

The main characters are Hank Allison, his wife Edith, and Father Joe Ritchie, a Catholic priest dying of cancer who renounces his vows and has an affair with Edith. The story also investigates the lives of a number of other men and women whom Hank and Edith choose as lovers. It is Hank who initially brings adultery into his and Edith's marriage, but when she discovers it, he immediately consents to her right to have extramarital affairs as well. The affairs they both have take their toll especially on Edith and make a sham of their marriage. The irony of the title—and the element that raises this story to the finest level of American fiction—is that Edith's adultery with a dying Catholic priest is not viewed by her or Father Ritchie as true adultery; the true adultery for her is staying in a marriage based on hypocrisy. Similarly, although this affair compromises Joe Ritchie in more ways than one, he and Edith both understand that their relationship is spiritually as well as personally the right thing to do; what worries Joe Ritchie most is that Edith might remain married to Hank, and he is relieved when she comes to him while he is dying to say that she is divorcing Hank. By deciding to divorce Hank, Edith upholds at least the *idea* of marital fidelity. Moreover, she realizes that her affair with Joe Ritchie has provided her with a new center for her life and that she would be unfaithful to herself and the belief in marriage to remain with Hank any longer.

"A Father's Story" • "A Father's Story," which was chosen by John Updike for the annual *The Best American Short Stories* in 1984, is in some respects Dubus's most important story. Smaller in scale than stories such as "The Fat Girl" or "Separate Flights," which each compress the story of several years into a few pages, "A Father's Story" focuses on a crucial incident in the life of Luke Ripley and his daughter Jennifer. Like many of Dubus's characters, Luke seems in many ways to be a version of the author, but in this case, a version that has achieved a deceptive veneer of simplicity. The opening line of the story, "My name is Luke Ripley and here is what I call my life," seems to present the voice of a direct, straightforward man. The life that Luke tells the reader about is one filled with a variety of contradictions: He is a devout Catholic but divorced; he attends Mass regularly but does not always listen; he enjoys talking to his priest but casually, preferably over a few beers, and what they discuss is mostly small talk; he is a self-described lazy man who dislikes waking up early but does so each morning to pray, not because he feels obligated to do so but because he knows he has the choice not to do so. Luke Ripley is a man who lives with contradictions and accepts them.

As such, when his daughter comes to him, frantically telling him that she hit a man with a car, he reacts almost instinctively. Rather than call the police or an ambulance, he drives to the scene of the accident to verify that the young man is in fact dead. When he knows that there is nothing that can be done to help the young man, he drives home and puts his daughter to bed, then takes her car out and runs it into a tree in front of the church to cover up the dent she had already created. The story ends with Luke recalling to the reader how he justifies himself to his God each morning, saying, "You never had a daughter and, if You had, You could not have borne her passion. . . . I love her more than I love truth." God replies, "Then you love in weakness," to which Luke responds, "As You love me."

The power of "A Father's Story" is that it captures perfectly the opposites that Dubus's fiction is constantly exploring. Luke Ripley's love for his daughter is both his strength and his weakness. Similarly, his love for his daughter moves him to deceive, even as his religion demands confession; and when he finds himself unable to confess his sin of covering up his daughter's crime, the story itself, it is clear, is his substitute for the confession that he cannot make to a priest. Like many of Dubus's stories, "A Father's Story" shows a person caught between the confusing, ambiguous demands of his human heart and the by-no-means-clear demands of a religion in which he believes but which speaks of an absolute he can only partially understand.

Thomas Cassidy
With updates by Charles E. May

Other major works

NOVELS: *The Lieutenant,* 1967; *Voices from the Moon,* 1984; *We Don't Live Here Anymore,* 1984.

NONFICTION: *Broken Vessels,* 1991; *Meditations from a Movable Chair: Essays,* 1998.

Bibliography

Breslin, John B. "Playing Out of the Patterns of Sin and Grace: The Catholic Imagination of Andre Dubus." *Commonweal* 115 (December 2, 1988): 652-656. An interesting analysis of the Catholic themes in Dubus's literature, written for a lay audience. Breslin focuses particularly on Dubus's trilogy of stories dealing with Hank Allison ("We Don't Live Here Anymore," "Adultery," and "Finding a Girl in America"), and "A Father's Story."

Cocchiarale, Michael. "The Complicated Catholicism of Andre Dubus." In *Songs of the New South: Writing Contemporary Louisiana,* edited by Suzanne D. Green and Lisa Abney. Westport, Conn.: Greenwood Press, 2001. Discusses Dubus's writing in the context of Catholicism and its role in the complex morality of his characters.

Dubus, Andre. "An Interview with Andre Dubus." Interview by David Yandell Todd. *Yale Review* 86 (July, 1998): 89-110. Dubus candidly discusses his decision to become a writer and the relationship between his life, his stories, and the authors who have most influenced him. He also considers what motivates his characters, creates their conflicts, and provides them with spiritual and moral significance.

Feeney, Joseph J. "Poised for Fame: Andre Dubus at Fifty." *America* 155 (November 15, 1986): 296-299. Using the occasion of Dubus's fiftieth birthday, the author provides a general introduction to the man, his writing, and his major themes. Written for an audience he assumes to be generally unfamiliar with Dubus's fiction, this article presents the major themes of Dubus's fiction without exploring them in depth.

Ferriss, Lucy. "Andre Dubus: 'Never Truly Members.'" In *Southern Writers at Century's End,* edited by Jeffery J. Folks and James A. Perkins. Lexington: University Press of Kentucky, 1997. Discusses several short stories with a focus on Dubus's concerns with Roman Catholic sexual politics, particularly in the context of his women characters and his connection with the literary tradition of the South.

Kennedy, Thomas E. *Andre Dubus: A Study of the Short Fiction.* Boston: Twayne, 1988. The first full-length study of Dubus's fiction to be published, this volume is by far the most helpful work for someone interested in Dubus and his fiction. Kennedy groups Dubus's stories together by their thematic content and analyzes them in separate chapters, which are each devoted to one theme. Also included are other critical evaluations, two interviews with Dubus, an extensive bibliography of primary and secondary sources, and a helpfully designed index. If there is a flaw, it is that Kennedy sometimes seems too devoted to Dubus's work to accurately evaluate its occasional shortcomings.

Lesser, Ellen. "True Confession: Andre Dubus Talks Straight." Review of *Selected Stories. Village Voice* 37 (January 17, 1989): 56. Lesser claims that "Dubus writes stories like a pilot pushing the envelope—continually testing fiction's effective limits." She praises his fiction for its deliberate unfashionableness and for its unsimplified Catholic sensibility.

May, Charles E., ed. *Masterplots II: Short Story Series, Revised Edition.* 8 vols. Pasadena, Calif.: Salem Press, 2004. Designed for student use, this reference set contains articles providing detailed plot summaries and analyses of these five short stories by Dubus: "The Curse" and "Dancing After Hours" (vol. 2), "A Father's Story" and "The Fat Girl" (vol. 3), and "Killings" (vol. 4).

Miner, Madone. "Jumping from One Heart to Another: How Andre Dubus Writes About Women." *Critique* 39 (Fall, 1997): 18-31. Discusses three stories—"Anna," "Leslie in California," and "Rose"—in terms of Dubus's ability to write empathetically from a woman's perspective, to speak with a woman's voice about women's experience, while still retaining his "maleness."

Rowe, Anne E. "Andre Dubus." In *Contemporary Fiction Writers of the South,* edited by Joseph M. Flora and Robert Bain. Westport, Conn.: Greenwood Press, 1993. General introduction to such Dubus themes as the passage from childhood to the adult world, failed friendships and marriages, and the individual's search for a meaningful center. Also includes an analytical survey of criticism of Dubus's fiction.

Yarbrough, Steve. "Andre Dubus: From Detached Incident to Compressed Novel." *Critique: Studies in Modern Fiction* 28 (Fall, 1986); 19-27. Argues that Dubus's short stories can be categorized in three different ways, of which the largest category is the compressed novel, which follows the course of characters' lives for several years. This article focuses on a number of short stories, including "The Doctor," "The Dark Men," "Townies," "In My Life," "Separate Flights," and "The Fat Girl."

Stuart Dybek

Born: Chicago, Illinois; April 10, 1942

Principal short fiction • *Childhood and Other Neighborhoods*, 1980; *The Coast of Chicago*, 1990; *The Story of Mist*, 1993; *I Sailed with Magellan*, 2003 (novellas).

Other literary forms • Stuart Dybek is known principally for his short fiction. He has also published three volumes of poetry: *Brass Knuckles* (1979), *Kiddie Corner* (1981), and *Streets in Their Own Ink* (2004). His only play, *Orchids*, was produced in 1990, and his short story "Death of a Right Fielder" was adapted to television in 1991.

Achievements • Editors have chosen many of Stuart Dybek's stories for inclusion in anthologies. He won a Special Citation from the Ernest Hemingway Foundation as well as awards from the Cliff Dwellers Arts Foundation, Friends of American Writers, the Whiting Foundation, and the Society of Midland Authors. In addition, he received a Nelson Algren Award, several O. Henry Awards, and the Church and the Artist Literary Competition Award. Dybek has been the recipient of a John Simon Guggenheim Memorial Foundation Fellowship and the National Endowment for the Arts grant.

Biography • Stuart Dybek was born on April 10, 1942, in Chicago, the son of Stanley and Adeline Sala Dybek. He grew up in a working-class, ethnic neighborhood, a milieu that figures prominently in his writing. After graduating from a Roman Catholic high school, he enrolled at Loyola University, but he interrupted his education to work in the Civil Rights and antiwar movements of the early 1960's. He earned a bachelor's degree from Loyola in 1964 and a master's degree in 1968. He married Caren Bassett in 1966.

After working as a case worker with the Cook County Department of Public Aid, teaching in a Chicago-area elementary school, and teaching high school on the island of St. Thomas as a VISTA volunteer, Dybek returned to school. He earned an master of fine arts degree from the prestigious University of Iowa Writers' Workshop in 1973. In 1974, he began teaching English and creative writing at Western Michigan University in Kalamazoo, Michigan. He served as a visiting professor at Princeton University in 1990 and began teaching in the Warren Wilson M.F.A. program for writers in 1985.

Dybek's first book-length publication was his collection of poetry and prose poems, *Brass Knuckles*. His first collection of short stories, *Childhood and Other Neighborhoods*, published in 1980, was well received by the critics. Likewise, his second collection, *The Coast of Chicago* (1990), received considerable critical praise. Beginning the mid-1970's, Dybek published a steady stream of stories in such important journals as *Ploughshares* and *TriQuarterly* and such popular magazines as *The New Yorker* and *The Atlantic Monthly*.

Analysis • Chicago has a long tradition of producing fine writers who use the city as their literary landscape. Gwendolyn Brooks, Carl Sandburg, Upton Sinclair, and Theodore Dreiser, among others, belong to this tradition. Stuart Dybek, while drawing heavily on the city for his settings, characters, and images, departs from the tradition with his dreamlike portrayal of life in a postmodern world. Some critics have identified his work with Magical Realism and have suggested a connection with Jorge Luis Borges and Italo Calvino. Dybek himself reports that after he wrote some of the early stories included in *Childhood and Other Neighborhoods* he began to read the works of Franz Kafka and Gabriel García Márquez.

In addition to exploring the intersection between dreams and reality, Dybek has pioneered the genre sometimes known as "sudden" or "flash" fiction. These stories are sometimes also called "short short" stories; sudden fiction can be just a few paragraphs long, and such stories are never longer than three pages. Consequently, readers of sudden fiction often find themselves in the middle of a situation well under way, a situation that will end but not conclude. Some of the prose poems in Dybek's poetry collection *Brass Knuckles* could fall into this category. *The Coast of Chicago* also includes several very short stories.

Many of Dybek's stories draw on his experiences growing up in a Polish-Latino neighborhood on the South Side of Chicago. His characters often have Polish surnames, attend Catholic churches, and carry with them the culture and mythology of Eastern Europe. Even when his stories are not overtly about the immigrant experience, their settings are rich with ethnic sounds, aromas, and sights. Churches frequently appear in the center of the landscape.

Dybek often places his characters in moments of transformation. Frequently this takes the form of a coming-of-age story, especially in *Childhood and Other Neighborhoods*. In a 1997 interview with Mike Nickel and Adrian Smith, Dybek says that he is always "looking for some door in the story that opens on another world." For some characters, this can be the world of adulthood; for others, it can be an entry into the world of magic or death. The entry into a different world can be a transformative moment for his characters, as well as for his readers.

Childhood and Other Neighborhoods • The eleven stories of the collection are about coming of age. With his title, Dybek deliberately suggests that there is both a time and a space to childhood; that is, he sees childhood in the same way one would see a neighborhood, as a place where interconnected people live out their lives, bounded by streets, houses, ethnicity, and religion. The main characters in this collection are generally young people, often second- or third-generation Poles making their homes in Chicago. Dybek himself identifies the subject of the collection as "perception," reminding his readers that children perceive the world in ways that are different from the ways adults do. For many of the characters in this book, their moment of transformation comes when they leave the familiar streets of their own neighborhood and venture out into the world at large. Sometimes these adventures end tragically, sometimes humorously. Often the world outside the neighborhood is a world infused with magic or horror.

The opening story of *Childhood and Other Neighborhoods*, "The Palatski Man" is about a young girl, Mary, and her older brother John. The story opens on Palm Sunday and continues to use religious iconography and imagery throughout. At the center of the story stands the nameless Palatski Man, a vendor who dresses in white and sells taffy apples and *palatski*, a confection of wafers and honey. There is a strangeness to this treat; Mary has never seen *palatski* sold anywhere else. For Mary, eating the *palatski* reminds her of Holy Communion, an image that recurs later in the story.

John and his friend Ray Cruz are fascinated by the Ragmen, who traverse their neighborhood collecting rags. John tells Mary about following a Ragman for a long way and discovering the place where all the Ragmen live. Ray and John are discovered by the Ragmen and become separated. Later, when John calls Ray's home, Ray denies that the adventure ever happened, and John is unable to locate the Ragmen's camp again. Later, John and Mary follow the Palatski Man and find themselves once again at the Ragmen's camp. In a mystical, frightening ceremony, the young people partake of a kind of Eucharist consisting of taffy apple syrup and *palatski*, which tastes surprisingly bitter. That night, Mary discovers that John has not eaten his portion. The story closes strangely with a scene that could be a real event, a vision, or a dream. The Palatski Man comes for Mary, and she knows that she must go with him. Dybek reports that he wrote this story while listening to the music of Polish composer Zoltán Kodály. The music suggested the strange, Eastern European images. There are also undercurrents of the Persephone myth, and readers should remember that this myth was a subject of a poem in Dybek's *Brass Knuckles*. In Greek mythology, Persephone eats pomegranate seeds offered her by Hades, the ruler of the underworld. As a result, she is bound to stay with him for six months of the year. Likewise, Mary's ingestion of the minute wafer given to her by the Palatski Man makes possible the final scene.

The Coast of Chicago • *The Coast of Chicago* contains both longer stories and very short stories, intertwined and interconnected by theme and image. Some reviewers suggest that the very short stories are lyrical in nature and may be autobiographical. Again, Chicago provides the setting for the stories, and again, Dybek has said that he listened to music, jazz this time, as he wrote the stories. Many of the stories in the collection have a dreamlike, legendary quality to them. Art and music figure in many of the stories. For example, "Nighthawks," itself a minicollection of tales within the larger collection, uses Edward Hopper's painting by the same name as its starting point. Likewise, "Chopin in Winter" draws on the music of the Polish composer. In all, the stories are often elegiac, somber, nearly hallucinatory. Again, Dybek seems most interested in showing the reader the way characters and settings change, often subtly, often before the reader's very eyes.

"Ant" • Appearing in the Winter, 1997-1998, issue of *Ploughshares*, "Ant" is a sample of Dybek's very short fiction and an example of the blend of fantasy and realism characteristic of many of his stories. In addition, the story features entry into another world and then back into the ordinary one. The story opens with Martin lying on a blanket under a tree with his lover. When an ant begins to drag him by his toe, Martin remembers stories read to him when he was a boy by his Uncle Wayne. His uncle, a veteran of an unnamed war, acted out the stories after reading them to Martin. The most memorable for Martin was "Lonigan and the Ants." His uncle, who had pretended that he was an ant and Martin was Lonigan, had begun to pursue him. All that saved the frightened Martin from the mad pursuit by his uncle was the reminder that Lonigan does not die, and the ants do not win; the "authority of the story" is enough to change his uncle's actions. Dybek seems to be playing with the boundaries of storytelling here. In the larger story, he exerts authority over his own story and writes a version in which one ant does win. Eventually, an ant works its way up Martin's back, grabs hold of his belt, lifts him off the ground, and carries him away.

Diane Andrews Henningfeld

Other major works

PLAY: *Orchids*, pr. 1990.

POETRY: *Brass Knuckles*, 1979; *Kiddie Corner*, 1981; *Streets in Their Own Ink*, 2004.

Bibliography

Cook, Bruce. "Walks on the Southwest Side." *Washington Post Book World* (January 13, 1980): 1-2. Places Dybek in the tradition of the Chicago writers, including Nelson Algren, Gwendolyn Brooks, and Saul Bellow, in a review of *Childhood and Other Neighborhoods*.

Dybek, Stuart. "An Interview with Stuart Dybek." Interview by Mike Nickel and Adrian Smith. *Chicago Review* 43 (Winter, 1997): 87-101. A revealing interview in which Dybek reflects on what it means to be a "Chicago writer," his ethnic background and how it influences his writing, and his ideas about form and writing.

_____. "Thread." *Harper's* 297 (September, 1998): 34-37. A brief memoir by Dybek recalling his Catholic upbringing and his first Holy Communion.

Gladsky, Thomas S. "From Ethnicity to Multiculturalism: The Fiction of Stuart Dybek." *MELUS* 20 (Summer, 1995): 105-118. Offers a brief history of Polish immigration to the United States followed by a consideration of Polish American writers before turning to an examination of Stuart Dybek in this context. Connects ethnicity and memory and discusses the role of Catholicism in Dybek's prose.

Kakutani, Michiko. "Lyrical Loss and Desolation of Misfits in Chicago." *The New York Times Book Review* (April 20, 1990): C31. Draws a parallel between *The Coast of Chicago* and Sherwood Anderson's *Winesburg, Ohio* (1919), noting similarities in characters, lyricism, and "emotional forcefulness."

Lee, Don. "About Stuart Dybek." *Ploughshares* 24 (Spring, 1998): 192-198. A profile of Dybek and his subject matter. Provides biographical information as well as considering Dybek's contribution to the "short short" genre of short stories.

May, Charles E., ed. *Masterplots II: Short Story Series, Revised Edition.* 8 vols. Pasadena, Calif.: Salem Press, 2004. Designed for student use, this reference set contains articles providing detailed plot summaries and analyses of these three short stories by Dybek: "Bijou" and "Blight" (vol. 1), and "Pet Milk" (vol. 6).

Shapard, Robert, and James Thomas, eds. *Sudden Fiction: American Short-Short Stories.* Salt Lake City: Gibbs M. Smith, 1986. The classic collection of the "short short" story. Includes Dybek's short short "Sunday at the Zoo" as well as an afterword by Dybek on the genre.

Ward, Robert. "A Review of *Childhood and Other Neighborhoods*." *Northwest Review* 18 (Fall, 1980): 149-157.

Weber, Katharine. "Windy City Dreaming." *The New York Times Book Review*, May 20, 1990, 30. Reviews *The Coast of Chicago*, connecting memory, dreaming, and the dreamlike nature of Dybek's stories.

Ralph Ellison

Born: Oklahoma City, Oklahoma; March 1, 1914
Died: New York, New York; April 16, 1994

Principal short fiction • *Flying Home, and Other Stories*, 1996.

Other literary forms • *Invisible Man*, Ralph Ellison's 1952 novel, is one of the most important American novels of the twentieth century. Ellison also published two well-received collections of essays, *Shadow and Act* (1964) and *Going to the Territory* (1986), which were combined into one volume in *The Collected Essays of Ralph Ellison* (1995). In 1999, a posthumous edition of his long-awaited second novel was published as *Juneteenth: A Novel.*

Achievements • Though he won a Rosenwald grant in 1945 on the strength of his short fiction, and though two of his short stories, "Flying Home" and "King of the Bingo Game," are among the most commonly anthologized short stories in twentieth century American literature, Ralph Ellison is best known for his 1952 novel *Invisible Man*, which won the National Book Award and the Russwurm Award. In 1975 he was elected to the American Academy of Arts and Letters, which in 1955 awarded him a Prix de Rome Fellowship. He received the French Chevalier de l'Ordre des Arts et des Lettres in 1970 and the National Medal of Arts in 1985. In 1984 he was awarded the Langston Hughes medallion by City College in New York for his contributions to arts and letters.

Biography • Ralph Waldo Ellison was born March 1, 1914, in Oklahoma City to Ida and Lewis Alfred Ellison, who had moved out of the South in search of a more progressive place to live. An ambitious student, he distinguished himself locally and was rewarded with a scholarship to attend the Tuskegee Institute, in part because the local white population did not want Ellison, an African American, to integrate the white colleges in Oklahoma. Unable to afford the fare to Alabama, he rode a freight train to Tuskegee, in which he enrolled in 1933. A voracious reader in college, he pursued interests in literature, history, and folklore. At the end of his junior year, Ellison, like the narrator of *Invisible Man*, was refused financial aid and so traveled to New York City, where he hoped to make enough money to finish his studies. While in New York, he met another African American author, Richard Wright, who encouraged Ellison's literary ambitions, and instead of returning to Tuskegee, he began to contribute short stories and essays to various literary journals and anthologies. From 1938 to 1944, he worked with the Federal Writers Project, and in 1945, he was a awarded a Rosenwald grant to write a novel. The result was *Invisible Man* (1952), a landmark work in African American fiction that won for its author numerous honorary degrees, literary awards, and worldwide fame.

Though Ellison would publish two well-received collections of essays, *Shadow and Act* and *Going to the Territory*, he would never follow up his first novel with a second in his lifetime. He began writing his next novel around 1958, and over the years he was to publish numerous excerpts from it as a work-in-progress. A fire at his Plainsfield,

Massachusetts, summer home destroyed much of the manuscript in 1967, causing him to have to painstakingly reconstruct it. Though he was to work on this project for the rest of his life, he never found a final form for the novel with which he felt comfortable, and it remained unfinished when he died of a heart attack in 1994. His literary executor, John F. Callahan, published his short fiction in one volume as *Flying Home, and Other Stories in 1996* and a self-contained portion of his final novel as *Juneteenth* in 1999.

National Archives

Analysis • Because most of Ralph Ellison's short fiction was written before his career as a novelist began, his short stories are often analyzed biographically, as the training ground for the novelist he was to become. This is not entirely unjustified because a biographical overview of his literary output reveals that he tried out the voices, techniques, and ideas that he was to present so boldly in *Invisible Man* and almost completely abandoned the form after his success as a novelist, devoting himself to his essays and to his never-to-be-completed second novel.

It is true that in his two most accomplished stories, "The King of the Bingo Game" and "Flying Home," he develops themes of the chaos of the modern world and the affliction of racial conflict that would later be combined and expanded in his famous novel. On the other hand, his earlier stories show him working out many of the same ideas from different perspectives. Although the voice that informs his most accomplished work is a mature voice that is uniquely Ellison's own, the voices in his other stories show more clearly the influences of Ernest Hemingway, Richard Wright, and James Joyce.

In relating his short fiction to his overall work, Edith Schor in *Visible Ellison: A Study of Ralph Ellison's Fiction* (1993) aptly observed that Ellison's short stories provided experimental laboratories for testing the translation of the forms and experiences of African American life into literature. In evaluating the stories themselves, however, Robert Bone best summarized their lasting value when he observed in "Ralph Ellison and the Uses of Imagination" (1966) that Ellison's short stories are about "adventurers" testing "the fixed boundaries of southern life."

Flying Home, and Other Stories • *Flying Home, and Other Stories* is a posthumous collection of stories edited by Ralph Ellison's literary executor, John F. Callahan, which brings together in one volume all of the principal short fiction Ellison wrote (excepting pieces that were published as excerpts of his novels). Callahan arranged the stories according to the age of the main characters, thereby highlighting the stories' thematic unity regarding the growth of young persons' ideologies, which might not otherwise be evident.

The collection opens with "A Party Down by the Square," a story told in an intentionally flat style by a young man from Cincinnati who visits his uncle in Alabama and witnesses a lynching on a stormy night. Confused by the cyclone that moves through the town, an airplane pilot mistakes the fire of the lynching for an airport flare and flies too low through the town, knocking loose a wire and electrocuting a white woman. Undaunted, the crowd continues with the lynching and the anonymous narrator watches a nameless black man being burned, marveling at the victim's resiliency but showing no moral awareness of the horror of the act.

Four of the stories in the collection focus on two young friends, Buster and Riley, as they explore their world and their friendship. The first story, "Mister Toussan," finds them making up imaginary exploits for Haitian liberator Toussaint L'Ouverture, a name they have heard but with which they have only vague associations and upon which they hang various fantasies. Similarly, "Afternoon" and "That I Had Wings" find the boys involved in imaginative games to stave off boredom. "A Coupla Scalped Indians" focuses on Riley, who has just been "scalped" (circumcised) at the age of eleven, having a sexually charged encounter with old Aunt Mack, an eccentric healer Riley sees naked in her shack as he is making his way home from a carnival. "All was real," Riley tells the reader after leaving her shack, in wonderment about his discovery of the encroaching adult reality.

"Hymie's Bull" and "I Did Not Learn Their Names" are stories about riding freight trains, and together with "The Black Ball" and "A Hard Time Keeping Up," they are about young men finding their way in a world that can be violent and harsh but that can also contain friendship and tenderness in unexpected places. The importance of learning to discern the tenderness amid the harshness of the world becomes the central theme of two of the most important stories in the collection, "In a Strange Land" and "Flying Home." "King of the Bingo Game," by contrast, is a story about a young man trying to make his way in a world that offers little in the way of tenderness and much in the way of danger. Though "Flying Home" and "King of the Bingo Game" are the most significant stories in this collection, the collection offers a startling group of works, each of which is a semiprecious jewel and which, when taken together, mark the growth of the author's artistry.

"King of the Bingo Game" • One of Ellison's most durable statements about the harsh chaos of the modern world can be found in "King of the Bingo Game." The main character is an unnamed black North Carolina man living in Harlem, who has wandered into a cinema in the hope of winning the door prize that might pay for a doctor for his wife. By playing his own and several discarded Bingo cards simultaneously, he manages to win the bingo portion of the game, which gives him the opportunity to spin the bingo wheel. While on stage, he spins the bingo wheel by pressing a button but is then unable to take the chance of letting the button go. Only double zero will win the jackpot of $36.90, and he realizes that so long as he keeps the wheel spinning, he has not lost, so he refuses to let the wheel stop. The wheel takes on the symbolic importance of a mandala, a wheel of life, something the main character realizes when he exclaims, "This is God!" Because he has taken much too long to let go of the button, security guards try to take it from him and knock him out in an altercation. The wheel stops at double zero, but as he fades into unconsciousness, he realizes that he will not get the prize he sought. Though this story is among Ellison's harsher fictions, it is also one of his most poetic presentations of the unfeeling chaos of the modern world.

"In a Strange Country" • Though not as artistically satisfying as the longer "Flying Home," "In a Strange Country" tells a similar tale of self-discovery through the acceptance of a previously despised group identity. Parker is an intelligent black merchant seaman who lands in Wales during World War II only to be promptly attacked by a group of American soldiers simply for being a black man. A group of Welshmen, led by Mr. Catti, rescues him but not before his eye is injured and begins to swell. Over several drafts of ale, Catti learns that Parker is a music enthusiast and takes him to a singing club. There, Parker is swept up in the emotions of the songs about Welsh national pride but reminds himself that he is from Harlem, not Wales. He feels at first alienated and then deeply connected to the men around him, who, he believes, see his humanity much more clearly than do his fellow Americans who are white. As the evening is ending, the band begins to play "The Star-Spangled Banner" in his honor, and he finds himself singing along with deep feeling.

On one hand, the "strange country" of the title is Wales, but on a deeper level, it is the part of himself that is opened up by the bonding of common humanity he shares with these Welshmen and which, for the first time in his life, disallows any easy cynicism.

"Flying Home" • Ralph Ellison's longest short story, "Flying Home," is also his most richly satisfying accomplishment in the form. At the center of the story is Todd, a young black man whose lifelong dream of becoming a pilot crashes along with his plane when he flies into a buzzard on a training flight. Jefferson, an old black man who comes to Todd's rescue after the crash, tells him the buzzards are called "jim crows" locally, setting up an important level of symbolism about what has really caused Todd's crash. In fact, Todd has been training with the Tuskegee Airmen, a group of black World War II pilots who trained at the famed Tuskegee Institute but were only reluctantly deployed for combat missions. For Todd, this crash landing on a routine flight almost certainly means he will never get another chance to fly and, in his mind, will become the common black man he considers Jefferson to be, the worst fate he can imagine for himself.

Despite the younger man's hostility, Jefferson distracts the injured Todd by telling him a story about dying, going to heaven, and flying around so fast as to cause "a storm and a couple of lynchings down here in Macon County." In his story-within-a-story, Jefferson is stripped of his wings for flying too fast and is sent down to earth with a parachute and a map of Alabama. Todd, seeing only that this story has been twisted to mirror his own situation, snaps, "Why are you making fun of me?"—which, in fact, the old man is not doing. A feverish dream into which Todd drifts reveals not only the depth of his lifelong desire to fly but also the power of his grandmother's admonition:

> Young man, young man
> Yo arm's too short
> To box with God.

To Todd, becoming a pilot means taking a position higher than the majority white culture wants to allow black men of his time to occupy; it is the equivalent of boxing with God in his mind. To have failed as a pilot means not only to have made a mistake but also to have let his entire race down, something he cannot allow to happen.

So when Dabney Graves, the racist landowner on whose property Todd has crashed, arrives at the site, Todd snaps at the man and places his own life in danger. Jefferson, though, saves him by intervening and telling Graves that the Army told Todd never to abandon his ship. Graves's temper is assuaged, and Jefferson and a young boy are allowed to take Todd to safety in a stretcher. The final image is of Todd watching a buzzard flying against the sun, glowing like a bird of flaming gold. This image suggests that though Todd will never fly again, his spirit will rise up like a phoenix from the ashes of his defeat, a victory made possible by the current of goodwill he can now allow himself to feel for Jefferson. Todd will begin to learn to love himself for who he is by loving others for who they are.

Thomas Cassidy

Other major works

NOVELS: *Invisible Man*, 1952; *Juneteenth*, 1999 (John F. Callahan, editor).

NONFICTION: *Shadow and Act*, 1964; *The Writer's Experience*, 1964 (with Karl Shapiro); *Going to the Territory*, 1986; *Conversations with Ralph Ellison*, 1995 (Maryemma Graham and Amritjit Singh, editors); *The Collected Essays of Ralph Ellison*, 1995 (John F. Callahan, editor); *Trading Twelves: The Selected Letters of Ralph Ellison and Albert Murray*, 2000; *Living with Music: Ralph Ellison's Jazz Writings*, 2001 (Robert O'Meally, editor).

Bibliography

Benston, Kimberly, ed. *Speaking for You: The Vision of Ralph Ellison*. Washington, D.C.: Howard University Press, 1987. Useful resource of responses to Ellison's fiction and essays. Also includes an extensive bibliography of his writings.

Bloom, Harold, ed. *Modern Critical Views: Ralph Ellison*. New York: Chelsea House, 1986. Though this widely available collection of essays focuses mainly on *Invisible Man*, it provides insights from which any reader of Ralph Ellison may profit, and Berndt Ostendor's essay, "Anthropology, Modernism, and Jazz," offers much to the reader of "Flying Home."

Bone, Robert. "Ralph Ellison and the Uses of Imagination." *Triquarterly* 6 (1966): 39-54. An important essay on the uses of transcendentalism and jazz in Ellison's fiction and of his writing's importance to the Civil Rights movement and black culture in general.

Busby, Mark. *Ralph Ellison*. Boston: Twayne, 1991. Excellent introduction to Ellison's life and work.

Callahan, John F. Introduction to *Flying Home, and Other Stories*, by Ralph Ellison. Edited by John F. Callahan. New York: Random House, 1996. Callahan's introduction to this collection of fiction is essential reading for anyone interested in Ellison's fiction, not only for the literary insights it provides but also for the basic editorial information about how these stories were selected and edited.

Jackson, Lawrence. *Ralph Ellison: Emergence of Genius*. New York: John Wiley & Sons, 2001. The first book-length study of Ellison's life. A good background source for the novelist's early life and career. Jackson, however, ends his study in 1953, shortly after the publication of *Invisible Man*.

May, Charles E., ed. *Masterplots II: Short Story Series, Revised Edition.* 8 vols. Pasadena, Calif.: Salem Press, 2004. Designed for student use, this reference set contains articles providing detailed plot summaries and analyses of these three short stories by Ellison: "Battle Royal" (vol. 1), "Flying Home" (vol. 3), and "King of the Bingo Game" (vol. 4).

Schor, Edith. *Visible Ellison: A Study of Ralph Ellison's Fiction.* Westport, Conn.: Greenwood Press, 1993. Published a year before Ellison's death, this is an excellent full-length study of the fiction that was generally available at the time, including his short fiction, which had not yet been collected in book form. This is probably the best place for the serious scholar of Ralph Ellison to begin.

Skerret, Joseph. "Ralph Ellison and the Example of Richard Wright." *Studies in Short Fiction* 15 (Spring, 1978): 145-153. An examination of the influence of Richard Wright on Ralph Ellison's short fiction.

Watts, Jerry Gafio. *Heroism and the Black Intellectual: Ralph Ellison, Politics, and Afro-American Intellectual Life.* Chapel Hill: University of North Carolina Press, 1994. Chapters explore critic Harold Cruse's influential interpretation of black intellectuals, the biographical background to *Invisible Man,* the relationship between the novel and black music, and the responsibilities of the black writer. Includes notes and a bibliography.

Louise Erdrich

Born: Little Falls, Minnesota; June 7, 1954

Principal short fiction • "The Red Convertible," 1981; "Scales," 1982; "The World's Greatest Fisherman," 1982; "American Horse," 1983; "Destiny," 1985; "Saint Marie," 1985; "Fleur," 1987; "Snares," 1987; "Matchimanito," 1988; *The Best American Short Stories 1993*, 1993.

Other literary forms • Louise Erdrich is probably best known for her novels, which include *Love Medicine* (1984), *The Beet Queen* (1986), *The Antelope Wife* (1998), *The Last Report on the Miracles at Little No Horse* (2001), *The Master Butchers Singing Club* (2003), *Four Souls* (2004), and *The Painted Drum* (2005). She is also the author of several collections of poetry, including *Original Fire: Selected and New Poems* (2003), and a number of children's books, including *The Range Eternal* (2002) and *The Game of Silence* (2004). In 1995, she published her first nonfiction book, a personal memoir of her daughter's birth, *The Blue Jay's Dance: A Birth Year* (1995). *Books and Islands in Ojibwe Country* followed in 2003.

Achievements • Several of Louise Erdrich's stories have appeared in the annual *The Best American Short Stories* and *Prize Stories: The O. Henry Awards* series. She received a Nelson Algren Fiction Award as well as a National Endowment for the Arts Fellowship in 1982, the Pushcart Prize and the National Magazine Award for Fiction in 1983, a John Simon Guggenheim Memorial Foundation Fellowship in 1985, and a Western Literary Association Award in 1992. Her *Love Medicine* received the Virginia McCormack Scully Prize, the National Book Critics Circle Award, the *Los Angeles Times* award for best novel, the Sue Kaufman Prize, and the American Book Award and was named one of the best eleven books of 1985 by *The New York Times Book Review*.

Biography • Karen Louise Erdrich was born in Little Falls, Minnesota, on June 7, 1954, the first of seven children of a German father and Chippewa mother. A member of the first coeducational class at Dartmouth College in 1972, she received her bachelor's degree in 1976. While teaching expository and creative writing on a fellowship at Johns Hopkins University, she earned a master's degree from The Johns Hopkins Writing Program in 1979. In 1980 she was a textbook writer for the Charles Merrill Company, and a year later, she became a visiting fellow at Dartmouth. On October 10, 1981, she married the writer Michael Dorris.

In 1981, Erdrich published her first short story, "The Red Convertible," in *Mississippi Valley Review*. Over the next two years, she published such award-winning stories as "The World's Greatest Fisherman" and "Scales." In 1984, she published her first collection of poetry, *Jacklight*, as well as her first novel, *Love Medicine*. In 1991, she coauthored *The Crown of Columbus* with her husband.

In 1981, Erdrich became writer-in-residence at Dartmouth's Native American Studies Program. She and Dorris later moved to Minneapolis and separated after fifteen years of marriage. During the divorce proceedings, Dorris committed suicide, on April 11, 1997. Although Erdrich has said that the success of her work was due in great part to the collaboration of her husband, she continued to be productive as a writer, especially in the long-fiction form. Between 1998 and 2005, she published five novels.

Analysis • Just as fiction in general has opened up to a diverse ethnic spectrum of writers, so too has short fiction, and Louise Erdrich's stories stand as excellent examples of contemporary Native American literature. Like Leslie Marmon Silko, Linda Hogan, and Paula Gunn Allen, Erdrich has taken a place as one of the prominent female Native American authors of short fiction. Even among American Indian stories, Erdrich's stand out for their multiethnic nature. Erdrich's stories include not only Native American characters but also characters of German, Swedish, and other European descent. Likewise, many of the stories' themes are not specifically Native American themes. Indeed, the themes of Erdrich's stories range from the effects of war on families and personal identity to loss of heritage and family and personal relationships.

Stylistically, Erdrich's stories reveal many similarities to the stories of writers she has said had significant influence on her. The distinct sense of place, of character, and of history that colors the works of Toni Morrison, William Faulkner, and Italo Calvino is similarly prominent in Erdrich's stories. She has said of Calvino that "the magic in his work is something that has been an influence," which is clear especially in stories like "Fleur" and "Snares." As Faulkner does with Yoknapatawpha County, Erdrich creates a world of the Chippewa reservation and the town of Argus, in which and around which nearly all of her stories occur. Many of her characters are employed repeatedly in her stories. Minor characters in one story may be the central characters in another or relatives of characters in one story are featured in later stories. Thus, most of Erdrich's stories connect to create a fictional world, which appears as true as the real world.

Erdrich has said that "the story starts to take over if it is good." Her stories fulfill this criterion, capturing readers' imagination and carrying them along on an intense mental ride. Her stories truly "touch some universals" that embrace readers of all ages, cultures, and beliefs.

"The Red Convertible" • "The Red Convertible" is Erdrich's first published story. Like many of her stories, this tale of two brothers later became a chapter in the novel *Love Medicine*. On the surface, the story appears to be merely a simple tale of two brothers and the car they share. Lyman Lamartine, a young Indian man with a "touch" for money, and his brother Henry save enough money to buy a used, red Oldsmobile convertible. Lyman tells the story, describing the early adventures he and his brother shared in the car. However, as the story progresses, it becomes clear that much more than the car is important in this story. Lyman describes how Henry changed when he returned home from the Vietnam War. While the family tries to help the deeply depressed Henry, Lyman tricks his brother into fixing up the car that he damaged. Although Henry does improve, even the car cannot save him, as he commits suicide in the end. In this story, the red convertible represents the freedom and innocence of youth, yet once those things are lost due to war in Henry's case and due to the altered Henry in Lyman's case, they cannot be regained; they must be let go. Although the story unfolds mainly on the reservation, part of its success is that the topic itself (the loss of innocence, the effects of war) is universal, which allows any reader to understand and be intrigued by the tale.

Michael Dorris

"Saint Marie" • Like many of Erd-rich's stories, "Saint Marie" also became a chapter in *Love Medicine.* "Saint Marie" is the story of a young Indian girl, who goes to the Roman Catholic convent near the reservation so she might prove she is better than the other heathen Indians. Marie tries very hard to keep Satan out of her life, yet one of the nuns, Sister Leopolda, believes Marie to be completely under the devil's control. Leopolda proceeds to torture Marie to the point of stabbing her with a fork in order to expunge the evil. Yet to cover her madness, Leopolda lies to the other nuns, telling them that Marie must be touched by God as she has the signs of the stigmata on her hand; Marie must be a saint. However, Marie uses her knowledge of the truth of what happened to intimidate and humble Leopolda. Once again, this is a story about loss of innocence, about the psychological effects of a traumatic event in a young person's life. Similarly, Marie's struggle with her beliefs and Leopolda's madness are not necessarily specific to Native Americans, so many readers can access the story and enjoy it.

"Destiny" • A story which later became part of *The Beet Queen*, "Destiny" describes Celestine Duval's visit to see her granddaughter's Christmas play. Wallacette, Celestine's granddaughter, is a large, strong, impulsive girl, who intimidates the other children in her school and town. The destiny of the title is Wallacette's destiny to be strong and independent, just like her grandmother. Celestine adores Wallacette, though she does not get along with Wallacette's parents very well. In particular, there is bad blood between Celestine and her daughter-in-law, whose gelatin molds with vegetables in them are a source of great disgust for Celestine. The story turns comic when Wallacette hits a little boy she likes when he does not cooperate in the play, and it ends on a humorous note as Celestine reveals that the secret dish she had taken to the play with her daughter-in-law's name on it was a gelatin mold with nuts and bolts in it. This story is very entertaining and universal in its depictions of family struggles and the pains of growing up. The psychological element still exists in this story, but some of the intense emotional pains are absent, which allows a humorous tone to come through.

"Fleur" • "Fleur" presents the story of one woman's multiple drowning experiences and her influence on the people around her. Told from the point of view of Pauline Puyat, this story later became a chapter in *Tracks* (1988). Pauline describes how Fleur Pillager drowned several times, and every man who rescued her ended up either crazy or dead. Pauline believes that Fleur has special magic powers, and she tells the story of the time Fleur left the reservation and went to the town of Argus. After beating a group of men at cards for a number of weeks, Fleur is attacked by the men in a smokehouse. Pauline stands by and watches the event, doing nothing to help Fleur. However, Fleur has her revenge when, in the midst of a storm that came from nowhere and touched nothing that Fleur valued, the men become locked in a meat freezer. Pauline believes that Fleur called up the storm. Although the story is about Fleur, it is also about Pauline. Pauline voices her own feelings and thoughts throughout the story, revealing the guilt she feels for not helping Fleur as well as the envy she feels toward this strong woman. Fleur is an enigma to Pauline, but she is also what Pauline seems to want to be in this story.

"Matchimanito" • Though it was published after "Fleur," "Matchimanito" is the story of how Fleur came to be the last living member of her family and what happened to her when she came back to the reservation from Argus. An old man, Nanapush, tells how he found Fleur amid her dead family and took her away to recover from the "spotted sickness." This story reveals that Fleur is different from everyone else from the beginning. She is quiet yet powerful. Upon returning from Argus, she lives alone in a cabin next to Matchimanito, the lake, which fuels rumors about her relationship with the lake monster, Mishepeshu. However, Fleur soon attracts a young man, Eli Kashpaw, and they live as husband and wife by the lake. Fleur becomes pregnant, and her pregnancy sparks more rumors, as the child's paternity is questioned. The birth of the child is difficult, and though many people believe that Fleur and her baby are dead, both live to prove them wrong. This is a powerful story because it demonstrates the strength of Fleur, the mixing of the old Indian ways with the new ones, the interaction of the community and individuals, and the history of both one person and a people. This story is particularly successful in its ability to show all of these things without force-feeding them to the reader.

Keri L. Overall
With updates by the Editors

Other major works

CHILDREN'S LITERATURE: *Grandmother's Pigeon*, 1996 (illustrated by Jim LaMarche); *The Birchbark House*, 1999; *The Range Eternal*, 2002; *The Game of Silence*, 2004.

NOVELS: *Love Medicine*, 1984 (revised and expanded, 1993); *The Beet Queen*, 1986; *Tracks*, 1988; *The Crown of Columbus*, 1991 (with Michael Dorris); *The Bingo Palace*, 1994; *Tales of Burning Love*, 1996; *The Antelope Wife*, 1998; *The Last Report on the Miracles at Little No Horse*, 2001; *The Master Butchers Singing Club*, 2003; *Four Souls*, 2004; *The Painted Drum*, 2005.

NONFICTION: *The Blue Jay's Dance: A Birth Year*, 1995; *Books and Islands in Ojibwe Country*, 2003.

POETRY: *Jacklight*, 1984; *Baptism of Desire*, 1989; *Original Fire: Selected and New Poems*, 2003.

Bibliography

Chavkin, Allan, ed. *The Chippewa Landscape of Louise Erdrich*. Tuscaloosa: University of Alabama Press, 1998. Collects original essays focusing on Erdrich's writings that are rooted in the Chippewa experience. Premier scholars of Native American literature investigate narrative structure, signs of ethnicity, the notions of luck and chance in Erdrich's narrative cosmology, and her use of comedy in exploring American Indians' tragic past.

Davis, Rocío G. "Identity in Community in Ethnic Short Story Cycles: Amy Tan's *The Joy Luck Club*, Louise Erdrich's *Love Medicine*, Gloria Naylor's *The Women of Brewster Place*." In *Ethnicity and the American Short Story*, edited by Julia Brown. New York: Garland, 1997. Discusses how Erdrich's *Love Medicine* is in fact a cycle of short stories. Suggests that each chapter is a story with a different narrator, but the narrators' voices combine to present a communal protagonist. An interesting concept and a useful way of understanding the stories as they stand on their own.

Erdrich, Louise. *Conversations with Louise Erdrich and Michael Dorris*. Edited by Allan Chavkin and Nancy Feyl Chavkin. Jackson: University Press of Mississippi, 1994. This is a collection of twenty-five interviews with the couple and includes an interview with Joseph Bruchac.

Ferguson, Suzanne. "The Short Stories of Louise Erdrich's Novels." *Studies in Short Fiction* 33 (1996): 541-555. An excellent discussion of four short stories—"Saint Marie," "Scales," "Fleur," and "Snares"—and how they were modified when they became chapters in the novels. Ferguson also argues that alone the short stories should be read differently than when they are presented as chapters in a novel. This is a good article for clarifying the differences between the short stories and their counterpart chapters in the novels.

May, Charles E., ed. *Masterplots II: Short Story Series, Revised Edition*. 8 vols. Pasadena, Calif.: Salem Press, 2004. Designed for student use, this reference set contains articles providing detailed plot summaries and analyses of these five short stories by Erdrich: "The Beet Queen" (vol. 1), "Fleur" (vol. 3), "The Leap" (vol. 4), and "The Red Convertible" and "Saint Marie" (vol. 6).

Rebein, Robert. *Hicks, Tribes, and Dirty Realists: American Fiction After Postmodernism*. Lexington: University Press of Kentucky, 2001. Study asserting that gritty realism has gained ascendancy over metafiction in American writing. Examines the works of Dorothy Allison, Annie Proux, Thomas McGuane, Cormac McCarthy, Larry McMurtry, and Louise Erdrich.

Smith, Jeanne Rosier. *Writing Tricksters: Mythic Gambols in American Ethnic Literature*. Berkeley: University of California Press, 1997. Thorough examination of ethnic trickster figures as they appear in the work of Erdrich, Maxine Hong Kingston, and Toni Morrison. Chapter 3 explores the trickster characteristics of Old Nanapush, Gerry Nanapush, Lipsha Morrissey, Fleur Pillager, and others.

Stookey, Lorena Laura. *Louise Erdrich: A Critical Companion*. Westport, Conn.: Greenwood Press, 1999. Good study of Erdrich's works. Includes bibliographical references and an index.

DATE DUE
